ONE WEEK LOAN

/ ... Regional Imperative

Regional Planning and Governance in Britain,
Europe and the United States

398

of related interest

Retreat from the Regions
Corporate Change and the Closure of Factories
Stephen Fothergill and Nigel Guy
ISBN 1 85302 101 6 hb
ISBN 1 85302 100 8 pb
Regional Policy and Development 1

Spatial Policy in a Divided Nation
Edited by Richard T. Harrison and Mark Hart
ISBN 1 85302 076 1
Regional Policy and Development 2

Regional Development in the 1990s
The British Isles in Transition
Edited by Peter Townroe and Ron Martin
ISBN 1 85302 139 3
Regional Policy and Development 4

An Enlarged Europe
Regions in Competition?
Edited by Sally Hardy, Mark Hart,
Louis Albrechts and Anastasios Katos
ISBN 1 85302 188 1
Regional Policy and Development 6

Sustainable Cities
Graham Haughton and Colin Hunter
ISBN 1 85302 234 9
Regional Policy and Development 7

The Regional Dimension of Transformation in Central Europe
Grzegorz Gorzelak
ISBN 1 85302 301 9
Regional Policy and Development 10

The Regional Imperative

Regional Planning and Governance in Britain, Europe and the United States

Urlan Wannop

Regional Policy and Development Series 9

Jessica Kingsley Publishers
London and Bristol, Pennsylvania

Regional Studies Association
London

The right of Urlan Wannop to be identified as author of this work has been asserted by him in accordance with the Copyright, Designs and Patents Act 1988.

First published in the United Kingdom in 1995 by
Jessica Kingsley Publishers Ltd
116 Pentonville Road
London N1 9JB, England
and
1900 Frost Road, Suite 101
Bristol, PA 19007, U S A
and Regional Studies Association (Registered Charity 252269)

Copyright © 1995 Urlan Wannop

Library of Congress Cataloging in Publication Data
Wannop, Urlan, 1931–
The regional imperative : regional planning and governance in
Britain, Europe and the United States / Urlan Wannop
p. cm.--(Regional policy and development : 9)
Includes bibliographical references and index.
ISBN 1–85302–292–6 (pb.)
1. Regional planning--Great Britain--case studies. 2. Regional
planning--Europe. 3. Regional planning--United States. I. Title
II. Series
HT395.G7W36 1995
338.9--dc20

British Library Cataloguing in Publication Data
Wannop, Urlan
Regional Imperative: Regional Planning
and Governance in Britain, Europe and
the United States. – (Regional Policy &
Development Series;Vol.9)
I.Title II. Series
307.12

ISBN 1–85302–292–6

Printed and Bound in Great Britain by
Athenaeum Press Ltd., Gateshead, Tyne and Wear

Contents

Illustrations

for Noreen

Acknowledgements

Sharon Galleitch of the Department of Geograhphy of the University of Strathclyde was skilful, patient and fast in preparing for publication both original and borrowed illustrations.

Permission to reproduce illustrations is gratefully acknowledged for Figures 1.2 and 1.12 (Avebury); Figures 1.3, 2.3, 3.1, 3.2, 3.3 and 4.3 (Crown copyright is reproduced with the permissions of the controller of HMSO); Figures 2.4 and 2.6 (Routledge); Figure 6.6 (Pinter Publishers. All rights reserved); Figure 4.2. (Strathclyde Regional Archives); Figure 8.1 (redrawn from B. Hogwood and M. Keating (eds) *Regional Government in England*. Oxford: Claredon Press).

Foreword

REGION = Indefinitely defined area (Franklin Language Master Dictionary and Thesaurus)

The Origins of the Book

Regional planning has been a mercurial and often ephemeral phenomenon. But there is an enduring imperative for it. Demands for regional planning and arrangements for regional governance sooner or later recur, in most regions. But most regions are impermanent; they shift and change. So most systems of regional planning and governance become progressively imperfect. And because new regional issues sooner or later arise across the boundaries of any newly-created system of regional governance, regional planning is never fully solved. It is always with us.

This book reviews experience in attempting to plan regions, primarily in Britain but also in some other regions of Europe and in the United States. And because governance is integral with regional planning, it is an issue penetrating throughout.

My own regional career began with colleagues on the Coventry–Solihull–Warwickshire Sub-Regional Planning Study, continued on the West Central Scotland Plan, and then in the setting-up and early development of the Department of Physical Planning of Strathclyde Regional Council. This experience was almost entirely engrossing, not just because of the intrinsic fascination of the planning issues and of their political contexts, but also because of the skill and commitment of some outstanding colleagues with whom I was fortunate to be associated.

Despite the great satisfactions of this experience, I hope that the book is fairly dispassionate and unprejudiced about the capacity and merits of regional planning and governance, in their different varieties. At least, I hope that readers find them discussed in a sufficient political and administrative context. Up to around 1970, a significant amount of planning practice around the world did originate from British experience. After that, Britain's contribution was appreciably less than that of the United States, in particular. But in regional planning, the United States and Germany pioneered approaches ahead of Britain. So, without attempting a world conspectus, the book sets British experience against that of other countries where regional planning has occurred in different political and administrative environments, and often in more ambitious ways.

Because my familiarity with British experience is fullest it is described most extensively, but not as offering any particular prime model, which it does not. Previous studies of regional planning in Britain have concentrated on the experience of Greater London and of South East England, with some but fewer accounts of the West Midlands. This book looks additionally at other regions, and at Scotland in particular. In thereby partly correcting the unbalanced record of British regional planning, I may also repay a debt to those who have set standards of professional and academic practice and understanding much higher than mine. Bob Grieve has been the most distinguished of all regionalists in the history of planning and of administrative action in the United Kingdom – from the Clyde Valley Regional Plan of 1946 to the formation of the Scottish Constitutional Convention in 1989. Donald Robertson crystallised the interest of economists in regional planning in the 1960s. Gordon Cameron had a similar clarity of mind and of expression, sustaining the Chair of Town and Regional Planning at Glasgow University which the Clyde Valley Plan actually proposed, and which Bob Grieve first occupied. In England, David Eversley notably helped write the history of British regional planning as a participant and as a researcher, policy analyst and commentator.

My gratitude is due to all colleagues with whom I have been fortunate to be associated when working as a regional planner, but particularly to Graham Harrison, Ian Turner, Martin Shaw, David Dare and John Randall. And to colleagues in Strathclyde, also, and to those of the working party on Strategic and Regional Planning which reported to the Royal Town Planning Institute in 1986.

I am indebted for help in many ways to Gerald Dix, Bob Grieve, Clyde Mitchell-Weaver and Bill Ogden. Dan Rich, Tim Barnekov and their colleagues at the University of Delaware gave accommodation and hospitality when the book was started. In visiting regions in Britain, Europe and the United States, I have been kindly received and given advice by many to whom I am indebted: particularly Martin Simmons and Geoff Steeley in Britain; Bob Mazanec, Bruce McDowell, Larry Ornan and Angelo Siracusa in the United States; Jean-Marie Ernecq and Joel Hebrard in France; Gloria Gonzalez in Spain; and Dr Friedrichs, Dr Lageman, Dr Hamm, Mr Schlieper and Dr Rechmann in Germany.

The Leverhulme Trust made a generous grant of a Fellowship Award which assisted in travelling, gathering information and preparing the book.

Others whom I have not noted as helping will correctly recognise that they should have been.

What Kinds of Region and Regional Planning?

Regionalism has been a persistent feature of politics in the United Kingdom, as in other European countries. Its roots are cultural and sometimes religious, growing from differences of physical environment and of economic development, and from the social and political ties they have fostered. The force of regionalism fluctuates, but it survives the intensification of the international culture transmitted by radio, television, compact disc and supermarkets.

Behind this deepest-seated political force of regionalism has arisen scientific analysis in geography, which has attempted to codify and delineate regions of many kinds and at different scales. As local government boundaries derived from medieval dukedoms have been overtaken by metropolitanisation and by new regional cities, there have been discontinuous, variously successful but repeated approaches to plan regionally. Yet, it remains that regional planning is more observed in the breach than in practice, and despite the adoption of regional councils in Scottish local government, regional planning of the classical kind is still a rare feature in UK governance in the late twentieth century.

What is Regional Planning?

There are many different understandings of what regional planning comprises. Like kinds of region, the kinds of regional planning are various. The long-involved US academic and regional planner, John Friedmann, has said that 'Regional planning' is often used as a phrase to describe a congeries of more or less unrelated activities', giving his own definition as: 'Regional planning is the process of formulating and clarifying social objectives in the ordering of activities in supra-urban space – that is, in any area which is larger than a single city' (Friedmann, 1963).

Perhaps most commonly in writing in the United Kingdom, regional planning is dealt with as the balancing of resources to modify standards of living and disparities in economic conditions as between different parts of the nation. This is often referred to as inter-regional or as regional economic planning, which has engaged economists particularly. Although since the early 1970s it has slipped behind as an activity of British governments, it has been sustained by the European Community. This book is not directly about that kind of regional planning, although it inevitably creeps in from the edge of our main field of vision.

Within the regions of the United Kingdom, another kind of regional planning has existed spasmodically. It has primarily attempted to resolve issues and local problems of growing metropolitan cities, spilling their population and their economic and social relationships and raising political disputes across their administrative boundaries. It has taken the form of consultants' reports to joint committees of local government or to government itself, it has taken the form of government planning teams, and it has produced standing conferences and supporting staff to monitor or advise upon developments. It led in 1975 to the reorganisation of Scottish local government into regional councils, although most administer areas not recognisable as regions at the UK scale and the three smallest were discreetly titled as islands councils. This kind of regional planning has frequently been described as physical planning, but sometimes as intra-regional planning.

Although most frequently associated with cities and metropolitan areas, this kind of intra-regional planning has also arisen in some sparsely populated regions of Britain with enduring problems of depopulation or of changing rural economies. Confusingly, it has sometimes been closely allied to economic planning as in the case of the regional economic planning councils which existed in England between 1965 and 1979, and sometimes largely separated from it as in the case of the Highlands and Islands since its Development Board was formed in 1965.

Also, of course, intra-regional planning has sometimes been wholly advisory as with the regional economic planning councils; sometimes it has taken the form of a government agency with resources and selective executive responsibilities as with the Highlands and Islands Board and, since 1975, it has existed in Scotland in the form of mainstream local authority administration. Its scale has varied from a population of 18 million in the case of the South East England Regional Economic Planning Council, to under 200,000 in the Highland Region of Scotland whose area is the greater. Indeed, in Scotland it has been possible to regard both the Borders Regional Council and the Scottish Development Agency as being agents of regional planning, although one has covered only 100,000 people in a part of the country and the other has served 5 million in Scotland as a whole.

Echoing Friedmann, Martins (1986, 3) defines regional planning as 'a type of public planning (state activity) which is specifically concerned with social space; with the "ordering" of activities and facilities in space at a scale greater than a single local authority and smaller than the state.' This definition covers a large variety of planning and a large variety of regions. It embraces plans with comprehensive scope and idealistic ambitions like the *Clyde Valley* and *Greater London* plans of the 1940s, as well as the bureaucratic and barely visible process of regional collaboration represented by the conference of South East England planning authorities through most of the 1960s and 1970s, when regional planning was at least more favoured by governments than it was in the 1980s. At an extreme, it covers the study of the future of the Yangtse Valley completed by the China Academy of Urban Planning and Design in 1990, and certainly one of the largest of regional plans anywhere.

In the contemporary era of economic unions of nations, of course, Martin's definition of regions as being smaller than states has been overtaken by supra-national regions, as within the European Community.

Some of the variety of conditions which explain the varieties of regional planning are described by Clout (1975, 315):

> National approaches to regional development then diverge from one another for three main groups of reasons. First, regional problems are in themselves highly varied and more importantly have been perceived in different ways by government institutions and planning bodies. Second, national systems of administration, government and planning vary enormously at the institu-

tional level. Third, national schemes of regional management vary in their stage of evolution.

The history and variety of regional planning in the United Kingdom will be traced in the course of evaluating its performance in its variety of contexts. Here and in cases from elsewhere, however, the purpose of the book is to consider intra-regional planning, and its relationship to its developing political, economic and social contexts. This means that the focus is not on 'physical planning' alone, because that should be merely one outcome of any adequate analysis of intra-regional problems.

What is a Region?

We come now to face the question of what is a region? The reader and critic will find that I take it rather as a constantly changing object, but this is its very nature. As Donald Robertson (1965, 121) wrote:

> The term 'region' has no very precise meaning. The geographers will most commonly infer from it some physical basis of similarity. For others the regional hypothesis may derive from a degree of cultural affinity or the sharing of common economic problems or possibilities. The physical planners tend to think of a region as related to their preoccupation with congested land use around a major city... Any one region will in practice owe its regional distinctiveness to a number of different possible sources of regional identity.

A listing of regional plans for any country is likely to quickly distinguish two basic kinds. Probably least common will be those plans covering what geographers or political scientists would recognise as regions – areas with unifying or homogeneous economic or cultural features, generally larger than established units of local government. But probably most numerous will be plans of a second kind, covering the area of at least two but commonly more local government units, being described as regions simply because they encompass problems perceived as larger than those of any one unit; this second kind of region may sometimes nearly coincide with a recognisable geographical region, but may frequently correspond only roughly.

This adoption by parties to regional planning of their own local definitions of regions and of regional planning causes much of the confusion over regional planning. Anyone looking for a single root and a constant base and definition will fail to find them. There are at least two roots and several stems, which sometimes intertwine and after many added grafts now flower in multiple variety.

From regional planning's geographical root comes the academic approach to classifying regions by categorical rules. Boudeville (1966) drew a simple distinction between two kinds of geographical region – the homogeneous and the nodal. Homogeneous regions are effectively constant in some principal characteristics, such as the flatness of East Anglia, the mountain ruggedness of Appalachia or the maize belt west of the Mississippi. Near homogeneity of landform may also be strongly associated with near homogeneity of crops or stock rearing, and be reflected in common cultural traditions. Nodal regions may nearly coincide with homogeneous regions in some cases, but are frequently heterogeneous. Their people and economic and social interests focus upon nodal centres for trade, administration and services, whether in rural market centres or metropolitan capitals.

Homogeneous regions tend to discreteness, whereas the fact that nodal regions are characterised by communications networks flowing upwards and downwards through a succession of service centres of varying significance, means that nodal regions group into successive tiers in a nesting pattern. Regions for planning and administrative purposes are most commonly of the nodal kind; they relate to labour or housing market areas as underlie the standard metropolitan statistical areas defined by the US Census, or similar journey-to-work area analysis in other countries.

Regions of both these geographical kinds are embedded in the history of regional planning – the Clyde Valley, the Tennessee Valley or the West Midlands. The great conurbation regions of Greater London or the Ruhr stem partly from this root but, like the great river valley regions of the Clyde, Tennessee and Columbia, their place in the history of regional planning arose from political factors rather than from geographical purity.

But in the context of regional planning, regions are primarily defined by political circumstances. They are not customarily defined from the academic standpoint of geographers' rules of a quasi-scientific nature – or at least of a consistent kind. They often emerge by their own internal logic, as for instance where a superior administrative authority wishes to find reason to intervene in the affairs of an inferior one; a 'regional' interest is consequently identified by the superior authority, justifying its interference at a more local level than it has been accustomed to do hitherto. As my definition of regional planning is that it customarily lies above the level of at least one tier of representative local govern-ment, or covers the jurisdiction of at least two significantly interested agencies of similar status, then it follows that the practice of regional planning inevitably runs against some political interest or other.

So, regional planning can customarily only be sensibly described within a context of political analysis, and only in that light can we satisfactorily assess the effectiveness of regional planning. Further, because of the political origins to so many cases of regional planning, there is no consistency between the kinds of region involved. The term 'region' has often been attached almost arbitrarily to plans or organisations. It is a term which politicians and administrators find expedient and use almost promiscuously. The term often hides more than it reveals. It is impossible to tidily classify regions through the eyes of those who describe them, or to categorise regional planning by the assumptions of those who practise it; there are no consistent definitions for either regions or for regional planning.

Writing about regional issues and regional planning is most extensive in Europe. Of the relatively rarer US studies, Ann Markusen's *Regions* (1987) records the interplay of local politics with economic and environmental pressures, the force and shifts of regional coalitions, and the development of regionalism in the US. Although she discusses regional planning only in an appendix, the breadth and detail of her account is skilful and without a UK counterpart of such quality. She describes four different frameworks in which regions tend to be described and discussed: first, regions viewed as areas of sectional, social character – of which the western 'frontier' is the classic American case; second, regions as organic areas, in which there is at least mutual dependency and at most homogeneity – like the Geddesian region; third, regions as analysed, synthesised and described by regional scientists; fourth, regions as employed in Marxist explanation. None of these frameworks quite meets the case of this book, because it is primarily concerned with planning and policy-making, and with public administration and action in regions. It is by the issues which do not satisfactorily fit the scope of the predominant, existing administrative structures that regions come to be recognised. They accordingly have three significant characteristics: first, that they are larger than the jurisdiction of at least the lowest tier of government in a country; second, that whenever governance is reorganised to better fit the area of a regional issue, this very fact tends to bring new regional problems to light at a higher level; third, that they never quite catch up with the significant trend to a generally wider scale of economic and social affairs.

These characteristics permeate UK experience of regional planning. Abercrombie prepared an East Kent Regional Planning Scheme in 1925 for an area that few planners would recognise as a region 70 years later – or even as a sub-region, perhaps. In countries of expanding urbanisation, metropolitan regions have only transitory boundaries. Regions are areas where some overriding interest does not fit the pattern of established governance. The misfit may exist either in the scale of the matter – as with London's growth which has never been capable of being all absorbed within its own administrative area; or it may exist in the view of a superior authority unwilling to entrust a matter to smaller administrations – as with the economic regeneration role of the Scottish Development Agency. In either event, the region covers an area embracing two or more authorities of equal administrative status, each in possession of powers in the matter but not capable of satisfactorily exercising them exclusive of one another.

Accordingly, by definition of observed cases in the UK, a region for the purposes of regional planning has commonly been an area larger than any one statutory planning authority with associated executive responsibilities. As in the US, it is true that regional planning in the UK has commonly been undertaken by often temporary alliances of agencies, either by local governments collaborating voluntarily, or more commonly under pressure from central government and sometimes with central government staffing and leading the exercise. More recently, administrative reorganisation has produced regional local government in

Scotland, *conseils régionaux* in France and autonomous regional governments in Spain. The German *Länder* and the US states have longer had the capacity to plan for administrative areas sometimes larger than some accepted geographical regions. We therefore also consider regional planning by executive regional authorities of this kind. However, we will later suggest that many of these administrative regions are highly unstable or are being overtaken by changing circumstances. Characteristically, they face difficulties in negotiating their plans and activities with a range of smaller local governments, each of which would wish to regard itself as having a significant interest in strategic issues. This is the nature of regional planning.

Taking this view, regions for our purpose might be defined as often transitory phenomena. They are fluid on either of two counts. First, as Friedmann (1956) emphasised, because the economic development of a region proceeds through different spatial arrangements, implying a different regional delimitation at each stage of development. Second, because no sooner is a 'region' consolidated by new governance arrangements, than it is likely to be destabilised as new 'regional' issues arise which surmount the consolidated area.

If regions are thus accepted as being inherently flexible, it implies that the pursuit of a perfect system of regional governance will never wholly succeed. Accordingly, consolidated regional governance should perhaps be thought of as a longer-lived variant of *ad hoc* regional planning, rather than as completely different to it.

By these definitions, I might be accused of almost falling back upon the old joke about a region being an area safely larger than the last one to whose problems no solution was found. It might be said against me that the US states are regions which have been stable for up to 200 years. But, as I will argue later, there and elsewhere experience has mostly been that contributions to regional governance have normally been overtaken by larger pressures. The old joke gains more truth as time passes.

Accordingly, because of its political roots, regional planning arises where established administrative and planning systems are overtaken by problems they cannot resolve. This confirms the two problems in the definition of regions. First, that they have as much variety as there is variety in the scale and character of administrative areas and the issues arising from them. Second, that because growth, change and decline progressively affect social and economic affairs in most regions, it is difficult to pin them down with permanently satisfactory administrative arrangements. They can be defined only relative to other areas, being distinctive through socio-economic and political differences as much as by more permanent geographical features. So because they are relative areas regions must tend to be unstable, because their external contexts will commonly shift.

What this book tries to do is to appraise regional planning and governance within some understanding of how regions are changing their form, and are being redefined by economic and political developments. It examines the experience of regional planning so as to assess its successes and failures, and the conditions which have influenced these. It gauges the case and the prospects for regional planning in the United Kingdom, with an eye on prospects for Europe and the United States. It suggests that regional planning and governance can never be perfectly arranged, except in the moment. But since regional issues are recurrent, regional planning and governance are essential arts in continually managing a constantly imperfect system of government.

CHAPTER ONE

The Rise of UK Practice

Preface: The Progressive Consolidation of the Regional Dimension

The rise of the regional dimension in planning and public governance in the UK has been irregular. But it has endured. False promise has recurred but, despite disappointments in practice, regional planning has been repeatedly revived by political circumstances and by social and economic necessity. Regional governance has a longer history. This chapter describes the course of initiatives in regional planning from 1909, tracing parallel initiatives in regional governance from the mid nineteenth century. Because developments in regional governance and in planning have been more closely related since the end of the Second World War, the account of administrative change since then is interwoven by connections with regional planning.

The Evolution of Regional Planning in the UK

1909–1939: The Experimental Era

Statutory planning in the UK began properly with the Housing and Planning Act of 1909, but there is argument about the substance of regional initiatives in the following thirty-five years. Massey (1989) describes this as 'the experimental era' for regional planning, noting how Frederic Osborn and Thomas Adams disputed its significance at the 1938 Town and Country Planning Summer School. Osborn was adamant that 'Regional and Advisory Committees do not work. Very little notice has been taken of Advisory Committeee Reports.' Adams eagerly opposed by asserting that 'I should flatly like to contradict Mr. Osborn, and to say that Advisory Reports in my own judgement, have proved worthy of representation as practical and useful.'

On the eve of the flowering of regional planning in the late wartime and early post-war period of the 1940s, these most dogmatic of pioneers of British planning could not foresee the impact of the plans of the coming decade. Osborn was to come to take a more kindly view of the Clyde Valley Plan, at least. Others have shared Adams's charity even towards the experiments prior to the blossoming of regional plans in the 1940s. Cherry (1980a, 14–16) suggests that 'the inter-war

Regional Reports can shed important light on the development of British planning thought and practice in that period.'

As late as the 1920s, surveys rather than plans dominated the regional field. Geddes and his contemporaries had pioneered civic surveys and descriptive studies in regionalism, to which planning and proposals for regional improvement were only occasionally attached. The Domesday Book had, of course, been probably the earliest of regional surveys in England. Although the plantation of Ulster in the seventeenth century may have been regional planning of a kind, it took until the twentieth century for surveys on the British mainland to develop into initiatives in regional planning. Even at the end of the twentieth century, indeed, surveys remained too often a substitute for planning.

The transition from surveys to plans began after the First World War. A Joint Committee for the South Yorkshire coalfield was established even prior to the South Wales Regional Survey Committee of 1920 (Cherry 1974, 87), but the latter committee gathering together Government, local authorities, industrialists and trades unions was more of a landmark. Its survey led to broad proposals to divert growth to the plains south of the mining valleys, and to establish new dormitory towns; a regional town planning board was recommended to prepare a detailed development plan.

Although he was associated with the South Wales Survey, Patrick Abercrombie's central participation in the rise of regional planmaking in Britain began properly with the Doncaster Regional Planning Scheme of 1922. The first significant regional plan of modern British planning history, it arose from the rapid development of the Doncaster coalfield and migration of miners into allied conditions of ill-housing and inadequate sanitation. Abercrombie's plan was more for growth than for renewal or rehabilitation, but it was the first comprehensive regional plan in the country. Covering 169 square miles and a population of 139,940, its scale would seem modest by comparison with regional plans only two decades later, but it regarded Doncaster as a city which was 'in the truest sense of the word, metropolitan' (Abercrombie and Johnson 1922). This may have been partly consultants' flattery of their councillor clients, but it went in hand with proposals to offset Doncaster's dominance with 'ten more communities, new or so changed as to rank as new towns complete in themselves but of moderate size, manageable in their loose texture.' This was a strategy which Abercrombie would prescribe again and again for much larger regions throughout Britain in the coming thirty years.

The reasons for regional planning arising in the 1920s and 1930s may commonly have been less strategic and visionary than narrow and local. Massey (1989) attributes the movement primarily to the wish of local planners to regulate locally within a convenient context. An example was the Manchester and District Joint Town Planning Advisory Committee, formed in 1921 after a conference representing 76 local authorities within a 15 mile radius of the city. Within four years, generally agreed outline proposals for regional roads, broad zoning and regional open spaces had been adopted by what had grown to become the South Lancashire and North Cheshire Advisory Planning Committee. It was decided that the best practicable course in order to prepare a detailed plan would be to set up a number of decentralised, statutory regional planning committees, under Section 2 of the Town Planning Act, 1925, enabling the formation of statutory committees to prepare and adopt joint planning schemes. The individual councils in membership of the Advisory Committee retained authority for interim development control, but were obliged to have regard to any preliminary proposals agreed from time to time between the regional committee and its members.

The Manchester Regional Planning Committee for the metropolitan core of the wider region met for the first time in 1928, comprising the City of Manchester and 14 other local authorities, all drawn from the county of Lancashire and excluding any authorities for suburban areas on the southern, Cheshire side of the conurbation. Other statutory regional planning committees formed, however, cooperating with the Manchester Committee through the South Lancashire and North Cheshire Advisory Planning Committee. With 14 participating sub-regional statutory planning committees in 1945, the Advisory Committee's history well reflected the multi-tiered complexity and dynamics of UK regional planning already well-evident in its experimental years.

Abercrombie dominated regional planning in this 'experimental' era. His work ran across all types of region. It was not primarily of the urban kind calling for prescriptions of new communities, and rural regions dominated his commissions by number – if not in significance. As late as 1932, the Cumbrian Regional Planning Scheme dealt primarily with the preservation of the traditional farmed and grazed landscape, and less seriously with the problems of the industrial coast. Nor did all the regional studies of the 1920s and 1930s combine survey and proposals in a balanced way. The Sheffield Civic Survey of 1924 remedied the deficiencies of underlying research and survey which Abercrombie conceded in his prior work in Doncaster. Moving on to the new East Kent coalfield, his prescription to support the opening of eighteen new pits was again for new small towns, eight of which would assist the modest expansion of older Kentish communities. This Regional Planning Scheme was less well regarded than that for Doncaster, at least amongst the local authorities. It was a case of organisational failure; the authorities pursued parochial priorities and lacked any sustained regional will to implement Abercrombie's planning scheme.

The practice of Adams, Thompson and Fry was second only to Abercrombie's in regional planning consultancy. A dozen or more regional plans came from the partnership, whose plans have been described as being:

> representative examples of their genre, notable for their lucid if wooden exposition, relatively unsophisticated analyses of physical, economic and social conditions in the sketchy surveys and straightforward recommendations which unashamedly had more to do with common sense than environ-

mental science. British regional planning had little intellectual rationale.
Simpson (1985)

Davidge was also engaged in several of the regional reports of the period, and
Mawson's practice encompassed regional planning too.

US planning techniques and practice had little influence on this earlier era of
British regional planning as came in the 1960s. Adams's eight years on the New
York Regional Survey and Plan he completed by 1931 was not reflected in the
work of his British practice. Economic, demographic and transportation analyses
and forecasting methods pioneered in the United States in this period were not
quickly transferred to Britain, perhaps because British practice was dominated by
those of an architectural or a surveying background. Indeed, methods of forecasting drawn from the economic and social sciences were still not widely taught in
British planning schools until the 1960s.

Abercrombie was perhaps not the catalyst for the regional planning to which
he contributed so much, although he was a consistent advocate for it in journals
and public places. If there was a single catalyst, it was George Pepler, principal
planner to Government from 1919 to 1946. As civil servant in the Ministry of
Health and as Hon. Secretary and President of the Town Planning Institute, and
as promoter and propogandist for planning, Pepler was in a position of greater
infuence than Abercrombie. His roles made him a sustained stimulus to local
authority action, to the launch of Regional Advisory Committees under the
provisions of the Housing and Town Planning Act of 1919, and to the commissioning of Abercrombie in so many cases. The Act enabled local authorities to
transfer their planning powers to the committees to prepare regional planning
schemes, but these voluntary arrangements stopped short of real machinery to
implement regional proposals on a collective and consistent basis.

By 1928, 55 town-planning regions were recognised by the Ministry of
Health, following the first created for the Doncaster region. Some of the regions
were contained within others, and they ranged in scale from the Midlands and
Manchester to Tonbridge and Leek. Many like the Chipping Norton and Rochdale
regions now seem mis-described, but it was only after the Local Government Act
of 1929 that county councils had a statutory right to plan, and before that the
regional committees were the principal means of planning at above the level of
small towns and urban districts.

Local political tolerance was needed if local authorities were to rise above their
own levels to join in wider planning, and the pattern of cooperation was inevitably
erratic and necessarily ad hoc. As Cherry comments: 'Regional planning... was
taken up by local authorities because its measures seemed not to hurt anyone, they
seemed full of promise, they cost little and offered cooperation rather than conflict'
(Wannop and Cherry 1994).

Slowly, the joint arrangements moved out of the less contentious advisory mode
to cover the more difficult processes of executing regional strategies. In 1926 there
were 33 advisory and only one executive joint committee. Four years later, in 1930,

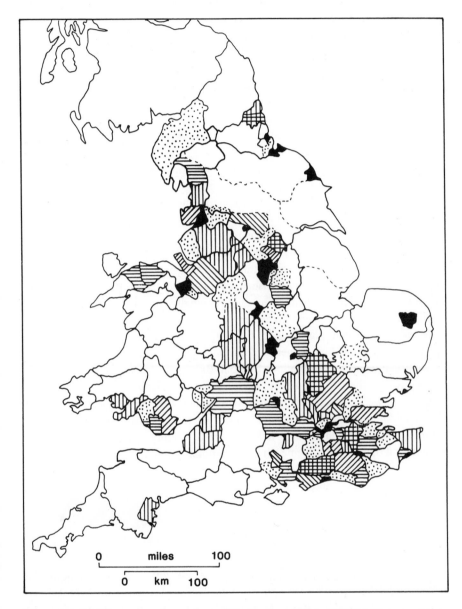

Figure 1.1. 104 Town planning regions of England and Wales 1930

there were some 60 joint advisory and 20 joint executive committees, involving some 880 local authorities (Hardy 1991, 188), although Fawcett (1930) accepted only two of the regions as being properly executive in character. Fawcett also noted some ten regional committees clustering within what later became the area of the Greater London Council, and other clusters in the West Midlands and in the traditional industrial parts of the North West and North of England. In 1931 a third of England and Wales was covered by joint committees, from Cumberland to Kent. By 1932 there were 60 advisory and 48 executive committees, from whom 30 regional planning schemes had emerged in England and three in Scotland. By 1938 the combined total of advisory and executive committees had reached 138 (Wannop and Cherry 1994). Not all committees were dependent on consultants. Some employed a few staff of their own, as notably the Manchester and District and Midlands Committees (Massey 1989).

When the economic depression came to dominate politics in 1931, the proliferation of joint planning initiatives brought a government departmental committee to examine them and particularly their planning proposals, as the possible basis for a programme of public works. Chaired by Lord Chelmsford, the committee concluded that the various reports did not add up to a coherent basis for a programme because they covered only 20 per cent of England and Wales, were unable to embrace redevelopment schemes for built-up areas, did not identify public works and were mostly advisory and interim in nature (Hardy 1991, 188). The joint committees had failed to plan regionally in a way which could have brought them political credit. Whether or not more could reasonably have been expected of regional planning in the 1920s, it had not met its first major opportunity to contribute to national development planning.

Regional planning's limitations in urban Britain were matched in the country-side. Only after the 1932 Town and Country Planning Act were local government's planning powers extended to rural areas, although there were instances as in the North Riding of Yorkshire where County Clerks were supportive of country planning. With the increasing involvement of county councils, there was an acceleration of planning schemes through regional committees from 1933 to 1937 (Massey 1989, 73). Thereafter, it would be six years before the establishment of the Ministry of Town and Country Planning in 1943 presaged a classic period of regional planning, and it would be a decade before the Town and Country Planning Act of 1947 made county development planning universal. After that, Tonbridge, Rochdale and Chipping Norton could no longer be regarded as British planning regions.

The transition from the modest regional planning of the 1930s to the ambitious and comprehensive plans which emerged in the mid and later 1940s was ensured by the (Barlow) Report of the Royal Commission on the Distribution of the Industrial Population. Appropriately published in 1940 as one decade turned into another, the Barlow Report gave strong answers to Government's questions about the economic and social impacts of industrial restructuring, and about uneven regional development. The Commission argued for an integrated linkage of the intra-regional planning for urban growth and conservation so assiduously fostered by Pepler, to the inter-regional unemployment and economic initiatives taken to quell the concern for the regions of the country most severely damaged by the 1930s Depression.

Government did not meet the Barlow Commission's case for a unified national planning authority to balance the distribution of industry in the UK, and to help decentralise people and industry from the congested and unfit metropolitan areas. When the Ministry of Town and Country Planning was established in 1943, its responsibilities embraced only land use planning and not industrial location, of which the Board of Trade took full charge in 1945. So the two main strands of regional planning were separated, and they were to remain uncomfortably so in a way which bedevilled all the subsequent history of regional planning in England, though not so much so in Scotland, Northern Ireland and Wales.

However, the Barlow Report did mark a change in the scale of and status of regional planning in Britain, and it opened the way to the classic period of the 1940s.

1940–1947: The Classic Vintage

Reformist imagination was liberated under the stress of war, when planning became for many not just the context for rebuilding bombed cities, but the path to social reform in housing, education, health and in all the social inequities of the 1930s. Whatever the primacy of the war effort, the Government could not ignore liberal pressures rising within the country and within the coalition administration. One response was to establish a Ministry of Town and Country Planning in 1943, and the new ministry became the stimulus to regional planning through the late wartime and early peacetime periods.

The first Ministry for planning was the opportunity to not only stimulate plans, but also to create new means of fulfilling them. It enabled moves towards legislation to build new towns through which regional development could be pursued, and to create national parks by which the finest landscape was to be conserved. And it was a stimulus not only within England and Wales. When the Secretary of State for Scotland soon after launched the Clyde Valley Plan, his motive was partly to preclude the new department for England and Wales extending its authority to control planning in Scotland.

A classic vintage of regional planning was now laid down, gathered over a period of only five years late in the war and in the early peace. Only a handful of plans, but significant beyond anything before and of enduring influence. No subsequent regional plans have had greater impact than those for Greater London and the Clyde Valley, and Abercrombie was author of both. And in other regions of Britain, there was a last flowering of the 30 year era of regional planning by consultancies.

Regional planning had begun to revive even before the Ministry of Town and Country Planning was formed, because the Government had already arranged for work to be started on Abercrombie's plan for Greater London. But the new ministry raised planning to a new status in government, although without the legislation enacted by the Labour government elected in 1945, regional planning's new substance would have faded through lack of machinery for implementation.

The *Greater London* and *Clyde Valley* plans were the peaks of the achievements of the period. Regional surveys or plans were made also for Hull, Merseyside, Manchester, South Wales and Monmouthshire, South Lancashire and North Cheshire, the West Midlands, the Black Country, North East England, Central and South East Scotland, and the Tay Valley. But these others were less dramatic than the two outstanding metropolitan plans. Some, like those for Manchester and for Central and South East Scotland, avoided the issue of new towns or left unresolved the question of where most overspilled metropolitan population would be re-housed. Others remained cast in the mould of the regional surveys characteristic of earlier times; the greatest by area and scope was the *West Highland Survey* by Fraser Darling (1954), completed in 1950 after six years of work. Only in the Manchester region was the plan's direction largely in the hands of local government; elsewhere, consultants were at least nominally in charge, whatever the background pressures and inputs from local government. Together with Abercrombie, Lock, Longstreth Thompson, Lloyd and Jackson, Mears, Pepler and Macfarlane, and Payne were all authors of plans for regions covering more than half of Britain's population.

The bloom on this classic growth of regional planning had faded by 1950, overtaken by the budding of the first development plans amongst the county councils, cities and county boroughs of Britain. The stem of regional planning would not flower again for another twenty years, but its classic vintage of the mid 1940s remains memorable. It was harvested from a crop of regional plans of unprecedented scale, force and scope.

1948–61: The Fallow Years

Regional plans by Pepler and MacFarlane for North East England and by Payne for the Tay Valley were not concluded until 1949; contention about regrouping settlements and about extra new towns for the North East caused that *Outline Development Plan* to remain unpublished (Hudson 1989, 211), and the *Tay Valley Plan* was a slight work. So 1948 can reasonably be regarded as the first of the fallow years of regional planning, following the great Town and Country Planning Act of 1947 (Wannop and Cherry 1994, 40).

Great progressive legislation that it was, the 1947 Act actually helped bring a suspension of regional planning. With a wave of plans behind it, the Government now turned to launching the new towns, urban renewal and other initiatives which the classic period of regional planning had crystallised. And local planning authorities turned to prepare development plans for the counties and county boroughs. So when in 1951 a Conservative government began thirteen years of continuous administration, its antipathy to planning and to regionalism and preoccupation with its promise to build more council houses than its Labour forerunners precluded any quick revival of regional planning. Initially, the political necessity to increase the output of new council houses caused the creation of eleven Regional Housing Production Boards, but these were later abandoned. Government departments progressively reduced or withdrew regional staff. By 1956, the abandonment of the Treasury's Regional Organisation Committee ended the procedures by which departments were obliged to obtain approval for expenditure deviating from the Standard Regional structure (Smith 1964, 22). Departments were now allowed to freely draw their own regional boundaries and to abandon any semblance of regional administration. The Ministry of Housing and Local Government had closed all its regional offices by 1958.

1962–71: The Regional Revival
1962–64: IN SEARCH OF REGIONAL PLANNING

The 1960s brought two rising pressures for regional planning. First, the government became acutely anxious about the electoral consequences of deteriorating economic conditions in Northern England and Scotland. Regional programmes abhorred in the 1950s now became a welcome means of advertising the Government's concern for voters in the region. Programmes could be anticipated by regional studies, prepared and published more quickly than any programme could be implemented. Secondly, projections of future national population growth came to far exceed the capacity of local authority development plans, or of the new towns being urgently launched or expanded. The assumptions of the great regional plans of the late 1940s had inevitably been overtaken by events, and government planners (Powell 1960) were publicly announcing the need for new frameworks for regional planning.

Government ministers did not immediately share the urgency of some of their planners (Powell 1978, 7). A range of regional studies was prepared in the early 1960s, but most fell far short of turning survey into plan. The Ministry of Housing and Local Government's South East Study (1964) documented the issues in the region, but did not propose a framework in which they might be tackled, although it did prepare the ground for the region's second generation of larger new towns planted in the middle part of the decade. The Study covered two-fifths of the population and economic activity of England and Wales, but its origins in the government's ministry for housing and land use meant that it largely excluded economic issues.

Lack of an economic dimension was not the case with the parallel studies in Scotland on Central Scotland: Programme for Development and Growth Scottish Development Department (1963a), and in England by the Department of Trade and Industry on The North East: A programme for regional development and growth (1963), which were positive planning programmes with both physical and economic dimensions. Although, as Powell (1978, 7) emphasises, these harbingers of a revived government concern for creative regional planning did not wholly marry physical and economic matters, they at least came between the covers of one planning document. Both plans would later be seen as seriously flawed in respects, particularly in the case of Central Scotland, but they marked the rediscovery of regional planning after nearly fifteen barren years.

1964–67: THE REGIONAL RESURGENCE

In 1964, the election of the first Labour government for thirteen years brought planning back to the heart of economic and social policy. Uneasy as was the marriage of its physical and economic components, regional planning and development became vogueish government activities. The first two studies completed in the new era were left over from its predecessor. The *West Midlands Study* (Department of Economic Affairs, 1965) was regarded as realistic because willing to discuss possible regional strategy without waiting for exhaustive data; but the *North West Study* (Department of Economic Affairs, 1965) was derided (Smith 1966, 251) because despite its wealth of statistics it was reluctant to come to strategic conclusions without further comprehensive survey. But both studies came from an old mould in which until 'we know everything about everything we cannot begin to understand what is happening, and therefore it would be foolish for us to presume to interfere' (Smith 1966, 252).

The attempted breakthrough to more dynamic strategic planning was led by the *National Plan* (Department of Economic Affairs, 1965), looking ahead to subsequent studies of how the regions could contribute to national growth, anticipating feasibility studies of possible estuarine cities to be developed on Severnside, Humberside and Tayside. More new towns were launched. Sub-regional studies were commissioned or encouraged in those industrial regions of England where expanding cities were most seriously in dispute with their surrounding counties about future growth. In the West of Scotland, the Scottish Office led local authorities in speculative land use studies to find possibilities for long-term urban growth.

Strategic planning followed rather than preceded many of these local studies and developments. The scale and urgency of the pressures for urban growth seemed so large that a full national framework would have to follow upon regional initiatives, rather than the other way round. Regional planning teams were being assembled for the South East, the West Midlands, the North West and for West Central Scotland. Twenty-five years after its last high tide, regional planning had again advanced fully into government favour. Bringing up the rear, an Inter-departmental Study Group under the leadership of the Department of the Environment was made responsible for a study of *Long Term Population Distribution in Great Britain*.

Reporting in 1971, the Inter-departmental Group observed that population projections had become less expansive than they had been ten years before. The national pressures for urban growth which had launched the wave of studies and plans of the mid to late 1960s were now easing, and although the North West of

England was still expected to suffer acutely, the demand for extra urbanisation might not now encroach as expected on the estuaries of the Severn, Humber and Tay.

The impetus for regional planning was also fuelled by the growth of land use transportation studies, which spread to most of the conurbation regions and to many lesser urban areas from the mid 1960s. These studies demanded long-term projections about future land use, employment, residential development and demography, although transportation consultants little appreciated the inherent uncertainties in such projections required to feed their computer models imported from the United States. Nor, generally, were planners reluctant to indulge in technically exciting but spuriously positive projections for many years into the future. Planners' professional collaboration underpinned transportation studies like those for South East Lancashire/North East Cheshire, the West Midlands and Greater Glasgow, all making assumptions about future regional growth implying regional planning strategies not approved as such. Subsequent regional plans were then faced with highway proposals, in particular, representing the sum of the ambitions of individual local authorities rather than any realistic programme of regional priorities.

1968–71: THE RE-INSTITUTIONALISATION OF REGIONAL PLANNING

As the resurgence of regional planning proceeded, it became almost wholly institutionalised. It was not a task now necessarily given to consultants as in the 1940s. Central and local governments were now stocked with professional planning staff – and a large base of geographers and economists amongst them. The Ministry of Housing and Local Government in England and Wales, and the Scottish Development Department in Scotland, wished to control the pace and framework of the plans. So the work was done largely by staff seconded from or appointed to the public service, however independent some of the planning teams succeeded in becoming.

In Yorkshire and Humberside and in the South West, the plans were authored by the Regional Economic Planning Councils; their narrow economic focus and insensitivity to many social questions betrayed their origin. In the West Midlands, the local authorities seized the initiative in strategy-making under threat of a government lead otherwise. In the South East, North West, East Anglia and the North, the arrangements were nominally tripartite – Government, local authorities and the regional economic planning council – but the Government pulled the strings to choose the teams' directors. Even so, Government's control was far from complete, for some regional teams produced some very radical proposals which some government departments found hard to accept.

The largest strategy was for the South East. For no other region was work so closely controlled, directed as it was by the Chief Planner to the Government, Wilfred Burns. So it was unsurprising that *The Strategic Plan for the South East* should have been so readily adopted. None of the succeeding English regional strategies

Year	East Anglia (EA)	East Midlands (EM)	Northern (N)	North-West (NW)	South-East (SE)	South-West (SW)	Yorkshire and Humberside (Y&H)	West Midlands (WM)
1964					'The SE Study' (MHLG) 'SE England' (Cmnd 2308)			
1965				'The NW- a regional study' (DEA)				'The WM- a regional study' (DEA)
1966		'The EM Study' (EMEPC)	'Challenge of the Changing North' (NEPC)	'An Economic Planning Strategy for the NW' (NWEPC)	'The Conference Area in the Long Term' (SCLSERP)		'A Review of Y&H' (YHEPC)	
1967					'A Strategy for the SE' (SEEPC)	A region with a future'- a draft strategy for the SW' (SWEPC)		'The WM- Patterns of Growth' (WMEPC)
1968	'EA: A Study' (EAEPC)			Strategy I: the NW of 1970's (NWEPC)				
1969		'Opportunity in the EM' (EMEPC)	'The outline strategy for the N' (NEPC)					
1970					'Strategic Plan for the SE' (SEJPT)		'Y&H Regional Srategy' (THEPC)	
1971								'The WM: an economic appraisal' (WMEPC) 'A Developing Strategy for the WM' (WMRS)
1972								
1973					'Strategic Planning in the SE: a first report of the Monitoring Group' (DOE)			
1974				'Strategic Plan for the NW' (NWJPT)		'A Strategic Settlement Pattern for the SW' (SWEPC)		'A Developing Strategy for the WM' (WMPAC)
1975	'Strategic Choice for EA' (EARST)			'Economic and social trends 1974' (NWEPC)				'A Developing Strategy for the WM : first monitoring report' (JMSG)
1976	'Stategic Choice for EA- first monitoring report' (EACC)	'A Forward Economic Look' (EMEPC)		'Economic and social trends 1975' (NWEPC)	'Strategy for the SE: 1976 review' (SEJPT)			'A Developing Strategy for the WM: second monitoring report' (JMSG)
1977			'Strategic Plan for the N region' (NRST)	'Economic and Social trends-1976' (NWEPC)				
1978		'A Forward Economic Look' (EMEPC)			'Strategic Plan for the SE' (DOE)	'Monitoring the Regional Strategy' (SWEPB)	'The Regional Development of Y and H' (SCCC)	
1979		'EM - a forward economic look 3rd edn' (EMEPC)	'First state of the region report' (NRJMT)					'Updating and Rolling Forward of the WM Regional Srategy' (JMSC) (WMEPC & WMPAC)
1980		'EM in Focus' (EM Forum)	'Second state of the region report' (NRJMT)		SE Regional Strategic Guidance (DOE)			
1981	'Regional Development Programme' (EACC)		'Third state of the Region Report' (NRCCA)		'SE Regional Planning- the 1980's (SCLSERP)		'Yorkshire Textile Action Area Plan' (RPCY & NI)	

Figure 1.2. Regional planning in England 1964–81: plans and major reports

were so quickly or so substantially absorbed by government. The reasons lay not only in the participation of the Chief Planner, but also in a concentration upon proposals almost wholly in the ambit of its sponsoring ministry. Despite a serious underlying economic analysis and the secondment to the team of staff from several government ministries, the significant proposals of the *Strategic Plan* were for the location of urban growth and for countryside conservation. It was less the first of the new wave of regional plans of the 1970s than a reminder of the plans of the 1940s. Indeed, Abercrombie's *Greater London Plan 1944* had been far more ambitious in scope.

The *West Midlands Regional Study* was the other major English regional plan of the period, and it escaped the Government. Managed by the local authorities and under the direction of an independently minded senior planner seconded by the City of Birmingham, it pursued a physical strategy for the region which became largely unacceptable to government officials and politicians. As in the South East, the region's major problem was to find room to house metropolitan growth. The solution recommended by the *Study* of small new towns detached from the conurbation was as unacceptable to some of the sponsoring authorities as to the Government, and after being completed in 1974 the strategy was recast and reissued as the framework for structure planning in the region.

Collectively of comparable significance to any of the full regional plans were the sub-regional studies and plans of this period. The most important were for the most pressurised city regions outside the metropolitan areas, particularly studies and strategies for *Leicester/Leicestershire* (1969), *Notts/Derbyshire* (1969), *Teesside* (1969) and *Coventry/Solihull/Warwickshire* (1971). The Government brokered these joint studies where tensions between local authorities had delayed strategies for inter-related growth. Local political sensibilities led to county council studies around Cambridge and Peterborough being described as sub-regional, although neither town was itself a local planning authority. For South Hampshire, two strategies were prepared in fairly quick succession.

There were some thirty other cases of sub-regional studies or plans in the resurgence of the 1960s and 1970s. Some were locally regarded as regional plans, although not as large as government plans and studies for the English standard regions. They spread geographically from the Belfast region to South West England, and to the Cambridge sub-region. Their status ranged from studies and plans on behalf of the Scottish Office and the Ministry of Housing and Local Government, to reports and planning proposals by local authorities and the regional economic planning councils. Their circumstances and their purposes greatly varied.

In Scotland, the close but not always parallel interests of economic and physical planners had produced a series of integrated regional reports from the late 1960s and into the early 1970s. Sometimes these were done by consultants as for the Falkirk–Grangemouth growth area, for the North East of Scotland and for the Borders, and sometimes primarily from planners of the Development Department as for Tayside and the South West of Scotland. The Highlands and Islands had their own development agency with its own strategy. Populous Central Scotland had had a programme of priorities and investment laid down in 1963, but not followed-up through the kind of interpretation of broad strategic guidelines by which structure plans would later bridge between National Planning Guidelines and local plans. Although joint local authority and Development Department land use working parties in the West of Scotland explored the feasibility of massive urban expansion, to cope with growth projected in the mid 1960s and also to pave the way for the designation of Stonehouse new town, the planning bridge for this most problematic region was not completed until 1974, when the *West Central Scotland Plan* presented the first comprehensive programme of action for the physical and economic restructuring of Clydeside since the *Clyde Valley Plan* of 29 years before.

The sub-regional plans particularly reflected the cultural transition occurring in this period. A generation brought up on Abercrombie's methods and classic plans directed the major regional plans of the 1960s. But their technical staff and the leaders of the sub-regional studies were social scientists, schooled in the newer analytical methods developing in geography and in the computerised techniques of land use/transportation studies. So the main report on the *Strategic Plan for the South East* (1970) was cast in the style of Abercrombie, but supplementary volumes reflected the new rising techniques of economic analysis, of objective setting, and of the generation and evaluation of alternative strategies. These new methods of 'rational' planning were even more visible in the *West Midlands Study* (1971) and came to the fore in the sub-regional studies for Teesside (1969), Leicester–Leicestershire (1969), Nottinghamshire–Derbyshire (1969) and for Coventry–Solihull–Warwickshire (1971). Concepts of flexibility and of systematic monitoring emerged, and the issue of resources took some plans close to budgetary planning.

1972–78: The Rebirth of Physio-Economic Planning

The new culture meant not only change in the emphases and methods of regional planning, but also in its political implications. Together with the *Strategy for the Northern Region* and the *West Central Scotland Plan*, the *Strategic Plan for the North West* raised very testing issues for government. All three plans aimed to help rectify their regions' comparative imbalances in housing, economic and environmental conditions. In doing so, they not only sought financial advantages for their regions, but they stepped on the responsibilities of departments of government other than that principally sponsoring them. Accordingly, the Government could accept some of the strategies' more central proposals only by adjusting national economic strategy, and by disturbing inter-regional political balances within the country. This was more than ministers expected from regional planning.

Like the *Strategic Plan for the North West* just before it, the *West Central Scotland Plan* called for national policy changes. But unlike the English plans, the special

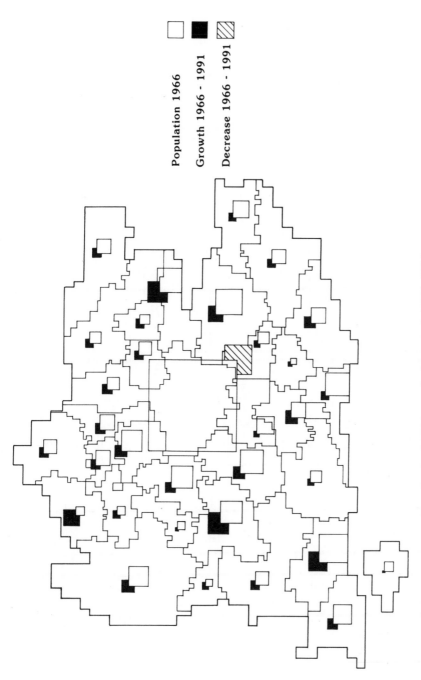

Figure 1.3. Strategic Plan for South East England 1970: population growth 1966–1991

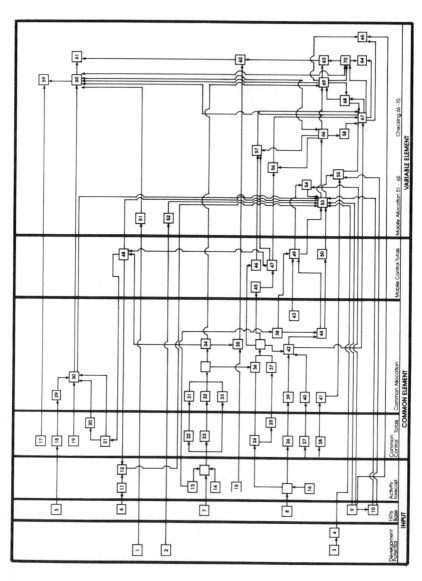

Figure 1.4. Systems circuitry: the technical process network for the Coventry–Solihull–Warwickshire Sub-Regional Study 1971

INPUT

a) Development Potential

1 Evaluate transportation implications of territory strategies (delineation of conurbation process)
2 Calculate industrial development potential surfaces 1969 and 1991
3 Calculate residential development potential surfaces for each strategy of 1969 and 1991
4 Produce residential development potential maps for 1976-91 strategy growth (km²)

b) 1976 Base

5 Add "certain" new links to Base Year Network (= 1976 certain network)
6 Sum 1969-76 land use change and add to 1969 developed land to give 1976 developed land (km²)
7 Add 1966-76 net change to 1966 population to give 1976 population distribution (km²)
8 Add 1966-76 employment distribution (km²)
9 Identify location of undeveloped land available for strategy growth (km²)
10 Identify outstanding commitments, residential and industrial at 1976 (km²)

c) Activity Forecasts

11 Estimate future densities and make allocation assumptions in relation to residential land, industrial land, and total land requirements 1976-91
12 Estimate total land requirements 1976-91
13 Population forecasts 1976-91
14 Household forecast 1976-91
15 Identify changes in household car ownership 1966-91
16 Employment forecast 1976-91

COMMON ELEMENT

a) Common Control Totals

17 Obtain Midland Regional Synthetic Traffic Model 1974 through/external trip matrices and assignment
18 Identify 1976-91 inter-urban trunk road schemes
19 Identify principal road schemes "already in pipeline" 1966-91
20 Calculate residual principal road expenditure for fixed population growth
21 Identify principal road expenditure 1966-91
22 Calculate adjustment factors to reflect 1976-91 mobile strategy growth
23 Calculate total housing replacement needs 1976-91
24 Identify split between centralised service jobs and population-based service jobs
25 Estimate deficiency in provision of centralised service jobs and population-based service jobs at 1976 and population-job ratios
26 Identify jobs displaced by redevelopment and voluntary industrial relocation 1976-91
27 Identify jobs fixed by site 1976-91 - mining manufacturing (part), services (part)
28 Identify mobile industrial jobs 1976-91

b) Common Allocation

29 Add 1976-91 inter-urban trunk road schemes to 1976 certain network
30 Add principal road schemes within residual expenditure to 29 (=1991 "committed" highway network)
31 Add 1976 population to 1976-91 change in household size and vacancy rate to give 1991 population within 1976 dwelling stock (TZ)
32 Estimate scale of local clearance need, future capacity of redevelopment sites and number of households displaced due to housing redevelopment (TZ)
33 Estimate increase in capacity of 1976 developed land area due to infilling 1976-91 (TZ)
34 Calculate 1991 population and households in 1976 developed land area (=fixed population) and disaggregate to (km²)
35 Calculate 1991 car ownership of fixed household distribution (TZ)
36 Allocate centralised and population-based service jobs to new residential areas and to jobs to areas of net population increase and to areas of net population decline within 1976 developed area (TZ) using population-job ratios (km²)
37 Allocate increments of service jobs to remedy relative deficiencies in provision 1976-91 (km²)
38 Identify natural increase of population by Local Authority areas, distinguishing separately the "rural" parts of rural districts

c) Mobile Control Totals

39 Allocate jobs lost to new service by redevelopment and voluntary relocation 1976-91 (km²)
40 Allocate jobs fixed by site 1976-91 (km²)
41 Identify approximate local authority share of mobile industrial jobs 1976-91 (LA)
42 Calculate new employment common to all strategies = fixed basic job growth 1976-91 (km²)
43 Calculate shift mobile projection of population distribution Strategy 906 only (LA)
44 Preliminary population and job allocation cycle
45 Calculate residual increases in population growth service jobs related to strategy population growth
46 Estimate proportion of growth of centralised services in central areas and in district centres
47 Estimate population-serving ratio for population-based jobs for strategy population growth
48 Calculate residential population and households to be accommodated in new residential areas (=mobile strategy growth)
49 Identify population to be allocated in each "greater" Local Authority area (LA)
50 Identify jobs to be allocated in each "greater" Local Authority area (LA)

VARIABLE ELEMENT

a) Mobile Allocation

51 Identify conceptual strategy road network
52 Identify possible development potential surface and outstanding industrial commitments (km²)
53 Allocate strategy growth in population to new residential areas relative to residential commitments, approximate graded development potentials, local authority population and job yardsticks, committed 1991 highway network tied job distribution and possible sites for new industry (km²)
54 Allocate population growth in rural areas and adjust shift (model control totals for Strategy 906 (TZ and km²)
55 Identify industrial sites and allocate mobile manufacturing jobs relative to industrial potentials local authority yardsticks, assumed origin of jobs outstanding commitments and preliminary allocation of population (km² population-based)
56 Allocate residual growth in population-based service jobs to new residential areas (km²)
57 Allocate residual growth in centralised jobs to central areas and district centres (including external centres) based on defined catchment areas (km²)
58 Allocate net growth in construction jobs, associated with road schemes new residential areas and redevelopment (km²)
59 Obtain MRSTM 1991 through/external trip matrices and assignment
60 Identify new principal road schemes to serve strategy growth; add to and adjust 1991 committed highway network where necessary
61 Identify 1991 trip generation rate assumptions for internal trips (TZ)
62 Calculate 1991 car ownership for strategy households and add to 1991 fixed car ownership (TZ)
63 Sum population data to 1991 traffic zones and convert to equivalent households (TZ)
64 Sum job data to 1991 traffic zones and adjust list for decline in agriculture and industries inadequately described (TZ)
65 Estimate distribution of developed land 1976-91 and check against original density assumptions and developed land pre-1976 : constrain developed land to single developed land totals (km²)

b) Checking

66 Modify strategy population allocation in light of field survey, changes in potentials (1966-91) objective weights, and possible new principal road links (km²)
67 Sum strategy growth in jobs for all sectors and add to common job distribution to give total 1991 population
68 Check population/job distribution against commuting assumptions
69 Sum strategy population allocation to 1991 fixed population to give total 1991 population distribution (km²)
70 Create 1991 traffic zones

Notes

1 The numbers refer to the attached diagrammatic network of the detailing process; their order does not represent the actual sequence of operations
2 Activity distributions were generally allocated to either local authority areas (LA), traffic zones (TZ) or kilometre grid squares (km²)

Figure 1.4. (continued) Systems circuiting: key to the technical process network

circumstances of Scottish politics and government enabled the major strategic recommendations of the *West Central Scotland Plan* to be quickly accepted and fulfilled. The *Plan's* proposal for an economic development corporation for Strathclyde was implemented by a new Labour government in the form of the Scottish Development Agency. And uniquely amongst regional plans in Britain, the *West Central Scotland Plan* was fortuitously succeeded by the creation of a regional council, fully embracing not only the whole area of the *Plan* but also its major proposals. So the Government was led to abandon the new town of Stonehouse and to turn to new approaches to regenerate Glasgow such as the GEAR project. Of all regional plans in British history, none was more quickly adopted.

The Northern Region team was the last to be instituted and to report, which it did in 1977. Under the direction of Bevan Waide, it followed the lead of the *West Central Scotland Plan* in compiling a profile of government expenditure for its region. The task in the Northern Region was technically as difficult, and was more so politically as there was no minister to fight the regional case in Whitehall. The Scottish Office was not only highly sympathetic to the *West Central Scotland Plan's* approach to economic policy, but it had long experience in fighting in Whitehall for Scottish interests. Civil servants in the Northern Region were perhaps more inclined to play a partisan regional role than colleagues in other English regional offices, but their first responsibility was to their departmental ministers and not to a regional minister like the Secretary of State for Scotland. So the significant proposals in the *Strategic Plan* for the North were too difficult for Government to accept. The strategic team called above all for changes in national measures to help the economy of the North; there were no significant accompanying proposals which could have been implemented without implications for other regions.

Fearing the example of the opaque response issued to the *Strategic Plan for the North West*, the Northern Region team called on government to definitively state what of the *Strategic Plan for the Northern Region* it actually approved. This was too optimistic a call. Government chose to make no official response to the team's report, whatsoever. Only after a Conservative minister came to office in 1979 was there a public announcement on the strategy submitted to his Labour predecessor two years before. It was stated that the strategy was a case of special pleading for the region, was too broad in scope and had been overtaken by circumstances.

The *East Anglia Strategy* was less immediate than the others in the sense that it assumed as a principal objective the raising of debate about the long-term quality of life in the region. As a region which promised to sustain major immigration far into its future, the strategy team under the direction of Tony Bird felt that East Anglia should face and debate some of the possible implications of this. It was therefore less preoccupied with the issue of short-term pressures for building land than was the *West Midland Strategy*, and less dominated by questions of poor housing and pollution than was the *Strategic Plan for the North West*. The East Anglia team uniquely employed a Delphi study to foresee some of the economic, social and technological changes which might impact upon the region's life and affairs.

Although the most exploratory and philosophic of the regional plans, the *East Anglia Strategy* also outlined the problems of disadvantage of rural dwellers and of their poor access to services. But the government's response to this was relatively less sympathetic than it had been to the North West team's case for recognition of urban disadvantage (Friend, Norris and Carter 1979). The *Strategy* displeased the local authorities too, who wholly opposed the suggestion that a body of civil servants was needed to plan and coordinate at regional level between central and local government. And the local authorities disagreed that substantial long-term growth in the region was inevitable.

Other significant innovations in the spirit of regional planning occurred in Scotland in this period. The most significant was the reorganisation of local government following a Royal Commission (1969) whose report put planning to the fore. Although only the Highland and Strathclyde regions were of a scale above that of an English county, all the new councils were required by the government to submit reports on their broad strategy not just for physical planning, but also for social and economic policy. This innovation of regional reports was accompanied by the start to a series of national planning guidelines issued by the Scottish Office, setting an all-Scottish framework for structure plans for the individual regions and island council areas.

The new emphases of UK regional planning in the 1970s changed the appearance of plan reports. It meant a progressive fading of the preoccupation with master regional diagrams of earlier periods. Many tables, figures and often distribution maps were bound into the texts, but no longer did the main report contain a pocket inside the end covers bulging with a regional master plan superimposed on an Ordnance map. And the technical appendices to the plans could occupy several volumes of economic analyses, or present abstruse accounts of mathematical models and other features of rational planning method.

1979–1990s: Regional Planning Scorned but Enduring

Even before Mrs Thatcher's government arrived in 1979 with an antipathy to planning unmatched since the Churchill government of 1951, regional planning had been receding. Population and urban growth had slowed, there was weakened confidence in longer term planning, strategic concern had shifted from overspill and new towns to the inner cities, and planners in the recently reorganised local authorities were preoccupied with preparing local and structure plans for their new areas.

The 'new right' ideology behind the new government scorned the decade of the 1960s, regarded as the source of consensual politics and all that was evilly permissive. As a feature of the 1960s, regional planning was damned for its supposed failure and transient fashionability. But as the decade progressed, political ideology was unable to suppress the need for regional planning. The return to planning came when the government's aim that developers might enjoy a free market to provide new houses in the countryside of South East England was challenged by its own supporters, anxious to protect their green belt backyards from building. And when builders demanded a sufficient supply of land and rational regional planning, ideology gave way to reality. Regional planning became a political necessity. This became even more obvious in the late 1980s, when London's transport problems intensified and the lack of an effective strategic planning authority was accentuated by the abolition of the GLC – and not wholly made up by the formation of the London Planning Advisory Committee.

Standing conferences of local planning authorities for South East England and the West Midlands had been continuous since the 1960s, but in other regions collaboration was less sustained or substantial until the mid 1980s, when a new willingness to collaborate spread to most regions of England and to Wales. The formation of the Standing Conference of East Anglian Local Authorities in 1987 led, two years later, to the completion of a strategy containing elements of regional advocacy, on which the Government's subsequent regional planning guidance for East Anglia published in 1991 avoided commitment.

In most cases, staffing of the regional conferences was slight and lacked permanency. Such as the East Midlands Regional Forum rotated not just the chairmanship but also the secretariat. The conditions did not help continuity or commitment. The *Regional Strategy for the East Midlands* for 15 years, published by the East Midlands Regional Forum in 1992, was characterised as comprising a shopping list of current proposals, pet projects and pious political expectations (Minay *et al.* 1992, 423). The Forum quickly turned to a review of the *Strategy* in 1994, following publication of the Department of the Environment's planning guidance for the region; but staff on short-term contracts were likely to be as preoccupied with their own future as with that of the East Midlands. In the North East, the strategic planning framework proposed to Government in 1992 by the county councils for Cleveland, Durham and Northumberland excluded the Tyne–Wear conurbation, for which the Department of Environment (1989) had already issued strategic guidance. Not only did the wider framework omit the economic and population focus of the region, but it barely referred to financial institutions, investment or travel-to-work areas (Minay *et al.* 1992, 425). At the opposite extreme of England, there was at least no arbitrary division of the South West region where the Conference's process of developing a plan engaged most of the region's interests.

When, in 1992, the local authorities of North West England at last formed a regional planning conference after years of failure, there was for the first time a complete coverage of England by standing regional conferences. They were of varying intensity and commitment, but they were an opportunity within which regional problems could be mediated as far as local government had the capacity to do so. Although in some cases formed only after long pressure from Government, these conferences met extreme disinterest when their planning led to claims for more public resources for their regions. And although such as the West Midlands Forum, in particular, had taken periodic initiatives towards coordinating their members' structure plans, the larger role of most of these cooperative arrangements tended to be in communication between the partners; policy initiation came to the fore less often.

In Wales, the Welsh Office took a positive lead in strategic planning by encouraging the Assembly of Welsh Counties to take a lead in coordinating development plans and programmes. It was also made clear that this would be done through guidelines, and not by anything describable as a regional plan. Even so, the scope of the Assembly's consultations in 1992 included at least two very political issues: how adequate or not were current approaches to economic development, and how could policies for affordable housing be employed to protect Welsh-speaking communities? These questions begged answers which might be as awkward for the Government as the issues of the 1970s, which had led to a decade's suspension of regional planning.

In Scotland, innovative ways in regional planning were succeeded by the formalities of statutory structure planning from the late 1970s. Although authored by regional councils, the plans were not distinguishable from structure plans by English counties. Indeed, on the government's abolition of Scottish regional reports after 1979, it could be said that with all their failings, the English conferences of local authorities thereafter achieved a wider regional perspective in strategic planning than did the Scottish councils. National planning guidance from the Scottish Office fell well short of the scope of work by the Assembly of Welsh Counties, or of the most ambitious of the English conferences of county councils. And facing the Scottish regional and islands councils was their abolition by the late 1990s, with no system of strategic cooperation considered with the options for their reshaping. So while again acceptable in the 1990s, the formalised system of British regional planning had very uneven substance, and without more responsibility being given it, it was questionable whether it could maintain impetus. The regional guidance issued by the Department of the Environment and its counterparts in Scotland and Wales seemed often tentative, was passive more than progressive, and made few promises of public initiative. It reflected the ambivalence of a government torn between an ideological abhorrence of intervention in the land market, and political awareness that some interventions were needed to capture the votes of key groups of people and of key localities. Strategic planning was accordingly complicated by government agencies introduced to intervene in politically sensitive issues of urban and regional development. This had been particularly the trend in Scotland since the 1930s, intensifying since the late 1970s when the Scottish Development Agency was sometimes superseding the strategic planning role of the regional councils. In England, the urban development agencies had been followed in 1992 by English Partnerships, bringing a new agency of even greater scope to influence regional development strategy.

The marked tendency to widen the responsibilities of its agencies was a move by Government to capture historic functions from local government. It meant also that Government was increasingly adopting a regional frame of influence, but not in a well planned frame of inter-considered actions. Local government had been given extra responsibility to initiate regional strategies, but now had lessened authority to implement them.

Figure 1.5 Chronology of principal regional plans and studies in the UK

1086	Domesday Book
1910	Board of Trade London Traffic Study
1910 (circa)	Civic Surveys of Greater London, South Lancashire and South Yorkshire
1920	Report of South Wales Regional Survey
1922	Doncaster Regional Planning Scheme (Abercrombie and Johnson)
1923	Deeside Regional Planning Scheme (Abercrombie, Fyfe and Kelly)
1924	West Middlesex Regional Planning Scheme (Adams, Fry and Thompson)
1925	East Kent Regional Survey (Abercrombie and Archibald)
1925	South Teesside Regional Planning Scheme (Abercrombie and Adshead)
1925	Rotherham Regional Planning Scheme Report (Davidge)
1926	Manchester and District Joint Committee Regional Scheme
1926	Wirral Regional Planning Scheme
1926	Leeds and Bradford Region Joint Town Planning Committee Preliminary Report
1927	Hertfordshire Regional Planning Report (Davidge)
1927	Chesterfield Regional Planning Scheme (Adshead)
1927	Lancaster and Morecambe Regional Planning Scheme (Forshaw)
1927	West Kent Regional Planning Report (Davidge)
1928	East Kent Regional Planning Scheme (Abercrombie and Archibald)
1928	North Middlesex Regional Planning Scheme (Adams, Fry and Thompson)
1928	North West Surrey Regional Planning Scheme (Adams, Fry and Thompson)
1928	Mid-Surrey Regional Planning Scheme (Adams, Fry and Thompson)
1928	South Bucks and Thamesside Region Report (Davidge)

1928	South Tyneside Regional Town Planning Scheme
1929	Greater London Regional Planning Committee. First Report (Unwin)
1929	North East Lancashire Regional Planning Report (Bruce)
1929	Mid Cheshire Joint Town Planning Advisory Committee Report
1929	Thames Valley Amenity Survey (Abercrombie, Adshead and Earl of Mayo)
1929	West Sussex Coast and Downs Regional Planning Scheme (Schofield)
1930	Wye Valley Regional Planning Scheme (Abercrombie and Kelly)
1930	Bath and Bristol Regional Planning Scheme (Abercrombie and Brueton)
1930	North East Kent Regional Planning Scheme (Adams, Thompson and Fry)
1930	Berkshire Regional Planning Survey (Davidge)
1930	Buckinghamshire Regional Plan (Davidge)
1930	Lake District (South) Regional Planning Scheme (Mattocks)
1930	South West Lancashire Plan (Sharp)
1931	Sheffield and District Regional Planning Scheme (Abercrombie and Kelly)
1931	North East Sussex Regional Planning Scheme (Davidge)
1931	South East Sussex Regional Planning Scheme
1931	West Surrey Joint Town Planning Committee Scheme (Adams, Fry and Thompson)
1931	Eastbourne and District Regional Planning Scheme (Adams)
1931	Midlands Joint Town Planning Advisory Council Regional Scheme
1931	Mid-Northamptonshire Regional Planning Scheme (Adams, Fry and Thompson)
1931	Oxfordshire Regional Planning Report (Abercrombie, Adshead and Earl of Mayo)
1931	South Essex Regional Planning Scheme (Adshead)
1931	North Tyneside Regional Planning Scheme
1932	Cumbrian Regional Planning Scheme (Abercrombie and Kelly)
1932	Gloucestershire Regional Planning Scheme (Abercrombie, Kelly, Trew and Falconer)
1932	Leicestershire Regional Planning Report (Allen and Potter)
1932	Brighton, Hove and District Regional Planning Scheme
1933	Greater London Regional Planning Committee. Second Report (Unwin)

1933	North Wales Regional Planning Scheme (Abercrombie and Kelly)
1933	West Essex Regional Planning Scheme (Adshead)
1934	North Riding Outline Report (Abercrombie)
1934	Cambridgeshire Regional Planning Report (Davidge)
1934	West Kent Joint Regional Planning Report (Davidge)
1934	Somerset Regional Report (W H Thompson)
1935	Buckinghamshire Regional Plan (Davidge)
1935	East Suffolk Regional Planning Scheme (Abercrombie and Kelly)
1935	Lincolnshire Coast Planning Scheme (Abercrombie and Kelly)
1937	Bedfordshire Regional Planning Report (Davidge)
1937	Amounderness (Fylde) Regional Planning Scheme (Mawson)
1937	Harrogate and District Regional Planning Proposals
1937	Highway Development Survey of Greater London
1940	Report of the Royal Commission (Barlow) on the Distribution of the Industrial Population
1943	County of London Plan (Abercrombie)
1943	Hull Regional Survey (Lock)
1944	Greater London Plan (Abercrombie)
1944	Merseyside Plan (Longstreth Thompson)
1945	Manchester and District Regional Planning Proposals
1946	Clyde Valley Regional Plan (Abercrombie and Matthew)
1947	South Wales and Monmouthshire Plan (Lloyd and Jackson)
1947	South Lancashire and North Cheshire Advisory Plan
1948	Conurbation (West Midlands Group)
1948	West Midlands Plan (Abercrombie and Jackson)
1948	Regional Survey and Plan for Central and South-East Scotland (Mears)
1949	North East Development Area Outline Plan (Pepler and Macfarlane)
1949	Tay Valley Plan (Payne)
1950	West Highland Survey (Fraser Darling)
1963	White Paper. London – Employment: Housing: Land
1963	White Paper. The North East
1963	Belfast Regional Survey and Plan
1963	Central Scotland: programme for development and growth

1964	South East Study 1961–1981
1964	Report on Land Use in the Highlands and Islands
1965	National Plan
1965	West Midlands Study
1965	North West Study
1965	Northampton, Bedford and North Bucks. Study
1965	Cumberland and Westmoreland: a sub-regional study
1966	Review of the South East Study
1966	South Hampshire Study
1966	Challenge of the Changing North
1966	Review of Yorkshire and Humberside
1966	East Midlands Study
1966	Lothians Regional Survey and Plan
1966	Highlands and Islands: statement of policy
1967	West Midlands: patterns of growth
1967	Draft Strategy for the South West
1967	A Strategy for the South East
1967	Wales: the way ahead
1967	Cairngorm Area Study
1968	Bedford, Milton Keynes, Northampton and Wellingborough Sub-Regional Study
1968	North West of the 1970s: strategy II
1968	East Anglia: a study
1968	Halifax and Calder Valley: an Area Study
1968	Moray Firth: a plan for growth
1968	Grangemouth/Falkirk Regional Survey and Plan
1968	Central Borders Plan (Johnson-Marshall and Wolfe 1968)
1969	Outline Strategy for the North
1969	Teesside Survey and Plan
1969	Leicester/Leicestershire Sub-regional Planning Study
1969	Notts/Derbyshire Sub-regional Planning Study
1969	Humberside Feasibility Study
1969	Huddersfield and Colne Valley Area Study

1969	Doncaster Area Study
1969	North East Scotland: survey of its development potential
1970	Strategic Plan for the South East
1970	Yorkshire and Humberside: regional strategy
1970	Deeside Planning Study
1970	North Gloucestershire Sub-regional Study
1970	Peterborough Sub-Regional Study
1970	Strategy for South West Scotland
1970	Tayside: potential for development
1970	Northern Ireland Development Programme 1970–75
1971	Severnside Feasibility Study
1971	Coventry–Solihull–Warwickshire Sub-regional Planning Study
1971	A Developing Strategy for the West Midlands
1971	Inter-departmental Study on Long Term Population Distribution in Great Britain
1972	North East Lancashire Plan
1973	Strategic Plan for the North West
1974	National Planning Guidelines for Scotland
1974	West Central Scotland Plan
1974	East Anglian Regional Strategy
1974	Cambridge Sub-Region Study
1974	Strategic Settlement Pattern for the South West
1975	The Pennine Uplands
1975	Yorkshire and Humberside: regional strategy review
1975	Northern Ireland Regional Physical Development Strategy
1975	Reading, Wokingham, Aldershot, Basingstoke Sub-regional Study (Area 8)
1976	Strategy for the South East: 1976 Review
1977	Strategic Plan for the Northern Region
1979	Strathclyde Regional Structure Plan
1980	West Midlands Strategic Review
1986	DoE Strategic Guidance for the South East
1988	DoE Strategic Guidance for the West Midlands
1988	DoE Strategic Guidance for Merseyside

1988	LPAC Strategic Planning Advice for London
1988	DoE Regional Guidance for the South East
1989	DoE Strategic Guidance for Tyne and Wear
1989	DoE Strategic Guidance for West Yorkshire
1989	DoE Strategic Guidance for London
1989	DoE Strategic Guidance for South Yorkshire
1989	DoE Strategic Guidance for Greater Manchester
1989	East Anglia Regional Strategy (SCALEA)
1990	A New Strategy for the South East (SERPLAN)
1991	DoE Regional Planning Guidance for East Anglia
1992	National Strategy for the Coastline commenced (DoE)
1992	Regional Strategy for the East Midlands
1992	Strategic Guidance in Wales: Overview Report
1993	Regional Economic Development Strategy for North West England
1993	DoE Regional Planning Guidance for the Northern Region
1994	Rural Development Commission 10 year strategy review
1994	National Planning Policy Guidelines for Scotland
1994	DoE Regional Guidance for the East Midlands
1994	LPAC Strategic Planning Guidance for London
1994	DoE Regional Guidance for the South East

The Evolution of Regional Governance in the UK up to 1945

A long historical perspective might place the Council of the North as the first modern regional administrative initiative in Britain. Established in 1537 as a form of devolved administration recognising the grievances of northern England, the Council was housed until its demise in 1641 at the Abbey of St Mary's at York whose Abbot, William Sever, led the Council for Henry VII. This landmark in regional governance has special amusement for a namesake of Robert Wanhope, Abbot of St Mary's from 1502–1507 and a predecessor of Sever. Later in the seventeenth century, Cromwell's Commonwealth was ruled through Major-Generals responsible for civil order and tax collection in regions of England.

The modern history of regional governance might be started in 1851, when the Census Commissioners amalgamated the counties of Britain into thirteen regions for statistical purposes; Wales was one region, Scotland was divided into two, and England comprised ten regions. Although the pattern for England south of a line from the Wash to the Solent had significantly changed and Greater

London was no longer itself a region, the skeleton of the 1851 regions remained a century later in the body of Standard Regions. The formation of government boards with responsibility for regional administration or development became familiar from the mid nineteenth century, although the Scottish Fishery Board established in 1849 had earlier origins. The Scotch Education Department was created in 1872, and the Crofters Commission in 1886.

Regional governance took more substance when the Scottish Office was created in 1885 and elected county councils followed in 1886. Regional administration for Scotland had begun after the Union of Parliaments in 1707 in the person of the Secretary of State for Scotland, and in the shape of various Boards and Departments preceding the establishment of the Scottish Office. In the eighty years after 1885, there periodic adjustments to this basic structure for reasons of war or the expectation of civil unrest, but only from 1964 were there significant changes impelled by issues of strategic and regional planning.

Boards and agencies with a regional role continued to proliferate. Dating from 1909, the Development Commission was a forerunner of the Highlands and Islands Development Board of almost 60 years later. The Commission's scope included fostering research and education in agriculture, forestry and rural industries; land reclamation; rural roads; harbours and inland waterways; and fisheries improvements. The Commission formed the Council for Small Industries in Rural Areas, and it began building factories from the mid 1960s.

Apart from Scotland, Greater London has been the most continuously disputed issue in regional reorganisation. The formation of the London County Council in 1889 only temporarily quietened the arguments. The case for further reform was fought over by local politicians, by reformers like H.G. Wells and by pressure groups. The issue rose high with the LCC's concern about the inadequacy of its jurisdiction to meet London's housing problems at the close of the Great War, when the Garden Cities and Town Planning Association (1918) called for a Greater London Town Planning Commission 'to exercise control with regard to housing, industrial and residential development and all means of suburban communication, over the whole region which is in direct and continuous economic dependence on London.' But although the Government acceded to LCC pressure by launching a Royal Commission on London Government in 1921, the Commission reported that opposition to a Greater London was so extensive that no reform should occur.

Regional initiatives have been strongly associated with war or civil strife. Harking back to Cromwell, the Esher Committee on War Office Reconstruction had proposed the restoration of Major-Generals for eight administrative commands in England prior to the 1914–8 war, when a rather haphazard regional administration was established to control production and distribution. Food supplies were regionally controlled, and labour was directed in a similar way. The post-war public housing programme was organised on the basis of Housing Commisssioners for each of seven English regions.

A more anxious problem in government arose with the prospect of the General Strike of 1926, when ten Civil Commissioners were to cover the regions of England and Wales, to maintain communications, power and food supplies, and to preserve health and livelihood according to the Government's priorities.

Other smaller regional devolution was occurring without immediate threat of internal or external strife; the schools inspectorate, electricity generation and employment exchanges were regionally organised. The Post Office was significantly devolved to regional management. Nonetheless, the Interim Report of the Departmental Committee on Regional Development of 1931, which was chaired by Lord Chelmsford, advised that there was no need for regional government. But the Government was driven to new kinds of regional action as economic depression spread across the United Kingdom in the early 1930s, blighting traditional industrial areas. In 1934, the Government sent investigators to report on conditions in four parts of the country which were exceptionally depressed – South Wales, North East England, the West Cumberland coast and Central Scotland. The following Special Areas (Development and Improvement) Act started the method of government regional economic programmes and direct regional initiatives, applied irregularly but still featured sixty years later. Two Commissioners were appointed under the Special Areas Act, one for England and Wales and the other for Scotland; the Commissioners were to act where government departments were not already involved, being encouraged to experiment in improving economic and social conditions. In practice, the Commissioners came to spend their energies and funds primarily on attracting and financing new industries. Influential in the setting up of the Royal (Barlow) Commission on the Distribution of the Industrial Population, the Commissioners' impact on subsequent eras of regional planning outlived their direct roles.

Out of the Depression of the early 1930s there also arose regional housing agencies for Scotland and Northern Ireland, to support local councils unable to adequately build for themselves and particularly to back local industrial initiatives. In the same period, regional agencies for factory building were established in the form of the Scottish and English Industrial Estates Corporations, with the latter confining its programme to northern England. The Highlands and Islands Board and the Scottish and Welsh Development Agencies later absorbed the tasks of developing and managing government's industrial estates.

The intermittent expansion of a regional tier of government in the inter-war period had three main causes (Saunders 1983, 3): expanding functions of government – as when the Ministry of Transport took over trunk roads from local councils in 1936; regional employment initiatives and Regional Commissioners of the Depression; and threats to civil order from either unemployment or fascist Germany.

Central government made some moves to reorganise its partners in local government in the same period. The case of Tyneside was a notable failure, when the Royal Commission which reported in 1937 was defeated by the unwillingness of the boroughs to be unified. But there were wider pressures for regional planning and governance. Although the Barlow Commission did not report until 1940, the evidence to it and the mind of its members anticipated a comprehensive approach to regional planning. No mere local reorganisations of local authorities could manage the task; government would have to lead. And however well the Government heard this message, the growing imminence of war was leading it to regional administration to meet the national emergency.

As early as 1932, Air Raid Commandants had been appointed in certain regions of the country to coordinate precautions against raids, and in 1938 a comprehensive regional organisation followed which came under the command of Regional Civil Defence Commissioners. The Commissioners were responsible for coordinating government departments in ten regions of England up to the point at which direct administration from London might collapse; thereafter, the Commissioners were to assume complete control within their regions. Scotland, Wales and Northern Ireland already had regional administrations with different degrees of self-containment. The ten English regions broadly fitted the pattern earlier established by the Post Office (Smith 1964, 12).

The Commissioners included the Master of Corpus Christi College, Cambridge, and representation from the House of Lords. Because London government held firm throughout the war, the Commissioners' role never grew from coordination to overall control of their regions, but they were effective in facing emergencies and in integrating war production. Government departments were organised under regional controllers managing transport, labour, supply and production according to the precedent of the 1914–18 war, guided by Regional Boards set up in 1940, comprising the senior regional officials of departments most concerned with industry. Stronger than even the regional economic planning councils and boards established under the Department of Economic Affairs from 1965, the Boards included co-opted representatives of both employers and unions, with irregularly effective support from advisory committees for the engineering, transport, building and iron and steel industries.

Although their first purpose was to better manage the domestic war effort and to prepare for any collapse of central government through bombing or invasion, the regional arrangements were seen as a long-term threat to local government. So the Regional Commissioners were quickly retired at the war's end in 1945. But devolved departmental administration was retained, and the Treasury oversaw a standardisation of departmental organisation through the Regional Organisation Committee, defining a pattern of nine Standard Regions merging the separate wartime regions of London and of the South East. Nearly all departments of government accepted a regional system, although each minister decided what degree of authority their senior regional official would enjoy. Senior officials represented their departments on inter-departmental regional committees, overseeing physical planning, building and distribution of industry.

Accordingly, the reforming Labour government elected in 1945 began its post-war programme of social and physical reconstruction with a unique basis for peace-time regional coordination. But it was a framework aloof from local government, and when in 1951 a Conservative government began thirteen years of continuous administration, its antipathy to planning and to regionalism soon suspended this dimension of government.

The Erratic Development of Regional Planning and Governance Since 1945

A Trail Winding and Unwinding

CENTRAL GOVERNMENT

Post-war direction of the inter-regional distribution of ew industry in the UK was pursued through the factory controllers of the Board of Trade, operating through the Regional Boards of Industry (Smith 1964, 18). The Ministry of Town and Country Planning also appointed regional controllers, whose responsibilities for the new system of development planning under the Town and Country Planning Act of 1947 brought tensions with their counterparts in the Board of Trade, still evident over forty years later.

Regionalism in government was integral to the Labour government's programme of post-war reconstruction, and was reflected also in the organisation of the National Health Service and of the nationalised industries. It was sustained by inter-departmental government committees, of which the Regional Distribution of Industry Panels and the regional Physical Planning Committees were significant in economic and land-use planning. The Scottish Office sustained its special interest in regional planning by creating the Advisory Panel on the Highlands and Islands, giving influential advice on use of resources and on plans by government departments, local authorities and other public agencies (Grassie 1983, 99).

Alongside this internal regionalisation of government, there was no reorganisation or regionalisation whatsoever in local government, apart from some joint consideration of regional plans commissioned by the government. Local authorities were preoccupied with housing problems and preparing the new development plans required of them. The Labour government did not move upon the report of the Local Government Boundary Commission (1947), which suggested a standardised reorganisation of councils in England into a system of counties, some of which would have a lower tier of county boroughs and others not. There was no suggestion of a regional structure.

With the succession of a Conservative Government in 1951, the regional dimension became less sympathetically viewed. Initially, the new Government's election promise to increase the output of new council houses caused the creation of eleven Regional Housing Production Boards, but these were later abandoned. Departments progressively reduced or withdrew regional staff and, by 1956, the abandonment of the Treasury's Regional Organisation Committee ended the

Figure 1.6. Standard regions in the United Kingdom 1964

procedures by which departments were obliged to obtain approval for expenditure deviating from the Standard Regional structure (Smith 1964, 22).

Departments could now freely draw their own regional boundaries and abandon any semblance of regional administration. The only remaining arrangements for regional administration upon which the government insisted were those to be instituted in a nuclear war; seventeen underground bunkers were built to house regional seats of government in England and Wales, the last completed in 1988 and the first being offered for sale as surplus in 1994.

After the ending of government-wide regional administration, the Ministry of Housing and Local Government had closed all its regional offices by 1958. But the nationalised industries and the Post Office kept regional structures, and the national strategic priority of food production was reflected by regional coordination within the Ministry of Agriculture, Fisheries and Food.

However, although some kept a regional structure, there was no compunction on departments to hold to the pattern of Standard Regions formalised in 1946. In the early 1960s, the Board of Trade and the Ministry of Agriculture each had seven regional controllers in England, while the Ministry of Works had five regional directors. There were eight divisions in the Ministry of Transport and nine in the Ministry of Health. Only in the Home Office were ten regions retained as in the 1939–45 system of administrative coordination. The Ministry of Housing and Local Government, of course, had nobody in the regions, measuring the political change of attitude to its responsiblity for planning.

The very large extent to which policy matters reverted to the centre during the 1950s was not matched by the total of civil servants withdrawn. Whereas the entire regional staff of the Ministry of Housing and Local Government was withdrawn to London, it comprised only 740 in 1953/4. By comparison, 20,000 staff in Agriculture, Fisheries and Food remained in the regions of England, Scotland and Wales in 1953/4, and still 10,700 in 1962/3, when 35 per cent of civil servants were employed in regions outside London. Although the regional offices of government planning and land use services were all closed after 1958, Manchester and Newcastle offices were reopened in 1962 to help local authorities with their housing programmes. This was even before the return of a Labour government in 1964, when a full system of regional offices and services was reinstated which has been continuous since.

The nationalised industries and services also incorporated regional organisation, but with different purposes and boundaries. The gas and electricity industries were regionally decentralised with the purpose of encouraging regional competition in prices, and although it was possible to have a Central Electricity Generating Board, a national grid for gas supply was not practicable until the exploitation of North Sea gas. The criteria for regionalisation in these two industries were, therefore, not the same as for other services. Ten gas boards were established which approximated to the Standard Regions, but their boundaries varied in detail and significantly so in the South East of England. Six regional railway boards were established and fourteen hospital boards. Synchronisation of boundaries has never been a strategic concern in subsequent reorganisations in these or other public services.

A fallow decade of regional interest in England and Wales ended in the early 1960s, when electoral anxieties turned the Conservative Government to a new interest in the regions. Its series of regional studies was supplemented by a special initiative in North East England, to which the extrovert Lord Hailsham was sent as a ministerial freelance to arouse instant action for long-standing economic difficulties. He would later (Hailsham 1992) admit to having believed that an elected regional authority was needed to support his plans. His colleague in government, the Minister of Housing and Local Government, was almost equally daring in his proposal for regional development corporations; these would have acquired and prepared land to accelerate major town expansion projects meeting the rising problem of national population growth (Cullingworth 1979, 203). But these ideas were beyond the mind of their government colleagues. And the general election of 1964 found that the Conservative Party had not convinced the outlying regions of the country of the depth of its new-found interest in them. It was the Labour Government then elected which was to initiate the most significant moves towards regional administration and planning in peacetime British history.

For Scotland and Wales and for each of now eight Standard Regions in England – a single enlarged South East region was created recognising the continuing spread of an integrated region including London – the new Labour Government established an economic planning council and an economic planning board. From 1964 to 1979, all regional offices of Whitehall departments were coordinated through the boards, whereby the civil service shadowed the regional economic planning councils of nominated industrialists, trade union officials, local politicians, academics and others with established regional loyalties.

The economic councils and boards were aimed at creating a regional machinery to help implement national planning. They were to establish broad strategy, help prepare regional plans and advise as these were implemented. They were to have no direct, executive responsibility, although their members would often be influential in executing departments or authorities. Although they were titled as 'economic' boards and councils, this tactic was to help placate suspicions that they would supersede the local authorities' job in physical planning. But George Brown (1971), their ministerial guardian, had no doubts but that they were born to combine physical and economic planning. Also, it has been claimed (Lindley 1982, 173) that ministers expected them to be duly transformed into a system of elected regional authorities. However, although influenced by French experience, they lacked the force of the French *prefectual* system.

Initially, the patronage of Brown's Department of Economic Affairs and their membership of public figures gave the councils a higher profile than the advisory regional boards for industry had enjoyed, established in 1940 to coordinate wartime production and persisting until their responsibility for preparing regional

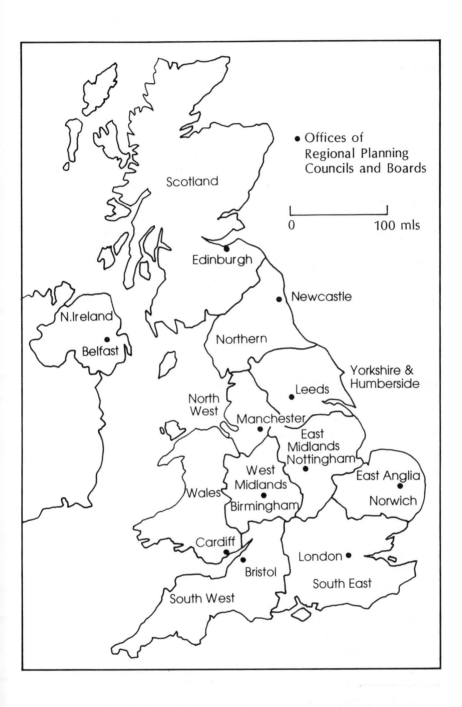

Figure 1.7. Economic planning regions in the United Kingdom 1975

plans was transferred to the councils in 1966. Of course, the transfer also allowed Government and the Treasury to dissociate themselves from any commitment to the plans, which could now be regarded as entirely advisory. Authorship by civil servants implied governmental commitment to any published proposals, as had ensued from the Scottish Office's *Central Scotland* programme of 1963, tying the Treasury's hands to an abhorrent degree.

Absorbing as it did the Board of Trade's regional development division, the Department of Economic Affairs might have patched over the persistent gap between physical and economic policy in Britain. A ministerial committee on Environmental Planning was formed under Brown's chairmanship, and a central planning unit drew staff from several departments to develop national and sub-regional planning studies. But the Department's bright flame was brief. It began to burn out when Brown left it in 1966, as deflationary policies wrecked the *National Plan*'s targets for economic growth. It closed in 1969, finally in the charge of a minister with no enthusiasm for substantial progress in regional planning. The idea of tightly connecting regional plans to public investment programmes had already been abandoned, although all economic planning councils had been launched on the task of preparing plans for their regions' development up to 1981, with an appraisal of prospects beyond.

The economic planning councils persisted for a decade after the strategies which all produced for their regions. But before the DEA expired, the Department of the Environment had already begun a programme to prepare physical plans for the major metropolitan regions of the country. So, the councils were progressively marginalised during the 1970s, when the influence of the planning boards upon government ministers became relatively more significant. The focus for regional planning shifted to the Department of the Environment, and the better connection between physical and economic planning promised in the mid 1960s failed to hold. The Department had no responsibility for economic affairs, and had little influence upon the departments which did. The economic planning councils had been effectively neutered.

Although none of the economic planning councils stamped an enduring mark on their regions, they had some benefits in their time. They could show a degree of naivety about physical planning, but this could stimulate local authorities to cooperate together or with government, to avoid having the councils preempt regional planning. Latterly, when they were at best only a helpful means of gathering information and views about regional economic prospects, this was yet a useful role, although government could be angered when it seemed to be played to claim regional favours.

This erratic system of regional planning was interleaved with the duties of local government. The connection was consolidated by the necessity for county councils to gain approval from the regional offices for their Structure Plans, and to earn Transport Supplementary Grant through rolling Transport and Policies Programmes. District councils required regional office approval for their Housing

Investment Programmes, and when inner city partnerships began in the late 1970s the role of the offices became even more closely entwined with the local authorities. The connection was extended through the planning and building of trunk roads, for which regional Road Construction Units were established in England in the late 1960s under the auspices of the Department of the Environment, and partially staffed from local authorities. However, only six regions were thought appropriate for road construction in England, whereas the parent Department of the Environment had eight regional offices as did the other major departments of government. Indeed, the Department of the Environment characterised the internal problems of coordinating government services, because its own services were organised in eleven different regional structures!

Although the Department of Agriculture most continuously found need for a regional presence, it was the Department of the Environment which found the regional dimension to be not merely administratively convenient but also functionally appropriate. This led to a situation in which as Young (1982, 78) points out, 'In so far as any point in central government exists which provides some sort of corporate link to local authorities, it is the regional DOE that most approximates to it.'

During the 1970s, constitutional reform in the UK became an issue beyond the mere internal organisation of government departments or the geographic divisions of local government. After over ten years of rising nationalist pressures in Scotland and of intense troubles in Northern Ireland, the Royal Commission on the Constitution reported in 1973 under the chairmanship of Lord Kilbrandon. Directly elected assemblies were proposed for Wales and Scotland, to which the majority of the Commission proposed legislative devolution for essentially those functions hitherto administered by the Secretaries of State for Scotland and Wales. In England, only non-executive coordinating and advisory councils would be established in each of the eight standard regions, comprising representatives of the local authorities and government nominees. A minority of the Commission disagreed with legislative devolution to the assemblies, and with the inconsistency between arrangements proposed for England and those for Scotland and Wales. The minority view was that five regions were appropriate to England, and that like those for Scotland and Wales their assemblies should execute government policy rather than originating their own.

Nothing came of constitutional reform. Only the slightest new regional dimension was introduced to government in the form of a parliamentary Standing Committee on Regional Affairs established in 1975. When the government put its proposals for Scottish and Welsh assemblies to Referenda in 1979, support in both countries was less than required by the voting rules. And a long list of government departments and agencies employed a disparate variety of regions for purposes of administration, erratically coinciding with the government's standard statistical regions. If inter-regional economic planning has been relatively continuous in the UK, substantially at the government's own initiative but sustained since the early 1970s by the necessities of membership of the European Community, intra-regional planning of either a physical or an economic nature has been discontinuous and fragmented by comparison. The two kinds of planning have connected only occasionally, being held apart not least by the long-standing and notorious lack of cooperation between the departments of government responsible for industry and for planning, housing and the environment.

From the mid 1970s, local economic development came to feature as a preoccupation of public planning in the UK as it had done in considerable areas of the US since at least 20 years before. Regional associations of local authorities, local industrialists and trades unions had been promoting new industry for many years previously. The North West Industrial Development Association had grown out of the Lancashire and Merseyside Industrial Development Association, and there were other notable associations for the North of England and for Yorkshire and Humberside. The rise of local economic initiatives went in hand with increasing attention to urban policy, coinciding with growing appreciation of the reduced prospects for inward investment to the UK and for transfer of industry from the more to the less prosperous regions, and an appreciation of how much manufacturing and wholesale employment had relocated from urban to peripheral rural areas in the 1960s and 1970s.

It was one of the more effective instances of regional planning in the UK – the *West Central Scotland Plan* (1974) – which marked the beginning of this period of adjustment to local enterprise in economic planning. Although less directly influential, the strategic regional plans for the North West and Northern regions of England also emphasised the need to foster the indigenous local economy, rather than to concentrate primarily upon attracting investment from outside the regions.

It was regional planning, therefore, which first recognised the importance of local economic initiative, and which fostered the rise of local development enterprise to stand at least equal with regional initiatives. So, although regional economic policy remains in the 1990s, it has been significantly modified and its impact has much reduced. Adapting and regenerating older urban and remote rural areas has come to seem the dominant strategic problem, to which regional economic policy makes only a marginal contribution in most parts of the UK. However, there is no paradox in concluding that regional planning and analysis is an essential context for local economic analysis.

Two lessons can be asserted from this readjustment of strategic views. First, that there were damaging side-effects in the long preoccupation with inter-regional economic policy of politicians and many strategic planners and academics. This helped delay for twenty years a sufficient emphasis on intra-regional economic restructuring and local economic development, which might have had greater benefits at an earlier stage in the process of Britain's de-industrialisation. Second, our experience of centralised government direction of strategy has lacked continuous regional participation. Only in Scotland, perhaps, have government strategies been given a sustained regional dimension, interpreted by a territorial minister with responsibilities across the fields of several secretaries of state in England.

GOVERNMENT AGENCIES

Alongside the regional restructuring of civil service administration in the 1960s, there were significant innovations of government agencies with regional planning and executive responsibilities. Nationalist movements and political tensions in the peripheries of the UK were commonly the origins of many government boards and agencies. The Highlands and Islands Development Board, launched by the Labour Government in 1965, had such unprecedented scope and ambitions that a former Conservative minister – and Highlands landowner – described it as 'Marxist'. But in action, the Board was so much less threatening that it became a permanent arm of subsequent Conservative governments.

What was given to Scotland it was necessary to give also to Wales, although in less substantial form. A Development Board for Rural Wales was delayed until 1977, and given more restricted tasks than was the HIDB in Scotland. Similarly, when the rising threat of the Scottish Nationalist vote helped the Scottish Development Agency into being in 1975, the Welsh Development Agency was formed with a relatively lower profile. But the history of corruption in land dealings by councillors in some South Wales councils led to the creation of a Welsh Land Agency, when elsewhere in Britain the Labour government of the mid 1970s looked to local authorities to manage the buying and disposal of land for development.

The Conservative government's curbing of local government in the 1980s brought major extensions in the use of government agencies for infrastructural development. Urban Development Corporations and City Action Teams, together with the selective spread of Enterprise Zones, saw the government directly intervene in the quality and spatial distribution of local development and urban renewal. In England, this had previously been the exclusive responsibility of local government. In Scotland, the Scottish Development Agency refined its role in strategic planning and development in the 1980s; translated in 1991 into Scottish Enterprise, the Agency contracted local initiatives out to local enterprise companies, whose spread of activities could sometimes seem to supersede the strategic planning role of the regional councils. Also, despite the degree of autonomy for the Countryside Commissions and the Government's divestment of some responsibility for several of the national parks, these bodies remained considerably dependent upon Government patronage. Indeed, the Government was moving in 1992 to reassert its interest in the national parks.

The free-ranging roles of the Scottish and Welsh boards and development agencies in economic development have been only palely shadowed in England, although the origins of the Rural Development Commission lie in the Development and Road Improvement Act of 1909. But from 1988, the Commission absorbed the Council for Small Industries in Rural Areas and was given an

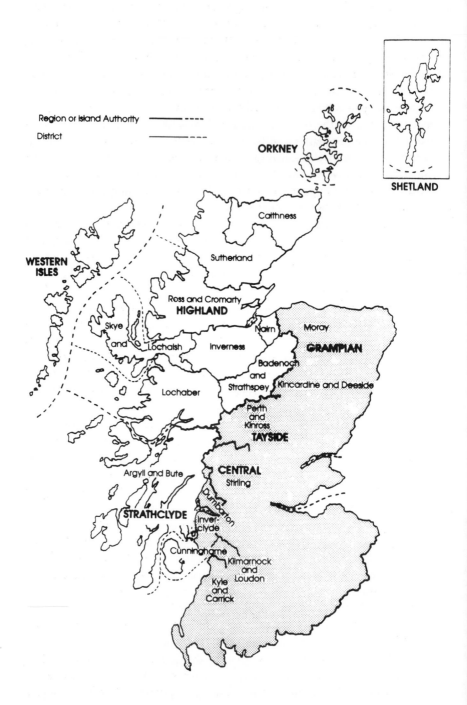

Figure 1.8. The Highlands and Islands Development Board Region 1965

expanded role to achieve annual job targets and to make rural integrated action plans. This merger of established functions was copied for primarily urban areas late in 1993, when what had been first announced as the Urban Regeneration Agency for England was actually launched as English Partnerships. Delayed by battles between government departments reshaping not just its title but also its earlier announced form, English Partnerships took over the government's established roles of promoting and funding derelict land and city grant projects, combining this with the work of the English Industrial Estates Corporation absorbed from the Department of Trade. Assuming also the task of building factories for the Rural Development Commission, the new agency was not to be tied strictly to urban areas; expediently, it was asked also to help regenerate the coalfield areas which the government was in the course of rapidly closing under its contentious mix of energy policies.

With only a small administrative centre in London, English Partnerships was to operate in a decentralised way from up to six regional offices. This compared with the ten regional offices in which coordination was to be reinforced for mainline departments of government in a contemporaneous development.

Despite its superficially broad regeneration objectives, English Partnerships seemed to have relatively fewer tools to mend urban decline than its nearest counterpart agencies in Scotland and Wales. It was largely confined to physical action. The Department of Industry withheld from it scope to directly link business and industrial development strategies to physical initiatives of land recovery, environmental improvement and building construction. The old divide between physical and economic planning remained in England, although less markedly in Scotland and Wales.

There was a similar schism in the machinery for coherent regional development in the fields of strategic public services. The strategic potential of the ten regional water authorities created in England and Wales in 1974 swept a mass of small water and drainage boards into executive regional authorities, of quite unprecedented scope and budgets. The Severn–Trent RWA stretched far beyond any previous region envisaged to contain the English Midlands, extending into mid Wales. Required to prepare 20, 7 and 5 year rolling programmes of investment, the RWAs were in charge of all aspects of the use and disposal of water, and for land drainage, pollution control and water-based recreation. The basis was created for more efficient water and sewerage services, at a scale which greatly clarified the issues for and the implications of regional planning. The ten RWAs combined the prior work of 187 water supply undertakings, of 1393 local authorities which had been responsible for sewerage and disposal services, and of 29 River Authorities dealing with water conservation and land drainage.

Although the RWAs were constructed upon the Geddesian principles of valley and catchment areas, it would have been more convenient if more than three of the ten authorities had substantially coincided with the boundaries of the Standard Regions of England and Wales. The RWAs all embraced at least two counties, and

Figure 1.9. The Regional Water Authorities of England and Wales 1974

the largest embraced several. Because local authorities acted as agents for the RWAs in sewerage schemes, there was an incentive for both sides to remain on good terms and to cooperate in regional planning. The potential for coherent regional planning was hugely improved, even if flawed in parts of the country where the RWAs were so large that it could have fostered some arrogance towards local councils.

By 1990, of course, Government had sold the RWAs into private ownership. A public Rivers Authority was created to oversee the standards of water management of the private water companies of England and Wales, but any obligation of the former RWAs towards regional planning had gone. Nonetheless, some county planning officers found the new private companies keenly interested in long-term development strategy as a key to their future profits.

The 1974 reorganisation of the National Health Service in England kept fourteen regional health authorities as had existed since 1959. Their boundaries were adjusted, and observing the principle that each would contain a teaching hospital ensured wide variation in the budgets and size of regions. The authorities' primary strategic role was to establish planning guidelines for district authorities, allocating resources and monitoring work in the districts. They also operated regional blood transfusion and management services, and in metropolitan districts ran ambulances. An 'arms-length' authority with a degree of discretion was preferred to a mere regionalisation of the Department of Health's administration. The system served to protect the interests of the traditional holders of power and prestige in health care – the medical profession and the hospital consultants in particular (Haywood and Elcock 1982, 142). So although fourteen regional authorities remained as an internal market for services was introduced to the Health Service in the early 1990s, the continuing role of the authorities was uncertain.

Scotland has consistently remained ahead of the rest of the UK in its exceptionally high degree of agency action. Up to the mid 1990s, the regional councils were to retain the water responsibilities wholly lost to English and Welsh local authorities twenty years before. The Scottish Special Housing Association and the Scottish Development Agency had enabled government agency participation in regional development prior to 1980, when opportunities were strictly limited in England, less fully developed in Wales, but were similarly possible in Northern Ireland. And the Civil Aviation Authority, British Rail, National Coal Board, the Electricity Boards, British Shipbuilders, the Housing Corporation and other agencies representing government have, of course, been very significant strategic influences in the location of economic activity in the United Kingdom. They have helped shape the intensity, location and permanence of regional economic activity, and of land use within urban areas and between the regions of the country.

It was a marked tendency of the early 1990s that agencies should widen their responsibilities. Government encouraged them to view their main purposes in a wider context. The abrupt adoption of previously neglected social and local community objectives by the London Docklands Development Corporation in 1988 was a vivid illustration. Another was the work of Scottish Homes to regenerate Scottish council housing being extended to include the setting-up of local employment projects. And in 1992, the Rural Development Commission started on three pilot projects to train young people, and to stimulate rural business and industry which could employ them.

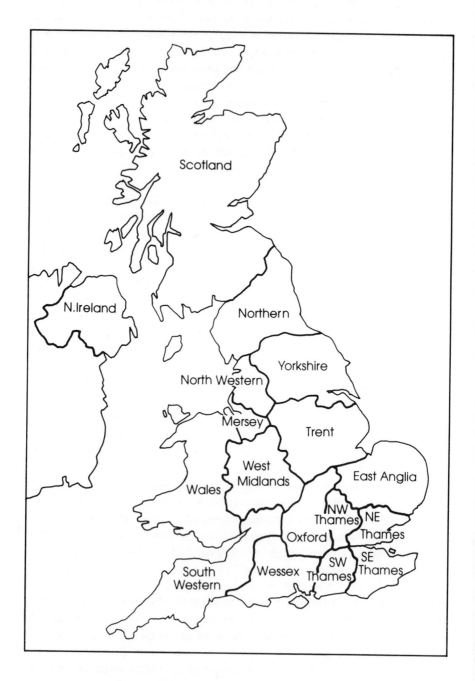

Figure 1.10. The Regional Health Authorities of the United Kingdom 1974

This may all have been a belated understanding that physical projects were often viable only with social and economic support. Or it could be seen as a further move by the Conservative Government to capture the historic functions of local authorities, pushing a Trojan horse deeper into the political territory of its enemy. Whatever its basis, the tendency meant that government agencies had more and more in common – at least at the margins of their work. This implied an even greater need for Government to coordinate.

But the Government's advances in its agencies and capacities for strategic planning and action in the 1980s were ad hoc, often disjointed and poorly coordinated. The means of intervention had proliferated, but the capacity for integrated action had been weakly managed.

LOCAL GOVERNMENT

The development of regional dimensions to local government administration since the 1950s has not entirely followed trends in central government. At a time when government departments were withdrawing regional staff, the Royal Commission on Local Government in Greater London was announced in 1957, and a Local Government Commission was appointed in 1958 to review the organisation of local government in England outside metropolitan London, and to consequently propose changes which it considered desirable for effective and convenient local government. The motives for change were notably political in the case of London, where the London County Council had fallen under near-continuous Labour control; the Conservative Government could hope for an occasional Conservative majority on the LCC only by altering the Council's boundaries and electorate.

The Royal Commission's report (1960) led to the London County Council being extended into an enlarged Greater London Council. The Local Government Commission had a more diffuse task and relatively less success. It made Special Review Areas of the conurbations, where it proposed to amalgamate boroughs to form extended metropolitan authorities in the case of Tyneside, Greater Manchester, the West Midlands, West Yorkshire and Merseyside. Only in the West Midlands did change ensue, but it was far from a strategic reform; Birmingham was left unchallenged and the changes merely reduced the fragmentation of the Black Country and failed to unify even there. Outside the conurbations, the amalgamation of boroughs into a new Teesside county borough was the most significant of the proposals to be acted on.

The Local Government Commission was dissolved in 1966. It had led to reorganisation in the Black Country and on Teesside. Elsewhere it either failed or envisaged relatively marginal boundary alterations. Its proposals were inconsistent, being more based on what might be seen locally as politically reasonable than on what was nationally rational. So, a continuous county council was proposed for Greater Manchester, but only a joint planning board for Merseyside. The two-tier system it proposed for Tyneside was rejected by the Minister of Housing and Local Government, who in turn proposed a single-tier county borough which he then did not proceed with pending the report of the Royal Commission on Local Government, which had just started work.

As the 1960s passed, the issue of English local government reorganisation had grown too large for the dissolved Local Government Commission. A comprehensive review was demanded from Royal Commissions on Local Government appointed for England, Scotland and Wales, reporting in 1969. The recommendations of the English Commission to the Labour Government would have grouped the 61 counties it proposed into eight provinces, for each of which an advisory assembly of county representatives would have been constituted. A minority report by Derek Senior drew on his earlier analysis of the regional geography of England and Wales, foreseeing a regional reorganisation of government administration which acutally arrived in 1994. But the Commission's proposals fell with the election of the Conservative Goverment in 1970, whose creation of regional water authorities in 1974 was yet a very significant regional initiative. And in Scotland, the Conservative Government did adopt the recommended system of regional authorities for the greater part of the country, although only the Strathclyde and Highland regions were of a size comparable to the provinces proposed for England.

Local authorities have taken joint regional initiatives in several other fields, apart from the spasmodic, tortuous and very uneven history of cooperative regional planning already outlined. Further education has been the most extensive case, with regional advisory councils established in 1946 in eight regions of England having a long and relatively successful history. Inter-authority coordination of local services only irregularly arose in other fields, such as the regional development associations for industrial promotion in the more disadvantaged regions, which in the 1980s were given a degree of government recognition by financial aid which simultaneously enabled a degree of government steering.

Since 1945, there have been perhaps fewer changes in the capacities for strategic planning in local government than have occurred within Government itself. Although local government in 1974 in England and Wales and in 1975 in Scotland was reorganised primarily because of the historic system's inadequacies in strategic planning, local government has subsequently contributed less than the Redcliffe–Maud and Wheatley Local Government Commissions of the late 1960s may have expected of it. The reasons underlying this hampered progress are several.

In retrospect, the nature of the strategic urban problems since the 1970s reorganisation – spatial inequality in local services, in the geography of social and economic opportunities in city and metropolitan regions, and in the financing and organisation of urban regeneration – have differed from the problems of urban expansion foreseen as the principal strategic issue to be faced by the new authorities. Boundaries and the division of responsibilities in the English metropolitan areas, in particular, met political rather than administrative or strategic criteria. The Royal Town Planning Institute and significant interests in strategic planning saw that the metropolitan county councils would have insufficient

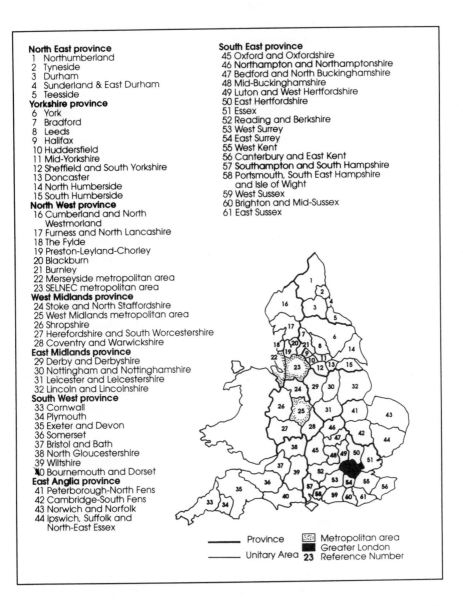

North East province
1 Northumberland
2 Tyneside
3 Durham
4 Sunderland & East Durham
5 Teesside
Yorkshire province
6 York
7 Bradford
8 Leeds
9 Halifax
10 Huddersfield
11 Mid-Yorkshire
12 Sheffield and South Yorkshire
13 Doncaster
14 North Humberside
15 South Humberside
North West province
16 Cumberland and North
   Westmorland
17 Furness and North Lancashire
18 The Fylde
19 Preston-Leyland-Chorley
20 Blackburn
21 Burnley
22 Merseyside metropolitan area
23 SELNEC metropolitan area
West Midlands province
24 Stoke and North Staffordshire
25 West Midlands metropolitan area
26 Shropshire
27 Herefordshire and South Worcestershire
28 Coventry and Warwickshire
East Midlands province
29 Derby and Derbyshire
30 Nottingham and Nottinghamshire
31 Leicester and Leicestershire
32 Lincoln and Lincolnshire
South West province
33 Cornwall
34 Plymouth
35 Exeter and Devon
36 Somerset
37 Bristol and Bath
38 North Gloucestershire
39 Wiltshire
40 Bournemouth and Dorset
East Anglia province
41 Peterborough-North Fens
42 Cambridge-South Fens
43 Norwich and Norfolk
44 Ipswich, Suffolk and
   North-East Essex

South East province
45 Oxford and Oxfordshire
46 Northampton and Northamptonshire
47 Bedford and North Buckinghamshire
48 Mid-Buckinghamshire
49 Luton and West Hertfordshire
50 East Hertfordshire
51 Essex
52 Reading and Berkshire
53 West Surrey
54 East Surrey
55 West Kent
56 Canterbury and East Kent
57 Southampton and South Hampshire
58 Portsmouth, South East Hampshire
   and Isle of Wight
59 West Sussex
60 Brighton and Mid-Sussex
61 East Sussex

Province — Metropolitan area
Unitary Area — Greater London
23 Reference Number

Figure 1.11. The unfulfilled proposals for provincial and unitary local government of the Local Government Commission for England 1969

resources of either land, revenue-raising potential or supportive executive responsibilities. The division of housing from other infrastructural responsibilities was seen as a major defect. The limited responsibilities and areas of the metropolitan councils were expected to be a severe disadvantage in raising and deploying local rate income to pay metropolitan costs and finance urban regeneration. This proved to be probably a greater disadvantage than the lost opportunity to plan for both urban renewal and urban expansion within the boundaries of a single authority, because the metropolitan counties excluded the new towns, new employment centres and suburban and ex-urban residential areas integral with the metropolitan social and economic systems.

Alongside restraints due to the form of local government reorganisation, government initiatives have strongly advanced at the expense of local government leadership in local physical and economic development. This was particularly evident under the Conservative Government after 1979, but was heralded during the preceding Labour administration. Coupled to financial incentives to encourage local authorities to cooperate with it, Government's role in strategic development established since 1947 through the new town development corporations was, with the curtailment of the new town programme, transferred to the older urban areas of the United Kingdom. Government gained a much increased influence in implementing plans in urban areas at a reduced cost in terms of real investment, despite specific initiatives with a high profile in the enterprise zones, through the urban development corporations, or in the Glasgow GEAR or area projects of the Scottish Development Agency. This trend did begin to moderate in the late 1980s, when government ministers began to speak again of partnership with local authorities in urban renewal.

Partially but not wholly because it excluded economic and social proposals and concentrated on land use as demanded by government, the development plan system was also a less effective means of strategic planning than might have been hoped before local government was reorganised. The strategic scene had a multitude of players at various levels of geography and governance. And two tiers of local planning authority and slow progress in local planning by many district councils divided what was originally intended as a unified system of development planning (Planning Advisory Group 1965). County and Scottish regional councils occasionally considered strategic priorities through statements of policy in informal reports published outside the statutory planning system, but they could rarely arrange to execute their proposals with the single-mindedness with which the area projects of the Scottish Development Agency were pursued, for example. This is not to deny such significant strategic policy initiatives as those of Strathclyde Regional Council to ameliorate social deprivation, or of several metropolitan councils in public transport operating policy, but structure plans were only an indirect route to strategic action. There were some initiatives in regional planning coordination, whose history has been outlined. The standing conferences of local planning authorities in South East England and the West Midlands have been continuous since the 1960s. After the two sub-regional planning studies for Leicestershire and Nottinghamshire were concluded in 1969, a full-time technical unit was briefly established to monitor the East Midland region's growth. But in other regions there was less sustained collaboration, although from the mid 1980s

Title	Purpose	Content		Accountability		Planning process (years)	
		Area	Scope	Initiating and implementing authorities	Approving authority and form of approval	Horizon	Frequency of presentation and review
Within the area of activity of the DOE							
Area management	Management	Sub-district	Service delivery	District[1]	District adoption	3	
Housing investment	Programming	District	Public sector housing	District[1]	DOE: programme approval	3/5	Annual roll-forward
Inner city	Programming and coordination	District	Variable	District	DOE	3/5	Annual roll-forward
Local plans	Indicative and coordination	District	Development and other use of land	District[1]	Counties: in accordance with structure plan	10/15	3/5
National Park management plans	Management and coordination	National Parks	Recreation and conservation	Joint or special planning district National Park committee	Park Planning Boards: adoption	5/10	within 5
Recreation strategies	Indicative and coordination	Region	Sport and recreation facilities	Regional councils for sport and recreation	Regional councils: adoption	10	3/5
Regional strategies	Indicative and coordination	Region	Economic, social and physical issues	Local authorities, DOE and Economic Planning Council	DOE	10/15	3/5
Rural action plans	Programming	Sub-district[2]	Industrial and infrastructural development	Counties	Development Commission: resource allocation	10	3/5
Structure plans	Indicative and coordination	County	Development and other land use	Counties	DOE: statutory approval	-	-
Water plans	Management and programming	Region	Water and sewerage	Regional water Authority[1]	DOE: and resource allocation	5 and 20	Annual roll-forward
Waste disposal	Management and programming	County	Finance	Counties	DOE: borrowing approval	5/10	Annual
Outside the area of activity of the DOE							
Public expenditure Survey Committee	Programming	National	Programme areas	Treasury	Cabinet adoption of White paper	3/5	Annual roll-forward
EEC regional development programmes	Programme and/ or indicative	Regions	Economic development	Department of Industry	EEC Commission: grant allocation	3/5	Annual roll-forward
Health Service plans	Management	District, area and region	Health care	District, area and regional health authorities[1]	Each tier approves the plan of the tier below	3 and 10/15	Annual and four-year roll-forward
Highways programmes	Programming	National/ regional	Inter-urban areas	Department of Transport[1]	Department of Transport: programme approval	10	Annual roll-forward
Regional tourist plans	Indicative and management	Regions	Facilities for tourism	Regional Tourist Boards	Regional Tourist Boards: adoption	10/15	-
Transport policies and programmes	Programming	National/ regional	Inter-urban areas	Counties[1]	Department of Transport: borrowing approval	3/5	Annual roll-forward

Notes:
1 Also implementing authority
2 Most usual area
Source: Department of the Environment (DOE) 1977

Figure 1.12. Policy planning systems and the scope of the Department of the Environment in England 1977

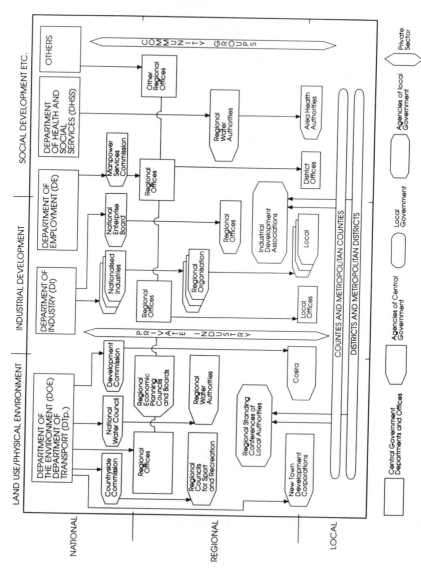

Figure 1.13. The institutional environment for regional development and planning in England 1978

came a new willingness to collaborate in most parts of England, and also in Wales. When the local authorities of North West England formed a standing regional conference in 1992 after almost 30 years of inability, the English regional mosaic was at last complete. The West Midlands conference, in particular, took periodic initiatives towards structure plan coordination, but the larger role of these cooperative arrangements tended to be in better communication between the partners; policy initiation came to the fore less often. And when staking claims to more resources for their regions, the conferences found government still unwelcoming.

Figure 1.14 Chronology of principal features in the development of regional governance in the UK

(Unless otherwise noted, the dates indicate the creation of new arrangements. Some arrangements may have had an occasional minor change of title, not all of which may have been noted.)

1707	Secretary of State for Scotland
1746	Abolition of Secretary of State for Scotland and replacement by Lord Advocate
1829	Metropolitan Police District for London
1845	Board of Supervision for Poor Relief in Scotland
1849	Fishery Board for Scotland
1851	Census Commissioners regionalisation of Britain
1855	Metropolis Local Management Act
1855	Metropolitan Board of Works for London
1872	Scotch Education Department
1885	Scottish Office
1886	Crofters Commission
1886	County Councils Act established elected councils
1889	Abolition of the Metropolitan Board of Works
1889	London County Council
1870	London School Board
1902	Metropolitan Water Board
1904	LCC succeeded the London School Board
1908	Port of London Authority
1909	Development Commission
1912	Scottish Board of Agriculture
1913	London Arterial Roads Conference

1919	Scottish Board of Health
1919	Electricity Commissioners and regional electricity supply boards
1921	Northern Ireland: Stormont parliament
1921	Manchester and District Joint Town Planning Advisory Committee
1923	Midland Joint Town Planning Advisory Council
1924	London and Home Counties Traffic Advisory Committee
1925	South Lancashire and North Cheshire Advisory Committee
1926	Central Electricity Board and national grid distribution
1926	34 Town Planning regions
1927	Greater London Regional Joint Town Planning Committee
1928	Manchester and District Regional Planning Committee
1928	55 Town Planning regions recorded in England and Wales
1929	Creation of Scottish Office Departments for Agriculture, Health and Prisons
1932	108 Town Planning regions
1931	Interim Report of Chelmsford Committee on Regional Development
1933	London Passenger Transport Board
1934	Special Areas Act and Commissioners for England and Wales, and for Scotland
1936	Greater London Regional Planning Committee dissolved
1937	Standing Conference on London Regional Planning established
1938	138 Town Planning regions
1940	Report of the Royal Commission (Barlow) on the Distribution of Industrial Population
1939	Transference of Scottish Office to Edinburgh and consolidation of Scottish administration under the Secretary of State for Scotland
1939	Regional Commissioners for Civil Defence
1943	Ministry of Town and Country Planning
1943	Clyde Valley Regional Planning Advisory Committee
1943	Central and South East Scotland Regional Planning Advisory Committee
1945	Board of Trade
1946	New Towns Act
1946	Advisory Panel on the Highlands and Islands

1947	London Transport Executive
1949	National Parks and Access to the Countryside Act
1950s	Regional Seats of Government established for civil administration in any future wartime
1952	Town Development Act
1958	Abolition of regional planning offices of Ministry of Housing and Local Government
1958	Local Government Commission
1962	Reconstitution of the Standing Conference on London Regional Planning (later the Standing Conference on London and South East Regional Planning)
1962	Post established of Secretary of State for Industry, Trade and Regional Development
1962	First reinstated (Newcastle) regional office of the Ministry of Housing and Local Government
1963	Greater London County Council
1964	Department of Economic Affairs
1964	Welsh Office
1964	North Regional Planning Committee
1965	Inner London Education Authority
1965	Reinstatement for all regions of England of regional offices of departments in membership of Regional Economic Planning Boards
1965	Regional Economic Planning Councils
1965	Highlands and Islands Development Board
1966	West Midlands Planning Authorities Conference
1966	East Anglia Consultative Committee
1968	Countryside Commissions for Scotland and England
1969	Passenger Transport Authorities
1969	Disbandment of Department of Economic Affairs
1973	Report of the Royal Commission on the Constitution
1974	Metropolitan and County Councils
1974	Regional Health Authorities (14) for England
1974	Regional Water Authorities (10) for England and Wales
1975	Scottish Regional and Island Councils

1975	Scottish Development Agency
1975	Welsh Development Agency
1975	Standing Conference on Regional Policy in South Wales
1977	Development Board for Rural Wales
1978/79	Regional Emergency Committees during national road haulage dispute
1979	Regional Economic Planning Councils abolished
1980s	English Regional Development Organisations (5 funded by Department of Enterprise – Northern Development Company; Yorkshire and Humberside Development Association; INWARD Ltd (i.e. the North West); West Midlands Development Agency; Devon and Cornwall Development Bureau)
1984	London Regional Transport
1986	Abolition of the Greater London and Metropolitan County Councils
1986	London Planning Advisory Committee
1986	Inner London Education Authority elected
1986	Association of Greater Manchester Authorities
1986	Yorkshire and Humberside Regional Association of Shire Counties and Metropolitan Districts
1986	West Midlands Regional Forum
1987	Standing Conference of East Anglian Local Authorities
1988	Rural Development Commission
1988	Completion of seventeenth and last Regional Seat of Government for administration in any future wartime
1989	South West Regional Planning Conference
1990	Abolition of Inner London Education Authority
1990	East Midlands Regional Planning Forum
1990	Planning Steering Committee for Wales; Assembly of Welsh Counties
1991	Scottish Enterprise and Local Enterprise Companies
1992	Regional Arts Boards for England
1992	North West Regional Association (completion of coverage of England by regional planning conferences)
1993	English Partnerships (Urban Regeneration Agency)
1994	Committee of London Authorities

1994   Coordinating directors for 10 regional offices of government services

1994   Disposal of Regional Seats of Government

Conclusion: The Uncompleted Regional Pursuit

The depth of experience of both regional planning and regional governance in the UK has grown progressively. When either has seemed to be in retreat at times, circumstances of one kind or another have sooner or later brought a revival. There has been a repeated pursuit of solutions to a wide variety of political, economic, social and administrative problems, all within regional contexts. But the form of the solutions has been repeatedly reshaped by changing conditions. And the regions themselves have also been reshaped; they have sometimes overlapped, and they have been repeatedly redefined at different times and for varied purposes. The pursuit has never been fully satisfied, nor has seemed likely to be.

CHAPTER TWO

Containment by Conference
South East England and the West Midlands

Preface: Planning by Conference

Although conferences of authorities have assembled from time to time in many regions of Britain, only in two metropolitan regions have they sustained a serious process of cooperative regional planning for more than ten years. There have been continuous conferences in South East England from 1962, and in the West Midlands from 1966. In both regions the conferences have fluctuated in their membership, in their preoccupations and in their methods of working. But uniquely in British experience, these regions have accumulated a long, unbroken practice of regional cooperation amongst equal partners.

Surviving for so long when cooperation in so many other regions has been short-lived or discontinuous, only the conferences of the South East and of the West Midlands provide sustained tests of the capacity of voluntary cooperative regional planning. Why have these two regions cooperated in planning for so long, so distinctively? They are the two most populous of UK metropolitan regions and, for most of the time, have been the two most prosperous. Their pressures for growth and expansion have been the largest, and their demands for building land the greatest. Sustained pressures and the considerable internal tensions they have wrought are principal explanations for their sustained experience of regional planning. Containment of their conurbations has been a principal aim of both conferences for much of their life.

The West Midlands also offers a case of effective regional planning undertaken by temporary cooperation. Sponsored by the planning authorities for Coventry, Solihull and Warwickshire, the planning study was nominally for a sub-region of the West Midlands. In all respects, however, it had the characteristics of regional planning in being fostered by politically separate authorities, aiming to resolve their strategic differences. The study well demonstrates the shifting ground commonly underlying regional planning, and the uncertainty of political contexts.

Greater London and the South East

Experiments in Regional Planning

The term 'Greater London' may have been first officially employed by the Registrar-General when, in 1875, he defined it as the area of the Metropolitan Police District (Freeman 1968, 150), which remained the statistical basis for the Census conurbation almost a century later. However, local government was reluctant to recognise that its functions should be unified despite growing description of London as a metropolis from around 1830. Metropolitan policing had commenced in 1829, followed by the Metropolitan Commission of Sewers in 1847, the significant creation of the Metropolitan Board of Works in 1855 and the Metropolitan Fire Brigade in 1865. But it was only in 1889 that twenty years of political dispute and a troubled history of the Commissions was ended by the formation of the London County Council, as part of the comprehensive reform of English local government.

But the unprecedently broad boundaries of the LCC were still not wide enough to contain the metropolis. London's economy continued to spread far beyond, to where newly settled suburbanites determinedly dissociated their home environment from the problems of the city which provided their living. The reform movement in town planning argued that new towns within a restructured metropolitan economy were the way to an efficient and wholesome way of living for London's people. Ebenezer Howard's inspiration launched Letchworth in 1903 and Welwyn Garden City in 1920. New towns were thereafter a main plank in most concepts of regional planning for London and the South East for more than half of the century, although only after 1946 becoming a public and not just a private initiative.

The London County Council

The LCC inherited 'a disarray of subsidiary local governments' (Foley 1972, 26). Rather greater order was brought to these in 1900, when they were replaced by 28 metropolitan boroughs. The boroughs were given extensive powers, and it was only later that the LCC assumed full status when it took over education, town planning and a concurrent responsibility for housing. But other functions were progressively assigned to authorities in which the LCC had no commanding voice. These separate agencies included the Metropolitan Water Board of 1902, the Port of London Authority of 1908, the London and Home Counties Traffic Advisory Committee of 1924, the Metropolitan Area Licensing Authority of 1930 and the London Passenger Transport Board of 1933.

The boroughs were jealous of their roles. They opposed a sustained campaign by progressive reformers to extend the LCC over the ever widening metropolitan region. They saw the launch of the London Arterial Roads Conference in 1913 as a surrogate means of introducing comprehensive regional planning, but Thomas Adams associated it with his proposition to have a central planning body to cope

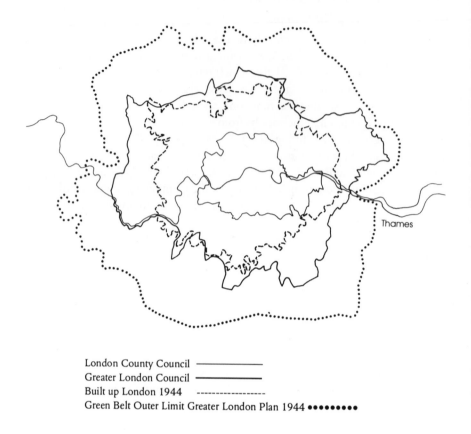

London County Council ————————
Greater London Council ————————
Built up London 1944   ------------------
Green Belt Outer Limit Greater London Plan 1944 ●●●●●●●●

Figure 2.1. Overtaken by London's metropolitan growth: the boundaries of the London County Council and Greater London Council

with the capital's population growth, transport and infrastructure needs and the rationalisation of fragmentary planning by London's boroughs and districts. Because the London County Council was already the largest local authority in Britain, the issue of regional cooperation inevitably raised suspicions amongst the London boroughs and neighbouring authorities. The Council's strategic planning capacity was curtailed by these political circumstances. Its boundaries were growing tighter as the metropolis spread and as building to relieve congestion and unfit housing became an increasing preoccupation.

During the First World War, the London Society – a voluntary and learned organisation – had prepared a plan for London which offered proposals for roads and open spaces. In October 1920, the Government's Unhealthy Areas Committee recommended that there should be a unified administration for the London region, and six months later followed by proposing that 'some competent person or persons should be at once authorised to prepare a plan for the reconstruction of London and the surrounding country, including the Home Counties as well as the Metropolitan and City Police Districts' and that 'an inquiry should be instituted without delay as to the nature, scope and functions of a new authority or combination of authorities to give statutory effect to such a plan, with such modifications as may be thought necessary, to control transport and to make such financial adjustments between the local authorities concerned as may be required.'

The immediacy urged by the Committee was not evident in action. The Government appointed a Royal Commission on London's Government, but it found widespread suburban and Conservative opposition to change and a majority of the Committee recommended against it. As far as a regional plan was concerned, the LCC had proposed in 1918 that a Joint Advisory Committee be formed for the metropolitan region (Young and Garside 1982, 148), to consider housing, town planning and communications. A first conference was attended by delegates from 92 authorities. Resolutions of good intent were passed, and the LCC hoped for a repetition of the good results of the earlier London Arterial Roads Conference. But the LCC was frustrated when councils from north of the Thames proposed that a regional housing authority be established for an area within approximately 13 miles radius of Charing Cross.

The LCC was totally unsympathetic to any regional housing authority, which was clearly a ploy by the councils on London's fringe to put the LCC in its place. The LCC had since 1917 been pursuing its own reviews of housing conditions across Greater London, as a basis for a large programme under its powers to build beyond its boundaries. Any new collaborative housing authority within the metropolitan area would be a means of curbing the LCC's housing role, and politicians on the LCC strongly opposed this attempt at a reverse takeover. So progress to metropolitan planning stuttered again.

A London and Home Counties Traffic Advisory Committee was established in 1924, comprising local authority representatives to advise the Minister of Transport. Joint town planning committees began to form amongst groups of local authorities in sectors of Greater London, but it took the Government to intervene to break the jam in action for the metropolis as a whole.

Encouraged by a deputation in 1926 from professional and voluntary groups, including the Town Planning Institute, the Royal Institute of British Architects, and the Garden Cities and Town Planning Association, it was Neville Chamberlain – who had chaired the Unhealthy Areas Committee and was now Minister for Health, supported by George Pepler – who at last brought the formation in 1927 of the Greater London Regional Planning Committee, representing 126 local authorities and chaired by Banister Fletcher, architect and member of the City of London Corporation. Chamberlain exhorted the Committee to look at the poor relationship between transport services and new housebuilding, at the allocation of land uses, and at the prospect for garden cities. The Committee established four sub-committees for General Purposes, Decentralisation, Traffic, and Open Spaces (SERPLAN 1992, 4).

Raymond Unwin was appointed as the Committee's advisor on his retirement from the Ministry of Health in 1929. He was aided by Adshead, Davidge and Longstreth Thompson, all regional planning consultants for parts of the metropolitan region. Unwin presented his rapidly prepared First Report later that year. His ideas on protection of open spaces, highways and ribbon development were not unexpected or unwelcome, but there was much disapproval of his propositions for an executive regional agency with powers to acquire land or to guide the voluntary pooling of landowners' interests.

The Committee was unable to reach any significant decisions, and by 1931 was being insufficiently funded to continue on a useful basis. Unwin presented his Second and more detailed Report in 1933, emphasising his concept of a green belt, and foreseeing that London's population growth might turn to a decline within ten years. In the same year, he was succeeded as Technical Adviser by Robert Hardy-Syms, and the Committee was reconstituted as a smaller advisory body under the 1932 Town and Country Planning Act.

The LCC's support for regional efforts further dwindled from 1934. The Labour Party had taken progressively stronger control of the LCC, which turned in on itself to consolidate its policies within its own administrative area. Slum clearance and building tenement flats for Londoners within the LCC boundaries was now preferred to out-of-county cottage estates, and when the LCC stopped contributing to the Committee's costs its impetus was deflated. In the words of Young and Garside (1982, 205), 'the Committee's work took its place, at best, alongside the 176 other town planning schemes in preparation for the London Planning Region.'

In 1935, a year prior to the Committee being wound up, the Technical Adviser reported on Greater London's need for airports and aerodromes for up to 50 years ahead. Although approved by the Committee, the report is said to have been a nail for the Committee's coffin when it was buried in 1936 (SERPLAN 1992, 5). Particularly unacceptable to the LCC was the report's proposal of an airport at Fairlop, to the north-east of London and where the LCC wished to build an out-county housing estate.

Dispute over Fairlop was followed by the LCC's withdrawal from the Committee. In public, the LCC argued that the Ministry of Transport had commissioned the London Highway Development Survey, and that together with the Council's direct action to protect a London green belt this left no effective work for the Committee. Unwilling to subject itself to an active regional effort beyond its adequate control, the LCC recommended that the dissolved Regional Planning Committee be replaced by a body which would initiate nothing, but only respond to questions raised by government or the constituent authorities. Such technical work as arose would be led by a seconded government official, supported by staff from the constituent authorities. So, regional consultation replaced regional planning in 1937 with the formation of the Standing Conference on London Regional Planning.

Abandonment of the Committee was more a political than a practical stance, and the LCC kept a private interest in regional planning. Satellite towns and industrial dispersal within the region remained longer-term strategic goals for some LCC politicians, and in 1935 the LCC had voted £2 million towards the formation of a London green belt, which was statutorily recognised in 1938 by the Green Belt Act. The LCC contributed to the green belt while the counties of Buckinghamshire and Hertfordshire did not. Praise for the LCC's benevolence helped deflect criticism of its abandoned role on the Regional Planning Committee.

The Standing Conference formed in 1937 lacked a permanent secretariat. The breadth of regional coordination and action which Unwin had sought was absent in this period. For example, the Highway Development Survey for Greater London completed for the Ministry of Transport in 1937 was divorced from town planning, and was no substitute for the comprehensive planning strategy which the LCC's interests required. And while the institution of the London Passenger Transport Board in 1933 brought rationalised operations in the metropolis, it simultaneously divorced them from other strategic functions still within the LCC's control.

Some of the suburban and Conservative councils may have been relieved at the LCC's withdrawal from formal arrangements for regional planning, but that again exposed the issue of reforming local government in Greater London. New interest in reform arose from senior national figures in the Conservative Party, who saw that an enlarged LCC area would much improve the Party's chance of recapturing the Council from Labour's tightening grip. But no move towards reform had been made before war began.

The LCC was not wholly against regional planning. But the narrowest view amongst LCC Labour councillors was reflected in its definition by Herbert Morrison, the Council's leader, who described it as 'merely good estate management on a large scale'. And at an open meeting of the Town Planning Institute in 1937, the Chairman of the Council's Town Planning Committee savagely attacked Patrick Abercrombie's criticism of the LCC for ignoring any regional context for its plans. Abercrombie was described as totalitarian, alien, un-British and fascist.

But the Conference which the LCC had caused to be born was simultaneously cumbersome and weak. It was exhorted not to initiate regional proposals but to confine itself to the London Traffic area and to matters referred to it. Yet the first report of its Technical Committee in 1939 called again for a regional plan for London (Young and Garside 1982). The call was backed by the near simultaneous completion of the Report of the Barlow Commission on the Distribution of Industrial Population, which provided an outlet for Patrick Abercrombie's views on London regional planning which had been so fiercely rejected by the LCC. The Government approved that ways and means should be considered of preparing a London Regional or Master Plan, and of examining the possibility of establishing a surrounding agricultural belt.

Although one of the reasons for the Barlow Commission had been the threat of bombing attacks on spreading London, the actual arrival of war in September 1939 suspended action on a London Regional Plan. It was not until 1941 that the Minister of Works and Buildings asked the LCC to prepare what would be published in 1943 as the County of London Plan, and in 1942 that he asked the Standing Conference to agree to his appointing an expert to prepare an Outline Plan and Report for Greater London. The expert would be Patrick Abercrombie.

The Greater London Plan

Although Abercrombie had a supporting Technical Committee already in position when he began on the *Greater London Plan*, completed between 1942 and 1944, he preferred to keep the local authorities at arm's length as he worked (Young and Garside 1982, 243). The *Plan* acknowledged the Committee's help, but Abercrombie saw it as impractical to work with 150 local authorities in the region, all empowered to prepare planning schemes. He was prepared to accept the LCC's claim that Londoners wanted to live in London and should not be shifted by the *Plan*, but he called for an executive Regional Planning Board to be appointed by government to ensure local authority cooperation through a number of Joint Planning Committees. The Board would have been able to set up executive agencies for the Green Belt, in the form of a Regional Housing Corporation, and to handle refuse disposal and other functions.

Massey (1989, 70) refers to the view of Gordon Stephenson – one of Abercrombie's team – that 'the Greater London Plan 1944 may be seen as a conclusion of work begun by Unwin and continued by Abercrombie', and that Unwin's Second report in 1933 for the Greater London Regional Planning Committee 'provided a challenge and a brief for Abercrombie, after lying dormant for a decade.'

A comprehensive strategic plan for London was not universally supported, however, nor everywhere regarded with high expectation. Some architects in high places argued that pragmatism, piecemeal patching and modesty should be the guides for London's rebuilding and growth; others thought the opportunity for London's planning and administrative reform had already been lost, although in the early war years government had already established internal committees to examine possible post-war administrative reform, including centralised national planning (Young and Garside 1982, 229–233).

Some of the tensions surrounding London's future were borne in on Abercrombie. Already started on a plan for the County of London commissioned by the LCC, which had insisted that he should not only protect the economic and political status of the County but also avoid any reduction in its size of population. On the other hand, Frederic Osborn and the Town and Country Planning Association

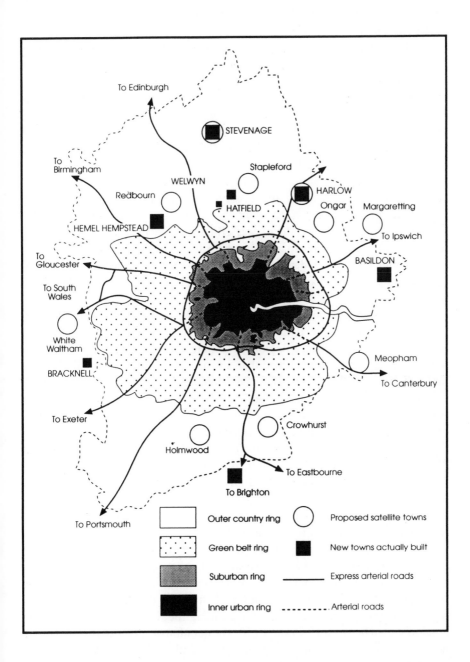

Figure 2.2. Greater London Plan 1944: the strategy for metropolitan containment and new towns beyond the green belt

demanded that London should decentralise through a major programme of new towns. Although there were strained relations with his clients during its preparation and they did not formally adopt it, Abercrombie's completed *County of London Plan* largely met the LCC's views. Consequently, the plan drew widespread criticism from the voluntarist town planning movement; Lewis Mumford (1946) was notably scathing. It was Abercrombie's commission for the *Greater London Plan* which enabled him to escape the LCC's influence and to shift his strategy to the ground of his recent critics. He now adopted a strategy of decentralisation amounting to over 600,000 people from the County of London, and over 400,000 from outer parts of Greater London.

There were implausibilities amongst Abercrombie's proposals. The regional housing programme included the cessation of building by some large local authorities, and much expanded building by some small authorities. And his London Regional Planning Board was criticised even by some of those long supportive of regional governance. It would have been government's creation, having nothing to do with democratic self-government, suggested Robson (1945, 110), the most profound academic advocate of regional planning and administration.

Even during Abercrombie's work, the Ministry of Town and Country Planning had turned against national direction of planning in favour of local control. Abercrombie's proposal for a Regional Planning Board was against the tide. No sooner had the *Plan* been published than any new impetus to a regional authority for London was quelled. The Government announced that there would be no major reform of London's government; local authorities would remain responsible for planning. And, as Young and Garside (1982, 246) show, the fact that the *Plan* had been produced was even used as an argument against reform. It was argued that the *Plan* had been produced despite the lack of such an administrative structure as Abercrombie had proposed. Moreover, as the *Plan* had been prepared with small resources it was argued that it rested on shaky premises, requiring much to be worked out in detail as it was implemented. This contorted argument led to the conclusion that reforming local government to implement the *Plan* would merely reveal some of its inherent inadequacies.

Although politics frustrated the *Plan's* administrative proposals, it was adopted in its other respects as the basis of government policy for South East England. It was given official status in 1947 by a ministerial memorandum, as the county councils of Greater London began on their first county development plans, but it was already the government's basis for planning the ring of new towns around London started between 1946 and 1950. The question of administration persisted, however, and the Government appointed a London Planning Administration Committee to advise upon how to achieve concerted action to implement a regional plan for London as a whole.

The London Planning Administration Committee did not report until 1949. It stressed the integration of the Greater London region, and emphasised the need for concerted action. It rejected the claim of government departments that they could do this effectively and carry out the *Greater London Plan*, but it found the local authorities unwilling to alter the status quo or to conceive of any form of joint planning. The LCC was opposed to any form of regional planning authority. Bereft of support, the Committee made no brave proposal but lamely suggested a Royal Commission to consider local government in the region.

But the Government had already partly by-passed the problem of inadequate regional governance. Having created the new town development corporations, it had hugely eased the difficulty of establishing a regional housing programme, which Abercrombie had seen as being developed through a Regional Housing Corporation. Taking the new towns wholly to its hands, the Government simultaneously reduced the potential scope for a Regional Planning Board. The role of the LCC in regional development was simultaneously constrained, which was a prime objective of the Minister of Town and Country Planning.

The LCC was only opposed to regional planning which was not on its terms. As the 1950s progressed, it grew increasingly dissatisfied with the new towns, over whose housing and industrial policies it had no control. The new towns were not helping to de-congest London's industries but were becoming replete with firms newly established or moving from elsewhere. So by negotiating to expand sympathetic towns in the outer South East region, the LCC was able to bypass the new towns and also the suburban councils which would not cooperate in its building programme for badly housed Londoners. The LCC did not need regional planning if it was able to manage its own programme of overspill.

The South East region was now spreading far beyond the Abercrombie limits. As early as 1953 it was evident to many that the Abercrombie framework was stretched under pressure. Significant parts of the *Plan* were being fulfilled in less than a third of the time expected. By 1958, the population of Inner London had reduced by as many as he had anticipated it would only in 50 years. Outer London had grown by many more than Abercrombie had planned. Powell (1960, 76–86) saw a new London Region with a radius of up to 50 miles.

The Conservative government of the 1950s declared its prejudice against planning, and like the LCC was not eager to initiate a new regional plan. Some county councils had exhausted their creativity by the effort of producing their first statutory development plans. But pressure grew from professional planners, both outside the civil service and some within it. Despite the apparent scepticism of the formidable Evelyn Sharp, Permanent Secretary of the Ministry of Housing and Local Government, the emergent regional planning conference was brought to life particularly by the support of Theo Durrant, Surrey's County Planning Officer, and of Sir William Hart, the Clerk to the LCC (SERPLAN 1992, 80).

Pressure on the green belt was a prime motivation for resumed regional cooperation. As the Ministry of Housing and Local Government began its *South East Study* in 1961, the Standing Conference on London Regional Planning was reborn. An initial 13 member authorities in 1962 grew to 19 in the London commuter area by 1964, and the following year the Conference was extended to coincide with the area of the new South East Regional Economic Planning Council; the title was accordingly changed to The Standing Conference on London and South East Regional Planning. The 33 London borough councils were represented by their association and not individually. Conference's constitutional responsibilities were to keep under review the principal planning issues affecting the region, to make recommendations for joint policy, to coordinate subsequent action and to consult upon all these purposes. A secretariat was appointed with Brandon Howell as Technical Secretary. The Conference was chaired by Sir Richard Nugent, Conservative member of parliament and former minister, who would keep his position for nineteen years through an alternation of Conservative and Labour governments.

Although Conference's initial flurry of activity was promising, a new regional plan was slow to emerge. No new Abercrombie was appointed. Conference argued that a master plan would be unsatisfactory when what was needed was a continuous growth of regional data, against which day-to-day decisions on regional development could be taken. When it arrived in 1965, the Economic Planning Council was less fastidious, crystallising in its reports some of Conference's tentative options for a new regional strategy.

These slow moves to regional planning were overtaken by a vigorous political tide, when after 20 years of internal struggle the Conservative government resolved to reform London's government. London Conservatives were chary of reform, but they were overridden by national figures in the party. On the basis of a White Paper published in 1961, the LCC was to be succeeded by the GLC. But long delayed as the reform was, it was neither driven by nor matched the need for coherent regional planning.

The Greater London Council

The GLC was established by a Conservative government which, as H.G. Wells (1903) had noted after an earlier Conservative government had created the LCC, came 'only to quarrel with it and hate it and fear it ever since'. Wells had himself quarrelled with what he regarded as the limited concept of the LCC, arguing that the London-centred region extended to the whole watershed of the Thames, to Sussex and Surrey, and across the eastern counties to the Wash. For this whole South East region, he proposed a 'mammoth municipality' which he saw as the means to 'revive the dying sentiment of local patriotism'. Otherwise, he suggested, he would prefer municipal trading, tramways and communications, telephones and nearly all such companies to be in the hands of companies, rather than those of 'petty little administrative bodies'.

At its abolition in 1965, just over 3 million people lived in the area of the London County Council. Sixty years before, the population had been half as large again. The subsequent spread of the metropolis had been recognised by various statistical and administrative arrangements. The Greater London Conurbation for Census purposes had a population of almost 8 million. The commuting region defined by the Ministry of Housing and Local Government contained 13 million, and covered seven times the Conurbation's area. The region of the Standing Conference on London and South East Regional Planning was more populous yet. And the area covered by the Government's *South East Study* (1964), made as the new Greater London Council was being created, had a population rising beyond 18 million and covering a region over 25 times more extensive than the Council would.

So, the Government ignored the wider strategic possibilities and chose the narrowest of the variety of metropolitan and regional contexts open to it. London's council became greater than before, but much less than effective strategic planning required. And, the new Inner London Education Authority was confined to the area of the former LCC and precluded from interfering in the outer boroughs of the new Greater London.

But the Conservative government's prime motive for creating the GLC was not to improve metropolitan or regional planning. London was reformed when other British conurbations with comparable problems of growth and change were ignored. The Herbert Commission (*Royal Commission on Local Government in Greater London* 1960) which recommended the GLC arose because the LCC presented particular political problems. There was the difficulty that some district councils – particularly in Middlesex – had grown large enough to claim the right to be detached from the county. The administrative structure of Greater London threatened to further fragment. And selective emigration to the suburbs of more affluent and socially mobile households had progressively reduced London's proportion of reliable Conservative voters. An internal study by the Conservative Party had confirmed (Barlow 1981, 75) that the chances of Conservative councillors regaining control of the LCC had been worsened by demographic change, so that the largest local authority in the country was at risk of lying permanently in Labour hands. And the LCC's County Hall stood provocatively across the Thames within full view of the terrace of the Houses of Parliament.

Some commentators have played down the significance of electoral politics in creating the GLC. But Young and Garside (1982, 308) firmly support the explanation, pointing to evidence over a long period and to 'a political decision taken at the highest level to create a metropolitan authority for London in expectation of Conservative control.' But a contemporaneous national swing against the Conservative government helped Labour win control at the first GLC election, and the Conservatives gained their goal only after the second council election.

The Royal Commission did consider the possibility of not replacing the LCC, and of having central government assume strategic control for the metropolis. The Commission rejected this solution. It came to favour a two-tier system with the GLC uppermost, and 32 reorganised boroughs and the City of London Council below. The LCC and the County of Middlesex were superseded, and small parts of other counties were bitten off. The Labour Party strongly opposed the reform for the same reason of party advantage as led the Conservative government to bring in the GLC.

The LCC's powers were not wholly transferred to the GLC. The status of the boroughs was reinforced. They had more resources than before, they had a greater role in planning, and the outer boroughs became education authorities. Later, they displaced the GLC in managing and building public housing. The capacity of the GLC to implement plans was hurt; the new council was in significant ways a weaker strategic planning authority than the LCC had been.

The GLC's strategic weakness was very evident in the arguments and evidence brought before the major public examination of its first *Greater London Development Plan* starting in 1970. A major concern of the *Plan* was to lessen the damage which decentralisation of activities to outer parts of the region caused through lost local taxes. The examination showed that the GLC's strategic responsibilities were widely divorced from the borough's local planning powers, and the regional context was too flimsy. Joint working parties talked, but their output depended upon political cooperation.

The transport component of the *Development Plan* had more substance than those on housing and other aspects, because the Council could start to directly implement a radical policy for public transport through the London Transport Executive and by its highway and parking powers. The GLC's responsibility for principal roads was a similarly direct means of implementing strategy. Indeed, it was the effectiveness of the Labour GLC's fares strategy for public transport which led some outer London boroughs to take legal action against the GLC in the 1980s, strengthening the will of the Conservative government to abolish the Council. But policy could not be so easily turned into action where housing was concerned. When both the GLC and government were in Labour hands, the wider boundary of the GLC offered the possibility that dwellings could be built to rehouse families from inner to outer parts of the Council's area. But when the Conservatives took control of the Council, they worked to protect the outer suburbs. The Council's housing role was chequered by political struggle throughout.

The South East Study and the Strategy for the South East

The region's local authorities had reconstituted their Standing Conference in 1962, but it had not brought great vigour to tackling London's strategic problems. It was the Ministry of Housing and Local Government which prepared *The South East Study* (1964), the first major appraisal of the region's planning problems for twenty years. Need for decentralisation remained the central issue, as the Ministry had already indicated in the White Paper of 1963 on *London – employment: housing: land*. The 20-year-old Abercrombie strategy had been only partially fulfilled, and continued national population growth was projected against his expectations and intentions. The *Study's* scope included East Anglia, to which London was now looking to help relieve its congestion.

The *Study* accepted that the region would continue to grow. An entire expected increase of 3.5 million people between 1961 and 1981 would have to be housed outside the conurbation. The new towns which had followed Abercrombie were still incomplete, but were insufficient for this scale of rehousing and growth. The *Study* envisaged an even wider dispersal and larger strategy, stretching up to a hundred miles beyond London. Around two-thirds of the growth was expected to be catered for through local authority development plans, but these left the region short of capacity for over a million people. Accordingly, new cities were suggested in the area of Southampton and Portsmouth, at Newbury and at Bletchley, and with differing backgrounds of local support; these proposals would later be translated into feasibility studies respectively for South Hampshire (Buchanan and Partners 1966), Reading, Wokingham, Aldershot, Basingstoke (Area 8 Study Team, 1975), and for Northampton, Bedford and North Buckinghamshire (Wilson and Womersley 1965). The new city for Bletchley would become the new town of Milton Keynes, but the other areas would not gain such status and would become persistent battlegrounds for development.

As well as to three new cities, the *Study* looked to six existing centres to expand on a very large scale – Swindon, Ipswich, Northampton, Stansted, Ashford and Peterborough. Other, smaller, towns were thought suitable for lesser growth. Swindon was already in the throes of a planned expansion, and feasibility studies were commissioned for Ashford, Ipswich, Northampton and Peterborough. New towns on new sites were now recognised as being more costly in their initial stages, at least, and Milton Keynes was to be the last of this kind. It was decided that Northampton and Peterborough should become new towns, with their development corporations in partnership with the borough councils.

The *Study* was born from a deathbed embrace of regional planning by an outgoing Conservative government. But it was difficult for the Government to unequivocally accept the *Study's* proposals without indicating where in the south-east the predicted growth of development would be located, and also without raising the ire of central Scotland and of the north-east of England, which both demanded the growth which much of the overstretched south-east would have preferred to be deflected (Cullingworth 1979, 200). A simultaneous White Paper on *South East England* nonetheless implied that the government would back the *Study's* proposals. It got no time to do so. The new Labour government elected in 1964 brought a much deeper enthusiasm for planning, and with it the new regional economic planning councils. The South East Council stretched its wings with its *Strategy for the South East* of 1967, embracing much but challenging some of the principal conclusions of the *Study* of three years before. Peter Hall (1966, 49) had criticised the *Study* for its lack of radicalism in sustaining the green belt, and not adopting the green wedge strategy being adopted elsewhere in Europe. Appointed to the Council, Hall's influence was clearly evident in the Council's proposal for nine corridors of growth radiating from London along the major transportation routes. Counter magnets more than 50 miles from London were to absorb an increasing share of growth in the metropolitan region (Hall, Gracey, Drewett and Thomas 1973, 474).

The Council's *Strategy* was a bold essay in physical planning, but it was not well received by all. It was perhaps more conscious of economic affairs than the earlier *Study*. But the local authorities in the Conference thought that it trespassed on their responsibilities for physical planning, and was also simplistic and insufficiently sensitive to local issues and knowledge. It was characteristic that as fragile bridges were built between economic and physical planning in Britain in the 1960s, it was the economists who most enthusiastically crossed over. They rushed to draw physical strategies with a cavalier boldness untypical of their economic analyses.

There was no consensus over regional strategy for the South East. The Council openly stood for growth in the South East, even against the spirit of government policy to foster the country's peripheral regions. The Standing Conference knew well that growth brought tensions in many localities, and it was now publishing a series of reports on the long-term future of the region differing from the Council's *Strategy*. The Conference and the Council were diverging. Yet, the Conference's belatedly published *Framework for Regional Planning in South East England* was slight and indecisive about how London might develop within its region. Government was dissatisfied that local authorities were failing to plan for the region, and were not matching government's initiatives to meet the pressures for regional growth.

A new joint study to establish or impose common ground seemed to the Government to be the solution. Although nominally sponsored in conjunction with Conference and the Council, the seconded team of government planners and economists and of local authority staff starting work in 1968 was firmly led by government officials, directed by Wilfred Burns, the Chief Planner of the Ministry of Housing and Local Government. And the officials were now aware that there had been some slackening in the growth of population occurring at the *Study* of 1964. The growth pressures of the 1960s seemed to be easing. But they remained significant, and the *Strategic Plan for the South East* (1970) now started on faced a larger region than Abercrombie found. The proposals which emerged became the most important statement of regional strategy since Abercrombie, and 25 years later became its major successor.

The Strategic Plan for the South East

The *South East Study* (1964), the *Strategy for the South East* (1967) and the *Strategic Plan for the South East* (1970) all embraced a functional region far larger than that of Abercrombie's *Greater London Plan* of over twenty years before. The region had more complicated internal dynamics than Abercrombie had recognised. Abercrombie assumed that new industrial growth within Greater London would be re-

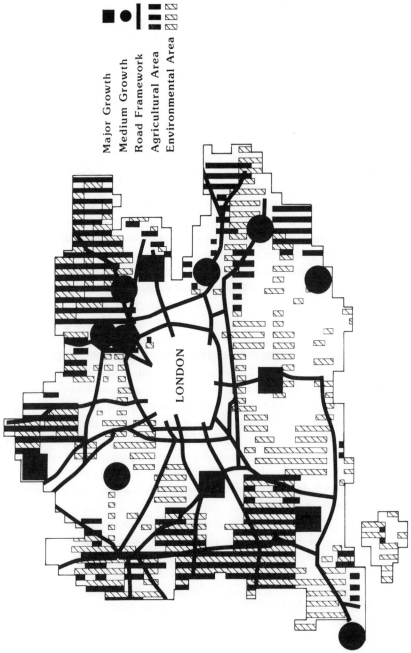

Major Growth
Medium Growth
Road Framework
Agricultural Area
Environmental Area

LONDON

Figure 2.3 Strategic Plan for South East England 1970: the strategy for the region's longer term development

strained, but the *Strategic Plan* of 1970 anticipated a decline by around 8 per cent in the following decade.

Abercrombie also assumed a turnaround from growth to a reduction of population in Greater London, and after 20 years experience of such a trend the *Strategic Plan* anticipated a further 6 per cent fall in the following decade. Where the 1946 and the 1970 plans differed was in the scale of population redistribution they accepted.

The *Strategic Plan* faced wider issues than Abercrombie had done. There were now problems of widespread regional growth as well as of overspill from London, and over twice as much land would have to be found for development as required by the *Greater London Plan*. When the background was of a possible fall in national population, Abercrombie had foreseen need to rehouse 1,033,000 people from metropolitan London in areas outside, of whom around 37 per cent would be housed in new towns, and some 100,000 even further afield. Against an altered background of projected national population growth, the 1970 *Strategic Plan* saw a shortage of 100,000 dwellings in Greater London by 1981, and a need to house an additional 750,000 households in the rest of the region – apart from replacing up to 200,000 dwellings possibly affected by slum clearance and redevelopment.

Although the *Strategic Plan* envisaged London's continuing redevelopment and its future as an international centre for finance, commerce and culture, its proposals were largely confined to the redistribution of population. So although facing larger problems in a wider region whose complex dynamics it better understood, its proposals left it a plan of narrower scope than the *Greater London Plan* of 25 years before. It identified five major and seven medium growth areas. The major centres would accommodate rather more than half of the region's growth by the end of the century. Their respective contributions were to be: South Hampshire (560,000); Milton Keynes/Northampton/Wellingborough (510,000); Reading/Wokingham/Aldershot/Basingstoke (700,000); South Essex (420,000); and Crawley (240,000). The areas of medium growth to accommodate collectively rather over 1 million additional people by 2001 were to be: Aylesbury; Bishop's Stortford/Harlow; Chelmsford; Ashford; Maidstone/Medway; Eastbourne/Hastings; and Bournemouth/Poole.

The *Strategic Plan* envisaged jobs continuing to disperse together with the people being rehoused outside metropolitan London. But dispersal was no longer acceptable to the largest local authority of the region, which published its *Greater London Development Plan* in 1969. The Greater London Council was coming to see a threat to its prosperity from the loss of skilled residents and of diminishing revenues from local industries. The Council was no longer willing to accept unrestricted loss of employment as a means of relieving congestion in London. The *Strategic Plan* took too traditional and narrow a view of regional planning for the Council's taste.

Several components of the *Strategic Plan* were already in place when it was completed. Northampton, Milton Keynes and Peterborough had become new towns. Expansion schemes and feasibility studies were proceeding elsewhere. Other decisions were being protractedly made over a location for London's third airport, and over the GLC's proposed *Development Plan*. In the background, the Registrar General was progressively lowering projections of national and regional population growth. Action already taken seemed to have been sufficient to cope with the some of the most pressing of regional planning issues. The formal responsibility of their Chief Planner for work ensured that ministerial expectations were met, and government approved the *Strategic Plan* in 1971 in general with only minor modifications. The medium growth area of Bishops Stortford/Harlow was dropped, partly to see how major growth developed in South Essex (Curry 1975, 28).

But although concluding nearly ten years of regional study and tentative planmaking, the *Strategic Plan* was not the long-term solution to the South East's problems that might have been expected. It was clear that the 1970 *Plan* lacked the sweep of Abercrombie's vision of 25 years before. Its message was less embroidered, and its text of 110 pages was scarcely half the length of Abercrombie's *Greater London Plan*. Yet, although the *Strategic Plan* was supported by an array of supplementary technical volumes which Abercrombie eschewed, its serious technical failings were soon revealed. Notably, the *Plan* failed to foresee the extent to which the average size of the region's households would shrink, and so the future growth of housing demand was seriously underestimated. The *Plan's* weaknesses lay too near to the surface to more than temporarily ameliorate the minor political crisis surrounding the lack of an agreed strategy for the South East.

Despite fairly early realisation that the *Strategic Plan* was misjudged in some fundamentals, at least another 25 years would pass without another such concentrated effort at attempting a unified and comprehensive regional strategy. The attempts of the 1960s to dictate a statement of coordinating strategy would give way to a process of protracted planning by conference. Regional planning became more than ever a process of technical and political negotiation between the councils and politicians of London and the South East. There was now a permanent regional planning conference supported by extensive technical committees, accumulating data and expertise from the counties of the region. This kind of framework had been absent or skeletal for most of the 25 years following the *Greater London Plan*. It included oversight of monitoring work, but was less than a continuing planning team.

But adopting regional planning by process rather than by the open drama of published plans was a shift from one extreme to the other. And the imminent reform of English local government would further divide the tiers of planning and do nothing to improve the basis for speedy regional agreement and unified action.

London itself was almost a hole in the *Strategic Plan's* regional proposals. The GLC had supported the preparation of the *Strategy* in exchange for the Ministry's agreement that London's future would be left to the GLC's *Development Plan*. But the GLC's proposals emerging in 1969 aimed at a significantly different future for

London than was implicit in the assumptions for the *Strategic Plan*. The *Strategic Plan* expected Greater London's population to fall until stabilising at 7 million, whereas the GLC sought to stem the outflow of people to achieve stabilisation at 8 million. Nor could the GLC accept that manufacturing firms should disperse to the outer region at the accelerated rate anticipated by the *Strategic Plan*. The *Strategic Plan* made evident how unresolved was London's future, but could not alone settle it.

Even for the outer South East on which its proposals focused, the *Strategic Plan* was soon in difficulty. It was not simply that a major regional development like the third London airport was left out of the *Strategy* (Damesick 1982, 98). Flaws in its own technical assumptions were soon revealed. Although knowing that there had been some slackening in the rate of growth since the early 1960s, the *Strategy* team assumed that the region's 1966 population of 17 million would grow by 1.7 million by 1981, with further growth expected to carry the region's population to over 20 million by 1991; by 2001 it was conceived to reach around 21.5 million. The team assumed that average household size would not alter in the 1980s.

The degree to which population growth was falling below expectations became increasingly clear as the 1970s developed. National and regional population projections were progressively reduced, and more of the assumptions underlying the *Strategy* became invalid. By the mid 1970s, projections suggested that the South East's population might grow little at all by 1991. Actual growth in the region up to 1981 turned out at around 800,000, whereas the *Strategy* had assumed that it would be over twice as much. But the *Strategy*'s failure to anticipate that average household size would reduce as it actually did was an appreciable mistake, countering the overestimate of population growth.

No major anxieties were expressed by the 1973 report of the Monitoring Group on Strategic Planning in the South East, which even senior civil servants agreed to be of disappointing quality (Curry 1975, 29). But by 1974 the Government came to accept that the *Strategy* was being challenged by events, including the arguments of the GLC's development plan. More than monitoring was needed, and a joint review team was formed from staff from government and the Regional Conference. An interim report (Department of the Environment 1976) showed how widely new economic and population projections differed from those of the 1970 *Strategy*, and it recognised that household numbers were growing to offset the lessened forecasts of total population. The report showed also how wide was the gap between the GLC's pessimism about the economic and social damage which continued trends and competition from the new towns could cause to London, and the sanguine view of economists from the Department of Industry who saw the capital's manufacturing decline as having relatively little impact on poverty and unemployment.

The review of the *Strategic Plan* concluded that despite continued significant population redistribution from London, there would be slight growth in the region as a whole. Although the Standing Conference had been reluctantly cooperating with the Government in a search for additional housing sites (Elson 1986, 42), the review suggested that only some locally significant adjustments were necessary, not a new strategy. So the review was able to turn to recognise London's difficulties of economic adjustment, over which the GLC had become so concerned.

The published *Review* (South East Joint Planning Team 1976) was still indecisive on the argument as to how to help London's economic and social problems. It took the view that it was too soon to substantially modify the 1970 *Strategic Plan*. It concluded that to support action to intensify the recovery of the Docklands and inner London, a five-year restraint could be put on housing growth in the outer region, but that it would be wrong to put a similar restraint on employment growth. The *Strategic Plan* was thought still appropriate for the outer region in the long term, at least.

The county councils of the outer South East were generally happy to see the possibility that pressure on them might be temporarily eased. But 'the Review implicitly acknowledged that regional planning does not exist in the sense of there being any power or machinery at a regional level to determine the allocation of resources in support of strategic objectives' (Damesick 1982, 105). Nor did government's response to the *Review* (Department of the Environment 1978) strengthen the region's planning. On the heels of its range of inner-city initiatives in the late 1970s, the government did nothing to reconcile these with the region's wider planning. The Standing Conference objected to the Government's response as being strategically unclear, and inadequate for its members' needs. In Conference's view:

> it became clear that no quantity of evidence or analysis was of itself adequate to influence central government politicians or officials who were either unaware or contemptuous of it; the statement altogether missed the point of the 1976 review, which had identified a whole set of new concerns with decline and decay in London's inner areas. (SERPLAN 1992, 20)

A close observer reviewed the effects of 40 years of regional planning in the South East at this time (Self 1982, 106):

1. Urban sprawl had been restricted and agriculture and rural areas had been protected, but a side effect had been to raise land and house prices, but to an uncertain extent.
2. The new towns had successfully dispersed people and jobs from London, but without a strategy for their continuous development or the creation of strong service centres.
3. Office employment had been substantially decentralised.
4. The countermagnet concept of the *South East Study* of 1964 was unfulfilled, due partly to a smaller increase of population than expected and partly to

bias of local planning authorities towards smaller and multiple points of growth.

5.   Planning for the South East and for London had been only weakly integrated, giving little help to London's restructuring.

So the *Strategic Plan* had brought a more temporary easement to the region's strategic problems than had Abercrombie's *Greater London Plan*. Events had overtaken both plans sooner than their authors anticipated, but Abercrombie's vision was the more durable. A vacuum of strategy grew in which nothing adequate was substituted for the *Strategic Plan*. The hiatus perpetuated struggles in the outer parts of the region over sites for new houses. And then, in 1979, a new government was elected which was not just equivocal about strategy but was ideologically antagonistic to planning. It was openly contemptuous of regional planning, in particular, being slow to see the difficulties for itself in neglecting a form of public intervention which contributed so much to the quality of life of so many of its supporters in and beyond London's green belt.

Greater London Streamlined

The new Conservative government was pressed by the Standing Conference to settle the uncertainty about regional strategy. A very short government statement was issued in 1980, but it left the uncertainties almost untouched. And the state of strategic indecision persisted as the Government struggled to reconcile its non-interventionist ideology with the facts of political life. Soon, regional planning was to become a stick with which to beat the South East's major council and the UK's largest.

The abolition of the GLC and of the six metropolitan county councils in England was an apparently sudden decision, reached by the Prime Minister on the eve of the 1983 general election. It was an earlier Conservative government which had created the GLC in 1965 and the metropolitan councils less than ten years before.

When in parliamentary opposition in the past, Ministers in the government of 1983 had spoken well of the GLC. But since the 1970s, a tide of suburban Conservative opinion had been running against the Council, anxious that Labour majorities would colonise the suburbs with council housing and Labour voters. There were divided views amongst Conservatives, even so, and when Sir Frank Marshall was asked to resolve these, his report of 1978 came down in favour of an even stronger role for the GLC. This unexpected conclusion represented a rare triumph of academic argument over naked political interest, and it caused a brief suspension of Conservative moves to dissolve the GLC.

The political pressures rose again in the early 1980s. Labour won the GLC elections of 1981, and Ken Livingstone became a leader too provocative for suburban taste – of which Mrs Thatcher was a connoisseur. There were immediate political tensions with suburban boroughs over the GLC's interests in housing and in subsidised public transport. The suburbs saw an electoral threat in new and unsympathetic migrant voters, and the direct expense of subsidising not just their own fares but those of others. For a government whose support was predominantly suburban, these and the GLC's creation of a London Enterprise Board for industrial development were unacceptable initiatives. But it was the failure of a Cabinet sub-committee early in 1983 to find an acceptable alternative to the rating system which possibly forced the abolition proposal. Failing in its main task, the sub-committee fell back on a recommendation to abolish the supposedly unpopular councils, and this became part of the Conservative election manifesto later that year.

The Government's case for abolition was set out in its 1983 White Paper on *Streamlining the Cities*. The ostensible grounds for abolition were that there was no practical role for the GLC or the metropolitan councils, and that they were excessively costly. They were argued to be strategically ineffective, and their struggle to make an impact had caused duplication and dispute with the lower tier of London boroughs and of metropolitan districts.

Most commentators from outside politics have rejected most of the criticisms of the GLC made in the White Paper, at least on its terms. Some recognised (e.g. Flynn, Leach and Vielba 1985, 32, Young and Garside 1982, 332) that the GLC had been built on shifting foundations and was inherently unstable. Its boundary arbitrarily excluded too much of its social and economic region. It could not effectively implement its strategic policies. Young (1984) put it that the GLC was too weak in its responsibilities, but too powerful to be ignored. But even those sceptical of the GLC's relevance to London and the region's problems rejected the White Paper as being blatantly political and factually misleading. The cumbersome quality of essential elements of the GLC's strategic planning was characterised by Peter Hall (1989, 171), who recorded how the *Greater London Development Plan* took four years to prepare, three to take through a public enquiry and four to be considered by the Secretary of State before he approved it. Although strategic planning is more than a statutory plan and much of the protracted process was beyond the Council's control, it left metropolitan London without binding strategic guidelines for over ten years.

The GLC's strategic failings were deep and real. The Government had sound grounds for saying so, even if it rather than the GLC had built the shortcomings into the Council's design. Its inherent deficiencies had helped the GLC fail 'to open up the suburbs during the first ten years of its life. It incurred successive defeats on land use issues in both inner and outer London, and the housing cut-backs of 1975 signalled the end of the third major attempt in the space of a decade to achieve a more equitable distribution of urban space' (Young and Kramer 1978, 213). Subsequently, the GLC handed the management of most of its widespread stock of housing to the boroughs, but it could not develop a new strategic housing role. Nor did the White Paper think there was need to. It derided strategic planning as an outdated fashion, and so avoided facing serious issues including London's transport problems and its future as a leading world financial and creative centre.

Whatever the strategic failings inevitable by the GLC's curtailed boundaries and functions, however, critics such as Flynn *et al.* (1985, 67) argue that conflict was less than the White Paper alleged. It existed, quite strongly and due to the GLC in some instances. However, conflict frequently reflected differences of interest existing within any metropolitan area. Abolishing the GLC would not remove proper differences of interest deserving to be heard. And conflicts between boroughs would remain without any upper-tier authority to occasionally mediate.

A fair assessment of the GLC's cost-effectiveness or profligacy in providing services depends upon qualitative comparisons with other authorities. Most comparisons show London's problems to be different in important ways. Where GLC services were relatively more costly, most studies have suggested that there were often very good reasons for this which government criticisms neglected.

Flynn *et al.* (1985, 60) suggest that government criticisms were not really to do with value for money but were about ideologically unacceptable policies and value judgements. It was the nature of the GLC's activities which sealed its fate more than any question of administrative overlapping and of inefficiency.

Of course, the abolition of the GLC occurred within a wider stream of centralisation of governance in Britain during the 1980s. The Government reversed the trend to devolved responsibility and wider trust of local authorities of the preceding twenty years. Control on authorities' discretion to raise expenditure locally was accentuated. The rate-capping penalty was introduced. Some significant strategic functions were switched from local government to agency hands. Others were sold off to private ownership. Routine administrative responsibilities were added, but significant policy and operational functions were withdrawn. The speed and simplistic ideology of much of what was done left a vacuum. And as time passed, it became evident that few of the supposed gains from the GLC's abolition were being won.

After Abolition: Growing Stresses

The Conference's structure had been reorganised in 1983 at the GLC's instigation, under the revised title of The London and South East Regional Planning Conference. Three years later, upon the GLC's abolition, the London borough councils were admitted to the Conference with an increased representation. But strategic planning was left uneasily divided between the Department of the Environment as the agent of government's interests, the London and South East Regional Planning Conference (SERPLAN) comprising the 33 London Boroughs and 12 counties in the region with 98 of their constituent districts, and the London Planning Advisory Committee representing only the London Boroughs. The Regional Conference now comprised 143 unwieldy authorities, all contributing elected councillors to full meetings. A Members Policy Group met to carry business

GREATER SOUTH EAST

SOUTH EAST

METROPOLITAN AREA

GREATER LONDON

INNER LONDON

Peterborough

Northampton

Cambridge

Ipswich

Milton
Keynes

Colchester

Oxford

Swindon

Reading

Southend

Southampton

Bournemouth

Brighton

Canterbury

```
0    20   40   60   80 km
├─┼─┼─┼─┼─┼─┼─┼─┼─┤
0   10   20   30   40  50 miles
```

Greater South East: constituent rings. Greater London, the area of the old Greater London Council, is part of a much larger London Metropolitan Area. But growth has now rippled right outside even this latter area – even, in fact, beyond the official South-East region, making it necessary to talk of a Greater South East.

Figure 2.4. Greater South East: constituent rings as described by Peter Hall in London 2001

forward, constituting a member from each of the twelve county councils, five to represent the London Boroughs and four to represent the district councils. SERPLAN's three functions were to monitor; to develop, maintain and review regional planning strategy; and to advocate strategy and issues to government and other bodies.

This congeries incorporated three different strategic interests struggling to find their roles. The Department of the Environment emerged after the mid 1980s to relearn skills in regional planning, as the Government was forced by pressures from its supporters to tolerate the revival of strategic planning, issuing Strategic Planning Guidance under the terms of the Act abolishing the GLC. SERPLAN attempted to assert the influence of local government – and of the counties in particular – against the threat of further government imposition of locally unwelcome growth targets. Finally, and with a fresh panache, the London Planning Advisory Committee established by the Act abolishing the GLC was charged to advise the 33 London Boroughs, and to represent their views to government and others.

At the time of the GLC's abolition, the Government's planning strategy for the region lay in policy planning guidance issued in 1986, and reissued as *Planning Policy Guidance Note 9* in January 1988. Credit for groundwork on the guidelines which related primarily to housing and the economy was claimed by SERPLAN, whose appraisal (SERPLAN 1985) of prospects for the 1990s was described (Brindley, Ridley and Stoker 1989, 53) as 'at its strongest, as seeking to guide rather than control growth'. SERPLAN took the South East's economic growth to be paramount, without any growth to be diverted as in the past to other regions of the country. This met the philosophy of the Secretary of State for the Environment, from the notably astringent right wing of the government who responded:

> At the outset it is necessary to recognise the limitations of the land use planning process. It is the private sector not the planning system that generates economic growth. But soundly based land use plans can help to facilitate development and investment. (SERPLAN 1986)

SERPLAN subsequently reviewed the strategy to take account of four or so more years of change, of a wider range of issues and of a longer future. The review was published in stages in 1989 and 1990 in three reports on *Into the Next Century, Progress on the Review of the South East Regional Strategy* and *Shaping the South East Planning Strategy*. Following thirty years behind other regions of Britain with longer experience of economic difficulty and of preparing regional development programmes, the reports asserted that perhaps their most important finding was that economic buoyancy and environmental improvement are inextricably linked. A 'lozenge of deprivation' was seen to have emerged across London from west to east, most intense in the inner east boroughs. But the former radial structure of the region predominantly focused on central London had transformed to a multi-centred pattern. It was argued that Inner London and the East Thames Corridor should provide new opportunities for growth, in an echo of the style of regional planning of the 1960s for North East England and Central Scotland. Indeed, the emphasis on reviving the economy of eastern sectors of Greater London also echoed themes heard in the *Strategic Plan for the South East* of twenty years before.

Whatever its greater sensitivity to acute local social problems of poverty and of weak employment opportunities, SERPLAN's analysis was still dominated by issues of economic overheating and of physical congestion, as for almost fifty years of prior regional planning for London and the South East. The symptoms were shortages and rising costs of labour, land and premises, all associated with an allegedly 'unsustainable rate of growth' (SERPLAN 1989, 10). Although more workers were now moving out to other parts of Britain than were moving in to the South East, the region's labour force was still expanding because emigration to other parts of the world had lessened. But within the region, labour markets had become segregated by skill levels, and also to a degree geographically. The huge increase of unemployed of the 1980s was unable to fill the surplus of jobs in the burgeoning parts of the region. Filling all the available jobs meant building more houses locally in the face of strong opposition by existing local residents. There were serious political dangers in what became known as the NIMBY ('not in my backyard') syndrome, and these had overcome the free market ideology which the Government had sought to substitute for regional planning in the earlier 1980s.

The emerging strategy had much in common with those of the past, although it vigorously encouraged a buoyant regional economy in which London's role as a world financial centre would be reinforced. It now sought to be cautious about moving more jobs out of the region, and it doubted that the Government's wish to still do so could be effective. But it wished more than it could deliver. It was long on intentions but short on the means to achieve them. It confirmed that because of congestion, it was mistaken to attract labour from other regions to overcome shortages. But it also argued that the region's own internal housing needs should be fully met by continuing the housebuilding rate of the 1990s beyond the year 2000, while failing to show why immigrants from other regions would yield to the deprived households of inner London to allow them their share of accommodation.

The wishfulness of much of the strategy perhaps reflected the disinterest of successive Secretaries of State for the Environment through the 1980s, distracted as they were by their prejudices against regional planning, by their preoccupation with abolishing the Greater London Council, and by the pressures of first disastrously replacing the local rating system with the community charge, and then of replacing the community charge with a reformulated version of the rating system. The abolition of the GLC, of course, had fragmented London's part in the Regional Planning Conference. The surrounding counties of the South East had now an even stronger opportunity to act in their own interests, whatever the rhetoric of SERPLAN's reports asserting London's vital needs and national role.

Late in 1990, SERPLAN consolidated its work and consultations into *A New Strategy for the South East*, which the Conference's chairman said was aimed at a better distribution of activity around the region; at measures to improve mobility and accessibility, with more emphasis on train and bus and less on the private car; at the conservation and enhancement of the environment in town and country; and at the provision of social and cultural facilities of all kinds readily accessible to all the people of the region. But the *Strategy* was short on detail. It could have been more convincing if it had reflected all the background sub-regional studies made for it. But not all counties would agree to those studies being published; Surrey was particularly sensitive about discussing the future of the area of Gatwick airport. And the *Strategy* also envisaged that the South East's growth might be encouraged to spill over into adjoining regions, where the scale of growth envisaged in the 1960s might at last be fulfilled.

But even the most forceful of new strategies could have only indirectly and protractedly helped improve the region's competitive advantages in the unfolding unitary European economy, as Conference's chairman hoped. And as the worthy exhortations of its Implementation Programme made clear, the *New Strategy* could not even direct how Conference's own members would interpret it, let alone the private sector or government agencies of one kind or another. Much could have been implemented through the Greater London Council, of course, had it remained in existence.

Receiving the *New Strategy*, the Government announced that it would review its regional guidance in the light of SERPLAN's statement and subsequently consult over new draft regional guidance. However, the *New Strategy* had accepted the assessment that previous government guidance had suggested about need for extra housebuilding, and it neither elaborated upon or even reproduced the Government's ideas about where the houses should go.

Independent views of the *New Strategy* were unfavourable. They supported such earlier criticism (Elson 1986, 125) as that SERPLAN's expectations that London's growth could be shifted from the west to the east were illusory, lacking any convincing indication of how this could be achieved. The Town and Country Planning Association claimed that the *New Strategy* sought only to shape trends, whereas it should oppose them where they were strategically unacceptable. The Association called into question the *New Strategy*'s fundamental effectiveness in refusing to envisage that economic activity might be decentralised, despite acknowledging that London's economy was becoming overheated and liable to labour shortages and congestion. The Association found the *New Strategy* vague about where the region's growth would be distributed; it urged the government to ensure that its regional guidance was substantial and coherent, fully capable of meeting challenges up to fifteen years into the twenty-first century, and not be just a diluted version of the inadequate SERPLAN document.

With such little surface substance, the *New Strategy* left more doubts than ever about SERPLAN's capacity to decisively lead in the South East's planning. When there had been an issue as large as the long debate over the location of the Third London Airport, SERPLAN had been incapable of reaching a unified regional view. Of course, the *New Strategy* could not reveal what went on in argument and adjustment of plans amongst SERPLAN members. A leading county planner in the South East (Steeley 1991, 6), emphasised the significance of collegiate and advocatory discussion alongside any published regional plans. Nonetheless, the impression left by the published *New Strategy* was that regional planning would be largely the sum of members' own plans. The only significant additions to government regional guidance lay in the implicit assertion that the regeneration of the East Thames Corridor had insufficient priority, and a question as to whether sufficient workers could be found to occupy the expected scale of office development in central London and Docklands. These were perhaps modest criticisms of inaction on the part of government and of some of SERPLAN's own members.

SERPLAN's constitutional lack of authority to fully deliver even government's minimum strategic expectations was reaffirmed in 1992, when Hampshire County Council declined to cooperate with the Conference's allocation to Hampshire of the largest share of the government target of 855,000 additional new houses in the region in 1991–2006. Hampshire threatened to leave SERPLAN if the Conference could not cut the County's expected contribution to regional growth. By political sleight of hand, the Government published new draft regional guidance early in 1993 both confirming the regional target and insisting that Hampshire house 6000 more people by 2001 than it wished to, but simultaneously refusing permission for a small new town for 13,000 people proposed in Hampshire by the Eagle Star Insurance company.

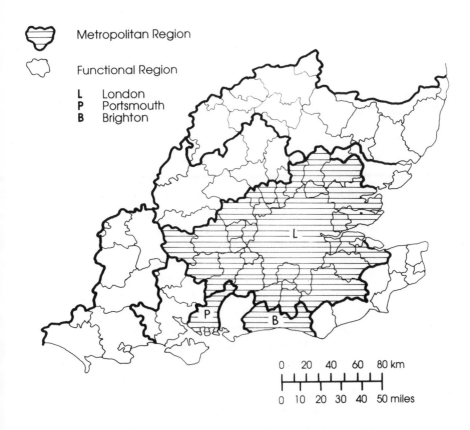

Metropolitan Region

Functional Region

L   London
P   Portsmouth
B   Brighton

0   20   40   60   80 km

0   10   20   30   40   50 miles

Figure 2.5. Greater South East: metropolitan and functional regions as described by the Centre for Urban and Regional Development Studies (CURDS), University of Newcastle upon Tyne

The return of Michael Heseltine as Secretary of State for the Environment late in 1990 had revived the impetus for regional action in the South East. Although most dismissive of planning in his prior term in the office ten years before, Heseltine's constituency was in a part of the region most prone to NIMBYism. He had run against his party's view in arguing for new support and resources for the regions of Britain traditionally favoured by regional policy. He had initiated the London Docklands Development Corporation, and he lived by grand gestures. In 1991, he brought in Peter Hall to advise him, and the idea of an Eastern Thames development corridor was given ministerial backing which it had failed to raise before. But two years and two secretaries of state later, growing national financial problems left doubts about the strength of the proposal and of its political backing. A consultant's preliminary work on the Corridor was succeeded by a government task force, aiming to prepare a strategic planning framework to be agreed and to be in place in 1994. This was a return to a regional planning style of the 1960s, but would resources follow and how consistently would the framework be filled-in by the many agents required? And what consistency and cohesion of policy and action would there be when, in only three years, the project had passed through the hands of three secretaries of state and several consultants, and faced possible further fragmentation upon the mooted abolition of the Essex and Kent County Councils in the later 1990s?

The Government's limp commitment to decisive regional planning was all too clear in March 1993 when it announced a package of potential developments to regenerate the East Thames Corridor. When untied by critics, the package was found to depend on improbable assumptions. The potential for 100,000 jobs and up to 128,000 new houses in the Corridor by 2015 depended upon preparatory action to remove contamination, improve degraded environments, ensure flood relief and create extensive new transport links. And strategically significant public investment depended upon following private capital. But in the aftermath of the market and public expenditure crises of the early 1990s, investment conditions seemed highly unfavourable. It was too much to expect sufficient preparatory public investment or an early redirection of private sector funding from more profitable opportunities in and to the west of London. The Task Force of civil servants to work with the 16 participating local authorities was no guarantee of real impetus for the Corridor. And when new regional guidance for the South East was confirmed in 1994 (Department of the Environment 1994a), the Council for the Protection of Rural England claimed that its roads programme would under-mine the objective of switching development to the east of London.

Government's indecisive and sometimes equivocal approach to the region's planning was mirrored in SERPLAN, which was internally divided according to interests and commitment. District councillors tended to be more active in SERPLAN affairs than were county councillors, but county planners dominated in officials' affairs. But the London districts were too disunited to contribute much, and those counties most under pressure by government to accept growth – Berkshire and Hampshire – were particularly unwilling to merge their interests in the greater regional good. In 1994, Berkshire insisted to the government that a maximum of 36,000 houses should be built in the county between 1991 and 2006; but government's draft regional planning guidance had proposed that 40,000 should be allowed for.

Other counties saw opportunity in cooperation; in northern parts of the region, for example, there was interest in working across the boundary of the South East with outside counties, diverting growth to other regions and considering the strategic impact of the major investment in transport infrastructure planned for the South Midlands and East Anglia. Aggressive long-term planning by the regional water authorities sold into private ownership provided an opportunity for strategic initiatives by some county planning officers. And in 1994, SERPLAN seized the opportunity of the Government's declared sympathy for policies of sustainability to pressure the Department of Transport in that direction; with support from industry, a rebalancing of investment was being proposed to strengthen the regional emphasis on public transport.

When a new secretary was appointed to SERPLAN in 1994, she looked to the possibility that the new strategic dimensions could be enlarged considerably: 'SERPLAN needs an economic strategy quickly. It has had a planning focus for 30 years. We see sustainable economic and transport strategies moving along together' (Morphet 1994, 16). These emphases reflected the more fully integrated kind of strategy which the London Planning Advisory Committee had been pursuing for London, but they were not in the SERPLAN tradition. Achieving them would meet some political difficulties, both within SERPLAN and with the Government.

So, SERPLAN has to be seen as an umbrella for only some of the strategic planning in the South East. New regions have been emerging on the flanks of the old South East; Kent's association with the Nord-Pas de Calais matched new links which counties like Hertfordshire were extending beyond the old region. And at the core of the South East, the Greater London Council had been succeeded by a new strategic planning arrangement in the form of the London Planning Advisory Committee staffed by a professional team whose strength would, by 1993, grow to around 30.

The strategic role of LPAC was in some regards even more difficult to play than had been that of the GLC. The Committee possessed statutory responsibility to advise but not to plan. The government's regional guidance note published in 1988 collated rather haphazard statements on policy, all issued prior to the Committee's opportunity to advise. By 1988, however, the LPAC planning team was able to compile comprehensive advice following substantial work and consultation. Remarkably, the 33 boroughs supported a common framework for London planning, incorporating a four-fold view of the metropolitan area as an economically buoyant world city, a social city of opportunities, a civilised city with a high quality of life, and an environmentally friendly city of stable and secure neighbourhoods. These were aims which all boroughs could readily support, perhaps, but there was understandable surprise that a consensus had been so quickly and effectively achieved. A heavy technical input by boroughs had greatly helped.

The framework incorporated policies to moderate the imbalance of prosperity and social conditions between the downtrodden east of the metropolis and the more prosperous west. This was a proposition which SERPLAN could quite readily support, because the prospect of shifting the pressures of growth was welcomed by Berkshire and the westerly counties on which they had fallen heavily in the past. And London's eastern boroughs were happy at the prospect of regeneration.

Having presented its advice to the Department of the Environment in October 1988, LPAC's Chief Planner, Martin Simmons (1990), records how the Committee was almost ignored as the Department proceeded towards its response. LPAC's criticisms of a preliminary draft (Department of the Environment 1989a) were scarcely met in the final version of the government's strategic guidelines, published as its *Strategic Guidance for London* (Department of the Environment 1989b).

The Department was thought to have paid only lip service to its exhortation that social and economic disparities between the depressed east and buoyant western parts of London should be ameliorated; it failed to recognise the strategic linkages needed for economic development. It also failed to adopt a clear development framework for the boroughs, with their relative roles established as a guide to strategic investment.

Disappointed with the Government's perspective of metropolitan planning, LPAC hoped that its influence could progressively rise as had the regional role of SERPLAN. It completed a review of its advice in 1989, and a further review in 1990. The Department of the Environment had agreed to a joint steering group of departmental and Committee officials to consider metropolitan matters under the control of government departments. This improved the routes through which the Committee could advise, but left it with a fuller vision of London's planning needs than the Government saw. The Committee aimed to bring the failings of collective strategy before the public and the Government in 1991, in publishing the conclusions of a research study on *London: A World City Moving Into The 21st Century* (London Planning Advisory Committee 1991). Aimed at an integrated strategy for development, the environment and transport, and set in a broad social and economic context and policy framework to retain London's status in Europe, the study's conclusions were difficult for the Government to evade. However, they had to be translated into 33 separate 'unitary' development plans if the boroughs were to satisfactorily prepare the ground on which the strategy must be built.

But there was no urgent response by the Government, and LPAC published a new discussion document on *Strategic Planning Issues for London* in 1992, summarising a dramatic weakening of London's economic and social conditions in only two years since the Government's strategic planning guidance. Regeneration of London's economy, a strategy for offices, the impact of the Channel tunnel and

the quality of London's green belt were amongst the issues raised, which challenged government performance and the defects of its strategic management.

LPAC struggled against insecurity and underfunding; during 1991, it was
proposed for abolition by the Conservative interests of outer London of the
London Boroughs Association – from mixed motives of party politics and pressure
for financial economies. Its Chief Planner (Simmons 1991) tacitly acknowledged
LPAC's vulnerability. He suggested that a planning commission appointed by
government could most logically replace SERPLAN and LPAC, overcoming many
of the inhibitions on effective planning.

Releasing a consultative draft of its advice on strategic planning guidance for
London in 1993, LPAC proposed that London should receive a level of public
investment to recognise the capital's significance to the national economy and in
setting national standards. The social and economic imbalances between much of
West and Outer London and much of East and Inner London must be more
effectively tackled by promoting urban regeneration, and sustainability must be
ensured. After consultations and six years after LPAC's first advice, the revised
strategic guidance (LPAC 1994) was sent to the Government as a basis for its
revised regional guidance. But there were limits to LPAC's influence on the
Government; encouraging London's regeneration meant restraining development
elsewhere, and LPAC staff saw themselves as representing 'an advisory body
advising a government that was not keen to set planning targets' (Gardner 1993).

Although its strategy had elements which might have divided them, LPAC
somehow kept the support of the 33 boroughs of the former GLC area for longer
than might have been expected, but cohesion was less in other matters. The major
groupings succeeding the GLC were the Association of London Authorities
representing the Labour boroughs of inner London, and the London Boroughs
Association representing the Conservative councils of outer London. Transport
matters were handled by these two associations, with the inner London councils
more supportive of cross-borough initiatives and the outer boroughs less so. In
this fragmented management of transport, the tendency was for strategic considerations to lose out to local ones; the development of an east–west cross-London
rail project was being held back at one stage by one borough objecting to the
location of a tunnel exit. Of course, the transfer of London's underground and bus
systems to London Regional Transport in 1984 had removed not just local control
of public transport, but also the possibility of a directly integrated planning,
transport and social policy for London.

Generally, the fragmentation of interests in London left planning and transport
badly divided, and the Government's Department of Transport gained stronger
centralised control of transport policy. But despite the Department's long familiar
disregard for a balanced transport policy fairly considering public transport, and
for any interests of the Department of the Environment for rational regional
planning, senior figures in London planning claimed that it was the Department
of the Environment which now least understood the relationship of transportation

problems to land use planning. This compounded the difficulties of balanced regional planning guidance for London and its region.

In addition to LPAC, there were more than a dozen joint initiatives to manage cross-borough issues in London in the early 1990s, of which the major was the London Fire and Civil Defence Authority, whose annual precept on the boroughs raised an operating budget of over £200 million. The London Borough Grants Committee spent around £30 million annually. Also, there was the London Ambulance Service; the London Arts Board; the London Boroughs Joint Ecology Unit; the London River Association; the London Strategic Policy Unit; the London Research Centre, which succeeded the GLC research and intelligence service; the London Waste Regulation Authority; the London Housing Committee; the London Committee on Accessible Transport; the Lea Valley Regional Park Authority which predated the GLC's abolition, managing a regional park running for 23 miles of the River Lea through two counties and several boroughs in East London; and others of lesser ambition. And wider interests like the South East Waste Regulation Advisory Committee and the regional group on minerals overlapped the metropolitan joint initiatives.

Some bodies were representative, others were nominated by various secretaries of state, and others were small and very much voluntary. Some dealt with problems close to daily life, like the London Boroughs Transport Scheme – popularly known as the 'London Lorry Ban' – which united 23 boroughs in attempting to restrict the flow and noise of heavy vehicles at nights and weekends, employing a Lorry Control Unit to contact vehicle operators, vehicle and component manufacturers, and their representative organisations.

The battery of post-GLC arrangements was so quickly introduced that it was bound to perform unevenly. Some arrangements have been moderately successful and others nearly failures (Travers, Jones, Hebbert and Burnham 1991). Least successful has been thought to be the London Borough Grants Committee which took over the funding of voluntary groups from the GLC. Requiring the support of two-thirds of the 33 boroughs for approval, the budget for 1991–92 was frustrated by lack of support from the outer Conservative boroughs, who wished a 14 per cent cut. Progress depended upon the Secretary for the Environment setting a spending limit, which then in turn required approval by two-thirds of the boroughs.

The joint cross-borough committees and units sponsored by the boroughs were topped by the cross-London arrangements directly responsible to the Government. The Metropolitan Police had long been in this position, but London Transport was taken under central control in 1984; subsequently, despite productivity improvements there was growing criticism of uncoordination in transport policy, and particularly of the drive to make London Transport pay its own way regardless of the costs imposed by this on London's efficiency as a whole.

Reviewing these patchwork arrangements, the Greater London Group of the London School of Economics (Travers *et al.* 1991, 44) came to five conclusions:

that because much of the control of cross-London matters was placed in government ministries, confusion arose because no elected body took direct responsibility and ministries failed to satisfactorily coordinate for London because they were preoccupied with their separate duties to England as a whole; that Conservative governments of 1979–92 had chosen to under-coordinate despite the potential to do much more; that although clumsy and unaccountable by comparison with the era of the GLC, the arrangements were not worse than for periods beforehand; that London's role as national capital brings unique pressures on the boroughs, which failure to meet would threaten national harm; and that London lacks a 'voice' to raise amongst those of the mayors of the world's other great cities, let alone amongst the other cities of Britain.

Several options for new strategic planning for London were advanced by different interests. The degree of elected control envisaged varied with political viewpoints. Late in 1990, the two Royal Institutes of Town Planning and of Architecture called for a Strategic Planning Authority to supersede the London Planning Advisory Committee, and they set up a group to consider and propose a constitution, powers and boundaries. Some proposed a government planning commission, and even LPAC's Chief Planner sympathised with the idea of a government commission to replace both LPAC and SERPLAN. The Labour Party proposed that if it were to win the General Election of 1992, it would establish a new, slim, effective and elected authority, which would be quite different to the GLC.

After its return at the 1992 General Election, the Conservative government remained under pressure to fill the vacuum in London governance. A junior minister was appointed to coordinate transport affairs in London; but a specially appointed Traffic Commissioner for London was insufficient for most critics. The Confederation of British Industry, usually reluctant to criticise Conservative governments, argued that one strategic body was needed to oversee transport, land use and the environment, where it counted over 60 different bodies to be taking decisions. And the London Boroughs Association (1993), representing councils controlled by Conservatives, called for its own government to massively increase investment in London's crumbling transport infrastructure.

Although so many critics emphasised that a major attack on London's strategic problems could only be tackled by a significant reconstruction of its means of strategic management, the London Boroughs Association supported the Government in opposing an elected capital authority. So, echoing the long history of US cities, a partnership of business and local authorities was launched in 1992 under the title of London First, led by the chairman of a UK-based international conglomerate. Harnessing a private sector membership to a minority of local government councillors, London First proposed to integrate London's approaches to transport, education and training, economic development, and its quality of life. The scope of interest of London First, but not its membership nor its executive powers, was very similar to that of the defunct GLC. But a parallel organisation with the same chairman and chief executive and title of London Forum excluded local councillors, and was potentially a tail to wag the dog. And a year later, London First was followed by a similar partnership – London Pride.

The vacuum of governance, and the Government's uncertainty over all but its refusal to create any form of elected body to succeed the GLC, was emphasised late in 1993, when the Secretary of State for the Environment launched his booklet *London – Making the best better*. This gesture was in effect a political defence against criticism by both the Government's supporters and opponents. Asserting what were London's assets, and setting out the Government's action for the capital, the booklet contained a questionnaire asking Londoners to reply with their views on what they most appreciated about London, what they felt to be most off-putting to visitors and how the capital could be improved. But it was clear that the Secretary of State would rule out answers calling for an elected strategic authority, and his approach had not been referred to either LPAC, the London Boroughs Association or the Association of London Authorities. No better demonstration of the shallowness and fragmentation of London's governance could have been arranged.

In 1994, local election results severely shrank the Conservative base in the London boroughs. A Committee of London Authorities was formed to represent the now wider range of boroughs in the control of other political parties. This offered the possibility of more unified action across metropolitan London – for several years at least.

The West Midlands

The Road to a Strategy

The Midland Joint Town Planning Advisory Council set up in 1923 covered a region of 2.5 million people and of 70 local authorities, the largest in area in the country. The Council structure was elaborate, its four committees for General Purposes, Regional Survey, Arterial Roads and Main Drainage, and Finance being assisted in preparing a *Regional Scheme* by six sub area committees for Birmingham, Coventry, Walsall, Warwick, Wolverhampton and Worcester. The *Regional Scheme* published in 1931 provided a zoning and road planning structure for the region. The *Scheme* was far-sighted; its suggested allocations for industry and housing, allied to land to be reserved for open space and recreation, were said to be 'indicative of the probable trend of development within the next hundred years' (Cherry 1980b, 45).

Four parts of the West Midlands were defined within which separate statutory joint committees were to prepare joint town planning schemes, implementing the *Regional Scheme* and supporting schemes already in preparation for other parts of the region. Later the Council was extended to include the whole of Worcestershire and Warwickshire, and became the Warwickshire, Worcestershire and South Staffordshire Advisory Planning Council.

The impetus of voluntary regional cooperation revived under the impact of German bombing during the Second World War, when the local authorities of the conurbation combined into six executive Joint Planning Committees for South East Staffordshire; West Bromwich, Smethwick and Oldbury; Dudley and District; Solihull and District; North Worcestershire; and Wolverhampton and District.

Birmingham would not cede its planning responsibilities to any joint committee, and in size of area and of population was larger than any of them. The City's Engineer and Hon. Surveyor to the Midland Joint Town Planning Advisory Council, Herbert Manzoni, was a member of the West Midlands Group which completed the *Conurbation* study in 1948. Although a voluntary group representing academic, industrial and civic interests, its work was supported by data and surveys provided by the 24 local authorities of the conurbation. The study was published, unlike the *West Midlands Plan* which the government commissioned from Abercrombie and Jackson and which was also completed in 1948. The *Conurbation* study assessed the scale of housing needs and argued for their relief by reconstructing the conurbation within green suburban settings, but it avoided specifying how many people might move into each of the suburban districts which were to be expanded.

Abercrombie and Jackson did not have the political constraints of a cooperative planning study. They adopted Abercrombie's principles for British metropolitan development of confining the conurbation by a green belt, beyond which 140,000 of the conurbation's population would be rehoused by expanding towns in the surrounding counties over a fifteen year period. No new towns were thought to be needed.

These two different approaches to regional growth paralleled the issue of peripheral expansion against detached urban growth which had arisen on Clydeside, and less significantly so in London. It was an issue which would still echo in the West Midlands 25 years later, when the Department of the Environment's principal planning officer for the region (Saunders 1977, 36) would regret that the wrong strategy had been adopted, rather than that of the West Midland Group.

After two years of consultation and reflection, the Government published a memorandum incorporating its decisions upon practical regional strategy. Abercrombie and Jackson's case was accepted in so far as the peripheral expansion of the conurbation would be limited, and overspill would be dispersed amongst existing towns. Four towns in Staffordshire which were short of labour and which could benefit from solely housing development were selected, together with Droitwich and Redditch in Worcestershire and three other towns where balanced industry and housing would be provided. The scale of dispersal would not be agreed until the feasibility of higher densities of redevelopment could be examined, and until the effect of new projections of population growth could be better anticipated (Friend, Power and Yewlett 1974, 68).

Abercrombie and Jackson had also recommended a new kind of regional authority. This was opposed by the local authorities, who argued that they had already established a joint regional conference to consider the *Plan*, and that the conference was supported by a technical committee to continue planning liaison between Birmingham and the three counties surrounding it.

As the conurbation expanded its economy, population and demand for built-up areas through the 1950s and 1960s, acute tensions grew between its overcrowded heart and its more spacious bordering counties. The Joint Planning Committees of the 1940s had withered with the coming of the counties as development planning authorities under the 1947 Town and Country Planning Act. A struggle over regional strategy began which would last for some 25 years. It engaged the City of Birmingham primarily with the counties of Staffordshire, Warwickshire and Worcestershire, but later also with Shropshire. The counties were not always or equally antagonistic to Birmingham, and the Ministry of Housing and Local Government and its successor, the Department of the Environment, was sometimes the initiator and sometimes the arbiter of regional proposals. After 1964, the Department of Economic Affairs had an influence which outlived its short life.

Party politics were perhaps not generally a more significant force than inter-institutional politics in the course of the struggles in the West Midlands from the 1950s to the 1970s. Nonetheless, the persistent Conservative majorities in the counties of Warwickshire and Worcestershire were clearly disinclined to import predominantly Labour voters to overspill estates established for Birmingham households displaced from slums and areas of urban renewal. At the same time, Conservative administrations in Birmingham had more to gain electorally from these exports than had alternating Labour administrations. So, relations between Birmingham and the counties could be as tense when all fell under Conservative administrations as when they did not.

The technical committee which had assessed the Abercrombie and Jackson *Plan* of 1948 operated through the early 1950s, as Staffordshire, Warwickshire and Worcestershire prepared their first development plans. It helped negotiate a proportionate balance between the counties in receiving Birmingham's overspill, and Worcestershire did suggest minor expansion schemes for Droitwich and Redditch. But the programme became bogged-down by government's refusal to meet the level of financial support which the counties claimed they required to assist. The protracted financial discussions left the technical committee of planning officers to handle only marginal planning matters. The hiatus was sharply interrupted in 1959, when the City Council made a planning application to build 14,000 houses over the outer edge of the City at Wythall, largely in Worcestershire but also encroaching upon Warwickshire.

The Wythall case is a *cause célèbre* in the history of British regional planning. The public inquiry called by government saw not only the county councils in opposition to Birmingham City Council. There was also a strong public representation by individuals and groups. The opposition groups were not unified in the outcome they sought, for the national Town and Country Planning Association and the regionally-based Midlands New Towns Society had objectives not altogether the same as those of the two county councils (Long 1961).

Most formidable amongst Birmingham's antagonists at the inquiry was David Eversley, secretary to the Midland New Towns Society, then on the staff of the University of Birmingham and later to lead strategic planning for the Greater London Council. Eversley's ability to confound both the statistics and the logic behind the City Council's case was a major contribution to undermining it. When the Government rejected the proposal almost entirely, it had two consequences. First, it warned the counties that government expected them to take more urgent initiatives to find means and places to help Birmingham rehouse its people. Second, it led to some disfavouring of the University by the City Council until Eversley left for London.

In the aftermath of Wythall, there was no markedly greater urgency amongst the counties to initiate proposals to help Birmingham. Further, Coventry's prosperity and rapid growth was threatening that it as well as Birmingham would require to overspill its boundaries. Worcestershire's planning officer had decided just prior to the Wythall proposal that it was technically possible to expand Droitwich, but not until 1964 was it possible to set up a Development Committee to manage the town's planned expansion. Other formal expansion schemes in association with Birmingham City Council under the Town Development Act of 1952 were launched at Daventry in Northamptonshire, and at Tamworth in Staffordshire. More significantly, the Government would designate new towns in 1963 at Dawley – later renamed Telford – in Shropshire, and in 1965 at Redditch in Worcestershire, which the County Council had earlier considered as a possible location for minor expansion. Warwickshire made no contribution on any scale until 1964, when Birmingham's proposal to build at Chelmsley Wood was accepted to the extent of 15,000 houses. So, not only were Birmingham's three adjoining counties contributing to its formal overspill programme by 1964, but two others further removed were also assisting. But although government had made plain its intention to impose regional planning when local government could not itself achieve it, the need continued to run ahead of the counties' initiatives.

The Labour Government returned in 1964 followed 13 years of a Conservative Government which had shown only a belated interest in regional planning. The creation of the Department of Economic Affairs brought both the reinstatement of ministry staff to a West Midlands office, but also *The West Midlands: a Regional Study* (1965). This study by civil servants indicated that there was still a large shortfall between the growth and rehousing expected from the conurbation, and the scale of overspill already committed to the counties and to new and expanded town projects. Ideas were floated of a possible new axis of 'national growth' along the border between England and Wales; there was reference to the imminent investigations of the feasibility of the Severn and Dee estuaries to develop to accommodate the expected large growth of Britain's population; a proposal to considerably expand the city of Worcester immediately drew objections from the City and County Councils.

The 1965 study was considered by the new West Midlands Economic Planning Council, which published its response in its report on *The West Midlands: Patterns of Growth* (1967). The Council used revised projections of population growth and proposed a fifteen-year programme of dispersal with a significant amount of associated industrial development. The long-term axis of growth suggested by the 1965 study was rejected, but in turn the government did not support the scale of industrial dispersal within the region favoured by the Council. It was still a time of vigorous diversion of growth to the lagging national regions. Government made it clear that the strategy for the West Midlands must focus more than the Council suggested upon overspill to places within commuting distance of the conurbation (Friend *et al.* 1974, 385).

The West Midlands Planning Authorities Conference and the West Midlands Regional Study

Alongside the new efforts of regionally-based civil servants and of the nominees on the Economic Planning Council, the local authorities found it expedient to form the West Midlands Planning Authorities Conference in 1966. Worcestershire had been persuaded by the Government's regional office to cooperate with Birmingham City Council to search for sites in the county for early housebuilding. The planning authorities in the wider region were encouraged by the Government to make a fuller review of longer term regional strategy. Despite the lingering reluctance of some to cooperate, the local authorities were collectively unwilling to have the Department of the Environment take the initiative as it had done in South East England, and as it would later decide to do in the North West, the North and in East Anglia. Since 1964, of course, the authorities had been collaborating with the Government in the West Midlands Transport Study, conducted by the consultants, Freeman, Fox, Wilbur Smith and Associates, and guided by a steering and a technical committee.

The Conference was to become of greater significance and have a much longer life than the grouping of local authorities petering out after its appraisal of the Abercrombie and Jackson plan of 1948. It was to be joined by all five counties in the West Midlands together with eleven county boroughs. Rather than accept a regional planning team led by central government, the regional Conference established its own team led by John Stevenson, a senior planner from the City of Birmingham, assisted by seconded staff from the authorities with assistance from government departments represented in the West Midlands regional office.

The *Regional Study* which was made between 1968 and 1971 became the only strategy for a British conurbation region which was led and largely staffed by the local planning authorities, rather than by government staff or nominees. A Technical Officers Panel formed a bridge between the Conference authorities and the Director of the *Study*.

Separately, a metropolitan region transportation team was established to follow-up on the consultant's initial strategic transportation study, and on the eve of the creation in 1969 of the West Midlands Passenger Transport Authority. Although also sponsored by the local authorities, the transportation team reported independently of the regional planning team. The regional team's interests were also overlapped by those of another separately directed study team, brought together late in 1968 in the sub-region comprising Coventry, Solihull and Warwickshire. The chief planning officers of these three sub-regional planning authorities held common membership of the steering panels of the regional and sub-regional studies.

Amongst this sudden and potentially confusing outburst of regional and sub-regional studies, there were particularly delicate relations between the Government's regional office and the Director of the Regional Study. The large turnover amongst local authority secondees to the planning team partly reflected ambivalence of attitudes towards the direction of the Study. A system of working parties employing middle and senior level staff representing local authorities and also academic interests only served to frustrate them. The Director drew upon consultants' help for some important parts of the Study, including an evaluation of alternative strategies. The process of the Study was opaque, however, and the Economic Planning Council complained that it was being largely excluded from it. Early in 1970, the Secretary of State, Anthony Crosland, wrote to the chairman of the Conference to stress his concerns. There was a subsequent meeting between representative officials of the Conference, the Council and the regional office to discuss cooperation, but it was resolved only to enlarge this on the basis of the team's completed work (Martins 1986, 50).

When the Study's final report on *A Developing Strategy for the West Midlands* was published in 1971, it advocated a principal axis of growth running through Birmingham from beyond Lichfield in the north-east to Redditch and mid Worcestershire in the south-west, together with associated islands of growth on the periphery of the conurbation but detached from it.

The Study's proposals for detached growth were clearly against the advice of the Government's regional officials. The *Developing Strategy* similarly clashed with the recommendations of the Coventry–Solihull–Warwickshire Sub-regional Study, completed earlier in the year. Finally, they clashed with political views in Birmingham City Council, which saw a threat to the city's economic future. The City Council's objections were taken to the length of leaving the regional Planning Conference for a period, and of withdrawing the Director and other staff who had been seconded from the City Planning Department to the regional study team. As for the Regional Economic Planning Council, its second major report on *The West Midlands: An Economic Appraisal* (1971) had drawn back from the extent of comment upon regional physical strategy of its *Patterns of Growth* report of 1967, focussing instead upon recommendations to the Government for economic policy

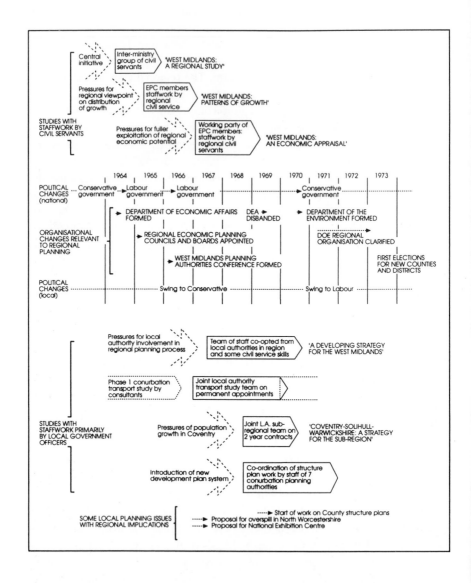

Figure 2.6. Main regional and sub-regional studies in West Midlands 1964–73 (Friend et al.)

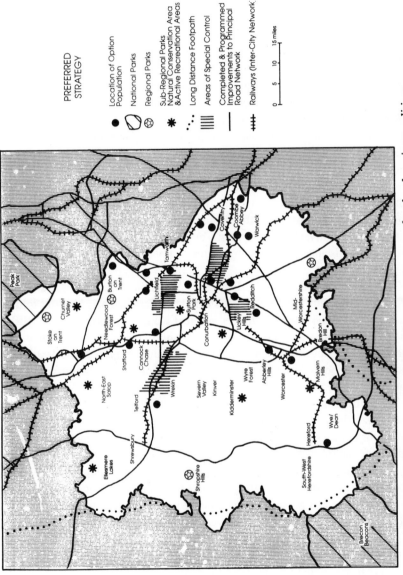

Figure 2.7. West Midlands Regional Strategy 1971: a preferred strategy soon overtaken by changing conditions

initiatives. However, the Council disagreed with the Study over its expansive assumptions about future growth and the mobility of industry.

As well as the serious political objections, criticism of the technical methods underlying the *Developing Strategy* came from the regional office of the Department of the Environment, and was laid also against the Study's alleged neglect of data in the hands of the region's planning authorities. Such points as the proposal that Droitwich should expand by less than the amount already negotiated for this town expansion scheme were used to undermine the Study's credibility. The new towns and some authorities argued that the *Strategy* actually underestimated the scope for dispersal from the West Midlands conurbation, contrary to their interests.

The *Strategy* came under sustained debate and negotiation. After the formal consultation period, the residual Study team combined with the Conference's panel of technical officers to report that no objection was sufficient to cause the *Strategy* to be rethought overall. Accordingly, a year after publication, the Conference concluded that it would advise the Secretary of State that the *Strategy* was broadly accepted. This sanguine view, however, quite ignored the fact that the structure plans now in preparation across the region collectively implied a far greater migration of population from the conurbation than the *Strategy* did. The shire counties were motivated to this partly by their wish for growth in the towns standing at a distance from the conurbation, rather than around its periphery in the green belt.

The Government's regional office and the Economic Planning Council were both dissatisfied with the Conference's bland conclusion. Their Minister told the Chairman of Conference that the Government would not approve the published *Strategy*. Conference was obliged to accept the ministerial view, and in conjunction with new and reduced estimates of regional population growth the *Strategy* was substantially modified. The scales of population and job movement from the conurbation were both reduced significantly.

The modifications rendered the technical method of the originally proposed *Strategy* scarcely relevant. The method had been to assume a common pattern of growth for the decade up to 1981, and to evaluate the relative merits of strategic options for the subsequent period of 20 years. The reduced growth upon which the modifications were based led to the abandonment of the horizon of 2001, and the earlier assumptions of growth up to 1981 were transformed to a range between the earlier figure and about three-quarters of it. The evaluation of options which had shaped the original *Strategy* had therefore been superseded.

The modifications also superseded some existing plans in some of the outlying parts of the region and in the new towns, which had come to seek much more growth than was now to be available to them.

As with the Abercrombie and Jackson plan of 1948, it had taken the government two years to issue a statement upon the *Strategy*. The statement resolved government doubts and objections from the local authorities and others. It left the Secretary of State to confirm that the authorities' structure plans properly interpreted the statement's guidelines. It was influenced by reducing projections of growth in the region, and it incorporated the strategy for the Coventry–Solihull–Warwickshire sub-region adopted by its sponsoring councils within only six months of its publication in 1971.

So, in 1974 the West Midlands came to possess its first formal, explicit and coordinated regional planning strategy. It had taken over 15 years since the pressures of demographic and economic growth had begun to seriously chafe against post-war local government boundaries. It was eight years after a regional planning conference had been set up, and six years after a full-time planning team began to prepare strategic recommendations.

Implementing and Developing the Regional Strategy

The foundation seemed to have been lain for a period of stable development in the region. There was an approved regional strategy, and before the new authorities were constituted in the spring of 1974, all except Shropshire of the region's outgoing planning authorities managed to submit structure plans for government approval and implementation by their successor authorities. Nonetheless, circumstances led to a much earlier review and updating of strategy than might have been expected.

The structure plans did not reflect a smoothly integrated system of strategic planning. Despite the Regional Study, the Conference and the formation of a West Midlands Conurbation Structure Plans Coordinating Group by the conurbation authorities, the submitted structure plans were inconsistent and uneven in style, in planning philosophy and in their horizons for allocating land for housing. Solihull and Warwickshire underprovided for households to move from Birmingham, whereas Staffordshire and Worcestershire overprovided. Strategic politics had led the counties into variations upon the strategic plan which they had earlier claimed to have broadly accepted. Furthermore, six of the structure plans came before their examination-in-public only after the conurbation authorities submitting them had been dissolved; and the newly established West Midlands Metropolitan Council had many modifications to propose in its own right, quite apart from those to which the Government was inclined.

The local administrative changes accompanying the reorganisation of English local government in 1974 were considerable and significant. They established a metropolitan county council for the West Midlands conurbation, and introduced two levels of planning in the larger region where there had been only one before. At the same time, the Severn–Trent Regional Water Authority was established which raised the level of water and sewerage planning and action far beyond the scale of even the West Midlands region, and also took it beyond the direct control of the Conference members. Similarly, the region shared in the national introduction of regional health authorities, and of regional councils for sport and recreation which followed in 1976. The battery of regional offices and organisations was formidable, although it was also untidy as Keating and Rhodes (1982) show.

The Planning Conference was reconstituted in conjunction with this most comprehensive administrative reorganisation in almost a hundred years of English local government. The Conference now comprised the five county councils of the region together with the seven district councils in the Metropolitan County and Stoke-on-Trent, the largest urban district council outside the conurbation. Simultaneously, the Conference joined with government's regional office and the Economic Planning Council in a Joint Monitoring Steering Group, by which government expected to be able to more continuously guide Conference than had been possible in the period 1968 to 1974.

The Monitoring Group was serviced by a joint Technical Working Group also combining local and central government, although its staff remained in the offices from which they were nominated. Mawson and Skelcher (1980, 156) note how this failure to bring the team together in one place left it fragmented; the members were torn by the influences of their separate agencies, independent ideas were few, and there was little resolution of the conflict of interests between the agencies. Despite the lack of cohesion in the Technical Working Group, it was able to see rapidly changing economic and population trends which clearly required an unexpectedly early review and update of the regional strategy.

The factors demanding a strategic review were outlined in 1976 in the second annual report of the Joint Monitoring Steering Group. Against a background of studies by the new West Midlands County Council suggesting that the region's thirty years of favourable post-war growth was at risk of ending, the Group reported that the strategy was in jeopardy because:

1. Population in the next ten years might grow by only a fifth of that assumed in the draft strategy of 1971, and might fall mostly beyond the Conurbation's green belt.

2. Overspill from the Conurbation was likely to be much reduced by trends including opportunities to renew housing within it.

3. There could well be a loss rather than a growth of jobs, and fewer might be able to relocate.

4. The social and economic problems of the inner urban areas required action not featuring in the earlier strategy.

The changing circumstances led the new West Midlands County Council to immediately review the plans of its predecessor councils. By quickly adopting the *Strategy for the Sub-Region*, the structure plans for Coventry, Solihull and Warwickshire had been the first in England to earn formal government approval. So with its prior statement on the regional *Strategy*, the Government had now confirmed in principle and detail where regional growth was to occur (Saunders 1977).

Some of the county councils of the region were not eager to share in a wider strategic review, however. A review would inevitably reduce the regional commitment to growth in the overspill schemes beyond the conurbation. But the changing economic and demographic conditions were only too obvious, and the review was begun in 1977 under the aegis of the tripartite Joint Monitoring Steering Group, comprised of representatives of government, of the Planning Conference, and of the Economic Planning Council. This, as Martins says (1986, 72), was not a circumstance in which independent recommendations were likely to arise.

The review was aimed to be completed in a year, but it took two and a half years and was concluded in 1979. During 1978, the review team developed a number of strategic and policy alternatives, but when these were circulated for consultation early in 1979 they were in two separate documents. The first report under the title of *A Developing Strategy for the West Midlands: Updating and Rolling Forward of the Regional Strategy to 1991*, outlined the options for physical planning in the name of both the Government's regional office and of the local authorities. However, government officials would not associate themselves with the second report on regional economic development, which appeared in the name of the Conference and The Economic Planning Council under the title of *A Developing Strategy for the West Midlands: Updating and Rolling Forward of the Regional Strategy to 1991 – The Regional Economy: Problems and Proposals*.

Although the local authorities were at one in arguing that the physical and economic components of strategy for the region were indivisible, they did not all wish the Government to adopt the same policy package. The shire counties suspected that government would insinuate policies against their interests, particularly to develop around the edge of the conurbation at the cost of prior commitments to more distant projects. This was not a concern shared with the Metropolitan County Council, which was in the course of preparing its own structure plan to replace the patchwork of plans prepared by the former county boroughs. However, the Metropolitan County wholly shared in the local authority view that regional economic prospects were much less favourable than government officials asserted (Martins 1986, 79), and in 1978 the Council submitted its first structure plan in the light of its faltering economy and problems in the inner city (Healey, McNamara, Elson and Doak 1988, 40).

The updating of the regional *Strategy* proceeded in this uneasy spirit, wherein the local authorities were collectively dissatisfied with government, the shire county councils were anxious to counter the ambitions of the Metropolitan County Council, and the metropolitan district councils sought back-door influence on the County Council's structure plan through their Conference membership.

As the various parties publicly responded to the alternative strategic options circulated early in 1979, some of the divisions of opinion were disguised, others were left for future resolution and a few were overcome by compromise. The difference between the view of the Metropolitan County Council that regeneration of the conurbation should have priority over wider regional economic growth was, for example, overcome by its acceptance that there were local problems of urban regeneration even in the shire counties. The Conference was therefore able to favour a strategy encompassing both urban regeneration and regional economic revitalisation, however vague it was and however much it left to be interpreted and disputed in subsequent structure plans.

The rise of unfamiliar economic difficulties in the West Midlands from the mid 1970s had, of course, underlain the local authorities' concern that economic policy must be part of regional strategy. The Conference was led to suggest the possibility of creating a Regional Development Board, responsible for not only the region's economic promotion but also for a regional economic development programme. The Economic Planning Council attempted to initiate a body of this kind during 1978, but the local authorities preferred to support an initiative through the Conference, and this was later fulfilled through the West Midlands Regional Forum.

The division over the place of economic policy in regional strategy was sustained in the middle of 1979, when the tripartite Steering Group decided to recommend acceptance of the Conference's favoured although rather imprecise physical strategy. Broadly, the strategy encompassed both housing and employment renewal in the conurbation, some relaxation of green belt policy and implicit growth within commuting range of the conurbation rather than distant from it. It had taken a degree of compromise for Conference, the Economic Planning Council and government to come to their agreed recommendation of approval. However, on the second, economic component of the strategy which both Conference and the Council thought essential, government would not compromise. Conference and the Council were left to issue their own statement regretting the inadequacy of government economic policy.

The 1979 general election intervened between the Steering Group's recommendation and the Government's response to it. So, it was a new Conservative government which in 1980 replied to the results of the strategic review started over three years before. The reply was confused in the view of the local authorities, and did little to resolve the ambiguities and unresolved issues of their submitted strategy. It spoke of the Government's favouring of private enterprise and disfavouring of planning constraints, and it spoke of need to assist industrial development around the periphery of the conurbation but of amending green belt boundaries only after careful justification. The mixture of political rhetoric and unresolved tensions was a flimsy outcome to the strategic update. Soon after, the Minister – Michael Heseltine – would tell the Conference that he was not prepared to discuss the issues raised by his reply, and he added that urban regeneration could not be helped by regional strategy but only by specific programmes and priorities. On the score of economic strategy, the Minister was no more cooperative than had been his Labour predecessor; furthermore, he had already disbanded the regional economic planning councils of England and abolished the Conference's ally in this interest.

It was soon evident that the updated strategy left room for argument and was certainly not comprehensive. The West Midland County Council's new structure plan examination-in-public in the spring of 1981 brought out some of the imprecision, as both the shire counties and the metropolitan districts challenged the feasibility of urban regeneration at the rate and scale assumed by the County Council. When regions up and down Britain urgently searched for sites for the rich prize of the Nissan car plant on offer early in 1981, none of the three proposed by the County Council were in its own structure plan, let alone anticipated by the strategy for the region.

The West Midlands Regional Authorities Conference

Despite the government's unwillingness to cooperate, Conference remained determined to find a role in economic policy. The loss of the Regional Economic Planning Council left a vacuum after 1979 which Conference stepped in to fill. This it attempted by reforming itself. Initially, it was proposed that the chairs and leaders of the five county councils together with two representatives of the metropolitan districts and two from the shire districts would form the West Midlands Strategic and Regional Planning Executive, which was to be advised by a West Midlands Regional Forum comprising all the region's county and district councils and new towns. A group of authority officers would give technical guidance to the Executive and the Forum, supported by a permanent secretariat. But the Metropolitan County Council did not wish to have lesser authorities with it on the Executive, and it got its way when it was decided that only the five counties would be represented on what would be retitled as the West Midlands Regional Authorities Conference.

The district councils objected to their lost influence at the top level. There were complaints that physical planning might take a back seat to economic lobbying, and the Government made it plain that local authorities should confine themselves to land use planning. The metropolitan district councils decided that if they were to be excluded from the Executive they would take no part in the new Conference either, excepting only Coventry. The shire county districts attended the first meeting of the Conference, but failed to overturn the decision to exclude them from the Executive. The county councils thereupon abandoned the stillborn Conference, forming what became the West Midlands Forum of County Councils upon which only they were represented. The district councils were to be invited to an annual consultation meeting, and intervening liaison would be the responsibility of each county council separately.

The constitution of the reformed conference leant towards economic advocacy, but it also added the task of monitoring and updating the West Midlands regional strategy. In 1984, a strategic planning conference held by the metropolitan authorities and the four shire counties led on to a review of regional strategy (West Midlands Forum of County Councils 1985), in which the once central issue of land for housing was now dominated by the problems of regional economic and physical regeneration. This was a much wider approach to the region's future than had been seen before, although the call for considerably increased government financial aid was not answered in the issue in 1987 of the Department of the Environment's first Strategic Planning Guidance under its new regional planning procedure.

The West Midlands Regional Forum

The dissolution of the Metropolitan County Council in 1986 created eleven structure plan authorities in the region in place of five. There was a new strategic game requiring new rules. The West Midlands Forum of County Councils had lost its central and largest player, and the remaining county councils were outnumbered by the newly empowered metropolitan district councils, all now equal with the counties as planning authorities. The outcome was the transposition of the Forum of County Councils into the West Midlands Regional Forum of strategic planning authorities, incorporating the four remaining county councils and the seven metropolitan district councils. The metropolitan district councils also established a West Midlands Joint Committee and a Planning and Transportation Sub-Committee which were serviced by officer groups.

The Department of the Environment's draft guidance on strategic planning for the region was published in November 1987. Although commonly regarded as perhaps the best in England, and much better received than the guidance for the South East, it was criticised by the West Midlands Joint Planning and Transport Sub-Committee. The local authorities on the Sub-Committee felt that they had faced up to a difficult issue in their strategy to release land for industry, whereas the Department in accepting the principle of more release had been reluctant to approve this in detail. But the final Guidance published in 1988 (Department of the Environment 1988b) remained less specific in some respects than the authorities wished.

By the end of the 1980s, the scope of cooperative interest in the region had much widened. The Regional Forum was now seen as giving the region a voice in the UK and Europe, as well as being a means of coordinating planning strategy in the West Midlands. The Forum was reconstituted in 1990, incorporating shire districts from the four counties of Hereford and Worcester, Staffordshire, Warwickshire and Shropshire. A technical secretariat serving the Regional Officers Support Group coordinated technical reports and papers, providing continuity and liaison between the planning authorities over the environment, waste disposal, economic development and transport.

In 1991, the Forum circulated a first consultation document to regional interests on *Asking the Right Questions*, and from the response went on to a 1992 report on *Making the Right Choices, The West Midlands: Your Region, Your Future*. The Forum was opening the region's affairs to wider view than common in other regions, and at a major conference in 1993, the Forum brought in a variety of public, private and voluntary interests to discuss the region's range of planning problems and issues. The conference was chaired by the recently retired chief planner of the Department of the Environment's regional office, whose own report to the Forum discussed opinions and issues with a candour untypical of government officials, retired or not.

The Forum did reflect some new attitudes to old doctrines gaining ground. Issues of West Midlands transport, green belt and urban growth were being looked at afresh. But more stayed as before. In 1980, Gordon Cherry had written:

> In the West Midlands more than fifty years of attempting to harmonise public sector investment and control private development in an integrated set of programmes on a regional scale have met with uneven results... There has been no shortage of technical input or imagination, but serious lack of political commitment within an ambiguous decision-making and implementation framework. The conclusion must be that we have failed to fashion an institutional framework for regional planning. (Cherry 1980b, 52).

Over a decade later, the same most experienced observer of planning in the region asked:

> How on earth did we get ourselves into such a plan formulation process, ostensibly so open to public debate and scrutiny, but in practice so tortured, so protracted, so restricted to fixed political and professional positions, so surprise free and ultimately so unrewarding?... *Making the Right Choices* has been expertly prepared, it is carefully crafted and no doubt is an astute balancing act between the political masters representing urban and rural interests. It is a report aimed to please most people and offend no one. (Cherry 1993, 468)

The Forum was plainly serving an unwieldy range of clients, but some old ideas about regional governance were being revived. At the Town and Country Planning Summer School in September 1990, Graham Shaylor, the recently retired Director of Planning for the City of Birmingham, called for a proper urban government to produce an overall plan for the metropolitan area of 2.5 million people. After 16 years as Director for the conurbation's core district, Shaylor had come to accept the necessity for strategic planning on a wider and more effective basis than that of the abolished metropolitan county.

The Coventry–Solihull–Warwickshire Sub-Region

The Sub-Regional Study

The Sub-Regional Study for Coventry–Solihull–Warwickshire (CSW), carried out between late 1968 and early 1971, was produced by an independent advisory team, steered by a joint committee of chief officers of the three financing local authorities. The terms of reference required the team to:

> prepare proposals for the major land uses in the sub-region, having regard to the development of population, employment, recreation and shopping in relation to each other and to transport. The purpose of the study is to serve as a bridge between regional considerations and the development plans of local planning authorities and to provide the authorities concerned with a common framework within which they can coordinate their plans and programmes. (CSW 1971, 184)

The study followed several years of sustained pressure by the Ministry of Housing and Local Government for the authorities to agree a strategy not only for Coventry's growth, but also for contributions by Warwickshire towards helping the housing needs of Birmingham and other parts of the West Midlands conurbation. Warwickshire was being squeezed by two landlocked cities which threatened boundary extensions into the County. The Department of Economic Affairs (1965b) had forcibly put the need for Coventry and Warwickshire to settle their differences and to adopt a joint strategy. The 1966 Review of the City of Coventry's development plan anticipated that all building land in the city would be developed by 1975. On its western flank, Warwickshire's objections had been set aside in 1964 when the Ministry had approved Birmingham's plan to build 15,000 council houses on the scale of a small new town at Chelmsley Wood.

The accentuating pressures finally persuaded the County Council to participate in the study. Birmingham City Council did not share in it, although like Warwickshire and Coventry the City was a partner with the other local planning authorities of the West Midland region in the contemporaneous and overlapping West Midland Regional Study (1971). Solihull County Borough Council did join the study to provide Warwickshire with the comfort of a sympathetic partner, similarly inclined in both politics and a disinclination to receive a further share of public housing to meet Birmingham's needs. Under the leadership of Urlan Wannop, a team was recruited specifically for the purpose of the study.

The Strategy for the Sub-Region

The team's recommended *Strategy for the Sub-Region* was published in May 1971, several weeks after being presented to the Steering Board. By the end of November 1971, all three sponsoring councils had adopted the *Strategy* – although it arose from an independent study to which none of the councils had any prior commitment. The three councils were thereupon the first in the country to be asked to prepare structure plans as introduced by the Town and Country Planning Act, 1968.

The preferred strategy of the West Midland Regional Study (1971) published in September 1971 differed clearly from that for the sub-region. The two studies agreed on the scale of housing for future overspill from Birmingham into

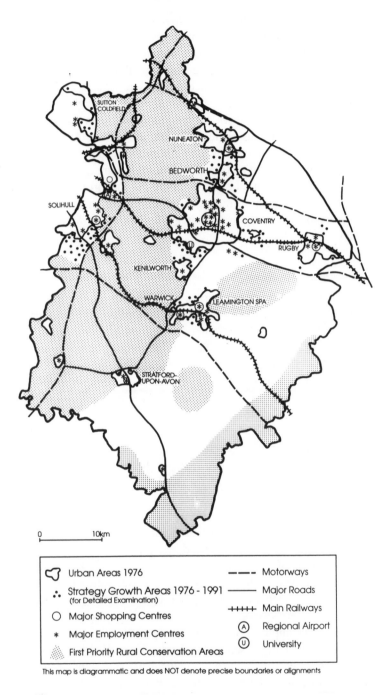

SUTTON
COLDFIELD

NUNEATON

BEDWORTH

SOLIHULL

COVENTRY

RUGBY

KENILWORTH

WARWICK
LEAMINGTON SPA

STRATFORD-
UPON-AVON

0   10km

	Urban Areas 1976		▬ ▬ ▬	Motorways
∴	Strategy Growth Areas 1976 - 1991 (for Detailed Examination)	▬▬▬	Major Roads
○	Major Shopping Centres	┼┼┼┼┼	Main Railways
*	Major Employment Centres	Ⓐ	Regional Airport
	First Priority Rural Conservation Areas	Ⓤ	University

This map is diagrammatic and does NOT denote precise boundaries or alignments

Figure 2.8. Coventry–Solihull–Warwickshire Sub-Regional Study 1971: the recommended strategy

Warwickshire, but they disagreed over where it should go. The Regional Study proposed locations detached from the conurbation, which divided it not only from the Sub-Regional Study but from the Department of Environment. It was to take over two years for government to negotiate and develop modifications to the regional strategy which would be concluded only in January 1974. What led to the rapid acceptance of the *Strategy for the Sub-Region*, particularly after a study later described as the high water mark of systems planning in Britain, a planning method often criticised for its neglect of political realities? At the outset of the Sub-Regional Study, the three sponsoring authorities held no common view as to the scale of growth to be planned for, nor as to what share each would accommodate, nor as to where it should be located. Why did the three councils receive the tacit approval of government to the recommendations of an advisory study team, over two years before a regional strategy for the West Midlands was fully established?

Why was the Strategy Adopted?

The route to the *Strategy*'s adoption has a significant lesson for understanding of the conditions for effective regional planning. The political context was critically important. But the political circumstances into which the recommendations of the Study emerged in 1971 were significantly different to those in which it was launched in 1968. It can even be supposed that elements of the *Strategy* which were acceptable in principle in 1971 might not have been acceptable, or might not have been so quickly supported, if there had not been unexpected changes in the political context since 1968.

The change of political circumstances followed the replacement of a Labour government by a Conservative government in June 1970, with the consequence of rejection of the Redcliffe–Maud proposals of 1969 for reorganisation of English local government. At the start and for most of the period of the study, the expectation of the sponsoring councils had been that Coventry and Warwickshire would be joined as a new unitary authority. It was expected that the Borough of Sutton Coldfield would be lost from Warwickshire, being an integral part of the West Midlands conurbation and separated by a green belt from Coventry and the greater part of urban Warwickshire. Socially and economically, Solihull was an integral part of the West Midlands conurbation as was Sutton Coldfield, but had won treasured independence as a county borough and had been lost to Warwickshire prior to the emergence of the Redcliffe–Maud proposals.

The Study team completed its report in early 1971 in ignorance of the pattern of local government reorganisation for England which the new Conservative government was about to announce. By coincidence, the team's draft report was delivered from the printer the day before the announcement that Coventry was to become a metropolitan council within a West Midlands Metropolitan County. This was an astonishing departure from earlier expectations that Coventry would be

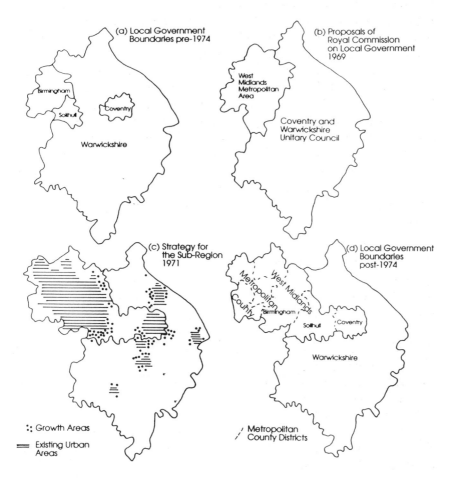

Figure 2.9. The politics of acceptance of a Strategic Plan: the strategy for Coventy–Solihull–Warwickshire and changing local government boundaries

united in a greater Warwickshire. On the advice of the Secretary to the Study's Steering Board, the draft report was circulated to the three sponsoring authorities without any late change to acknowledge the reorganisation proposals.

The immediate response of some local officials was that the recommendations of the study report had been effectively killed, because the westerly political attachment of Coventry to the West Midlands Metropolitan County Council would negate the report's strategy to consolidate the historic north–south axis of Warwickshire towns running through Coventry. The same point was put to Team members by leading Coventry councillors at public meetings to publicise the Study's recommendations (Wannop 1985, 204). The Team's answer was that a north–south axis had developed over several centuries, despite the historic administrative separation between the central city and its expanding and intimately linked neighbouring towns to the north and south. The Team argued that the unexpected outcome of local government reorganisation did nothing to deny the economic, social and environmental logic of the recommended strategy, whatever the disadvantages of continued administrative separation between Coventry and Warwickshire.

Notwithstanding this turmoil of political realignment, the three local authorities took only a few months to conclude that their advantage lay in the same direction as the Study Team's rationalisation of the relationship between its strategy and the future pattern of sub-regional local government. Why was this? There were five strands of political rationale behind the authorities' acceptance of the sub-regional strategy recommended to them.

First, for varying reasons all three councils were united in an urgent wish to preserve the green belt between the West Midlands conurbation and the Coventry belt of towns on the north–south axis through the city. Warwickshire wished to limit the eastward encroachment of the conurbation into the County, which had already encompassed Chelmsley Wood and could threaten further loss of territory to other administrative hands. Neither did Coventry wish to see any narrowing of the green countryside belt between it and the conurbation, although it was willing to become just one metropolitan district amongst several rather than the focus of a greater Warwickshire, in order to retain its status as an education authority together with other functions afforded only to metropolitan districts. Solihull also wished to protect the larger part of its green belt, so as to conserve its environmental privileges and simultaneously deny Birmingham the opportunity to rehouse council tenants and likely Labour voters in the district. Second, although Solihull had been a county borough with unitary status for several years, its position was not totally secure in the face of some of the proposals for local government under consideration in the late 1960s. Its size of population was at the borderline of acceptability for some of the administrative patterns under discussion. Although the scale of growth proposed for Solihull by the Sub-Regional team might have seemed unduly large if the borough were to be extinguished, as the Redcliffe–Maud proposals would have ensured, the arrival of a Conservative government during the Study raised hopes of reprieve. In these new circumstances, it became to Solihull's advantage to expand sufficiently to lift itself safely above the threshold size for an acceptable metropolitan district. Later, however, when its district status had been assured, Solihull would attempt to scale down its expansion when it came to prepare its structure plan.

Third, although the Government's reorganisation would slightly ease the boundary strait-jacket which was curtailing Coventry's growth, it did so only to the west where the city was determined not to expand. Choosing to protect itself by the green belt from being engulfed by the much larger urban mass of the conurbation, Coventry could only substantially expand by opportunities to the north, east or south. So, Coventry remained as dependent upon Warwickshire's cooperation to find opportunities for growth as it had been at the outset of the

Sub-Regional Study. Whether or not the Study's proposed growth was located exactly where Coventry itself would have preferred, the scale was adequate. The City Council was bound to accept the proposals or face the cost of continued and probably fruitless dispute with the County Council.

Fourth, Warwickshire had been thrown into extreme anger by the unexpected pattern of local government reorganisation being thrust upon it. The County had assumed the prospect of its unification with Coventry, even though it would increase the likelihood that the traditional Conservative majority on the shire Council would sooner rather than later fall to a Labour administration. However, by simultaneously losing Sutton Coldfield and failing to gain Coventry, Warwick-shire's population was so reduced that with one blow it was swept down from the upper to the lower ranks in the league table of English counties. This was the very language in which Warwickshire figures discussed the County's fate. These unexpected and unwelcome circumstances made Warwickshire eager to grow quickly to restore something of its lost status. The recommended sub-regional strategy offered the County both growth and a means of rapidly legitimising it in a statutory structure plan.

Fifth, the strategy accorded with the Department of the Environment's princi-ples for the growth of the West Midland Region, and it offered its Minister the hope of reduced political tensions in a part of the West Midlands.

These, then, were the different rationales which led the three local planning authorities to accept the recommendations of their independent study team, and to do so with the tacit approval of government. The common context was of political considerations unexpectedly and substantially altering during the period of the Study. Had the Labour government of 1968 when the Study began continued until 1971, the Team's proposals would have been seen in quite a different light. A Labour government would have much more closely followed the Redcliffe–Maud proposals to merge Coventry and Warwickshire, and it is possible that the Study's acceptance would have been neither so rapid nor possibly so complete as achieved by the arrival of a Conservative government.

After the Strategy: Structure Planning in the Sub-Region

After the *Strategy's* quick acceptance, the Department of the Environment invited the three sponsoring councils to prepare England's first three structure plans. It then became clear that the councils would each interpret the *Strategy* as it chose to. When considering the three structure plans submitted to him, the Secretary of State had therefore to resolve differences arising in the individual interpretations.

Coventry claimed that more of the city's people would now have to find homes in Warwickshire. For its part, the County Council preferred not only to limit Coventry's further expansion to less than envisaged in the *Strategy*, but wished also to limit growth in rural Warwickshire to little more than the natural increase of rural dwellers. The Solihull Council was prepared to have growth on a scale which met the Secretary of State's expectations, and so in 1975 he modified the Coventry and Warwickshire plans to compromise between the two in regard to the expansion of the city.

In the following years, declining prospects of economic and population growth allowed Warwickshire to continue to press for cuts in Coventry's claims for additional land and housing. The County Council remained determined to prevent growth which could justify expanding the boundaries of the City of Coventry or of the West Midlands County Council, to further reduce the area of Warwickshire. But there was continuing pressure on Warwickshire, emphasised when the first *West Midlands County Council Structure Plan* was published in 1980. The *Plan* doubled Warwickshire's then estimate of demand for houses for migrants from Birmingham and Solihull, and also increased the estimate of demand from Coventry.

A report on the state of housing in the region (West Midlands Forum of County Councils 1981) recommended that the county councils should make a periodic analysis of strategic issues in the various parts of the West Midlands, including housing needs and demand. The results of this analysis should, it was said, be discussed with the district councils. So the process of regional planning had become divided; the county councils had formed a Forum of their own and had separated their interests from those of district councils in both the metropolitan and the shire county areas. The Sub-Regional Study of 1971 had looked to a planning horizon of 1991, but accepting the *Strategy* could not prevent recurrent disputes between its sponsoring councils about its implementation as conditions unfolded over the years.

Conclusion: Only Relative Stability

These two most major regions were also the most prosperous and expansive in the UK when their standing conferences became permanent in the 1960s. Urban expansion for new housing was the outstanding issue in common. Both regions have since experienced significant economic and local government change. Each has seen the arrival and later departure of a metropolitan authority.

As economic confidence was dented in both regions in the 1970s and 1980s, causing economic regeneration to be added to their longer established priority of satisfying housing needs, the conferences diverged in their emphases. The West Midlands conference broadened its scope to include a more direct part in supporting the region's economic development than occurred in the South East, where SERPLAN continued to focus primarily on land use and physical planning of a more traditional kind.

CHAPTER THREE

Adversity and Innovation
Strathclyde and North West England

Preface: Regional Regeneration by Innovation in Adversity

There has been a less continuous history of collective regional planning in the West of Scotland and the North West of England than in the South East and the West Midlands of England. Yet, as two of the UK's major metropolitan industrial regions, the West of Scotland and North West England have long suffered similarly adverse and extensive problems of economic and environmental regeneration. Their sustained problems might have been expected to stimulate collective regional initiatives, but those which have been internally fostered have been only spasmodic.

Yet, these two regions have had quite different experiences in regional planning. In North West England, divided between metropolitan Manchester, metropolitan Liverpool, and the counties of Cheshire and Lancashire, regional planning has been a very occasional and diffuse process, frustrated for much of the time by mistrust amongst the authorities. In the West of Scotland, after failure to persuade effective local cooperation in regional planning over a long period, the government imposed the Strathclyde Regional Council at the local government reorganisation of 1975.

Strathclyde has been a unique experiment in regional governance; the only metropolitan regional council ever introduced in the UK, and with an exceptional range of services by which to support its strategies. Unified strategic planning for Strathclyde has contrasted with North West England, where the separate county councils for the region's two metropolitan areas were each constrained in size and functions, and neither were capable of a significantly greater strategic role than had been the city councils they replaced.

The differences of strategic approach and of local government reorganisation in these regions in the 1970s stemmed wholly from the special experience in regional planning of the Scottish Office. After further reorganisation in the 1990s, Strathclyde will be abolished and both regions will be fragmented. But Strathclyde will have been a unique regional experiment by comparison with the rest of the UK and with other countries.

Clyde Valley to Strathclyde

The Developing Idea of a Region in the West of Scotland

Of all regions in the UK, the West of Scotland has had the most varied experience of regional planning and governance. Its strategic growth has been influenced by four major regional plans – by the *Clyde Valley Plan* of 1946, by the *Central Scotland Programme for Development and Growth* of 1963, by the *West Central Scotland Plan* of 1974 and by the structure plan of Strathclyde Regional Council since 1975. And entering the 1990s, the Council remained the only regional and metropolitan local authority ever instituted in the United Kingdom. It was a unique experiment and an exemplary illustration of the impermanence of attempted solutions to regional governance. For the Council was to survive for only a year beyond its twentieth birthday in 1995.

So, although notably influential and effective, this distinctive experience of regional initiatives in the West of Scotland serves to confirm the inherent volatility of solutions to regional issues. The Clyde Valley region of 1946 became the West Central Scotland region of the 1960s, and in 1975 grew further to become the Strathclyde region. As the scale of regional issues continued to spread in the 1990s, they outgrew even the wide area of Strathclyde. And although significantly different to the kind of regional authority proposed by the *Clyde Valley Plan* of 1946, the Council's experience vindicated the *Plan*'s conclusion that because regional planning must be a continuous task, its own proposals were 'not final'.

The Clyde Valley Plan

A plan after the style of Abercrombie's analysis and prescriptions for Greater London, his *Clyde Valley Regional Plan* was the first significant stage and perhaps the most important event in regional planning in the West of Scotland. The *Plan*'s proposals were vivid and of such comprehensive scope as to quickly and enduringly earn a visionary reputation.

At the heart of the *Plan* team – and 40 years later still central to debate on strategic issues in the region – was Robert Grieve, the most distinguished of all regionalists in the British experience. He had been associated with the small cooperative regional planning team established by the local authorities in the 1930s, for whom the scope of regional planning was centred on landscape planning for arterial road projects. Within less than ten years, a much wider scope for regional planning had been accepted through the *Clyde Valley Plan*, initiated in 1944 by Tom Johnston, the outstanding Secretary of State for Scotland.

The *Plan* faced the most severe concentration of slum housing in the United Kingdom. Twenty-five years earlier, in 1919, it had been estimated that 57,000 new houses were needed to meet Glasgow's needs. There had been a major public housing programme between the two World Wars, but conditions remained deplorable and the *Plan* raised the estimate of need to 100,000 houses. Already, many had come to accept that the City's problems of unfitness and overcrowding

HOUSING 87

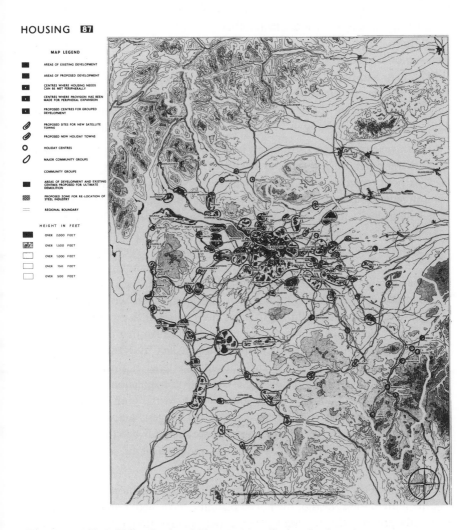

MAP LEGEND

AREAS OF EXISTING DEVELOPMENT

AREAS OF PROPOSED DEVELOPMENT

CENTRES WHERE HOUSING NEEDS
CAN BE MET PERIPHERALLY

CENTRES WHERE PROVISION HAS BEEN
MADE FOR PERIPHERAL EXPANSION

PROPOSED CENTRES FOR GROUPED
DEVELOPMENT

PROPOSED SITES FOR NEW SATELLITE
TOWNS

PROPOSED NEW HOLIDAY TOWNS

HOLIDAY CENTRES

MAJOR COMMUNITY GROUPS

COMMUNITY GROUPS

AREAS OF DEVELOPMENT AND EXISTING
CENTRES PROPOSED FOR ULTIMATE
DEMOLITION

PROPOSED ZONE FOR RE-LOCATION OF
STEEL INDUSTRY

REGIONAL BOUNDARY

HEIGHT IN FEET

OVER 2,000 FEET

OVER 1,500 FEET

OVER 1,000 FEET

OVER 750 FEET

OVER 500 FEET

*Figure 3.1. Clyde Valley Regional Plan 1946: relieving the slums by new towns
and decentralised housing developments*

should not be solved within its relatively generous boundaries, but the City
Corporation still wished to try.

Accordingly, the *Plan* was assembled in the context of dispute about the ability
of the City Corporation to solve Glasgow's problems. The Scottish Town and
Country Planning Association had for several years argued for new towns divorced
from the built-up area of the conurbation. The tide of planning thought was
towards regional planning, and government ran with it. The commissioning of the
Plan was placed in the hands of the Clyde Valley Regional Planning Advisory

Committee, comprising seventeen of the region's local authorities but under the dominating influence of the Scottish Office.

Within Glasgow, the ruling Labour politicians were divided. Some had long seen regional planning as inseparable from planning for the City. Jean Mann (1942), who had been Convenor of Housing on the Corporation and – like Sir William Whyte, secretary to the Regional Planning Advisory Committee – a long-term member of the Scottish branch of the Town and Country Planning Association, wrote critically in 1942 of recent developments, asking:

> Can we contemplate carrying on in the old way, transferring the population to the outer fringes, without regard to time and money spent on travel; without regard to Location of Industry?... Well-meaning civic patriots are already planning to make their ugly fat cities larger still by boundary extensions... If Scotland's housing requirements are 400,000 houses, these should be planned in new towns, to which industry should be directed, and/or directed to existing small Burghs which, on survey, indicate the need for further development... Even now, Glasgow is planning 6500 houses at Castlemilk (twice the size of Knightswood) without the slightest regard to industry or the increasing value of the land which will surround their development, and swell the private owner's purse; or to the theft of Ruther-glen's green belt... Some pseudo planners still plan that the workers shall be near such works, building in the centre of the City 10-storey tenements. The road engineer rejoices in a beautiful arterial highway (which cuts through the centre of a housing estate with a population of 50,000). An expert architect announces that the solution to the problem of the over-crowded city is overhead transport. Another suggests houses underground. Like the rehoused family they insist that we should live in the kitchen. They promise to plan it for us, beautifully and compactly, so that we sleep comfortably on the pulleys?

The struggle in the City Corporation between civic and political aggrandisement and the more selfless ideas of the liberal planning movement broke to the surface in counter-proposals to the *Clyde Valley Plan*, published by the City Engineer, Bruce, in 1945 and 1946. Bruce proposed to rebuild Glasgow – including the whole city centre – within its conurbation of contiguous burghs. Unreal as it was, the prospect led the City Council to object to East Kilbride – the first of the *Plan*'s new towns – and to accept a spillover of Glaswegians only later in 1952.

The *Plan* had 76 Conclusions or Recommendations. The strategy to meet Clydeside's persistent overcrowding of rooms, and the congestion and unfitness of the dwellings in which they were meanly housed, was decentralization from redevelopment areas on the model of Greater London, as previously advanced by the consortium of lay and minority councillor opinion sustaining the Town and Country Planning movement through the wartime period. East Kilbride, Bishop-ton, Houston and Cumbernauld were to be the new towns whose attractions for

Estimated Decentralised Population from Redevelopment Areas		
Location	Estimated Population	Decentralised Population from Redevelopment Areas (Approximate figures)
City of Glasgow	1,127,948	550,000
Large Burghs		
Airdrie	27,860	3,500
Clydebank	47,912	17,500
Coatbridge	45,045	10,000
Dumbarton	22,214	10,000
Greenock	81,297	39,000
Hamilton	39,315	11,000
Motherwell and Wishaw	67,693	11,500
Paisley	91,167	28,500
Port Glasgow	19,785	9,500
Rutherglen	25,441	9,000
Small Burghs		
Barrhead	12,265	6,000
Johnstone	13,882	4,000
Milngavie	6,400	nil
Renfrew	16,509	7,000

Figure 3.2. The Clyde Valley Regional Plan 1946: restructuring Clydeside by redeveloping the slums and almost halving their population

Glaswegians and for people from Greenock, Paisley and eleven other old towns on Clydeside would divide the Regional Planning Advisory Committee, helping frustrate the *Plan*'s advance for almost twenty years. In retrospect, after forty years' development of planning on Clydeside and in Scotland, the new towns seem not such a dominating element in the *Plan* as they appeared to be at that time. Indeed, setting aside half of Houston's full capacity which was to be built only if the steel industry of North Lanarkshire were to transfer to the navigable Lower Clyde, the other new towns were to house a maximum of only 190,000 of the 500,000 people to be decentralized from Glasgow and of the 166,500 to move out of redevelopment areas elsewhere on Clydeside. The major contribution to rehousing the people of the teeming tenements of Cowcaddens, Govan, Maryhill, Dalmarnock, Paisley, Motherwell and the old burghs would be in the historic way, by outward extension of contiguous urban areas. Glasgow's spread was to be curtailed by a green belt but, even so, at least 250,000 of the 550,000 – half the City's population – who were to leave the then built-up area through the decentralization programme, were to resettle on the periphery of the City.

Understandably, at a time of large visions in social and physical planning which were little restrained by speculation about long-term resources, majority opinion in the City Corporation fought the *Plan* on the issue of the new towns and of the constraint of the green belt, which removed much of the massive capacity for rehousing provided by the boundary extensions of less than a decade before. Yet, the new towns were intended to absorb under half the number of Glaswegians which the *Plan* intended should find homes in new peripheral estates around the City. Furthermore, while the green belt would have constrained building over much of the City's long-pursued extra territory won prior to the War, it lay beyond the boundary at other points where the City Corporation might have foreseen future building and further boundary extensions. The opposition of the Corporation to the new towns has subsequently been represented as a dispute principally over long-term strategy, with the Corporation's case for the City to hold most of its population represented by Bruce's (1946) Second Planning Report. The more immediate justification lay in Glasgow's plans for Easterhouse and Drumchapel, substantially advanced by the Corporation's architects during wartime, but jeopardized by the green belt which the *Plan* had thrust over these areas of the City. Although Pollok and Castlemilk – the other two of what would become the four major post-war peripheral housing estates – were not so impeded by the *Plan*'s green belt, the impetus of Glasgow's building programme was seen to be seriously threatened by the green belt's advance in the north-east and north-west sectors of the City.

The *Plan* saw the new towns and the restructuring of Glasgow neither as overwhelming all other proposals and recommendations nor, after the flowering of its influence since the early 1960s in the second half of its life, can these be seen as other than part of a wider design for continuous regional planning and governance.

It was not on the *Plan*'s call for an enquiry into its proposal for a Regional Authority that the Advisory Committee failed to agree, but rather on the shorter-term issue of where early housebuilding should be located. The concluding chapter of the *Plan* on Local Government Administration was written by Robert Grieve at the instigation of Sir William Whyte, the Clerk to the Committee. It asserted that the water-tight compartments of the then system of local government areas were inadequate for the best development of the Clyde Valley; a Regional Authority was not only a desirable but necessary representative of the various local authorities, relying on them for its income to manage its functions of acquiring and controlling land for the green belt; regional parks; conservation of water resources; the establishment of new towns; oversight of local planning schemes and supervision of the Regional Plan in an advisory capacity, including advice on the distribution and location of industry. Prior to passage of the New Towns Act of 1946, the *Plan* envisaged a Regional Authority which would not merely municipalize the green belt but would develop the new towns, therefore embracing more than the narrower conurbation area to be administered by the English metropolitan counties of 1974– 86, but less than the regional hinterland of Clydeside which Strathclyde Regional Council would cover from 1975. In functions too, the *Plan*'s

Regional Authority was not assigned any of the personal services of social work, education or consumer affairs which Strathclyde would later administer.

The *Plan* made a case for a confined regional administration which rested first on the compactness of the industrial, economic, commercial and cultural ties of the conurbation and their coherence under Glasgow's domination. The reasoning was that 'a reasonable line must be drawn to include only such areas as have outstandingly common interests and problems. It appears to us that the compact integration and great population of the Clyde Basin form the really convincing argument for treating it as a Regional Administrative Unit.' Second, it rested on the geographical separation of the rural counties and on the national concerns which their coastal and recreational issues were thought to be. In contradistinction to the Clyde Basin and its 'great congested area where the threat of complete fusion and close development are imminent', the *Plan* posed the situation of Ayrshire, 'geographically separate from the Conurbation', and the coastal holiday aspect 'which is being more and more looked upon as a national concern rather than as a local or even a regional one.' Implicitly, the *Plan* anticipated the responsibilities of the Countryside Commission for Scotland and the Scottish National Planning Guidelines which, 30 years later, would be amongst the array of strategic agencies and interventions amongst which the new Strathclyde Regional Council would have to establish its own role in regional planning and development.

The Influence of the Clyde Valley Plan, 1944–75

In 1960, after its first fifteen years of life, the *Plan*'s influence was not just incompletely developed but seemed also to be fading. Yet, in the next fifteen years the *Plan*'s robustness became increasingly evident as the inevitability of its prescriptions were borne out.

Though the *Clyde Valley Plan*'s proposals had been only slowly implemented between 1946 and the early 1960s, they were then fulfilled in quantity. By 1976, 11 of the *Plan*'s 15 key proposals had been implemented, as had 39 of 61 other recommendations of lesser significance. This was a tribute to the *Plan*'s depth and foresight, both in terms of substantive policies and on the need for institutional structures to carry them through. In the 1960s, when the Wheatley Commission began to examine Scotland's local government system, the *Plan*'s influence could still be seen not just on the physical development of the West of Scotland, but on the face of Scottish public administration.

Influential and increasingly seen to be so over a life of 30 years, why did the *Plan*'s reputation endure, and why was Scottish experience of regional planning and governance different to that in England?

Through the 1950s, the Scottish Office kept faith with the potential for regional planning, at a time when collective planning was out of favour except as a tool to reach increased targets for public sector housebuilding, and without its strongest adherents finding the wider support and open political sympathy which revived nationally only in the 1960s. Robert Grieve had joined the Scottish Office when the *Plan* was completed, to become Chief Planning Officer of the new Scottish Development Department created in 1962. James McGuinness, later to build what would become the Scottish Economic Planning Department, was an administrative civil servant in the Scottish Office associated with the *Plan's* production; his influence would intertwine with Grieve's through thirty years of innovation and reform in Scottish regional development and in government, centrally and locally. Backing could be earned for proposals and ways of thinking not openly acceptable by the Conservative government by engaging the support of the non-party lobby of Scottish interests, in which commerce, industry, local politicians, unions, employers and academic representatives sank positional differences for Scottish advantages.

The convictions of Grieve and McGuinness of the potential of regional planning would have been insufficient without the detachment from Whitehall of the Scottish Office and of Secretaries of State for Scotland; rivalries between Scottish Office departments existed, as between the Development Department and the Agriculture and Fisheries Department in the formative years of the Highlands and Islands Development Board, but the Secretary of State spoke in Cabinet for a collective Scottish interest against the narrower interests of Whitehall Ministers for functional departments like Industry, Education or Transport. With a geographical rather than a functional base and with the rise of political nationalism through the 1960s, the Secretary of State for Scotland pressed a partisan case for investment in regional development as no other Cabinet Minister was so inclined to do. Sponsorship of regional planning and of programmes for regional development became of great political advantage to both Labour and Conservative Secretaries of State for Scotland.

If the *Plan* can be seen as highly successful in so many of its proposals, this does not mean that it was right, even in its fields of greatest influence. The perspective of such a long history even allows the *Plan* to be challenged in what was for long seen as the significant failure of government to curtail Glasgow's early intrusions into the green belt. The ill-repute into which Glasgow's four post-war peripheral housing estates of Drumchapel, Easterhouse, Castlemilk and Pollok fell has commonly been seen as arising from the City's unwillingness to observe the *Plan's* principles, not only of a tighter green belt but also of community development.

It has been shown (Smith and Wannop 1985, 222) that the *Plan* assumed greater resources than would actually become available to support the reconstruction of Clydeside to the standards of community services, transport and recreation which it recommended. That standards would be lower in the event does not negate the *Plan*, either in its other elements nor in its ambitions. In the significant case of Glasgow versus the new towns, however, it might be argued that events have shown the *Plan* to be wrong in its objection to the peripheral housing estates of Drumchapel and Easterhouse.

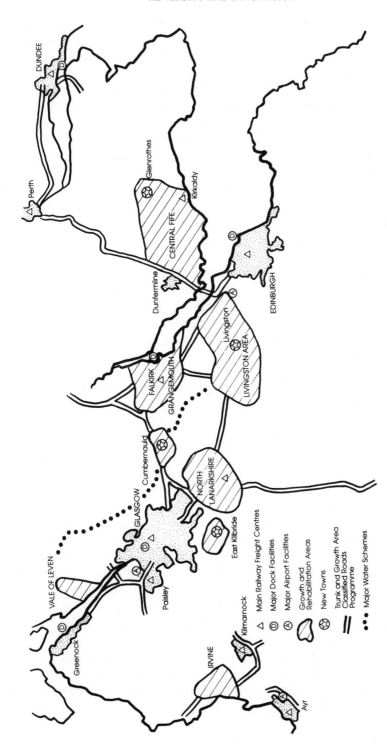

Figure 3.3. Central Scotland Programme for Development and Growth 1963: a programme unfulfilled in its expectations of growth and by the failure to rehabilitate as fast as new towns were developed

Commonly, the history of the City's peripheral estates has been seen as justification for the *Plan*'s objection to Glasgow's peripheral encroachment on the proposed green belt. The estates' deterioration as houses were abandoned, the paucity of shops and social facilities, the savage rise of unemployment in the economic depression of the later 1970s and early 1980s, the high cost of living and of travel on Glasgow's outskirts, have all been blamed on the failure of the City Corporation to provide the quality of social and economic environment of the new towns. On this comparison, the *Plan* might seem to have been right.

But a fairer interpretation may be that Glasgow had relatively fewer resources than had the new towns, and whatever the history of poor management of Glasgow's peripheral housing estates, their residents would have had no better opportunity of work by living in a new town, no better ability to pay probably higher house rents, perhaps less disposable income despite better and more accessible shopping, and would certainly have faced higher travel costs and a less sufficient service of public transport. Life in a new town would have little affected the skill level and competitive ability in the labour market of Drumchapel and Easterhouse residents. The evidence (Wannop 1985b) shows new towns to have no less unemployment than could be expected from the relatively high social and employment status of their populations; transformation from a home in Easterhouse to one in Cumbernauld would not improve the lot of an unemployed person in this respect. In the perspective of forty years of history, it may well be that Glasgow's capture of sections of the *Plan*'s green belt was a rather better solution for the residents of Drumchapel and Easterhouse than would have been their transfer to East Kilbride, Cumbernauld, or to either of the *Plan*'s new towns which were not built.

The Regional Planning Advisory Committee had disbanded after Glasgow Corporation's failure to agree on a role for new towns, suspending collective pursuit of most of the *Plan*'s proposals through the unsympathetic years of Conservative administration from 1951 to the early 1960s. If East Kilbride was the principal initiative to be credited to the *Plan* in its earliest years of influence, its conception of the administrative framework required to fulfil regional planning also embraced control over industrial location in Britain, regional water schemes, electricity supply, coordination of railway companies and either regional or national management of other public services, whose achievement during the life of the Labour government of 1945–51 was through larger political movements than the *Plan* could create. The establishment of Cumbernauld in 1955, however, perhaps more significantly reflected the strength of the *Plan*'s analysis and the continuing support it carried in the Scottish Office than did even the designation of East Kilbride, which had come on the rising tide of a new town programme throughout Britain. Cumbernauld came at the furthest retreat of the tide under the Conservative government of 1951–64, which had to be persuaded of the exceptional severity of Glasgow's housing problems and of the uniqueness of Clydeside conditions, to accept a further new town when no other was being permitted elsewhere in Britain.

The political emphasis on housebuilding by the Conservative government of this period, and its acceptance of a massive contribution by the public sector to its targets allowed Cumbernauld to become established, but industrial intervention and regional economic development were not to become politically opportune until the early 1960s. In this period in which government policy was ostensibly to dismantle the industrial nationalisation of the Labour government of 1945–51, the Scottish Office nonetheless collaborated with the Scottish Council (Development and Industry), an association of industrial, trades union, local authority, commercial and public interests with origins in Scottish reaction to the Depression of the early 1930s. Until the arrival in the mid 1970s of the new regional councils, the Scottish Development Agency and the Scottish Economic Planning Department, the Scottish Council was a significant source of economic proposals, initiatives in industrial promotion, reports and plans, which commonly moved ahead of the Scottish Office and were frequently inspired by it.

The report of a Committee of the Scottish Council on Industry (1961) which reviewed the Scottish economy, was perhaps the most significant case of the by-passing by the Scottish Office and Scottish Ministers of blockages in their direct relations with Whitehall and the Cabinet. The Report laid the basis of the Scottish Development Department's (1963a) strategy of economic growth poles for Central Scotland, grafted onto the established programme of new towns, comprehensive development areas and Scottish Office infrastructural investment in 1963, when the Conservative government's conversion to planning in its dying years permitted the Scottish Office to publish the first review of strategic planning for Clydeside for almost twenty years. Significantly, this new strategy for Central Scotland was accompanied by a move towards local government reorganization also published in 1963 (Scottish Development Department 1963b), although the theme was not sustained in the subsequent White Paper of 1966 on the Scottish Economy 1965 to 1970 (Scottish Office 1966).

The impetus towards administrative reorganization which the *Clyde Valley Plan* had seen as essential to continuous, positive regional planning accelerated through the 1960s. The Scottish Economic Planning Department took responsibility for the new town programme and later for the Scottish Development Agency – whose financing of land reclamation, environmental improvement and area development projects would come to be a strategic influence on regional development policy in the first half of the 1980s. This resulted in an uneasy division of responsibility for regional planning between the departments for Economic Planning and for Development. The Scottish Development Department's National Planning Guidelines and responsibility for supervising and obtaining approval for regional councils' structure plans, would be indirect influences matched against the more direct intervention in strategic development of its child grown to maturity – the

Economic Planning Department. But the widest administrative reorganisation was to be in local government.

Although not fulfilled until 1975, local government was reorganised on the basis of the report of a Royal Commission (1969) whose analysis echoed that of the *Clyde Valley Plan*; Hugh MacCalman, who had been Chairman of the Clyde Valley Regional Planning Advisory Committee and author of the preface to the *Plan* of 1946, was a member of Wheatley's Commission. The Commission's report drew quotations from the *Plan* on which to rest the case for a unified administrative region. But the *Plan*'s arguments were used selectively and wrongly. The *Plan* had specifically rejected the whole Clyde Valley as a unified administrative area, which was seen as reasonably including only the conurbation of Greater Glasgow and the Lower Clyde and its Green Belt. The *Plan*'s careful distinction between the wider Clyde Valley and the narrower area of the conurbation was ignored. Recommending an extended region, the Commission echoed the *Plan*'s analysis but distorted its conclusions.

Nonetheless, the Wheatley Commission helped introduce a regional council for Strathclyde which was appropriate to the form and circumstances of the region at the time of the Commission. But having reported in 1969, Wheatley was already six years behind events at the creation of Strathclyde in 1975. Just as the West of Scotland region had been redefined between 1946 and 1969, it was already being redefined by altering circumstances in the mid 1970s. By the early 1990s, circumstances were as far ahead of Wheatley as he was of the *Clyde Valley Plan*. With the Plan of 1946 so largely fulfilled, a new context for strategic planning was emerging in the *West Central Scotland Plan*, completed on the eve of the birth of the new Strathclyde Regional Council.

The West Central Scotland Plan

Begun by a team of planners and economists seconded from the Scottish Office, the later stages of the *West Central Scotland Plan* were directed by Urlan Wannop in association with Colin Buchanan and Partners and Professor Kenneth Alexander, repeating the pattern of the *Clyde Valley Plan* through the authorship of consultants. The *West Central Scotland Plan* had a different focus to its predecessor, the *Clyde Valley Plan*, reflecting changing preoccupations on Clydeside and would differ too in the timescale of its impact, which would be immediate.

The origins of the *West Central Scotland Plan* lay in worsening economic conditions on Clydeside in the early 1970s, and in the accumulating discontent of the Scottish Office with the quality of Glasgow's urban renewal projects of the 1960s, as the Corporation's programme of 29 comprehensive development areas fell behind expectations both in progress and quality. The surrounding counties were persuaded to cooperate in the Steering Committee of public and private representatives which – infrequently – sat alongside work on the *Plan*. However, not until problems of finding sites for petro-chemical industries came to concern

Figure 3.4. West Central Scotland Plan 1974: an action programme to rebalance the strategy for a declining region

local politicians in Ayrshire and Renfrewshire was there a sufficient coverage of authorities to enable work to proceed for what was effectively the same area as the *Clyde Valley Plan*. The Wheatley Commission's recent proposals for regional local government can reasonably be supposed to have helped the local authorities accept government's case to make a regional plan because, unwilling to be dissolved into a new Regional Council, the four counties of the West of Scotland could not readily argue against Wheatley if they were to neither themselves instigate a collective regional plan nor associate with it when fostered by government.

The principal proposals of the *West Central Scotland Plan* were to establish an economic development agency for Strathclyde (SEDCOR), to create a Task Force for environmental improvement in the region and to defer the start to the newly designated new town of Stonehouse. This was within a programme of building and renewal which accepted that continued expansion of urban Clydeside was wastefully stretching resources, and flying in the face of a new but sustained trend of dwindling population and employment in the region. Begun before Parliamentary debate on the Government's proposals to adopt the regional scale and major elements of Wheatley's proposals, the *West Central Scotland Plan* was concluded after government had cast the die for local government reorganization. The members of the new Strathclyde Regional Council were to be elected barely weeks after the *Plan* was published. The *West Central Scotland Plan* was thereby presented with much of the machinery for regional local governance for which the *Clyde Valley Plan* had to argue in a concluding chapter; the need for an economic development agency remained, however, and it was in the case for this by which the *West Central Scotland Plan* carried forward the linkage between regional planning and administrative innovation.

In May of 1975, Strathclyde Regional Council assumed full responsibility for strategic local government services and the Scottish Development Agency was instituted as an arms-length agency of the Scottish Office. Regional governance was introduced with collective responsibilities which were distinctive in the United Kingdom, for two regions – Strathclyde and Scotland – which were functionally complete to an extent to which none of the English metropolitan county areas were. The distinctiveness of these circumstances became unique in 1986. How has experience of almost 20 years of the most complete form of regional planning and governance introduced in the UK compared with the preceding 30 years of planning and development for Clydeside?

The *West Central Scotland Plan* proved as influential in the short term as the *Clyde Valley Regional Plan* of almost thirty years before had in the long term. Unlike its predecessor, the *West Central Scotland Plan* found immediate machinery by which it could be directly implemented. Political conditions in the mid-1970s were favourable to the launch of the Scottish Development Agency, which broadly resembled the economic development agency for the West of Scotland proposed in the *Plan*. Similarly the thinking of the new Strathclyde Regional Council was shaped by a new awareness amongst policy-makers that the greatest challenge lay not in the traditional field of housing policy but in the decline of the basic economy of Clydeside.

Although not formally adopted either by its joint steering committee or by the Regional Council, the themes of the *West Central Scotland Plan* matched the instincts of the leading politicians in the new Strathclyde, and helped the new Council assert itself as a force for coordination of regional planning and development. The Council made it a special early priority to persuade government to abandon its proposed new town at Stonehouse, supporting a strategic proposal of the *Plan.* Pursuing the abandonment of Stonehouse marked the intention of the new Regional Council to supersede the Scottish Office in regional planning. The area of the new Strathclyde housed new towns at East Kilbride, Irvine and Cumbernauld, all already well-established. In regional conditions wherein both jobs and population were dwindling, and in which claims to rehabilitate and renew infrastructure and services in the older areas limited the resources available for urban expansion, a further new town was argued by Strathclyde to be unnecessary and wasteful.

Strathclyde Regional Council 1975–1996: Regional Local Government

The Regional Council was designed on very different principles to the metropolitan county councils established in England a year earlier. It reached far beyond the built-up limits of its central conurbation, which circumscribed the metropolitan counties. It embraced a larger population in remote rural areas than did the Highland Region. Its population of almost 2.5 million was less than that of several of the metropolitan counties, but its functions were significantly greater and its annual budget was second only to the Greater London Council. It faced the problem of as many as nineteen lower-tier district councils, but its functions were wide and contained effective tools of strategic control:

Strategic Planning	Social Work
Sewerage	Consumer Protection
Water	Electoral Registration
Public Transport	Rating
Roads	Police
Education	Fire

The most significant exercise of the Regional Council's scope to dictate strategy by its control over infrastructure was its successful pressure on the government to terminate Stonehouse new town, achieved in 1976. The infrastructural thresholds which the new town had to overcome were so high that the Council's pressure overcame initial government reluctance. Subsequently, the Regional Council and government were generally in accord that strategy should focus development on existing urban areas, where new infrastructure was not a big issue. Where in cases like expanding the Roche plant in north Ayrshire or new holiday villages on the

Argyll coast, there was no spare infrastructural capacity, both the Council and government were sympathetic to providing it. Where the Regional Council opposed government over the expansion of East Kilbride new town, little infrastructure costs fell on the Council and government decided for development without need of the Council's infrastructural backing.

So, when urban expansion in the late 1970s and in the 1980s was much reduced by comparison with that of the 1960s, the Regional Council's infrastructural responsibilities were less a means of restraining unwelcome development than might have been expected. This begs the question as to how far they were able to foster strategy by stimulating welcome development. And that is part of the larger question of how significant was the Council's *Structure Plan* by comparison with other strategic influences.

The overriding principles behind its *Structure Plan* (Strathclyde Regional Council 1981) were the Council's objectives of alleviating social deprivation and of improving employment conditions. These led to a physical strategy to help reduce the flow of population and employment from established urban centres; the main ways of helping were seen as assistance to urban renewal, particularly in deprived areas, and help to improve the attraction of Strathclyde for investment. The *Plan* established the restraints to be applied to urban expansion where urban renewal was an acceptable alternative but, as to the action to be taken within urban areas and as to where lay the priorities for renewal, the *Plan* was oblique. Notwithstanding the Regional Council's dominant role in capital and revenue investment in the conurbation by the public sector, the *Plan*'s indication of priorities for renewal action related merely to the distribution of vacant land, disregarding problems of re-use of buildings, of improvement and demolition of housing, and of relocation of activities within the changing structure of the metropolitan region. The areas of the conurbation indicated for urban renewal were so extensive as to be plainly beyond comprehensive action within the five-year horizon of the *Plan*.

Accordingly, as a means of indicating priorities for physical change within metropolitan Clydeside, the *Structure Plan* seemed a pallid strategic influence. It appeared to lack the strengths of an effective strategic plan by offering little information about the future social, economic or physical environment of the metropolitan area; by failing to give guidance on priorities connecting with the local scale at which urban renewal occurs; and by not even indicating how departments of the Regional Council might coordinate investment to support the most beneficial form of metropolitan restructuring and renewal.

It has been said that the *Structure Plan* had relatively little impact (Keating 1988, 96). Certainly, it contained little original strategic analysis and few significant proposals not originating from or already in the hands of others. Despite very effective environmental and recreational projects initiated and carried out by the Planning Department, its *Structure Plan* was in the oblique style of county development planning of an earlier era. It did not advance the planning approaches of

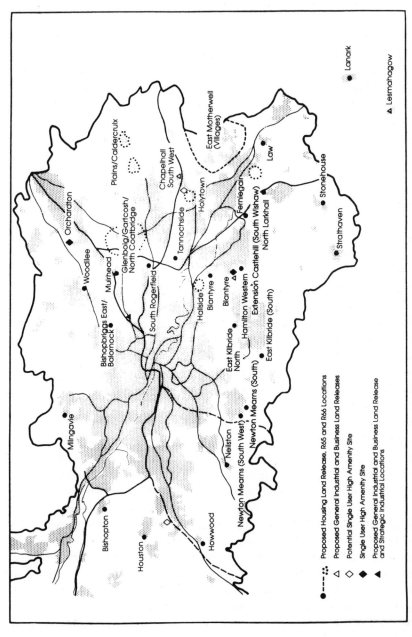

Figure 3.5. Strathclyde Structure Plan 1992: a strategic regional local authority releases land for housebuilding and industry

its predecessors, the plans for the *Clyde Valley, Central Scotland* and *West Central Scotland.*

The *Structure Plan*'s reversion to a traditional mould occurred when regional planning issues were becoming much less concerned with past preoccupations with urban expansion, and much more with economic and metropolitan regeneration. The Regional Council's principal political strategies were to aid social deprivation and employment. And a collective of government agencies – notably the Scottish Development Agency, the Scottish Special Housing Association, the Housing Corporation and the new town development corporations – gave government an effective control of strategy through direct intervention.

So, a new dominating preoccupation with urban regeneration, which had been no more foreseen by the Wheatley Commission in Scotland than by the Redcliffe–Maud Commission in England, led to strategic planning being redefined almost as local government was reorganised in 1975. It became more urgent to stimulate development than to restrain it. Planning had to work harder for obvious returns. In such a large reorganisation as that for Strathclyde, whereby four counties and Britain's third city were combined, the largest change in the nature of established local government functions was in planning. The scale of administration of other functions vastly increased, but the purpose of the service did not. The new regional planning was not expected to be only an inflated version of the old county planning; it was conceived of as qualitatively different. But as recruitment to the new Regional Council was initially confined to staff of the former authorities, the experience they brought was mostly of an older style of development planning.

The new Council's central emphasis on strategies for deprivation and employment also led to questions about the extent to which the *Structure Plan* was significant to those objectives. And it caused cultural tensions between younger and older staff of the young Department of Planning, subsequently helping lead to the transfer of social and economic analysis to the Chief Executive's Department.

Why did the Regional Council survive the abolition of the GLC and the metropolitan county councils in the mid 1980s? Probably above all it was because Strathclyde, Scotland's major council, had not abruptly challenged the government on ideological issues. Strathclyde's political leaders undoubtedly preferred to avoid the kinds of action which government was able to characterize as 'irresponsible' on the part of the GLC and English metropolitan councils. Perhaps, too, the established intimacy of principal figures in Scottish public affairs continued to produce alliances over Scottish national interests, tending to suppress confrontations in internal affairs. And the Secretary of State for Scotland for the first half of the decade, George Younger, had grown up in politics in the late years of the old local government system, knowing its failings and the incomparable improvements of the system which he had helped shape.

But significant also must have been the the battery of government development agencies in Scotland, by-passing local government and far exceeding experience in England. By initiatives such as GEAR (Glasgow Eastern Area Renewal), the area projects of the Scottish Development Agency and the housing renewal programme of the Scottish Special Housing Association, government simultaneously directly led strategy and also bought the quiescence of councils in return for supplements to their Rate Support Grant and spending limits.

So, until the later 1980s, there was little public criticism of the form of local government from either government or any significant other source. There were no public campaigns to restructure it. Such complaints as there were were mostly unsupported by evidence, and where existing between the two tiers of local government this was potentially constructive (Midwinter, Keating and Mitchell 1991, 126).

The Strathclyde Council's greatest strategic significance was probably its capacity to raise resources over a wide area, redeploying them to selected points or purposes within the metropolitan region. The scope for strategic intervention of this kind was notably evident in equalising prior imbalances in the distribution of teachers, and in elements of public transport policy including concessionary fares and interchange of tickets. In strategic planning with a physical output, the Council's opportunities seemed to be less well or so consistently fulfilled. There were too many players on the strategic scene for the Council or its *Structure Plan* to play the dominating role originally envisaged. And there was never an effective integration of land-use and financial planning (Midwinter, Keating *et al.* 1991, 127). But the uniqueness of this British experiment in strategic physical planning was recognised by the European Community when the EC award for regional planning for 1990/91 was given to the Strathclyde *Structure Plan*.

In 1993, however, the Secretary of State for Scotland announced the shape of a new reorganisation of local government. 28 unitary single-tier councils would replace Scotland's 9 regions, 3 island areas and 53 districts. But this was essentially fragmentation of local government, not a new gigantism. Only a few of the more rural regional councils in Scotland were retained. The largest, including Strathclyde, would be abolished. It was a move parallel with the concurrent proposals to abolish the English county councils, and it belatedly completed the government's drive against metropolitan Labour local governments following the coup in England in 1986.

Clothed in rhetoric about gains in cost savings and local democracy – the Prime Minister, John Major, had notoriously described Strathclyde as 'monstrous' – the new Scottish reorganisation was nakedly partisan, as that of 1975 had not been to such an extent. By 1993, only two councils in Scotland had a majority of Conservative councillors. The new reorganisation was designed to increase this number, and also to prospectively increase the number of parliamentary constituencies which might fall into Conservative hands.

Although there was no pressure for local government reorganisation in this form, except from Conservative interests in a permanent minority in Scotland, the Government intended to have it in place in 1996, before the next expected general election. Whatever the governing party, however, a new local government system would certainly exist before the end of the century. Not only the Labour and Liberal Democrat parties but also the Scottish Nationalists knew that their own ideas for a Scottish Assembly or Parliament were incompatible with the major regional councils, and most obviously with Strathclyde.

Pluralism in Regional Planning

Even at the inception of the Regional Council in 1975, the concept of regional planning which had driven the proposals for Strathclyde had already been modified. The creation of the Scottish Development Agency (SDA) occurred only six months after the Council took office. It presaged a progressively increased central government presence in the strategic planning and development of Strathclyde, particularly from about 1980. Although the Agency's investment in urban renewal, environmental improvement and in local economic development did not grow to be more than a small part of the total public sector effort in the region, it was profoundly strategic in its influence.

The SDA was innovative in the ways in which it spent public money and it levered extra expenditure from local authorities for Agency priorities; it was directed to central government priorities. The Agency clearly viewed the statutory structure plans by which the Scottish regional councils most publicly represented their planning role as insignificant to its key concerns: urban regeneration, area projects, environmental recovery, the revival of Glasgow's City Centre, the Glasgow Garden Festival, the development of the Greenock and Dundee waterfronts, the Clydebank Enterprise Zone and the multiplicity of other initiatives by which the Agency strategically intervened in Scottish development.

In its first five years, the new Strathclyde Regional Council did have a relatively clear run in strategic planning. Having not only the areas of the new towns within its boundaries, but also additional responsibilities for water, sewerage, social work and education, Strathclyde Regional Council enjoyed powers to influence strategic regional planning lacking to the Greater London and English metropolitan county councils.

Although the launch of the GEAR project in 1976 (Wannop, 1990) was not followed immediately by other strategic initiatives, by 1980 a variety of other local interventions were emerging under the direction or patronage of the SDA. The Agency became a *de facto* regional planning body for Scotland alongside the local authorities. It sometimes picked up and implemented projects conceived by the authorities, and at other times conceived of its own. Pluralist regional planning had emerged, with the Government playing several parts simultaneously. The field of strategic planning became crowded with players in precisely the manner which the Wheatley Commission, with its clear conception of the vertical division of labour between central regional and local governments, had sought to avoid when it recommended reorganization into large areal units.

By the late 1980s, central government had advanced much further into local government responsibilities. The Community Charge and the National Business Rate were about to further reduce local financial discretion. The break-up of the very large role of district councils in Scottish housing was to be achieved through a new government agency – Scottish Homes – designed to considerably displace local authority management of selected housing estates in Glasgow and other areas. Scottish Homes absorbed both the Scottish Special Housing Association and the Housing Corporation for Scotland, assuming new responsibilities for urban regeneration, including economic as well as housing action.

Redefining the Region: The West of Scotland in the 1990s

Even by the same socio-economic principles as underlay the *Clyde Valley Plan* and Wheatley, some redefinition of the West of Scotland region would have been necessary in the 1990s, let alone through political change in local–central government relationships running for the previous decade or more. Indeed, in the case of the West of Scotland at least four dimensions to contemporary regionalism could be identified.

First, significant features of the old metropolitan regions remained. Although no longer recognised for Census tabulations, the old Clydeside Conurbation still constituted one of the United Kingdom's most extensive metropolises, with an extensive range of social, cultural and administrative functions. However, because of suburbanisation, the dispersal of manufacturing and distributive industries, and the shift of middle and higher income households to new towns and areas beyond the Conurbation, it had become progressively less able to generate the revenues required to rebuild and maintain itself. So the metropolitan area remained a dominating focus in the region's planning.

Second, Strathclyde Regional Council survived after the dissolution of the Greater London Council and of the English metropolitan counties. It was a regional and not merely a metropolitan authority. For its first dozen years of life, the Regional Council had suffered relatively little public criticism by either government or press – certainly not of the kind which assaulted the Greater London and English metropolitan county councils in the early and mid-1980s. The Conservative government and its Secretaries of State for Scotland appeared to prefer the regional councils to a return to all-purpose city councils on the pre-1976 model. By 1988, however, strong pressures surfaced in the Scottish Conservative Party to have the regional tier of local government removed, and these intensified in 1991.

Third, after the general election of 1987 had reduced Conservative representation to only one in six of Scottish parliamentary seats, the Scottish Office was more open than for many years to criticism that it was returning to its initial role as a quasi-colonial arm of Parliament, dominated by English political interests. Certainly, having failed in the Devolution Referendum of 1979 to vote sufficiently for the degree of administrative autonomy offered, Scotland had slipped within a

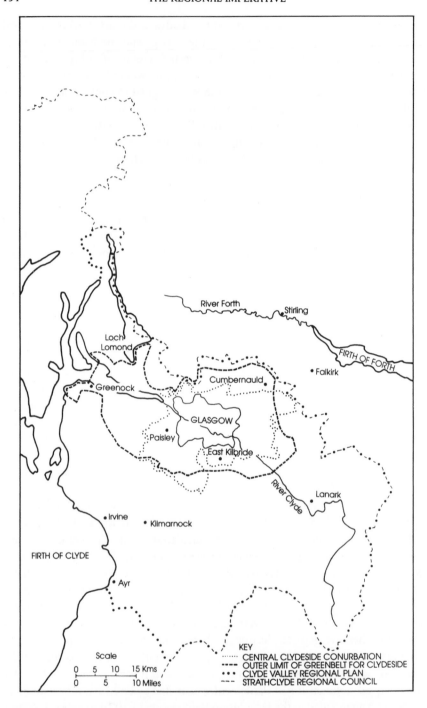

Figure 3.6. The evolution of regions in the West of Scotland 1946 to 1975: the Clyde
Valley Regional Plan to Strathclyde Regional Council

decade to being more nearly than for many years an administrative region of the United Kingdom. Within that region, government was reinforcing its role in executing as well as shaping policy for regional development. Through its battery of agencies for economic, housing, countryside and infrastructural development, government was progressively displacing local government for the internal regions of Scotland by regional agencies for the whole of Scotland.

Fourth, and overlapping the dimension of the Scottish Office, came the revival of nationalism, as supported by about a quarter of Scots in the early 1990s. After its rebuff in the 1979 referendum, nationalism's force was reduced both by disappointment and the disregard of a centralising Conservative government with little sympathy for any kind of regionalism.

As well as overt nationalism, the conditions of the 1980s encouraged those supporting the less extreme option of regional government for Scotland. The Campaign for a Scottish Assembly, founded in 1983 to strive for the 'creation of a directly elected legislative assembly or parliament for Scotland with such powers as may be desired by the people of Scotland', developed a broader base of support than had been achieved for devolution in the 1970s, embracing the unions and local government interests, and (according to polls) a 77 per cent majority of the population. The increasing credibility of an assembly added to the uncertainty over the future of the regional councils. The Scottish Nationalist Party had always argued that, with the establishment of a national assembly, local government should be organised into a single tier of unitary authorities and the regions abolished. The ruling Labour group on the Strathclyde Regional Council accepted this as an inevitable consequence of any Labour government's institution of a Scottish Assembly. And in 1991, the Conservative government at last announced its intention to adopt single-tier local government.

The West of Scotland and Regional Idea

Three themes have underlain this account of the unique case of the West of Scotland. First, that Strathclyde Regional Council has been a conception of regional governance far larger than the models for England and Wales advanced through the Redcliffe–Maud Royal Commission on Local government in the late 1960s, let alone the metropolitan county model actually introduced to England in 1974. Second, the Regional Council has nonetheless been less dominant in its regional planning role than the Wheatley report on Scottish local government envisaged in its recommendations of 1969. The Council came to share the field of regional and strategic planning with a range of agencies unforeseen by Wheatley. The conception and implementation of key strategic elements of regional development occurs through several agencies, rather than by the exclusive lead of the Council or of its *Structure Plan*. Third, these circumstances reflect the progressive redefinition of the West of Scotland region centred on Clydeside, and of the priorities of regional planning and action. Changing economic, social and political circumstances over the course of almost 50 years have progressively altered the planning case for the region, and have enlarged its scale.

For the purpose of strategic planning and action, the significant region became no longer the river valley system of Patrick Geddes and of the *Clyde Valley Plan*, and certainly not the metropolitan core for which the *Plan* considered a regional authority to be appropriate. The significant European region was now larger than that of Strathclyde Regional Council, although this stretched 200 miles from north to south by ferry and tortuous lochside roads, from Iona in the inner Hebrides and nearly to England.

Strathclyde has undoubtedly proven the feasibility and potential of regional planning and of regional governance. It has been a successful case in significant respects. But also, overtaken by changing regional geography and evolving national politics, it has finally proved the impermanence of the region.

Greater Manchester and the North West

Manchester Regional Planning

Following a conference of 76 local authorities from within a 15 mile radius of the city, a Manchester and District Joint Town Planning Advisory Committee met first in Manchester's Town Hall on 14 January 1921 (Manchester and District Regional Planning Committee 1945, 5). The Committee's scope covered over 1000 square miles from Warrington in the west to Chapel-en-le-Frith in the east, and from Rawtenstall in the north to the southern edge of Cheshire.

In 1925, the Advisory Committee was extended into the South Lancashire and North Cheshire Advisory Committee, which recommended that decentralised statutory planning committees should be immediately established. As a whole, the region covered four counties, seven county boroughs and 89 smaller local authorities. Seventeen executive Joint Town Planning Committees were established to prepare and adopt joint planning schemes under Section 2 of the Town Planning Act, 1925. For a framework, the Advisory Committee adopted in 1926 a plan of generally agreed outline proposals for regional roads, zoning in broad outline and regional open spaces (Wannop and Cherry 1994).

Whatever the immediacy urged by the Advisory Committee, the statutory Manchester and District Regional Planning Committee was not constituted until 25 January 1928. The Manchester and District Committee was authorised to prepare and adopt a joint planning scheme for the area of its 14 local authority members – the county boroughs of Manchester and Salford, the municipal boroughs of Eccles and Middleton, the urban district councils of Audenshaw, Denton, Droylesden, Failsworth, Irlam, Prestwich, Stretford, Swinton and Pendlebury, Urmston and Worsley, and the rural District of Barton-upon-Irwell. Other bodies also had places on the Committee. At 1945, there were represented also the Lancashire County Council, the Lancashire Rivers Board and the Ministry of War Transport. The Manchester Chamber of Commerce had provided the Committee with the services of the Chamber's Planning Consultative Committee, which offered advice on warehousing requirements, shops and industry.

The new statutory committee for Manchester and District covered a population of about 1.3 million, hugely outweighing that under any of the 13 other statutory committees for the South Lancashire and North Cheshire Advisory Committee region of 1945 – for Oldham and District, Chorley and District, Rossendale, Wigan and District, Bolton and District, Bury and District, Rochdale and District, Leigh and District, North East Cheshire, North Cheshire, East Cheshire, Mid Cheshire No. 4, and Mid Cheshire No. 5.

There was thereby created a three-tier local government planning system, of which the two upper tiers were both described as being regional. The upmost level of the South Lancashire and North Cheshire Advisory Committee was the means by which research findings could be exchanged between the constituent regional planning committees, unnecessary duplication of research could be minimised, and studies could be made of wider aspects of planning. The Advisory Committee was also intended to help coordinate and assist where difficulties arose between adjoining regional committees. The 14 statutory regional committees were authorised to prepare and adopt joint planning schemes, to which the lower level of individual local authorities were obliged to have regard when exercising their powers of interim development control. For the most important of the regional committees and the largest local authority, there was the convenience that Manchester Town Hall housed the planning staff for each of the Advisory Committees, of the Manchester and District Regional Planning Committee and of Manchester Corporation.

A preliminary statement approved by the Regional Planning Committee in 1931 led to preparation of a draft scheme. Work on the scheme was expanded under the influence of the Town and Country Planning Act, 1932, but a provisional draft joint scheme was not submitted to the Regional Planning Committee until December 1937. Consideration of the draft was protracted. By the outbreak of war in September 1939, the two principal members of the Committee – Manchester and Salford – had yet to approve the scheme, although all others had done so with the exception of Irlam.

By 1938, government officials were dissatisfied with progress, particularly towards proposals for a green belt around Manchester which was divided between different regional committees. George Pepler, Chief Town Planning Inspector to the Ministry of Health, informed the Manchester and District Joint Town Planning Advisory Committee that a green belt around Manchester was desirable in the light of planning proposals made to the Ministry by certain of the planning authorities of the area. In December 1938, Pepler met the chairman of the Committee, and in consequence he convened a conference of representatives of the Advisory Committee together with representatives of the three county councils of Lancashire, Cheshire and Derbyshire, across whose fringes the green belt would lie. Subsequently, it was the Ministry of Health which chaired an informal technical sub-committee formed to draw up a green belt scheme. The sub-committee involved the county surveyors or planning officers of Cheshire, Derbyshire and Lancashire, but only conferred with the regional committees rather than incorporating them. The limitations of the regional committees and of the Advisory Committee's coordinating role had become too evident.

The outbreak of war in 1939 interfered with preparations for the Manchester green belt, whose priority was overtaken by groundwork for post-war planning and reconstruction. This had become a national issue of government concern by August of 1941, when Lord Reith attended a meeting of the Regional Planning Committee to ask it to prepare a provisional plan for redevelopment. The Committee agreed, and directed its Surveyors' Sub-Committee to proceed with work which included re-examination of the draft scheme begun ten years previously. It also included an interim report on the green belt submitted in November 1943. So, in July 1944, tentative regional planning proposals were brought

Figure 3.7. Manchester and District Regional Planning Committee 1945

forward to the Committee, which were published in 1945 as the *Manchester and District Regional Planning Proposals* with the classic reservation that:

> this Report does not, therefore, necessarily represent the unanimous report of the Surveyors' Sub-Committee, that it is in no way binding on the individual members of the Surveyors' Sub-Committee so far as their own authorities are concerned, and, further, that it has not been considered or approved by the Regional Planning Committee. It has been prepared and is published for the specific purpose of bringing before the members of the constituent local authorities and all other interested parties proposals upon which opinions are sought by the Surveyors' Sub-Committee and the Regional Planning Committee, in order that, in preparing and completing the regional planning scheme, such opinions may be properly taken into account

These tentative proposals included a precisely defined green belt; a scheme for an inner, intermediate and an outer ring road; neighbourhood facility planning standards; and an assessment of the numbers of people to be overspilled by redevelopment. A quarter of the erstwhile population of Manchester, Stretford and Salford could not be housed after redevelopment; barely a third of the houses they needed could be provided within other authorities in the area of the Regional Planning Committee. The balance of some 42,500 houses or nearly 140,000 people would have to be provided for outside the Committee's area of responsibility.

The last contribution of the old order of regional planning was the publication of Nicholas and Hellier's *Advisory Plan for South Lancashire and North Cheshire* in 1947, in the same year as the reforming Town and Country Planning Act launched a new system of development planning. The *Advisory Plan* for the wider region was entirely consistent with the *Manchester and District Proposals*, as could have been expected when the City's Surveyor, Nicholas, was author of both. Dispersal of up to 250,000 people from overcrowded inner Manchester was proposed, to be rehoused outside the city principally at Middleton and Worsley in Lancashire, and at what would effectively be new towns at Lymm and Mobberley in Cheshire. Dispersal from Manchester would impact most heavily on the county of Cheshire, and Lancashire would provide most considerably for Liverpool's overspill. But some of the locations for growth and its distribution were unacceptable to the Cheshire politicians, in particular. So there was no agreement on the proposals, which were lodged as the City of Manchester's bid for delivery by Cheshire County Council in its forthcoming development plan.

The planning authorities accordingly turned to their responsibility under the 1947 Act to produce their first development plans, without any agreed framework as to where or how the Manchester conurbation's overspill would be housed. Although the Labour government of the time was sympathetic to new towns, none was designated in the region before the Conservative government of 1951 was elected. Against the background of the new government's disapproval of new towns, proposals for one at Parbold in Lancashire and one at Congleton in Cheshire fell from the respective county development plans (Cullingworth 1960, 128). The Government was willing to foster town expansion schemes under the Town Development Act but, as delay occurred, relations between Manchester and Cheshire County Council became particularly difficult. Manchester struggled to hold its overspill of households within the city's social and economic hinterland, if not within its administrative boundaries. But although willing to receive a share of emigrant Mancunians, the counties preferred them to break their ties with the conurbation by mostly resettling in relatively self-contained towns beyond easy commuting distance. Expanded towns were preferred to new towns, and Cheshire was particularly strongly opposed to the *Advisory Plan*'s proposals for Lymm and Mobberley.

Through the 1950s and into the early 1960s, Cheshire County Council fought against Manchester's bids to capture the most sensitive sites in the county. Cheshire became reconciled to the fact that Mancunians would largely commute back to Manchester, but it wished to assimilate most in smaller numbers in numerous places around the fringes of the city. Cheshire did pick Congleton as a prospective new town, being well beyond comfortable commuting range of Manchester, but this made the City Council unwilling to accept its merits. So the 1950s was a sequence of bids and rejections, with Lymm and Mobberley the principal points of contention. First, Manchester moved to build a new town itself at Mobberley, then withdrew in the hope that the Government would do so under the new legislation for new towns. Successive governments turned somersaults over proposals; several lesser expansion schemes proceeded, but the issue of a new town persisted without resolution.

Because the Conservative governments of the 1950s disfavoured more new towns, Congleton did not become one. Nor because of the poor financing available did it go ahead under the legislation for expanded towns, despite the Government's willingness to support it on that basis. So the framework of the Advisory Committee's regional strategy of 1947 was only erratically developed, lacking its central structure of new towns. The Government thwarted Manchester by rejecting its repeated proposals of new towns at Lymm and Mobberley. Tension between Manchester and Cheshire hardened. And a statutory green belt could not be established because the strategy for Manchester's growth remained incomplete.

A new Labour government in 1964 was one of the events to change the context of planning in Manchester's region in the mid 1960s. The preceding Conservative government had already come to accept that more new towns were needed for Britain's conurbations; Skelmersdale and Runcorn had been started to help Liverpool, and the idea of a new town at Warrington came forward, which could be some help to Manchester. Then a new County Clerk arrived in Cheshire, followed not long after by the designation of the area of Leyland–Chorley for a new town in northern Lancashire. And in the background a national downturn in birth rates was emerging, implying reduced projections of long-term population growth and overspill from all of Britain's conurbations. The frosty politics of metropolitan regional planning were about to thaw.

The Thawing of the Regional Frost

By 1947, the strategic issues of the green belt and of population overspill had already clearly outgrown older administrative and geographical concepts of regional planning. The new development plan system of 1947 minimised the fragmentation of regional planning, but had been unable to fully rationalise it. To the contrary, having fewer and more significant partners ran the risk that even one standing too much on its dignity could thwart the others. So the overspill issue caused intensely difficult relations to persist between Manchester and Cheshire right up to the mid 1960s. The problems were not wholly due to boundaries arbitrarily dividing from each other the two ends of a single problem. This could be seen when relations would remarkably improve after the arrival of John Boynton to the post of County Clerk of Cheshire in the early 1960s. As much as any other of the changes of the decade, that single change of personality helped melt the frosted relationship between Manchester and Cheshire; it perhaps rationalised regional affairs more than did the later arrival of the Greater Manchester Council.

So, in the decade before metropolitan reorganisation in 1974, strategic transport and regional planning was revived in Manchester's region. In November 1963, a conference of local authorities agreed to support the Ministry of Transport in a *South East Lancashire North East Cheshire Transportation Study (SELNEC)*, centred on Manchester. Then, in 1965, came the *North West Study* from the new Department of Economic Affairs, and the Regional Economic Planning Council followed up with its *Strategy I* and *Strategy II* reports of 1966 and 1968. However, none of these appraisals introduced any new measures of regional planning strategy.

The *SELNEC* study was protracted. Its final proposals were not published until March 1972, by which time there been established not only a Passenger Transport Authority and a Passenger Transport Executive for the area of the study, but also a planning team which had started in 1971 on an overarching *Strategic Plan for the North West*. The roads emphasis of the *SELNEC* proposals was predictably criticised by the passenger transport interests, and by the regional planning team which had yet to publish its report and wider proposals. Like many transportation studies elsewhere, large assumptions were made about the future of the *SELNEC* region, leading to ambitious proposals which the regional planners found premature and misguided – neglecting the need for public transport and excessively emphasising new highways, which were neither wholly practicable nor likely to find sufficient funding.

Strategic Plan for the North West

Begun in 1971, the *Strategic Plan for the North West* had been preceded by a pattern of planning studies similar to that which had occurred in the South East region. The *North West Study* (1965) had come from the new Department of Economic Affairs, and the Regional Economic Planning Council followed up with reports in 1966 and 1968 respectively described as *Strategies I and II*. However, none of these appraisals introduced any new measures of regional planning strategy. Nor was there any comprehensive examination of the issues of living standards and of quality of life in the region, which the *Strategic Plan* considered its central strategic themes.

Also inherited from the 1960s were the SELNEC transportation study and its counterpart for Merseyside, the MALTS study. Like transportation studies elsewhere, both had made assumptions about the region's future leading to ambitious proposals which the *Strategic Plan* found premature and misguided.

Although there was such a legacy of studies, there was no standing conference of local authorities in the region. So, as in South East England, the *Strategic Plan* was nominally sponsored by the Government, the local authorities and the Regional Economic Planning Council. Although central government was again in charge, however, the team found itself more able to move outside the conventional bounds of land use planning than had its immediate predecessors in the South East.

Together with the subsequent plans for the Northern region of England and West Central Scotland which also spread their proposals well beyond the narrower limits of physical planning, the *Strategic Plan for the North West* raised testing issues for the Government. By implying that the region's relative deficiencies in housing, economic and environmental conditions should receive special government aid, the *Plan* not only sought financial advantages for the North West, but stepped also on the responsibilities of departments of government other than that principally sponsoring it. Government would have been able to accept some of the *Strategic Plan's* central proposals only by adjusting national economic strategy, by disturbing inter-regional political balance within the country, and by increasing the influence of the Department of the Environment.

The Department of the Environment had provided the director of the team – Geoffrey Powell – but had no responsibility in several aspects of the action recommended; it was responsible for administering Rate Support Grant which the team proposed to be revised, but there was no obvious authority to handle the small regional fund which the team proposed should be made available to be distributed from within the region itself. The Treasury would have wished to stay such independent action, not to mention the Cabinet. Similarly, the Departments of Trade and Industry and of Employment, local authorities and the passenger transport executives were all indicated as agents for various proposals. Not least, the transport division of the Department of the Environment had the reputation of being a ministry within a ministry, and would not be easily persuaded of the

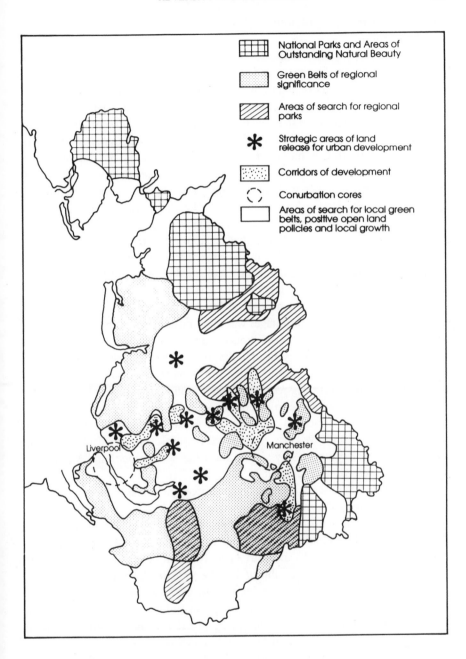

National Parks and Areas of Outstanding Natural Beauty

Green Belts of regional significance

Areas of search for regional parks

Strategic areas of land release for urban development

Corridors of development

Conurbation cores

Areas of search for local green belts, positive open land policies and local growth

Liverpool

Manchester

Figure 3.8. Strategic Plan for North West England 1974: a physical plan complicated by its proposals affecting the responsibilities of several government departments

merits of the strategy's wish to restrict car usage and to favour public transport in the conurbations.

The team proposed that future development should be concentrated within the Mersey Belt between Manchester and Liverpool, especially in mid south Lancashire and along the corridors of public transport. It was suggested that the Central Lancashire New Town might develop more slowly than had been planned, and would serve as a longer-term strategic reserve. The *Strategic Plan* accordingly turned away from the indications of the preceding studies, which had suggested that north Lancashire and south Cheshire might be focal areas for future development.

The Government took 20 months to produce an opaque response to the *Strategic Plan*, which 'read together with the *Strategic Plan* where necessary, sets out the approved Regional Strategy.' As an experienced civil servant, the team's director (Powell 1978, 11) later wryly commented that government would be aware about how this would mislead in deciding what the approved strategy actually was. The North West was a region in which it was particularly necessary to skate over the thin ice of proposals going well beyond established government policy. But there did appear to be approval for the *Strategic Plan*'s emphasis upon the Mersey Belt, and it has been suggested (Friend *et al.* 1979, 16) that the strategy's evidence of the North West's urban disadvantages was more positively endorsed than was the East Anglia team's claim for recognition of rural disadvantage, for instance. But Friend's study (1979, 58) notes the unwillingness of the Department of Trade and Industry to accept the *Plan*'s proposal that the Department should fund improvement of run-down industrial environments as a stimulus to new employment. Nor was the *Plan* wholly welcome to the North West. The structure of advisory and steering committees associated with the *Plan* lacked the status to approve and implement it on a collective basis. And the *Plan*'s physical strategy broke relations amongst the local authorities by setting the cities of Liverpool and Manchester against Lancashire County Council.

The *Plan* wished to see Manchester recuperate from its loss of employment and population, by concentrating regional growth on the Mersey plain. But although the north of the plain in Lancashire was favoured rather than southern parts in Cheshire, Lancashire County Council felt that the strategy would frustrate its commitment to the Central Lancashire New Town and to the mid and northern parts of the County. Lancashire objected to the *Strategic Plan* as being naive and a threat to investment in its established urban areas. The Council's Chief Executive had a long-standing involvement with strategic planning in Lancashire, which the *Plan* threatened to undermine. His antipathy to the *Plan* and to further regional planning persisted to the brink of his retiral in 1990.

This mistrust of the *Strategic Plan* prejudiced Lancashire, and for almost twenty years frustrated the revival of regional planning in the North West. And into the confusion following the *Strategic Plan* entered two new strategic metropolitan planning authorities, one to construct a plan for Merseyside and the other for Greater Manchester. Not only was the region fragmented without any means offered for effective strategic planning, but the two metropolitan counties were both significantly smaller than the real metropolitan areas in which they lay; the Greater Manchester Council covered only 62 of the 90 local authorities which the Royal Commission (1969, 220) had considered 'should be administered as a whole for the purposes of land use planning, transportation and major development.' Particularly, the new Council was abruptly truncated to the south, where Cheshire County Council had won the political battle to save itself from extinction. In winning, it held on to such a significant district of suburban Manchester as Wilmslow, which in the 1960s had been intended for major expansion to rehouse households from inner Manchester. So the new Greater Manchester Council found itself planning for an arbitrary metropolitan area.

The Greater Manchester Council

In its early life, the Greater Manchester County Council followed the policy lead of the *Strategic Plan for the North West* in pressing government to restrain the growth of the Central Lancashire New Town. Anxious to avoid resources being diverted from Manchester's regeneration, the County Council looked upon the new town much as Strathclyde Regional Council did upon Stonehouse. But Strathclyde Council had direct responsibility for the local authority services required for Stonehouse, whereas the Greater Manchester Council's strategic influence was much less because the new town lay beyond its administrative area.

As the Government cut back its new town programme in the later 1970s, however, the issue receded and was no impediment to the Secretary of State's approval to the Greater Manchester *Structure Plan* in 1981. Modifications subsequently proposed by the County Council were approved only shortly before its abolition in 1986.

During the later 1970s, a regional association of county councils had linked the Lancashire and Cheshire county councils with the Merseyside and Greater Manchester Metropolitan County Councils. But when all four councils turned from Conservative to Labour control in 1981, the two metropolitan authorities declined to continue with the association. The Merseyside metropolitan area then turned inwards, preoccupied with internal politics in Liverpool.

Some of the regional issues of earlier periods had faded, of course. Pressures within the North West had significantly abated since the 1960s. Because the need to rehouse slum dwellers beyond its boundaries had collapsed, the Greater Manchester Council had no need to fight for land in the surrounding counties as its predecessor had done a decade before. To the contrary, the Council established a major programme of environmental action jointly with Lancashire, bringing metropolitan resources to its neighbour's benefit and ameliorating Lancashire's anxiety about being deprived to pay for Manchester's regeneration.

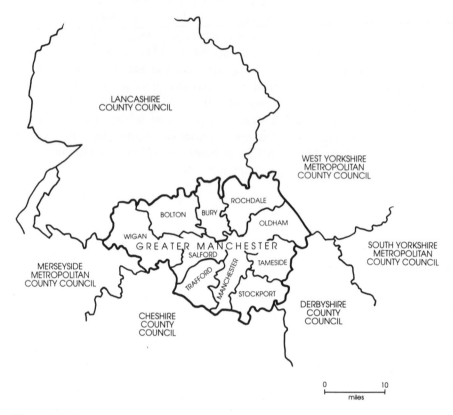

Figure 3.9. Greater Manchester Metroplitan County Council 1974–1986 and its Metropolitan District Councils

Manchester Streamlined

During the life of the Greater Manchester County Council, collaborative arrangements had started which were able to be readily continued after the Council's dissolution in 1986. The principal continuing collaboration was the Association of Greater Manchester Authorities, representing the ten district councils of the former metropolitan area.

Four committees were confirmed to serve the Association: the Joint Grants Committee; the Joint Highways and Transportation Committee; the Joint Planning and Countryside Committee; and the EEC Information Service. Comprising the chairs of the planning committees of the councils, the Planning and Countryside Committeee was advised by a Greater Manchester Chief Planning Officers' Group. A Greater Manchester Research and Information Unit was retained and funded by the ten districts, jointly. Also retained were a Countryside Planning Unit and a Minerals and Waste Disposal Planning Unit. Each unit was led by a different metropolitan district council. Smaller units for archaeology and acid rain were recognised.

A test of the cohesion of the ten councils came early in 1987, when government circulated its initial ideas on the regional guidance to which it expected the councils to fit their unitary structure plans. The Joint Planning and Countryside Committee responded by indicating to government the ideas upon which the district councils were agreed; separately, the councils responded where they could not all agree or where they had specific local concerns.

There was no such cohesion in the North West beyond metropolitan Manchester. The wider region remained fragmented through the 1980s. Cheshire County Council did favour regional planning but carried less political weight than Lancashire, which was not persuaded to assume a regional interest. Lancashire county councillors were unsympathetic to regional planning whether Conservative or Labour was in control, and sympathetic officials could persuade neither their Chief Executive nor their political leaders to change their set minds. What was more, both county councils particularly mistrusted Liverpool and Merseyside, and the regional office of the Department of the Environment brought little force to bear to heal old sores.

A revival of regional cooperation was heralded in 1987, when a meeting chaired by a government official of the regional office of the Department of the Environment was attended not only by the ten district councils of the former Greater Manchester county area, but also by the three adjoining county councils and other government departments and agencies. This led the metropolitan councils to develop a statement of advice for Greater Manchester, for the Government to elaborate in its draft statement of regional guidance.

Differences of emphases now began to show; the districts were not unanimous on how to achieve urban regeneration, or on what should be the strategy for out-of-town shopping centres, or on to what extent Manchester could provide for new housing (Glasson, Lloyd, McMillan and Wood 1990). There were also issues which concerned the metropolitan districts about the future of areas beyond their collective jurisdiction, calling for discussion with the surrounding counties and new towns. And transportation issues were now bedevilled by a fragmentation of responsibility for roads, railways and now deregulated bus transport.

A joint report was nonetheless produced in which the metropolitan districts put their strategic views before a second regional meeting on Greater Manchester in 1988. The Secretary of State was called on to clearly declare his policies on urban regeneration and out-of-town retailing. At the end of the year, the Secretary of State published a draft of his intended regional guidance. The districts replied that the 13 pages of guidance were thin in number and in substance. In the autumn of 1989, the final guidance was published, but the districts still thought it to be bland and to leave a good deal unsaid. Even so, it had taken government over two and a half years to turn the districts' proposals into generalised guidance, rather than a year as intended.

Some (Glasson *et al.* 1990) have suggested that the districts cooperated more fully than opponents of the abolition of the Metropolitan County anticipated. This may have been helped by the common service from their joint research and intelligence unit, by the fact that eight of the ten districts were Labour controlled, by the network of contacts amongst planning staff from the dissolved Metropolitan Council now working in the districts, and by a collective reluctance to give government the excuse to interfere in issues of mutual agreement. Of course, these were circumstances in which strategy might also tend to reflect the lowest common denominator of agreement, and to lack strong coherence and direction. This seems to have been the tendency in Greater Manchester, but not necessarily more evident since the abolition of the Metropolitan County Council than before.

New regional groupings emerged as the Metropolitan County faded to a memory. Significant was the North West Business Leadership Forum, launched in 1989 and combining some 30 of the region's business leaders, collectively responsible for over 300,000 employees. The leaders declared their commitment to the long-term prosperity of the North West, which they aimed to ensure by pressing government for improved transport infrastructure, by promoting inward investment, by supporting environmental and urban regeneration projects, and by what they described as strategic support for a variety of key projects in the region. The idea of a regional development agency was strongly backed by some in the Forum.

In March 1990, the Chief Officer's Group of the Association of Greater Manchester Authorities indirectly pointed to the limited strategic role and capacity of the dead Metropolitan County Council by reporting that:

> In the 1970s, the Strategic Plan for the North West was produced, which placed the 'Mersey belt' at the heart of its policies. There has been no update or revision of that strategy since then, but the region's problems have not diminished – indeed, there is today an even greater need for some form of regional strategy or planning mechanism. For too long the North West has stumbled along without an effective local authority regional voice at Westminster or Brussels, and key strategic issues have gone uncoordinated and decisions taken in isolation.

Although some chief executives of the Manchester districts may have been sceptical of regional planning, seeing it as a restraint rather than a help to development, they were prepared to accept it if it led to an action programme for the special issues of the time.

Professional planners in the region set out their view of the region's shortcomings after twenty years of neglect of regional planning (Royal Town Planning Institute, North West Branch 1990). Insufficient land was being set aside for housing and urban growth; green belts required reviewing; key industrial sites were critically few; transport planning was in a vacuum, with motorways planned without relation to rail policy; growth of regional airports was being restrained by government decisions. There was a pressing case for strategic planning after 16 years without a review of regional strategy.

Barriers to real regional cooperation were now being pushed aside across the the North West region, and not just around Greater Manchester. Lancashire was dissatisfied over the issue of where in the region to locate a rail terminal for traffic to the new Channel Tunnel, and wished to gain more strategic influence than it had had on the public/private North West Channel Tunnel Group which had advocated a site outside the county. At last, in 1990, the Government itself openly accepted that regional guidance for structure planning was desirable throughout England, and that this would be helped by regional cooperation amongst local planning authorities.

Government's revived sympathy for regional planning influenced a change of heart in Lancashire's Chief Executive, but only on the eve of his retiral. It was his successor who helped crystallise a new basis for regional cooperation, although the Council's leader was reluctant almost to the end. But early in 1992, a North West Regional Association was formed with a potential much greater than of such a regional planning conference as Lancashire had long resisted. The Association comprised 27 representatives of the region's three counties and a larger number of district councils, with the latter collectively dominating the membership. Five committees were initially established to pursue the North West's interests in planning guidance, transportation, economic matters, Europe and the possibility of bringing the Olympic Games to Manchester.

Why did the county and district councils of the North West come to collaborate in such a potentially major regional association when, for so long, they had been unable to form even a standing conference on physical planning? By 1992, all other regions of England possessed at least a planning conference, and the Midland and South East regions had sustained regional planning teams for 25 years or more.

Collaboration had been thwarted by the region's internal politics for many years. The notable tension of the 1960s between the Manchester and Cheshire councils was succeeded in the 1980s by tensions over Liverpool's Labour council, when other Labour councils in the region preferred to distance themselves from the Government's political whipping boy. Lancashire thought that regional planning would be against its best interests. The metropolitan county councils did not feel an urgent need for it. Later in the 1980s, however, new circumstances arose. Liverpool's politics became more moderate. The Government became encouraging of self-help regional planning. It became evident that regional associations were a means to earning benefits from the European Community. And there grew the real prospect of a future Labour government which might replace the county councils with regional assemblies, which both Lancashire and Manchester Labour councillors supported and which an association could foreshadow. The formation of the Association was directly encouraged by the European Community and by the North West Business Leadership Forum. The Forum and the EC both offered to help the Association finance the preparation of a 20 year strategy for the region.

The Association's planning officers recommended that a strategy should be prepared to show how investment could be attracted to the region from South East England and Europe, how the region's external communications could be improved, and how strategic environmental issues could be tackled. There had been no commonly approved regional framework through the 1970s and 1980s.

Early in 1993, a *Regional Economic Development Strategy for North West England* prepared by the PIEDA consulting group was sent by the Association to the EC in Brussels. Echoing its predecessor, the *Strategic Plan* of 1973, its emphasis was on clearing blockages to the growth of the regional economy, seeking still to raise skills, help small firms, clear dereliction, reduce water pollution, improve transport infrastructure, and to provide sites to draw inward investment and polish the region's image. The updated strategy had less need to dabble in issues of urban growth and land supply than had its predecessor of 20 years before, but its other targets were enduring ones.

Within a year, lost time was rapidly made up as the North West Regional Association followed its regional economic strategy by a regional transport strategy, and then by the region's own advice to the government on regional planning under the title of *Greener Growth*. Seeing changed conditions, the new planning strategy put relatively more emphasis on regenerating the region's older urban areas than had the *Strategic Plan* of 20 years before. There was a switch of emphasis of growth from the east–west corridor of industry and transport between Manchester and Liverpool, to the region's north–south spine of the M6 motorway and mainline rail route; the switch was probably necessary to continue Lancashire's revived enthusiasm for regional cooperation.

The region's Business Leadership team was associated throughout with this resurgence of strategic planning. After 20 barren years for cooperative planning in the North West, it seemed that the region might have built a broader and deeper foundation for strategic planning into the first decade of the twenty-first century than had any other in England.

Conclusion: Opposite Directions

The economic and social histories of the North West of England and the West of Scotland have been perhaps more similar than for any other two of the UK's more prominent industrial regions. But after the government sponsored plans for each region in the early 1970s leading to comprehensive proposals for physical, economic and environmental regeneration, subsequent arrangements for regional planning differed extremely.

Political attitudes between local authorities in the North West frustrated any revival of sustained regional cooperation for twenty years. But in Strathclyde, the only comprehensive metropolitan regional authority in UK history was at practice in the same period. The circle was completed during the mid 1990s; an association of North West councils resumed a form of regional planning in conjunction with industrial and business interests, when the unique Strathclyde experiment in regional planning and governance faced closure without real regard for continued effective strategic planning.

CHAPTER FOUR

Has Regional Planning in the UK Been Successful?

Preface: A Failure or Sometimes Successful?

The variety and contexts of regional planning have been so many and the history so long that no easy judgement of its effectiveness is possible. Some categorisation of the varieties is necessary for even a tentative evaluation. But judgement must be qualified because of the twists and turns of political contexts, differences of kind even within a basic categorisation, and the impossibility of sufficient knowledge being gathered on each case. But because protagonists are commonly sweeping in their dismissal or approval of regional planning, some answer must be attempted to the question of whether it can be successful, in what circumstances, and of what kinds? This requires us to consider the origins and variety of the UK's regional initiatives, the form of their shortcomings, and the circumstances in which even their successes may have been under-regarded.

The Variety of Initiatives in Regional Planning and Governance

Central/Local Relations and The Role of Government in Strategic Planning

The tides in regional initiatives in the UK have ebbed and flowed with changing government views of their political, economic and administrative potential. There have been four kinds of regional approach.

First, four main surges of extensive regional physical planning, of which the first began after the First World War and ran up to the beginning of the Second, when most of its impetus was lost. This was 'the experimental era'.

The second surge emphasised the major conurbations, commencing in the Second World War and concluding by 1948. Although containing major proposals for economic management, the central purpose of regional plans such as those for *Greater London* and the *Clyde Valley* was for government to launch programmes to relieve urban congestion. The plans accordingly represented only the initiation of policy, although in underwriting a significant part of the new town programme they also established government's control over regional development.

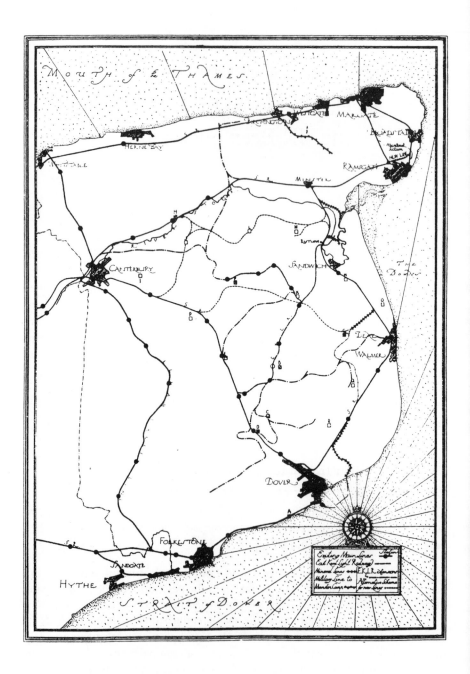

Figure 4.1. East Kent Regional Planning Scheme 1925: proposals for a regional railway scheme

*Figure 4.2. The roots of the Clyde Valley Regional Plan 1946: decayed Glasgow
tenement housing 1945*

The third surge and reassertion of regional physical planning came as the national birth-rate and population projections rose in the early 1960s, when government again took the initiative in fostering sub-regional and regional studies for most major cities and conurbation regions, as well as for potential growth areas. This surge began with the *Teesside Survey and Plan* in 1965, and might be said to have concluded a decade later with the *Strategic Plan for the North West* and the *West Central Scotland Plan* of 1974. The *National Plan* of 1965 saw regional planning as having a key role in supporting economic growth.

The regional and sub-regional initiatives of the third surge were frequently managed by local authorities, although government sooner or later exerted its authority where it was unsympathetic to emerging strategic policy. And local authorities in the South East and West Midlands of England in particular kept a candle continuously burning for regional planning through the 1970s and 1980s, when in most other regions the light was dimmed in those times.

The fourth surge came in the 1990s, after the retreat from regional planning had turned in the late 1980s. Government's policies for the National Health Service and for withdrawal of schools from local authority control implied that it must retain or possibly expand its regional administrative structures. The tools for a more fully integrated and effective system of regional planning and governance were being gathered into the hands of government, while it encouraged local authorities to be more active in cooperative regional planning.

Second, a long wave of intra-regional economic planning which arose in the early 1960s, and which although ebbing from the mid 1970s left its mark on UK governance. Departmental studies of economic, demographic and social conditions in the major regions followed government concern about employment conditions in the industrial periphery of the UK in the early 1960s. The first substantive regional economic initiative to arise was the *Central Scotland Programme for Development and Growth* of 1963. The high point of the wave came perhaps two years later in the *National Plan*, which was a classic case of policy being communicated without adequately effective means of control, notwithstanding the associated creation of the Highlands and Islands Development Board, of the National Economic Development Council and of the regional economic planning councils. Although the force of regional economic planning had much faded by the mid 1970s, elements remained as in the enterprise agencies into which the Highlands and Islands Development Board and the Scottish and Welsh Development Agencies were reshaped in 1990.

The reinforcement of the Development Commission for England in 1984 confirmed the permanancy of the several arms of government control in aspects of regional economic development. By 1985, however, government's physical initiatives for economic development had been largely transferred from the new towns – where they had been centred for almost 20 years – to the towns and cities. In England and Wales there had been installed Urban Development Corporations, Enterprise Zones, Task Forces, City Action Teams and Partnership and Programme arrangements, and an urban regeneration agency as late as 1992; Scotland had the

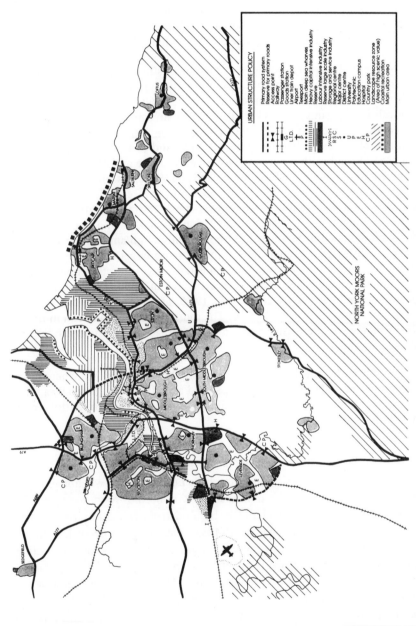

Figure 4.3. Teesside Survey and Plan 1969: urban structure policy for a sub-metropolitan region

Glasgow Eastern Area Renewal (GEAR) initiative and a range of Area Projects initiated and coordinated by the Scottish Development Agency. Although there was only indirect economic content in some of these initiatives, the tendency until the late 1980s was to down-play their social content; thereafter, social objectives became acceptable again, with the turnaround being most remarkable in the case of the London Docklands Development Corporation.

Third, four principal reorganisations of systems of strategic and regional governance. The expansion of the area of London County Council to become the Greater London Council and the creation of the Teeside County Borough in the 1960s were localised reorganisations within the broader streams. The first principal surge included the creation of the Countryside Commission, of the regional water authorities, of the passenger transport executives and of a new administration for regional and local health services; it overlapped with the mid 1970s wave of local government reorganisation which, in England and Wales, discarded the metropolitan regional representative governance proposed by the Redcliffe–Maud Commission and replaced it with the more narrowly-spread, elected metropolitan county system. In Scotland, the Wheatley Commission's proposals of a full metropolitan region were initiated in Strathclyde, although only Highland amongst the other top-tier Scottish regional councils was in any sense larger than a small English county. The third surge of strategic administrative reorganisation came with the creation of the London Regional Transport Board in 1984, the abolition of the English metropolitan county councils in 1986, and the abolition of the Inner London Education Authority in 1990. The fourth surge began to run in the mid 1990s, with the comprehensive moves to reorganise local government in England, Scotland and Wales.

Fourth, Northern Ireland has suffered unique political conditions, wherein what amounted to a regional assembly was dissolved after 1968, succeeded by a special history of reorganisation of public agencies and direct government control for most local administration.

The Motivations and Limits to Regional Action

The waves of regional physical planning have been strongest when major urban regions of the country have been most strongly in need of room to expand. The demand to clear the slums and rebuild the bomb-damaged cities inspired the classic vintage of regional planning in the 1940s; a Labour government led the programme and backed it with new towns to ensure that the plans could be fulfilled. Public action and housing was the centrepiece of strategy, and both policy and control was taken into the Government's hands. Then, during the fallow years of regional planning under Conservative governments of the 1950s, metropolitan pressures grew to bursting within the boundaries of the major cities. But the pressures were largely for rented council housing, which Conservative ministers were reluctant to impose on their supporters and the parliamentary constituencies in the shire counties. In the 1960s, the added pressure of alarming projections of potential national demographic and urban growth led another Labour government to again raise a high wave of regional planning, backed by a new programme of new towns.

Conservative governments have generally but not always had low enthusiasm for regional physical planning. They were led to it in the early 1960s as electoral anxieties grew, when regional studies could be represented as tokens of government concern for regional problems. But the studies were nearly all survey and very little plan. Again, when anxious to accelerate private housebuilding in the 1980s, Conservative governments were reminded that real regional planning could help resolve the tension between two of their groups of keenest supporters – between the housebuilders who sought more countryside to build on, and those already-established suburbanites who wanted no more households to follow their migratory example. These mutually exclusive views were reflected in a luke-warm approach, whereby the Government of the early 1990s achieved comprehensive coverage of regional planning in England and Wales, but contributed too little direction in policy, communicated weakly, and added nothing to help local government control regional strategies.

Over the long development of regional planning, a distinction can be drawn between that form involving primarily the production of occasional plans, dependent for success upon control of or observance by those required to implement proposals, and that form involving a process of sustained political and technical persuasion, negotiation and adjustment. The two forms were fairly well characterised by the *Strategy for the South East* completed in 1970, laying a framework of diagrams and tables which were relatively well integrated, as opposed to the subsequent process of 25 years of partial statements and reviews of planning policies and programmes for the South East region, occasionally surfacing from a sustained process of bartering and coercion, unseen, unreported and with little public sight of any underlying coherence or comprehensiveness. Indeed, the revival of regional planning in the 1990s was based more on negotiating processes than on formal plans.

Difference of ideology might have been expected to separate Conservative and Labour governments more considerably over the role of economic than of physical planning. And it has been true that, under Labour governments, regional economic policy has more often emerged in discussion and in proposals alongside regional physical isssues. In Scotland, of course, most Conservative ministers of the Scottish Office have been distinguished from their colleagues in England by their tolerance of aspects of economic planning, which has been an occasional tool with which to carve out benefits for Scotland.

So the impacts of regional economic planning in England have significantly differed from those in Wales, Northern Ireland and, particularly, in Scotland. This was evident when research in the 1970s into the effectiveness of past regional economic policy came to question earlier conventional analyses of regional problems. The policy implications were increasingly recognised by regional planners in the 1970s, who emphasised the need to improve the local economic environment and stimulate the indigenous sector. The nurturing of the indigenous, the small and the new was seen to require local knowledge and contacts. Civil servants of a centralised ministry were not well placed to do the job and to directly administer economic aid. Assistance had to be selective not only in the instruments employed, but also over which industries, firms, areas and people were to be helped in order to achieve local economic regeneration. The need to establish new agencies was implied.

This approach emerged most significantly in the *West Central Scotland Plan* of 1974, which contributed importantly to the case for creating the Scottish Development Agency. Although established in 1975 under a Labour government, the SDA might well have emerged in some form or other under a Conservative government. In England, however, political conditions were less favourable. Even a Labour government was unable to accept or even welcome the kind of regional economic proposals arising from the regional strategies for the Northern and North West regions.

But when presented with economic proposals, both Conservative and Labour governments have regarded economic policy as a government responsibility, not to be devolved to the regions so as to give any the opportunity to independently improve its competitive advantages. So, the *Strategic Plan for the North West* and the *Strategic Plan for the Northern Region* were both set aside where they tampered with the responsibilities of the Department of Trade and Industry. Similarly, indeed, did the *West Central Scotland Plan* fail where it proposed changes in financial incentives to benefit its region, despite the *Plan's* contribution to the creation of the Scottish Development Agency. No governments have been prepared to relinquish economic policy and control, despite allowing a cloak of economic colour to clothe regional planning at times of acute economic and electoral difficulties.

Regional reorganisation has similarly had limits, although again set wider by Labour governments. Only a Labour government has come to the brink of offering regional devolution as with the potential Scottish and Welsh Assemblies of 1979, but in practice regional governance has advanced little further under Labour than under Conservative governments. Both have employed regional agencies of government, and both have had recourse to extensive regional administration.

After deliberate disinterest in the 1980s, government in the 1990s again recognised the need for strategic planning and control in aspects of regional development. And in health services, in the arts, in the organisation of the police and potentially in schools and education administration, the government's central control was confirmed through existing or new arrangements for regional administration of public services. But through the 1980s, regional offices of the Departments of the Environment and Transport had been deprived of sufficient staff to adequately contribute to regional planning by either government or local authorities. Overwhelmed by the administration of fragmentary urban initiatives and with little time for deeply considered regional guidance, the regional offices had some greater responsibilities but a diminished capacity to help. The issue for the future was less whether government saw the need for strategic planning and more how that need could be met. How could policy be more effectively and far-sightedly prepared, how could its purpose be more widely communicated in a fragmenting system of governance, and how could participation of local and regional interests be arranged?

Who Made Regional Planning Work?

But successful processes of planning depend upon influence and authority, which is not a simple function of the amount of staffing in regional offices of government, or in joint local authority planning teams. Nor does success follow automatically upon the high quality of the technical inputs to a regional strategy or policies.

Smith (1969) emphasises the opportunity for influence of the chairs of the regional economic planning councils, at their most active in the latter half of the 1960s, and Painter (1972) has written of this too. The chairmen had the ears of the ministers who had appointed them, as well as an accompanying regard from senior civil servants. Depending upon their background, they could earn respect from regional industrialists or even local politicians. As the councils comprised a variety of public and private interests, they could contribute to a regional consensus. How much of an impact that had would be a matter of circumstances and personal abilities. After 1979, the abolition of the regional economic planning councils cut the link between the regional consensus and senior ministers. But in South East England, the government's continuing dependence upon SERPLAN in negotiating the scale of housebuilding in the counties of the region must have owed much to the political connections of its successive chairmen, all members of the House of Lords.

The organisation of the regional offices of government is noteworthy. They were led by an under-secretary, who chaired the economic planning board and was typically drawn from the Department of Economic Affairs during its lifetime. After the demise of the DEA, the Department of the Environment provided the regional director in the offices, supported by regional controllers for planning, housing and transportation respectively. Nearly 30 years later, in 1993, the Department of Industry joined the consortia of interests in the regional offices; the senior civil servant coordinating the government's various efforts in urban regeneration for each region now got the opportunity of reporting to a senior government minister, chairing a ministerial committee in Whitehall and setting national priorities.

So, the communicative role of regional offices of Whitehall departments has been quite well sustained, backed by tools of executive control. But the power of deriving policy has generally been held close to ministers' hands in Whitehall, however inconstantly and carelessly it has been exercised. So economic policy has not been regionalised, except in the marginal ways possible within Scotland, Wales and Northern Ireland at the discretion of their Secretaries of State, or in England through the development corporations and agencies being added to in the 1980s.

Effective regional planning, therefore, has customarily depended upon inside influence at a high level of politics and of governance. It has normally required the agreement of several significant local authorities, or of different departments of government. It may require changes of government policy, and it may call for special allocations of national resources. Its success less often depends primarily on the contribution of the professional planner than in most fields of planning. Because its implications are bound up with party and institutional politics, senior administrators and senior politicians are commonly at least as significant to it as the technical planner.

So the history of regional planning is notably bound up with figures of administrative and political influence. A few planners have moved into this role: Pepler and Abercrombie in England from the 1920s to the 1940s; Grieve in Scotland from the 1940s to the 1970s; Burns in England in the 1960s and 1970s. But politicians have been significant as at least hand-maidens in the regional process: Johnston in Scotland in the 1940s; Brown in England in the 1960s; Younger in Scotland in the 1960s. And amongst their other roles, that of controllers of the government's regional offices, and of under-secretaries in the Scottish Office such as James McGuiness, have been notably significant in regional planning. Regional planning is a political construction in more dimensions than most forms of planning, and its design more than usually dependent on political sensitivity and support.

The Shortcomings of Practice

Failings of Governance

THE PARTICIPANTS IN THE REGIONS

The studies and plans of the 1960s were largely imposed on the regions of the UK, because however local authorities and regional interests may have complained about the insensitivity of government to their region's problems and needs, it was government which was most able to coerce support for a collective study or plan. Local interests were often reluctant to face the likelihood that a common strategy would curtail some sectional ambitions. Nonetheless, some authorities did see cooperative planning as a means of achieving their ends, or at least of controlling their destiny; the reconstitution in 1962 of the Standing Conference on London and South East Regional Planning came largely by the initiative of Surrey County Council (Young and Garside 1982, 306), supported progressively by the clerks of the other counties in the region, at a time when the Ministry of Housing and Local Government was working on its *South East Study* (1964).

Accordingly, the participants entered into the studies and plans with varying degrees of suspicion of each others' motives. They were perhaps not always convinced of the sincerity of the case put by the *National Plan* (1965, 84) that:

regional policy has a key role to play in the achievement of faster growth. One of its major aims is to make use of the reserves of labour in some regions of the country and to speed up industrial growth where it is lagging.

The *National Plan* (1965, 85) also warned that:

'regional policies will not be concerned with bolstering up small areas which have no economic future' even if it was also concerned with the 'problem of securing a more balanced regional development of industry and housing in the context of a rapidly growing population. On present forecasts the population of the United Kingdom will grow by 20 million over the rest of the century'

Whatever the prospect that government might allocate a share of this growth to underwrite the future of some of the peripheral and less prosperous parts of the country, there were tensions and jealousies in both prosperous and lagging regions about how this growth would be internally distributed. Some local authorities did not wish to share in population growth, and others had high hopes which they did not wish to be frustrated.

Against this background of massive projected national population growth, the Labour government elected in 1964 moved to translate into plans the regional studies which its Conservative predecessors had turned to as the election had loomed. The new government had little sympathy for the Conservative county councils which had resisted overspill from the principal English conurbations, and the projected national need for urbanisation plainly required growth in the established metropolitan regions, as well as exploration of the potential of the great estuaries including particularly Severnside and Humberside. There seemed to be an acute urgency to release metropolitan growth.

The regional economic planning councils established to advise the regional economic planning boards had been given responsibility to prepare the regional plans. This arrangement also placed responsibility with the Department of Economic Affairs rather than with the planning division of the Ministry of Housing and Local Government, from which initiatives in regional planning had previously derived. But while partly reflecting the kind of arrangements through which France operated economic planning, the new DEA lacked representatives in the regions as influential as were the *préfets* in the French regions. The role of the chairmen of the English regional boards was weakened by the uncertain authority of the new DEA in relation to the Treasury, and by the diminishing force of its minister, George Brown, in the Cabinet.

Only the *West Midlands* (1965) and *North West* (1965) Studies were completed under the auspices of the DEA, before responsibility was switched to the economic planning councils from the economic planning boards. The switch turned subsequent studies into advocacy documents rather than official plans for government investment and development policy. As Martins (1986, 184) points out, the switch meant that government need not be financially committed to any proposals in the plans. The shift of responsibility anticipated the abolition of the DEA, and Lindley (1982) explains it as also partly the consequence of the Government shying away from further commitments to the regions on the scale of those implicit in the plan to expand the Scottish economy (Scottish Office, 1966), and partly by difficulty in coordinating government departments inhibiting both the preparation and the implementation of plans.

Although some question the priority which the DEA gave to regional planning (Wright and Young 1975), the collapse of the *National Plan* and of the DEA reinforced the independence of departments and weakened regional coordination. It also weakened the link between economic and physical planning, because only in the lagging regions of the country did economic issues remain a central part of the regional plans subsequently prepared, until they returned strongly throughout the UK from the late 1970s.

The economic planning councils were not wholly successful as planning agencies. The West Midlands Economic Planning Council was criticised on occasions for special pleading on behalf of predominantly industrial interests, being insensitive to issues outside its preoccupation with economic growth (Painter 1972, 467). Its capacity to systematically analyse alternatives and to follow the rigours of a meticulous planning process were also doubted. Other councils – like that for South East England – were also cavalier in their style of strategic planning, echoing the approach of the architect planner consultant impresarios of the 1940s more than that of the modish systems analysis attractive to professional planners in the late 1960s and early 1970s. There was also some naivety about the councils' initiatives on occasions, which sometimes seemed not familiar with realities of politics and of public administration.

Notwithstanding a limited overlap of membership and the merits of having a wider range of issues coming forward for debate, uneasy relationships between local authority conferences and economic planning councils caused difficulty for ministers in the Department of the Environment. The influence of the councils could not have been expected to be even. Painter (1972) suggested that the West Midlands Economic Planning Council had only a marginal effect upon government allocation of public resources; accelerated construction of a motorway link between Telford new town and the national motorway system was one of the Council's larger influences. Nor were local authorities much more happy to accept guidance from unelected bodies. The Standing Conference for London and the South East considered the *Strategy for the South East* published by the Regional Economic Planning Council in 1967 to duplicate Conference's work, and the West Midlands Conference was disturbed by the 1967 *Patterns of Growth* report by its Regional Planning Council.

So, the regional economic planning councils had been only briefly given their head before the Department of the Environment resumed the initiative in regional planning. In the West Midlands, it was decided that the Conference would take the lead in developing a planning strategy for the region, although through a team constituted for the purpose at arms-length from local political interference. The outcome was unsatisfactory to almost all interests; the team's strategy was 'irrelevant to a derisory degree', as Martins put it (1986, 186). In the South East, where because the Conference was older it had a longer history of underachievement, the government decided that it would itself prepare the strategy under the leadership of the chief planner of the Department of the Environment. Although the local authorities and the Economic Planning Council of the South East shared in a formal supervisory committee, technical direction and the shape of the strategy was firmly led by government officials.

Martins (1986, 109) suggests that the single most important result of the long process of preparing, modifying and adopting the West Midlands strategy was the creation of a commitment to a continuous process of regional planning. But the process was protracted, frequently indecisive, and the authorities repeatedly backtracked upon implicit principles in sometimes ambiguous strategic agreements. Nor did the fault lie entirely with the local authorities. Martins emphasises that government's cooperation in joint planning with the authorities was sometimes secondary to its need to conceal interdepartmental policy rivalry.

So, the experience of the later 1960s and early 1970s in England was that neither the regional conferences nor the economic planning councils were reliable agents for responsive and sensitive regional planning, clearly and quickly able to determine balanced priorities. Moreover, when too exact expenditure proposals emerged, they could severely embarrass government. In 1972, the responsible minister in the Department of the Environment implicitly confirmed that government would lead future regional strategies, when he announced that they would be prepared in collaboration with the regional economic planning authorities and the local authorities. Government also lowered its expectations of regional planning (Crosland 1974, 447) to achieving a framework only for county structure plans, and for major investment or environmental decisions by public bodies.

These were modest expectations by comparison with what had been sought from regional planning in the mid 1960s. The coordinating framework for structure plans could be little more than consistent population and housing projections assumed by local authorities. As other government departments and statutory authorities stood as at least equals with the Department of the Environment, the force of a coordinating framework for them could accordingly be only slight, omitting many significant regional decisions to be settled separately.

THE GOVERNMENT'S ROLE

What have been the weaknesses of the government's role in regional planning, in essence? The two greatest were its sustained tolerance of a fragmented and outdated structure of local government which derived from the geography of the 19th century, and a government structure which was largely inimical to continuous regional planning. Against these difficulties, it was almost more notable that regional planning occurred than that its impact was so variable and even absent in some leading cases.

These weaknesses were greatest in England and Wales, but they existed also in Scotland despite such exceptional experiences as those of Strathclyde Regional Council, the Highlands and Islands Development Board and the Scottish Development Agency. They have underlain discontinuity in regional planning in all parts of the UK, as they have the usually poor marriage of physical and economic analysis and proposals.

A place for economic policy in regional strategies was hard fought for against inter-departmental rivalry on many occasions over a long period. Differences between the Departments of Trade and Industry and of the Environment were a sustained brake upon the integration of physical and economic strategy. There was a long history of an inability of these two departments to fully integrate their policies. The tension was evident in the late 1940s, when the Board of Trade's policy to divert jobs to the older industrial areas competed with the Ministry of Town and Country Planning's ambitions to support the new town programme in the South East (Self 1982, 96). There was also stress between the departments over the location of new industry within the decentralising metropolitan areas, which was repeated in West Midlands planning in the 1970s and the 1980s.

The *Strategies* for the *North West* and the *Northern* regions attempted to integrate physical, environmental and economic dimensions in their proposals, but their reception suffered notably by the inter-departmental problem. Only in Scotland did the more unified purposes of the Scottish Office allow the familiar divide between economic and physical planning to be fully overcome. Physical and economic analyses had been linked in regional planning in the Scottish Office from the early 1960s, where although falling to different departments these were united by common responsibility to the Secretary of State for Scotland. So, backed by distaste for the Department of Trade and Industry, the Scottish Office keenly encouraged the establishment of a regional economic development agency as the centrepiece of the *West Central Scotland Plan*.

The Department of Economic Affairs might have come to bridge the gap in England, but was too short-lived to do so. Popularly regarded as a failure, the DEA fell partly by the idiosyncratic behaviour of its Secretary of State, George Brown, but also by its inability to command the higher rate of national economic growth towards which it wished the country and other government departments to aim. But the DEA helped launch a flood of planning initiatives, and it was party to a period of unprecedented intense planning for regional problems and issues. A kinder judgement on its record is certainly due in this than in some other of its roles. In 1968, for instance, it set out a framework for relations between the regional economic planning councils and the emerging regional standing conferences of local authorities. The councils were assigned responsibility for advising the government on the implications for the regions of national economic policy, and for advising on how national economic policy might be adjusted to special regional circumstances. However, the councils were not to be so overcome by their responsibilities as to avoid close cooperation with local authorities.

The creation of the Department of the Environment was ostensibly to better integrate mutually-related policies previously developed and applied by separate government departments, and by the transport and planning ministries particularly. The aim was never satisfactorily met. The very large size of the new department was cumbersome for the Secretary of State to manage and blend. Also, not only did the staff of the former Ministry of Transport remain together in an almost autonomous division, but notoriously they remained more sympathetic to the interests of the national road building lobby than to those of public transport, or indeed to their colleagues in the planning divisions.

The strains of managing such a large and varied department might well have led its ministers and senior officials to avoid forcing regional planning into its mainstream. Regional planning could affect so many divisions of the Department of the Environment that it required a sustained effort of belief and will to cultivate. But even if sometimes a useful opportunity to step upon the responsibilities of rival departments of government, regional planning was not a ready vote winner at constituency level and was resisted by some powerful divisional interests in the Department. Painter (1980) confirms this by reporting how centralised coordination of the Department's divisions progressively gave way to looser management. Concurrently, headquarters in London was reluctant to devolve to regional offices decisions whose regional impact might have been better seen in the regions.

So the leading role adopted by the Department of the Environment after the demise of the DEA was inhibited, not only by its steady state of conflict over regional policy with the Department of Trade and Industry but also by divisional responsibilities within it, whereby national rather than regional programmes took precedence. The Department was perhaps less able to control within government than it was amongst local authorities. The authorities had an incentive to converge on the Department's wishes in regard to regional planning, because they were ultimately dependent on the Department for approval to their structure plans.

The ambiguities of elements of the plans and also of the position of the Department of the Environment, made government responses to the plans and strategies difficult to compile. There was no response at all to the *Strategy for the Northern Region*, and responses emerged only after 18 months in the *North West* and in over 12 months in *East Anglia*. The responses skated over difficulties which government wished to avoid and they were equivocal, particularly where the Department of the Environment touched on matters which were the responsibility of other departments. This lack of clear government commitment to strategies much weakened their influence upon statutory agencies such as the regional water authorities.

The regional economic planning councils lingered for a surprisingly long time. As a government initiative, they have been given credit (Self 1982, 97) for the incidental benefit of stimulating local government to an interest in regional planning, aiming to rival initiatives by the councils. But the councils lost their impetus as the 1970s went on, and they might well have been dispensed with sooner than by the arrival of the Conservative government of 1979, simultaneously dismissing the councils and the idea that economic planning had any place in the regions. Ministers asserted that economic planning was bound to be relatively ineffective at regional level, being capable only of being properly taken into account in national planning of infrastructure and other spending programmes. Under English administrative arrangements in the 1960s and 1970s this was a fair conclusion, but it ignored experience in Scotland and did not consider whether there might be merit in finding better arrangements than England had enjoyed.

What the period of attempted integration of physical and economic planning showed was that if the scope of regional planning is to be as wide as attempted in strategies like those for the *North West* and *East Anglia*, it can only be fully worthwhile if some adjustment to the means of local and central government is made to match it. No planning can expect to coordinate many spending programmes spread between a large number of largely autonomous authorities and agencies, except by having sufficient significant leverage upon them.

This weakness of UK experience lay largely in England, where responsibility for regional planning lay with only one department among many, amongst whom several had higher status. Only during the short life of the DEA was there a possibility of regional planning coming right to the fore. The weakness was characterised by a senior official of the Department of the Environment, speaking as a major review of the *Strategic Plan for the South East* began only five years after its completion: 'Regional plans are so quickly overtaken by events. We have had the [Third London] airport saga, the Channel tunnel decision, Department of the Environment land use circulars, and the change in the economic climate' (Curry 1975, 31). So much change, not only beyond the scope of the *Strategic Plan* but by strategic decisions in which the Department of the Environment was only a bit player.

But as in other countries, effective leverage in the UK has been achieved in cases and without comprehensive regional governance. Leverage has been applied through alternative forms: regional local government on the Strathclyde model was one form; that of the Scottish Development Agency was another, comparable to the French *conseils régionaux* in its topping-up of the funds of agencies willing to cooperate.

What Kind of Executive Agency is Needed for Regional Plans to Succeed?

Some of the most influential and decisive advances in regional planning have been achieved without regional governance of matching sophistication. Influential plans for Greater London, the Clyde Valley and for West Central Scotland were each undertaken because their regions had long lacked a formalised governance. Although in West Central Scotland a unique regional council soon followed to help implement the *West Central Scotland Plan* more quickly and completely than might otherwise have happened, the case merely reinforces a serious question. How necessary is regional governance to effective regional planning, and what alternatives are practicable?

The disappointing experience of the GLC and of the English metropolitan county councils as strategic planning authorities was wholly predictable. It was due to an inadequate design for governance. Established within boundaries containing a disproportionately large share of their regions' economic and social problems, the councils possessed a disproportionately small share of regional resources of finance and land by which to ease them. Strategic planning in the regions of the GLC and of the metropolitan counties depended heavily on the goodwill of the metropolitan districts and of the shire county majority. Some would see the protracted progress and inadequacies of English regional planning as reason to create powerful regional local government, as a Working Party of the Royal Town Planning Institute (1986) did. But there are different ways of empowering regions. The most significant and powerful example ever attempted in the UK has been Strathclyde. Perhaps unfairly, therefore, an answer to the question of whether powerful regional local government is needed to make regional planning work in the UK must rest primarily on the Strathclyde experience.

Incomparably superior to prior arrangements in the West of Scotland, regional planning since the advent of Strathclyde Regional Council has been continuous and in many ways responsive to sudden regional issues. But we have seen that there were many partners in Strathclyde's planning, including several government development agencies with specific and significant influences. The Council's Department of Physical Planning crystallised the regional *Structure Plan* to which local plans throughout the 19 district council areas of Strathclyde were expected to conform; it was able to advise the Council on decisions on the few but significant planning applications 'called in' from the hands of district councils; it took initiatives to guide district councils, government agencies and private investment towards regional planning objectives; and it initiated and executed projects for environmental recovery, for countryside protection, and for leisure and recreation.

Nonetheless, the Regional Council's planners took only a small – but valuable – direct share in executing regional strategy for Strathclyde, and of investment in it. And key elements of the *Structure Plan* were contributed by government agencies, executive departments of the Regional Council, or were largely dependent upon the vagaries of private sector investment. If these circumstances are compared with those in England, Strathclyde is exemplary so far as strong political leadership and corporate management gave potential to directly support planning strategy by investment and departmental programmes for transport, main drainage schemes, water supply, social and education services. But the evidence of the parallel programmes of economic and environmental action pursued by the SDA suggests that its leverage on local authorities through financial aid to selected projects was at least as effective in supporting regional strategy. And, in respects, the SDA was able to twist strategy to its own targets.

Looking also at experience in the US and in France, we can see too that it is not essential to unite regional plan-making and the execution of principal supporting programmes of public services under the same administrative roof. Regional planning can be quite effectively fulfilled by means other than by unified, comprehensive regional government. What is needed is effective leverage by those responsible for strategy, which can be arranged through financial support for strategic initiatives. And which particular political conditions can also provide. It is not imperative for the guardians of strategy to have a hand directly on every lever of implementation.

Nonetheless, regional planning of the 1960s and 1970s in England in particular was imposed upon an administrative and political system not designed for it, and its dependence upon inputs and accord from many parts of the system was an inherent weakness. The *Strategic Plan for the North West* and the *Strategic Plan for the Northern Region* derived from teams sponsored by the Department of the Environment, which had no authority to implement some of the key proposals of the plans because they fell within the responsibility of other government departments, or demanded resources which the Treasury would not release. The *West Central Scotland Plan* might have met a similar fate had it not emerged within a uniqely favourable political context, favouring its proposal for a regional economic development agency as well as providing Strathclyde Regional Council to implement its significantly new physical strategy. And the *Coventry–Solihull–Warwickshire Sub-Regional Study* met unexpectedly favourable circumstances of local politics, which were less kind to some of its contemporary sub-regional studies.

But it could only be said that inadequacies of political support failed English regional planning at particular times if that planning's technical methods were wholly sound. And flawed methods undoubtedly swelled the political turbulence in some cases.

Methodological Development

Between the two World Wars, although regional conferences of local authorities spread across significant urban and rural regions, no professional planner could be regarded as being engaged on full-time regional planning. Some staff were seconded to cooperative local authority teams to plan regional highway and parkway projects; this was architecture writ large, scarcely even landscape design. Pepler propagated the merits of regional planning amongst the local governments of England and Wales, but his duties precluded his sinking himself into technical methodology. None of the consultants from whom plans were commissioned worked exclusively on regional planning; many were architects, whatever their contacts with ideas of regional surveys taught by Geddes and Branford. Indeed, surveys often seemed a substitute for analytical planning. Plans were little concerned with administrative impediments to implementation.

When regional planning became a tool for reconstruction after the Second World War, its methods and prescriptions consolidated rather than advanced on what had gone before (Cherry and Wannop 1994). The teams were led by Abercrombie or others whose methods had been developed before the War. Proven ways and means were employed, and the scope of proposals understandably echoed the Barlow Commission and the inter-war campaigns of the Garden Cities and Town Planning Association and of the Town Planning Institute. The plans disposed densities for reconstruction and for new residential neighbourhoods. Railway stations were relocated, helicopter stations were introduced, idealised urban land use structure and communication networks were planned, and green belts and leisure facilities served the cities. Decentralisation of city populations was a keynote. Resources were regarded as the tool and not the master of ideology. But although Abercrombie's plans for Greater London and the Clyde Valley were seriously concerned about means of implementation, his matured philosophy of new towns beyond a metropolitan greenbelt in these two great plans was underlain by intuition as much as by scientific method.

The idealism of this planning method was borrowed freely from the spirit of geography and sociology, but scarcely from economics. The methodology was not seriously challenged until the 'systems revolution' of the 1960s. A relatively unsophisticated progression from initial surveys to proposals was blurred by value judgements and idealised prescriptions. Abercrombie's *Clyde Valley Regional Plan* prescribed the massive redistribution of people from the slums of Clydeside. This was inevitable, but the proposal that the City of Glasgow should be reduced to 1 million people was based, as Robert Grieve has recalled, on Abercrombie's belief that this was an optimum city size. Planning dogma of an instinctive and unscientific kind lay at the heart of the *Plan*.

Nonetheless, the conclusions of the plans of the period commonly commanded popular support from overcrowded citizens if not always from their councillors, to whom decentralisation and population redistribution was a threat to their cities' status as much as it was a threat to their counterparts outside.

So, by the 1940s, regional planning for metropolitan regions was typically a strategy to thin out and decentralise population with a following movement of industry, frequently supported by a circumscribing green belt. The strategies seemed to be cast in timelessness. The plans had simply to unfold like the pages on which they were printed.

The fallow decade of the 1950s saw most of the leading pioneers in regional planning fade from practice. So when problems of urban congestion persisted and the shire counties of England remained reluctant to help relieve it, technical work in regional planning fell to a generation without prior experience. And it was a generation increasingly dominated by younger planners trained exclusively in planning, or first in geography, sociology, economics or another of the social sciences, which came to displace architecture, surveying and engineering as the paths to planning practice.

So, new methodological attitudes were creeping into the foundations of planning as the 1960s arrived. And although old problems of urban sprawl continued, projections of future national population growth now far exceeded the capacity of local authority development plans and of the new towns being urgently launched or expanded. The scale of regional problems was increasing, and they were allied to rising unemployment and anxiety about the economic condition of the UK's peripheral regions.

The new generation of regional planners cut their teeth initially on regional studies rather than regional plans. The Ministry of Housing and Local Government's *South East Study* of 1964 documented the issues in the region, but did not propose the framework in which they might be tackled. Yet, although it covered two-fifths of the population and economic activity of England and Wales, its origins in the ministry for land use and housing meant that it largely excluded economic issues. Similarly, studies for other key regions like the North West (1965) and the West Midlands (1965) surveyed but lacked prescription.

The economic dimension was, however, dominant in parallel studies for development and growth in Central Scotland and North East England, both published in 1963. In these two regions, civil servants acted more as advocates of their regions' interests than as dependents of the government in Whitehall. Ministers allowed a degree of licence when political necessity called for it. So positive planning programmes were produced with both physical and economic dimensions. The studies would later be seen as flawed in respects, particularly and seriously so in the case of Central Scotland, but they marked the start of a revival of regional planning after nearly 15 barren years. Being led by political pressures, the plans were longer on goals than on grass-roots practicalities. They also displayed the characteristic weakness of plans led by economists, a Panglossian dislocation from hard reality when looking to futures beyond the usual short-term horizon of financial planning.

The outstanding example from this mould of economic planning was the *National Plan* of 1965, adopting the approach of indicative planning pioneered in France and other countries. It assumed subsequent studies of how the regions could contribute to national growth. Scotland's contribution to the national effort was set out in a five-year programme for the period 1965–70. Within this new framework of economic planning and led by the DEA, a ministerial committee on Environmental Planning was established (Cullingworth 1979, 224), with a central planning unit set up to accelerate studies of potential growth areas. There was no available context of up-to-date regional plans matching the scale of national population pressures now foreseen. As Cullingworth (1979, 225) has commented:

> The problem, however, was of a national rather than a regional character. No previous attempt had been made to determine a national strategy for long term development... New developments would need to be planned in terms

of their total scale and 'the increasingly close-knit national context that will affect them in terms of communications, technological change, etc.' It would be necessary to plan major expansions as national growth centres which might attract population from outside the region in which they were located.

The imminent pressures seemed too great to permit a stately progress from preparation of a national strategy to the confirmation of regional plans, and then to the designation of new towns and local growth areas.

The shortlived DEA which had initiated the *National Plan* might eventually have patched over the persistent gap between physical and economic policy in Britain. But the Department expired in 1969 when the idea of tightly connecting regional plans to public investment programmes had already been abandoned.

The impetus for regional planning in the 1960s had also been fuelled by the growth of land use/transportation studies, encompassing most local authorities in the regional conurbations and in many lesser urban areas. Demands from these studies for comprehensive data about the future stimulated new methodologies in metropolitan and regional planning, some of which had been pioneered in new town planning, particularly in Cumbernauld. However, transportation consultants in the 1960s little appreciated the uncertainties inherent in the long-term employment and population projections required to feed their computer models. So planners were often willing to indulge in technically exciting but spuriously positive projections for many years into the future. Planners' professional collaboration underpinned transportation studies like those for South East Lancashire/North East Cheshire, the West Midlands and Greater Glasgow, all making assumptions about future regional growth implying regional planning strategies not approved as such.

The refinement of planning methodology ran behind the rate of spread of US transportation planning methods. The watershed between the older and the newer generation of regional planning methodology lay in the *Strategic Plan for the South East* of 1970. It concentrated its proposals almost wholly in the ambit of its principal sponsor, the Ministry of Housing and Local Government, and it was directed by the government's two most senior planners. So despite its associated economic analysis and the secondment to the team of staff from several government ministries, its significant proposals were for the location of urban growth and for countryside conservation. Its main report was less the first of the new wave of regional plans of the 1970s than an echo of the plans of the 1940s. Indeed, Abercrombie's *Greater London Plan* of 1944 had been more ambitious in its width and depth. But its supplementary reports showed the new scope and methodologies of regional planning coming through.

Regional planning of this period reflected a cultural transition. A generation brought up on Abercrombie's methods and the classic approach directed the major regional plans. But their technical staff and the leaders of the sub-regional studies were schooled in or attracted to newer analytical methods developing in geography, and in the computerised techniques of land use/transportation studies. Whereas the *Strategic Plan for the South East* was cast in the style of Abercrombie, new methods of 'rational' planning underlay the *West Midlands Study* and surfaced strongly in the sub-regional studies for Teesside, Leicester–Leicestershire, Nottinghamshire–Derbyshire and particularly for Coventry–Solihull–Warwickshire. Concepts of flexibility and of systematic monitoring emerged, and the issue of resources took some plans close to budgetary planning.

So 1971 was a turning point for the issues and style of regional planning. Plans produced subsequently were not dominated as before by problems of overspill from the cities, but now turned their attention to economic, environmental and regional budgeting proposals alongside older physical questions of new towns and land use. Metropolitan areas were generally consolidating now, rather than exploding. The switch of emphasis was associated with the new generation of planners coming to lead regional teams.

As the 1970s developed, both population growth and economic expectations continued to sharply reduce. As pressure for long-term urban expansion eased, social problems in the inner cities took more political attention. The cultural shift amongst regional planners was concluded, reflected in the phase of plans meddling in resource allocation and economic policy, causing confusion within government and contributing to the distaste in which regional planning would be held by Thatcher governments of the 1980s.

The full regional plans after 1971 were the *Strategy for the Northern Region*, the *West Central Scotland Plan*, the *East Anglia Strategy* and the *Strategic Plan for the North West*. All raised testing issues for government. They aimed to rectify inter-regional imbalances in housing, economic and environmental conditions. In doing so, they not only sought financial advantages for their regions but stepped on the responsibilities of other departments of government than that which principally sponsored them.

From the mid 1970s, local economic development became a widespread preoccupation of public planning in the UK, as it had been from time to time in regional planning. The *West Central Scotland Plan* of 1974 marked the beginning of this period of adjustment to local enterprise in economic planning, and the strategic regional plans for the North West and Northern regions of England also emphasised the need to foster indigenous local economies. So, paradoxically, it was regional planning which anticipated the rise of local development enterprise to stand at least equal with regional economic initiatives. And regional planning thereby was seen as having downgraded its own significance.

The new emphases of regional planning meant a progressive fading of the preoccupation with master regional diagrams of earlier periods. Many tables, figures and often distribution maps were bound into the texts, but no longer did the main report contain a pocket inside the end covers bulging with a regional master plan superimposed on an Ordnance map.

And a new model for the regional process emerged in Scotland, where a special feature of the new local government system begun in 1975 was the requirement for all regional councils to prepare a regional report. The reports were expected to overview each region's physical, economic and social problems, without the cumbersome procedures and limitations of statutory development plans. Although most councils failed to follow-up on their first reports before the approach was quashed by the incoming Conservative government of 1979, the format was much envied by English planners.

The 1980s brought a government ideologically opposed to planning and dismissive of regional planning as an undesirable vogue of the 1960s, on which the government blamed so many of the trends of which it disapproved. But as government supporters came to complain that lack of regional planning threatened green belts, house prices, traffic congestion and the environment, political realities brought tacit government acceptance of the need to maintain elements of regional planning.

In this redemption of regional planning, regional plans themselves were absent, but by 1992 the whole of England was for the first time covered by regional conferences of local planning authorities. Government published regional guidance by which structure and local plans were coordinated in the regions. Whatever the justifiable criticisms of its irregular quality and frequent failure of foresight, the early 1990s saw a process of regional planning fully institutionalised across all England and for the majority of the United Kingdom.

The process and methodology of regional planning was again redirected, however. They did not yield the drama of master planning as in the 1940s, nor the arcane aproaches of mathematical modelling, systematic evaluation and other rationalist methods of the late 1960s and early 1970s. More than ever, the process was of political negotiation, bullying and bartering to exhaustion. Plan-making itself was the least of the tasks. The West Midlands and South East conferences, in particular, took periodic initiatives towards structure plan coordination, but the larger role of these cooperative arrangements tended to be in communication and reaching political settlements between the partners; policy initiation was at the fore less often.

When, in 1992, the local authorities of North West England formed a standing regional conference after years of frustration, there was for the first time a complete coverage of England by standing regional conferences, of varying intensity and commitment, providing forums in which regional problems could be mediated as far as local government had the capacity to do. Idealism, ideology, determinism and abstract methodologies had been squeezed to the margins of regional planning. As SERPLAN (1992, 21) saw it for the South East:

> all strategies and plans, with the possible exception of the Abercrombie Greater London Plan, have in some degree blended the deterministic and normative. Determinism assumes that there is a sequentiality and linearity in events: that the future will develop in direct line from the past; the basic tool is extrapolation. The normative approach, on the other hand, treats the future as being able to be shaped, as a matter of choice rather than inevitability.

Yet, it is tension between the two views of what is possible or desirable which demands that plans and policies contain flexibility, the attribute which so many claim but so few can show when called on.

Professional Method: The Critical Issue of Flexibility

As a channel of planning practice only occasionally navigated, and commonly so by ad hoc teams of planners drawn away from their regular experience, regional planning has not developed a continuous and sophisticated methodology. It has sometimes been clumsy, and the political tensions surrounding it have on occasions been exacerbated by methods which were technically as well as politically naive. The critical methodological failure has been to ensure that plans have been genuinely flexible, able to remain valid and robust when meeting often predictable disturbances to smooth implementation.

The protracted preparation and negotiation of a West Midlands strategy during the 1970s was bedevilled by the issue of the scale and location of population dispersal from the conurbation. Some more distant parts of the region hoped to expand by importing families from Birmingham, particularly to towns in Staffordshire and the new town of Telford. So as regional population projections fell, and as private housebuilding in the conurbation began to compete with building beyond the green belt, the periphery of the region feared that its ambitions would evaporate. For a period, the regional conference's planning team held together a crumbling coalition of councils, employing the device of maintaining the originally expected ambitions of growth as the upper end of a possible range for each authority and town, of which the lower end was scaled to the new projections of regional growth. Each council could thereby maintain the belief that it might, after all, reach its earlier expectations of growth. This was collectively impossible, of course.

This device of West Midlands planning has been employed elsewhere. A variant on it was used in the *West Central Scotland Plan*. It has been a ploy which can bridge troubled political waters. But it can be argued that if the West Midlands had faced the unavoidable uncertainty about population growth from the start, some of the difficulties of reaching an agreed strategy might have been anticipated. They might have been either earlier faced or avoided. The original decision to rest the whole technical work of designing a strategy upon a single projection of long-term growth proved to be politically unwise in the long run, as well as being technically unsound. It led to a preferred strategy which was evaluated against only one condition of economic and demographic growth, and when this proved so wrong in the event it left the evaluation as worthless.

Although simultaneous with the *West Midland Regional Study* of 1971, the *Coventry–Solihull–Warwickshire Sub-Regional Study* was perhaps fortunate to gain early political approval, before the West Midlands region faced decisively falling population projections. It also based most of its strategy-making upon a single future condition of growth of population and employment, but significantly incorporated tests of flexibility in evaluating alternative strategies. To this extent, it faced the possibility that growth might considerably diverge from the best projection of the time which underlay the alternatives evaluated. This approach was taken further in the *West Central Scotland Plan*, which regarded the high and low ends of a projected range of demographic and economic conditions as being equally possible. It consequently evaluated strategic alternatives against each of these two possible conditions, finding the same alternative to be the best in each case.

The approach of the *West Central Scotland Plan* took it further than the *Coventry–Solihull–Warwickshire Study*, and overcame the methodological weakness of the *West Midlands Study*. Also, in circumstances in which neither government nor local councils were ready to publicly accept the probability that the West of Scotland was turning from growth to sustained decline, the method of evaluating strategy against both possibilities was politically successful. It allowed those political interests unable to openly accept that people and jobs could both decline to simply ignore the prospect. By the time this comparatively robustly assembled and evaluated strategy was incorporated in political decisions in the two years after completion of the *Plan*, political circumstances had altered and decline could be faced. In 1981, ten years after the base year for the *Plan*'s projections, the actual population of the region fell just within the lower end of the projected range; in 1991, the actual population had fallen further than the lowest projected level.

While in each case the approach helped maintain political coalitions for plan-making, that in West Central Scotland had a methodological strength absent in the West Midlands. The political lesson from the comparison may be that the unpalatable is better tasted early, but can be diluted by methods which are both methodologically and politically sensitive.

The most significant failure to adequately consider the technical implications of flexibility in regional planning was in the *Strategic Plan for the South East* (1970). The *Plan* was quite aware of the issue. It referred to failure of some of the assumptions underlying Abercrombie's *Greater London Plan* of 1944, and its Preface asserted (p. ix) that it dealt with the region's pressures 'not by recommending a rigid master plan for the region – but by outlining a flexible framework.' But although observing (p. 83) that without detailed projections including study of household size, it would be very difficult to say what London's population might be beyond 1981, the *Strategy* assumed that the South East's share of national population growth up to the year 2000 would be in proportion to the region's share of national population in 1966. It was acknowledged that the level and inter-regional distribution of national growth was uncertain, and could lead to higher or lower levels of growth in the South East, but 'The team considers, however, that the recommended strategy should be able to cope satisfactorily with either eventuality.' The team assumed that the region's households might increase by 550,000 by 1981 (p. 24), after which average household size would not alter in the 1980s (p. 58).

The *Strategic Plan* made two basic mistakes. The first was to neglect the coming decade of the 1970s and to be 'primarily concerned with the emerging regional situation after 1981' (p. 84); it was supposed that the region's development in the 1970s was already determined by established plans. The second error was that the demographic assumptions were badly founded.

In the event, actual regional population growth fell well below expectations. By 1981, it actually amounted to only half that expected in the *Strategic Plan*, and by 1991 real growth in the region outside Greater London fell over 2 million below what the *Plan* implied it would be. On the other hand, there was a real and marked shrinkage in average household size in all parts of the South East, contrary to the *Plan*'s assumption. So whereas the *Plan* expected the number of households requiring dwellings in Greater London to fall by 200,000 between 1966 and 1981, the number actually housed fell by only 112,000; and in the rest of the region in the same period, the number housed grew by 705,000 when it had been expected to grow by 750,000.

The errors in these two assumptions were offsetting, causing the real increase in demand for new houses to be proportionately much greater than the growth of population. And there was a further real departure from the *Plan*'s expectations, for five major areas for growth earmarked by the *Plan* collectively absorbed a notably smaller share than expected. So, despite slower real population growth the demand for new building land remained high and in dispute in the region beyond Greater London. And the tensions became severe within just a few years of the *Strategic Plan*'s publication, long before the end of the 1970s for which it supposed the South East's development to have been already determined. In that decade, the annual average rate of building in the region outside Greater London was some 42,500, not far short of what was implied in the *Strategic Plan*. And the *Plan*'s expectation of a demand for an additional 42,000 houses a year in the 1980s compared with an actual average annual building rate of some 48,000, with construction falling steeply after running at over 50,000 a year up to 1987.

So experience of UK regional planning shows that flexibility has to deeply underpin a regional plan. Confident assumptions about the future are impracticable except within a quite a wide range of reasonable uncertainty. To be a real attribute of planning policy, flexibility has to be a fundamental component, embedded in technical processes and its implications sustained throughout the plan's design and proposals. It is the most necessary attribute of robust regional planning.

Why Has Regional Planning Been Under-regarded?

Components of Underestimation

Regional planning had lost the prominence it had in urban and regional development in the UK from 1962 to the early 1970s even before it became scorned by the Government in the 1980s, when even former friends considered it to be in possibly terminal decline.

Why did regional planning come to be so under-regarded? Why could it be dismissed by some as a presumptuous vogue of the 1960s, or be more justifiably supposed by others to be no longer necessary when urban expansion was so much reduced in so much of the UK?

Being so many things to so many different ideologies and interests, regional planning probably suffered from several changing circumstances, which led to both its record and its future being underestimated. There were changes in politics and of political ideology, external to regional planning but profoundly affecting its opportunities. There were its relationships to political trends in the old nations of the UK; to the centralisation and nationalisation of local affairs under Conservative governments after 1979; to the decline of budgetary planning outside Whitehall; to the fragmentation of local government; to social and economic restructuring in the regions; and to the decline of regional economic policy in the UK.

Regional Nationalism

Regional planning's political implications have been most extreme where they have borne on the issue of devolution of government power. Whether through loss only of national coherence of economic policy, or by transfer of central resources and major functions of government to the control of regions, some modes of regional planning have seemed to threaten centralised government. Defence of national unity in the face of nationalist movements in Scotland and Wales has made Conservative governments particularly suspicious of regional planning, accentuating ideological mistrust of planned intervention in economic and free market affairs. The scorn in which regional planning was held by Conservative ministers in the 1980s was certainly tied in to their rejection of regional government, as well as to their general distaste for planning of any kind.

There is a long history to the association of regional planning with regional nationalism, for one of the reasons for the *Clyde Valley Regional Plan* being undertaken was the wish of the then Secretary of State for Scotland (Johnston 1952, 166) to preclude any rival initiative in Scotland by his colleague in the Cabinet responsible for town and country planning in England and Wales.

As regional governance of some kind has become a policy of both the Labour and the Liberal Democrat parties, and was an aim of both in their campaigns at the 1992 general election, the implicit association with regional planning continued to damn the latter in the mind of some ministers of the Conservative government.

Centralisation and the Nationalisation of Local Affairs

In their fourteen years of life, the regional economic planning boards were able to bring more responsibility to the decentralised level of the regional offices. But senior civil servants and ministers wishing to uphold their status in Whitehall are likely to limit the extent to which they will devolve decisions on policy. Coordination within regional offices implies give-and-take, and the amount of give which Whitehall departments tolerate is slight. Self (1975, 468–471) saw the regional coordination as being marginal and, just as the regional economic planning councils were being buried, the House of Commons Environment Committee (1980, para. 4) said of the boards that 'REPBs did not seem to provide the level of coordination between departments and areas of policy achieved by the Scottish and Welsh Offices for their respective countries.'

As for the regional economic planning councils, they were primarily intended to advise government on regional issues and to obtain a consensus amongst participating interests in support of government policy. But the councils had no executive power, they were not accepted by local authorities as equal partners, and when they occasionally became advocates against government policy they lost their value to ministers. Originally meant to be a support to the Department of Economic Affairs, helping its aggressive founder – George Brown – attack the dominance of the Treasury in expenditure policy and pursue strong regional policy, the councils' status was much reduced by the abolition of the DEA and their transfer to the patronage of the DOE.

The regional standing conferences of planning authorities have been meetings of equals, or at least ostensibly so. Although the county, metropolitan district and Scottish regional councils have statutory responsibility for structure plans and strategy for their areas, district councils can object and take their case to the government minister. However, in practice, not all are equal. Party politics give particular authorities more clout than others, and the geography of development and of resources gives some less influence on events and others more. Yet conferences have inevitably shown a general tendency to settle for the lowest common denominator of agreement.

So the abolition of regional economic planning councils together with the modest role played by most of the planning conferences left the regions without forceful voices. The regions were less vocal advocates of their own interests than they might have been. And the low profile of regional planning was accentuated by the move from the publication of recognisable and comprehensive plans as in the 1960s and 1970s, being replaced by the largely invisible negotiatory processes of the 1980s and 1990s. It has been too easy to under-regard what has been done in regional planning.

The Decline of Regional Budgetary Planning

The peak of activity in regional planning in the 1960s matched the peak of ambition for regional dimensions to national economic and budgetary planning. The 1970s added to the problems of adopting regional budgets because of the Public Expenditure Survey Committee system of rolling projections. The introduction in 1976 of the cash limiting system compartmentalised spending, limiting it not only within sectors but also in discretion to adjust between them. The basis for integrative regional planning was weakened.

Through the 1980s, centralised control of local government finance intensified. Late in the decade, local councils in England still raised 55 per cent of their funds, but by 1993 the proportion had dropped to as little as 15 per cent in England and to lower than 10 per cent in Wales. The shrinking of local control had come with the strengthening tendencies of a severely centralist government, whose measures included an end to locally determined tax rates for local services to businesses. Local budgetary discretion had been radically reduced.

With more central control of local budgets and with a higher share being directly disbursed by the government, it had become more possible for any government which chose to establish a system of regional budgeting. But the potential for this was certainly not being exploited under Conservative governments from 1979 onwards, except so far as to increasingly channel local and regional financing through agencies responsible to the Government. It was estimated (Ferguson and Wylie 1993) that as much as 39 per cent of the budget of the Scottish Office was allocated to agencies of government, ranging from health boards, Scottish Homes, the local enterprise companies and the Scottish Tourist Board to higher education. This was indeed regional budgeting, but its shape was imposed upon Scotland and was not arranged by any elected regional forum.

So the possible links between regional development planning and budgetary planning being explored in the decade up to the mid 1970s were subsequently neglected. Only in North West England in 1993 did any regional conference of local authorities at last resume the exploration. But after years of government disinclination to adopt regional budgeting, its neglect had to be blamed equally upon lack of initiative from local governments in the regions.

Fragmentation of Metropolitan and Regional Governance

In the 1980s, the Government justified the abolition of the metropolitan counties and the GLC on the criticisms that strategic planning was an outmoded fashion, and that an upper tier of local government was a costly duplication. In the 1990s, cost, duplication and remoteness were again the Government's grounds upon which moves to eliminate a tier of Scottish local government began.

Were the failings of the upper tier so great that local government could be fragmented without serious loss? Was the case for strategic and regional planning made for decades before the 1974/75 reorganisation so failed by actual performance?

Recognising the upper tier's difficulties, Flynn *et al.* (1985, 78) suggest that in several respects the metropolitan counties significantly improved on previous arrangements. At least, having public transport, highway and land-use planning under one authority let the metropolitan councils determine transport priorities over whole metropolitan areas with a decisiveness rarely achieved prior to 1974.

But in the larger field of planning, the conditions for decisive and effective strategy were undoubtedly weak. The experience of the GLC had shown this before the metropolitan councils were created. The GLC had struggled with the London boroughs over its *Development Plan* and local development with strategic implications. The GLC had more responsibility than power, as was very evident (Rhodes 1972, 337, Marshall 1978, 15), and the metropolitan counties were given no more authority.

In practice, a mutual tolerance frequently grew between the metropolitan counties and their districts, deriving from collegiality between professional planning officers. The metropolitan counties were sometimes more in accord with their metropolitan districts over strategy than with neighbouring shire counties, as was true of the West Midlands. And whether strategically significant development applications were to be decided by the metropolitan or the district councils was usually the choice of the respective professional planning officers. The officers would commonly make tactical choices according to shared professional ethos and the strategic consistency of their respective politicians (Flynn *et al.* 1985, 79). Of course, those who damned the two tiers for sometimes arguing might also damn mutual tolerance as being merely comfortable duplication.

Just as the GLC struggled with its boroughs to define its strategic interests where legislation was imprecise, so were there struggles between the metropolitan counties and districts. Some focused on development applications, and in Scotland this was characteristic also in the early relationship between Strathclyde Regional Council and Glasgow District Council. The investment which several metropolitan councils put into environmental regeneration led to disputes over their right to prepare local plans for the purpose, as notably in Greater Manchester. And where executive responsibility was clearly with the districts, as in housing, the metropolitan council could yet properly argue that this was the largest land use in its area and inevitably an issue of vital strategic concern.

Clearly, the experience of the two metropolitan and regional tiers can be more justifiably criticised for ineffectiveness than for duplication. Planning issues in the metropolitan and regional areas do run at more than one level, and to dismiss strategic planning because it has involved disputes is to be ignorant of economic and social dynamics. Some duplication is necessary for a clear view of issues, provided that they occur at scales of governance approximating to those into which the issues divide.

The inherent administrative inefficiencies of the UK's local government reorganisations of 1974 and 1975 made it certain that regional planning would also be inefficient. And the reorganisations being planned for the later 1990s were no remedy for the difficulties. In these circumstances, it was unsurprising that regional planning languished and that confidence in its potential should have run low.

Restructuring of Social and Economic Regions

Realisation in the early 1970s that the decline in national birth rates had undermined earlier projections of population growth also undermined confidence in regional planning. Projections were progressively reduced, and the consequent turmoil in planning in the West Midlands has been described. Other regions felt the impact, which was first worked out in new policies in the *West Central Scotland Plan* (1974). Later, of course, the rapid formation of new households in a declining population brought back problems of growth in South East England which were as contentious as ever. In most regions, however, the dominant issue of distributing new growth gave way to a twin focus on renewal and a more modest scale of metropolitan dispersal.

The rising emphasis on urban regeneration and relative decline in most of the UK in the urgency of metropolitan expansion lowered impressions of the merits of regional planning. This was understandable in the narrower view of its scope, as when new towns and population overspill were its dominating preoccupations. And when governments frowned on and tried to quell the economic content which came into regional planning in the mid 1970s, its remaining physical content was seen as having less urgency than before.

Decline of Regional Economic Policy

The disfavour into which economic policy outputs from regional plans fell from the mid 1970s went in hand with decline in the significance of inter-regional economic policy in the UK. The decline accelerated through the 1970s, and continued through the 1980s.

Many politicians from all parties must find it impossible to distinguish between regional economic planning for policies for inter-regional financial and policy aid, and regional planning for intra-regional action. Both kinds would be seen as regional planning, and collectively favoured or disfavoured by political inclination. So as the significance of UK regional economic planning declined, many must have been led to disregard the continuing opportunities for self-help intra-regional economic planning, of the kind spreading widely in Europe in the 1980s.

A Failure or a Flawed Success?

There has been too wide a variety of experience of regional planning in the UK to make a single, sweeping judgement on it. And too few judgements on it have shown any depth and width of knowledge. Most commentators tend to see it sympathetically but with regrets about its erratic impacts. The Nuffield Inquiry (1986, 72) into Town and Country Planning in the UK noted much criticism of governments for failing to provide a regional structure for planning, or to use one to implement national policy for matters such as population distribution, boundary problems, airports or power stations. But the system of regional planning guidelines subsequently introduced by the Department of the Environment has also been much criticised. So although only by the recurrent stimulus of successive governments has there been any significant history of regional planning in the UK, governments have also failed to consolidate their role to ensure an enduring framework for effective regional planning.

The lack of a sure governance context for regional planning has been only one of many uncertainties surrounding it, which even such an important plan as the *Strategy for the South East* of 1970 failed to sufficiently build in to itself. The problem was characterised by Ravetz (1980, 114):

> regional plans... were in themselves powerless to compel such [economic] growth to come to their region. Their forecasting had in fact something of the same realism that we find in weather forecasting in the uncertain conditions of the British climate. That is to say, their arguments were sound and sensible, given existing information.

Because it is customarily infrequent, broad in scope, speculative and looking to a distant time horizon, the uncertainties surrounding regional strategic planning means that it involves acute issues as to what strength of policies to adopt, by what means they can be translated into action, and how strategic control can be exercised in the long-term. These are issues at any scale of planning, but particularly so at regional scale. They reflect Gillingwater and Hart's (1978) distinctions between the three components of fully effective regional planning: policy, communication and control. It is useful to keep these functions in mind in considering what may have been successful, and in what regard. The nature, permanency, origin and variety of initiatives in regional planning have certainly shown differing degrees of strength in policy and in communicating and controlling it.

While plans with strong policies like those for Greater London and the Clyde Valley have become widely regarded as significant regional influences, their communicative role being followed by significant and extensive action over extended periods, regional plans have been too often weakly translated into consistent strategy. Means of control have been inadequate. In the hundred years of regional initiatives in the UK since the late nineteenth century, there has been widespread failure to maintain impetus by continuous reviewing of strategic issues and policy – a minimum requirement for effective control. And administrative reorganisations which have arisen have commonly failed to observe principles of effective control of implementation.

But have the failures been due to intrinsic faults of policy in such regional plans as have emerged, or have they been disappointed by subsequent failure to act and to control them effectively? In retrospect, we can see that some of the least successful regional planning was sometimes allied to shortcomings in the technical method of preparing plans, although more usually to a lack of means to effectively translate plans into action. The political and administrative controls of regional planning have customarily been missing, or flawed at best. Notably, the 1974 reorganisation of local government in England and Wales failed to observe the principles of effective strategic governance; more so the 1986 abolition of the GLC and the Metropolitan Counties and the prospective abolition of the county and regional councils in the later 1990s.

Discontinuous regional planning has undoubtedly exacerbated some contemporary problems in the UK, notably that of inner city decline, whether this is seen as a socio-economic problem or as one of land and property. Furthermore, the role of local government in strategic and regional planning has been progressively diminished as central government has more extensively involved itself in local affairs with strategic implications. And these interventions have often been disjointed and not obviously coordinated; major policy differences between the Environment and Industry Departments in England have persisted for much of the post-war period, and have been highly significant for regional planning. It was predictable that the circumstances of the 1990s would make the case for effective regional strategic planning more widely recognised. But neglect and not lack of experience wasted the opportunity to arrange effective means of regional planning.

Regional planning has persisted because regional planning issues endure, and because however the process of planning may be improved it can never be arranged to perfectly anticipate and cover all issues. The flaws in regional planning have been most frequently failures in governance, and in the weak political backing which plans have received.

Nonetheless, it is inherent in the circumstances of regional planning that many regional plans have not been implemented, and that others have been missing when required. Regions and regional issues tend to be impermanent. Once regional issues are responded to by a new structure of governance or administration, new regional issues inevitably arise across the boundaries of the new region.

There have also been damaging technical flaws in the way in which some regional planning has been undertaken. Policies have been insufficiently robust on occasions, when unsound projections of population change or false assumptions of economic growth have destroyed the realism of some regional planning. This is not a unique feature in regional planning. It has been equally true of statutory structure and of local planning. It has been true of the management of some new towns. It has been true of the Treasury's financial planning and of Budget statements of innumerable Chancellors of the Exchequer. It has been true of planning in industry and for the failed development projects of many in the field of private commerce. Its appearance in regional planning is no reason to condemn the art and science of this.

Seeing the experience of regional planning and governance in this light, it can be suggested that the record of regional planning has been as reasonably good as conditions have allowed it to be. On occasions, it has been profoundly influential, not just in several of the major conurbation regions of the United Kingdom, particularly Greater London and Clydeside, but it also has been appreciably effective in rural regions through government agencies such as the Highlands and Islands Development Board and the Countryside Commission.

It is also clear that some of the best and most effective regional plans were conceived outside a regularised regional governance, through relatively casual arrangements. They were prepared sometimes by ad hoc and temporary planning teams, or by consultants, or sometimes in conjunction with cumbersome steering committees of disparate and occasionally unwilling partners. Despite these potential disadvantages, the quality and vision of this stream of regional planning has been satisfactorily high.

This leads to another suggestion. Perhaps the limits to which regional governance is pursued should be set primarily by considerations other than those of regional planning. Indeed, should the pursuit be attempted at all? A perfect region for all purposes can never be achieved, and there have been circumstances in which imaginative and sometimes highly effective regional planning has been successfully superimposed upon established and fragmented administrative arrangements.

Conclusion: Confusion Over More Than a Fashion

Two deep questions arise from the experience of the UK. Perhaps its staunchest advocates expect too much of regional planning, and perhaps its critics unreasonably expect to judge it against too tight a model of an interlocking system of policy, communication and control.

It may be the real nature of much regional planning to be a form of crisis management. Regional issues may be often too volatile to be stabilised or fully controlled by initiatives in planning and governance. As an enduring but inconstant feature of public affairs, regional planning has been well able at its best to ease blockages of policy and to quell mutual problems of the kind irregularly arising between different levels and areas of mainstream governance.

And regional governance in many varieties has inevitably followed upon sustained problems of regional planning. Its potential has been commonly bounded by the inevitable circumstances and compromises of politics. And in the experiential definition of regional planning, its dimensions will always spill over the boundaries of any established system of regional governance.

On this understanding, regional planning in the United Kingdom can be seen as having too frequently proved its worth to be dismissed as a mere fashion. Confusion over its nature has caused much misjudgement of its performance.

CHAPTER FIVE

Regional Planning and Governance in the UK in the 1990s

Preface: The Return From Neglect

In the 1980s, regional planning and governance in Britain were commonly regarded as lost causes. But behind government rhetoric dismissing regional ideas, political pressures encouraged a revival of the regional dimension in strategic physical planning and in varied aspects of government administration. Despite continuing antipathy to elected regional local government or assemblies, the Government was forced to accept that regional issues and problems of top-heavy centralised government demand regional dimensions in physical, social and some economic planning. So although the progressive absorption of the dimensions into government affairs has been random, ill-considered and ill-coordinated, the potential base for regional governance is being widened in the 1990s.

The Alleged Demise and Unexpected Resurrection of Regional Planning and Administration

Premature Intimations of Mortality

In its 1983 White Paper *Streamlining the Cities* (Secretary of State for the Environment 1983), the Government damned regional planning as a fashion from the 1960s, but it was neither made clear what that fashion comprised nor what were its failings. Being motivated almost wholly by party politics and aimed at disposing of the GLC and the English metropolitan counties, the White Paper found it unnecessary to describe the regional planning in mind, or to analyse its real record.

So, when in the 1980s the imminent demise of regional planning was widely assumed, the new forms into which it was being shaped were overlooked. Too much was read into the dismissive comments of government ministers, and too little was observed of actual practice and events. For the potential for strategic and regional planning was being reinforced, often unwittingly and generally incoherently. When their Secretary of State for the Environment privately met backbench Conservative Members of Parliament in the late 1980s, he told them that unless their counties and districts prepared realistic development plans, the minister would be unable to systematically dismiss appeals against refusals of planning permission for housebuilding. And realistic local planning required realistic regional planning, particularly in the contentious South East of England, where Hampshire County Council was notably reluctant to grow as much as expected by the Government and the majority of partners in the London and South East Regional Planning Conference (SERPLAN).

Abolition of the Greater London and English metropolitan counties caused so much political noise as to obscure some positive developments in regional and strategic governance in the 1980s, many of which introduced a regional dimension to government administration. They were still being added to in 1994, when much strengthened coordination of the Government's departmental offices was introduced in the English regions. And although the Government was intent on abolishing Scotland's largest regional councils in 1996, this was not as full a retreat from regional planning as critics supposed. Only the Strathclyde and Highland regions were of a scale and construction comparable to those commonly recognised in England, and Strathclyde had become a less appropriate regional area than when designed almost 30 years before.

The motivations to reinforcing forms of English regional administration since the mid 1980s have been many and different, and some developments were as politically expedient as was the abolition of the GLC. Yet, without there being any coherent or real government enthusiasm for regional administration and planning, many developments added up to an appreciable flow of regional initiatives. This was shown in health administration, it was being threatened for the police, it seemed inevitable for schools, it was being introduced in urban regeneration, and it was even being anticipated in the allocation of EC funds.

But emerging regional initiatives seemed not part of any strategy for comprehensive regional governance. They were separated, of different origin and inconsistent (Breheny 1991). And most were above the head of local government, as with the privatisation of the public water industry in 1989. Privatisation had some small merit for strategic planning in that the ten new water companies in England and Wales lost some of the privileges which the RWAs had sometimes employed to place themselves above the scope of structure and strategic planning. But the water companies' monopoly, and their special relationship with the government which had created them, left them still privileged in the matter of strategic planning. Similarly, the former nationalised electricity and gas boards were unable to accept that they should now be liable, like any other private company, to full control under local authority planning. Indeed, as public corporations previously they had been beyond direct influence by the government ministers responsible for planning.

But there was strategic potential in the creation of a National Rivers Authority, responsible for environmental and river water standards. Previously, the RWAs had acted as judge and jury in their own cases. In 1991, the Authority's corporate plan introduced catchment management plans, which would examine the links between hydrology and land use over parts of England with a collective population of six million. Although initially tentative, the plans had the capacity to better inform structure and local development planning – and certainly to conflict with it on occasions.

A potential effect of the continued sale of public utilities to private companies in the early 1990s was to bring new power stations, reservoirs, oil and gas developments more than before within the influence of public planning authorities. But the areas of the new companies were ill-fitted to each other and to the pattern of local authorities. Their boundaries gave no help to the new companies or to local or central goverment for preparing better and more efficient strategies for essential services. And privatisation was also a potential rod for the Government's back because it could potentially release criticisms in regard to failings in strategic planning; whereas chairmen of public corporations did not openly criticise the politicians who appointed them, private companies could criticise more freely. The Chief Executive (Morton 1993) of the Eurotunnel company was scornful in the extreme towards the 'tragi-comedy' of the government's inept planning for a high-speed rail link from the Channel to London.

Regional Planning Risen From the Bier, and the Spread of Regional Administration

So the context for strategic planning was notably altering in the 1990s. It was changing in both the socio-economic and political realms. The strategic planning problems of the 1960s underlying the 1970s reorganisation of local government had been primarily urban congestion and overspill. But these problems had been transformed: local economic development had become central to urban strategy; urban regeneration had replaced clearance and urban renewal; government agencies had become integral to both strategic planning and strategic development, as notably through the Scottish and Welsh Development Agencies, the urban development corporations, Scottish Homes and the English Regional Development Associations; central–local relations including financing had changed; and the EC had come to expect that regions would have a political as well as a planning status.

The regional consolidation spread into important areas of government administration. In the early 1990s, reform of the National Health Service was expected to lead to the dissolution of the fourteen regional health authorities on the creation of local health authorities; but in 1993, the Health Secretary announced that eight regional offices of the Health Service management executive would replace the former regional authorities. This maintained a central influence in the regions against the wishes of many managers of the newly formed local hospital trusts, but the Secretary argued that a 'strategic overview' was needed. The 10 English regional arts boards set up in 1991 were assigned further responsibilities, added to those already devolved from the English Arts Council. And unified administration of UK universities was divided when a Scottish Higher Education Funding

Council was established, following the transfer to direct government control of those higher education institutions managed up to the end of the 1980s by local government.

The regional coordination of urban regeneration policy in England from April 1994 had real potential, being led by new directors in 10 regional offices overseeing work previously managed exclusively by the four Departments of Employment, the Environment, Trade and Industry, and Transport. A Single Regeneration Budget was created combining 20 previously separate budgets from within the four departments. Closely associated with the new directors would be the equally new English Partnerships agency, nationally led but drawing funding from the Single Regeneration Budget, which would also finance urban development corporations, housing action trusts and locally sponsored regeneration projects.

The new regional system was far from a considered initiative to redress years of disjointed regional planning and budgeting in England. It had two significant advantages for government. It disguised a large overall cut in funding for the 20 categories of spending unified in the Single Regeneration Budget. And it also disguised the fact that the European Commission had called for a single programme document from each region competitively bidding for EC Funds. Britain in particular had to better order its approach to the Community's regional imperative.

Nonetheless, each regional director was now to prepare an Annual Regeneration Statement setting priorities for regeneration and economic development. Enthusiastic directors with political skill had the opportunity to arrange some real regional planning.

The new regional arrangements for England only faintly echoed the character of the Scottish, Welsh and Northern Ireland Offices. The regions lacked the support of their own Secretary of State in Cabinet. The Government undoubtedly expected the new emphasis on competitive funding to help it divide and rule amongst local authorities in the English regions, but it also gave skilful local politicians an unprecedented opportunity to influence regional priorities and investment programmes.

The Government's campaign to have schools opt out of local council management also portended more regional administration, to shed the centralised weight of direct funding assumed by the Department for Education. But as opting-out slowed in England in 1993 and failed to excite Scotland, comprehensive regional administration for schools seemed likely to be delayed until the dissolution of county and regional councils. But long regional experience made the Scottish Office keen not to be outshone by English initiative, so plans were laid to merge the pollution control duties of the river purification boards and of local authorities in a Scottish Environmental Protection Agency, echoing the centralisation and allied regional administration of local functions so vigorous in England.

Also in 1993, the Home Secretary sought to break the long-standing alliance between policing and local authorities, aiming to take the police wholly into national government hands and more than halve the 43 existing forces in England. Although rebuffed by strong resistance, it was inevitable that the Government would return to attempt to regionalise the police forces when it dissolved counties of England and the regions of Scotland later in the 1990s.

So regional administration in Britain was being reinforced, but this was a modest step towards significant regional governance. And while regional planning of a rather low-key kind was being tacitly reinstated from the mid 1980s, it was generally less ambitious than even the tentative kind of regional economic planning first featuring in the 1960s, and refined in the *West Central Scotland Plan* (1974) and in the *Strategies* for the North West (1974) and the Northern (1977) regions of England. What was re-emerging was mostly planning from the mould of the 1960s, its physical emphasis only lightly touched by economic planning. But if the UK government baulked at economic issues, the European Commission was quite prepared to encourage 20 year regional strategies with economic dimensions, as prepared by consultants for the Regional Association of local authorities of North West England in 1992.

There were two important aspects to the growing emphasis on regional action; it was a scaling-up in the level of planning and action in many social and economic dimensions of public interest, and it represented a significant switch of control of both planning and action from elected local councils into the hands of government offices and agencies. So it was a loss for local democracy and a growth in central authority. Because nothing was devolved from central government, it was a rise in regional administration without any popular participation. It was regional governance in its narrowest form.

The scale of the centralising shift in Wales had reached the level at which 34 per cent of the Welsh Office's budget for 1993/94 was estimated to be channelled through quangos (University of Wales 1993). A comparable estimate for the same year was that 39 per cent of the Scottish Office's budget was spent by quangos, by government appointees double in quantity to the number of elected local councillors (*Scotland on Sunday* 1993).

As the regional imperative reasserted itself, the 1990s were building upon trends arising in the 1980s. It was clear that:

1. Strategic intervention had advanced on several fronts in the 1980s, customarily represented by local action by government and its proliferating agencies in what, prior to the mid 1970s, were normally local authority responsibilities.

2. Government was providing only a fragmentary strategic framework for the extended regional planning, which was failing to satisfy many of its intended customers.

3. The transfer of electricity, gas, water and services to the private sector had, in respects, potentially increased opportunity for regional planning to influence and support development. But the prospective break-up and part-privatisation of rail services promised to damage metropolitan and regional planning. However, even in the public sector these services did involve substantial problems of coordination.

4. Government's rising dominance in strategic planning was denying an important part of the basis for the local government reorganisation of Britain in the mid 1970s. But the new reorganisation begun in 1986 and being further pursued in the 1990s seemed likely to greatly weaken the potential for local government in regional planning, with no sign that the Government could convincingly fill the strategic void.

5. Leading regions in Europe had been taking strategic initiatives in planning and development which most British regions were unable to match, and which local government reorganisation was going to put further out of reach as the 1990s progressed.

6. Yet, despite some braver cases, local government has commonly been too self-centred, unambitious or painfully slow to either initiate strategic planning or to collectively execute it. Even Scottish regional councils have been too often satisfied to depend on government to institute major physical and economic initiatives of strategic significance.

7. The advancing scope of government's spatial influence on physical and economic development in the United Kingdom was reinforcing major policy inconsistencies. The long-standing differences between the Departments of Trade and Industry and of the Environment were paralleled by newer differences between Agriculture and Environment. And, over all, Treasury pressure on all Departments had produced anomalies in several fields.

8. While the Scottish system of local government did develop some capacity for regional planning, the English system contained serious inherent defects. Accordingly, the abolition of the metropolitan counties actually did less strategic damage than their defenders suggested; because the counties had an inadequately substantial base for strategic planning at regional level, the strategic vacuum was simply enlarged.

9. The experience of strategic planning had shown that the need for it was characteristically accepted too late. Where its performance disappointed, the fault lay commonly in weaknesses in the structure for planning and implementation, frequently wholly foreseen in advance.

Although flawed and with perhaps unrepeatable opportunities being wasted, the flow of regionally significant initiatives helped avert the supposedly imminent death of regional planning and governance. By the early 1990s, although its quality was criticised by local authorities, regional planning guidance had been adopted as a government duty, and the authorities themselves had formed regional planning conferences throughout England, as had never been the case before. The enduring London and South East Regional Planning Conference perhaps claimed too much credit for itself in suggesting that 'the Government has been sufficiently impressed with the utility of the system to extend it to the rest of England and Wales' (SERPLAN 1992, 20), but SERPLAN must certainly have been seen as more success than failure to encourage replicas in every region.

The universal spawning of regional planning conferences in England was perhaps also a reaction to government shortcomings in regional planning, characterised by such cases as the North East, where the regional guidelines of 1993 had a hole at their heart where the metropolitan county council of Tyne and Wear had been; separate guidelines of 1989 for the former metropolitan county left questions not only over their consistency with the regional guidelines, but over the Government's case for abolishing the metropolitan county.

But as regional planning conferences at last became universal in England in 1992, the ground was shifting beneath them; questions were arising about possible changes to the pattern of Standard Regions which governments had employed for many years. A Royal Town Planning Institute (1986) working party had pointed to the new regions emerging from the dynamics of economic and social geography. The Chairman of SERPLAN convened a meeting with all adjoining regions in 1992, to discuss the spillover of interests from South East England; the South East was still spreading its regional connections. The overlap between regional interests became even more obvious in July 1992, when government announced that it supported the need for a national strategy for the coast, meeting parliamentary criticism of the lack of coastal zone planning. No British region could be self-contained in the 1990s. Yet, while certainly short of perfection, a more comprehensive basis for regional planning than previously existed had been born in England. Whether the will and the techniques were also at hand for a healthy and effective growth of regional planning was less certain.

Against these developments in cooperative planning, the abolition of the GLC and metropolitan county councils could be seen as done primarily from political malice, even if there were some good supporting and apolitical reasons. But it was seriously mistaken to abolish the councils without any coherent means to replace and improve their contribution to strategic planning, as the Government came to tacitly recognise by its later initiatives.

So in the early 1990s, the Government's declaration of 1983 that regional planning was a fashion of the 1960s was itself becoming a quaint historical attitude. The Government effectively confirmed the poverty of some of its own arguments for abolishing the GLC's strategic planning role when, in July 1992, a junior minister was appointed to chair a working group to coordinate public transport in Greater London. And a senior government minister was said to have privately admitted that regional planning was again acceptable in the 1990s – but on condition that it was described as neither 'regional' nor as 'planning'.

But there was a limit to the Government's acceptance of the regional dimension. It was not to incorporate locally accountable politicians. In 1992, a then junior minister, John Redwood, publicly denied any future for regional government in Britain. The minister's argument was suported by arbitrary estimates of cost reminiscent of those raised to damn the idea of a Scottish Assembly. But the Government's purpose had perhaps more to do with maximising its political control of UK affairs than to do with reducing costs.

The Conservative government of the 1990s remained as adamant as its predecessors of the 1980s that there was to be no real devolution of power from Whitehall, particularly to Scotland. Centralisation, not devolution or greater local responsibility, would proceed. Retaining parliamentary power despite barely exceeding 40 per cent of the national vote at general elections, the Government faced a country in which Conservative councillors dominated in only a diminishing minority of local governments. So when ministers argued that major road and rail routes in Britain should be planned at national level, and that regional governments might not be able to ensure a coherent answer, they were being disingenuous at best and autocratic at worst.

The Context for the 1990s

Changing Regional Economic Problems

The state of the world economy considerably controls the potential for economic growth and for employment change in the United Kingdom. The speed of economic change within many UK regions accelerated during the 1980s and 1990s, particularly under the impact of two deep economic recessions. And the tendencies of enterprises to organise themselves internationally has made them even less responsive to local or national policies. International companies have been able to trade production locations between European governments, who have often seemed as much supplicants for investment aid as any third world nation.

What is clear is that the uncertainties over regional change and futures are deep, and perhaps intensifying. But the more the uncertainties and the power of macro-forces, the more the case for a strategic capacity for regional responses. And the more need that the kinds of local economic initiative most commonly taken within urban areas since the 1970s should be spread more widely outside. Coordination of initiatives within labour market areas reaching into semi-rural and rural hinterlands beyond the cities and inner conurbations has seemed increasingly sensible. So it was arranged in the most coherently designed of the local enterprise companies in Scotland and of the training and enterprise companies in England. The nature of weaknesses in urban and regional economies varies and, as local and national policy initiatives proliferate, participants and sponsors need rationalised policies and streamlined regional networks.

However, the government's view was that regional planning was to be responsive and not creative in economic matters. The relationship was defined in para. 6.30 of the White Paper on *This Common Inheritance* (Secretaries of State 1990):

> The government's regional planning guidance sets broad strategic policies for land use and development... Such policies are not the prescriptive economic planning of the type attempted in the past, but flexible guidance on ways of responding to economic forces to help local authorities plan for their areas.

But however unwelcoming of regional economic analyses and policy initiatives the government might be, these were again developing in the early 1990s. The regional association of local authorities in North West England commissioned an outline programme of regional priorities, and the EC Committee of the Regions starting work in 1994 seemed likely to offer an alternative outlet for regional economic strategies, outflanking central government. So the prospects for regional economic strategies were brightening. And in looking to channel a proportion of EC funding through a 'Regional Challenge' competition, the UK government was – amongst other motivations – seeking to have strategies flow through its hands rather than to run direct to the European Parliament, to EC Commissioners or to the Committee of the Regions.

So there has been a trend for regional economic policy to separate into a stream of national policy measures including aid to the defined areas of assistance, and a complementary stream of regionally based initiatives aimed at financial, physical and training problems in regional economies. This anticipated more 'self-help' approaches to regional development, incorporating a closer relationship between urban and economic planning than customary in the UK since the 1970s.

There were forerunners of the trend, as when after the regional economic planning councils were abolished in 1979 the West Midlands Regional Economic Consortium was formed in 1983, associating the Forum of County Councils in the region with the CBI, the TUC and Chambers of Commerce. North West England followed suit with its Business Leadership team in 1989. In Scotland, the Glasgow Action project to foster the potential of the city centre launched in 1985 had some characteristics of the American model for collective urban economic development, as had the whole reorganisation of the SDA into a pattern of local enterprise agencies in 1991. But the trend comprised often random events.

There were few outward signs that the government recognised that there were potential gains from self-help planning in the regions, from directly relating national public expenditure to strategies for regional and local development, from frameworks to provide industrial investment funds using new sources of finance and controlled within each region, from better integrating regional economic policy and regional planning within national government, from fuller linkages between regional policy and other policies of local government, and from minimising confusion of interests amongst agents in regional development such as the regional health, energy and water bodies.

A school of political ideology with some more knowledgeable academic support (Evans 1988) has asserted that the economy is hampered and partly impoverished by the planning system. But some sympathetic to some of this line of argument also argue that the lack of a viable regional administrative tier compounds national problems (Cheshire, D'Arcy and Giussani 1991). They suggest that there is a void between local and national government at the level of coherent regional socio-economic systems, whereby most of Britain suffers a competitive disadvantage with other European countries which are regionally organised. The reasoning is not convincing in all respects, but it puts a rare economic case for regional planning and governance.

The regional case is also supported by many in the development industry. When the government had been unenthusiastic about regional planning in other respects, the Department of the Environment had led a National Coordinating Group which sustained regional working parties on the supply of construction aggregates; the government accepted that assured supplies of sand, gravel and rock for construction of many kinds required regional planning. But industry has called for wider regional planning yet. The House Builders Federation calls for regional guidance and clearer national guidelines to allow soundly based investment (Royal Town Planning Institute 1991, 5). Bodies like the Institution of Civil Engineers, the British Road Federation and the CBI repeatedly make the case for increased investment in the physical infrastructure. Regional planning is a context and sometimes the means of confirming the scale of need for construction and investment for programmes in all these interests. The gas, electricity and telecommunications industries have been less accustomed to raise problems which regional planning may help, although their production and processing installations cause serious strategic issues.

Major and long evident problems with infrastructure lie in the railways, London's underground transport, and the antiquity of the largely subterranean water supply and drainage systems, with which is associated a still increasing concern to improve the quality of water effluents into rivers and seas. Maintenance and renewal works could eat up very large resources; the great difficulty remains in predicting just how much longer the assets will last. Sustained failure to sufficiently invest since the 1970s has reduced the quality of infrastructure, down to levels requiring accelerated action to meet the environmental and service standards expected in the 1990s. A regional perspective is an essential part of economical and productive reinvestment.

Regional Social and Metropolitan Structure

Metropolitan regions have extensively restructured since the end of the Second World War, with dispersal of many activities reducing the central city focus for

REGIONAL AND METROPOLITAN STRATEGIC ISSUES 1980's	Implications of lack of Strategic Guidance or Intervention	Opportunities for Strategic Management and Policy	Current means of Public Strategic Management
LAND RESOURCES • Availability for development	• Overbidding by local authorities and private sector (on behalf of both public and private sectors) for land e.g. industry in W. Yorks., housing in Strathclyde • Conflict of narrow private with wider public interest e.g. Greater London green belt	• Resolution of competition for alternative uses of land e.g. planning control • Development planning	National Planning Guidlines (Scotland) Regional Planning Conferences and Fora. Structure Plans and Local Plans Local authority initiatives e.g. Woodham Ferrers, Essex Department of Environment, Scottish Office, etc. i.e. Public Enquiries
QUALITY OF ENVIRONMENT • Legacy of public and private conservation of heritage of land and buildings • Quality of air and water • Disposal of wastes • Housing	• Derelict land and buildings e.g. London Docklands • Despoliation of areas of outstanding beauty • Ill-health • Fouling of industrial supply • Toxic poisoning of domestic water supply • Urban decline and blight	• Support for agriculture and forestry (e.g. Halvergate Marshes) • Environmental impact appraisal • Financial support for conservation and environmental control • Financial support to relocate environmentally damaging activities • Housing investment policy	Countryside Commissions, Norfolk Broads Management Committee National Parks Historic Buildings Commissions EEC Environmental Policy Regional Water Authorities HIP's and Housing Plans County, Regional and District Councils
INEQUITIES OF SPACE • Differential access to public facilities • Differential access to opportunities to improve wealth and income • Blighting effects of public and action • Differential distribution of personal income • Differential distribution of opportunities for local tax revenue	• Excessive costs imposed on selective groups; unequal access to education • Uneven distribution of costs of travel and costs of change • Unequal distribution amongst local authorities of costs of services • Unequal capacity of local authorities to undertake renewal	• Transport policy • Regional economic policy • Local development policy • Relocation of urban and rural facilities • Sports facilities • Administrative reorganisation • Distribution of local services	New Towns Urban Development Corporations Regional Development Grants Sports Councils Passenger Transport Executives Inner London Education Authority
STIMULI TO ECONOMIC IMPROVEMENT • Fostering economic opportunity • Conserving resources	• Underuse and lack of land and infrastructure • Insufficient support for entrepreneurship and innovation • Neglect of incipient problems e.g. 'inner city' and land shortage problems	• Major infrastructure • Sectoral economic policy • Local economic initiatives • Labour market policy (I.T. training policy)	Scottish Development Agency Welsh Development Agency Central Electricity Generating Board Regional Electricity and Gas Boards National Coal Board British Rail
INFORMATION • Economic environment • Social environment			

Figure 5.1. Regional and metropolitan strategic issues in the United Kingdom in the 1980s: their range, their management and the implications of neglect

homes and for manufacturing, but reinforcing the focus for many financial, business and administrative functions. The outcome has been of extended urban systems in which economic and social relationships have strengthened across urban and metropolitan boundaries, encompassing new towns and significant rural hinterlands. These social and economic trends have created new perceptions of environmental issues, frequently at strategic scale.

The spreading nature of metropolitan regions has been reflected in the way in which governments have progressively redefined the region centred on London. In the Second World War, a London region of some 7 million people was assigned its own Regional Commissioner. At the War's end, this London region was combined with four counties to its south east into a London and South Eastern region of 11 million people; separate Southern and Eastern regions incorporated the counties in the other two of three sectors surrounding London. In 1974, all were combined into a single South-East region incorporating thirteen counties and over 17 million people. The progressive consumption by the London region of others around it led directly to a new East Anglia region being defined. But there were adjustments throughout England. Only the West Midlands region remained constant from the end of the Second World War.

The shift of new manufacturing and some service activity to rural and peri-urban areas in recent years has seen new kinds of growth region emerging, less strongly centred on the conurbations than was the case up to the 1980s. In certain of these new regions, like the M4 corridor or the area of landfall of the Channel Tunnel, infrastructure planning and resource priorities have raised issues beyond the capacity of individual authorities to satisfy by piecemeal action. Some of these regions may require intensive regional planning and regional action for only a relatively short period of history; others may be nearly permanent features of British geography.

In remoter rural areas, economic developments have led to authorities for regional action. For conservation of resources of landscape, wildlife, woodland and vegetation, there have been established the Countryside Commission, the national park planning boards and the Nature Conservancy; and for economic redevelopment there was created the Highlands and Islands Development Board and the Development Commission. Contemporary trends in agricultural economics suggest that need for regional action may increase as farming retreats.

In looking to future regional change, the defunct regional economic planning councils and metropolitan county councils showed that – whatever their limits of effectiveness – they could identify and foresee problems which government could not. The West Midlands County Council's *Time for Action* appraisal of 1974, and the South West Economic Planning Council's (1967) crystallisation of priorities for rural development, both took a strategic view of regional priorities and prospects of the kind which government was reluctant or incapable of doing. In the 1980s, industry, commerce and the public sector cooperated in the *Futures Study* for the West Midlands, anticipating the future environment for investment. And in the 1990s, business, industry and structure planning authorities combined in North West England to prepare a 20 year vision of the region's future. Speculative as they were, approaches like this were of a kind upon which rival regions in Europe were accustomed to build seriously.

The Changing Context of the European Community

Regulation (EEC) No. 1787/84 on the European Regional Development Fund required member states to submit a report on the implementation of regional development programmes every two and a half years. Coupled to this stipulation was the intent to further increase the proportion of funding to be applied to programmes rather than to projects.

But in 1984, both regionalism and regional programmes were out of favour with the United Kingdom government, which was then intent on abolishing the GLC and the English metropolitan county councils, with the assertion that regional planning was an outdated fashion. Regional policy which had been in decline for over a decade was being further reduced. From the start of its membership of the EC, the quality of most regional programmes submitted by the UK to the EC had been of weak quality; they were scrambled from the hands of civil servants without any depth of reflection. Only when Integrated Operation programmes came to be compiled did the EC receive UK programmes of evidently considered scope and cohesion, but such as for Strathclyde were assembled by local authorities and not by civil servants.

But as the 1990s came, the Government found regional planning more necessary, even if reluctant to call it such. Nor did the Government admit to how the growing centralisation of public administration was reinforcing the pressure for regional governance in the central government sector. There was a massively increased dependence of local government on Exchequer financing, caused particularly by government's centralisation of control over education and the collection of local business rates. So, the power of government to discriminate amongst local authorities and to play politics with the financing of local government was significantly increased. The trend was naked in discrimination in the government's exceptional financing of selected Conservative 'flagship' boroughs in London, but took on a regional dimension in 1993, when local authorities in the south of England were favoured to offset the rising electoral risk in parliamentary constituencies normally bastions of Conservatism.

So, in the early 1990s, some tendencies in the UK were actually converging with the EC's sustained pressure for more considered regional planning. There was a growing imperative for regional administration within central government, in a country where centralisation of power was being hugely strengthened. Indeed, although ideologically incapable of recognising it, the Government's centralisation of public affairs and its financial policies and measures had features in common with the centralised planning of the former Soviet Union. And as the Government's

control of local affairs and planning was being reinforced, this was only manageable by an intermediate tier of central administration, with or without the
appointment of some form of government-financed agency.

This trend and its potential to match EC ambitions for regional programming
became quite obvious late in 1993. Just as part of local government financing had
previously been channelled into the City Challenge competition, advantageous to
the Government because discrimination amongst cities could be legitimised on the
grounds of matching resourcing to organisational competence, the Government
was now considering how to manage a Regional Challenge scheme, to be
sponsored by the Department of Trade and Industry. When more details were
announced in 1994, the amount of the UK's allocation of aid from the EC Regional
Development Fund to be distributed through competition between local authorities in association with the private sector had been cut from up to 50 per cent to
only 10 per cent. The EC funding would, however, be linked to the UK's Single
Regeneration Grant consolidating many previously separate funding schemes.

The new Regional Challenge competition together with an unprecedented
degree of coordination amongst government regional departments begged large
practical and political questions. The EC regions of industrial decline do not
correspond to the UK Standard Regions, for which regional planning conferences
exist in England and Wales; what new planning groups would be required, and
would they merely emphasise the vacuum left by the Government's abolition of
the metropolitan county councils? Would the Department of the Environment's
entrenched determination to deny that land use planning had any economic or
social connections be exposed for the blinkered absurdity that it was? And could
the Government really overcome its long-standing antipathy to regional economic
planning, exposing the needs of the regions and laying claim to government
resources?

But, whatever the paradoxes in the Government's new tolerance to aspects of
regional economic planning, and whatever its demands that the UK should be
freed of EC intervention in regional affairs, the idea of Regional Challenge was
yet another sign of UK convergence with approaches to strategic and regional
planning which the EC had long encouraged. Just as the EC's rising emphasis on
metropolitan and urban contributions to economic development and regional
policy had been matched in the UK from the late 1970s. For the future, the chief
executive of the Confederation of British Industry foresaw that 'there could be a
need even under the Conservative government for some kind of regional groupings
which can influence the development of European regional policy' (H. Davies
1993, 93).

Who Wants Regional Planning and Governance?
The planning profession and all the aims of its Institute's charter were anathema
to the new right politics swept into government in 1979. Planners were certainly

long on ideals but their practice was short on proven theory. And where the whole merits of planning were being challenged in the 1980s, the value of a regional contribution to strategic planning was an issue little evaluated and readily disputed.

As a poorly formalised process, regional planning was more readily pushed aside than was the mainstream of planning. Later in the 1980s, as government came to ride the mainstream it also gave token encouragement to regional planning, albeit under restricted terms. Yet, regionalism in any guise remains scarcely acceptable not only to new right, libertarian philosophy, but also to some academic observers of government. Who, then, wants regional planning?

In local government, the administrative ramifications of the local government changes of the 1980s were still being felt in the early 1990s. But the changes introduced a new system only for some areas, leaving two different forms of organisation existing side by side in the former metropolitan and in the remaining shire counties. The anomaly was untenable, and all three principal political parties proposed to remedy it.

The basis for a Conservative reform was set out in government consultation papers in 1991. It was proposed to introduce unitary local authorities throughout England, Scotland and Wales. The scale and duties of authorities and any role for community or other very local councils was to be set out later. But there would be no question of any regional tier of governance; although a few English counties or the Scottish Highland region might become new, unitary authorities, the historic upper tier of local government was to be widely dissolved. The development planning system which had been extensive since the early 1930s and comprehensive since 1947 was to be shattered. With whatever contribution from the increased number of generally smaller local authorities, guidelines for regional planning would remain in the hands of civil servants, directed by Ministers.

After several years of unresolved differences between interests in the Labour Party, its attitude to local government reform and regional planning was better unified for the 1992 general election. The Party (Labour Party 1991a, b) then committed itself to an initial regional devolution of government administration, followed by the election of around ten regional assemblies with underlying district authorities. The regional assemblies would produce regional plans and have an input into national planning and expenditure decisions. The proposals were substantially driven by the promise to launch an elected assembly in Scotland in Labour's first year of office, and particularly by the need to assure the Northern region of England that no disadvantage for others would ensue.

Solving the Scottish problem only raised a new difficulty for Labour. A comparable assembly for the South East would represent anything up to half the population of England, and it would swamp the party's wish to bring Greater London back under Labour control. So a strategic authority for metropolitan London has been a constant in Labour policy. Responsible for only the selected functions of transport, planning, the environment, tourism and policing, the

Greater London authority would yet involve uncertainties over its relationship with any assembly for the wider South East, Britain's most populous region.

Committed like the Conservative Party to abolishing many upper-tier councils, Labour's proposals have been substantially different by aiming to reinforce the role of locally elected government. Yet, the depth of Labour's commitment to regional assemblies in England has been widely questioned, and many have believed that its interest would fade quickly after establishing assemblies for Scotland and possibly for Wales.

The Liberal Democrats have been clearly committed to federalism for the United Kingdom, though traditionally divided on whether England or its regions would be the constituent units, alongside Scotland and Wales and, perhaps, Northern Ireland. But like Labour and the Conservatives, the Liberal Democrats have sought a single tier of local government. Although the party's favouring of elected regional government has been clearer than in the case of Labour, it has had a protracted timetable to introduce a system if ever able to do so. Six years would be required, as local income tax and a comprehensive pattern of town, community, parish and neighbourhood councils would be introduced alongside the regional government.

So, unanimity amongst the political parties has existed only in looking generally to a single tier of local government, albeit widely differing on the form and boundaries of councils. And although Labour and the Liberal Democrats have been committed to regional planning, regional governance and regional development agencies, there has been no consensus on the form which these should take.

Professional planners have continuously pressed for regional planning, but less concertedly for regional governance. The report leading the Royal Town Planning Institute (1986) to accept a policy favouring regional local government was adopted against the views of county planning officers amongst its members. And in strongly advocating regional cooperation, the County Planning Officers' Society (1990) sought regional guidance rather than regional plans, arguing for voluntary regional planning conferences rather than elected regional councils. Later, the Society (1992) published its call for *Competent Strategic Planning* and dismissed the possibility that voluntary conferences of district councils could replace the strategic work of county councils; but the Society ignored the equal criticisms applying to the voluntary regional planning conferences of county councils which they expected to retain.

Local governments protect the status quo when reform is in the air, and chief planning officers protect their jobs. Chief officers' juniors were similarly unable to contemplate administrative reform, but were characteristically braver in arguing for a system of government-led regional planning, along lines reminiscent of the 1960s (South East Branch RTPI 1991).

The Unstable Legacy

A Decade of Mismanaged Reorganisation

The repeated fluctuations in the successions of regional initiatives and governance in the UK reflect recurrent instability. There have been several causes for this erratic progress. Practical redundancy has been a factor. This has sometimes occurred when the purpose of a regional initiative has been served, as with the production of many regional studies or regional plans. But arguments that higher tiers of local governance have become redundant have commonly been a political ploy, as when Conservative governments of the 1980s and 1990s came to abolish much of the upper tier of local government. Created by the Conservative government of the 1970s, the upper tier had come to be comprehensively dominated by opposing parties. Party political tensions surrounded the GLC in the 1980s particularly, and they intensified in the traditional shire counties of England until in 1993 all but one had been swept out of majority Conservative control.

Some old regions have become redundant or been considerably redefined by changing economic circumstances, as in South East England and in Strathclyde. But should new regional levels of governance always become cuckoos in their central government's nest? This fear of Conservative governments in Britain is little justified by the cases of Germany and Italy, where there has been no fundamental shift of power from the centre, due considerably to the manner in which government departments have protected their sectoral interests from being undermined by the regions.

Rather than being overtaken solely by changing voter distribution and political relations, it can be argued that the GLC and the metropolitan councils were faulty at their conception. Their reform was inevitable, because their responsibilities and administrative areas were both unbalanced, as many foresaw at their outset. Similarly, there was an instability in the Scottish system of regional councils, particularly in Strathclyde.

But whatever the inherent faults of metropolitan England, its supposed streamlining in 1986 left far too many gaps and rough edges in the new system of English unitary councils. And sufficient proposals for reorganisation of the English shire counties had been published by the Local Government Commission by early 1994 to suggest that they would be replaced by perhaps greater inconsistencies of discretion and capacity. The Commission was torn between its own inclinations and the heavy hand of the government's guidelines to it. When making public statements, the Chairman seemed to lack confidence in some of the Commission's proposals, and the Government and many in local government, industry and public affairs certainly did. As in England, the proposals for Welsh and Scottish reform harked back to fragmented government of the kind which, for much of the twentieth century, had plagued coherent urban and regional planning and inhibited an efficient economic infrastructure. Reverting to a design for local governance of the kind which had failed the social and economic needs of the country in the past was unlikely to bring a new stability.

ENGLAND: AFTER THE ABOLITION OF THE METROPOLITAN COUNCILS

Although the strategic capacities of the metropolitan county councils were greater than those of the arrangements by which they were replaced, they were all inherently unsatisfactory to a greater or lesser degree. They were inherently unstable. They were badly designed in their areas, in their functions, and in their relationship to district councils, government agencies and private interests.

The metropolitan county councils were all much smaller than even recognisable city regions. Arrangements for strategic cooperation had to be struck not just between county councils and surrounding shire counties, but including two metropolitan counties in some cases. The Mersey Basin Campaign established by the Department of the Environment in 1984 joined the efforts of the Greater Manchester and Merseyside county councils with many other councils in North West England in a 25 year programme of water, environmental and economic action.

But the post-1986 arrangements have been as unstable as those before, as seen in the way in which strategic problems have been acted upon no more convincingly than prior to 1986. This has been naturally most strongly recognised in Greater London, where transport problems, widespread criticism of the capital's lack of a coherent and decisive strategic voice, and the poor prospects of cooperative effectiveness amongst joint boards and committees signify the growing case for further reform.

The continuing hiatus has not been for lack of widespread recognition of the strategic issues. It may even be that by serving all the London boroughs, the London Planning Advisory Committee approach has produced a fuller consensus on some aspects of Greater London planning than the GLC was able to achieve. London's traffic problems were quickly made a priority for advice by the new LPAC, adopting some of the strategic concern of the abolished GLC. But in response, government showed little sign of altering established programmes, although abandoning studies for some possible major new road schemes. And LPAC staff stressed their limitations, having neither the capacity nor the powers to act as strategic planners could do in a strategic authority (Dolphin 1993).

Noting in 1980 that the GLC had been unable to force a coherent programme of transport investment for the metropolitan area and the surrounding region, and that the inertia of established programmes was powerful, the House of Commons Transport Committee had concluded that coordination was imperative to a balanced transport strategy for London. Ten years later, the Committee was seeking to set up a forum within which transport agencies might jointly examine common issues; and a senior Conservative who was chairman of the London Tourist Board complained that an industry worth £5 billion a year to the capital was at risk because of piecemeal and uncoordinated transport planning.

There have been no convincing signs of the Government adopting real vision, forward thinking, strategy or dynamic planning for Greater London. Such flag-ships as the government have helped launch have seemed leaky and accident-prone:

the Docklands enterprise had been a lesson in unbalanced strategic planning; the East Thames Corridor project seemed insufficiently substantial to bear comparison with urban projects in many non-capital cities in other countries; and the protracted story of deciding on terminals and entry routes for the Channel Tunnel rail link has been a comedy in many parts without a convincing conclusion.

Abolishing the English metropolitan counties without a viable replacement was a retreat from the kind of strategic metropolitan planning and governance occurring in most dynamic metropolitan regions in Europe. The legacy of neglect included:

1. The lack of any influential and effective organisation able to coordinate planning with transportation and other matters at a metropolitan level.

2. Representative metropolitan regional planning conferences lacking executive powers or resources to plan and to invest in essential infrastructure, or to decisively support urban economic regeneration.

3. All decisions above district and borough level having to be taken by ministers, civil servants or joint bodies on a basis of voluntary cooperation.

4. Highway planning and implementation at metropolitan scale becoming a ministerial responsibility, with the separation of transport planning from other metropolitan functions.

5. The number of structure plan authorities increasing in 1986 from 6 to 36 in metropolitan England, and from 1 to 33 in the GLC area. After 1996, the shrinking or abolition of more county councils will further fragment strategic planning.

6. Break-up of specialist teams for strategic programmes for reclamation, minerals, waste disposal, historic buildings, intelligence, and other functions.

Experience after abolition naturally differed. The metropolitan areas did not seize-up through lack of governance but, as Leach and Game (1991, 142) say, not all was 'streamlined' as government had implied it would be. There was disruption, complexity and further instability. Greater London was left with 30 different ways of administrative division, and with 75 bodies providing public services in addition to the 33 boroughs. In the areas of the former metropolitan counties, any previous confusion over the respective responsibilities of counties and districts was succeeded by greater confusion or ignorance over the new joint bodies and authorities.

In reviews of post-abolition experience in metropolitan England, only the West Midlands has earned unequivocal credit for facing strategic issues squarely through joint working by district councils. Fuller awareness of issues and appreciably less banality in government's regional guidance has been attributed to a particularly active and experienced regional planner of the Department of the Environment, and to supportive contributions by the counties of the region surrounding the metropolitan area.

By 1993, all counties in England had come to participate in regional planning conferences, forums, or other associative regional arrangements. This belatedly fulfilled 70 years of erratically pursued effort by government, but the scope and quality of planning was uneven. The quality of the Department of the Environment's regional guidance was commonly criticised as being slight, and in South East England was widely condemned for its poverty by comparison with the more ambitious appraisal of the London Planning Advisory Committee. In 1990, regional guidance was claimed by one contributor to a Royal Town Planning Institute conference on strategic planning to be little more than the sum of its county parts. Davies (1993) pointed to the unduly narrow view of regional planning taken by government, focusing on land use and preferring to exclude many analyses which an experienced regional planner would expect – such as of the dynamics of housing conditions influencing changing pressures for land.

The regional revival of physical planning was paralleled by new regional agencies, and by confirmation that existing regional levels of government administration would be retained – even if reduced from fourteen to eight from 1994 as in the National Health Service. Against a background of internal and external dissent, the Arts Council was being erratically steered by a rapid succession of Arts Ministers towards devolving much of its funding programme to newly formed regional arts boards, adapting the Council's centralised, national funding structure by 1992. The new boards were to bring policy and funding to regional levels within England – as had previously existed for the Scottish, Welsh and Northern Ireland regions – but creating a closer relationship with local government interests.

This regionalisation of arts funding was certainly not entirely aimed at giving the regions more say in deciding which arts were dearest to them. What was being done was consistent with other of the Government's initiatives towards local financial management, whose benefits were not only reduced bureaucracy overall, but also an offloading of responsibility for many locally unpopular decisions.

NORTHERN IRELAND: SHADOW LOCAL GOVERNMENT

After local government was displaced in 1968 from functions in which it had been discredited by nearly 50 years of sectarian discrimination, Northern Ireland has been centrally ruled with only minimal local government. The reform of the province's governance has been indefinitely deferred, and the question of regional instability has dimensions fortunately absent in most of the UK.

SCOTLAND: THE END OF THE REGIONAL EXPERIMENT

Since 1975, Scotland's local government base for effective strategic regional planning has been probably more rational than in any other part of the United Kingdom. Strathclyde, the only truly metropolitan regional council ever established in Britain, survived when the English metropolitan county councils were dissolved. But in 1996, Strathclyde will be abolished by a Conservative government, and no alternative government would be likely to restore such a large council.

The Scottish Conservative Party called for the elimination of a tier of local government at its annual conference in 1988, although the commitment of the Secretary of State to reform was unsure until June 1991 when the government declared its intention to proceed. Some saw the transformation of the Scottish Development Agency in 1990 into over 20 local enterprise agencies as a stalking horse for the reform proposals, but when they were announced (Scottish Office 1993), the 28 unitary councils did not match the 23 agency areas. The three islands councils were all to be retained, as were two of the regional councils, including the Highland region. But Strathclyde would be swept away and its nineteen district councils reduced to ten. Altogether, 65 councils were to be succeeded by 28.

But whereas strategic planning had been confined to 12 top-tier councils since 1975, structure plans would from 1996 be divided amongst the single tier of 28 new councils. The fragmentation would be most significant around the four major cities of Glasgow, Edinburgh, Aberdeen and Dundee. Metropolitan Clydeside, for which successive governments had since 1944 accepted the need for repetitive integrated strategic planning, would cover all or part of at least ten independent councils. The Secretary of State's only recognition of this inevitable need was to suggest that he would:

> specify those areas where he considers that a structure plan should cover more than one local authority. He will expect the authorities in those areas to work together to prepare and maintain such structure plans... He would also be able to use his general power to establish formal joint boards. (Scottish Office 1993, 8)

The government's attitude to strategic planning had reverted to that of the 1930s, sixty years before. All the lessons of the intervening years had been forgotten. Whatever the fact that many of the past issues within Scottish regions had now risen to be of all-Scottish significance, independent strategies remained necessary for the major urban regions for transport, industrial development, office location, housebuilding, leisure and recreation. And there were no signs that the Government would provide a more substantial strategic planning service at the Scottish level. The Chief Executive of the Scottish Council for Development and Industry, an organisation active as a stimulus for strategic planning since its formation by an apolitical spread of private and public interests in the 1930s, complained about the unacceptable scenario of local development agencies attempting to co-exist with local authorities with few common boundaries to ease the task (Morrison 1993).

Nonetheless, Scottish local government and regional planning was to be reformed, regardless of the party in government. The Labour Party had gone further than the Conservatives, sooner, when its intention to move to a single tier of local government in conjunction with the institution of an elected assembly in Edinburgh was confirmed in February 1990. It was implicit that strategic planning of the regional kind would become a responsibility of a Scottish Assembly, whose scale would be comparable to the Labour Party's apparent intentions for regional assemblies in England.

Although it is political developments which are going to reshape local government and strategic planning, there are other good grounds for suggesting that the Scottish system has served its time. Events have already considerably overtaken the strategic planning role envisaged for the regional and islands councils prior to 1975. Two circumstamces are particularly significant.

First, the Government's agencies have become progressively more involved in strategic initiatives. When they have failed to persuade, the agencies have over-ridden regional council policy when they have chosen to force issues. Senior officials of the SDA privately scorned and publicly challenged regional council structure plans, pursuing development initiatives in different strategic directions – as with the Dundee waterfront, Glasgow's Parkhead Shopping Centre and Aberdeen's Bridge of Don exhibition complex. When Scottish Homes was formed, it similarly added to the range of strategic initiatives made independently of regional councils. In 1994, the agency's chairman (Scottish Homes 1994) implicitly criticised almost twenty years of local government planning, calling for long-term visions and action plans to link housing, economic and social development in urban Scotland; he argued that competitive success required 'a clear understanding of the long-term future of all our cities and towns'.

Second, easier travel and new social and commercial tendencies have increasingly transcended regional boundaries. Some strategic planning issues have risen above the level of even Strathclyde and Lothian, the two most populous of Scottish regional councils. Neither region was large enough to contain all the planning or political implications of the shopping megacentres proposed there in the late 1980s, when the planning decisions were taken by the Secretary of State into his own hands because their scale had grown from regional to national.

This tendency for leading metropolitan and urban centred regions to progressively expand is international. And because inherent in the notion is the implication that some regions will disappear as others encroach on their territory, institutional politics are a natural brake on the acceptance of change. An early initiative of the new Glasgow Development Agency in 1991 was to host a discussion on the complementary relationship of Edinburgh and Glasgow, attended and sympathetically contributed to by the leaders of the two city councils. But though the Clydeside region of the *Clyde Valley Plan* (Abercrombie and Matthew 1949) had swelled by the 1990s beyond the boundary of Strathclyde Regional Council's *Structure Plan*, the prospect of unified local government for a central Scotland region embracing both Glasgow and Edinburgh was politically unacceptable.

These have been substantial changes in local–central relationships and in the scale of strategic planning issues and priorities for action. They have much reduced the relevance of the analysis underlying the Scottish local government system introduced in 1975, which began with the need for strategic development planning. And if the opportunity to redistribute resources in education and in social services has perhaps proved the greatest benefit of the regionalisation of 1975, the scope for more of this kind of redistribution was considerably reduced when the Community Charge and then the Council Tax came to replace the Rating system.

So there have been convincing grounds upon which to reconsider at least the geographical scale of the Scottish regional councils. But the single-tier pattern of reorganised local government which the Government proposed in 1993 and aimed to institute in 1996 harked back to the mid nineteenth century as much as it looked forward to the twenty-first. It gave no weight to strategic planning, despite the special lessons of over 50 years of Scottish experience. And as in England, the geographical shapes of the proposed councils had the incidental benefit for the government of seeming likely to minimise the number of Labour councils, and of maximising the number which might come under Conservative control.

In any political and economic conditions, however, there would be a strong case to redefine the scope of strategic planning in Scotland and to reinforce the contribution to it of the Scottish Office or of any elected Assembly in Edinburgh. This would be appropriate for any pattern of single-tier local government, and even if an intermediate planning level were established on a joint basis or as an elected authority as proposed by planners in Strathclyde (Department of Physical Planning 1991).

WALES: NEW TEETH FOR THE DRAGON?

In 1990, a Strategic Planning Steering Committee was formed by the Welsh Assembly of Counties, encouraged by the Secretary of State for Wales. Subsuming the standing conferences for North and West Wales, and for South Wales, the Committee was invited to advise the Welsh Office, and to consult district councils and conservation and other planning interests through a Strategic Planning Forum, representing also the district councils and the three Welsh national parks. The county councils were asked to consider the main strategic planning issues which might affect Wales over a future of up to fifteen years.

By early 1992, the Committee was consulting on the issues and modifications to strategic guidance for structure plans published by the Secretary of State for Wales two years before. The Committee's chairman claimed that the objective was not to produce a regional plan for Wales, but only guidelines for authorities' development plans. The form of regional plan which was specifically dismissed was *Wales: The Way Ahead* (Welsh Economic Planning Council 1967); the government clearly wished the Welsh regional planning revival of the 1990s to exclude politically embarrassing economic content. In fact, economic issues were lightly touched on in the consultations and the subsequent observations by the Assembly on the Government's development planning guidelines.

The Welsh Office was quite willing to recognise physical, economic and social interlinkage when allocating funds for local development. In 1994–95, it instituted a Strategic Development Scheme (Welsh Office 1993), bringing together the previously separate Urban Programme, Rural Initiative and schemes for Projects of Regional and National Importance and Special Projects. In applying for aid under the integrated Scheme, local authorities were expected to show how their prospective initiatives would promote sustainable local economic development, benefit socially deprived areas and local communities, and reinforce partnerships between the public and private sector. Logically, this approach should have been matched by similarly integrated dimensions in the parallel revival in Welsh regional planning.

Government's Regional Schizophrenia

So while the Government fostered a revival of regional planning conferences in the 1990s, it divided local government whose capacity to participate effectively was much reduced. And as government spawned agencies for strategic intervention, it gave them semi-autonomous authority making difficult the kind of regional partnership which it wished to introduce in the spending of EC funds. And as some government ministers denied any future for regional government in the UK, growing centralisation of public administration and services reinforced regional levels of administration in central government, marked by the institution in 1994 of new arrangements to coordinate inter-departmental affairs in the 10 regional offices of government.

There is a real schizophrenia about the Government's view of regions and of regional planning and governance in the 1990s. There has been a reviving need and some awareness of the merits of regional administration, but no comprehensive framework for such a system. The new interdepartmental coordination introduced in England in 1993 embraced only five government departments. Since the 1960s, most departments had slipped from the good intentions that regional coordination should be improved. There had been low use of Standard Regions as a systematic basis for departmental administration (Hogwood and Lindley 1982). Although the slippage may be partly explained by the fact of different functions imperfectly fitting standard packaging, by functions which have altered and by administration that has had to be recast from time to time, it remains that regions for their own sake had little interest for departments.

Throughout the 1980s and further in the 1990s, there was a significant increase in the amount of planning and strategic action being placed in the hands of agencies, beyond the influence of local government and of its councillors. Task forces, urban development corporations, hospital and health management boards, training and other agencies, and the sale of the regional water authorities, were all developments moving local development and services away from the managerial influence of elected representatives. In some respects, the transfer of assets from ownership by the population at large to a relatively few private hands brought them more under the influence of planning, because nationalised industries such as electricity, gas, and even water to a degree, had a status which took them

The new regional offices 1994, to oversee a combined Goverment 'single regeneration budget' previously administered under 20 separate programmes through five departments

Figure 5.2. The new regions of 1994

considerably beyond the planning controls to which industry and the private housebuilding industry was liable. So what was lost in one direction of influence was partially compensated in another. However, the autonomy of some of the agencies has been doubted. The planned allocation of resources by the regional water authorities (RWAs) could be significantly influenced by local authorities, Saunders thought (1983, 41). But although Payne (1978) suggested that the RWAs followed rather than led in regional planning policy, despite such as the Severn–Trent Authority which spanned several of the Standard Regions of England, others were less sanguine. Hickling, Friend and Luckman (1979) considered the RWAs at least lukewarm to the development plan system, and likely to encourage building where it was economical for them rather than where it best suited regional strategy.

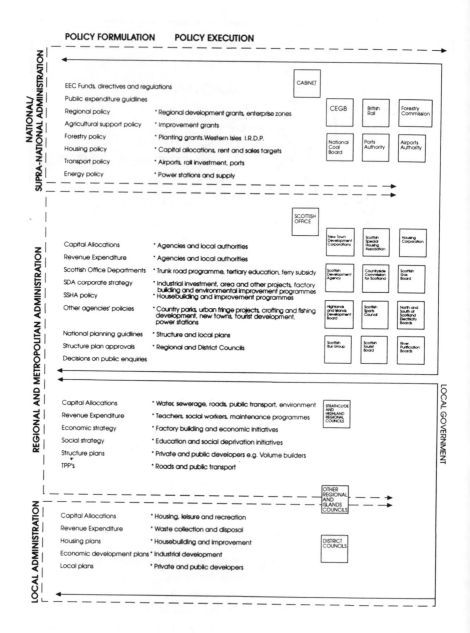

Figure 5.3. Regional and metropolitan adminstration in Scotland 1985: the levels and divisions of responsibility

Senior officials of the Scottish Development Agency in the 1980s were contemptuous of structure plans, which were regarded as of no importance where the SDA had different strategic objectives.

This is an apparently confused state of affairs, developing without any basic consideration of the role of regions within the economy, of the relationship of one kind of region to another, or of the principles of effective administration. Regional planning has seemed to be the last thought in the Government's mind, when many knowledgeable or active in local economic development and urban regeneration have admired the spread of regionalism elsewhere in Europe, or even the Scottish model of Strathclyde.

The better opportunities for formalised regional planning and governance in other countries of Europe have been a significant tendency. But it can also be seen that some regions of Europe unburdened by the cares of comprehensive administration and of 'statutory' planning have been more far-sighted and imaginative than others with heavy responsibilities. Politicians in regional organisations whose ambitions are greater than their executive capacities may seek to consolidate their role by reaching beyond the vision of administrative bureaucracies. They may wish to create international linkages, or to establish long-term scenarios for their region's development. This is a creative strategic role of great potential value, but experience suggests that it does not always fit comfortably within an organisation with substantial executive responsibility. Responsibilities for 'doing' tend to overwhelm any inclination to 'think' and to imagine the future; the present is burden enough for administrators without adding future cares.

The Significance of Inter-Government Relations

If any elected regional assembly or other-titled regional level of governance were to be introduced to the UK, it would be necessary to consider at least five possible major dimensions to the issue of inter-governmental relations. First, those between a regional assembly with legislative and – perhaps – tax-raising powers and central government; second, those between a regional assembly and local government; third, those between any regional local government and central government; fourth, those between a regional and a lower tier of local governments; fifth, those between a cooperative or appointed regional authority and the local governments within its area.

How do these dimensions enter the question of the link between policy-making and its execution? It has been seen as a weakness of British regional planning that it has mostly separated the two functions. But there is a contrary argument. It can be suggested that the larger the organisation which combines the two functions, the greater the difficulty of ensuring that they fit. This does not deny the potential advantages of placing both functions within one organisation, but it may have associated difficulties.

The case of Strathclyde Regional Council illustrates the problem. Neither the Council's original *Regional Report* (1976) nor its subsequent *Structure Plan* (1981 *et seq.*) caused early significant adjustments in inter-departmental priorities in expenditure. Progressively, demographic changes and political shifts did bring largely marginal changes in departmental priorities and budgets. The process of regional planning, however, was not such a central or a coordinating influence upon the programmes of departments as the concept of Scottish regional councils had envisaged (Royal Commission 1969). The Council's Departments of Roads, Sewerage, Water, Education and Passenger Transport had budgets, commitments and sometimes political strength much exceeding that of the Department of Physical Planning.

The formation of a large Chief Executive's Department with responsibility for corporate management displaced the coordinating role of the planners and of their Strathclyde *Structure Plan* to an extent, of course. However, the stronger political base and much greater capacity to coordinate resting with the Chief Executive's Department still faced the self-interest of major service departments. Furthermore, the Chief Executive's department was so very large that it had to be managed through a divisional structure. By this necessity, the process of corporate management was made harder; it had to be internally coordinated before ever meeting the major departments for whose consistency it was designed.

It may be that a small authority with a limited executive role will tend to have more incentive to achieve internal coordination within the sphere of the authority's interests. Internal vested interests may be less jealous of each other because they do not derive from executive responsibilities allied to large budgets. Because its status depends upon its influence upon others, the authority may tend to be more motivated to internal cohesion. That will raise its morale and possibly improve its status in its battles with external interests.

Strathclyde illustrates another problem of coordinating major spending departments within a large regional council. Departments may share greater linkages and common interests with outside bodies than with others within their own organisation. This is common with highway departments throughout British local government, whose professional relationship with trunk roads engineers in central government has been notably close. The relationship has gone beyond the professionally necessary in many cases, to collusion in a common interest in road-building regardless of corporate or strategic planning. The consequence is an inter-governmental alliance between parts of two levels of government, which is sometimes stronger than the process of planning internal to either level.

Now for the issue of inter-government relations in development planning. The 'statutory' status of structure plans has often been misinterpreted by local authority planners as conferring autonomy and authority. This is largely illusory. The statutory basis of local authority plans lies only in their preparation being required as of statute. The real status of structure and of local plans depends primarily upon the degree to which they are actually supported by government, rather than by the courts. Government is involved from an early stage of their preparation, and it will normally have steered them towards the outcome which ministers wish. If not, government will modify policies when a recalcitrant plan comes forward for approval. In the 1990s, the move towards councils adopting their own structure plans will make no difference to the decisive hand which government will play where plans do not conform to government's regional guidelines.

Shrinking Local Government

The grand fiasco of the system of Community Charges and of a Uniform Business Rate which ignominiously collapsed in 1990, proved the rule of policy dynamics that to each and every new initiative there is an almost equal and opposite reaction. As it recovered from the collapse, the Government pushed on to more extensively shrink the functions of local government. Education was the prime service to diminish, having much the largest employment and largest revenue expenditure of any sector of local government. Reordering the management of education was government's key to the extreme peripheralisation of local government it wished. But of all the overturning of historic functions of local government, that of education had perhaps the most implications for regional governance.

Reconsideration of the channels of funding for local education followed upon already significant changes to school management started in the 1980s. The management reponsibilities of local education authorities had been divided and significantly curtailed. Central government assumed the prior responsibility of local authorities for school curricula and assessment procedures, and boards of governers took charge of schools' financial management. Although only a minority of schools chose to entirely opt-out of local authority control, the administrative responsibilities of elected councils were severely curbed. The Inner London Education Authority was abolished.

At the higher level of education, polytechnics and advanced colleges of similar status were taken from the control of local education authorities late in the 1980s, passing to the Department of Education and Science or to the Scottish and Welsh Offices.

These largely irreversible changes raised questions as to whether central government would crumble under the weight of administering school funding, and how schools could obtain support services which they could not reproduce individually. The Government's failure to blame the disaster of the Community Charge upon local authorities added to the temptation to it to take on all the costs of schooling. Funding through income tax rather than a local tax was in principle less regressive than the Community Charge. It also promised to tend to reduce the local bureacracy which Conservative governments believed to stifle education administration, and it would remove opposition parties from a role in education – at least during the lifetime of Conservative governments.

However, the merit of much of the change begun in the 1980s and still being adjusted to in the 1990s does not necessarily justify the nationalisation of education. Being antipathetic to regional government of any kind, there was no intermediate level of governance at which the Conservative national government could settle education once it had decided that the established level of counties, unitary boroughs and regional councils was unacceptable.

If school funding were to widely remain a task for local governance, the role of local education authorities is even so likely to be permanently reduced. They would remain strategically important, but there would be a strong argument to reduce their number. The reasons for regional governance would become more. Indeed, collaborative regional planning was already under way amongst further-education colleges in the early 1990s. Professor David Hargreaves, chief inspector of the Inner London Education Authority before its abolition in 1989, argued that regional education authorities would be the rational solution. Some 104 locally elected education authorities might be replaced by perhaps 12 to 20 regional authorities, each chaired by a person appointed by the Secretary of State. Each would have a membership equally contributed by nominees of local authorities, by election from the region's teachers and headteachers, from the chairs of schools' governing bodies, and from nominees of the Secretary of State. Hargeaves argued that such a regional system would reduce conflict within education, offsetting the local insensitivity inherent in government's growing centralisation of education funding and policy, and providing support services which had been becoming increasingly specialised. It would produce more equity in school financing, maintain satisfactory local control, and allow for consultation and accountability.

But as its loss of major responsibilities has overwhelmed the few added by the Government, local government's frustrations have not been widely redirected into exciting regional planning. A critic looking at the West Midlands in the 1990s commented:

> So this is what regional planning has come to... Planning is reactive, no longer proactive; it is an iterative, incremental management of process, whereby at fairly regular intervals statistical updates are made of housing demand and perhaps one or two new planning features introduced. Planning has become extraordinarily conservative and risk-free. The novelty, the imagination to be different is missing. It is all competently done, but it doesn't exactly set the pulse racing. (Cherry 1993, 468)

Conclusion: Instability Revived

Ad hoc as it has often been, the experience of regional planning and governance in the United Kingdom, Europe and the US has not been inadequate as some hypothesise that it must be. Regional planning is not an anomaly but a part of the mainstream of public affairs. It was a widespread feature of public administration in the 1990s.

Although experience suggests that effective regional planning is entirely possible without a wholly complementary system of regional governance, this does not deny convincing arguments for a recognisably regional scale of governance. This may be justified on other grounds of public administration and enterprise, or of politics.

By definition, regional planning will persist in the UK, because much of it arises because of cross-boundary issues and tensions inevitable with any pattern of governance, regardless of whether or not it matches geographical regions.

CHAPTER SIX

A Europe of Regions in Flux

Preface: Regions in Flux

Regional governance has been reinforced or introduced in most countries of western Europe since the 1970s, and the European Community has developed its own strategy of European integration, fostering new trans-European regions of common economic and social interests, each comprising old regions from several nations. In eastern Europe, 40 years or more of authoritarian centralist governments failed to quell regionalist forces, which brought violent resurgences of ethnic regionalism after the political upsets of 1989.

Amongst the varieties of regional governance, the Nord-Pas de Calais of France has taken outstanding advantage of regional reforms placing elected conseils régionaux *alongside the historic system of delegated prefectual administration; in the Ruhr in Germany, Europe's oldest and most sustained association for regional planning illustrates a repeated return to regional cooperation, but the successive reshaping of it under changing political circumstances; in Spain, the Andalusian autonomous* Junta *exercises exceptional devolved powers comparable only to those of the German* Länder.

In eastern Europe, regionalism which had been confined to an administrative dimension under Communist governments prior to 1989 rose bitterly to the surface afterwards in Yugoslavia and the Soviet Union, and inevitably but less violently so elsewhere. But even under Communist regimes, the regional dimension was recast at intervals. The dynamics of regionalism and of regional governance were also evident under totalitarianism.

The Europe of Regions

The Shifting Mosaic

European regional governance since 1945 has grown from four roots (Keating and Jones 1985, 2). First, from the administrative necessity to decentralise load from governments' headquarters offices; policy differences between departments can be mediated by regional civil servants, generally unencumbered by any regional level of local government. Second, in regional economic policy emerging in all countries, publicly asserted to be a means of achieving internal economic efficiency and equity. Third, in regional economic and cultural pressures causing internal political tensions, quieted either by regional economic policy or by a degree of devolved administration. Fourth, by the re-emergence of historic, political regions, concealed for many years under the pattern of countries arising from the nationalist movements of the nineteenth century and the post-war political settlements of the twenty-first century.

Regional governance is more extensive in Europe in the 1990s than at any time since it was submerged by nationalist movements of the nineteenth century. Regionalist forces have dominated the late twentieth century as nationalist movements did much of the nineteenth century. Hebbert (1987, 240) suggests that there are commonly five grounds to the regionalist cause: that a national territorial distribution of power is unbalanced; that regional governance is an alternative to federalism; that regional reform will benefit political integration; that it can correct imbalances in political economy; that a Europe of Regions is a means of supporting the future of a Europe of Nations. But expressed in this way, the regionalist cause seems far removed from the violence of action or speech sometimes surrounding it. In the Soviet Union, regionalism has carried into federalism, and in Yugoslavia it has gone beyond to independence and to a new imperialism. But the tide of regionalism over Europe has not eroded its much older feature of very local government. And the persistence of parochial local self-government by the multiplicity of communes in many European countries explains, as Bennett (1993, 4) suggests, the parallel tradition of regional administration by central government. This is reflected in the legacy of the Napoleonic prefectual system, shared by France with other countries of Europe falling under French influence in the past. But as Bennett (1993, 10) also goes on to emphasise, exposure of ethnic or cultural regional tensions in the aftermath of the ending of authoritarian regimes has been destabilising. This has been seen following fascist regimes in Spain and Portugal, as well as after the communist regimes of eastern Europe.

Enlarging the scale of local or sub-national government has been general in Europe, with the notable exception of Britain and some specific exceptions such as the cancellation of cooperation of levels of government in the region of Greater Copenhagen (Bours 1993, 110, 126). It is suggested (Barlow 1993, 136) that the tendency to regional governance has had three common stimuli: by administrative regionalism, where central governments have devolved functions to regional offices and may also have borrowed functions from local government; sub-national elected governance, particularly for cultural or ethnic regions; and metropolitan governance in the face of a globalising economy and of competition between metropolitan areas.

The Council of Europe (1991) has seen five kinds of scale enlargement as afoot in the Community:

1. Addition of member states to the EC.

2. Enlargement of state territories, as in Germany.

3. Insertion of a regional layer, as in France and Italy, or by the adoption of the
    71 European Statistical Regions.

4. Deletion of a layer of governance and transfer of some of its functions to cen-
    tral government, as in Britain.

5. Amalgamation of lower levels of governance, as in Sweden, Denmark and
    Britain, or new arrangements for metropolitan or regional cooperation as in
    the Netherlands, Italy and France.

Some of the enlarging scale of governance has clearly been stimulated by the
European Commission, whatever other factors have contributed in specific countries. Greece introduced a level of thirteen administrative regions following
national legislation in the late 1980s (Georgiou 1993, 53); although headed by
government appointees, the regions were a small step in devolving the highly
centralised Greek administration, but also matched the expectation in Brussels that
EC aid programmes would be monitored within the regions benefiting. The
Republic of Ireland was led to launch eight regional authorities in 1994, nominated by the constituent counties, coordinating government services in the regions
and being also responsible for monitoring the implementation of EC programmes.
While antipathetic to any regional governance with local politicians participating
as in Greece and Ireland, the UK government nonetheless internally reorganised
its departmental affairs in the English regions. This reorganisation of 1994 went
some way to bridge the previously widening gap between the UK and the
Commission over the principal of regional economic planning.

But dilemmas arise as scales of governance enlarge. Elected regional councils
have commonly added to the complexity of governance, for when established to
work alongside or to replace government regional administration, they have been
generally very remote from the communes (Marcou 1993, 56). Consequently,
regional reform in Europe has customarily added to the tiers of elected governance
rather than displacing one. And as the economic imperatives for metropolitan
government strengthen, there is the question of whether it should be part of local
government or be absorbed into a regional government (Barlow 1993, 142).
Europe's metropolitan areas have been crossroads on the routes to reform of
governance, at the junction between demand for local responsibility and of
opportunities for economic initiative and efficiency through regional management.

Although not yet the standard, regions have become a common element of
administrative reform in western Europe (Marcou 1993, 54). The region has
become a full level of governance in France, Italy and Spain, and in Belgium has
become effectively a form of federal governance as existing in the German *Länder*
since 1949. In the early 1990s, regions were being established in Portugal and
Greece, were being considered for the purposes of strategic planning and regional
development in Hungary and in Poland, and were an implication of possible EC
membership for the Scandinavian countries. Even in Britain a new although partial

system of regional coordination of government departments was introduced in England in 1994, driven considerably by EC practice.

As EC policies have been increasingly structured to fit a more sophisticated categorisation of social and economic regions, the significance of national frontiers has been progressively reduced. The Commission has created a pattern of trans-European regions fragmenting nation states, creating cross-frontier alliances of common interest, encouraging regional politicians to give their regions – and themselves – a supra-national status.

The regionalisation of Europe has been matched by the progressive rise of new international assemblies of regional representatives. Some groups have been vitally concerned with EC issues, like the Association of European Border Regions. Two major groups have been the Council of European Municipal and Regional Authorities primarily composed of local government associations, and the Assembly of European Regions dominated by regions with their own parliaments, like Catalonia and Flanders. Keen rivals, these two groups jockeyed to dominate the EC Committee of the Regions as it was established in 1994. Just over half of the 189 members of the Committee nominated by their governments represented local rather than regional authorities, and only from Germany, Belgium, Spain and Italy were regional representatives in the majority.

The rise of these international groups ran with the spreading sense of the arbitrariness of most national boundaries to the contemporary economic geography of Europe. The reality of the geography of common interests was expressed by a leading European bank:

> The economic interests of cities like Milan, Frankfurt, Paris, and London have far more in common with each other than any of them has with, say, Cornwall, Limousin or the Mezzogiorno. They might form a rather stable monetary union of their own, if it were practicable. (Credit Suisse First Boston Bank 1992)

One club of regions formed in 1986 comprised the Rhône-Alpes from France, Baden-Württemberg from Germany, Lombardy from Italy and Catalonia from Spain. Known as the 'Four Motors of Europe', this was a club for the rich.

The number of clubs to which some regions belonged almost defied credibility. A relatively late enthusiast for inter-regional cooperation, Catalonia not only joined in European networks but made cooperative agreements with Wales, the State of Illinois and with the Provincial Government of Buenos Aires in Argentina. Lombardy had international agreements to cooperate with regions in China and Canada (Borras 1993, 169).

Amongst outer regions fearing that they might suffer by the consolidating economic strength of the core metropolises of Europe, the new assemblies have contained a strong measure of regional self-protection. In the 1990s, the long-standing view of economic geographers of a 'Golden Triangle' across parts of France, Germany, Britain, the Benelux countries and of Italy, was being succeeded

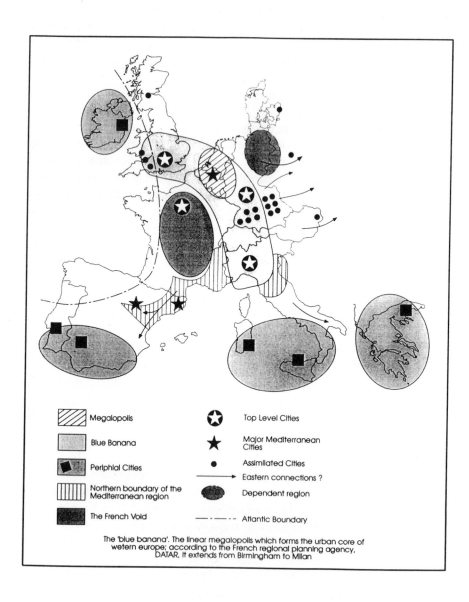

The 'blue banana'. The linear megalopolis which forms the urban core of wetern europe; according to the French regional planning agency, DATAR. It extends from Birmingham to Milan

The 'Blue Banana'. The linear megalopolis which forms the urban core of western Europe; according to the French regional planning agency, DATAR, it extends from Birmingham to Milan.

Figure 6.1. The Blue Banana: a view of the western European urban system in the 1980s

by the notion of the 'Blue Banana' – a favoured arc of rapid growth running north-west from Lombardy through Switzerland, southern Germany, the Benelux countries, northern France and south-east England. The images may have been trite and flawed in parts, but they had significant political impact. As EC policy put increasing emphasis on the economic potential of metropolitan regions in and near the 'Blue Banana', even the sunrise economies of the northern Mediterranean felt the need to assert themselves; significantly, in 1993 the Assembly of European regions drew its president from Spanish Catalonia and its vice-president from adjoining French Languedoc-Roussillon.

Of regions and regional groupings within the Community apparatus, the German *Länder* have had unique status as special observers at meetings of the Council of Ministers. Other regions had to wait for formal representation until 1988, when the European Commission established the Consultative Council for Regional and Local Authorities, from which 42 representatives could directly comment on the regional and local implications of Community policy. In 1991, the Maastricht Treaty agreed to reform the Consultative Council as the Committee of Regions and Local Authorities, with a membership of 189, to which the United Kingdom, France, Germany and Italy would each contribute 24. The Committee would be consulted by the Council of Ministers or the Commission over the activities of the three structural funds – regional, social and agricultural – and of the new Cohesion Fund.

So new associations of regions have been created by the Commission, forming new spheres of common political interest across Europe. There has been a shifting mosaic of often overlapping regions. The overlaps reflect different purposes and terms of definition of the different patterns. In the Regional Policy Directorate's report on *Europe 2000* (European Commission 1991), for example, eight supra-national regional groups were defined:

Atlantic Regions (UK, Ireland, France, Spain, Portugal)

Central Capitals (London, Bonn, The Hague, Brussels, Luxembourg, Paris)

Alpine Regions (Germany, France, Italy)

West Mediterranean Regions (Spain, France, Italy)

Central Mediterranean Regions (Italy, Greece)

North Sea Coastal Regions (UK, Netherlands, Germany, Denmark)

Inland Continental Regions (France, Spain)

East Germany

This particular pattern of supra-national regions has been criticised (Gripaios and Mangles 1993, 749) as poorly justified, because the regions lack sufficient socio-economic homogeneity. It is also argued that Community policy should aim to link peripheral and central parts of Europe, rather than setting them apart. The

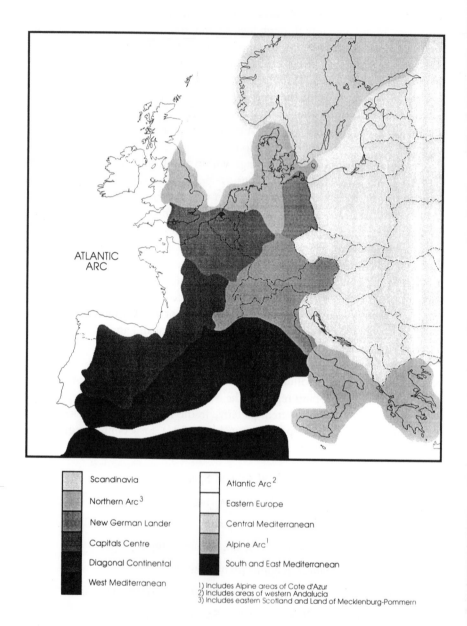

ATLANTIC
ARC

Scandinavia		Atlantic Arc [2]	
Northern Arc [3]		Eastern Europe	
New German Lander		Central Mediterranean	
Capitals Centre		Alpine Arc [1]	
Diagonal Continental		South and East Mediterranean	
West Mediterranean			

1) Includes Alpine areas of Cote d'Azur
2) Includes areas of western Andalucia
3) Includes eastern Scotland and Land of Mecklenburg-Pommern

Figure 6.2. EUROPE 2000: the EC's perspective of regional grouping in the current and future Community

origin of the pattern was geographical proximity and developing political relationships between parts of the regions, but there was probably more promise in the different approach of sponsoring networks of often widely separated areas with more narrowly defined interests under the European Regional Development Fund (ERDF). Furthermore, the eagerness of eastern European countries to join the already declared list of applicants for EC membership promised a significant future extension of Community geography.

Anticipating the enlarged Community, a revision of the *Europe 2000* document was soon under way. The Commission regarded regional planning as an essential tool in European integration, by which the economic and social programmes to offset inter-regional disparities could be advertised and used to justify political cohesion. It was likely that the 'Golden Triangle' and the 'Blue Banana' would have to be succeeded by a new symbol, politically necessary to reflect the east-west axis inevitably developing as the new and wider European economy consolidated.

As the regional linkages proliferated, they did so most vigorously under Article 10 of the ERDF. Under the Regions and Cities in Europe (RECITE) programme, local or regional authorities with populations as small as 50,000 were able to participate in RECITE networks, all aimed at promoting common economic interests. The goals of the programme were to help less-favoured regions, transfer expertise from the better developed regions and realise economies of scale through cost-sharing. Economic development, urban planning, transport, rural development and public services were principal areas of concern. The ERDF could meet up to 75 per cent of project costs of RECITE projects, which by 1992 fell under 37 different networks involving cities and regions in Community countries:

Atlantic Regions – cooperation of remoter coastal regions

Coast – environment and employment issues in nine coastal areas

Chambers of Commerce and Industry – vocational training, information and local economic observatories

Communications Technology – six cities and regions with under-used telecommunication networks

Compostella Forest – tourism in south-west European forest regions

Demilitarised – replacing dependency on military installations

Dionysos – technology transfer between French, Italian, Spanish and Portuguese wine-growers

Economic Cooperation – business, research institute and local government links

Ecos and Ouverture – two projects to link less-favoured cities and regions with counterparts in Eastern Europe

Ecowat – water conservation and renewable energy

Environet – exchange of expertise in urban planning and environmental protection

Eurisles – islands linkage to overcome problems of isolation

Euroceram – regions with ceramic industries

Eurocities – cooperation of 40 large cities over common interests

Eurogateway – collaboration of development agencies to expand services for small and medium sized enterprises

European Urban Observatory – data bases for metropolitan cities

Eurosynet – tourist, commercial and urban planning projects

Finatlantic – venture capital projects in Atlantic coastal regions

Hydre – management and improvement of water quality in Mediterranean coastal regions

Idee – re-integration of people in difficulties

Less Favoured Regions – resource centres for economic growth

Mediterranean Tourism – new opportunities to offset the trend of decline

Medium-Sized Cities – development and urban renewal, engineering, science and technology parks

Motor Vehicle Manufacturing Cities and Regions – regions affected by restructuring of the motor industry

Polis – new technology for mobility within 25 urban areas

Public Transport – fostering of urban public transport

Quartiers en Crise – multiple social problems in 25 urban areas

Rebuild – solar energy in the reconstruction of seven historical city centres

Regional Development Agencies – liaison between agencies

Resigmur – geographical information systems for urban planning and property tax matters

Roc Nord – Danish advice to Crete on economic and environmental planning

Science Centres – technological skills for five cities and regions in southern Europe

Sealink – interchange of maritime experience between northern German, Greek and Italian ports

Strategy for Medium-Sized Cities – selective development of cities disadvantaged by size and location

Technology Transfer – strengthening competitive base of enterprises in six regions

Transport in the Mediterranean – eight Mediterranean ports developing potential for coastal shipping

Universities and Regions – diffusion of research on European regional and urban problems.

Other EC schemes with regional implications operating in 1991 were *RECHAR* (conversion of coal mining areas), *RESIDER* (conversion of steel areas), *RENAVAL* (conversion of shipbuilding areas), *ENVIREG* (environment-friendly economic development), *STRIDE* (research and production), *INTERREG* (cooperation across national borders), *PRISMA* (product quality standards and public procurement), *REGIS* (extremely remote regions), *REGEN* (energy supply networks), *TELEMA-TIQUE* (data transmission services) and *LEADER* (rural development).

Alongside the European-wide linkages, general assemblies and committees of regions and of local authorities formally recognised by the Commission, self-selective groupings have persisted outside the Community's aegis, representing special geographical or social and economic interests. Transcontinental regional alliances have formed, sometimes amongst neighbouring regions across international frontiers, and sometimes between regions widely separated on the map but close in economic and political interest. Sometimes the groupings seem likely to benefit only the self-importance of politicians, but progressively agreements have been struck for inter-regional cooperation for economic, education, research, cultural and other objectives.

The Conference of Peripheral Maritime Regions and RETI (Régions Européennes de Tradition Industrielle) were two of the earliest groupings. But the groupings changed as the economic geography of Europe was reshaped. The most enthusiastic of RETI's members at its formation in 1984 was the Nord-Pas de Calais, which chose to reorient itself in the 1990s as its perspective of itself was changed by the Channel Tunnel, the TGV and the modernisation of its regional industrial base. Being already linked to Kent since 1987 in a Trans-Manche regional partnership endorsed by the EC, the Nord-Pas de Calais became in 1991 the hub of a trans-Channel region extended to include all Belgium's three regions of Wallonia, Flanders and Brussels. A Euroregion of 15 million people was recognised, embracing three countries and programmes of cooperation in economic and technological development, land use and transport planning, the environment, promotion and exchanges and a comprehensive survey for possible joint action.

Elsewhere the Saar, Lorraine, Luxembourg and Belgium's most easterly region were associated; three prosperous regions bordering Switzerland – the Rhône-Alpes, Baden-Württemberg and Lombardy – stretched their association to include buoyant Catalonia. And Baden-Württemberg was in turn linked to the counties of Wales.

The EC has sponsored other new linkages with regions in Eastern Europe, whereby through the *Ouverture* programme the Strathclyde region oversaw connections as wide as Europe itself, interchanging experience between east and west in local economic development, local government, planning and the environment. Capital cities and small towns have had their own networks separate from the regional ones, and professional and trading groups also have access to the Commission and may be consulted by it. The UK government's Glasgow Development Agency has been partly funded by the EC in a link with local economic development agencies in the Hérault area of France and North Rhine-Westphalia.

Although many linkages may not go much beyond the kinds of communal ceremonial typical of town-twinning, their proliferation in the 1990s suggested that some might develop real significance. And in doing so, the effects would not always include better integration within Europe. Combined with devolution and regional government within European nations, some of the more productive transnational linkages may help increase internal disparities in wealth – Catalonia's advance within Spain, for example. International links between fast-growing regions may allow some to reinforce their ability to pull further ahead of those which are lagging.

The Incongruity of European Regions

Europe's latticed regional networks sometimes overlap and are sometimes discrete. Breaking the old rigidity of national political frontiers, the new patterns of European regions often better reflect contemporary cultural and economic geography, creating new interest blocs wider than the widest of European nations. But the patterns remain incongruous in some of their detail. They are unable to perfectly combine the regions and administrative units of the EC member countries, which vary so widely in size of area and of population, and also in status. No uniform system exists which is observed by all countries and is capable of serving all the purposes of European regional planning equally well.

Building on this inheritance of member states' different national patterns of regions and other units of internal governance, the European Commission's NUTS (*Nomenclature des Unités Territoriales Statistiques*) scheme imposes a broadly systematic pattern of regions across Europe, at three different levels. Even so, this comparative scheme links the English county of West Sussex to the neighbouring counties of East Sussex and Surrey in a single NUTS level 2 region, despite about a fifth of level 2 regions in Europe housing fewer people than does West Sussex alone.

Any pursuit of a systematic level and pattern of regions in Europe must be inevitably complicated by political and cultural factors. And different directorates within the Commission have employed different regional patterns; notoriously, the directorate for competition policy (DG IV) has supported national regional aid policies according to a map of regions appreciably different to that employed by the directorate for regional policy (DG XVI) for support under the Community's

Correspondence Between Community Regions (NUTS Levels)
and National Administrative Divisions 1992

Member state	NUTS 1		NUTS 2		NUTS 3	
Belgium	Regions	3	Provinces	9	Arrondissements	43
Denmark[1]	–	1	Groups of Amter	3	Amter	15
Germany[2]	Länder	11	Regierungsbezirke[3]	31	Kreise	328
Greece	Groups of Development regions	4	Development regions	13	Nomoi	51
Spain	Agrupación de communidades autonomas	7	Comunidades autonomas and Melilla & Ceuta	18	Provincias	52
France	Zeat	8	Régions	22	Départements	96
	& DOM	1		4		4
Republic of Ireland	–	1	–	1	Planning regions	9
Italy	Gruppi di regioni	11	Regioni	20	Provincie	95
Luxembourg	–	1	–	1	–	1
Netherlands	Lansdelen	4	Provincie	12	COROP-Regios	40
Portugal	Continente & Regioes autonomas	3	Comissaoes de coordencao regional & Regioes autonomas	7	Grupos de concelhos	30
United Kingdom	Standard regions	11	Groups of counties[4]	35	Counties	65
European Community		66		176		829

1 A breakdown of Denmark into three regions is given in most of the tables and maps
2 Regions of the former GDR are not included (5 Lander, 15 Bezirke, 218 Kreise)
3 26 Regierungsbezirke and 5 Länder not subdivided into Regierungsbezirke
4 Grouping for Community purposes

Source: Commission of the European Communities/Eurostat

Figure 6.3. The EC's NUTS classification: correspondence between the Community's NUTS regions and national divisions of governance

Objective 1, 2 and 5b programmes. The discrepancies and the criteria for the regional maps have irked several member states; France has long and severely criticised the DG IV map for its insensitivity, and others have complained that NUTS 3 level regions are so big that region-wide data obscures severe local problems of industrial restructuring.

The pressures on EC pattern-making have been primarily from four directions. First, from previous regional systems designed by the EC including: the 66 regions at NUTS 1 level, 174 regions at NUTS 2 level and 829 regions at NUTS 3 level; the regions defined for Structural Funding; or the number of regions implied by a nation's allocation of seats on the EC Committee of Regions, to which the UK, France, Germany and Italy each contribute 24 of a total membership of 189.

Only Germany amongst EC nations has a system of elected sub-national government at the NUTS 1 level; Belgium, Spain, France and Italy have elected councils at NUTS 2 level. The highest level of elected UK council is at NUTS 3 level, where there are around 100 county, regional and metropolitan district councils. This gap encouraged the UK government in its eventually unsuccessful attempt to marginalise local government influence on the Committee of Regions by itself nominating the UK members.

Second, from the powerful forces asserting cultural and ethnic identity prevalent in many parts of Europe in the 1990s; these have been translated into regional governance in several countries, but others remain volatile while cultural identities are denied.

Third, from the inheritance of historic administrative arrangements still stamped on several EC countries; an indelible impression of Napoleonic administration remains in parts of Europe.

Fourth, from the forces of socio-economic dynamics often overrunning traditional regions, creating larger or even new regions; the spreading nature of UK metropolitan regions has been reflected in the way in which governments have progressively redefined the region centred on London. In 1939, the region included 7 million people. After 1945, this London region was combined with four adjoining counties into a London and South Eastern region of 11 million people, to which in 1974 were added two previously separate adjoining regions to form a single South East region incorporating thirteen counties and over 17 million people. These pressures press and pull against each other. The EC presses from above and inherited administrative systems press from below; cultural and socio-economic forces pull from the sides. The possibilities for resolving these pressures in a systematic way differ greatly in different countries. The incongruity of European regional boundaries will persist.

The Development of Community Policy

The Commission's work contains strong elements of coordination and policy integration. But however long discussed, regions have only become a dominant context for EC funding in the 1990s. Expenditure upon agriculture has dominated the Comunity's budget since the 1950s, and almost forty years later continued to crowd-out the full implementation of other areas of policy. Thus, while coordination and integration remain as good intentions, there have been serious doubts about the effectiveness of many policies in regional development.

Emerging in 1973, the Community's Regional Development Fund (ERDF) followed a declaration by the Heads of State that structural and regional imbalances must be modified or might otherwise affect economic and monetary union. While aimed at applying regional economic policy, the Fund had implications beyond the availability of a new category of financing. It led to studies of comparative economic and social conditions by which patterns of regions were drawn across the countries of the Community. This did not merely permit fair comparisons of need to be made, but also recognised regions or groupings of authorities and gave them a status which national governments sometimes resented.

Starting with the ERDF, regional dimensions in EC policy and funding grew slowly. Regulation (EEC) No. 1787/84 on the European Regional Development Fund stipulated that member states must submit a report on the implementation of regional development programmes every two and a half years. Coupled to this stipulation was a further increase in the proportion of funding to be applied to programmes rather than to projects. At the EC summit meeting in December 1990, the possibility was raised of a new European structure of regional government, and the possibility became stronger at the subsequent Maastricht meeting. German *Länder* already had the right of representation at the Council of Ministers where their interests were represented. Minority regions without such a basis saw a new structure as giving them representation on a new policy-making assembly, offsetting the dominance of capital cities inherent in central governments' participation in EC affairs.

The Maastricht Treaty of 1992 marked the consolidation of EC policy and funding around the regional level. It instituted the Committee of Regions as a participant in Community affairs, and it anticipated that from the late 1990s all EC funding would be based on regional bids and regional allocations. Single programming documents rather than sectoral bids would be expected. Most member countries of the Community already had some form of regional governance through which programme plans could be prepared, but the UK in particular lacked any adequate or experienced arrangements and responded by reorganising coordination of regional offices of government in England.

In the 1990s, a Cohesion Fund sympathising with the difficulty of poorer countries in keeping pace with the growth of richer members was added to the established Structural Funds comprising: the Regional Development Fund to reduce regional imbalances; the Social Fund to promote jobs in regions of persistent employment difficulty; and the Agricultural Guidance and Guarantee Fund to help rural and agricultural areas. In support, the European Investment Bank provides long-term loans for balancing developments, and the Coal and Steel

Community offers grants and loans to coal and steel regions suffering problems of adjustment.

Funding is shaped by the Community's objectives and categorisation of regions: Objective 1 regions are those 'lagging' on the European periphery, drawing the bulk of Regional Development funding; Objective 2 regions are those seriously hurt by industrial decline; Objective 3 and 4 regions relate to employment and training programmes under the Social Fund; and Objective 5 regions are those with rural and agricultural concerns.

So far as it has gone, the EC has still to fully superimpose a level of planning upon member states. The process of constructing supra-national strategic legislation has been difficult, depending on member states allowing the Community more autonomy than it yet possesses. But notwithstanding the difficulties, the Community has introduced the idea of a programmatic approach to regional development; environmental policy now has the potential to deal with pollution in a comprehensive manner, and the Social Fund has supported innovative strategies for training and reducing unemployment. Yet, within the Community there are many instances where policy has hurt local and regional areas, although set against negative effects are instances where Community support has stimulated comprehensive planning action, the Belfast Integrated Operation being an example.

Although in 1979 a 'European Indicative Planning Agency' was proposed to superimpose a European tier of regional planning on member states, requiring them to demonstrate a real capacity for strategic planning and implementation, it was only after a first meeting of Regional Policy and Planning Ministers in 1989 that the EC directly involved itself in what it termed 'spatial planning'. Previously, regional policy was matched to the expectation that Community members would bid for financial aid on the basis of regional plans and programmes. Some members, notably the UK, submitted regional plans of only a rudimentary and almost derisory character. Other countries had systems and areas of governance producing more considered and convincing regional plans.

Spatial planning in the Community's meaning combines strategic and regional planning (Martin 1992, 18), at levels above those of national responsibility for town and country planning. Town and country planning is regarded as not a Community interest, being defined as planning for individual towns or areas which are less than regions at EC scale (Davies 1993, 243). Although the Commission remains without any formal responsibility for spatial planning, it has been led to it by awareness of how widely and significantly European territory is being restructured by the forces of economic change and of an enlarging Community with an Open Market. Trade patterns are altering, capital is more mobile, industrial and business locations are shifting. The distribution of prosperity within Europe is altering, and many peripheral regions are more vulnerable than ever in the new economic geography. There are changes in the effectiveness of EC policies. And as national boundaries have less significance to investors, to economic forces and to would-be migrants in Europe, issues of strategic and regional planning increasingly escape the control of individual national governments.

Recognising member states' common interests in this new geography, the Commission turned to investigate its possible strategic and regional impacts. Studies in spatial planning joined others on inter-regional and inter-urban networks, cross-border cooperation and urban pilot projects. Initial studies in spatial planning were into European demographics up to the year 2015, urbanisation and the functions of cities in Europe, new industrial location factors and the spatial impact of the Channel Tunnel. The studies led to the Commission's (1991) appraisal of *Europe 2000*.

Europe 2000's overview of European demographic and urban trends looked forward to the completion of scenario studies for transregional development in Europe's Atlantic Regions, its Northern Seaboard, Central NW Europe, the Central Mediterranean, the Western Mediterranean, the Alpine and Peri-Alpine Region, and the Interior Regions of France and Spain.

Three additional studies of the impacts of change on countries to the south, east and north-east of the Community extended the framework within which governments could plan for individual regions. And to support regional planning in member countries, the Commission was to launch a Committee on Spatial Development to systematically exchange information. These initiatives were to lead to a follow-up to *Europe 2000*, filling out the framework for planning.

So strategic legislation for European regional planning exists in part, with good intentions abounding. But the Commission's aim to extend the content and scope of its economic, social, environmental and regional policies has been restrained by the limits to its budget, by the unwillingness of member states to agree on a common agenda for reform, and by the difficulty of agreeing difficult policy options.

Regionalism in the Community

Devolution and Regionalism in France, Netherlands, Spain, Italy and Germany

The twelve EC member countries of the early 1990s displayed a range of conditions in regionalism and devolution of governance. The UK has been at the extremity at which strong centralising trends in government have refused any devolution of power to regions. At the opposite extreme, Germany was joined in the 1980s by Spain, where substantial power including wide legislative discretion lies with regional assemblies. Belgium's cultural divide has been as sharp as any in Spain, accentuated by religious differences which have led to a state of near-federated regions. Most member countries have tended to develop towards the devolutionary extreme, although fairly slowly in Portugal and particularly so in Greece.

In this Europe of incongruous regions, five cases illustrate something of the variety of arrangements for governance. France, where after almost 200 years, Napoleonic regional administration was counter-balanced in 1986 by the introduction of elected regional councils; the Netherlands, where a highly structured system of national governance and planning was adapting in the 1990s to metropolitan reorganisation of local government for the Rijnmond; Spain, where much of the centralised authority of Madrid was devolved to the *juntas* for the autonomous regions formed by 1983; Italy, where elected regional authorities were established from 1970, being suffused in the bureaucratic and political corruption of Italian government to become marginal players in events; and Germany, where for over forty years the *Länder* have been as significant a level of regional governance as Europe has attempted, with a unique status in the Community.

FRANCE

Napoleonic administration and the prefectual experience of France is outstandingly important; it is a system which has survived for 200 years in important respects.

The 95 European *départements* established by Napoleon remain as branches of central administration, superimposed upon a local government of 325 *sub-départements* or *arrondissements*, 3075 *cantons* and 36,433 *communes*. Little change occurred when the conservative government of the 1970s encouraged the amalgamation of *communes* (Gilbert and Guengant 1989, 242), and significant devolution of government did not occur until the Mitterand presidency of the 1980s and the election of *conseils régionaux*.

The multiplicity of *communes* have cooperated in joint councils – or *syndicats* – for one or more services of mutual interest. There were over 13,000 *syndicats* in 1986, with their own taxation arrangements.

Between the *régional* and the *commune* levels, a number of metropolitan authorities – *communautés urbaines* – had been formed by the late 1960s. Those for the largest metropolitan areas of Bordeaux, Lille, Lyon and Strasbourg were mandatorily established in 1961, and those for Brest, Dunkirk, Le Creusot-Monceau-les-Mines, Cherbourg and Le Mans were subsequently set up by local choice. The functions transferred from the *communes* have been decided by local agreement, but are normally limited to planning and infrastructure, including housing, urban renewal, roads, recreation and the arts, schools and colleges. The Lille *Communauté* combines 87 communes with a population of over a million people; its joint initiatives have included a new town, an Olympic standard sports stadium and a museum of modern art. With the later formation of the *conseils régionaux*, it might have seemed that the strategic role of the *communautés* would be challenged. However, the view of some in the *conseils régionaux* is that the *communautés* have consolidated metropolitan interests in a helpful way, and better enabled negotiation over regional priorities.

Figure 6.4. The conseils régionaux *of France 1982*

Above the level of the Napoleonic or Jacobin local government, the rise of national economic planning and of regional voices led in 1959 to 21 *régions de programme* being recognised, working within the policy framework of the *Délégation à l'Aménagement du Territoire* (DATAR) established in 1963. The regions comprised from between two to eight *départements*, with populations ranging from under a million in Limousin to nine million in the Parisian region. A regional social and economic plan was to be compiled for each region by an interdepartmental committee of officials, chaired by the regional prefect in consultation with a 'regional expansion committee' of local representatives. In 1964, the arrangements were considerably refined. Regional prefects were appointed to prepare five-year economic development programmes, drafted by officials of *missions économiques régionaux*. Each *préfet* had the support of a parallel *conférence administrative régionale* and of a *commission de développement économique régionale*, which were echoed by the regional economic planning boards and councils introduced in England a year later.

For five of the regions in which *métropoles d'éqilibre* were clustered to counter-balance Paris's growth, special planning teams were formed in 1966. These *organismes d'aménagement d'aires métropolitaines* (OREAM) were responsible for plans for Lille-Dunkerque, Nantes-St. Nazaire, Nancy-Metz, Lyon-St. Étienne and Marseille-Aix. Action had been organised to coordinate growth and change in the French regions, to strengthen eight of their capitals, to give incentives for economic development, to invest in infrastructure and to build new towns (Palard 1993, 194).

After the government's approval in 1960 to a relatively short term plan for the next ten years of the Paris region's growth, a permanent planning body for the Paris region was set up in 1961 under its *Délégué-Général*, working with a consultative regional assembly and a representative board of local and central government to oversee a budget sufficient for a selection of regional projects. The newly approved plan was severely criticised for having unreal expectations of halving immigration and curbing the capital's growth, and for its weak regional dimension. Within four years, the *Délégué-Général* produced the *Schéma Directeur d'Aménagement et d'Urbanisme de la Région de Paris*. Despite the imminent fostering of *métropoles d'équilibre*, it was now accepted that Paris would remain an expanding capital, and the *Schéma* incorporated large new towns on axes tangential to Paris which continued as a basis for strategic metropolitan development for the next twenty-five years.

The emerging system of regional programming and planning was coordinated from the centre. The *Commissariat Général du Plan* had supreme responsibility for the national plan, assisted by the *Commission Nationale d'Aménagement du Territoire* which made longer term appraisals of population and economic change and of urban and regional strategy, and by DATAR which coordinated regional plans and had a significant budget for investment to support them. After 1967, the *Commission* was absorbed into the *Commissariat*.

The strategic policy of *métropoles d'équilibre* was unable to attract sufficient economic activity and investment to make them a serious counter-balance to Paris, at least in the conditions of the 1960s. Only later did improved transport and communications, and burgeoning telecommunication and computer links provide a convincing basis for the deconcentration and redistribution of French industry. The economic map of France was transformed, and the old distinction between centre and periphery disappeared (Claval 1990, 26).

Changing economic geography made the regional system outdated. Although providing a framework for national planning, the regions were less functional than merely convenient to long established administrative practice. They were control-led by the French administrative elite and not by locally elected politicians; and those regional politicians and industrial figures favouring a modernised and decentralised administration were at risk of being institutionalised into the regional economic and social development commissions, and thereby marginalised.

Only in 1972 were representatives of the *départements* and *communes* introduced to the regional processes, but they were nominated and not directly elected; the councils could spend nothing on their own initiative, but only support others' initiatives, and they could employ no staff directly. There were continuing demands that Paris devolve responsibilities, which led to the prefects who initially headed the councils being succeeded by regional politicians in the late 1970s. There were strong tensions within the councils between state and regional figures, and until the Mitterand presidency the government strongly constrained the councils. Even so, regions like the Nord-Pas de Calais dominated by socialist politicians used the councils as a new power base, turning to associate with regions in other countries whereby they could find a fraternal status which Paris would not permit them in France.

So, as new economic potential arose in cities such as Bordeaux, Nice, Toulouse and Grenoble, regions which in the 1960s had much depended on the redistribution of Parisian wealth were building their own resources. They were much less in need of central support and better able to manage their own affairs in their own contexts. Not just economic but also political relationships were altering. Conditions were now allowing for more regional autonomy and less central governance.

The arrival of the Mitterand presidency promised a rapid advance in authority for the regions. Although drawing back from the scale of devolution some had envisaged, the Decentralisation Act of 1982 built upon developments over the two prior decades. 21 regional councils were to be wholly elected, and were so by 1986. Elected presidents displaced the *préfets* as chief executives of the *département* councils, although the *préfets* retained many important powers as well as responsibility for coordinating state functions. After being briefly dropped, the title of *préfet* was restored to the state's principal administrator.

The reforms of 1982 considerably advanced decentralisation of responsibility from Paris to local government. *Conseils régionaux* were enabled to take responsibility for funding projects of direct regional interest, and for allocating the proportion of regional development aid previously distributed by the *préfet*. They could also take holdings in regional development and mixed economy companies. The municipalities and regions gained reinforced planning responsibilities. The need to help cities beyond Paris to contribute to national development was better recognised. This decentralisation went in hand with the disappearance of national planning of the 1960s style, and with a switch in government preoccupation from internal problems to concern about France's possible marginalisation in the new Europe (Motte 1991).

The greater empowerment of the provinces of France was dominated after 1985 by an emphasis on aggressive metropolitan planning strategy. Supported by a national strategy for communications, including the network for *trains à grande vitesse* (TGV), these metropolitan strategies were backed by new planning organisations for the metropolitan agglomerations. The metropolitan strategies were locally fostered, as for Lyon and Lille-Roubaix Tourcoing, but their context was the new Europe and the social and economic opportunities which could be seized by infrastructure programmes and far-sighted but flexible planning. And despite slower population and economic growth than expected in the original Paris master plan, adopted in 1976, the Director of the Greater Paris Regional Planning Institute was in 1990 able to regard the capital's growth as having been 'rather coherent and organised'.

A major new draft regional plan for the Paris region prepared for the Government in 1989 came from a part-private and part-public organisation, not one as fully under official control as was the team under Paul Delouvrier which had prepared the earlier *Schéma Directeur*. The draft plan was heavily criticised by most of the region's planning authorities, as was a later version published in 1992.

The disagreements over the Paris plan left the city's future role vague. Paris still remained the pre-eminent national focus for manufacturing industry in the 1990s. Past restraints on Parisian growth and policies for outlying regions had coincided with some weakening of France's centre–periphery polarity. The new distinction was between cities and regions highly accessible to the international circuit, and those which were not. Accessible regions adapted to changing economic conditions, while the others struggled (Claval 1990, 28).

The *conseils régionaux* and the French Government were very conscious of the new economic geography of the Europe of the Single Market. The concept of competitive metropolitan regions and of regional planning was a strong influence. And the scale of regions within the system given elected status only in 1986 was already in doubt. So a law of 1992 to foster inter-regional cooperation in planning reflected French acceptance of the significance of regional organisation and initiatives in national economic restructuring. Agendas of the Interministerial Committee for Structural and Regional Planning had already noted issues of further decentralisation of public services from Paris (Palard 1993, 193). Not only was state centralisation being cut, but the French government was encouraging the regions to strengthen by cooperating against their competitors in Europe.

Some of the regions were outstandingly open to the new planning opportunities. There was strong inclination to envision the future: 'The aim is to define the central issues, to propose alternative scenarios capable of dealing with them...; these strategies form the basis of negotiations on future state–region contractual planning' (Palard 1993, 196).

So, in 1992 the French government also assembled the *conseils régionaux* for a first, collective meeting to discuss regional priorities. The *présidents* of the *conseils* met with the *Commissariat du Plan* to announce their regional targets. But in the same year, the position of the *départements* was reinforced by new responsibilities and resources, and it was confirmed that cooperation rather than merger would be the means of covering the cracks in France's fragmented territorial governance (Marcou 1993, 55).

However, although freed from much central direction and with more discretion to spend on local priorities in recent years, local government's tax bases had been narrowed. Central taxes had been displacing local ones to a degree, as when Value Added Tax took over from local turnover tax in 1968. The proportion of local expenditure met by government grant had accordingly grown.

But moves to push responsibilities into the regions continued, and the government of the right replacing the socialists in 1993 had its own particular political interest in these. This was seen with the issue of a new plan to end the hiatus over a strategy for Paris which had existed from 1992 until 1994. Much of the draft of 1989 remained; consensus over the scale and the general location of growth continued between the *conseil régional* and the government's regional office, acting as the strategic planning authority because the *conseil régional* for the Paris region had not the status of those elsewhere in France.

Where the 1994 plan shifted the emphasis for the Paris region was in its relationship to the rest of France. The new government was seeking to show its loyalty to rural France where it aimed to consolidate its political support (Newman 1994, 167). So a new gesture was added to the those which had gone before, declaring anew the aim that the outlying regions of France should take a larger share of national growth in which Paris had dominated for so long. A motivation for so curbing Parisian growth was to gain votes for the rightist candidate at the 1995 presidential election, and the plan accordingly shaved proportions off the previously expected size of population of the capital region in 2015, off its share of places for students, and off its expected urban spread.

Cooperation amongst the *conseils régionaux* was now envisaged by the government as on the scale of seven super regions. Under the national economic development plan, each new region would house a particular state function under a national decentralisation programme. The north region would receive either the customs or the housing administration services; consumer affairs would go to Loire-Armorique; and the judiciary would go to the south-west. The new regions were certainly designed in the light of national politics as of the needs of inter-regional competition in the new Europe; lagging coastal districts with particular difficulties in economic restructuring were linked with more secure inland areas, reducing their statistical isolation.

France was therefore consolidating the role of its regions in the 1990s, but was doing this in a way confirming the instability of regional patterns and their underlying economic and political dynamics.

NETHERLANDS

As in other European countries inheriting the Napoleonic code, the subsequent history of governance in the Netherlands was much occupied with modifying the strongly centralised tradition. Dilution in the Netherlands began relatively early, in the mid nineteenth century, when the lowest level of the municipalities was reinforced in relation to the provinces from which the Dutch federation had been formed. Subsequently, there has been sustained support to a principle of uniformity between the now reduced number of 714 municipalities, while the 12 provinces have become progressively less relevant to some of the special issues of planning and governance for the most urbanised groups of municipalities.

The government's central authority is sustained so far as it appoints the chairs of the provincial and municipal councils, although in practice the municipalities are rarely interfered with (Norton 1983, 4). The provincial councils make regulatory ordinances, including some in physical planning, but within these ordinances the municipalities have substantial discretion.

The National Physical Planning Agency (*Rijksplanologische Dienst*) is matched by a National Physical Planning Advisory Council comprising representatives of many development and environmental interests. However, the only plans in the Netherlands which all are bound to observe are the zoning plans (*bestemmingsplans*) of the municipalities, albeit that they require provincial approval. The National Physical Planning Reports which began in 1960, and Structure Schemes and provincial Structure Plans, show the strategic intentions of each of these levels of government, but they do not tie the others except when supplemented by infrequent directives.

The First Physical Planning Report of 1960 described the principles of Dutch urbanisation policy and the Second of 1966 set out a strategy for action. Both were of the style of blueprint planning (Voogd 1982). The Third Report of 1973 concentrated on instruments to implement the principles and strategy, emphasising the process of planning rather than its physical targets. It has been argued that the attention to process was pretentious (ter Heide 1992, 141), but the Report incorporated financial incentives to help fulfil strategy and structural outlines and schemes were later elaborated and subsequently interpreted through regional plans. Reviewed every ten years, regional plans are not binding, but are a basis for negotiation on local detail and investment between various levels of governance.

Over the course of the first three Planning Reports, the definition of national planning problems changed. The original priority for new and expanded towns arose from the perceived saturation of the older towns by congestion of people and housing. Overspill was the thrust of strategy. Then, sprawling suburbanisation became a prime issue to be managed by focusing growth on selected centres outside the cities; this was the policy of 'concentrated deconcentration' to which the Third Report gave practical, financial support. But soon after, the philosophy of 'compact cities' came to dominate and to displace the emphasis on deconcentration. The major cities had lost more population than was necessary to create good environmental standards, and energy conservation had become a popular objective. Rotterdam and Amsterdam both adopted the compact city philosophy (Van der Heiden, Kok, Postumu and Wallagh 1992, 127).

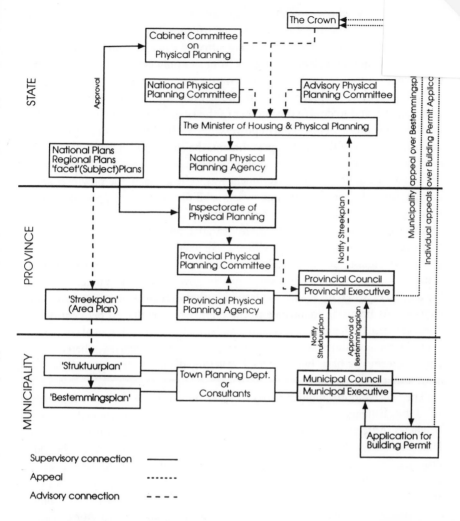

Source: Thomas D. *et al.* 1983, p.34

Based on W. Brussard 'The Rules of Physical Planning in the Netherlands'

Figure 6.5. The planning system of the Netherlands 1983

So, the Fourth National Physical Planning Report of 1988 and the Fourth Report Extra of 1990 brought new ideas about spatial planning (Altes 1992, 103). Economic and population growth were both declining fast. Centralised direction of strategy was argued to be no longer appropriate when local economic and social regeneration was the new priority, not nationally managed urban growth. Environmental issues and the position of the weaker of the Dutch regions were emphasised, particularly in the Extra Report which followed a leftward shift in the coalition government.

In a country whose respect for 'rule and order' is yet associated with such administrative irregularity, building a consensus has become an essential skill of Dutch governance and planning, widely admired even by Dutch academics (e.g. Van der Heiden *et al.* 1992). During the brief and only period of post-war Labour government in the 1970s, it brought forward a scheme for 44 city–regional public administrations to displace functions from both the municipal and provincial governments, and to double the number of the latter. The scheme would also have involved devolution of government powers, but it fell with the Labour government. Yet, after the fall of the Labour government, the succeeding Liberal governments felt it necessary to initiate improvements for regional cooperation. Although a third tier of administration below government was to be avoided, the provinces should assume some hitherto centralised responsibilities and be responsible also for assuring improved sub-regional cooperation.

Continuous attempts at Dutch administrative reform have had three principal characteristics (Blaas and Dostal 1989, 233): amalgamation of municipalities, by which the number of municipalities has reduced by almost a third since 1948; rearrangement of financial relations between government, the municipalities and the provinces, whereby against the trend in other European countries government increased its financial dominance to the point where under 10 per cent of local resources arise from municipal taxation; and initiatives in sub-regional cooperation between municipalities within or across provincial boundaries, whereby about 1500 agreements have been reached covering planning, transport, health and many other local services.

The procedure for municipalities to agree on specific initiatives was meant to avoid the challenge which multi-purpose regional organisations would pose to the provinces. Agreements to municipal cooperation have related to particular issues. They have tried to cover for the regional level of action missing in the Dutch structure, but consciously avoiding the addition of a further tier of general governance. The independence of these initiatives has been complicated by the extensive system of regional and sub-regional offices created by government, associated with its overwhelmimg role in financing municipal activities.

But the agreement procedure was not adequate for the Rijnmond, the Netherland's major metropolitan area. The Government established an elected Rijnmond council in 1964, linking Rotterdam with fifteen neighbouring municipalities. The council's principal concern was guidelines for physical planning, which the municipalities were obliged to follow except where they have successfully appealed to the province. The guidelines covered land use, housing, economic affairs, traffic and transport, the environment, recreation, disaster planning, education and waste disposal. But the council's only significant direct responsibility for implementation was to allocate government housing subsidy.

But the Rijnmond council failed to overcome its inherent restrictions. Although covering a metropolis with over a third of South Holland's population of 3 million, the council arrangements fell short of a smoothly articulated linkage of strategy and action. A level of planning had been interposed without the province and the municipalities correspondingly readjusting. The Rijnmond lacked control in port and economic affairs. It was squeezed between the province and the Rotterdam municipality, leading to questions as to whether the Rijnmond should become a full province in its own right, or whether the municipalities should yield some of their executive functions. Its anomalous administrative relationships helped lead to its dissolution in 1986.

In 1985, the Joint Regulations Act specified 62 regions in which inter-municipal cooperation was to be encouraged, but it left doubts about the match between these regions and some of the essentials of strategic planning. Only exceptionally were specified regions allowed to cooperate with others; Groningen, Utrecht, the Hague and other large municipalities were divorced from their functional hinterlands, and Amsterdam uniquely was excluded from the pattern of regions. Municipalities were also required to abandon old agreements for cooperation, although in places these had reached an effectiveness which the new regions could not quickly provide.

Giving provincial status to the Rijnmond would have increased the council's resources and reinforced its strategic role in Rotterdam's metropolitan region, but it would have done little to streamline implementation. It would have left the execution of policy to the municipalities, who have been erratic and insufficiently willing to make cooperative agreements. But the Dutch Government persisted in seeking to reform territorial governance to improve the quality of strategic management; the Government had advice (Netherlands Scientific Council for Government Policy 1990) that some form of metropolitan governance was necessary if Rotterdam and other cities were to hold their own in a Europe of dynamic, competitive city regions. The Government then put the problem to the seven metropolitan regions: what would they propose? (Van den Berg, Van Klink and Van der Meer 1993, 102)

The local authorities for Greater Rotterdam moved fastest on the Government's invitation. Rotterdam had already taken an initiative in partnership with neighbouring municipalities to produce a physio-economic strategic vision for the metropolitan region. And late in 1991 the partnership produced a scheme for a two-tier administration, which was approved both locally and in Parliament within three months. In the background was the threat that the Government would proceed with a scheme in the absence of local action.

The Rotterdam region was given provincial status in 1993, and in the mid 1990s a Greater Rotterdam regional government is being introduced. It will be directly elected and will replace the provincial administration and the Rotterdam municipality, absorbing existing regional transport and police authorities. It will manage the port and key areas like the city centre of Rotterdam, raising the lower tier of boroughs in the city to the status of the existing suburban municipalities. Some argue (Van den Berg *et al.* 1993, 114) that although the new body will have a more robust base than the failed Rijnmond approach, it will suffer by covering less than the true functional region.

Despite the frustrations of the Rijnmond experience, strategic planning in the Netherlands has been determined and sustained. It is argued to have been relatively successful (Faludi 1992, 90), reflecting consensual Dutch support for 'rule and order'. So – overlapping on the Rijnmond – the strategic concept of a 'Randstad' dominated for many years, whereby a 'Green Heart' has been enclosed by the four urban areas of The Hague, Amsterdam, Utrecht and Rotterdam. In 1991, the provinces of North Holland, South Holland and of Utrecht reached an agreement to coordinate what has been called the Greenheart Metropolis. Employing the project team previously engaged on an urbanisation strategy for the Randstad, the arrangements have been seen as not adequate by some in the Netherlands. The means of coordination lacks clout with government (Priemus 1994, 52), not least because as the Fourth Report on Physical Planning of 1988 had noted, the core of the Netherlands now spreads wider than the area of the Randstad and includes two-thirds of the Dutch population (Faludi 1994, 487). So the Randstad concept had been considerably superseded by economic change, and in 1992 the Minister for Physical Planning called for the Prime Minister to take overall responsibility for coordinating the future of the wider Randstad.

SPAIN

Spain sustained strong regional cultures around its periphery for centuries after the unification and domination of the country by Madrid and Castile. Suppressed during the Francoist regime, these regional identities were released by the administrative reforms after the ending of the Franco regime and the subsequent constitution of 1978.

Prior to 1978, a level of 50 provincial administrations and 7 islands councils was interposed between central government and Spain's several thousand munici-palities. On the French model, the provincial adsministrations acted as agents of the centre, although after 1925 they became more partners of local government than controllers of it. The multiplicity of municipalities are grossly uneven in size and resources, but before 1978 had similar responsibilities (Solé-Vilanova 1989, 209). The system was severely stressed, and its poor capacity to cope with major urban growth was compounded by the characteristic disinclination of Spanish municipalities to cooperate with their neighbours.

In few cases were voluntary joint boards established to overcome the historic fragmentation of municipalities. For Madrid and Barcelona, however, special measures were taken. The Madrid municipality did expand by incorporating a number of adjoining municipalities, but a metropolitan government was not created. Instead, government established the COPLACO agency in 1963 for the purpose of planning the larger conurbation of Madrid, retaining direct ministerial control over the capital's development. In Barcelona, however, a unique metropoli-tan multi-purpose authority was created, financed by the local governments and covering 27 municipalities and a population approaching two million, for whom planning, transport, parks, water and sewerage could be jointly managed at conurbation scale.

After Spain abandoned long-term macro-economic planning in 1973, it moved to produce statutory regional plans rather than the earlier, advisory and unsuccessful regional and provincial planning (Teixidor and Hebbert 1982, 26). But this still centralised planning was overtaken by regional reform. The 1978 constitution retained the two-tier local government of provinces and municipalities, but offered the possibility of regional government without specifying its nature or insisting upon it for all of Spain. Regions could claim autonomy at either a higher or a lower level of responsibility. It was expected that the regions with strongest identity and historic impetus to devolution – Catalonia, the Basque country and Galicia – would choose the higher level of devolved responsibility, but perhaps few others. It was expected that some parts of Spain would not seek to have a regional government.

The outcome of the constitution was that all parts of Spain chose to adopt regional government, either in combination with others or in some cases individu-

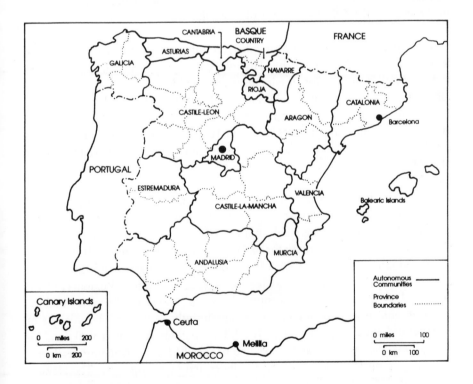

Figure 6.6. The autonomous regions of Spain 1983

ally. It was possible to directly absorb the old provinces into the new regional autonomies where only a single province was involved. Only the two Spanish towns on the Moroccan coast remain beyond the 17 regional autonomous governments established between 1979 and 1983. Seven of the autonomies have the higher level of responsibility, and ten the lower. The differences of responsibility are substantially in regard to education and health.

Each regional *junta* has legislative authority, equal to that of the government in principle but not to override it in basic areas including education, health, law and order and matters of general national concern. The *juntas* have the capacity to reform local government, which they resource in conjunction with central government. The provinces remain where regions have combined two or more of them; Andalucia, for example, covers nine provinces and 764 municipalities, of which the largest is Seville with a population of 650,000, but 645 have fewer than 50,000. The Catalonian *junta* particularly sought to minimise the role of its provinces; it was not prepared to continue the Barcelona multi-purpose metropolitan authority, and it substituted for that a metropolitan district for transport and a larger district for water and refuse disposal. To the contrary, the *junta* for the Valencia region has established a multi-purpose county for metropolitan Valencia. In the capital, the COPLACO arm of government has been superseded by the Madrid *junta*.

Education and health remain provided through government except in the seven regions with higher responsibility. Highways, transport, housing, social services and financial incentives for development are provided primarily by central and regional governments, but also by provincial and municipal authorities. Sports, cultural and community facilities are provided by all three levels below central government, while municipalities have main responsibility for planning and urban development, parks, sanitation and water. Ambiguity in the Local Government Act of 1985 has left overlap between the roles of the municipalities and the provinces and regions.

There has been a very real shift of governance from the centre to local government, and particularly to the autonomous regions. Between 1982 and 1986, one in five civil servants were cut from central government, more than balanced by the increase in staff working for the regional *juntas* (Hebbert 1990, 124).

But administration is not the whole power of governance, and the Spanish government has remained the overwhelming agency for taxation. Regional or local taxation depends on government approval. Taxing powers are the same in fifteen of the seventeen autonomies, but differ significantly in the troubled regions of Navarre and the Basque country. The fifteen regions receive central funding through tax-sharing grant and the ceding of specified taxes including death and gift duties, property transfer tax, stamp duties and gambling taxes. The Navarre and Basque regions also receive ceded taxes, but their basic income deriving from personal income tax, corporation tax and value added tax is contracted rather than shared. The regions with higher responsibilities receive appropriately higher allocations. *Juntas* may surcharge on ceded taxes as well as on personal income tax. This government-based income has been supplemented by provincial funding in six regions. Opportunity to add additional revenue from sources untapped by government has been taken in only a few regions; regional taxes have been variously put on betting, oil and land.

As in other nation states of Europe, the modern tide of Spanish regionalism swelled from historic ethnic, political and cultural divisions of the country. And as in other European countries, the Spanish regions have been constituted in a period when the national government has been looking to consolidate its place in the European Community.

So the regional *juntas* have not broken the power of Madrid. The effect of Spanish entry to the EC has been centralising (Hebbert 1987, 248), and central government has continued its important role of redistributing resources to the regions not enjoying such rapid economic expansion as Madrid and Catalonia. Madrid has coupled economic strength to cultural dynamism, becoming for the first time in Spanish history the true national metropolis (Hebbert 1990, 137).

The municipalities, however, continue to suffer for their traditional dependence upon local resources, and marked disparities in the quality of basic services persist through insufficient equalisation. The other outstanding issue is that of Spain's lesser metropolitan areas, which except in the case of Valencia nowhere receive a sharply focused administrative emphasis. Metropolitan structures may even divide a region's strength. Seeking to rise above its autonomous region, Barcelona established its plan for the year 2000 in the context of a region which it claimed to stretch to Toulouse, Montpellier, Saragossa, Valencia and Mallorca, embracing not just parts of several other Spanish regions but also of France as well.

ITALY

Italy's governance has paralleled Spain's insofar as local administration has been seen as a defence against the return of fascism (Norton 1983, 43). Regionalism advanced only erratically, being mistrusted by Christian Democrat governments which feared that it would sap their power. However, it was impossible to delay decentralisation to the fiercely independent peripheral regions of Sicily, Sardinia, Val d'Aosta, Trentino-Alto Adige and Friuli-Venezia Giulia, which were successively recognised by statute as 'special' regions after World War II. Elsewhere in Italy, government ministries held their power tightly to themselves. In the south, the *Cassa per il Mezzogiorno* was a pioneering example of a regional infrastructural agency, with extensive powers to develop and help finance agriculture, irrigation and industrial development.

As had already happened in France and as was occurring in the UK at the same time, regional economic planning committees were set up under the Ministry of Labour in 1964–65 to support the National Economic Plan. Plans had been produced for all but one of the regions by 1970, when a full system of 'ordinary' regions was instituted for the Italian mainland, completing the regional tier of governance begun in the 'special regions'.

Elections in 1970 in all of the twenty Italian regions established legislative assemblies with authority in regional planning, agriculture, forestry, small industry, health, transport, tourism and schools. But there was an erratic decentralisation of central authority, only reluctantly leaked from Rome. Government departments were slow to cooperate, holding power to themselves or dissembling through the creation of subsidiary agencies. Regions remained heavily dependent upon central government funding. They were fragmented by political connections between selected ministries and councillors. The ineffectiveness of the provinces and the weight of problems in the communes led to congested regional governance, unable or unwilling to sufficiently devolve wholly devolvable functions. Corruption heavily stained the scene.

Figure 6.7. The regions of Italy 1970

It was inevitable that the work of the regional assemblies would add to bureacratic complexity, because they added a tier to Italian governance. So although substantial devolution of decision-making was reinforced by improvements in 1975–77 (Arcangeli 1982, 59), more streamlining or efficiency was not always achieved. The regions were closer to local pressures and were obliged to take more time to consider them. And a crisis in national economic planning hampered the development of local initiatives to succeed the earlier model of large-scale regional projects, epitomised by the discredited *Cassa per il Mezzogiorno* (King 1987, 341).

The impediments to more effective regional planning did not lie wholly within the regional tier; a parliamentary commission of 1980 blamed the government for failing to set proper goals for regional planning, for not reforming the organisation or financing of local authorities and other public bodies, for persisting in sectoral planning by ministries without regional coordination, and for inadequate resourcing for regional development planning (Arcangeli 1982, 65).

But the possibility of major overhaul of Italian governance from the top in Rome to the bottom in the communes was drowned by the persistent crises of Italian politics. The crises burst wide open during 1993. The corruption which was exposed embraced the highest in politics, some of the highest in industry and finance and, allegedly, the highest in crime and in the Mafia. Behind the moral crisis grew a crisis of the regions, particularly where the Lega Nord rose from its base in Lombardian populism to become the leading party of the whole of the prosperous north of Italy. The Lega's leader, Umberto Bossi, sought to reassemble the 20 Italian regions into only three, detaching the North from the Centre and the South. Each of the new regions would raise its own taxes and pay Rome for very much reduced central services; freed of the cost of supporting the slower-growing regions, the north would enjoy an even faster rise in prosperity.

The powerful pressures for decentralisation of government and the reduction of central power and corruption pointed to the likelihood of a major reformation of Italian governance in the 1990s. The solution of the Lega Nord would amount to devolution and near federalism. The issue is not of what levels of sub-national governance will operate, but is of who controls them. In the 1970s and 1980s, the regions and provinces were relatively weak levels, squeezed between the dominant central administration in Rome and the traditional base of local government in the communes.

The system of governance has been overloaded with bureaucracy and corruption. Between the regions and the municipalities, the persistence of a provincial level of administration casts a long shadow of the Napoleonic system. This is as far as Roman bureaucracy has been decentralised, which has combined with local political interests to make the provinces a notable force for interference, if not for action. Each of the levels of municipal, provincial and regional government has an executive board, nominated by the elected councils. In the provinces, a centrally appointed prefect matches the president of the elected provincial council. As metropolitan problems have accumulated across Italy, the significance of the provinces has been threatened by the rise of metropolitan administrations. Initially voluntary and frequently ineffective, the rise of metropolitan government has been staccato. Metropolitan land use plans – *piani intercomunali* – were prepared in some areas, but there was no larger administrative reorganisation. The government prepared legislation in 1982 which defined metropolitan areas as those of over a million population, with a central municipality of at least 400,000. Metropolitan provinces would be set up to embrace all municipalities in their areas, adopting the powers of a province and also the planning and general development interest of the municipalities. But party political considerations prevented the bill's passage.

It was only in 1990 that legislation for metropolitan reform was finally enacted (Mazza 1991, 143). It was much in the mould of the ideas of 1982. Together with a strengthening of the provinces, new metropolitan provinces were to be established for Turin, Milan, Venice, Genoa, Bologna, Florence, Rome, Bari and Naples, all within boundaries to be drawn in 1991 by the regional governments. The act did not specify whether the outer edge of the new provinces would lie just beyond metropolitan urban perimeters, or reach into their regional hinterlands. This would be left to the politics of the regional governments.

With all the delay and impediments to consolidation of regional and metropolitan government, it promised to change the face of Italian governance. The *Cassa per il Mezzogiorno* was terminated in 1991, its agency functions being fully displaced by elected administrations in the south of Italy. But as these moves to greater regional and metropolitan rationality were being made, Italian political affairs were being more and more exposed as almost terminally corrupt. And this seriously threatened the already unsure prospect of central government's attempts to establish a national urban strategy. In 1992, the Ministero dell Ambiente (1992) had published an official ten-year Plan for the Environment (DECAMB), based upon the preceding Quadroter project sponsored by the national research institute in association with the Ministry.

The Quadroter studies had shown that while artificial statistical boundaries suggested that the population of some metropolitan areas was declining, this was certainly less true of metropolitan economic attractions (Archibugi 1986). The data suggested that congestion and declining environmental standards were likely to intensify in the overloaded urban areas of Milan, Turin, Bologna, Genoa, Florence, Rome, Naples, Bari, Palermo and Catania. Declining medium-sized urban areas were being overshadowed by the burgeoning metropolises, and cities of historic and cultural interest needed to have action to stem migration.

So, a national strategy was postulated to reorganise the metropolitan areas by deconcentrating their cores, to foster a new system of 80 intermediate cities of much enhanced economic and social attraction to lessen migration and metropolitan pressures, and to create a framework for policy and investment to support the rehabilitation of Italy's historic and cultural heritage lying in its small, depopulated towns. Although there was an echo in the strategy of the style of classificatory geographical method which, in some countries in the 1950s and 1960s, had substituted for a dynamic understanding of underlying urban forces, yet the Quadroter project was in effect just the frontispiece to many necessary subsequent volumes of regional and metropolitan plans.

So Quadroter was only a beginning, and an ambitious one. But however uncertain the future of such a national strategy prior to 1993, the political turmoil of that year put it in greater doubt. It was, nonetheless, an appraisal of a kind which few other European countries had attempted in such a style. Its ambition and sweep was more typical of strategic planning for a third world country than for a European nation.

GERMANY

Germany's administrative structure has been exceptionally decentralised. The contemporary system is underlain by the Basic Law of West Germany of 1949, establishing strong *Länder* governments to counter Federal power, limiting central government's capacity to restore the totalitarianism of the Nazi era (Bahrenberg 1989, 255).

The *Länder* are interposed between the federal government and the counties (*Kreise*) and communes (*Gemeinden*), both regulated by the independent *Länder* legislatures whose law-making powers lie largely in local government, education, police and the media. After 1949, the autonomy of the *Länder* was trimmed but their influence upon federal affairs has concurrently increased. Widening social and economic inter-connections between regions of West Germany has led to developing cooperation between the *Länder*, particularly in education and in economic and rural development, in which the government has participated jointly with the *Länder*.

The federal government has also legislated to establish a federal framework for regional planning (*Raumordnung*), but prime responsibility for regional planning is assigned to the *Länder*, and may be divided between the administrative regions (*Regierungsbezirke*) within the larger *Länder*.

Communities may band together into counties when they are too small to separately exercise functions, and some of the largest cities function as city-counties with all of a county's powers. Between 1967 and 1980, the number of communities was reduced by amalgamation by two-thirds, the number of counties by almost a half, and the number of city-counties by over a third. Against a background of relatively weak government, the complexity of local decision-taking had led many to argue that there was need to strengthen central government. This contrasted with the more common argument in other European countries that more decentralisation was required.

The *Länder* and local governments are financed by taxes under a federally controlled sharing scheme incorporating grant adjustments, and by charges for services. 70 per cent of *Länder* income arises from taxes, and the balance from grants, charges and other sources; local government draws only 40 per cent of income from taxes. Bahrenberg (1989, 265) regards the financial problems and

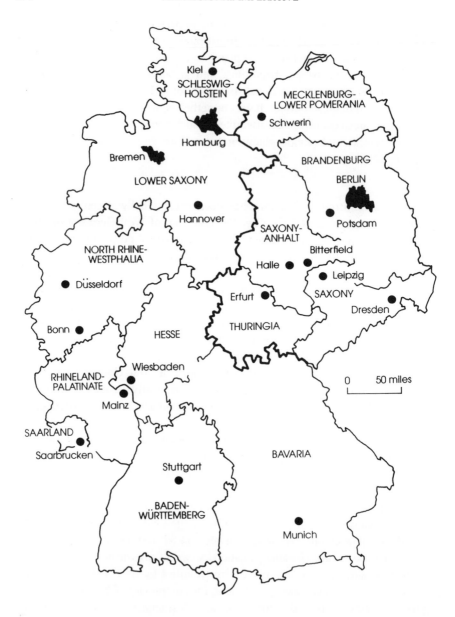

Figure 6.8. The German Länder *1990*

dependency of local government as the acute difficulty of West German governance. The business tax which is the main local tax is volatile because business
conditions are so, particularly in the older industrial areas. The *Länder* have
generally a more resilient financial base, although it partly rests upon local
government revenues. Nonetheless, there are disparities between the *Länder*,

although they have opposed suggestions by Federal ministers that some of the smaller might be amalgamated into a more equally-sized system.

Regional planning in Germany has a relatively long history. The *Zweckverband Gross-Berlin* was a Common Purpose Planning Authority for Greater Berlin established in 1910 in a metropolitan region of 3.5 million; in 1920, Old Berlin was merged with 93 suburbs to form Greater Berlin, by area then the second largest city in the world. The *Siedlungsverband Ruhrkohlenbezirk* (SVR), however, has greater distinction as the first significant regional planning agency in the world of the modern period. Founded in 1920, the SVR had powers for regional development, including cooperation in preparation of town plans, transportation planning and financial support for local projects. In a region of 10 million people, the SVR was appreciably successful in transportation planning, in recovering degraded environments in the Ruhr and in its recreational strategy. It has experienced several major transformations in its long history. In the 1970s, when economic and political circumstances had much changed from its earlier years, its relationship to the *Länder* and to the city authorities of the region became too unstable, and it was replaced in 1975 by the *Kommunalverband Ruhr*, a cooperative organisation active in landscape improvement, but whose role in planning was much less than that of the SVR.

Following the 1965 Federal Act for Physical Planning, *Länder* were required to allow regional planning associations to be formed where considered necessary. The population of the areas of associations varied up to several millions. Only three associations were formed under the Act to cover the whole of North Rhine-Westphalia, but sixteen associations were created in Baden-Württemberg.

Elsewhere, metropolitan planning advanced. Hannover established a metropolitan organisation composed of representatives of the local authorities, exercising a strategic role through its financing of public transport. In Frankfurt, a metropolitan Union established by the Hessen *Land* incorporates two cities and three counties with a combined population of over 1 million. The Union's principal function is physical planning, supported by joint projects for recreation, waste disposal, water supply and economic promotion. The councillors of the Union are directly elected, presenting a structure plan for the approval of an upper Chamber of Municipalities, comprising representatives of the 43 communities in the Union. To be prepared within the context of a regional plan – formally a *Länder* responsibility – the structure plan has brought equivocation over the degree to which the Union might participate also in the regional plan. Too much leadership by the Union might have too much established its authority, and threatened the municipalities.

Although regional planning is the responsibility of *Länder*, it is the responsibility of the Federal Minister of Planning, Housing and Urban Planning to regularly revise the framework Federal Regional Planning Report, which is done customarily every four years. Responsibility for regional economic policy is shared between the *Länder* and the Federal government. However, the Federal Report merely outlines spatial trends and problems in development and influences rather than dictates planning policy within the *Länder*.

From 1972, the Federal government supported regional projects in the *Länder* by equally shared financing in accord with agreed priorities for regional economic restructuring (Waniek, 1993, 468). But an attempt in 1975 to establish a federal spatial development programme (*Bundesraumordnungsprogramm*) was rebuffed, when Baden-Württemberg and Bavaria were particularly unwilling to sink their interests for wider benefit, while other federal ministries were also unwilling to suffer coordination by their planning colleagues. Remaining federal intervention in *Länder* planning goes only so far as a regular report to the Federal Parliament on spatial development trends in Germany.

Constructive regional planning in Germany accordingly originates substantially at the level of the *Länder*, or at that of their decentralised administrative *Regierungsbezirke*. But in several *Länder* the arrangements give groupings of local authorities a significant influence, where regional planning is not merely a subsidiary part of *Länder* planning. Customarily presented at a scale of 1:50,000, regional plans are of a detail greater than has been common in British practice; they may look 15 years ahead. The experience, suggests Kunzmann (1990, 48), reflects political weakness at the federal level, incomplete marriage of physical and economic planning, and a lack of cooperation between major competitive urban areas. Nonetheless, Kunzmann argues that regional planning in Germany has been successful, despite the emphasis having been on communication of information rather than of policies. He points to the evidence of little scattered development by comparison with other countries, a well functioning hierarchy of urban settlements associated with policies explicitly based on central place theory, and to lesser disparities in urban and social conditions than in other densely populated European regions.

Regional plans in Germany have progressively changed their nature, as Fürst (undated) notes. Their style has shifted from one profoundly influenced by Christaller and the German school of central place theorists from the 1930s up to the 1960s, when the geometry of the geographical theorists was proving an unsuccessful basis for development policy. For a decade thereafter, the inter-regional equalisation of infrastructure became the focus, and plans took on the shape of comprehensive action programmes. But in the 1970s it ceased to be possible to expect resources to be available on demand, and regional planners were forced to retreat from investment planning by ministries jealous of their sectoral interests. In the 1980s, the green movement strongly coloured regional planning, and ecological protection rose as a major regional issue (Fürst, undated).

The fragility of cooperative arrangements for planning for metropolitan regions in Germany is unsurprising where, as Norton (1983, 24) emphasises, five main levels of government already jostle each other. A sixth and voluntary level is a cuckoo in an already crowded nest. The experience of the SVR is a prime example, pioneering in the world but at last subverted by the inherent instability pervading regional arrangements.

Looking to the 1990s and unification in Germany and also in the European market, some (Ache and Kunzmann 1991) have seen the possibility of a fresh attempt to coordinate planning in the *Länder* from the new federal capital of Berlin. Economic and social disparities between the regions of West Germany have been overwhelmed by those between them and East Germany. The implications for migration, for transport and for urban growth are so considerable and so rapid that regional planning is not only urgent in the federal interest, but may be acceptable to some of the previously reluctant *Länder*.

Nord-Pas de Calais

The region of the Nord-Pas de Calais has outstandingly characterised the developing scope of regional planning and governance in France. Dominated by politicians from the left, with more political affinity to regions in countries such as Italy and to the French Walloons of neighbouring Belgium than to D'Estaing's Parisian government of the right, the Nord-Pas de Calais aggressively sought to raise its economic and political status from the the mid 1970s. Looking to its future in a Greater Europe for both economic and political reasons, the region was developing Pan-European associations strongly prior to the French regional decentralisation of 1982.

The circumstances in which the French *conseils régionaux* were empowered in 1982 were different to those in which the English metropolitan and Scottish regional councils had been established several years before. After two centuries of centralised administration in France, there were fewer territorial interests on which the new *conseils régionaux* might tread. The new *conseils* could seek opportunities to introduce a regional dimension in the face of the highly centralised, conservative and sectorised Parisian administration. Of course, the *conseils* met difficulties with Parisian administrators reluctant to act as flexibly as the new circumstances demanded, and the *départements* were similarly suspicious of the threat to their traditional power.

Although responsibilities cascaded to the *conseils* after 1982, there were not resources to match. The *conseils* were not providers of comprehensive services as were those in Scotland. Finance could be contributed only at the margins of regional priorities, but nonetheless the *conseils* had real ability to 'lever' support for regional objectives. In the Nord-Pas de Calais, senior regional planners regarded the development of more coherent public transport as one of their major strategic contributions. Derelict land comprising about 1 per cent of the region's surface area and environmental improvement became priorities which the communes had never tried or been able to tackle. And the emphasis on leisure and cultural facilities – such as the Lille Orchestra – were priorities which Paris would not have independently emphasised so much.

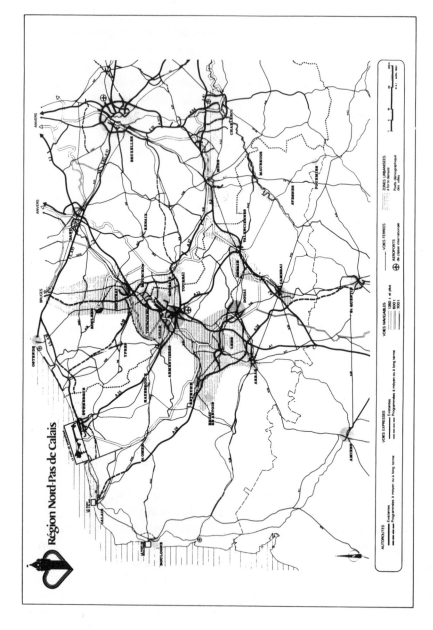

Figure 6.9. Région Nord-Pas de Calais 1982

In 1992, the *Établissement Public Foncier Nord-Pas de Calais* was created as an agency for land recovery and environmental improvement financed directly by the government. As a unique agency in France, the independent *Établissement* was probably less a failure to strengthen the direct responsibilities of the *Conseil Régional*, than a means of specially favouring the region and of ensuring that the minister would earn credit for this. It was also a French example of the pronounced British tendency for government to place its own agencies in the regional scene.

The *Communauté Urbaine de Lille* was formed in 1966, but despite its 3000 employees, an innovative tax-redistribution scheme and the merit claimed for it in consolidating otherwise fragmented metropolitan interests, it has lacked ambition (Van den Berg *et al.* 1993, 66) for most of its life. It was insufficient for longer term planning, and nor did the *Conseil Régional* provide a planning framework in sufficient detail. So, as for other French metropolitan areas, the *Agence de Développement et d'Urbanisme de la Métropole Lilloise* was established in 1990, coordinating physical planning for Lille, Roubaix, Tourcoing and the new town of Villeneuve d'Ascq by a metropolitan structure plan. The objectives of the agency particularly recognised the area's relationships with London and Brussels, and the need to progressively reinforce its metropolitan character.

With a staff of only 20, the *Lilloise* agency's board was nominated by the *communes* and chaired by Pierre Mauroy, original *Président* of the first *Conseil Régional* and subsequently Prime Minister of France before returning to regional politics, where from 1989 he took over leadership of the *Communauté Urbaine de Lille.*

The growing battery of regional organisations includes two industrial promotion agencies, together with a regional development agency. Promotion is pursued by the Lille Metropolitan Area Economic Promotion Agency (APIM) on behalf of the Lille Urban Community (CUDL), and in the remainder of the region by *Nord-Pas de Calais Développement* for the *Conseil Régional* and in association with DATAR. Established by the *Conseil Régional* in 1982, the Regional Development Agency (ARD) advises on regional economic policy and the *Plan Régional*, and in liaison with the Regional Business Creation Task Force (*Mission Régionale pour la Création d'Entreprises*), it advises budding entrepreneurs.

The earliest trans-national links of the Nord-Pas de Calais were consolidated in RETI (*Régions Européennes de Tradition Industrielle*), a grouping of Europe's old regions of coal and heavy industry created in 1984. But seven years later, the region's view of itself was recast by the Channel Tunnel, the TGV and progressive modernisation of its regional industrial base. Through an agreement in 1991, the Nord-Pas de Calais joined in a self-styled Euroregion with Kent from England, and with Wallonia, Flanders and the Brussels capital region – comprising the whole of Belgium. With a combined population of 15 million people, the Euroregion envisaged programmes of cooperation in economic and technological development, land use and transport planning, the environment, and promotion and exchanges; the real substance of this Euroregion remained to be proven. The dissolution of internal borders in the European market in 1993 would end many centuries of the Nord-Pas de Calais as a border region; in the later 1990s, new alliances would have to be struck outside the borders of the unified European market.

The Ruhr

Established in 1920 and being replaced only in 1975, the *Siedlungsverband Ruhrkohlenbezirk* (SVR) has been the longest-lived regional planning organisation of significance in modern experience, in any country. The local authorities of the Ruhr ceded their powers for regional development to the SVR, notably over cooperation in preparing town plans, transportation planning and financial support for local projects. When the decline of the coal and steel industries left comprehensive pollution, dereliction and damaged environment, the SVR planned the regeneration of the region's landscape by networks of recreation areas and parklands.

The origin of the SVR lay in the Great War. There had been ideas of regional planning previously, but it came because of the peace settlement imposed on Germany by the Allied Powers and the tribute of coal demanded by them. Coal production from the Ruhr had to be vastly increased, and 150,000 miners migrated to the pits. The task of planning was beyond any one local authority, and the SVR was founded in 1920 to tackle the problems of new settlements, traffic and road planning, and protecting open spaces.

The SVR was to this extent imposed on the Ruhr. But it was simultaneously a potential threat to its instigators – Germany's occupying powers. An elected authority raised the threat of a 'Red Ruhr'. So the SVR was representative, but unelected. Its interests were divided. Its representation was fractured between areas of industry and of rural communes, and between industrialists and workers. Like the Ruhr itself, the SVR was never a firm entity.

. But uneasily as it sat beside the fragmented politics and local governments of the Ruhr, and resented as it was by the two Prussian provinces on which it encroached, the SVR survived. It outlasted the Third Reich and change amongst wider political forces.

After the evacuation of the occupying forces and sweeping away of the Weimar republic, the SVR was continued by the new Nazi administration. The representative parliament was swept away, and a leader imposed so that ideas of planning and of new procedures could be transferred from the SVR to apply elsewhere in Germany. The SVR was also a means of indirect control of affairs in the Ruhr, where possible opposition to Hitler might emerge.

The role of the SVR as a tool of outside interests continued after 1945, when to remove taint of Nazism the British re-established a parliament comprised only of commune representatives under the direction of Philip Rapaport. Again a means of post-war reconstruction, the SVR was expected to develop growing signifi-

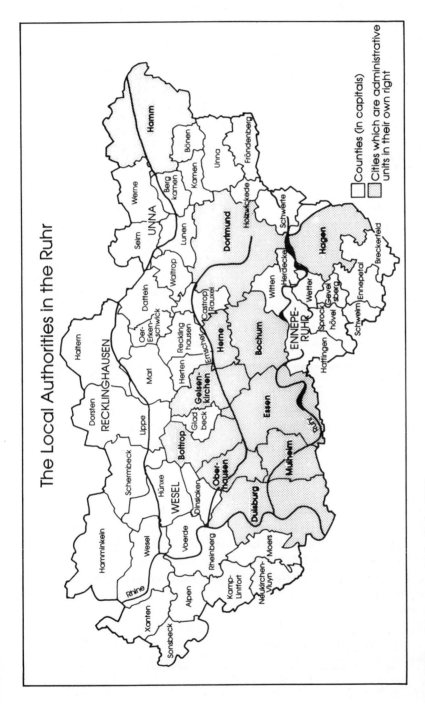

The Local Authorities in the Ruhr

Counties (in capitals)

Cities which are administrative units in their own right

Figure 6.10. Local government in the Ruhr 1990

cance. But it was not until 1958 that a more fully representative parliament was established.

At its peak of influence before threats to its future heightened in the early 1970s, the SVR was funded for 80 per cent of its ordinary budget from local government, and only 10 per cent from the *Länder*, 10 per cent of its funding came from the Federal government or from its own sources. 60 per cent of the assembly's members represented local authorities, and 40 per cent were co-opted from lists compiled by chambers of commerce, trade unions and other groups. The responsibilities of the SVR were for establishing policies and statutes, drawing up regional physical and general development plans, and for establishing a regional budget. It administered all matters promoting settlement activity, including green belts, regional traffic networks, collaborative physical plans, recreation and intermunicipal refuse disposal.

In a region whose population had grown to five anda half million people, the SVR had had a very appreciable impact on the Ruhr's development and transformation over its life of more than 50 years. It was successful in most of its purposes, but its authority was curbed with the connivance of the local authorities for whom it was created. It held together for a long time, despite constant internal tensons between industry and the communes, and between big and small towns. Its longevity was aided by extraordinary external political circumstances, which had also created it. As the oldest of European regional organisations, it eventually met redundancy.

By the 1970s, economic and political circumstances had much changed since the earlier years of the SVR. Established under Prussian Law, it had passed through the Third Reich and the massive economic and political developments of post-war Germany. But its relationship to the *Länder* and to the city authorities of the region had become unstable. Three principal explanations of its demise have been asserted.

First, perhaps most prominent of the pressures on the SVR was that from the *Land* government of North Rhine Westphalia, which chose in the mid 1970s to devolve more executive authority to the level of its *Regierungsbezirke*. Rather than establish the Ruhr as a region of the *Land*, under an administrative head whose status might vie with that of the *Land* itself, the Ruhr was divided between the three *Regierungsbezirke* of Düsseldorf, Münster and Arnsberg.

Second, some of the principal cities of the Ruhr had an equivocal relationship with the SVR, like parents jealous of their child's growing status and independence.

Third, the economy of the Ruhr had changed in 50 years; its common interests were no longer dominated by coal and steel, and its population was now declining as employment progressively fell from a peak in 1961.

So the pressures of changing political contexts led to the SVR's planning powers being cut in 1975 and transferred to the *Land's Regierungsbezirke* of

Düsseldorf, Münster and Arnsberg. In 1979, the title SVR was supplanted by that of the KVR (*Kommunalverband Ruhr*).

The KVR remained a consortium of 53 local authorities of the Ruhr, but was deprived of the role in regional planning which its predecessor had played for such an exceptional time. The KVR was expected to provide services to support the municipalities, but not to lead them in planning. It lost its role in planning transportation, but kept its work of mending the old despoiled landscape of heavy industry and coal mining. Its main duties were now to help promote the Ruhr's reputation as a 'new' economy, to support creation of new recreation facilities, to help manage the problem of waste disposal through a very profitable public company, to foster a green belt, to manage the woodlands of which it was the largest owner in Germany, and to undertake planning work under commission from the local governments and in conjunction with open space conservation on urban outskirts. Regional initiatives by the KVR remained important, although implementation was primarily in local authority hands. And whereas the SVR had had considerable authority, the KVR had now to arrange a consensus around its programmes.

Like the SVR before it, the KVR was not initially much concerned with recycling land for industrial and commercial development (Kunzmann 1990, 27). But in 1980 the *Land* government established a Ruhr Real Estate Fund to buy, rehabilitate and resell land for industry, business, housing and recreation. In response, the KVR presented a strategy in 1985 to protect the Ruhr's green areas and to encourage the re-use of unproductive land and buildings. And the wheel of politics was now turning again, so that the reviving significance of the KVR gained new impetus.

As its tertiary economy advanced in the 1990s, some argued that the Ruhr was becoming no more integrated and had indeed always been less of a region than outsiders thought. It had six distinct labour markets (Klemmer 1988, 514). Düsseldorf remained outside it and was still resented by many inside the Ruhr. But because of political change in Europe, the regional imperative was reasserting itself in the Ruhr in a fascinating way. European Community policy was strengthening the emphasis on regions in Europe, and it begged the question of what was the Ruhr's region.

There were different answers to this question from different interests. The *Land* government of North Rhine-Westphalia had chosen to segment the Ruhr between three administrative divisions – dividing and ruling it in the eyes of staff of the SVR and KVR. The privileged position which a *Land* government enjoys in EC affairs would be diminished if the Ruhr rose in status in the Community. On the other hand, staff of the KVR had always taken the view that although administratively fragmented, the Ruhr remained tightly integrated in its social and many of its economic linkages. It was in staff's interest to accentuate the integrity of the Ruhr and to potentially gain greater EC recognition.

Between these two views of the Ruhr, the local authority membership of the KVR was pulled in two directions. The larger authorities had reduced the SVR in 1975 so as to gain greater independence. But in the 1990s, most preferred that the EC should recognise them rather than the *Land* government as the agents for regional planning for the Ruhr. So, only 15 years after having reduced the SVR, local politicians of the Ruhr became willing to increase their commitment to the KVR. The Ruhr authorities could use their collaboration in the KVR to claim themselves as the true region, stealing status and influence from the *Land* government. And there was a new incentive for the *Land* government to by-pass the KVR.

The struggle over the region's future was being fought by the Ruhr authorities on a double strategy: by a growing budget for the KVR to promote economic potential in the Ruhr, including a large emphasis on its cultural development and its new social face; and by moves to create a regional economic development agency working closely with the cities of the Ruhr, complementary to the broader role of the Economic Development Corporation of the *Land* government, which has shifted its emphasis from selecting and promoting industrial sites to direct initiatives to stimulate industry and business, and to back them with advisory and support services.

The contest for regional supremacy in the Ruhr between the *Land* government and the KVR authorities has particularly surrounded economic development. In the early 1990s, the *Land* government's ZIN (*Zukunftsinitiative für die Regionen Nordrhein-Westfalens*) initiative instituted new linkages with chambers of commerce in North Rhine-Westphalia, under the level of the *Regierungsbezirke* which represented the *Land* government. Chambers and local interests were invited to bid for funding for local economic projects within five fields of *Land* policy. By 1992, projects had been agreed in fifteen regions, such as an initiative in metal-coating technology in Siegenland involving the local university. This approach shifted the emphasis from *Land* programmes to projects initiated within regions. But whereas North Rhine-Westphalia had long been divided into five administrative regions, the *Land* government's new policy created a more fragmented pattern of fifteen smaller regions for economic development.

While some saw the ZIN initiative as an attempt to decentralise previously over-centralised economic development policy, it could also be seen as a possible ploy to reinforce the authority of the *Regierungsbezirke* and of the *Land* government. And although the fifteen ZIN regions fitted both to *Regierungsbezirke* and chamber of commerce boundaries, they were criticised as being more for administrative convenience than to match real local economic linkages (Waniek 1993, 472). Equally, the regions might have been seen as conveniently cutting across natural political linkages between local authorities.

So, while some interests in the Ruhr wished to see North Rhine-Westphalia losing status as the map of European regions was redefined by the EC, the *Land* government was trying to reinforce itself by intensifying its patronage over an underlying pattern of regions. And six of these regions covered the Ruhr, which the *Land* had previously cut only three ways! The *Land* government of North Rhine-Westphalia certainly wished to exorcise both the name and old, damaging reputation of the Ruhr, and some argue that the parts of the Ruhr should seek separate economic futures and not a collective one. Nonetheless, local authorities have ensured that a body for economic promotion of the whole Ruhr continues, linked to the KVR by having the same president.

Andalucia

The major of Spain's problem regions, Andalucia has a population of close to 7 million divided between 8 provinces and 764 municipalities. To develop a role in the region, the regional planners of the *Junta* have had to struggle to establish a place for themselves in a fragmented and evolving administrative system.

Figure 6.11. The Andalucian autonomous region 1983

The regional planning division of the *Junta's* Department of Public Works and Transport has been squeezed from three directions. First by central ministries with their only loosely coordinated programmes for regional infrastructure, second by the established provinces and municipalities, and third from within the *Junta* itself.

Lack of coordination amongst ministries was an early problem for the Andalucian *Junta*, as for others in Spain. The ministries remained largely autonomous in their infrastructural competences, although opportunities for coordination improved as some boards were established and as a government commission was created for the major Spanish cities, including Malaga, Seville and Cadiz. Through initiatives such as a survey and strategy for the Bay of Cadiz, the *Junta* attempted to influence ministry priorities and programmes where it had no authority to intervene. And it was able to make agreements over local projects to jointly invest with the municipalities, and with government ministries.

Structure planning for the cities and other municipalities remained a municipal responsibility. Only for the Donana National Park had the Government prepared a PDTC framework plan, but the model was considered to be too inflexible for the *Junta* to adopt as it looked to planning issues in the major urban areas. So, as they looked towards legislation to create a system of appropriate plans, the regional planners sought a lighter framework than that of the national PDTCs, with less detail and financial commitment.

Prior to obtaining legislation and to drawing up sub-regional and other plans, the regional planners were able only to ride on the backs of others. An early move to create an Andalucian Solidarity Fund by which the regional planners could participate in and influence the *Junta*'s programmes failed. So although part of its largest department with around 50 per cent of the *Junta*'s budget, the regional planning division has had no direct financial power.

Nor have the regional planners been secure within the *Junta*. Facing the greater strength and disputing priorities with the economists of the *Junta*, the division was for a period demoted to the status of a research group. The planners' priorities for help to declining inland areas of rural poverty were at odds with the economic advisers' priorities for investment in coastal areas of tourist and industrial potential. Restored to executive status, the regional planners remained short of effective tools until the *Junta* could adopt a regional framework plan. In 1992, the division was preparing legislation for the *Junta* to adopt to allow:

1.   A regional framework plan

2.   Integrated plans for local areas

3.   Topic plans

4.   Observance by other departments of the *Junta* and of the government

Passage of the legislation would leave the regional planners still considerably dependent on persuasion to achieve their wishes and plans, at least with government departments. In disputes on the plans, the backing of the national constitutional tribunal would be required to ensure that plan proposals were mandatory.

Plans would be prepared by a variety of arrangements. Some would be commissioned from consultants. Plans would be managed by local groups of authorities, except where the *Junta* declared a special metropolitan area, as in Granada or Malaga. By 1992, only for the sub-region of Seville had a *Junta* plan been established, which was mandatory on lower authorities but not on government ministries. But special metropolitan arrangements were delayed for Seville, impeded by the political tension between the nationalist city council and the socialist *Junta*.

So, regional planning in Andalucia had to fight to create a role and a political base, both on behalf of the regional *Junta* and inside it. The experience has been characteristic of new regional administrative systems in many countries.

Europe Beyond the Community

Switzerland

Perhaps more than any other European country, Switzerland is a national region whose topography has helped maintain sufficient national identity despite the ethnic differences between its 26 cantons. Formalised national strategic concepts for Swiss development are a special case of regional planning within a Europe of regions. The Federal Spatial Planning Report of 1987 was followed in 1989 by a start to prepare guidelines for national spatial development (Ringli 1991), whose dominant policies are to focus urban and business growth within existing towns and cities, and to foster public transport for environmental reasons. Marking Switzerland's position as a region at the centre but not of the European Community, the guidelines aim to control the environmental damage of commercial and industrial traffic crossing between community member states. The guidelines also recognise that European economic growth is fastest in the major urbanised regions, and they aim to strengthen the functional links between Swiss cities to create a joint urban force which none are large enough to achieve alone.

Developments in Eastern Europe Prior to 1989

Prior to 1989, sub-national administrative reforms in eastern Europe had a territorial rationality which was much less the case in western Europe. Eastern Europe worked upon post-1945 structures based on the Soviet pattern of regional, district and commune levels. The reforms sought some degree of mass participation and equity as Bennett (1989, 39) suggests, but they too rigidly bound the economy and society and thereby veered to inefficiency.

Not of the Soviet Bloc, Yugoslavia was a special case until 1989, diluting a centralised hiearchical autocracy at a much earlier stage. Even so, the regional basis for economic reforms established in the Bloc countries was echoed in a regional dimension to centralised Yugoslav administration. Whereas other eastern European countries formalised the regional dimension for both economic and administrative purposes, Yugoslavia observed it in a shadowy way by eliminating it in the republics but reproducing it in government in Belgrade.

A characteristic of east European administrative reforms from the late 1950s onwards was the tendency to squeeze or eliminate district government, at the level between the equivalent of the county scale in England and Wales and the lowest level of town councils or rural communes. Elimination occurred in Bulgaria, Hungary, Poland, Romania and Yugoslavia.

The general tendency of thirty years of reforms up to the political transformations of 1989 was for diminution of local autonomy in rural areas of eastern Europe
in particular. The towns took on administrative responsibilities for rural areas,
together with a focal role in economic development. The implications for rural
villages included neglect in programmes for housing and the improvement of
services, leading to social decay. Such tendencies have also existed in many rural
areas of western Europe, of course, even without administrative reform and the
economic policies pursued by east European countries between 1960 and the late
1980s.

BULGARIA

Fifteen regions and a larger number of districts were established in Bulgaria in
1949, but both levels were replaced in 1959 by a pattern of 27 administrative
departments together with an administration for Sofia. Simultaneously, the number
of local communes was halved, and in 1979 they were cut again by three-quarters.
Ostensibly, the purpose was to reinforce national policy of balanced regional
development by strengthening towns in the backward regions. However, in 1987
a further reform grouped the departments into nine administrative regions coinciding with the country's economic regions.

The 1987 initiative displaced the departments which primarily represented
state administration, and it implicitly recognised a devolution of administrative
responsibility to the basic level of town councils. The administrative regions also
became ostensibly autonomous, although together with their assigned administrative powers they were expected to coordinate municipal development in line with
the state's regional policy.

The regions were to play a two-way role between Sofia and the municipalities.
They were to participate in drafting guidelines for national development, and to
interpret it in regional strategies for social and physical development. They would
organise and coordinate action amongst the municipalities.

CZECHOSLOVAKIA

The more limited reform of Czechoslovak territorial administration prior to the
1980s has been attributed to the dispersion and fragmented pattern of rural
settlements in the country. This explanation is not wholly convincing when a
comparison is made with experience in other eastern European countries. However,
Czechoslovakia certainly made only small steps towards administrative amalgamation of small communities when other countries reformed much more substantially.

Substantial reform began in 1983, and four years later the rural communes had
been shrunk by amalgamation to one-tenth of their previous number. Simultaneously, a system of citizen's neighbourhood committees was created. Amongst the
towns and cities, growth and the varying intensity of problems produced a five-part
categorisation of administrative committees, reflecting status. The reforms did not

comprehensively link larger towns to their hinterlands, and despite their aim of devolving powers and integrating responsibilities to urban committees they left centrally directed enterprises working alongside the committees in an uneasy relationship.

With the flowering of the new democracy after the second 'Prague Spring' in 1989, Czechoslavakia's two federal parts eased themselves from the constraints of central control. The breaking of the ice let the floes separate. Slovakian nationalism sought extensive devolution of federal responsibilities to the Slovak parliament, with separate management of railways, postal services, fuel pipelines and the media, and a separate branch of the central bank. The Czech parliament was opposed to extensive devolution, its interests being dominant in the federal parliament whose authority the Slovaks wished to narrow. But on 1 January, 1993, the federation divided into separate Czech and Slovak republics.

EAST GERMANY

East Germany retained a system of 15 administrative and economic regions from 1952, ranging from a half to two million in population. This tier was strictly administrative and lay over a pattern of some 200 urban and rural districts.

Territorial administration of government educational and welfare services stood alongside sectoral organisation of the economy, and alongside less centralised but still sectorally organised national services including construction, post and telecommunications, water and transport. The territorially administered services were responsible to the local government councils at that level, as well as to their parent ministry. Such an arrangement of dual loyalty would tend to be fraught with tensions in western Europe. Prior to 1989, at least, it offered East Germany the opportunity to harmonise locally assessed needs with nationally determined objectives and programmes.

Both regions and districts had planning commissions to integrate economic and infrastructural development, aiming to harmonise both horizontally and vertically according to targets set by the next higher authority. As a design, the system was perhaps the most streamlined of the eastern bloc. It might seem an ideal form to anyone unfamiliar with the human inefficiencies which corrupt perfect administration. In the context of the country's political history, it was certainly incapable of achieving a perfect quality of creative interaction between levels of administration.

In October 1990, German unification was immediately succeeded by elections in the five *Länder* restored to bring the East into line with governance in its Western partner.

HUNGARY

The largely inherited territorial boundaries for administration established in Hungary in 1950 were found to be too numerous for the government's purposes, and subsequent reforms led to a reduction or grouping of local councils in predominantly rural areas. As this lowest level of governance was raised and the distance between it and the top level of 20 regions was narrowed, the intervening level of district administration was progressively squeezed until abolished in 1984. In the course, a network of larger towns became centres of administrative responsibility for sub-regional clusters of local councils.

During the mid 1960s, progressive moves to economic reform included some freeing of local government from direct restraints by government ministries. Rather than being a direct disaggregation of sectoral ministry plans, local development became regulated but not directed by ministries. There was delay, however, in reforming administration to match the philosophy of greater local discretion. Regional self-development was not achieved, and up to the late 1980s the 19 regional councils continued to act as agents of central government with limited scope to exercise real regional initiative. They lacked influence not only upon economic enterprises in the regions, but also upon centralised planning from Budapest. The consequences included a sustained lag in infrastructural investment. The regions also had become ill-fitting to the pattern of functional areas developed in the country since 1945.

While government in Budapest remained decisive in planning for settlements, liberalisation and economic crises after 1986 made it necessary for local councils to themselves raise finance to support local development. In the circumstances of the time, however, this has not benefited their practical ambitions. They have remained dependent upon central government for half their income, and a further 30 per cent or so derives from profits and taxes from local firms and organisations.

POLAND

Major administrative reforms occurred in Poland in the 1970s. In 1973, district administration was abolished when the lower commune level was made more significant, and the controlling role of people's councils was also separated from the executive role of a state official appointed by the regional administration. In 1975, further reform established a two-tier administration of regional and local levels, aimed at consolidating economic regions organised around urban centres.

By 1983, local people's councils became of such significance that they were given responsibilities for planning, managing and coordinating local economic and social affairs. So far as they were able to raise resources, they were able to act without their regional authority's intervention. The scope for local revenue raising was very limited, however.

In 1988, the role of the people's councils was further strengthened relative to the state administration. At the level of the 49 regions, budgets to which central government contributed 80 per cent of revenues in the early 1980s drew under 40 per cent from this source in the late 1980s. By this time, the centre was negotiating with the regions to transfer control of further enterprises from which – if profitable – regional revenues could be expanded. Potentially, this decentralisation obviously raised the authority of the regions and made them dominant in territorial governance.

ROMANIA

A sustained sequence of reorganisations of territorial administration took place in Romania in the 1950s. The motivations were political rather than to refine any policies of regional development. Policies of that kind did arise in the 1960s, however, coupled to embryonic economic reforms. They reached as far as the creation of state enterprises which reduced the dominance of the sectoral ministries, and of a larger scale of administration at the commmune level.

Romania streamlined its administration in 1968 to eliminate one of the three territorial levels, leaving 39 departments and the city of Bucharest together with a system of communes. Again ostensibly to reduce imbalances in regional development, the reform strengthened the scope for the highly centralised, personal and corrupt autocracy of the closing years of the Ceaucescu regime. Settlements were classified for development or neglect within a strategy which echoed practice in some rural counties of England or, notoriously, in the declining pit districts of Durham. Medium-sized towns which could be most economically served with infrastructure were the basis for the national strategy for the regions. The strategy became discredited outside Romania when it appeared to be coupled to a policy of persecution of peasants of Hungarian connection.

SOVIET UNION

Each republic of the Soviet Union had discretion to establish its own structure of governance, including any autonomous or other regions within the republic. In 1987, 7 of the 15 republics had no regions, but there were altogether 174 administrations immediately below the republic level ranked as autonomous republics, autonomous regions, autonomous areas, territories or – most numerously – regions. Two further tiers of more local administration fell below this first, sub-republic, level.

Fitting irregularly with this administrative structure with its confusing terminology, the Union's planning was organised into 19 economic regions. In each region there were networks of territorial production complexes. Complexes differed in kind: they may have combined production plants from several economic sectors with comprehensive social and political linkages, or were systems of settlements for economic and environmental development. Complexes had their own administrators, inevitably causing tensions with the larger and longer established structure.

Regional organisation of economic enterprises was regarded by some as relatively effective in countering insensitive sectoral management in the republics. Since 1977, the republics had had responsibility for comprehensive economic, social and physical planning. The previous separation between territorial planning and sectoral economic management was overcome, and an integrated rationality

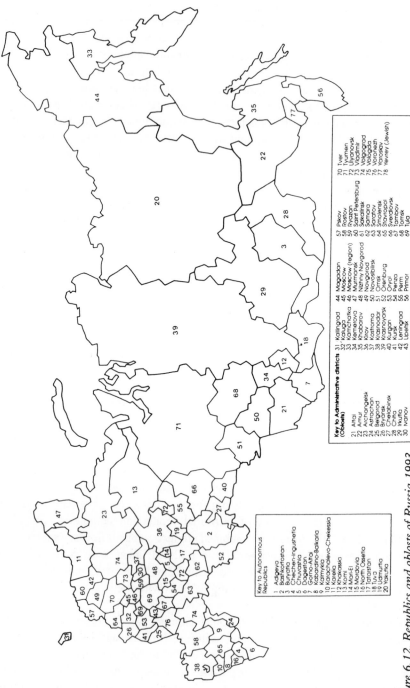

Figure 6.12. Republics and oblosts of Russia 1993

became possible. There was substantial devolution of economic, social and budgetary planning, and a progressive increase in the raising of local revenues. It became
a duty of ministries and of institutions to consult regional and local administrations
over industrial plans. Local soviets took responsibility for exploiting and conserv-
ing resources of land, water and forests, and for wildlife, air and environmental
protection.

Regional policy remained a strong feature of the Union. Exploiting the Asiatic
republics was coupled to a policy of income redistribution, dominated by the
demands of high demographic growth in republics with continuing large dependence on central funding. The social fund contributed up to 40 per cent of central
funding for some republics.

YUGOSLAVIA

Administrative reform in Yugoslavia was sustained from the 1950s, fuelled by the
country's suppressed ethnic and regional tensions. Regional structures were
contained within each of the six republics and two autonomous provinces created
in 1949, but were abolished in 1952 when decentralised communal self-government was instituted at local, settlement level. But when subsequently fostering this
decentralised self-government, central government replaced sectoral by regional
administration of its functions. And in the mid 1960s, a form of regional planning
appeared as in Hungary and Romania and, indeed, as in Britain at the same time.
The Yugoslavian government thereby retained its role in affairs in the republics,
by which it was more strongly challenged than in any other country of eastern
Europe.

But Yugoslavia was to fragment more violently than was any other country of
eastern Europe. Having for centuries been captured, colonised and divided into
regions of successive European empires, Slovenia's independence as a nation state
of Europe came in 1991. Death and destruction fell on other ethnic regions of the
Yugoslavian state formed by the Allied powers after 1918, as the centralised
Serbian-dominated government fought to hold control and to consolidate Serbian
territory.

Eastern Europe Since 1989

The crumbling of totalitarian governments already under way in Hungary and
Poland became a comprehensive collapse in the autumn of 1989. The demand for
popular representation and local community control ran alongside urgency for
economic reform, which required centralised action. The coincidence of these two
apparently contradictory processes of decentralisation and of centralisation (Welch
1993, 72) left a vacuum between them. Some form of regional governance was
inevitably necessary to fill the vacuum in most countries, but it lay between the
levels of immediate priority for action.

But as ethnic divisions led to bloody struggles, particularly in the former
Yugoslavia and Soviet Union, and as Czechoslovakia too divided into new

republics, the resilience of regional cultures emerged. National boundaries formed after 1919, either by revolution in the Soviet Union or by the Allied powers in the Slav countries, had been often clumsily imposed upon a disordered patchwork of fragmented ethnic territories.

So the regional issue inevitably resurfaced in the post-1989 eastern European countries, not only by ethnic resurgence, but also by the imperative of bridging between central and local governments, and by awareness of their potential in fostering economic development.

In the often violent regional fragmentation of the Soviet Union into the Confederation of Independent States in the 1990s, 21 former autonomous republics became independent between Eastern Europe and Far Eastern Asia.

A regional approach to self-government developed by a variety of mechanisms in the CIS, the former Soviet Union. The approach was unsteady, because of the differing degrees of sovereignty and independence of the 14 new republics (Ushkalov 1993, 300). A level of regional self-government was added in the Ukraine. The new Russia was divided into 78 regions, of which 20 were autonomous republics and 58 had the lesser status of administrative districts; for the first time a special role was defined for regional soviets, separate from local government and with elected heads.

The Russian regional soviets were regarded as of equal status to central state organisations, being given authority to enter into agreements with other Russian regions and republics, and being able to to deal with questions of administrative and territorial structure within their regions (Lysenko 1993, 286).

In Poland, the district level of local government abolished in 1973 is being restored as a level of local government between the local communities and the counties (*voivodies*). But the first step was to establish almost 2400 municipal councils through local elections, after which debate argued whether the country's 49 provinces should be displaced by at least 8 regions. General opinion favoured 12–14 regions (Regulski 1993, 206).

In Hungary, an act of 1991 rationalised the previous local government system by affirming 7 prefectual regions, each containing either two or three counties of diminished status. The prefects supervised the host of local governments, leaving at issue the question of if and when their function as state officials would be displaced by the succession of elected regional governments.

In Czechoslovakia, the system of local and regional governments prior to 1989 emulated that of the Soviet Union. After 1989, the 10 regional committees were abolished, with consequent severe difficulties when the previous trend of a reducing number of communes was succeeded by a trend of their proliferation! Calls came for regions or up to five republics to bridge the governance gap, but the division of the country into separate Czech and Slovak republics in 1993 took precedence over sub-national reform.

Conclusion: Continuing Turmoil in the Europe of Regions

Eastern Europe's turmoil of regionalism released in the early 1990s overtook regional change at a lower key running through Belgium, France and Spain during the previous decade. But turmoil rather than evolution was being threatened by Italy's political crisis, with the unity of the nation threatened by a strong regional political movement.

The continued force of the EC's drive to a Europe of the Regions has at the same time been challenged by the member states asserting the authority of the Council of Ministers against the Commission.

Regions and regional planning will remain central issues in the EC's future and of Europe's political development. Regionalism has been a widespread and persistent tendency. Its motivations have combined differently at different times in different European countries. The consequence has often been unstable regional governance, but the tendency promises to recur and to reshape continuously a Europe of Unfinished Regions.

CHAPTER SEVEN

United States, But Enduring Regionalism

Preface: More Loose Than Tight

The US has led Europe in important aspects of regional planning and governance. But there have been many contexts for regional planning in the US, and many varieties and different roles for it. And regional governance has been a recurrent feature in national politics and in relations between federal, state and local governments.

Two notable but contrasting experiences of regional planning have been for the fast expanding metropolitan regions of Minneapolis-St. Paul and of the San Francisco Bay Area. The Twin Cities Metropolitan Council for Minneapolis-St. Paul has been almost unique, incorporating as systematic and formal an approach to continuous and effective regional planning as has developed in the US. The Bay Area of San Francisco reflects all the fragmentation and vested interests characteristic of US metropolitan regions, but has developed a sustained structure of organisations for regional planning and management, backed by unusually committed and effective voluntary campaigning interests in regional planning.

The Twin Cities and the Bay Area are not extreme and opposite cases in all respects, but they highlight the impediments to fully effective regional planning in most of the US, illustrating its wide range from tightness to looseness.

The Enduring Regional Dimension

Regional planning and regional initiatives in the US in the modern mould preceded the First World War, whereas in Europe they generally followed it. Classic steps like the Tennessee Valley Authority, the New York Port Authority or metropolitan regional transportation planning in the 1960s, were strong influences on European practice. Regional planning and regional governance have repeatedly reasserted themselves. But their guises and motivations have differed at different times.

What was commonly represented as regional planning in the US up to the 1970s, has since as frequently gone under the title of growth management. And the instigation for collective regional governance has sometimes been from the federal government, sometimes from local governments, recently from state governments, and since the nineteenth century rise of the modern industrial economy also commonly from private sector interests in industry and commerce.

Twentieth century economic and urban growth in the US has occurred without the local administrative reform which has been infrequent in most European countries, but which has been often extensive when it has come. In the US, however, states' rights and the historic privilege of local determination have frozen sub-national governance into a mould cast in the eighteenth century.

These circumstances have ensured the persistence of regional issues in the US. Population shifts, economic restructuring and exploding urbanisation have brought dramatic changes in the nation's economic and social geography since the potential of regional planning and analysis was advocated by Mackaye (1962) in the 1930s, or later by Friedmann and Alonso (1964). Re-emerging as 'growth management' in the 1990s, after a decade of retreat, regional planning remained alive although requiring nurture.

Regionalism has been a prominent feature in the political economy of the US, and has been a significant historical force in US politics. Of contemporary studies, the concise quality of Ann Markusen's (1987) account of the political economy of regionalism in the United States could not be bettered. Her interpretation of the interlinkages of regional culture and of regional economics is exceptional, but in such a sweeping study she could only touch on the dimensions of regional planning and of regional governance.

Regionalism in a Federacy

Marble-Cake Federacy and the Origins of Regional Planning

US government is founded on the separation of functions and of powers: presidents and mayors propose, while the congresses and councils dispose. But the tiers of federal, state and local government responsibility intermingle, characterised by Grodzins (1978, 265) in the image of a rainbow or marble cake, with 'an inseparable mingling of differently colored ingredients, the colors appearing in vertical and diagonal strands and unexpected whirls.'

The vivid image of the marble cake also matches the way in which US regional planning has developed. Friedmann (1956) describes the concept of the region as a planning tool as having originated in the Great Depression, but it had rooted much earlier. Its first widespread flowering did come in the 1930s, however, since when five types have been seen in theory and practice (Hufschmidt, 1969): that focused on metropolitan areas as earliest on Chicago and New York; that aiming to manage natural resources, as through the TVA or Columbia Basin projects, or by thirteen reports by the National Resources Planning Board between 1936 and 1943 for regions including New England, Alaska, the valley of the Arkansas river and metropolitan St. Louis; that embracing cultural regions, shaped by physical geography and social history as was the Old South; that undertaken through mathematical modelling, by the regional scientists led by Walter Isaard; and that of the development economists of various shades, to whom John Friedmann built a bridge for planners.

But by describing only the focus of regional plans, Hufschmidt neglected the way in which regional planning initiatives are born of political dynamics, and almost as often die by them. So, the histories of regional planning and of regional organisations in the US do not fit tidily into Hufschmidt's typology. They have to be intertwined and seen in the light of progressive economic, social and political change.

As early as 1790, special districts were being established in the Philadelphia area to administer prisons, schools, public health and the port. Metropolitan boards were created around New York for police in 1857, and for health in 1866. Massachusetts had district commissions for sewerage, parks and water by the 1890s (Jackson 1985, 153). First amongst regional organisations of the twentieth century was the Boston Metropolitan Improvement Planning Commission of 1902 (Advisory Commission on Intergovernmental Relations 1973, 53), following upon a Boston Regional Park Commission of nine years before. The Improvement Planning Commission had comprehensive regional planning responsibilities, and it anticipated by a few years the more celebrated and notably effective *Plan of Chicago*.

Sponsored privately by the Commercial Club of Chicago and driven by the force of a self-made tycoon, Richard Dyer Norton, the *Plan of Chicago* prepared by Daniel Burnham between 1907 and 1909 arose – like the work in Boston – from city boosterism and voluntarist enthusiasm for city improvement and more beautiful environments of the early twentieth century. The 'city beautiful' movement was not all it might seem at first sight, and has been associated by some (Rondinelli 1975, 24) with progressive reformers opposed to the political machines of the big cities. The reformers sought to separate planning from the corruption and interests of city government. So began a tradition of planning commissions within but not wholly controlled by local government.

Burnham's *Plan for Chicago* encompassed 4000 square miles and parts of three states. It proposed a network of regional roads and railways, a regional park system extended to 60,000 acres, and a grand design for Chicago's shore on Lake Michigan incorporating parks, public facilities and Lakeshore Drive. Within less than 20 years, the City of Chicago had invested around 300 million in developing the *Plan* (Friedmann and Weaver 1979, 52). But the *Plan* had no social concern. It was for Chicago's greater growth, not for the issues of slum housing and inner city congestion observed by Park, Burgess and the Chicago school of urban geographers.

As a motivating force for regional planning, the city beautiful movement marched alongside the movement of corporate interests. America's industrial corporations were consolidating and nationalising their consumer markets and production systems, but were often impeded by the fragmentation of local governments in the swelling metropolitan areas. Better roads, water supply and industrial infrastructures were required to minimise the costs of production and distribution of the burgeoning corporations, who early and eagerly fostered regional planning and governance (O'Connor 1973). Regional or metropolitan bodies often were formed to provide public utilities for major industrial concentrations (Boyer 1986, 180). The Lucas County Planning Commission in Ohio coordinated parks and highways, and in ·the same state in 1915 the Miami Conservancy District was organised for flood control. In California, the East Bay Municipal Utility District of 1921 provided public services for Oakland's metropolitan region; 70 years later, the Bay Area Council was pursuing the cause of regional planning for the still expanding metropolis on behalf of a wholly private consortium of national and international companies in banking, the oil industry, gas and electricity supply, management consultancy and electronics.

Through the 1920s, regional planning commissions spread across the United States (Scott 1971). In 1923, the Boston Metropolitan Planning Commission was re-formed to advise on transport and public utilities for the metropolitan area, and the Los Angeles County Regional Planning Commission was created to advise on highways, water conservation, sanitation, zoning and parks. In New York State, five regional groups were established in the form of the Niagara Frontier Planning Board, the Onandaga County Regional Planning Board, the Capitol District Regional Planning Association and the celebrated *Regional Plan of New York and its Environs*.

The origins of the *Regional Plan of New York* lay fully in private concerns, mingling the streams of corporate and civic interest rising earlier in other American metropolitan areas. The opening of the Panama Canal in 1914 greatly increased demands on the port of New York (Boyer 1986, 182), leading to the creation in 1921 of the deceptively titled Port of New York Authority, whose responsibility to plan for the port's physical development would later spread into many aspects of metropolitan development.

The strategic context would take several years to emerge, and it would be privately sponsored by the Russell Sage Foundation – 'patrician progressives' as Simpson (1985) called them. Helping crystallise this private initiative was Richard Dyer Norton, so satisfied with the dramatic regional perspective of Burnham's Chicago plan that, on moving to New York, he worked to instigate a comparable study. A committee spurred by Norton was formed in 1922, and late in 1923 the Scotsman, Thomas Adams, already deeply active in planning affairs in the United States, was appointed as General Director of Plans and Surveys for the *Regional Plan of New York and its Environs*. Comprising two volumes published in 1929 and 1931, and backed by eight subject reports, the *Plan* anticipated the region growing from its then population of 9 million to 21 million in 1965. The detail of the *Plan* was broad, a framework for others to fill by detailed planning and action. The framework was of what Adams called 'recentralisation', the shaping of growth into localised, self-contained residential and working communities. These centres of growth would be strung like beads at intersections of an integrated system of roads and passenger transport. A regional park system would intersperse with the new communities. The private sector would achieve most of the development; urban renewal and low-income housing were not issues for public intervention, in the *Plan's* view. Even so, the *Plan* contained social statistics and an approach to control of land use absent from its predecessor for Chicago.

Whether the *Plan* would have met Norton's ambitions can only be guessed at; he died in 1923. It certainly did not satisfy Lewis Mumford, who found it to supinely accept the inevitability of massive population growth, and who found recentralisation a concept suborning his ideals of comprehensive decentralisation. Mumford spoke with the support of the Regional Planning Association of America, an evangelical forum since 1923 for architects and planners including Clarence Stein and Henry Wright, regional visionaries like Benton MacKaye and Mumford, and housing reformers including Catherine Bauer. Mumford declared Adams's *Plan* to be a monumental failure. He criticised it for lack of radicalism, and for accepting the inevitability of both megalopolitan excess and of minimal public intervention in private control of the land market. He found it seriously short on the principles of decentralisation and of public new towns of Henry Wright's *New York State Plan*, completed in 1926 during the long gestation of Adams's proposals. But over half a century later, criticism would take a quite opposite viewpoint (Fitch 1993), Adams being accused of inciting New York's collapse by fostering industrial decline and starving the city's economic arteries.

But unlike the plan for Chicago, that for New York had probably little impact on events. Although a Regional Plan Association for New York was founded to promote Adam's work, it was the older Regional Plan Association of America which through writing, personal influence and the work of its practitioner members, left more of a mark on Roosevelt's New Deal (Friedmann and Weaver 1979, 29).

Mumford's criticisms of unconstrained growth in the Tri-State region had little effect, but the Association was significantly influential in helping bring about the road parkways and regional park system built by Robert Moses in the 1930s. Later, however, the Association turned against Moses when his projects came to seem inimical to the quality of life in the city and state of New York.

The celebrity of the plans for Chicago and New York and the historical interest of their private sponsorship tends to obscure the more enduring roots of twentieth century US regional planning. There were also private or civic club initiatives in Philadelphia, Minneapolis-St. Paul and San Francisco, but public regional planning was rising behind them. From 1913 to 1915, state law of Pennsylvania authorised a Suburban Metropolitan Planning Commission to plan to coordinate highways, sewerage and waste disposal, water supply, housing, playgrounds and other public improvements. The first metropolitan county planning commission was established in Los Angeles in 1922, advising the County Board of Supervisors. In 1923, the Ohio State legislature passed legislation enabling local governments to arrange to plan jointly. Between 1924 and 1929, at least eleven more regional planning agencies were established at county level or above. The New England Regional Planning League of 1929 later grew into the six-state federally sponsored New England Regional Commission, and the councils of government of twenty years later were anticipated by arrangements such as the Allegheny County League of Municipalities, formed in Pennsylvania in 1929, which in turn preceded a long history of cooperative planning and action in the Pittsburgh region.

The Depression of the 1930s crystallised into action ideas of effective regional planning not previously feasible. The New Deal 'allied itself passionately with the regional idea' (Graham 1976, 312). President Roosevelt gathered advisors sympathetic to planning, including Rexford Tugwell whose involvement in regional planning would be sustained for forty years. A new regional discipline entered federal affairs. From 1933, the Federal Emergency Administration of Public Works had required bids for finance to indicate whether they fitted any approved regional programme. Also in 1933, a National Planning Board was launched, soon evolving into the National Resources Committee, which in 1935 published a report discussing the regional concept in national planning 'as thoroughly perhaps as has ever been done in an official government document' (Weaver 1984, 68). The report dwelt prominently on the four major river basin projects associated with the New England Regional Commission, the Colorado River Basin Compact, the Pacific Northwest Regional Planning Commission and the Tennessee Valley Authority (TVA).

The National Planning Board aided states to draw up long-term plans for state development, and it strongly pursued regional planning. But the TVA was its only direct initiative in regional planning and development, and was both the first and last of regional development agencies launched in a wide spirit. But the spirit evaporated as the Authority's role narrowed under the leadership of David Lilienthal to selling electricity, to flood control and to serving industry, rather than to achieving balanced social development. The TVA had more impact in supporting urban growth than in expanding rural incomes; polarisation of prosperity increased (Weaver 1984, 71).

No more authorities were created like the TVA, although another ten possible valley authorities were identified by Roosevelt's advisory National Resources Committee when succeeding the National Planning Board (National Resources Committee 1935). Rather than a development authority, a Pacific Northwest Regional Planning Commission was established over four states and 226 more local planning commissions were fostered (Advisory Commission on Intergovernmental Relations 1973, 54), aiming to exploit power from the Bonneville and Grand Coulee dams associated with the Columbia River Basin Project sponsored by the Federal Bureau of Reclamation.

Regional initiatives were not wholly for specified areas, even as large as the Tennessee or Columbia river valley basins. The short-lived Resettlement Administration, set up in 1935 under Rexford Tugwell, had a roving brief for its life of a year and a half. Tugwell's Greenbelt New Towns programme and his espousal

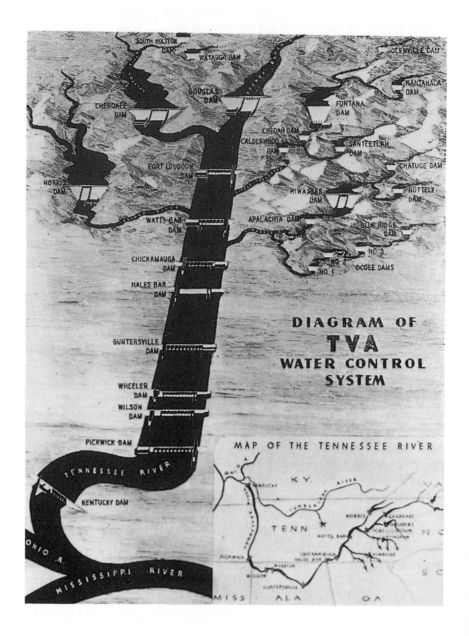

Figure 7.1. The Tennessee Valley Authority: controlling floods and making electricity

of metropolitan planning for economic purposes were influential, at least upon planning doctrine (Friedmann and Weaver 1979, 72). But where the Resettlement Administration had hoped to build fifty new towns, it started only three in Maryland, Ohio and Wisconsin, before expiring after the US District Court of Appeals in New Jersey declared it unconstitutional in 1935 (Weaver 1984, 67).

The number of strategic planning agencies swelled hugely during the mid 1930s. There had been only four states with long-range comprehensive planning agencies in 1931, but by 1936 these existed in all states except Delaware. However, the planning had generally a physical focus, was occupied with surveys and reports more than action, and had little influence on events (Rothblatt 1971, 30). At the metropolitan level, the St. Louis Regional Planning Commission spread into two states. By 1937, there were 506 metropolitan planning agencies at county level or above, and metropolitan or regional planning agencies covered at least 30 major US cities by 1939.

The President's Committee on Administrative Management of 1937 had advised that the executive should create an agency to coordinate federal departments and programmes. This aroused criticism that central authoritarianism would flourish. No new agency emerged, but the National Resources Committee lingered until, in 1939, it was again reshaped as the National Resources Planning Board for its final four years of life. Roosevelt meant the Board to promote regional and metropolitan development programmes, paving the way for post-war coordination of federal departments. It produced analyses at a high intellectual level on a range of social, economic and resource issues. But it was too elevated and far-sighted to earn credibility with the working bureacracies, and it raised fierce departmental and political jealousies; the Army Corps of Engineers particularly resented its involvement in regional water resource planning. But there were much deeper difficulties. Nine regional offices were to have decentralised federal policy-making, and Congress and federal departments conspired to defeat this challenge to their status. The Board was the President's creation, but was brought down by his opponents.

Planning lost its grand patron upon Roosevelt's death, but the regional planning which had arisen in the depressed 1930s did not all recede in the 1940s. The common purpose of wartime perhaps helped dissolve inhibitions upon regional cooperation, facing still-growing metropolitan problems of urban blight, rapid suburban growth, airport construction, public transport, water supply and sewerage. Citizen planning committees were reinvigorated and at least seven new public regional planning bodies created. The activity was so much that at times and at places it duplicated effort, overlapped surveys and brought conflict between plans. So, there was less convincing action in the wartime period than there was variety of regional initiatives. The birth of a number of privately dominated regional planning councils was possibly the most significant trend of the period.

The first and historically most significant in the resurgence of private initiatives was the Allegheny Conference on Community Development, founded in 1943.

Associating individual figures from business, government and labour unions, the Conference employed the private Pittsburgh Regional Planning Association to undertake its research and, in turn, it was financed by the Pittsburgh Civic-Business Council. The Allegheny initiative was quickly followed by similar private regional organisations in San Francisco, Boston, St. Louis, Cincinnati and Kansas City. The Kansas City Citizens Regional Planning Council combined parts of two states, included the mayors and presidents of the chambers of commerce of four cities, and was mainly financed by some 200 business firms. And a group of the most significant interests in downtown Los Angeles formed Greater Los Angeles Plans Incorporated, to promote the 'recentering' of the exploding regional metropolis (Davis 1990, 72).

The Second World War was one of the watersheds in the development of regional approaches. Several tensions broke to the surface. One was between the rural traditional bias of much regionalism of the 1930s and the view of urban economists that the US depended upon its cities for technological progress in the post-war era (Friedmann 1956); it was argued that metropolitan regional planning was as much a case of resource planning as any in the rural US. There was simmering stress between central and devolved planning, whether devolved to departments of the federal government or to a local level. There was stress also between planning by planning commissions or semi-private bodies and planning by state and local governments.

As the War ended, state and local governments increasingly seized their rights. First, the Michigan state legislature authorised the state planning commission to create regional commissions for homogeneous areas. By the end of 1945, seven other states had followed Michigan's lead. Central Lane Planning Council in November 1945 was the first voluntary regional cooperation of peacetime. Covering the single county Eugene-Springfield area of Oregon on the model of many of the councils born in the War, it was a planning-oriented council of local government officials.

The bi-county Atlanta Regional Metropolitan Planning Commission of 1947 was the first multi-county body to be supported entirely by public funds. Also in 1947 were established the Detroit Metropolitan Area Regional Planning Commission, the Northern Virginia Regional Planning and Economic Development Commission, and the Regional Planning Commission of Reno, Sparks and Washoe County, Nevada. In 1950 there were some 18 regional planning bodies, and the number grew to nearly 40 by 1953. Half, however, operated in regions of fewer than 150,000 population, and few significantly influenced the planning of their participating municipal and county governments. The metropolitan commission for Tulsa, Oklahoma, was exceptional for this period, in that all counties and cities of the metropolitan area were required to refer to it all proposed improvement and subdivision projects.

The regional commissions were severely limited by the divorce of their planning duties from the executive responsibilities of the local governments they served. State legislatures had established a widespread framework for regional planning, but this could not circumvent unsympathetic local governments. But when Washington made it a requirement that much federal financial aid would depend upon competent regional planning, the pressure for this brought the era of the flowering of councils of government.

The Flowering of Councils of Government

Matching 50/50 Federal grants for the costs of metropolitan planning were introduced by section 701 of the Housing Act of 1954. By 1959, bids for funding came to exceed the financing available, although the planning it supported did not automatically guarantee subsequent funding for implementation.

The New York Metropolitan Council and the Puget Sound (Seattle) Governmental Conference were two of the more significant councils of government in this early period of their development. States passed enabling legislation either requiring or permitting planning agencies over local government areas, although the State of Maryland created a planning council for the Baltimore region without recourse to legislation. The federal government maintained its pressure for effective regional planning. The Housing Act of 1959 broadened the eligibility for funding, and the Bureau of Roads of the Department of Transportation used the tool of transportation studies to force the pace of regional cooperation. Increasingly refined methods of transportation planning necessarily looked across many local government areas, and looked to time horizons for land use and socio-economic change beyond the range of consistent planning amongst fragmented local governments.

The stimulus of the Bureau of Roads for major regional and metropolitan transportation led to some major contributions to regional planning history. The Penn-Jersey Transportation Study established in 1959 was perhaps the most notable, combining the interests of the States of Pennsylvania and New Jersey, the City of Philadelphia, eight counties and the Bureau of Roads. The Study was of an almost unmanageable sophistication. It helped lead to the formation of a Regional Council of elected officials, comprising a representative of each of 388 general purpose governments in the region. This Council with its intended width of political legitimacy was not more wieldy than the Study's intricate technical methods, however, and it soon failed. Its collapse was accompanied by that of the Pennsylvania–New Jersey–Delaware Metropolitan Project Inc., a private body to foster regional studies and interests funded in its five years of effective life by the Ford Foundation and by regional business, civic and research interests. From the ashes of these short-life regional initiatives rose the Delaware Valley Planning Commission, appointed following a contract between the States of New Jersey and Pennsylvania, and surviving in a curtailed form in the 1990s.

President Kennedy's promotion of the Area Redevelopment Act of 1961 marked a small revival of federal enthusiasm in regional intervention, absent in

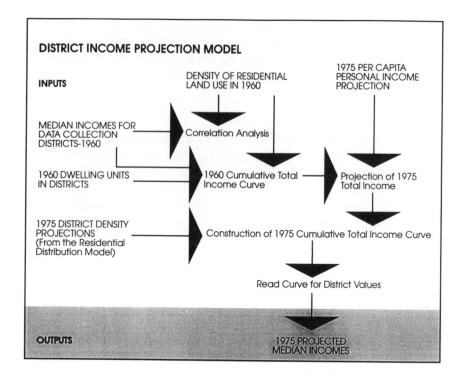

Figure 7.2. Feeding transportation planning: income projection model for the Pennsylvania–Jersey Transportation Study

sub-national economic policy for almost twenty years; major groups and parts of the US opposed it. The Act produced a four-year programme of limited aid by the Federal Area Redevelopment Commission to locally formed agencies, aiming to help rather than merely plan for people in poverty in economically distressed regions. The programme was disappointing, but did not dissuade the Administration from deciding that long-term regional action was feasible (Estall 1977, 342). Congressional disputes over the Area Redevelopment Commission led to its being wound up at the end of its four-year term, when the Public Works and Economic Development Act of 1965 created the Economic Development Administration to fund local and regional planning agencies in areas of low income and high unemployment. But although senators from regions such as the upper Great Lakes pressed for equal treatment and seven other commissions were formed, touching on twenty-nine states, these fell away. Only the Appalachian Regional Commission obtained federal funding, for a major programme of action across thirteen states.

Created under its own Act of 1965, the Appalachian Regional Commission was firmly constrained to achieve economic efficiency, investing to raise regional per capita income rather than for wider social benefits. The overwhelming majority of its initial funding was for highway construction, causing sharp criticism that this was not the most effective way of realising the potential of Appalachia's resources of people. But the Commission was seen by some as the most significant regional initiative since the Tennessee Valley Authority, and as the most promising of regional development institutions in the US (Rothblatt 1971, 192).

But the promise of the Appalachian Commission was not borrowed elsewhere, although the Economic Development Administration organised regional development programmes for over 800 counties. The local agencies created to implement the programmes performed very variably. An evaluation of its work in 1972 concluded that the Economic Development Administration had brought minimal benefits to depressed areas, and that the impact of its strategy of growth centres was indiscernible. Nonetheless, both the Administration and the Appalachian Commission remained in place 20 years later.

The 1964 Housing Act offered grant aid to the production of town plans, and cooperative, comprehensive and continuous regional planning became a prerequisite for federal aid to inter-state highways in metropolitan areas; from 1965, construction funds were released in urban areas of over 50,000 population only where regional transportation and development plans had been prepared.

The Urban Renewal Administration was similarly insistent. In 1968, the Federal Bureau of the Budget called for a network of state, regional and metropolitan planning and development clearing houses to gather information and coordinate development. Suddenly, regional planning was a widely desirable activity. Councils of government had to be formed for substate regions so that their local governments could attract federal funding.

The whole governmental structure of the United States was changed by the interposition of these substate regions between local and state governments (Advisory Commission on Intergovernmental Relations, 1982). The councils of government became eligible for planning funds under the Housing and Urban Development Act, and for economic development under the Public Works and Economic Development Act. The requirement for metropolitan planning to ensure federal transportation grants was extended to funding for other public facilities. Health planning and law enforcement councils were amongst the variety of regional initiatives instigated by federal funding policy. Another eighteen nationwide federal programmes were helping fund regional councils throughout the US by 1971.

Councils of government (COGs) were not an instant means of comprehensive planning for the US metropolises and regions of fragmented governance. On the eve of the great flowering of the COGs, Martin (1963, 49) had commented that they were the:

> weakest kind of alliance conceivable, one which has no sanctional authority with regard to its members, one from which a participant may withdraw without citing cause. It is not a body politic or corporate, nor could it by any reasonable definition of the term be called a government.

As to the metropolitan planning agencies, the Joint Center for Urban Studies (1964) regarded them as being severely handicapped by insufficient power to control development, by lack of clear statutory direction, and by small and uncertain budgets.

This foresight was later confirmed by Rondinelli (1975, 15), who commented that:

> From a traumatic decade emerged a painful lesson: the most widely accepted principles and assumptions of American planning theory proved inadequate to meet the complexities of implementing urban and regional development policy. Despite government expenditure of millions of dollars in the twentieth century to produce a myriad of master plans for urban development, few cities in the United States have been developed or substantially redeveloped in accordance with a comprehensive plan. Large-scale policies designed to ameliorate major urban social and economic problems have been criticised as being either ineffective or perverse. Attempts to require comprehensive planning in federal housing, transportation, regional economic development, anti-poverty, and community development programs have not succeeded.

Disappointment over the councils was typified by the New York Metropolitan Council. First organised in 1956 and reaching its peak of activity in the early 1960s, it incorporated 9 New Jersey counties, 11 New Jersey cities and towns, 6 Connecticut towns, 6 New York counties and 5 New York cities. Aron (1969) argued that the Commission was weakly led, under-resourced and suspect to local interests objecting to centralisation. The Commission was almost dead by 1966. With federal help, cooperative planning was revived in the Tri-State Transportation Commission of 1965, which combined the three states of New Jersey, New York and Connecticut.

But despite gathering disappointment, planning did not close down with the end of the Democratic 1960s of Kennedy and Johnson. The new Nixon Administration did not put an immediate Republican damper on planning in the 1970s. It adopted a national Urban Growth Policy for 100 new towns and 100 new cities in the last 30 years of the century – all by private builders and supported by federal funds. An Urban Affairs Council was established to develop a national urban policy, and to coordinate 400 separate federal programmes affecting metropolitan areas (Graham 1976, 197). And Nixon attempted to strengthen his presidential authority over government departments, extending the coordination of federal activities to metropolitan and local levels.

But coordination was really a euphemism for cutting federal expenditure, and there was little sympathy for regional planning under the Nixon Administration. Funding for regional and area programmes was curtailed. There had indeed been unfavourable evaluations of many (Weaver 1984, 98). And despite early rhetoric about achieving more balanced growth in America, Nixon's programmes quickly ran into sandbanks of mistrust. Yet, a range of environmental legislation in the

1970s did motivate some regional cooperation between local governments. Federal legislation for Clean Air, Clean Water, Safe Water, Coastal Zone Management, Flood Disaster and other environmental issues was matched by a wave of state laws on mining, power plants and other local environmental concerns. There was local opposition also to the regional dimension. A National Land Use Policy and Planning Assistance Bill to foster statewide land use planning was proposed by a senior senator in 1970. The threat to local governments and to private interests brought accumulating opposition, and despite presidential, gubernatorial and much business support, Senate killed the Bill in 1974 (Friedmann and Bloch 1990, 595).

The Stirring of Growth Management

But if unpopular and difficult to sustain under the title of regional planning, imperatives for the process remained. It began now to pass in the guise of 'growth management', the philosophy developing from the 1970s onwards to more comprehensively direct urban growth, and to conserve resources from its more damaging impacts. By 1992, thirteen states including Vermont, Oregon, Colorado, Hawaii, California, North Carolina and Florida had legislated for state-wide or special area land use planning, as for coastal or mountain areas. It was environmental concern more than metropolitan stresses which launched these plans. Their first wave ran from 1970 to 1978 (DeGrove 1991), followed by a second wave arising in 1985 in Florida, running on through New Jersey, Maine, Rhode Island, Vermont, Georgia and Washington State. In Florida, the Governor's 1989 task force on growth management advised that the doubling of the State's population since 1970 required a strategic urban policy for the future, to combat urban sprawl in the State. But although plans were frequently underfunded and troubled by ambiguous political support, they elevated regional planning to a concern in a growing number of state governments.

So almost the entire US had become covered by regional planning organisations by 1980, overseen by councils preponderantly comprising elected councillors but also containing co-opted interests, including appointed officials. In 1961, there had been only 36 COGs, including 25 amongst the 212 metropolitan areas of the US of which around two-thirds possessed metropolitan planning commissions at that time. In 1966, the stimulus of extra federal funding had swelled the total to 119 councils, of which 71 were metropolitan. The impetus was sustained. By 1971, all of the by then 247 metropolitan areas had official regional planning, mostly under the aegis of elected COGs. By 1978, there were 659 councils in the nation, of which 292 were in metropolitan areas; 44 of these councils operated in regions of over a million people, but most had less than a quarter of a million. Staff averaged 44 in councils in the greater of the metropolitan areas, but only 13 in areas separated from them. Most COGs became official public agencies established under state law. A large majority of states drew compatible boundaries for substate districts, by which they administered their own responsibilities on a framework similar to that of the regional councils.

Federal encouragement for systematic boundaries did not preclude their overlap. Nor did it avoid the presence of several single-purpose organisations in some regions. Single-purpose councils came to predominate nationally, although not in all states. And some regions crossed state boundaries. But the councils generally had little or no power. They were tellingly characterised as 'clearing houses' by their enabling federal legislation, although the extreme case of the Minneapolis-St. Paul Metropolitan Council raised taxes and carried out measures of anti-pollution, solid waste disposal, zoning and noise abatement. Councils' priorities greatly varied. In rural regions, councils often derived from prior organisations for soil conservation, cooperative farming and resource management.

General-purpose councils growing from these earlier initiatives helped provide technical skills to small, poorly staffed local governments, giving them greater leverage on their states through regional planning. They were a channel for federal funds for programmes including economic and rural development, housing, historic preservation, recreation, fire protection, employment and training, water quality and airports.

The COGs adopted a variety of titles. They were variously called regional councils, regional planning councils, planning district commissions, regional planning and development commissions, and area planning and development commissions. Environmental politics in Portland, Oregon, helped bring the first transformation of a representative council of government into a directly elected metropolitan government, responsible for a staff of 200 and for strategic planning, operating the transit system and disposing of solid waste, amongst a limited range of other functions. Covering a region of over one million people comprising over 40 per cent of Oregon's population, the Portland Metro was still the only directly elected regional government in the US in the 1990s, but some observers (DeGrove 1991) felt that it had yet to realise its full potential.

The tax-raising powers of Portland's metropolitan government made it the model which the Advisory Commission on Intergovernmental Relations (1982, 280) considered to be the ultimate solution to US regional problems. However, there has been no sign of the model spreading widely. The Commission noted (1982, 295) that federal support had been a very significant and vital factor in such success as the regional councils had had, but that the growing complexity, unstable features, and deteriorating amounts of federal financing raised questions about reliance on the model in the long term.

So there was a gap between the intent of federal legislation and practice in regional planning. Political realities made it difficult for Washington to withhold funds from even the most tokenist of councils of government. The Demonstration Cities and Metropolitan Development Act of 1966 called for a wide variety of development projects to be submitted for review to:

any area-wide agency which is designated to perform metropolitan or regional planning for the area within which the assistance is to be used, and which is, to the greatest practicable extent, composed of or responsible to the elected officials of area-wide government or the units of general local government within which jurisdictions such agency is authorized to engage in such planning.

Reviews were to 'include information concerning the extent to which the project is consistent with the comprehensive planning developed or in the process of development.'

Commonly, comprehensive planning was more in the process than actually developed, because councils were reluctant to prepare any regional plan interfering with members' individual interests.

The regional councils were far from uniform. McDowell (1985b) described them as of ten different kinds, ranging from those which were in name only because their sole purpose was to channel federal funds through a post office box number or a room in a town hall, to those staffed to provide regional services and stopping just short of tax-raising and law enforcement. In 1982, the two principal categories each possessed around a third of all councils; councils in the regional broker category were engaged in resolving local–regional disputes brought to them, keeping a low profile but having high public credibility; councils in the local entrepreneur category had a similar role in resolving disputes, but these would sometimes arise because the council itself actively initiated regional programmes. The remaining third of councils were predominantly executive in character.

During the 1970s, regional groupings formed not just within states, but amongst the states. As the rate of growth of broad regions of the US sharply diverged (Markusen 1987, 159), three great political coalitions formed at a scale far larger than that of any conventional regional planning. The Southern Growth Policies Board embraced 12 growing states, the Northeast-Midwest Congressional Coalition combined 17 with problems of severe economic adjustment, and the Western Governors' Policy office covered 11 on the old American frontier where energy was overtaking cows and grain as a staple product. Only ten states of the Union remained outside these regional groupings. The Southern Board aimed at a six-yearly 'Statement of Regional Objectives', and at interstate and regionally significant initiatives for population distribution, comprehensive land use plans, and for new and redeveloped communities. Whatever the unprecedented scale of the South, the phraseology of conventional regional planning was being employed.

The Republican Retreat from the Cities and Regions

In the 1980s, the Reagan and Bush administrations severely and particularly reduced federal aid to metropolitan areas. Regional planning was seen now as a state or local responsibility. The states gained influence. All but two of the twelve big federal block grants were fed through the states, tending to spread them more evenly and to disconnect them from metropolitan or regional planning (McDowell 1985a). So joint planning for metropolitan areas generally subsided as the 1980s proceeded, although the federal Department of Transportation still arranged much financing of urban transportation planning through regional councils in metropolitan areas. But in some states, regional collaboration became perfunctory. Where it remained, it had to sell its merits and services to the local governments subscribing to it. Councils could more economically purchase supplies and equipment, hire specialised staff, or arrange training or joint programmes of a similar kind.

The changes to cooperative regional planning in the 1980s and the new entrepreneurialism forced on council staff were typified in the Delaware Valley, where the Regional Planning Commission formed in 1965 between the states of Pennsylvania and of New Jersey oversaw a region of 5 million people and of 3833 square miles. Incorporating representatives of the two states, eight counties, the City of Philadelphia, three other cities and the federal Departments of Transportation and of Housing and Urban Development, the Commission was curbed in the 1980s when its roles were restricted primarily to transportation planning and to proposals for federal funding, a strategy for solid waste disposal, forecasting, data banks, and the sale of information and of consultancy services to local governments and the private sector. It was an almost wholly advisory agency without executive responsibility.

Older regional initiatives remained as in the Chicago area, where the private sector's historic involvement in metropolitan planning was continued through the Metropolitan Planning Council. But the Northeastern Illinois Regional Planning Commission and the Chicago Area Transportation Study had long been ineffective in persuading the local governments funding them to also implement their proposals. In Pittsburgh, where a tradition of civic leadership through business and political partnership persisted still in the 1990s after 50 years of life, incentive remained to uphold the city's transformed reputation. Pittsburgh's regional partnerships continued to work alongside one other: there were six partnerships respectively concerned with planning, research and community development; land and building development; regional promotion; help in entrepreneurship, education and training; and small business and start-up management guidance.

Elsewhere, civic interlinkages less strong than in Pittsburgh meant a shrinkage of regional councils. Their transportation role was shrunk in scope and foresight. Councils' duties to the federal government were progressively eliminated. In his 1987 programme for continuing cuts in federal aid, President Reagan proposed to abolish eight national programmes together with the major Appalachian Regional Commission, which spanned several states as did new regional lobbies like the Western Governor's Policy Office (Markusen 1987, 35). McDowell (1986) observed how the states had grown much more capable since 1960, being better able in the 1980s to assume what until Reagan's presidency had been federal responsibilities, exercised through councils of government and framed within comprehensive plans. The survival of the regional councils accordingly depended upon their states adopting comprehensive planning, or upon their entrepreneurialism in providing strictly local services according to local needs.

As the tide of regional planning subsided in the early 1980s, previous sympathisers became willing to discuss its limitations. It had striven in the 1970s for comprehensiveness, was very expensive, and relied on large quantities of often outdated data to feed cumbersome data-processing routines. It was primarily designed to meet federal aid requirements. The whole process tended to be slow and unresponsive. Ambitiously comprehensive and visionary plans were often rigid and unyielding, and the councils of government were generally too fragile to implement contentious proposals (McDowell 1985c, 8).

Despite the extent to which councils of government came to cover the US, the movement did not carry over into any widespread reorganisation of local governance. Metropolitan government could not be imposed as it was in Britain in the 1970s, and the metropolitan governments actually created for Dade County (Miami) and for Nashville were exceptions. Unlike the British case, US inner cities were not generally aggrandising and seeking to incorporate suburban local governments. Having only just achieved a breakthrough of black mayors, few former city minority groups were likely to be willing to succumb again to the white majorities which would have resulted from incorporating suburban districts. The suburbs were similarly reluctant to take on the bill for inner city social and physical regeneration.

Superimposed upon this history of regional and metropolitan initiatives with definite geographical boundaries were other Federal programmes which many (Friedmann and Bloch 1990, Markusen 1987) regard as being regional in kind. These programmes had no defined boundaries and their impacts were widely diffused. But they significantly restructured the spatial economy of the United States, both nationally and within the metropolitan regions.

The three federal programmes dominating this regional and inter-regional restructuring of the United States were those to manufacture military equipment, to explore space and to build the interstate highway network. The military and space programmes spread new industry to the south and west, and into New England; the seaboard states from Massachusetts to Florida and California to Washington became propelled by defence expenditure. The weight of spending finally became so great that some of the older industrial cities of the north-east and the Great Lakes came to share in it, but its most significant impacts were in fostering new industrial regions on the former economic periphery. The interstate highway programme from the mid 1950s to the early 1990s had fostered metropolitan decentralisation, better connecting regions across the US and providing conduits of communication, which crystallised growth corridors as centres of activity decentralised and grew in the metropolitan suburbs.

But as an older context for regional planning faded in the 1980s, a new one was showing in parts of the US. The stimulus shifted from federal financing to state management of resources and of the environment. Some (Friedman and Bloch 1990) could see US planning in the 1990s as again being able to raise itself above the fine-grain to reconsider the regional scale. Intensified environmental concerns, growing traffic congestion and local demands to control growth led both states and local governments to realise the merits of metropolitan planning and manage-ment. Growth management became an electoral issue in many areas. California originated growth control, whose adoption in Petaluma in 1973 led other local governments and commissions in the Bay Area to try to tighten the screw on growth pressures in the region; the era of growth control in the US was founded.

Growth control sailed on murky waters; some developers opposed it, while it created profitable local land monopolies for others. It brought windfall campaign funding for some politicians to whom developers turned for favourable planning decisions. It worried many commercial and industrial interests, to whom regional strategic planning seemed a way out of threatened local impasses. In the mid 1980s, the growth-favouring Mayor of Los Angeles turned to the US tradition of strategic planning by blue-ribbon groups representing the major corporations and city elites. The resulting report of 1988 on *L.A. 2000: A City for the Future* was criticised (Davis 1990, 82) as a 'manifesto of a new regionalism', based on rationalised growth management within a regional goals consensus but assuming an economy of 'endless growth. There is no consideration whatsoever of possible contradictions within this perpetual growth machine.' The contradictions soon surfaced in the Los Angeles riots of 1992 and the failing Californian economy.

Popular demand for environmental protection was already forcing states to plan for coastal and other areas of pressured environment. And industry and commerce had a strong interest in ordered regional development which minimised the costs of labour, production and distribution. The Bay Area Council had pursued these ends around San Francisco since the Second World War, and they were embedded in the Los Angeles strategy of 1988.

The two characteristics of the trend were that states were now instigating plans, rather than being merely partners in frequently limpid associations with local governments, and that the new regional planning went under the euphemism of 'growth management'. Growth management had a suitably businesslike ring about it, whereas regional planning sounded like a constraint on free enterprise.

The Consolidation of Growth Management

From the mid 1980s, a second wave of growth management consolidated on the first wave which had risen in the 1970s (DeGrove 1991). The states stepping in to assert their strategic planning role were mostly on the Atlantic or Pacific coasts, where environmental risks raised popular anxieties. Californian and Pacific North West lifestyles and the tourist economies of the New England states depended upon conservation. So growth management initially arose from concerns for the physical environment, although the second wave of the 1980s was driven by wider pressures when transportation gridlock had spread from central metropolitan areas to their suburban hinterlands. The better quality of life for which people had fled the cities was being overtaken by dispersal of the problems from which they had hoped to escape. The difficulties of metropolitan areas which had stimulated regional planning in earlier decades were now being extensively spread. Metropolitan areas were losing their coherence as activities spilled out to new suburban foci. Such administrative cohesion as metropolitan councils had was being eroded. State legislatures were now more widely regarding traditional metropolitan problems as states' issues. Growth management was reformulating the scale and the degree of states' involvement in regional planning.

The states' emphases and motivations to growth management differed. Hawaii's motivation to assert itself as a state planning authority was the rapid loss to building of its fertile agricultural land; Vermont was being pressured by development; Florida was drowning in urban growth; Maine's coast had become an asset of perhaps greater profit for tourism than for fish; Californians saw risk of being cut off from their beaches and coast, and Georgia could see the fate of Florida nearby; Oregon was anxious to hold back the debasing tide of what was called 'californication'; New Jersey was already the most urbanised state in the US in the still consolidating Bos-Wash megalopolis, in whose path lay Rhode Island.

The state programmes of growth management of the 1980s had six characteristics (DeGrove 1991). They focused on: strategies for funding and implementation; balancing environmental protection and economic development; increased emphasis and state funding for affordable housing; matching infrastructure to the impacts of development; mandated strategies for implementation; rural and wetland protection.

The means of growth management have differed (Cullingworth 1991). Hawaii was not too large to introduce statewide zoning by the state government; Vermont's tradition of local democracy brought citizen district commissions to administer a system of development plans; Florida's 1985 Growth Management Act introduced state controls in 'areas of critical concern' and where developments had 'regional impact'; California's response was to establish a coastal planning system; Oregon established state planning goals for a comprehensive system of local government planning; New Jersey's Office of State Planning was established in 1986 under a State Planning Commission, empowered to prepare and adopt a State Development and Redevelopment Plan every three years; Arizona and Texas introduced statewide growth management even where space for development might have seemed ample.

The tide of growth management was uneven and sometimes disturbed. The evolution of New Jersey's first Plan was fraught with controversy. After New Jersey's Supreme Court had decided in 1980 in the Mount Laurel case – which resounds in the history of US planning practice – that a particular form of exclusionary zoning was illegal, the State Governor within days abolished the State Development Plan Guide upon which the Justices had rested their decision. The State and Regional Planning departments which had produced the Guide Plan were dissolved. It took six years to restore a department of statewide planning.

Has growth management been a real revival of regional planning, after substate organisations had so shrunk in substance after Reagan had withdrawn federal funds from the cities? Not equally in the eight states implementing their growth management legislation; some have a centralised scrutiny of locally prepared growth management programmes, while others involve regional bodies in the process of analysis and approval (Gale 1992, 427). The fourteen regional commissions in Vermont are required to prepare their own plans, and in Georgia the regional bodies similarly have a higher profile than in the majority of growth management states, where local communities have a more significant input to the states' programmes. But as experience spread, it was argued (Bollens 1992, 462) that those states initially practising top-down planning tended to accept greater local inputs in cooperation with local communities.

But DeGrove (1991) argues that growth management gave new life to the otherwise declining activity of strategic planning. State funding gave purpose to the new planning. Growth management aimed at real questions of resources and facilities, through significant proposals and a will to impose consistency upon local plans. In Florida, for example, inundated by excessive growth, all new development in the state must be accompanied by matching infrastructure for transportation, drinking water, sewage and stormwater disposal, solid waste and parks and recreation. State legislation required all local governments to produce comprehensive local plans. Local plans were reviewed and approved for consistency with the *State Comprehensive Plan* by the Florida State Department of Community Affairs; consistency was also required with an intervening level of comprehensive regional policy plans mandated from eleven regional planning councils, each composed of two parts of local government representatives and one part of nominees of the Governor. The regional councils were established under Florida's Environmental Land and Water Management Act of 1972. Their duty was to mediate between cities and counties and to review developments of regional impact, giving technical help to smaller cities and counties, including plan preparation. The councils also staffed six of Florida's now twenty-one metropolitan planning organisations (DeGrove, 1991). So, the rise of states' growth management programmes reinvigorated regional planning under a new guise. DeGrove suggests that it may prove to have been a prime tide in the history of US planning. Its significance was to tie regional agencies into state-wide planning systems. Regional organisations which were becoming moribund were being assigned real duties in planning and in implementation. The degree of funding and of constraint inherent in the systems made them effective. States were stepping in where federal government had withdrawn much of the impetus it had brought to regional planning twenty years before.

But in 1991, federal encouragement to regional planning revived through the long familiar, but indirect, route of transportation planning. The Intermodal Surface Transportation Efficiency Act reformed the system of federal transportation grants, allowed unprecedented flexibility to switch funding into environmentally friendly transport projects, and especially emphasised the potential of mass transit and the importance of economy in spending on interstate highways. The Act required statewide transportation plans in addition to the metropolitan transportation plans required since 1962.

The potential effect of the Act was great. Urban Transportation Management Areas were made responsible for linking transportation planning to relief of traffic congestion and to energy conservation, clean air measures and land use. The aims seemed to be to produce plans reflecting local political commitment to relieving traffic congestion, and through these plans to allocate federal funding to a variety of state and local agencies for land development and the environment.

Is the Regional Imperative Inevitable?

Regional issues and pressure for regional planning in the US are inherent in the fragmented complexity of its local governments. Competition and self-interest arises in a local system ill-fitted to the social and economic geography of the late twentieth century. So without prospect of comprehensive reform such as European countries arrange periodically, familiar regional issues must persist in the US because they will never be subsumed into the everyday practice of unified local government.

There is no prospect of extensive reorganisation of fragmented US local governments. But this is only one amongst several persistent stimuli for outbreaks of regional planning and cooperative regional governance in the US. Seven principal stimuli have recurred and mixed in different proportions at different times:

1. Problems of enduring fragmentation of local governments in the most urbanised parts of the US, under pressures of development affecting regional issues from water supply and sewage disposal to traffic gridlock.

2. The economic interests of industry and commerce, from Chicago in 1909 to the Bay Area of the 1990s.

3. National political crises, from the economic depression and the New Deal to pressures of war-time, and on to problems of economic adjustment as in the 1970s Rustbelt.

4. Resource development as typified by river basin planning from the Tennessee Valley to the Columbia River from 1933 to 1945, and on the Atlantic and Pacific seaboards more recently.

5. Environmental movements – from the Sierras Club to the Greenbelt Alliance of the Bay Area.

6. Times of advancing federal intervention and support for the cities and metro-
    politan regions, coupled to the rise of new techniques for strategic land use
    and transportation planning.

7. Times of retreating federal intervention and support for the cities and metro-
    politan regions, with a relatively increased role for the states in regional
    planning.

At different times the pressure for regional arangements has been mixed in different
ways. The federal government has been the initiator at certain periods and in
particular ways. State governments have been more concerned since the 1980s.
But the regional dimension in US planning and governance endures. Only its guises
vary.

Tight and Loose: Two Varieties of Regional Planning

Minneapolis-St. Paul: The Metropolitan Council of the Twin Cities Area
A DISTINCTIVE US GOVERNMENT

Established by the Minnesota State Legislature in 1967, the Metropolitan Council
for the Twin Cities of Minneapolis and St. Paul is a distinctive form of organisation
amongst the metropolitan regions of the United States. No other metropolitan area
in the US, suggests Markusen (1987, 41), has been able to fashion as far-reaching
an organisation with such grace.

As transportation, waste disposal and other metropolitan problems accentuated
in the 1950s and 1960s, the metropolitan regions of the US generally chose not
to reorganise to pool their own resources and collectively overcome their difficulties. At a time when federal aid was more available, local governments turned to
these resources rather than pooling their own. Few regions were prepared to face
any local reorganisation, but the Twin Cities did. When federal funds were being
withdrawn under the Reagan Administration of the 1980s in particular, the states
and the metropolitan regions were thrown upon their own resources. They lacked
the organisational advantages built by the Twin Cities since 1967.

Other metropolitan regions in the United States have formed councils of
government, composed of representatives of the local governments of the region,
but the Twin Cities Council is entirely responsible to the State Legislature. The
Council does not depend upon achieving a consensus at the lowest common level
of agreement between participating units of local government. Naftalin argues
(1986, 2) that this makes it responsible to the people of the region rather than to
a collective of local governments.

The chair and members for the 16 districts of the Council's area are appointed
by the Governor of Minnesota, and the Council's staff are appointed by the Council
itself. Although unelected, the Council's members have area responsibilities within
its seven-county area of 3000 square miles, with a population rising above 2
million and comprising half that of the State. Within the seven counties, there are

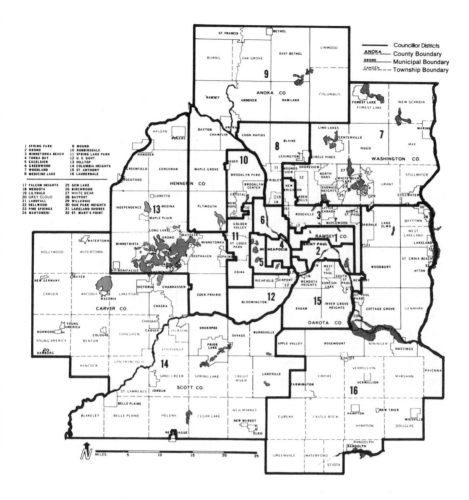

Figure 7.3. The Twin Cities: the region of the Minneapolis-St. Paul Metropolitan Council

in addition to the cities of Minneapolis and St. Paul some 290 other units of government, including 25 cities, 105 villages, 68 townships, 77 school districts, and 20 special service districts.

In preparing an overall plan for regional growth – the *Metropolitan Development and Investment Framework* – and more detailed regional plans for the systems of sewers, transportation, airports and parks, the Council has differing degrees of oversight of six metropolitan executive agencies. It has direct oversight of the Metropolitan Waste Control Commission, the Regional Transit Board (itself overseeing the Metropolitan Transit Commission) and the Metropolitan Airports Commission; there is fiduciary oversight of the Metropolitan Sports Facilities Commission but the Metropolitan Parks and Open Space Commission is actually

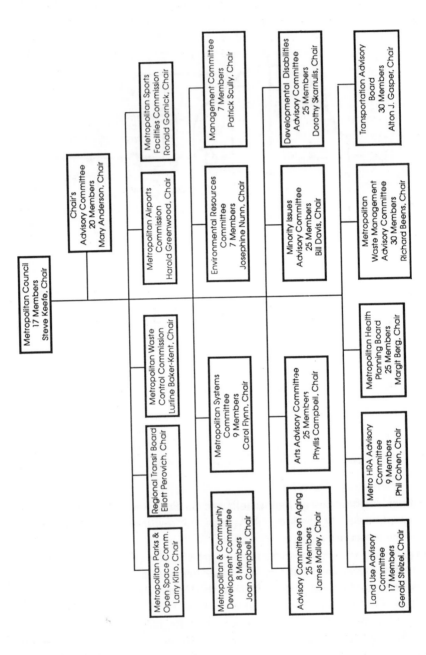

Figure 7.4. The Twin Cities: the committees of the Metropolitan Council 1988

staffed by the Council. In 1989, these commissions had combined budgets of around $300m.

With a budget of $12.4m and a professional staff of 214 in 1989, the Council sets regional policies within the scope given it by the State Legislature, but has no powers to directly encroach upon the authority of the 189 elected city and township governments and the 49 school districts of its region, except with the support of the State Legislature. The range of the Council's recommendations to the State Legislature can be nonetheless considerable. In 1989, for instance, the Council sought authority to require any of the region's seven counties to amend its solid waste master plan to reduce its call upon landfill, in accord with the Council's 20 year plan; it asked for authority to approve separate and self-interested light rail proposals which counties were advancing competitively; it proposed to continue to work with the Metropolitan Airports Commission to plan for the expansion of the Minneapolis-St. Paul International Airport, and for its possible replacement in the early twenty-first century; it sought an increase in the State's contribution to maintaining regional parks from 9 to 14 per cent, and it noted the demand for the Metropolitan Parks and Open Space Commission to invest $67m in acquiring further parks.

In addition to the traditional fields of physical planning, the Council has also become involved in planning and grant support for health, housing and emergency medical services, the arts, programmes for the elderly and the emergency telephone system. In 1990, the Council was making a historic turn to redeploy resources towards human services.

THE COUNCIL'S ORIGINS

The foundations for the Council had been laid over a period of over 30 years prior to its inception. A voluntary planning association for the metropolitan area was organised briefly in 1927. The first joint undertaking on an official basis was the Minneapolis-St. Paul Sanitary Sewer District of 1933; this was followed in 1943 by the Metropolitan Airports Commission which dissuaded the two cities from each building their own airport, and in 1958 came the Metropolitan Mosquito Control Commission.

In 1953, the executive director of the League of Minnesota Municipalities had begun to lobby for a metropolitan planning commission, leading to the creation of the Twin Cities Metropolitan Planning Commission in 1957.

Much like a council of governments, the Metropolitan Planning Commission was representative of the cities, towns, five counties and special districts of its area, but it reported to the State Legislature and had no authority to implement policy. A Metropolitan Area Sports Commission followed in 1956 for the purpose of building the stadium which brought major league baseball and football to the Twin Cities, intensifying the identity of the region. In 1959, the Minnesota Municipal Commission was established to rule upon municipal boundary changes in the State. Indicative of widespread recognition of the chaotic growth of municipalities – 130 of the cities of the metropolitan area had fewer than 500 residents as late as 1975 – the Municipal Commission signified consensus upon the need to minimise the fragmentation of the region's governance. A Joint Transportation–Land Use Program involving the Metropolitan Planning Commission followed between 1961 and 1967, after the State Department of Highways had published proposals for ten freeways focusing upon downtown Minneapolis, clashing with plans for land use.

So, by the mid 1960s there had been a progressive development of associative planning and action in the metropolitan region. There was prior experience in acting over common interests, but their scale and intensity was increasing. There were continuing mutual problems over sewage and solid waste disposal, urban sprawl, transportatation and open space protection. Minneapolis and St. Paul feared that they would have to unfairly meet the cost of overcoming the sewerage problems of the suburbs. Failure in four successive sessions of the State Legislature to agree a comprehensive waste treatment and disposal policy was perhaps the major factor in accelerating political support for metropolitan planning. When refused the services of the Minneapolis-St. Paul Sewer District, the suburban town of New Hope threatened to build its own treatment plant and discharge the effluent into streams that ran through Minneapolis's parks. Unequal tax bases amongst municipalities had also caused common problems, particularly in the case of a large power plant built at Stillwater in suburban Washington County. Environmentally destructive and opposed by areas outside Stillwater, the plant was supported by local people because of the tax revenue it brought to them. The case added significantly to the impetus for the Metropolitan Council, and to the adoption of a unique Twin Cities tax-base-sharing programme dampening the effects of unequal distribution of metropolitan wealth in terms of both residents and activities. There was an almost even balance between the central cities and the suburban areas in terms of both population and of property valuation (Horan and Taylor 1977, 172).

The layers and complexity of US governance and the specific case of the Twin Cities area were illustrated by the Advisory Committee on Intergovernmental Relations (1973). The City of Fridley was locked into the northern suburbs of the Twin Cities in 1966, on the eve of the Council's formation. The 15,173 residents were also tied into 11 layers of government:

1. City of Fridley
2. Four Independent School Districts
3. North Suburban Sanitary District
4. Minneapolis-St. Paul Sanitary District
5. North Suburban Hospital District
6. Soil Conservation District
7. Anoka County

8. Minneapolis-St. Paul Metropolitan Airports Commission

9. Metropolitan Mosquito Control Commission

10. State of Minnesota

11. Government of the United States

When instituted in 1967, the Council was able not only to adopt some established commissions but also to inherit a climate of mutual action and debate. It also extended the metropolitan area from five to seven counties, adding to the scope of the preceding Planning Commission. Its predecessor had won acceptance in the Twin Cities, but its legal and geographical extents had opponents, primarily the conservative rural areas of Minnesota, the economically favoured city of Bloomington on the fringe of the Twin Cities, and the seven counties. The rural areas wished to perpetuate their majority position in the State Legislature, but their strength was reduced by redistricting in 1966 which gave the metropolitan region almost half the seats in the Minnesota State Legislature. Support from outside the Legislature came principally from the Citizens League, the business community and city officials grappling with common problems. The Citizens League was central to the campaign for the Council. The Legislature's acceptance of the Council must have owed something to Minnesota's underlying attitudes of Scandinavian liberality and rationality, as well as to the origin and home in the State of 29 of Fortune magazine's top US companies – characteristically supportive of regional affairs. Only a casting vote in the Legislature in 1967 made the Council an appointed rather than an elected body.

THE WORKING OF THE COUNCIL

Established as a planning and policy-making body, the Council's duties have been substantially widened during its life (Naftalin 1986). It has taken on some operating duties, although to only a limited extent by comparison with its responsibilities for strategic guidance. Its authorised functions are fivefold:

1. To prepare a long-range growth and development plan, policy plans for the metropolitan commissions, and a regional solid waste disposal plan.

2. Where judged necessary, to suspend for up to a year those projects of metro-politan significance incompatible with its long-range plan; to approve local governments' long-range development plans; to approve capital pro-grammes by the metropolitan commissions; and to approve certain applica-tions for state and federal funds.

3. To issue bonds to develop regional parks, sports and transit facilities, the re-gional sewer system and solid waste landfills, and other specified capital im-provements.

4. To administer directly: in housing through authorisation to serve as the Met-ropolitan Housing and Redevelopment Authority; the acquisition and devel-opment of regional parks, with advice from the Metropolitan Parks and

Open Space Commission; in health, as the federally designated Health Systems Agency in conjunction with the Metropolitan Health Planning Board; and the allocation of Federal funds for older people and state funds for the arts.

5. To give advice and assistance in the arts, criminal justice, disaster and local physical planning, care for the elderly, telecommunications, and regional trends in demographic and other data.

The Council is financed from four sources. A levy placed on all property in its area gave the Council 59 per cent of its funding in 1991, when 20 per cent came by Federal support, 7 per cent from the State, and 14 per cent from chargebacks, investment income and other sources. Federal grants had provided almost 67 per cent of Council funds under the Carter Administration, but fell towards 20 per cent under Reagan.

ENSURING REGIONAL POLICIES AND STANDARDS

The Council can compel action to only a limited degree, except for its specific authority over the several commissions. But it has four levers of influence: the *Metropolitan Development and Investment Framework*; administration of the Metropolitan Land Planning Act; authority to review plans and, if necessary, to suspend projects of regional commissions; authority to review proposals involving federal and state directives.

The *Metropolitan Development and Investment Framework* of 1986 remained in force in 1990. It aimed to channel most of the region's growth into four zones of the metropolitan heartland: the central business districts of Minneapolis and St. Paul; other areas of regional business concentration with large employment bases and sales volumes; the remaining fully developed areas of the central cities and the first ring suburbs; the developing area surrounding the metro centres where growth is to be focused.

The Council implements its *Development and Investment Framework* principally by ensuring that all local government physical development plans are consistent with it. It has responsibility for this under the Metropolitan Land Planning Act, matching local investment with regional system plans for sewers, transit and highway projects, parks and airports. The capacity to suspend commission plans is also effective; it has been employed to veto a second major airport, a fixed-rail subway system and an experimental plant to recover energy from sewage sludge.

By choice of the State Legislature, the Council has also become the Metropolitan Housing and Redevelopment Authority, and the authority to both plan and fund regional parks. It administers federal and state housing programmes for suburban communities on request, including almost 4000 houses in 77 communities, a demonstration rehabilitation programme and others for low and moderate income households.

Through expediency, the Council has accumulated further responsibilities for special programmes for which its political position or area-wide coverage fitted it.

Through the Program on Ageing, the Council awards federal grants for nutrition programmes and services for the elderly. The Developmental Disabilities Program gives technical and demonstration support to some 50,000 disabled people, the Emergency Telephone Program produced the first unified multi-county service in the United States, and the Arts Program finances local arts groups. Local cable systems are dealt with by Regional Telecommunications Planning, as is a regional public service channel and the impact of telecommunications policy on the metropolitan area.

IS THE COUNCIL BUOYANT?

Unlike most regional bodies in the United States, the Council has unified backing because it is empowered by the State Legislature. Why has it remained distinctive? Kolderie (Lim 1983) attributes its origin and persistence to the Twin Cities' prominence in the State; the metropolitan region possesses half of Minnesota's population and twenty times more than its second ranking urban area. The Legislature was perhaps simultaneously attempting to balance the Twin Cities' interests with those of the rest of the State, helping to ensure that its outstanding metropolis kept pace with developing competitors in other states.

Nonetheless, while the Council is stable and has held its position while metropolitan reform has failed to gather any impetus in the US, the Council's support from the Legislature and the Governor has wavered on specific issues. The Council was by-passed when the Governor appointed task-forces to examine the need for an international trade centre and a Minnesota convention centre, although the Twin Cities area was most likely to house both. Similarly, the Legislature has been cautious of over-extending the Council's powers. The Metropolitan Sports Commission established in 1977 was made independent of the Council, as was the Minnesota Racing Commission empowered to locate a racetrack without the Council's right-of-approval. In 1982, the region's 44 secondary watershed districts were required to prepare plans to reduce surface water run-off, but the Council was again deprived of right-of-approval.

Minnesota's governmental system has tended towards a strong state legislature, a rather tightly controlled local government and generally weak counties. After the formation of the Council, the counties were less inclined to remain as effectively administrative agents of the state (Horan and Taylor 1977, 175). As the state bureaucracy was restrained from interfering in its affairs, the Council's inception brought some transfer of activity down to lower administrative levels. Nonetheless, the Council has been regarded by some (Naftalin 1986) as having been sometimes culpable in weakening its position with the Legislature. It may not have consistently pressed its own legislative programme, and may not have resisted all attempts by the state commissions to increase their autonomy. Of course, this could have reflected political trade-offs, the inherent limitations of a system separating a planning agency from executive agencies – although the Council appoints a majority of members to the Waste Control and Parks and Open Space Commissions, and to the Transit Board – or wholly accidental circumstances. It may have reflected disengaged leadership, for with new and particularly experienced and engaged chairmanship, the Council appeared to have reasserted itself with new force in the mid 1980s.

Unlike the widespread US model of councils of government, local governments have no representation on the Metropolitan Council. But they considerably involve themselves with it, because their local interests are widely affected – the cities even more than the counties. The cities are directly affected through their obligation to make their development plans conform to the metropolitan framework, and the counties through their duties to dispose of solid waste and to develop and operate parks in accord with Council plans and funding.

In its impact on local governments, Novak (1974, 20) considered that the Council stimulated:

> governmental action, especially by the major urban counties in social service activities such as community health and criminal justice planning... it has also saved some expense by curtailing the over-zealous construction programs of the single purpose districts.

What has worked well for the Council is compared by Martin (1993) with what she thinks to have been less successful. The longstanding issue of airport growth and possible replacement she considers to have been better handled by the Council than it would have been otherwise. Sewerage services have been handled with similar strategic success, and while the Council's *Development Guide* and *Framework* have been significantly helpful in fostering the regeneration of the business cores of the two central cities, she implies that the Council may have failed to face the strategic issues underlying a proposal to build a shopping mega-mall in the metropolitan suburbs. And while suburban growth has not leapfrogged its planned limits within the metropolitan region, it has been more intense than anticipated and has spilled beyond the Commission's region into counties beyond. This spreading of the functional metropolitan region beyond the scope of metropolitan governance is seen by Martin as a major threat to the Council.

Because it is not elected, the Council has no direct constituency. The councillors have assigned areas of geographic responsibility, but this is potentially as much a means of fragmenting and dispersing popular discontent as of giving it rein. The Citizens League for the Twin Cities has perhaps been the most significant focus for connections between the Council and the metropolitan population. The idea of the Council was crystallised with the active encouragement of the League, which remains a major connecting channel. It combines 3000 individual and 600 corporate members.

Latent opposition to the Council remains – particularly in outlying areas of the region. Amongst supporters, there is divided opinion on whether the Council should remain primarily a policy-setting body, or should extend its role into substantial implementation. The Legislature appears unlikely to add substantially to the operating responsibilities already passed to the Council. There has been concern that the Council was becoming too bogged in detailed approval of applications and plans. But a strong minority opinion in the highly supportive Citizen's League believes that separation of policy and action makes the Council much less effective than it could and should be. The Council has not stopped the Twin Cities' suburbanisation, and its views have been shouldered aside in such highly political cases as the location of the new stadium, the regional shopping mega-mall and trade centres.

Outsiders enthusiastic for government and business partnerships for communal development have approved of the Twin Cities model. Its rise has been explained (Gappert and Knight 1987) partly by the relative isolation of the Twin Cities from other metropolitan areas, by the lakes and parks which keep well-to-do residents in the attractive urban environment, and by prolonged snow-bound winters conducive to public meetings rather than individual recreation. Perhaps more convincingly, they point also to the region's cultural inheritance from Yankee, Scandinavian, German and Polish immigrants, bound to the work ethic and high standards in education. Markusen (1987, 41) supports this notion of an egalitarian and liberal tradition contributing to readier communal action than has generally arisen elsewhere in the US. She credits the permanancy of the region-wide tax-sharing arrangement to Scandinavian heritage, upper Midwest populism, and the success of the Democratic Farmer-Labour Party. However, although Minnesota is a competitive two-party state, Horan and Taylor (1977, 174) stress the lack of partisanship at both local and state elections.

The Council's relative stability has been earned through a system designed deliberately to be able to resolve conflict of policy between local governments. Notwithstanding some operational functions added to it, the Council was conceived of as a means of coordinating local governments which were wholly competent to execute policy, but not wholly willing to agree what was in the metropolitan rather than in their local interest. The Legislature forced the Council away from involvement in operational detail to remain at the level of strategy. And because its relationship to the Transit, Waste, Airport and other State commissions has been firmly established, the Council's capacity to influence essential aspects of metropolitan policy has been real. The Council's role may have been advisory, but not in the word's weakest sense.

Yet it may be an open question as to whether the Council can so well handle the increasingly diverse and less manageable metropolitan problems of the twenty-first century (Rothblatt and Jones 1991, 18). The dilemmas raised by the functional spread of the metropolitan region and its internal restructuring are strong. The two old city centres have regenerated and retained their strength in business offices quite well, but have been more vulnerable to the metropolitan redistribution of shopping. And the future of the burgeoning airport and its possible replacement far outside the Twin Cities has set the metropolitan region not only against itself, but against distant parts of the State. When the new state governor was elected in

1991, he asked the Council to convince him of its own purposes within two years or to face abolition.

The Bay Area

GOLDEN GATEWAY TO THE OVERGROWN GARDEN

The history of growth politics and of regional planning around the Bay is vivid. And it revolves around some distinctive and long-established regional pressure groups of a very interesting kind. The Bay Area's three central cities of San Francisco, Oakland and San Jose lie within a metropolis housing over 6 million people in 1990, spread over almost 7500 square miles and expected to grow by a further 1 million within 15 years. It is a fragmented metropolis, where there has been significant regional planning and cooperation over the environmental and transport problems iaround the Bay. But although a bill proposing regional growth management for the Area was put before the California State legislature in 1991, the prospects of extensive reforms to regional planning for the Bay Area were unpromising.

A movement to create a Greater San Francisco local government swelled in the years following the earthquake and fire of 1906. It was strongly resisted outside the city and particularly in Oakland, across the Bay, where a new city was forming which was disinclined to be subordinated to the interests of San Francisco.

Frustrated in expanding on the East Bay, San Francisco turned to a possible annexation or consolidation with San Mateo County, its southern peninsular neighbour. This possibility was pursued through the 1920s, but was voted down by San Mateo's residents in 1931 (Barlow 1981, 243).

As in many other cases in the US, the idea of a Bay region was sustained more eagerly by private groups than by the city administration of San Francisco. A Regional Plan Association established in 1923 strongly represented San Francisco business, and argued for coherent planning across the whole Bay Area, served by an agency to gather data and plan on the basis of it.

But the Regional Plan Association did not last into the 1930s, and it was not San Francisco but the local governments of the East Bay which cooperated increasingly through the 1930s in the fastest growing sub-region of the whole Bay Area. They created special districts to arrange water supply first, then the disposal of sewage and finally the preservation of open land for parks. But however this may have eased problems of growth in the East Bay, it deferred effective coordination over the whole Bay region. An East Bay Municipal Utilities District operated separately from an East Bay Regional Park District. Each held land with recreation potential, for instance, but one behaved almost as a private utility company while the other pursued wider community interests. Barlow (1981, 247) suggests that this example of special districts for separate functions and for only parts of a natural metropolitan region symbolises the weakness of the special district approach.

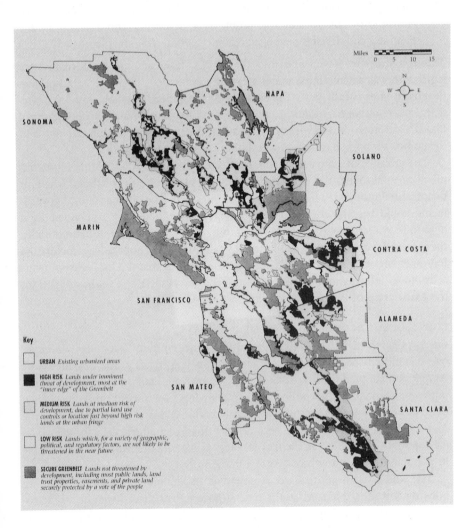

Figure 7.5. Campaigning for conservation in the Bay Area: the Greenbelt Alliance taking a strategic lead in a fragmented region.

What happened on the East Bay was a lost opportunity to guide the growth of the Bay Area, stemming from:

> the failure of San Francisco and the East Bay to unite on a plan for providing the major concentrations of population... with a common water supply,

[being] an outstanding example of the independent special district that enormously complicates the problem of achieving coordination in the planning and development of a great metropolitan region. (Scott 1959, 181)

Through the late 1940s and into the 1950s, however, the Californian state legislature was assembling a wider array of commissions to plan for and protect the environment of the state. The commissions included the whole Bay Area, even if by sub-regional divisions. So, the Bay Area Regional Water Quality Control Board was formed in 1949, the Bay Area Rapid Transit Commission in 1951, and the commission for Bay Area Air Pollution Control came in 1955.

The advance of state commissions reflected the State of California's growing involvement in what the cities had previously seen to be their affairs, whatever financial help they may have welcomed to aid them. The cities and local governments could see the threat to their independence, and they responded by a new-found eagerness to be seen to be planning collectively and regionally. Initially, the 9 counties of the Bay Area thought to call their new cooperative structure the Bay Area Metropolitan Council. But this title implied that the local governments cede more authority in their cooperation than they wished, and so they settled for the Association of Bay Area Governments (ABAG).

THE ASSOCIATION OF BAY AREA GOVERNMENTS

On its creation in 1961, ABAG opened its membership to 9 counties, 98 cities, over a hundred special tax districts and 24 transit agencies in the Bay Area. The Association adopted the functions of studying metropolitan problems, of originating recommendations for policy and of reviewing government proposals. When the region's dominant cities of San Francisco and Oakland belatedly joined, the Association had the potential to become the official planning agency for the whole metropolitan area which, in the first 30 years of ABAG's life, would almost double its population by a growth of over 2.5 million.

But ABAG has never realised its potential. Its ambitions in regional planning grew during the 1960s, when the federal government placed weight on metropolitan and regional planning as a context for the allocation of federal funds. ABAG itself moved to have the State legislature enact a bill to make the Association a multi-purpose statutory authority for the Bay Area, responsible for regional planning, refuse disposal, open space and parks, and regional airports. There was much support in the Area for an enhanced regional authority, but the passage of legislation was suspended. There were differences over whether the authority would be directly elected and separate from existing local governments, or would be representative of them. And despite repeated attempts in the 1970s to pass legislation to create various forms of multi-purpose authority, all failed.

ABAG did produce an initial regional plan in 1970 which was amended in 1980, envisaging a 'City Centre Region' to concentrate housing at higher density and save green space between. But the plan had limited success (Rothblatt and Jones 1991). Within twenty years it was a 'dead letter' (Lewis 1991, 36), overtaken by the forces of urban dispersal and of ambitious local tax-earning development projects stimulated by the effect of Proposition 13 on revenues. City governments were driven to attract commercial building and to push residential developments to the metropolitan periphery. Local governments sought to make up lost property tax revenue by fostering development contrary to sound regional planning.

As growth burgeoned, reaction set in. San Francisco restrained office construction in the city centre within limits more stringent than its planners had recommended. Some suburban communities abruptly curtailed further residential development; other local governments persisted with growth. The context for regional planning was anti-collective; the individual agendas of local governments precluded a unified strategy. ABAG was neutered.

After substantial withdrawal of federal funding in the 1980s, ABAG branched into earning revenue by servicing local governments and working under contract for the private sector. It provided advice on preparing for earthquakes, and it administered insurance and worker's compensation schemes for public agencies. Its original purpose of comprehensive regional planning shrank as attention was allowed to only selected strategic issues including regional trails, water quality, earthquake safety, air quality, hazardous spills, solid waste management, jobs and economic development, and housing (Jones and Rothblatt 1993, 406). But ABAG has no authority to directly implement any policy it may conclude.

As ABAG's planning functions shrank, so did its significance alongside the Metropolitan Transportation Commission and other California State single-purpose regional commissions, notably the Coastal Commission, the Bay Area Air Quality Management District responsible for the regional *Air Quality Plan*, the Bay Regional Quality Board and the Bay Conservation and Development Commission – which had quite effectively protected the Bay from being filled-in in the absence of sufficient support in the councils of government for adequate legislative protection. The fragmentation of the region's management was reflected in the 24 special transit districts and authorities, and the 108 additional special districts for parks, water, sewerage, fire and other purposes.

So, looking back from the 1990s, ABAG can be seen to have been rarely more than the sum of its parts. It has been subordinate to the individual interests of its members, and particularly of its suburban local governments. It is regarded as having no value to San Francisco, and as having taken no initiatives to make itself significant to what remains the Bay Area's major focus, although San Jose is now more populous. Like other regional organisations in the US, ABAG's influence has subsided since the mid 1970s. The adoption of Proposition 13 by Californian voters in 1978 led to a halving of ABAG staff in five years. Of an ABAG planning staff of 15 in 1992, the majority worked on data analysis and information systems and only 6 on policy studies.

The many state commissions are considerably interlocked. They have authority which ABAG has never matched. The 1982 *Bay Area Air Quality Plan* requires the Metropolitan Transit Commission to delay projects which might have an adverse effect on air quality. The Transit Commission's *Regional Transportation Plan* of 1983 was a detailed plan resting on ABAG forecasts of employment and population change. But there has been no comprehensive and binding regional strategy to which the commisssions and their plans can directly respond.

In 1990, ABAG's Executive Board did adopt a statement on a *Proposed Land Use Policy Framework* for the Bay Area. It advocated a city-centred concept of urban development, with 'balanced growth guided into or around existing communities in order to preserve surrounding open space and agricultural land, as well as environmentally sensitive areas' (ABAG 1990). But the *Framework's* five policies were equally unexceptionable to most of ABAG's membership, who were merely encouraged to: direct growth where there was capacity in regional infrastructure, and where natural resources would not be overburdened; foster development which minimised commuting by car and increased access by other means of transit; establish firm boundaries for urban growth; support housing for all income levels; establish new communities along transit corridors with spare capacity.

The proposed *Framework* was an overt attempt to fend off the State government, offering the faint prospect that local governments would support state agencies to achieve effective regional growth management. But ABAG's regional strategy planning was in practice little more than sum of the separate plans of its individual members, moderated within the limits of regional growth forecasts. In 1991, more than half of the Bay Area's local governments limited their growth by regulations supplementing land use controls. Limited subregional planning amongst groups of local governments occurred, but although Californian State legislation required that municipalities prepare a general plan, ABAG was politically incapable of setting growth targets for individual local governments. Yet this put it in a vulnerable position when the State Governor had established an Interagency Council on Growth Management, charged with the job of proposing a statewide mechanism for regional growth management.

However, if ABAG had become more reactive than it was far-sighted and had only limp ambitions to plan regionally, other interests had stronger intent. Popular and corporate concern about the Bay Area's intense problems of traffic gridlock and deteriorating quality of life had fostered a host of public and corporate initiatives urging alternative directions forward. All argued for regional action, but for different agendas. More enduring successors and influences than had been the Regional Plan Association of the 1920s, the Greenbelt Alliance and the Bay Area Council remain the two longest standing and most creative of the interest groups. But whereas the Greenbelt Alliance's view of the metropolitan future sought to curb sprawl and implicitly to restrain growth, the Bay Area Council saw growth as the basis for a strategy which would even so also curb sprawl.

THE BAY AREA COUNCIL AND THE GREENBELT ALLIANCE

The two most senior of the Bay Area's interest groups mixed with several others of only temporary life or of narrower regional interest. The Bay Area Economic

Forum combined high-level public and private representatives, sponsored by ABAG and the Bay Area Council and openly favouring growth. The Forum has sought to market the region's potential beyond the region and to press within it for more action on its traffic problems. The California Business Roundtable represented corporate chief executives, attempting to produce a statewide coalition for action on growth issues. Traffic problems were the focus of pressure from groups including Californians for Better Transportation and the Bay Area Commute Alternatives Alliance.

Founded at the end of the Second World War, the Bay Area Council is a consortium of over 200 regional, national and international, industrial and commercial interests, including oil companies, banks, electronic industries and management consultants. Its 1988 report, *Making Sense of the Region's Growth*, clearly showed the Council's motivation to reduce the damage which lack of regional planning threatened to its members' financial interests. Fragmented planning had brought an inefficient and inadequate infrastructure for transport, sewerage, water supply and other services, on which economical and continuing economic, population and urban growth depended. The Council wished to see more rapid transit projects, a green belt, enough waste disposal sites, pooling of water supply and planning for it, and a streamlined process of regional development permits. Lack of regional planning curtailed growth, and growth was the Council's business.

Regional planning's potential benefits to the members of the Bay Area Council were not all explicitly stated. Affordable housing, compact development and easier and cheaper transportation would reduce employees' costs, and reduce wage and salary needs. The problem of polluted air has threatened freedom of transportation. So industry and commerce have had much to gain from regional planning, and their goals and policies to achieve it have had a surprising amount in common with those of the conservationists and the supporters of the Greenbelt Alliance.

The Bay Area Council has been led into many strategic initiatives to help its members. It has participated in a campaign to get local governments to fairly help meet the housing needs of minorities and low income households. It has helped to link schools to industry and commerce. It has encouraged training programmes. It has analysed future regional employment trends. It has pressed for reform of water supply. It has linked with the group of Californians for Better Transportation to foster more effective congestion management programs.

Although sustained primarily by a membership of foundations with environmental interests and private citizens, the Greenbelt Alliance has won a remarkably significant position in Bay Area affairs. Originating in 1958 as Citizens for Recreation and Parks and translated into the Greenbelt Alliance in 1987, the Alliance promotes effective protection of the Area's green belt, actively defends open land against development proposals, initiates or supports campaigns for new parks and trails, promotes coastal protection projects and argues the case for more compact urban growth and for strategic planning. A bridge of personal confidence

**Bay Area Council
Executive
Committee**

Chairman
George M. Keller
*Chairman of the Board
and CEO
Chevron Corporation*

David A. Bossen
*Presiden and CEO
Measurex Corporation*

Albert Bowers
*Chairman and CEO
Syntex Corporation*

James T. Clarke
*Regional Managing Partner
Coopers and Lybrand*

Richard A. Clarke
*Chairman of the Board
and CEO
Pacific Gas and Electric
Company*

A.W. Clausen
*Chairman and CEO
Bank of America*

Paul M. Cook
*Chairman of the Board
and CEO
Raychem Corporation*

Myron Du Bain
*Chairman of the Board
SRI International*

Sam Ginn
*Chairman and CEO
Pacific Telesis Group*

James R. Harvey
*Chairman of the Board
and CEO
Transamerica Corporation*

Paul Hazen
*President
Wells Fargo Bank*

John M. Lillie
*Chairman and CEO
Lucky Stores, Inc.*

Charles A. Lynch
*President and CEO
Levolor*

Richard B. Madden
*Chairman and CEO
Potlatch Corporation*

Cornell C. Maier
*Director and Consultant
KaiserTech Limited*

Robert T. Parry
*President and CEO
Federal Reserve Bank
of San Fransisco*

James A. Vohs
*Chairman and President
Kaiser Foundation Health
Plan, Inc.*

Ex Officio
Angelo. J. Siracusa
*President
Bay Area Council*

**Bay Area Council
Project Staff**

Project Manager
Thomas B. Cook
*Director of Housing and
Land Use*

Brigitte LeBlanc
*Vice President
Communications*

Stephen E. Barton, Ph.D.
Policy Analyst

Bay Area Council
847 Sansome Street
San Francisco
CA 94111

*Figure 7.6. Campaigning for economic efficiency in the Bay Area: the top people in
US business and industry support the Bay Area Council*

EXECUTIVE SUMMARY

PUTTING GROWTH ISSUES IN CONTEXT

The region's growth patterns have been undergoing a fundamental shift. Job growth is no longer focused on central cities, but is distributed among multiple suburban employment centres - a pattern of "deconcentration" being experienced by nearly all major metropolitan regions in the U.S. To avoid worsening growth problems, our planning systems must adapt to this change.

Resolving growth problems is critical to our future quality of life and economy. The Bay Area's prosperity is strongly linked to our unique quality of life - and our quality of life is made possible in part by our economic strength and affluence. If the current growth trends and climate are not improved, we risk losing the advantages Bay Area residents have come to take for granted.

UNDERSTANDING GROWTH PROBLEMS

Bay Area job growth has been shifting to the suburbs for some 40 years. San Francisco has not had a majority of the region's jobs since 1947. The Bay Area's unique geography, the development of major freeways, the emergence of the high-tech industry in the South Bay, and business' growing tendency to follow the workforce have all fueled the development of multiple job centres in the region. Since 1980, most of the region's new jobs and office space have been created outside San Francisco, Oakland, and San Jose.

Fiscal forces have been a major factor in suburban job growth, and in the severe shortage of housing near job centres. Since Proposition 13, communities have had a strong financial incentive to encourage revenue-generating office, industrial and commercial development, rather than new housing. Some communities have welcomed new job and retail centres regardless of their ability to handle added traffic and housing needs, a practice that has done much to incite public resistance to growth.

The planning for growth has been based on traditional values and development patterns, not on the realities of a deconcentrating region. Responding to citizens' preferences for single-family housing and the desire to minimize the impacts of development, suburban communities have tended to zone for low-density residential and industrial development. This pattern has pushed development into outlying areas, while pushing up the cost of suburban housing. It has also had a major effect on traffic, creating criss-cross commute patterns and scattering job sites and homes beyond the point where they can be effectively served by transit or van pools.

Land use decisions have been divorced from planning for infrastructure. Suburban development patterns have not been designed to make efficient use of available transportation, sewer, and water services; at the same time, growth has often been approved for areas where adequate urban services have not been available - and as a result, has had to for greater negative impacts than would have come with the necessary systems in place.

Our ability to fund infrastructure is lagging ever further behind demand. The growth of the '80s has been made possible by the infrastructure investments made in the past, but the Bay Area has been living off those assets without providing for future growth. Many communities are reaching the capacity of transportation, wastewater, and solid waste systems.

Each Community makes growth decisions in isolation. Policies that make sense at the local level often don't add up at the subregional or regional levels, and one city's traffic levels or housing needs can be dramatically affected by another city's unilateral decisions. Yet communities have devoted more energy to competing for revenue-producing growth than to coordinating their plans, and current State law gives cities little incentive to work with their neighbours.

LOOKING AHEAD

Regional forecasts anticipate slower growth and continuing deconcentration in the future. They also point to a worsening shortage of housing, a need for major investments in transportation, and a worsening mismatch between the location of new jobs and new housing. These problems, and their effect on the supply of skilled labour, raise serious questions about the region's economic wealth in the future.

The deconcentration of jobs has resulted in problems, but it could be an opportunity. The lack of planning to guide deconcentration has meant dislocations in housing, more traffic, and changes in community character. But if well planned, deconcentration can increase economic, housing, and recreational opportunities while easing pressures on central cities.

Growth problems demand immediate, practical solutions. We cannot wait to achieve radical changes, such as weaning Americans from the automobile. Instead, we must move to adopt and improve the management of growth in a variety of ways. Among key planning objectives: a better balance of housing and jobs, more clustering of homes and employment centres, more funding for infrastructure, better coordination of infrastructure and land-use decisions, and a restructuring of fiscal incentives for local growth decisions.

The greatest need: a new framework for dealing with growth problems that transcend local boundaries. Many local leaders and the public strongly agree that more coordination among community land-use and infrastructure decisions is needed. Growth problems can be solved, but only if all concerned can work toward the same ends.

TAKING ACTION ON SOLUTIONS

Our system of planning must be overhauled to support and motivate more cooperative planning by local governments. The planning framework must be altered enough to give communities a strong reason to make and enforce difficult multi-jurisdictional decisions, but not so much as to undermine local authority.

Neither a voluntary approach nor a "top-down" mandatory approach to cooperative planning will work. Voluntary cooperation breaks down when communities feel they are being asked to compromise too much, and voluntary decisions are difficult to make and enforce. On the other hand, State level planning would be too far removed from local concerns, and creation of a strong regional planning agency is fraught with political and technical difficulties.

Moving toward a subregional framework for planning could be the answer. At least for the near term. It is at the subregional level that communities are likely to have the greatest mutual understanding and the biggest stake in reaching agreement.

To be effective, subregional planning must be formalised and adequately funded, with strong incentives for cooperation. Perhaps the best incentive available would be to tie state funding for transportation and other community improvements to the completion and adequacy of subregional infrastructure plans. While the state should not make growth decisions, it alone can set ground-rules for effective planning. But the authority to review plans and allocate funds need not rest with the State; other options include creation of a special body of local representatives.

The planning of growth can be improved in many other ways in the meantime. Local governments have the power to pursue many planning goals, particularly the creation of more affordable housing to match job growth. Regional level decision-making could be strengthened. And the State should provide more resources for infrastructure, strengthen current housing and planning requirements, and reward communities for better growth management.

The Bay Area is at on a clearing with issues of growth.

Even though the region's patterns of growth have some serious adverse effects: rapidly worsening traffic congestion, a shortage of affordable housing, changes in the character of our communities, and widespread public resistance to growth.

Yet based on our current population and job base alone, the region will continue to grow. And at least some growth is needed, not only to house our residents and maintain the health of our economy in the future, but to help ease pressures caused by inadequate housing and transportation.

The time for action is now. Regional systems are beginning to reach the breaking point, and failing to act would be an advice with devastating consequences for our quality of life and, ultimately, our economy. Creating a subregionally based planning framework will not solve growth problems overnight. But it is an evolutionary approach that will allow us to move toward better management of growth, and a better future for the Bay Area.

Figure 7.7. Growth issues in the Bay Area: the Bay Area Council summarises the issues in regional growth management

between the Alliance's Director, Larry Orman, and the President of the Bay Area Council, Angelo Siracusa, spanning from the Bay Area's environmental to its the industrial and conmmercial interests, was a major contribution to the *Bay Vision 2020* initiative.

Although the Bay Area Council and the Greenbelt Alliance formed a strong association in favour of much improved regional planning, tensions between those for growth and those against it have been extreme in a region with a strong tradition of environmental action. But by initiatives to seek common ground to reconcile growth and anti-growth factions, the major groups formed investigative coalitions. The Greenbelt Alliance and the Bay Area Council formed the joint Regional Issues Forum. The Council and ABAG formed the Bay Area Economic Forum, and ABAG, the Metropolitan Transit Commission and the Air Quality Management District combined to commission a study of how the Bay Area might develop over the coming 30 years, as far ahead as the year 2020. This study was given the title *Bay Vision 2020*.

Industry and business had come to the idea of regional planning to minimise confrontation with local governments deciding to protect their residential environment, or limiting the costs of building roads or other public facilities often required because of growth of adjoining cities. Local governments at Petaluma in 1972 and Walnut Creek in 1984 had been amongst the first in the United States to limit residential and commercial growth respectively.

The demand for regional planning and the control of its underlying problems spread into the cities. San Francisco had been the first major city in the nation to set an annual limit to office building, and many interests in the city called for regional planning for the future. Local interests mostly preferred this to be done cooperatively by the area's local governments rather than by intervention by the State of California. Others had different motivations to propose regional governance. In 1990, the speaker of the State Legislature proposed to merge regional agencies into seven regional governments for the State of California, including one for the Bay area. Some saw this as a move favouring developers (Lewis 1991, 142).

A NEW VISION FOR THE BAY?

The incoherence of Bay Area strategy was unsatisfactory to interests beyond ABAG, and to some within it. The hiatus encouraged separate initiatives by the Metropolitan Transportation Commission and by the Regional Issues Forum, which had been sponsored by the Bay Area Council in association with the Greenbelt Alliance. Each initiative sought to shape a coherent view on the region's problems, and through it to find policies and the means to manage regional growth in a collective way. Regional planning was being asserted as an interest not just of local governments, but equally of private business, industry, citizens' groups and of the established Commissions for the major Bay-wide activities of Metropolitan Transport and Air Quality Management.

The two initiatives combined in the Bay Vision 2020 Commission, launched in 1989 and comprising 'blue ribbon citizens' appointed in association with ABAG, the chairs of the boards of supervisors for the Area's nine counties and the mayors of the three major cities. Chaired by a former Chancellor of the University of California at Berkeley and with a staff of only six, the 31 temporary commissioners came primarily from the ranks of business, politics, the housing and land development industry and high technology interests in Silicon Valley, rather than from the Bay Area's general citizenry.

Reporting in 1991, the Commission suggested how to avoid a 'region that emulates Los Angeles'. Its paramount conclusion was that the Bay Area had plenty of government, but without the organisation that the future required. There were single-purpose agencies for air quality, water quality, Bay filling and transportation, but no multi-purpose agency which could effectively relate these problems to regional land use and activity issues. The region was continuing to disperse into counties beyond the recognised nine of the old Bay Area, and was doing so at unsatisfactorily low density. Environmental quality was deteriorating in some respects, and was connected to issues which were not being tackled regionally. And the core of the Area contained insufficient affordable housing for lower income households.

The *Bay Vision* was that the key to improved management of regional issues would be democratic and accountable regional governance, not 'vertically' arranged as in the established single-purpose agencies, but horizontally organised in a consolidated commission combining the Bay Area Air Quality Management District, the Metropolitan Transportation Commission and ABAG. Later, the Bay Regional Water Quality Control Board, the Bay Conservation and Development Commission, waste management and other agencies might also be absorbed. The new permanent Commission would prepare a regional plan integrating the work of the merged agencies, and would submit it for approval by the State Governor and Legislature.

After the regional plan had been approved, it would be implemented by the new Commission, which would not operate or build such things as transportation systems, but could prevent local development interfering with or inconsistent with the plan. And the Commission would be able to recommend financial penalties if local governments disregarded regional goals and policies.

Some essential issues stood out from *Bay Vision 2020*: what part would the Commission play in arranging regional tax-sharing; to what extent would sub-regional planning persist – a euphemism for parochial planning by local government; could the merged agencies be effectively combined to a unified purpose; would the Commission be elected or nominated; and would the *Vision* be supported by the State legislature?

The Bay Vision Action Coalition formed to pursue the *Vision* immediately helped place a bill before the State Senate to initiate regional growth management for the Bay Area. A Regional Commission would be created from January 1994 by merging ABAG, the Bay Area Air Quality Management District and the Metropolitan Transportation Commission. The Commission would be required to prepare a regional strategy for conservation and development, in consultation with planning associations for each of the nine counties of the Area based on the recently created congestion management agencies. The Commission would work to help establish urban growth boundaries in the counties, and the measures of its plan should coordinate infrastructure planning and funding, achieve federal and state standards for air and water, protect agricultural and open land, restore the ecological health of the Bay Area, promote development which was compact and which supported mass transit, encourage affordable housing, and propose fiscal strategies for the State to adopt. The Commission would have the status of a state-mandated local programme.

Over the following year, the bill passed from the Senate to the State Assembly, suffering amendments as opponents and doubters trimmed its sharper edges. It was made explicit that the Commission would have no powers or authority to tax or to control land use not already existing, and local government powers would not be affected. The bill sustained the *Vision* of compact, affordable and environmentally sensitive development in the Bay Area. But although city representatives on the Commission would dominate politicians from the counties, it seemed unlikely that the Commission could readily escape the constraints which neutered ABAG.

Despite its opponents, the bill retained key elements of an effective planning machinery. A study of alternative population growth scenarios for 2020 was to be undertaken. The Commission would also analyse current projections about population, employment and housing growth, recommending policies to reconcile them with regional criteria for efficient and environmentally acceptable growth. There would be ample ground for dispute there, if the Commission were to flex its muscles. Similarly, there was room for bitter argument in the invitation to make fiscal proposals to smooth inequities in sales and tax revenues arising from land use policy.

But it seemed that the bill might sink or run aground in the storms of Californian politics in the early 1990s, brought on by the delayed effects of state and federal Reaganomics savagely eroding California's finances. Preoccupation with deep cuts in state spending pushed growth management in the Bay Area behind others of the Governor's problems. It seemed unlikely that the Bay Area bill could be passed before 1993, if at all. It lay in danger of being sidelined as the initiatives in regional government of 20 years before had been.

The Bay Area issue was unlikely to be derailed for long, however, as the regional interests of the Bay Area had significant friends in the region's economy. In the fastest growing southern sub-region of the Area, the Santa Clara County Manufacturing Group established in 1978 had been showing much the same concern for transport congestion, the environment and housing that the Bay Area Council had longer held. There were also other regional pressures in California, with demand in the north of the state to secede from the south and to create two Californias. One way or another, regional issues would persist in the most populous of the nation's states.

Conclusion: Enduring Regional Initiatives

Regional issues creating pressure for regional planning are inherent in the environment of fragmented complexity of US local government. Competition and self-interest arise in a local system ill-fitted to the social and economic geography of the late twentieth century. Without prospect of comprehensive reform such as European countries arrange periodically, regional issues will never be subsumed into the everyday practice of unified local government.

As in other countries, the mix of regional stimuli changes. At times, the federal government has initiated new moves to plan and govern regionally. In the 1980s, state governments were the bolder. But whether formally recognised as regional planning or in the guise of growth management, the regional dimension has endured. Only its scales and its titles have changed; initiatives in regional planning and governance will inevitably recur in the marble-cake federacy.

CHAPTER EIGHT

Regions and the Nature of Regional Planning
A Cross-National Comparison

Preface: The Ubiquitous Region

The regional planning which has been described has occurred within many different contexts, has been stimulated by a variety of issues, and has been associated with many different forms of regional governance.

Before drawing conclusions about the nature of regional planning, some of its types and of its relationships with governance have to be identified. Although such a typology must be arbitrary to some degree, some framework must be employed if the comparative performance of different cases of regional planning is to be fairly assessed.

Also, we have to carefully choose the criteria by which we measure performance. Some unfavourable criticism of regional planning may have had unreasonable expectations of it. So a reasonable evaluation requires the grounds for analysis to be set against distinguishable criteria. And criticism must be informed by an understanding of the kinds of stimuli causing regional planning to insistently recur.

Typologies of Regional Planning and Governance

Regions of Multiple Variety

Compiling a typology of regional planning and governance raises the dilemma of how to mix and match cases of great variety. Plans and processes have been of many styles and differing degrees of substance and ambition. Previous typologies of regional planning have been prevailingly uni-dimensional, focusing primarily on geographical scale, or on relativities between the authority of sub-national levels of governance, or on the style of regional planning involved. And typologies of governance have had little regard to planning.

The most widespread categorisation of regions in official use is the European Community's NUTS system, imposing a unified system of regions on the map of Europe, where the internal regions of member states differ greatly in status and scale. So the system's principal emphasis on geographical scale means that NUTS regions fall under widely differing arrangements for governance in the different countries.

At the largest scale of NUTS level 1 regions, only Germany, Belgium, Spain and Portugal of the twelve EC member states have sub-national elected autonomous governments. There are similar inconsistencies at the successively smaller scales of NUTS level 2 and NUTS level 3 regions. And if a Transatlantic comparison were attempted by integrating the United States into the NUTS system, further problems would arise. The NUTS system could not really accommodate the size of California, for example, despite US state governance being otherwise quite comparable to that of the German *Länder* or of the autonomous regions of Spain.

Focusing more on forms of regional governance, a basic typology like that of Rhodes (1974) distinguishes: regional administration, which is the breaking down of central government into geographical divisions, as with the Scottish Office or the partially coordinated regional offices of government in England; regional economic planning, which is government's recognition that special measures are necessary in selected regions of the country, with or without any geographical rearrangement of administration; regional government, which involves the passing of some government power to a reorganised local government; and regional devolution, which is regional government raised to the status of a legislative assembly.

This simple categorisation of Rhodes's is concerned with means of organising the execution of policies, but it specifies only regional economic planning, which in the UK has been largely distinct from regional planning for metropolitan and urban development. Omitting strategic physical planning thereby neglects a principal stimulus for the reorganisation of local government in Britain up to 1975.

A start to crystallising measures by which to compare and analyse the effectiveness of different kinds of practice might be to initially employ Gillingwater and Hart's (1978, 8) three distinctions, which are between the *making*, the *communication* and the *control* of policy. It is one thing to make good policy, another to ensure that the policy message is clearly passed on to those who expected to share in applying it, and an altogether different thing to effectively implement it.

The planning process can be described in other ways. For example, Martins (1986, 190) describes four dimensions of: the *sponsoring organisations*, an *appraisal and approval network*, an *intelligence network* and an *influence network*. In Martin's taxonomy, the sponsoring organisations together with the appraisal and approval network are equivalent to Gillingwater and Hart's process of plan or policy making, the intelligence network to their communication process, and the influence network to their control process.

These are very various ways of describing regions, governance and regional planning. They have to be somehow related if cases of regional planning are to be understood within their different contexts, so that the comparative performance of regional planning can be fairly evaluated. It is necessary to account for its political context and the degree to which it is linked to executive capacities. But before constructing a typology which somehow links regional planning and governance, some aspects of these should be explored.

Regional Planning
THE SIGNIFICANCE OF CONTEXTS

The significance for regional planning of different political contexts can be illustrated by comparing the UK and the US, although the context in each country has contained a rather different mix of components at different times. Choosing only the period of Thatcher and Reagan government in the 1980s, the respective political contexts were as shown below.

United Kingdom	United States
Inherited obligations to the dissolved kingdoms and to old 'national' identities	Rapidly shifting population and fewer debts to internal 'nations'
No significant devolved legislative capacities	Significant devolution to state legislatures
Regional agencies of government as placebos and to assert government hegemony	Retreat of regional agencies of federal intervention
Displacement of local government so as to unify local policy and reduce local government spending	Increased emphasis on states' responsibilities by cutting federal aid
Limited experience of councils of regional government and of recent regional cooperation	More experience of councils of regional government and of recent regional cooperation
Long practice of regional rather than local economic policy	Longer practice of local but little of regional economic policy
Brief practice of major regional development projects	Considerable practice in big regional development projects
More experience of integrated regional plans	Scarce recent experience of integrated regional plans
Over-representation of urban areas in Parliament	Historic under-representation of urban areas in Congress
Dissolution of metropolitan strategic planning with minimal replacement at regional scale.	Reinforced emphasis on state planning at strategic and regional levels.

So differences of political context help explain why the 1980s brought different experiences in regional and strategic planning to the UK and the US, despite both countries being driven in the period by ostensibly similar political ideologies. Both governments abhorred the idea of 'regional planning', and the practice generally declined in both countries. But it actually advanced in the US at the level of state government, whereas in the UK it tended to retreat as metropolitan government was dissolved.

THE SUBSTANCE OF REGIONAL PLANNING

Contextual differences in different cases of regional planning are commonly associated with differences of substance. Different times mean different economic or social priorities, while different sponsors have different concerns. Varying contexts of governance provide varying strengths of political support for planning proposals.

As basic as any of the differences in the substance of regional planning is that between its economic and physical forms. Although combined in some cases and in some countries, there is a long history of tension between these two kinds. There has frequently been serious incomprehension between practitioners of the two kinds, notably on the part of economists dictating the regional components of plans for developing the sectors of a national economy. Much confusion arises by those seeing regional planning as only of the one kind, or by those who see two but wholly separate kinds.

But, of course, there are varieties within physical and economic planning and in the ways in which they may combine. The terms *regional economic planning* and *regional development planning* are commonly interchanged, although the former tends to imply training, financial or other measures of support for business and industry, while the latter tends to imply a programme with a large component of physical infrastructure. Weaver (1990) traces the international history of regional development planning in three stages, each of different substance; he distinguishes a first phase of comprehensive river basin development planning, exemplified by the TVA in the US and by the Aswan High Dam project in Egypt, succeeded by a phase of spatial development planning in which growth centres, external control and optimum models of urban systems were expected to stimulate growth in underdeveloped or depressed regions, followed by a third and current phase of decentralised development planning, in which the weaknesses of the earlier approaches are to be mended by stimulating more local initiatives to strengthen the indigenous base of regional economies.

Glasson (1980) draws distinctions in the substance of four kinds of planning. He first distinguishes *physical* from *economic planning* before following Friedmann's distinction between *allocative* and *innovative planning*, then distinguishing *multi* from *single objective planning* and *indicative* from *imperative planning*.

Alden and Morgan (1974, 192) note the difference between *functional* planning in which the planner regards him or herself as essentially neutral, and *normative*

planning in which the planner is politically engaged and proposes value judgements. Within *normative* planning, there is a further distinction between *advocacy*
and *innovative* planning. *Innovative* planning goes beyond mere *advocacy*, because
it makes proposals about the means to achieve its ends; it combines policy with
implementation.

A classification of some British regional planning studies of the 1960s by
Cowling and Steeley (1973, 15) distinguished between those helping decisions
on the *allocation* of resources, and others more concerned with *coordinating*
decisions by other organisations. This is a useful distinction, although most
contemporary regional planning implies something of each characteristic.

These various distinctions relate to substance in regard to the political weight
and style of plan proposals rather than to their scope. But even in one region, the
scope of regional planning may significantly vary at different times. The *Greater
London Plan* of 1944 illustrated on an Ordnance Survey map the locations of the
new and expanded towns to which London's congested households were to
decentralise, and it suggested a Regional Planning Board for Greater London with
overriding powers. No such specific proposals in these aspects has ever emerged
from the SERPLAN conference in over thirty years of life. But the *Greater London
Plan* had no conception of the issue of priorities in transport policy which
SERPLAN faced 50 years later, and shifting concerns and contexts made for other
differences in the substance of regional planning at the two periods.

Regional Governance

Some use the term *regional governance* to describe only regional administration by
government departments, regional government and regional devolution. They (e.g.
Jones 1988) neglect any of the many instances of long and significant involvement
in regional governance by local government, up to such cases of regional local
authorities as Strathclyde Regional Council or the *conseils régionaux* of France.
Others take a wider view. Barlow (1981, 21) summarises six strategies by which
a regional dimension may be achieved where local governance has been fragmented:

1. *Consolidated governance* by creating a single unit which wholly eliminates
    fragmentation. The difficulties in doing so are initial opposition from units
    wishing not to be merged, and the later difficulties in satisfying localities
    that big governance can meet local needs.

2. *Transfer of local functions* to a higher level of government. This was
    significant in the UK during the 1980s, when London Regional Transport
    and other new agencies adopted several previous local government func-
    tions as in higher education, public housing and local economic initiatives.

3. *Transfer of revenues* between units of local government can smooth
    unevenness in their comparative wealth. This can be done either by a local
    revenue-pooling scheme as in metropolitan Minneapolis-St. Paul, or may

be arranged entirely by central government, as in the UK. From the mid 1980s, the transfer to central government of local functions and of payment of business rates brought a massive transfer of local revenues in the UK. While allowing the possibility of fair redistribution of revenues to match clear local needs, such an upwards transfer is also open to political distortion, as very certainly occurred in the UK in the 1980s when selected local authorities in Conservative control were favourably funded so as to minimise local taxes.

4. *Special-purpose authorities* may be of two broad kinds. They may be on the US model and be established by sub-national governments, either by states as for the Bay Area Metropolitan Transit Commission in California, or by local governments as for the many sewerage and water supply authorities in the US, and for authorities in the UK such as that for the Lea Valley Park in London and as was set up to manage the environmental problems of the Norfolk Broads. Or they may be established by central government, as were the Tennessee Valley Authority in the US, the Etablissement Public Foncier Nord-Pas de Calais in France, the Highlands and Islands Development Board in Scotland, and the National Parks Boards in England.

5. *Inter-government* co-operation, either wholly local or involving central government. The development of regional planning in the UK has been substantially by this means, and when complete coverage of England by conferences of local planning authorities was achieved in 1992, this model seemed likely to prevail in the UK for most of the rest of the decade.

6. *Two-tier government* on the model introduced for most of the UK's urban area in the local government reforms of 1974 and 1975. It is one of the most prevalent of systems. But it has many varieties, and it is a pattern which has become complicated in such countries as Germany, France, Spain, Italy and Canada, where collaborative authorities have been introduced for strategic purposes in some metropolitan areas. And in the US, county governments complicate the picture of the two-tier system of states and municipalities, quite apart from the question as to whether states are regarded as being really a regional level of governance.

An alternative categorisation is by Keating (1982), who sees regional governance being arranged alternatively by:

- *Central government*, as an extension of its departments into regions
- *Local government*, by either cooperation or unified regional authorities
- *Mediating institutions* intermediate between central and local government, and considerably representative of and dependent on both
- *Regional institutions* of central government brought under the direction of elected regional assemblies

- *Elected regional assemblies* on a federalist model, absorbing powers devolved from government, and substituting for it in relations with local government.

European levels of government are categorised by Bennett (1989, 12) as:

- *Central Government:* overall national or federal government
- *State Government:* in federal systems, as German *Länder* or Swiss cantons
- *Regional Government:* within a state, or groups of states or of local authorities
- *Upper Tier Local Government:* province, county, *département*
- *Lower Tier Local Government:* municipality, district, commune.

Such a categorisation stratifies governments according to their relative constitutional and administrative roles. This is a helpful but necessarily simplified approach, with two principal limitations. First, it does not exactly reflect the responsibilities of the different levels, whose powers relative to one another will differ from one country to another and even within individual countries – as in the four parts of the United Kingdom. Secondly, it is inevitably inconsistent about geographical scale because politics rather than geographical consistency determine administrative divisions, and because there are no consistent international terminologies. For instance, Strathclyde Regional Council would be categorised only as an upper tier local government, although in most respects it has been more deeply and widely involved in its region's social, economic and development affairs than *conseils régionaux* in France, which would be categorised as regional governments.

The dilemma in trying to unify geographical and administrative approaches to regions cannot be perfectly resolved. The geographical region is defined by rules of homogeneity or association. These can be fairly consistently transferred from one country to another. But administrative regions arise from political and administrative history which widely differs from one country to another.

Bennett's categorisation implies that regional government is either a branch of central government within a country – as with the Scottish, Welsh or Northern Ireland Offices or the French *préfectures* – or an institution intermediate between central government and local authorities – as in the Spanish autonomous regions or the French *conseils régionaux*. This fits the definition of a region as an area where political necessity led to a planning or executive initiative, at a level not provided for by the customary central and local government arrangements for the country as a whole.

However, we have also seen that regional roles are played in many varieties of dress, significance and dialogue. Grodzins's image (1978, 265) of 'marble-cake' government is universally appropriate. Regional planning and governance cannot be described simply in terms of their levels in practice. We have to consider their varieties of purpose and their varying political contexts, as well as their scale within larger administrative systems.

Flynn *et al.* (1985, 38) outline three broad roles which metropolitan authorities may assume:

- *First*, a *functional* role in which certain services are provided at or about their optimum level, e.g. fire, public transport, water and sewerage.

- *Second*, a *strategic* role with various degrees of allied capacity to implement policies. The strategy will integrate many elements, few if any of which can be treated in isolation. But the authority may have its hands on few levers for direct implementation.

- *Third*, a *resource allocation* role with sufficient levers in the authority's hands to itself implement strategy quite effectively.

Europe shows the most complete and versatile range of means by which metropolitan and regional government may be arranged to support planning through functional, strategic and resource allocation roles. In the United States, regional arrangements have often transcended the state level, as with the Tennessee Valley Authority, the Appalachian Regional Commission, the Delaware Valley Planning Commission, and regional economic development and water planning commissions. Several of the states approximate to regional governments, and either whole state or sub-regional planning has been operated through coastal zone management, farmland preservation, flood plain control and other approaches (Lim 1983, 9).

US arrangements for planning for metropolitan regions and sub-regions of states (Advisory Committee on Intergovernmental Relations 1973, 50) illustrate less satisfactory arrangements by which the three roles may be attempted, very incompletely at times. There are:

- *Councils of government (COGs)*, which are single or multi-functional voluntary regional associations of elected local officials, or of local governments represented by their elected officials. The governing body is composed predominantly of elected councillors representing their member political jurisdictions, and at least partial funding has come from local public sources. COGs have no governmental powers or operating responsibilities, their existence resting explicitly on the goodwill of the constituent local governments. Resource allocation is normally the least of a COG's ambitions, and their functional roles are usually modest.

  Councils of this kind flourished extensively in the US after 1965, including such as that for Metropolitan Washington and the Association of Bay Area Governments (ABAG), but all were far short of the significance of Portland's directly elected metropolitan council, which grew out of a prior council of government and was a pioneering – but lonely – example of what the Advisory Commission on Intergovernmental Relations suggested (1982, 280) was the ultimate solution for US regions.

- *Metropolitan, regional, areawide or joint planning agencies or commissions (RPCs)* are sometimes defined in terms of the representation on their governing bodies. But instead of elected local officials, their members are citizens co-opted by the state government or localities involved. They are public planning bodies authorised by a state legislature under a specific act or enabling legislation. But their strategic role usually lacks the assured support of parallel commissions with functional and resource allocation capacities, as in the Bay Area where the transit and water quality commissions have a substance which ABAG has never achieved, or in the case of the Port Authority of New York and New Jersey.

- *Development district agencies* are sometimes encouraged by the federal government, and sometimes instituted by the states. Such agencies may have considerable potential to combine strategic, functional and resource allocation roles, but their political contexts commonly put constraints on their independence.

- *Hybrid areawide organisations* essentially fit the COG or RPC definitions, but such as the Twin Cities Metropolitan Council having special attributes not generally associated with either, and with powerful patronage enabling the playing of several roles at the same time.

The Twin Cities Metropolitan Council stands out in US experience. It plainly has the admiration of US planners and of many observers, although with little evidence that it is likely to be widely emulated in the United States. If it is an unattainable model for most of metropolitan America, are its merits worthwhile and replicable in the more ordered and malleable local governments of Europe? We should first translate it into more familiar terms. It is really an area committee appointed by the State Legislature, comprising co-opted and unelected members. In UK terms, it is comparable to a quango appointed by a county or regional council; it has small similarities to the regional economic planning councils for England of the period 1965–79, but with far greater capacity to guide or divert central or local government programmes.

The Twin Cities Council is a top-down approach, in essence. It maintains State authority rather than ceding influence to a council of governments, as the federal government might have preferred. It is even so a filter, not a valve controlling development and programmes. It depends upon retaining the Legislature's confidence, as well as that of the local governments in its jurisdiction.

Hogwood (1982, 13) suggests a simplified illustration of three models of regional government. Of these, his first two have been reflected in French experience, and his third by practice in England. None of the three has been reflected in US experience.

(a) Ideal type 'prefect' model

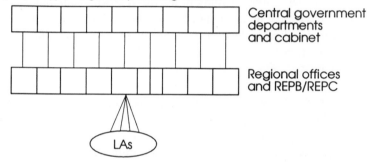

(b) Ideal type 'regional planning' model

(c) Simplified description of actual English regional arrangements

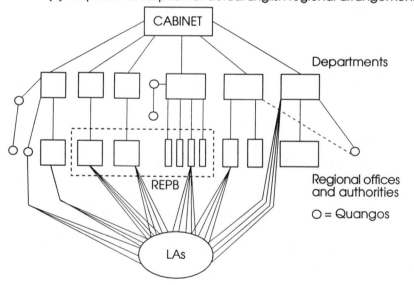

Figure 8.1. Models of regional government and arrangements in England 1965–79 (Hogwood 1982)

Typologies

The wide variety in which regional planning and modes of regional governance can by typified reflects their variety of meanings for different people. Often, it also reflects an approach of abstract categorisation rather than observation of experience. Our purpose is to typify cases from experience in several countries in some very different contexts, and without it being possible to pursue all the subtleties of all cases.

Devising a new typology might start by recognising the variety of stimuli giving rise to regional plans and forms of regional governance. Technocratic stimuli may be provided by philosophers of civic improvement or of rational planning, from Richard Dyer Norton in Chicago and New York to Britton Harris of the Penn-Jersey Transportation Study, or the Royal Town Planning Institute Working Party; stimulus may lie in the political opportunism of a government, from the consular regionalism of the Roman Empire up to the creation of the GLC in 1964 and its abolition in 1986; and there may be stimulus of popular demand for representation in regional affairs as led to autonomous regions in Spain in the 1980s.

So, the stimuli to regional initiatives must be given weight in a typology, because they help determine the substance of regional planning and the status of forms of regional governance. And as there is no substance to regional planning if it is not effectively implemented, then a significant aspect of governance to be taken into account is capacity for implementation. However, we have seen that effective implementation may occur in the absence of an agency designed to directly execute regional plans and policies; this will be evident when cases are fitted into the typology.

We might accordingly regard four dimensions as being notably significant in relations between regional planning and regional governance. Stimuli and substance being the notable dimensions of regional planning, and form and capacity for implementation being the notable dimensions of regional governance.

Pairing these dimensions, two typologies can be devised into which we can be fit the cases reviewed:

- *First*, of cases of regional planning including regional governance with a special planning content, categorised according to their stimulus and substance.

- *Second*, of cases of regional governance; categorised according to whether created primarily to exchange information, to derive policy, to allocate resources or to implement directly.

STIMULI x SUBSTANCE IN REGIONAL PLANNING AND IN GOVERNANCE WITH A SPECIAL PLANNING CONTENT

Voluntarist and reformist groups were a main stimulus to regional planning in the earlier twentieth century; they remain so in parts of the US and were re-emerging in the UK in the 1990s. Some have come from the side of environmental concern,

		PRIMARILY ECONOMIC		PRIMARILY PHYSICAL	
		MANDATORY/ALLOCATIVE	INDICATIVE/COORDINATING	MANDATORY/ALLOCATIVE	INDICATIVE/COORDINATING
ADMINISTRATIVE AND TECHNOCRATIC PRESSURES	ADMINISTRATIVE DEVOLUTION	NHS Regional Administration Regional Ahs Boards	Government Regional Offices (1965)		
	TECHNOCRATIC DEMANDS				Penn-Jersey Transport Study Greater Glasgow Transport Study SELNEC Transport Study
LOCAL POLITICAL CRISES	INTER-LOCAL GOVERNMENT GROWTH MANAGEMENT				Standing Conference on South-East Regional planning London Planning Advisory Committee West Midlands Forum
	FAILURE OR LIMITATIONS OF LOCAL GOVERNMENT	Columbia River Basin Project (US)	West Central Scotland Plan Strategic Plan for the South East	Countryside Commission	South East Joint Planning Team Leicester-Leicestershire Sub-regional Study Coventry-Solihull-Warwicks Sub-regional Study Derby-Derbyshire Sub-regional Study
	CENTRAL/LOCAL STRUGGLE	Local Enterprise Companies Conseils Régionals (France)		English Partnerships	
POLITICAL CRISES AT THE CENTRE	WAR AND OTHER CRISES	Länder (Germany Autonomous) Regions (Spain)	Greater London Plan Clyde Valley Plan Government Regional Directors (1994)	Air Raid Commissioners	
	DEMOGRAPHIC CRISES			Humberside, Severnside and Tayside Studies	
	ECONOMIC CRISES	Central Scotland programme for Development and Growth Scottish Enterprise Highlands and Islands Enterprise Appalachian Regional Commission Tennessee Valley Authority (US)	National Plan West Central Scotland Plan Regional Economic Planning Councils and Boards		
VOLUNTARISM	SOCIAL AND ENVIRONMENTAL INTERESTS		Growth Management (US)	Greenbelt Alliance (US) Conurbation (Birmingham and Black Country)	
	ECONOMIC INTERESTS	Bay Area Council (US)		Chicago Plan (US)	

Figure 8.2. Typology of forms of regional governance: according to stimuli and substance

others have represented the interests of business and industry. Similarly detached from direct party politics have been technocratic or administrative stimuli, from groups concerned for rationality in their professional operations; professionals of town and country and of transportation planning have pressed for regional planning and have initiated it, and administrators in strongly centralised bureaucracies such as those of the UK in the 1980s and 1990s have been often associated with measures of devolved regional administration, sometimes strongly reflecting political ideology.

Direct political initiatives have been the principal stimuli to regional planning, however, arising from political crises of various kinds and at various levels of governance. Crises may occur at the centre, arising from national or regional economic threats to a government's electoral future, from demographic trends implying exceptional demand for urban growth, from a war's implications for civil defence or emergency administration, or from conditions calling for widespread political devolution. Or the crises may be more localised, lying in particular local political circumstances or a lack of capacity amongst particular local governments to effectively fulfil regional needs; or long-term growth management may call for semi-permanent arrangements for regional planning to forestall local crises.

The substance of regional planning is described in the typology as primarily physical or primarily economic, and in both cases as either indicative and coordinating in nature or as mandatory and allocative. Examples of regional planning which are indicative and coordinating are normally associated with forms of governance emphasising information and policy; those which are mandatory and allocative are usually more closely linked to forms of governance with a fair capacity for direct implementation.

FORMS OF GOVERNANCE x CAPACITY TO IMPLEMENT DIRECTLY
Together with a simple division of governance into central, local and intermediate sub-national levels, we must recognise the role of external voluntary or pressure groups in the experience of regional planning. Some have been sources of regional data and others have been advisory or advocacy groups. As in the Bay Area of the US, they have been at times highly active in regional politics and capable of forcing regional issues onto political agendas. So the typology must include at least four contributions to governance.

An inbuilt capacity to implement proposals is no guarantee that a form of regional governance will effectively fulfil a regional plan, nor is it a prerequisite for fulfilment. Different contexts of politics and of interplay between levels and bodies of governance may be crucially influential. But the less able it is to directly implement, the more a source of regional planning proposals must depend on political patronage, on indirectly influencing resources, and on such other levers it can engage to bear on events beyond its own capacity to realise.

	CENTRAL GOVERNMENT	SUB-NATIONAL GOVERNMENT	LOCAL GOVERNMENT	EXTERNAL
IMPLEMENTATION	AGENCIES Lake District national Park London Regional Transport Cassa per il Mezzogiorno (Italy) Columbia River Basin Project (US)	AGENCIES Twin Cities Transit Board (US) Bay Conservation and Development Commission (US)	AGENCIES Yorkshire Dales National Park Greater Glasgow Passenger Transport Executive COUNCILS OF GOVERNMENT London Fire Metropolitan Police	
ALLOCATION AND IMPLEMENTATION	REGIONAL OFFICES Scottish Office Roads Department AGENCIES Appalachian Regional Commission(US) Scottish Homes Regional Water Authorities Etablissement Public Foncier Nord-Pas de Calais (France) Local Enterprise Companies Highlands and Islands Enterprise	DELEGATED OFFICES Regierungsbezirke (Germany)	ELECTED LOCAL GOVERNMENT Highland Regional Council Strathclyde Regional Council Greater Rotterdam Regional Government (Netherlands) Communautés Urbaines (France)	
POLICY AND ALLOCATION	SUPRA-NATIONAL GOVERNMENT Council of Ministers (EC) European Commission (EC) REGIONAL OFFICES Scottish Office Doe Task Force Regional Directors AGENCIES COPLACO (Spain) Countryside Commissions Scottish Enterprise Welsh Development Agency	ELECTED LEGISLATURES Republics (Soviet Union) Länder (Germany) Autonomous Regions (Spain) States (US) Regional Assemblies (Italy) ELECTED NON-LEGISLATURES Conseils Régionaux (France)	ELECTED LOCAL GOVERNMENT Greater London Council Frankfurt Metropolitan Government (Germany) COUNCILS OF GOVERNMENT Hanover Metropolitan Union (Germany)	
INFORMATION AND POLICY	NATIONAL PLANNING DATAR (France) National Physical Planning Agency (Netherlands) REGIONAL OFFICES DOE Regional Guidelines Scottish National Planning Guidelines PRIVILEGED ADVISORY GROUPS North West Joint Planning Team Quadanter Project (Italy) South East Joint Planning Team West Central Scotland Plan Clyde Valley Plan OREAM (France)	PRIVILEGED ADVISORY GROUPS Twin Cities Metropolitan Planning Commission KVR (Germany) Regional Development Agency for The Nord-Pas de Calais (France)	ADVISORY GROUPS Coventry-Solihull, Warwickshire Sub-Regional Study KVR (Germany) Leicester, Leicestershire Sub-Regional Study Greater Glasgow Transport Study COUNCILS OF GOVERNMENT Planni Intercommunal (Italy) Association of Bay Area Governments (US) London Planning Advisory Committee Standing Conference on SE Regional Planning Delaware Valley Regional Planning Commission (US)	ADVOCACY GROUPS Greenbelt Alliance (US) Bay Area Council (US)
INFORMATION	ADVISORY GROUPS Ecos Ouverture (EC) Rechar (EC) Regional Economic Planning Councils and Boards East Midland Study South East Study	ADVISORY GROUPS Committee of the Regions (EC) COUNCILS OF GOVERNMENT Assembly of European Rights	COUNCILS OF GOVERNMENT Scottish Local Government Information Unit	ADVISORY GROUPS Planning Exchange London Research Centre Greater Manchester Research

Figure 8.3. Typology of forms of regional planning: according to roles and capacity to implement policy

TYPOLOGIES AND THE 'SUCCESS' OF REGIONAL INITIATIVES

The merits of realism in typologies derived from practice in regional planning and governance will be tempered by the distortions attending empirical observation. Some cases can be fitted into both frameworks, because some regional governance has been designed primarily for regional planning. And as they are frameworks, some subtleties will inevitably escape them.

Nonetheless, the typologies show that 'success' has occurred in a variety of circumstances, and cases with relative lack of success are similarly dispersed across the frameworks. Closeness to central government is understandably a major potential advantage, but we have seen how this may be eroded by inter-departmental tensions. And the lack of the capacity of an organisation with strong ideas to directly execute its regional plan does not always mean a lack of effective influence on those who have the powers to implement.

Of course, if the degree of 'success' of a new regional initiative cannot be directly predicted from where it might fit into the typologies, this is some reflection of the way in which those are constructed. It indicates that the chosen measures are insufficiently subtle or not fully tuned to measure the grounds for success. But although it is impracticable to comprehensively assess the success or failure of every instance of regional planning and of regional governance we have reported, this does not preclude some valid general conclusions and individual judgements.

We are not suggesting success to be all accident or to depend on factors invisible to any researcher. Different political circumstances favoured plans for Coventry–Solihull–Warwickshire and for West Central Scotland, when contemporaneous plans for Leicester–Leicestershire and for the Northern Region were not similarly favoured. It has been noted that the *Greater London* and *Clyde Valley* plans were influential over long periods, when plans prepared with equal care in the North West and in East Anglia had less impact. It has been seen how significant in some regional planning and governance have been personalities and politics. But these elements are often hidden, and it has not been practicable to investigate them across the full range of our cases.

However, if we cannot go so far as to deduce a formula for invariable regional success or to exactly measure its extent in all our cases, we cannot reasonably avoid discussing the criteria by which success might be systematically measured.

What is Successful Regional Planning and Governance?

What Criteria?

REGIONAL PLANNING

Because regional planning is so many things to so many people, it can be judged by many criteria. And when associated with regional governance the potential measures of its quality become numerous.

Evaluations of cases of regional planning and governance have been various. Measurements of its performance have been perhaps more limited in developed than in less developed countries, where both theory and the evaluation of regional policy has been more sustained and intensive. Metropolitan plan-making has been examined by Boyce, Day and McDonald (1970), but their accounts of several US examples make little or no retrospective appraisal of the plans' effectiveness. In the UK, Greater London's case has been best recorded, as well through the eyes of regional economists (e.g. Damesick 1982), historians and political scientists (e.g. Young and Garside 1982), as by critics of planning method and machinery (Self 1962, 1971). Peter Hall (1969, 1989) has combined all roles, as an incessant futurist, commentator and critic of London's planning and development, documenting its lumbering history of strategic planning.

Several studies of the process of regional planning in England have involved John Friend and colleagues associated with the Institute of Operations Research. After the pioneering work in plan evaluation of Friend and Jessop (1969), the Institute's studies included an examination of Droitwich's development in its regional context (Friend et al. 1974), proceeding to a wider review of changing processes of regional planning. Sometimes (Friend et al. 1979), the Institute's work has tended to make regional planning appear more opaque than clear.

The European Commission's linking of regional concepts to Europe's economic future has been paralleled by much independent economic commentary, sometimes explicitly linking regional governance to economic planning (e.g. Cheshire et al. 1991), but not always wholly convincing that only effective regional governance can fully exploit regional economic potential.

The Scottish experience of regional planning has been discussed by Diamond and Spence (1983) largely in regard to inter-regional economic policy, but in their review of the impact of the *Clyde Valley Regional Plan* over a period of almost forty years, Smith, Wannop and colleagues (1985) traced the development of Clydeside since 1946. They assessed the extent to which the *Plan's* proposals were implemented, and concluded that it was remarkably influential over a period of at least thirty years.

Taking the Gillingwater and Hart (1978) approach to the components of regional planning means separately analysing the policy-making component of cases, the means of influencing those through whom the policies will come into play, and the means of controlling the policies in action. Policy-making is the deepest form of regional planning, but depends first upon good communication which is mixed with issues of coordination, politics and administration, and then depends upon controlling and implementing policy, squarely raising a range of issues of governance.

Although these distinctions between *policy-making, communication* and *control* may be considerably blurred in many cases, they are helpful. For example, they would allow such a significant case of regional planning and governance as Strathclyde Regional Council to be studied not only as a highly developed administration controlling the implementation of policy. The quality of the Council's regional policy-making could be separately evaluated, as could the effectiveness with which these policies were translated from the structure plan of the Department of Physical Planning into the policies and programmes of the Council's principal implementing departments.

Characterising the distinctions, we may see *policymaking* as indeterminate, because 'Each of the many participants has limited control over conflicts... Since means available for solving problems change over time, calculation must be incremental and is bound up with processes of political interaction – groping, uncertain and experimental' (Rondinelli 1975, 212). From study of regional development programmes in the 1960s in Appalachia and Pennsylvania, Rondinelli describes policy as having the following characteristics:

1. Comprehensive policy analysis is constrained by 'spillover effects' from past decisions, externalities from current activities, and unanticipated consequences.

2. Policy-making is synergistic, whereby diverse organisations pursuing various uncoordinated goals produce cumulative results.

3. There are transaction costs to participating in policy-making and implementation, limiting the degree to which political conflict can be restricted.

4. Problems of regional development are complex, amorphous, and difficult to define concisely. Their solutions change over time, as do relations in the political environment.

5. There are long lead and lag times in perceiving problems, and in responding by forming and implementing policies.

6. Demands for policies and programmes are influenced by the availability of means to fulfil them.

7. Evaluating policy is complicated by the difficulty of knowing what are its real outputs.

8. There is an indeterminate number of possible alternative ways to ameliorate problems, evolving by political interaction.

9. Those making and implementing policy have each only a limited capacity to evaluate it.

10. Data used to evaluate policy alternatives are interpreted according to preconceived specialised interests.

11. Objectives are adjusted to expectations of success, and are pursued by organisations through strategies of incremental expansion.

Asking questions about policy in regional plans means examining documents commonly incorporating a composite of policies derived from various sources. A typical strategy like that of the *Strathclyde Structure Plan* includes policies of which some are original and others are borrowed from other sources; sources may be other strategies at a higher level – like the *National Planning Policy Guidelines* for

Scotland, or at a similar level – like the strategic policies of the Housing Corporation or of the Glasgow Development Agency, or at a lower level – like housing strategies of district councils. But apart from the question of how far the authors of the *Structure Plan* are responsible for the quality and scope of policies within it, there is one to be asked about whether the *Plan* uses and effectively employs all the powers of the Regional Council, and another to be asked about the uncertainties which the policies may face.

Communication of policy is significant because regional plans and policies have to be persuasive over their implications for a congeries of institutions, both public and private. This may be true also within individual institutions, where the interests to be harnessed may be as diverse as those of separate institutions. The case of the *Junta* for Andalusia has shown the conflicts of internal approaches, calling for more than persuasion to resolve. The experience of the major metropolitan and regional councils of Britain is similarly revealing.

Effective communication must cover not just the presence of regional policies and their clear statement, but also their validity and the implications of non-compliance. A regional structure plan like that for Strathclyde will make assumptions about population growth, employment change, land availability and other characteristics of land use and social and economic activity. Such data may sometimes have little policy content, but may help coordinate, guide or give confidence to those whose support will contribute to the plan's wider fulfilment. In this role, the plan's effectiveness may be partly related to the reliability of its information and to the extent to which probabilities of error are indicated. Those to be communicated with and persuaded will ask if the data is sufficiently relevant, and if it relates to their timescale of investment decisions.

Some planning such as that for the Clyde Valley or the original basis for the Tennessee Valley Authority earned and has long held a reputation as being visionary. This is highly effective communication, outlasting the bare content of written documents and the basic data of regional planning.

In *Control of Policy*, we have seen that effective implementation does not simply depend upon an agency financed and with the authority to directly execute all a plan's proposals. At the least, however, there must be legislative support for the plan's principal objectives; or legislation must follow, as with the *Clyde Valley Plan* it did intermittently over a long period of 30 years subsequent to the *Plan's* completion.

So, effective control of a regional plan will depend on some or all of the following: upon a legislative basis for the control of development, for local planning and for other statutory procedures by which other parties can be bound to observe the plan; upon the initiators being able to themselves initiate significant of the plan's elements directly, or through agents of their political backers, since legislation may give only negative and not positive control; or upon the planners being able to lever support for their policies through financial or political patronage.

REGIONAL GOVERNANCE

When the effectiveness of regional governance is assessed, it has to be considered to what extent the given responsibilities of a unit of governance are appropriate to its scale, and also to its relative position in its country's structure of governance.

Four often conflicting criteria are noted by Ostrom, Tiebout and Warren (1961) as significant in designing large-scale governments: control, efficiency, political representation and local self-determination. Control requires that administrative boundaries sufficiently match those of the events and issues being managed; efficiency in the technology of providing services and economies of scale may suggest even wider boundaries; political representation requires the appropriate range of political interests within the area and machinery of governance; and local self-determination expects that local groups and issues will not be obliterated by larger interests.

There are up to four tasks which a regional organisation may perform, suggests Hogwood (1982, 9):

1. Direct services, as with selective financial assistance offered through the Department of Industry's regional offices.

2. Supervision of the organisation's more local offices.

3. Strategic allocation of resources to organisations at a more local level, as has been the relationship between Regional and Area Health Authorities in the UK.

4. Coordinating oversight over other authorities at a more local level, as applied by the regional offices of the Department of the Environment to planning by local authorities.

Young (1982) describes the UK government's regional administration as playing several roles. It: has formal executive responsibility; coordinates Whitehall's efforts in its regions; actively promotes government policies; intervenes to 'mother' local authorities; arbitrates between agencies or authorities; lobbies in support of local authorities; and acts as the eyes and ears of government in the regions.

Where a regional organisation performs one or more of these tasks by statute or by delegation from a statutory authority, the effectiveness of its performance can be measured by ordinary criteria of administration. But many regional organisations lack this inherent authority. As we have seen, some organisations are formed to seek consensus where administrative arrangements are inadequate to solve a regional problem; others arise as pressure groups to persuade or seek favours of authorities with real powers and resources. These regional organisations without statutory authority can only influence by force of reason, by transmitting information, or by cajoling with such political muscle as they can generate. It may be hard to evaluate the effectiveness of these organisations, which is not often measurable in terms like the number of miles of road built, applications for planning permission processed, or other obvious outputs.

So the regional influence can be hard to trace; it does not always leave fingerprints. It may be frustrated by almost immovable forces, or it may be difficult to judge what would have happened if it had not been brought to bear. Sometimes the main influence of a regional organisation may be not on central government, or on some outside organisation, but upon the behaviour of the individuals or bodies incorporated in it. In these circumstances, its influence may be unseen, because the organisation may hide its internal pressures and politicking.

There are seven principal theoretical criteria for administrative appropriateness in Bennett's view (1989, 55). These relate to sense of community, technical efficiency, economic efficiency, preference structures, administrative constraints, mass participation, and resource distribution. No one level of administration can be found to optimise all criteria. But the more the number of levels created to separately optimise the criteria, the more this is likely to increase difficulties of coordination, restrict economies of scale, widen financial disparities in expenditure and revenues, and confuse rather than clarify lines of accountability.

1. *Sense of community.* Communities are not uniform. They can have collective identity as strong as in a cultural region such as Scotland, or as with the residents of any commuter village or small town defending themselves against expansion of housing for more of their own kind. But collective sense of communal values does not necessarily become most intense at smaller scales, where the degree of stability varies widely with the economic and social character of the community.

2. *Technical efficiency.* The technical efficiency of providing services was a research question examined for the Royal Commission (1969) into the reorganisation of English local government. It has been a focus for much research in the United States. Optimising the area covered by a service is particularly a means of increasing efficiency, where the costs of distributing the benefits of the service are a high proportion of the costs of running it.

3. *Economic efficiency.* This criterion incorporates technical efficiency into a wider economic view, which encompasses matters of resource allocation, social distribution and economic stabilisation. This wider view of the external effects of local investment and efficiency will necessarily be taken from a level at which macro-economic or investment policy is decided.

4. *Preference structures.* Buchanan's (1966) theory of public choice spans the criteria of community and economic efficiency. It implies that a pattern of smaller communities can better meet the variety of popular preferences, can better provide consensus, and can better limit the need for regulatory control. It recognises, however, that local action has external impacts which may justify collective initiatives in regard to spillover effects. Collective action may be acceptable up to the point at which the costs of working together come to exceed the benefits to individual collaborators.

5. *Administrative constraints.* Bureaucracy is the drag to which any administrative structure succumbs to a degree. The larger a form of governance the more it will tend to departmentalise, and the more it does this the more are the potential problems of internal coordination. But bureaucratic constraints do not necessarily multiply as do the overall size of administrative units. Ultimately, it is the generosity of outlook amongst staff and sympathy for overriding organisational goals which determine the degree to which bureaucratic drag interferes.

6. *Mass participation.* It might seem that the larger a unit of governance the less significant would be each person within its area. But the quality and responsiveness of staff administering services are likely to be as critical as the sheer size of the unit which they serve. In the circumstances of the diversity of peoples within a major urban area such as London or Philadelphia, it is likely that education and social services can be more sensitively attuned to the variety of ethnic and other characteristics within a widespread authority than by a patchwork of administrative units. Extinguishing the Inner London Education Authority in 1990 in favour of 13 separate borough education authorities seemed unlikely to sustain ILEA's variety of services attuned to a population speaking some 150 languages. And although the larger an administrative unit the less chance has any individual of speaking to the leader of the council or to the director of education, it is not the case that this is the measure for most people of their capacity to effectively participate. There are many models of participation, of course, and New England town meetings or schools councils and boards of governors are particular local modes, ones which are quite compatible with strategic governance by larger administrative units.

7. *Resource distribution.* It is a paradox that the more a central government is in sympathy with decentralisation of authority, discretion and independent action, the more its dilemma over resource distribution and scope for raising local revenues. The more room it gives for local responsibility, the more it may have to reveal about the detail of its allocation formula and lose its power to stabilise the national economy. If all is decentralised, the centre cannot hold to a national policy, because the sum of local actions has macro-economic and macro-political implications. Also, national governments' tax and budgetary policies differentially affect different local government areas. Adjustments are customary to reflect the uneven regional distribution of economic activity, property and of personal incomes, but regions will claim unfairness if their per capita allocation is overall less than average. The tension arises in all countries, and not just those in which there is such antipathy to local governance as the centre in the United Kingdom displayed in the 1980s.

Evaluating Performance
EFFICIENCY AND EFFECTIVENESS

Effective regional planning and governance requires more than efficiency in its components. The processes are never self-contained, and the contributory parts must perform effectively with one another and not be merely efficient in themselves.

As we have seen, regions in the practice of regional planning customarily cover several areas of local government, where some common interest has been found to override a fragmented pattern of governance. The main issues for governance which arise in such cases have been suggested (Barlow 1991, 19) to be:

1. *Efficiency* in avoiding the duplication of services, in minimising interference in achieving economies of scale, and in observing the spillover from one administrative area to another of the benefits of services.

2. *Effectiveness* where services are poorly coordinated, and where administrative areas are arbitrary for many services, e.g. fire protection.

3. *Equity* where different levels of service are determined not by comparative need, but by the relative wealth of property and of the tax base.

But the prime conditions for regional planning in situations of fragmented metropolitan or regional areas are the lack of coherent strategies, and rivalry or near warfare between administrations. These are secondary problems to a student of governance (Barlow 1991, 19), who in comparing five cases of metropolitan government ranked them in descending order of sophistication as London, Manchester, Toronto, Melbourne and San Francisco. A comparative order of sophistication in regional planning would also have placed London ahead of San Francisco, even if others in a larger choice of cases might have outshone London, or been less well developed than San Francisco.

Increased size for increased efficiency was a basic criterion underlying the Redcliffe–Maud Royal Commission's (1968) recommendations for local government reform in England. There have been many who have disagreed. Consultants have normally been able to provide a case for any size of authority which has wished to claim that it is at the optimum for the cost of providing its services. No systematic correlates of size can be found, as Bennett (1980) shows. He concludes that they are invariably evident where infrastructural services like water supply, electricity, gas, sewerage and sometimes road provision are concerned, but they seldom consistently operate where people are participants in the service. Bureaucratic overload, distance from the participants and problems in adapting services to individual needs all seem to impede increases of efficiency in line with increased scale of service.

Managerial effectiveness is an avowed target of government administration, but it has its limits where regional planning cuts across departmental interests. The difficulties of the Department of the Environment in getting other departments to accept that English structure plans might have any coordinating role for government programmes were matched in the 1970s by the Scottish Development Department's similar difficulties over regional reports. The promise of the Scottish system of regional reports of the 1970s, in which regional councils interrelated their regions' social, economic and physical problems, was cut short partly because other departments of the Scottish Office were unwilling to concede to the Development Department an interest in affairs beyond its direct responsibility. The problems of departmental protectiveness were evident also in West Germany in the early 1970s, where it was a federal ministry rather than local authorities which authored the proposals touching upon other ministers' responsibilities.

Glasson (1980, 321) highlights the difficulty of government departments in adapting from the 'vertical thinking' of headquarters in Whitehall, to the 'lateral thinking' desirable to coordinate in the regions. In this regard, the regional staff are perhaps expected to show greater flexibility of mind and reticulist ability than their seniors at headquarters. Also, as John Mackintosh (1972) observed, some civil servants in the regions regard 'posts there as temporary sojourns in an administrative siberia, promotion being back to Whiltehall where there are not only senior posts but where a degree of initiative is permitted or even encouraged.'

Coordination has several dimensions of possible ineffectiveness. The size of the network may be greater than allows the coordinator to sufficiently cultivate all its necessary contributors. There may be opposition between scarcely reconcilable interests. There may be insensitivity to interests which might be amenable to skilled negotiation. The policies or actions which are the purpose of coordination may be inherently flawed, or they may be misunderstood or ineffectively conveyed to the network. The effort of achieving consensus may leave too little time to consider the most imaginative but least familiar of ideas.

IMPLEMENTATION

The history of failures of regional coordination demonstrates how fragile is the process. Perfect coordination faces the ten standard requirements for perfect implementation described by Gunn (1978). Translated into the context of regional planning, they would be:

1. There must be no crippling external constraints on the planner.

2. The plan must be supported by adequate time and sufficient resources.

3. There must be no overall constraint of resources, and the required combination must be available at each stage of the plan.

4. The plan must incorporate valid theories of cause and effect.

5. Cause and effect must be directly related, with none or few intervening links.

6. If the plan is not implementable entirely by the planning agency, the dependency upon other agencies should be minimal in number and importance.

7. The objectives of the plan must be completely understood and agreed upon throughout its life.

8. The detail and sequence of each participant's tasks must be exactly specified.

9. There must be perfect communication and coordination between the elements and agencies implementing the plan.

10. Those behind the plan must be able to obtain perfect compliance.

Gunn's rules of perfection might seem to preclude regional planning ever becoming extensively successful. But it has often succeeded sufficiently, and has certainly not been uniformly unsuccessful. We can seek to explain differences in the effectiveness of regional planning if, with help from Lichfield (in Lichfield and Darin-Drabkin 1980) and Sieber (1981), we consolidate Gunn's principles into a Framework of Potential Impediments to Implementation.

Figure 8.4. Framework of potential impediments to implementation

Technical inadequacy of the plan:

- unbalanced emphasis on one or a few of a large number of interconnected factors
- wrong diagnosis of the situation
- invalid theory of the cause and effect
- theory of implementation incorporates too many intervening links
- attempting to achieve too much
- failure to abandon obsolete policies
- misclassification of policies or areas in terms which tend to worsen stigma which policies are meant to alleviate

Insufficient legal framework:

- crippling external constraints

Inadequate institutions:

- crippling external constraints
- too many dependency relationships

Lack of accord with authorities or plans at a higher or lower level:

- incomplete understanding of objectives
- incomplete specification of tasks for participants in the implementation process
- imperfect communication amongst agencies

Goal Displacement:

- means gradually become ends; policies pursued for themselves regardless of purpose

Inadequacy or maldistribution of economic resources:

- goals beyond the resources available, or unavailable as required at each stage of implementation
- inadequate financial resources for compensation

Inadequate time available:

- crippling external constraints

Lack of political backing:

- crippling external constraints
- inability of authority to obtain compliance
- failure to follow through on policy
- policy exploited to the advantage of the implementers

Lack of public backing:

- crippling external constraints
- exploitation of the plan and policies to the advantage of those at whom it is targeted
- public reaction against a principal policy
- public apathy to principal policies

Figure 8.4. Framework of potential impediments to implementation (continued)

Within this framework, regional plans and planning processes can be analysed. We can discern which factors have caused less than perfect implementation – as to a greater or lesser degree must be inevitable in such an ambitious pursuit. However, the result may be merely a slight stumble or an irrecoverable fall. The case of the *Clyde Valley Regional Plan* of 1946 can usefully show how the framework can be applied.

Over a long period, the *Clyde Valley Plan* had some two-thirds of its major recommendations adopted. But in the first 20 years after being announced in 1946, relatively few of its proposals were adopted. The administrative and legislative tools which the *Plan* saw as essential to support its proposals were slow to be forged. The problems which held it back were primarily of governance, as the *Plan* had anticipated. There was also a technical difficulty in that the *Plan* had assumed that there would be no growth in the region's population, but there was considerable early growth. After East Kilbride was begun in 1947, governments delayed a further new town at Cumbernauld for a decade, allowing Glasgow to spread

PROBLEMS INHIBITING IMPLEMENTATION	CLYDE VALLEY PLAN 1946	
	1946 - 66	1966 - 90
Technical inadequacy of the plan • unbalanced emphasis on one or a few of a large number of interconnected factors • wrong diagnosis of the situation • invalid theory of cause and effect • theory of implementation incorporates too many intervening links • attempting to achieve too much • failure to abandon obselete policies • misclassification of policies or areas in terms which tend to worsen stigma which policies are meant to alleviate	unexpected population growth	
		Scottish Office overemphasis on new towns
Insufficient legal framework • crippling external constraints	lack of regional coordination	
Inadequate institutions • crippling external constraints • too many dependency relationships		
Lack of accord with authorities or plans at a higher or lower level • incomplete understanding of objectives • incomplete specification of tasks for participants in the • implementation process • imperfect communication amongst agencies	lack of CVPAC	
Goal Displacement • means gradually become ends: policies pursued for themselves		Scottish Office overemphasis on new towns
Inadequacy or maldistribution of economic resources • goals beyond the resources available, or unavailable as required at each stage of implementation • inadequate financial resources for compensation	regional parks green belt acquisition	
Inadequate time available • crippling external constraints	encouragement of Glasgow's periphial estates	
Lack of political backing • crippling external constraints • inability of authority to obtain compliance • failure to follow through on policy • policy exploited to the advantage of the implementers	fragmented local admin. lack of administrative reorganisation	
Lack of public backing • crippling external constraints • exploitation of the policy to the advantage of those to which it is targeted • public reaction against a policy • public apathy to a policy		

Figure 8.5. Problems inhibiting the implementation of regional planning: the experience of the Clyde Valley Plan 1946

much further into its green belt than the *Plan* thought right. But particularly in the first ten years after 1966 and before the coming of Strathclyde Regional Council, inhibitions delaying the *Plan's* progress were progressively removed. A cascade of the *Plan's* proposals came into being after 1966, when the *Plan* could be seen as not only visionary, but also as realistic and of profound influence.

So it is fair to say that satisfactory implementation of regional plans and policies is possible without a near perfect model of regional governance. At least, not at the level of the region itself. For example, the case of the Twin Cities suggests this, and that of Strathclyde supports the view. But as other cases we have discussed have demonstrated, political support is imperative at the next level above the regional one. The Twin Cities Commission depends upon the support of the Governor and the Legislature of the State of Minnesota, because it seeks to influence other State commissions as well as the multiplicity of local governments. Strathclyde's major strategic policies of curtailing the population growth of the new towns, of stopping the new town of Stonehouse and of reinforcing the renewal of the Clydeside conurbation, all depended primarily upon government support and upon government's direct action. It might even be suggested that the strongest regional influence in the abandonment of Stonehouse was not the Strathclyde Council's planning, financial or executive powers. Rather, the strongest influence may have been direct pressure on the Scottish Secretary of State following a change of heart amongst Labour Party colleagues, who on being elected to the Regional Council reversed the support they had given to Stonehouse in the councils they had previously represented.

The Stonehouse case in Strathclyde is perhaps comparable to the issue of a new airport for the Twin Cities of Minneapolis-St. Paul in scale and regional significance. If so, it begs the question as to whether effective discussion, examination, formulation and implementation of regional strategy demands a full regional local government on the Strathclyde scale. Does regional policy making have to be directly linked to the supply of water, highways, sewerage, schools and social services to be effective? Superficially, the Strathclyde example suggests that it is at least helpful if it is. Deeper reflection and the case of the Twin Cities suggests that it is not imperative.

Accountability

Accountability is a concept with highly political undertones. Politicians demanding accountability amongst local governments commonly infer that they should respond less to the opinions of the majority of local electors, and more to the interests of the politician's supporters who are in a local minority. This attitude was strongly evident in the abolition of the Greater London Council and the English metropolitan county councils in 1986, and behind the selective 'capping' of local council expenditure commencing in the UK in the 1980s.

The two basic categories of internal and external accountability in local government are indicated by Foster (1988), separating internal managerial issues from issues of responsiveness to external interests. He suggests that internal accountability requires that activities are freely viewed, that it should be clearly established who is responsible for what, and that individuals should answer for those working to them. These are the precepts for administrative efficiency. On the other hand, external accountability lies in four dimensions. These are that of the taxpayers contributing to the administered services; that of local businesses, industries and other activities which have no vote; that of higher levels of government; and that of accountability to the local electorate.

The means of accountability, the relative weights allowed to different factions and the range of factions recognised are, of course, highly contentious. Foster's categorisations raise many political issues.

Accountability raises the lesser question also of independence in the preparation of plans and policy. British experience up to the 1960s was predominantly of consultants preparing regional plans. During the 1960s and early 1970s, consultants took a lesser part, although participating in the *West Central Scotland Plan* as late as 1974. From the late 1960s, however, the planning teams were predominantly either recruited by a group of sponsoring authorities as in the sub-regional strategies of the period, or were seconded from government departments or from local government.

It is arguable as to what degree these different kinds of planning team gained or took advantage of such independence as their origins provided. Consultants are not commonly commissioned to produce proposals which are markedly independent of their sponsors' expectations. Consultants are sensitive to their clients, and even when appointed by a disparate group of interests they will be aware of where power lies. Abercrombie's record of regional planning showed his awareness of the preferences of the more influential of his clients; his switch of emphasis from retaining population in the *County of London Plan* to dispersing it in the *Greater London Plan* clearly reflected the LCC view in the first instance, and the ministerial view in the second.

The three major sub-regional studies of the late 1960s undertaken by teams specially recruited by the sponsoring local authorities did, in two cases at least, produce largely independent proposals. In the case of the *Leicester–Leicestershire* study, the consequence was that the team's proposals were considerably recast by the County Council, which was able to assert its own wishes in the subsequent structure plan. In the case of *Coventry–Solihull–Warwickshire*, the planning team was perhaps fortunate that political circumstances changed unexpectedly during the study to favour a strategy which might otherwise have been found to be too independent. The *Nottinghamshire–Derbyshire* study was perhaps more aligned than the others to the strategy which, from the outset, was likely to find favour with the two county councils who held the whip hand in implemention.

Amongst the regional strategies staffed by secondees from government departments, that for the *North West* undoubtedly took directions which were independent of government policy of the time. The team was prepared to make it uncomfortable for departments in regard to priorities for government spending. This had not been the case with the *Strategic Plan for the South East*, which was led by the Chief Planner of the Ministry of Housing and Local government and was much closer to government in two senses. The *Northern Regional Strategy* team was considerably recruited from outside government departments, and perhaps more even than the *North West* team it produced proposals which challenged government policy, and did so in the field of regional economic policy for which its sponsoring planning ministry was not responsible.

The *West Central Scotland Plan* combined seconded staff from departments of the Scottish Office with staff from the consultants introduced at the mid-point, all under a director separately appointed. The *Plan's* proposals were wholly independent in the direction of suspending the new town of Stonehouse, which the Scottish Office had had in train for several years, but the proposal for an economic development agency for the region was much favoured by the Scottish Office.

The *West Midland Regional Study* was the only major UK regional study led by local authorities and largely staffed by them, including the directorship. The independence which ensued was not wholly to the liking of the principal authorities, and certainly not to government. The independence certainly lacked realism in its waywardness in the face of political realities, and it would be hard to argue that it represented a clearer view of what was good for the region than did the modified strategy later adopted.

The Case Against Regional Governance

Redundant and Dangerous?

Some critics are vehemently against regional government. Jones (1988, 11) dismisses it as 'redundant and dangerous', borrowing from the White Paper on Streamlining the Cities (Secretary of State for the Environment 1983) to describe it as 'a fashion' drawing functions from both central and local government, having its own tax, being directly elected, and never having being tried in Britain. By such a narrow definition, it is correct to say that regional government is untried in Britain, as it has been approached only in the schemes for Scottish and Welsh Assemblies which fell after the referenda on devolution in 1979. But this fails to recognise the case of Strathclyde Regional Council or even of the Highland Regional Council, both in separate ways significantly different to the Greater London or metropolitan county councils which Jones mistakenly regards as having most approximated to a regional model. It may be correct to assert that the metropolitan county councils and that for Greater London were wasteful, unnecessary and little lamented by the public, but others would argue that they were ineptly designed for effective regional planning or implementation.

But regional governance has been widespread in Europe and taken various forms in the United States. Composed soon after the abolition of the GLC and the metropolitan councils, Jones's criticisms were for Britain and lacked the advantage of the longer hindsight of the 1990s, when parliamentarians, industry, business, transport and other private interests increasingly argue for a form of strategic coordination and leadership for Greater London, in particular. But although the government then established simple arrangements for a degree of better coordination in Greater London, they were far short of being intrusive and their effectiveness was in doubt. Jones's view that strategy was a mythical need was blinkered when lack of effective regional planning and investment was so palpably sustaining the intensification of London's traffic problems of both public and private transport, when the spatial economic and physical impacts of the Channel Tunnel and of entry of the European Community to a wholly open market were being so inadequately considered in the early 1990s, and when tensions about where new houses should be built had been endemic for so many years amongst the counties of south-east England, and in other metropolitan regions of the UK.

Other arguments against regional governance – of whatever kind – are that regional cultures and regional perspectives are absent, and that it is villages, small towns, suburban enclaves, or middle and upper class urban 'villages' by which people identify with a 'community'. There is also an additional allegiance to a state in the US – preferably Texas – and to an ancient county in England – preferably not Staffordshire. These arguments in favour of old allegiances against potentially new ones have a romantic footing, but mobility within nations reduces their strength. Regional identifications were clearly altering in the late twentieth century. County sides were still competing for the cricket championship of England in 1994, but every one was drawn from birthplaces reaching beyond the county boundary – and in some cases from several countries. In English rugby, the county championship gave way to a divisional championship in the 1980s. Manchester United supporters in the 1990s no longer came largely from Manchester as in 1939, but travelled regularly from Dublin, London and places far afield. The regional television contractors had established new spheres of common interest and awareness, superimposed upon circulation areas of longer established local newspapers and transcending historic local political boundaries.

So, better arguments must be found to dismiss regional government than the beguiling proposition that small is likely to be more beautiful in public administration. Arguments like Jones's against regional government commonly incorporate fallacies and misconceptions. It is a vigorous case which has much to commend it in parts, but which is distorted in the whole. By failing to consider whether a regional scale could be adopted for local government rather than adopting a new level between it and national government, a straw man is attacked, neglecting possible and significant variants upon one particular form of regional governance. This denies both what might be possible and what is real experience.

Unitary, multi-purpose local government has everything to recommend it as an abstract concept. It offers the hypothetical attractions of perfect integration of local services, of minimal need for external coordination, and of clarity of accountability. But the abstract concept loses its perfection when it is applied to the irregularity and variability of real circumstances.

Does Regional Planning Imply Full Regional Governance?

Criticism of regional planning is frequently implicit criticism of regional governance, the greater bogey to some political scientists and to many politicians. But this is a confused view, not recognising that regional planning can be and has been profoundly influential even when not directly matched by a system of regional governance. Political circumstances alone may conspire to support a regional strategy. Although matching regional governance may in instances be greatly helpful in adding support, it is not the only means whereby the main features of a strategy may be imposed on a region.

The case against big regional government is accordingly not a case against regional planning, nor necessarily against 'small' regional government. There are those, indeed, who recognise the weaknesses of the *ad hoc* and weakly resourced regional systems of the US and the UK (Self 1982, 119), but point also to their potential strengths. Where a variety of organisational interests sponsors regional planning, none may have an overriding pull. The capacity to make imaginative plans may be improved. Absence of an elected controlling body may remove impediments to joint planning between levels of government. So, it can be argued, there are real merits in advisory planning.

This line of argument has supporting evidence, from the *Greater London Plan* through the *Coventry–Solihull–Warwickshire Study* and the *West Central Scotland Plan*. But not all plans from the advisory mould are influential. What is required for any plan from any source is that it has leverage to foster implementation which is consistent with its policies. Regional plans from within large regional organisations of governance may find support hard to raise from other departments of their own organisation, and may have only tenuous control over outside agencies and events.

Leverage for regional plans and policies may be ensured by events and by means other than full-blown regional government or major administrative reorganisation. Effective regional planning can be achieved by a variety of arrangements. It can be achieved even without a directly matched form of regional governance, which as the case of Strathclyde shows may become unstable in changing circumstances.

The Irregular but Insistent Regional Dimension

The Politics of Regionalism

WHY REGIONALISM?

The need for regional planning is not constant, but the pressures for it are recurrent and insistent. Like regional governance, its re-emergence is commonly bound up in politics of various kinds. Examples of regional governance are certainly to be more often explained by political circumstances than by pure administrative theory.

Surveys for the European Commission in 1991 suggested that Europeans can identify themselves with their regions (Commission des Communautés Européennes 1992). In Spain, Greece and Portugal, regional affiliation was found to be as strong as national affiliation. And only in Belgium was regional attachment weaker than that to villages. His or her region was, of course, what each interviewee regarded it to be, and not necessarily as their neighbour might have thought. Even in the UK, regional affiliation appeared only a little less strong than national affiliation, although it is problematical what the Scots and Welsh regarded as their region and what as their nation.

Yet, a higher degree of regional identification was revealed by these surveys than might have been expected, including in the UK, where even those favouring regional planning and governance have found it hard to answer criticisms that they have no strength of regional identification to build on except in Scotland, Wales, and perhaps in the Protestant community of Northern Ireland.

But a regional case continues to re-emerge even in England. Barlow (1991, 306) suggests that this is just because England lacks a state or provincial level of government as in other countries, where the regional issue is often argued at a smaller scale than in the UK.

WHY REGIONAL INITIATIVES?

Whether the basis of regionalism lies in cultural or economic history, either is an aspect of politics. And politics is the most common basis for government intervention in regional planning and governance. The pure aim of efficient and sensitive coordination of interrelated aspects of governance has been a relatively rare motivation. When regional structures of government administration were being introduced and consolidated in the UK in the 1990s, the roots lay in the government's sustained political attack on administration and policy and decision-taking by locally elected representatives. Regional administration and agencies became functionally necessary as a consequence of the progressive transfer of power from local to central hands.

In the first half of the twentieth century, individual reformers and voluntary groups were prominent in the slow march to regional planning. As Weaver (1984, 2) records, US reformists pressing to stop flooding metropolitan growth in the 1920s drew on the ideas of earlier civic reformers and libertarian socialists, seeking to revitalise rural regions by decentralising new economic activities and by modernising social and other services in rural America. David Dale at New Lanark and Ebenezer Howard had been forerunners of new communities and social advancement in Britain. But the reformist tradition underestimated the strength of metropolitan agglomeration and of its underlying capitalist forces. Governments with entirely capitalist sympathies would not sponsor regional development threatening metropolitan economies.

The Great Depression between the World Wars brought pressures for governments in the US and the UK to be seen to attempt to alleviate poverty and unemployment in decaying regions. The initiatives primarily fostered industrial growth, even in the Tennessee Valley in the US, and the evidence of this encouraged governments after the Second World War to initiate regional development programmes graced by emerging economic theories which were variants on Perroux's strategy of 'growth poles'. The increasingly evident external diseconomies of metropolitan locations for industry made decentralisation policies more palatable to most politicians, aided by the overwhelming aim of those with a social conscience to spill overcrowded and poorer city dwellers out to green field estates and new towns, leapfrogging the earlier flight to the suburbs of more wealthy citizens.

In the late twentieth century, Weaver (1984, 8) suggests that capitalist imperatives often overlap rather than oppose those of the unemployed and the poor. At least where both are contained with a single region, where both the economic elite and the underprivileged share an interest in withstanding the vagaries of multinational economic restructuring. When allied to the reassertion of regional identity in an ethnic or quasi-nationalist movement, blight on a peripheral regional economy may therefore first stimulate a demand from the region for a regional planning programme, and secondly encourage a government to placate the region by offering one. This stimulus of cultural regionalism for regional planning was particularly obvious in the United States in the 1930s, and in Scotland and Northern England in the 1960s. But as Weaver regrets, it led not to regional planning in the control of the regions, but to its firm direction by national government.

So the long development of regional planning owed much originally to academic exploration and voluntarist enthusiasm, and in parts of the United States still depends heavily on the latter. But governments came to dominate in regional initiatives in most countries, before in some permitting differing degrees of devolved responsibility. We can define five common grounds for central government initiatives:

1. To sustain central government authority in significant matters of long-run political interest: e.g. the Scottish Development Agency/Scottish Enterprise; Scottish Homes; English Partnerships; the Applachian Regional Commission,

2. To cover for a political crisis: e.g. the White Paper and allied initiatives in North East England in 1963; wartime measures to organise output or civil defence.

3. To overcome stalemate in local government over strategy for urban growth: e.g. the sub-regional planning studies in metropolitan England in the late 1960s and early 1970s.

4. To manage national assets: e.g. the National Parks in the US and in England and Wales; the Countryside Commissions; coastal planning.

5. To spread pressures on central administration: e.g. regional offices for the government's ministries; regional management of the National Health Service; regional boards for the Arts Council.

In many countries, an intermediate level of government is enshrined in the national constitution as it is in the United States and Germany. In other nations, like France and the many countries she has influenced, central government has a defined pattern of systematic territorial administration. These intermediate levels of government or administration are to be explained in terms of national politics, as are the arrangements successively established for Scotland, Northern Ireland and for Wales. Indeed, the absence of such arrangements in England has also a political explanation, reflecting the reluctance of predominantly unionist governments to hint at federal governance threatening the unity of the UK as a whole.

The persistence of a regional dimension in UK administration since the Second World War is explained by Hogwood (1982, 17) in terms of governments' progressive accumulation of what had previously been local authority functions. First, as more administration has been amassed by central government, it chose to decentralise it regionally rather than draw it all into London. Regional offices were preferred to the risk of swamping headquarters departments of central government with a multitude of local decisions. Secondly, despite losing health, water and some other responsibilities, English local government adopted some new duties and extended others. Central government wished to supervise these duties, and regional offices were a convenience in doing so.

POLITICAL IMPLICATIONS AND SUPPORT

Why are governments motivated to initiate or permit regional planning, and why may they suppress it? During the Second World War, it was associated in Britain with the drive to prepare for post-war reconstruction of bomb-damaged cities, and for a simultaneous and long-delayed effort to eliminate the worst of the unfit housing, lack of open space and pollution of the industrial conurbations. Regional planning was an element of the social revolution for which the ground was being laid through governmental committees and commissions, when there was no certainty that a British government would exist when the war was done. Much of what was done implied very different or hugely accentuated political priorities compared with those prior to 1939. Much was designed for a radical government unlike any of the inter-war period.

When a radical Labour government was elected in 1945, it inherited initiatives in regional planning with whose physical and social objectives it was wholly in accord. Amongst the Government's wave of legislation for economic and social reconstruction, measures like the New Towns Act were integral to fulfilling the aims of the regional plans, but there was no administrative reform or other measures which directly stimulated regional planning. The great Town and Country Planning Act of 1947 created a system of effective development planning and the means to control development, but it did nothing to instigate continuity in regional planning.

Why was there no major reform to establish regional planning after 1945? The Government had a large legislative programme, and Abercrombie's regional plans for the three major problem conurbations of Britain had been achieved without any administrative reform. The requirements for continuous regional planning were perhaps not evident. Perhaps some thought the plans for Greater London and the Clyde Valley complete for ever. The LCC was strongly opposed to being subsumed in a London regional authority, and its former leader, Herbert Morrison, was now a central member of the post-war Labour government, although he recognised that the capital's local government was in a muddle.

Regional planning can run against party political objectives. It can run against institutional politics. It has run against the sectoral interests of government departments. Not only in the early post-war period in Britain, it has frequently run against the local interests of established political bases such as the proud and active LCC. In the late 1940s, it was also at risk of diluting or running against the strong centralised initiatives of the reforming Labour government. There were reasons enough to defer local government reform and the institutionalisation of regional planning. As Bours (1989, 74) indicates:

> The scale on which government has to operate is prescribed by the way in which society operates. Although constantly changing, the tensions of scale between the organisation and its environment are intrinsic; the incongruency between the scale of societal needs and the scale of government organisation seems to be permanent.

Regional organisations may thus be a means of central government trying to control local political problems, or of local interests combining to better counter the centre. Markusen (1987, 35) notes the Appalachian Regional Commission embracing several US states, and established by the federal government to provide special aid and treatment for the deprived Appalachian populations; she also notes the Western Governors' Policy Office set up to press regional claims on Washington. These being two regional organisations looking to influence from opposite directions.

Administrative Compulsions and Other Stimuli

If a case is to be made for regional government to pursue regional demands and interests, Hogwood (1982, 5) argues that it needs the support of an explicit theory to demonstrate that such a government could make the pursuit more effective. Conversely, he suggests, it is not necessary for there to have been any pre-existing regional characteristics or identity to make the case; there may be justification enough in the inadequacies of either central or local government, or in a theory of the allocation of powers within the state.

The concepts of region and of regional demands and activities do little to explain the existence of regional institutions in England, Hogwood (1982, 5) goes on to suggest. He explains regional organisations as deriving from four sources: the convenience of administering national services from sub-offices rather than from a single, central location; technical requirements including economies of scale; avoiding swamping headquarters offices of government with administrative routine; and passing certain government functions to regional public boards or corporations, particularly to avoid local government claims on the functions or to meet the expectations of strong professional interests.

Hogwood's explanations refer primarily to England, of course, although they might also partially explain administrative arrangements for Scotland, Wales and Northern Ireland. Administration in those parts of the United Kingdom has a stronger basis in politics than in mere administrative convenience. Indeed, as the way in which national administration is exercised in Scotland, Wales and Northern Ireland has become a more serious political issue in the late twenieth century, it has had its influence upon England. The Northern region of England, particularly, has regarded itself as deserving comparable administrative status with Scotland. And the major political parties have all seen that devolution of powers to any elected assemblies in Scotland or Wales would justify similar assemblies for English regions.

Pure administrative theory has little influenced the geography of European administration, even in modern reforms. The Napoleonic division of France derived from the stamina of the horses by which prefects rode to the limits of their prefectures; the limit of a departmental prefect's responsibility is still that of a day's ride from the prefectual capital, just as it was 200 years ago. Many of the counties of England instituted in 1886 were territorially unaffected by the 1974 reform, despite the rise of the telephone and of a range of means of communication unavailable a century before; it was at the lower, district level that most boundary adjustments occurred.

It is commonly asserted that governmental tasks should be performed at the lowest possible level appropriate to their nature and spread of concern, which is the area of the resident or working population affected. For different concerns the spread may differ considerably, and objectives like the development of underdeveloped regions or water management cannot, by their nature, be pursued without a strong regional level of planning.

Absorbed into European Community agreements, this aim of devolving decision-taking to the lowest appropriate level is known as the principle of 'subsidiarity'. It is allied to the EC strategy of developing regional levels of policy-making and implementation within Europe. But while ostensibly an approach of defining appropriate levels of government primarily in terms of consumers' interests, it is a principle very differently interpreted by governments in the light of their own particular political circumstances. Interpreted by the German and Spanish governments as a means of consolidating the roles of the *Land* and the autonomous regional governments, it was interpreted by the UK government as means of consolidating its authority against any potential for regional or local government.

In thirty years of reforms of local government and of shifting government attitudes in the UK, two concepts of relationship between levels of governance have dominated. As Foley (1972, 180) and Flynn *et al.* (1985) observe, the hierarchical concept has opposed the doctrine of separate powers. Subordinate levels in a hierarchy operate to guidelines imposed from above, and functions frequently overlap. The hierarchical principle was reflected in the distinction between structure and local planning in the two-tier system of local government introduced in Britain in 1974/75. The opposite doctrine expects separate levels to have clear and separate responsibilities. The concepts were perhaps combined in developments after 1979, when central government openly subordinated local government and moved to establish a single tier with reduced and circumscribed responsibilities.

Instability and Inertia
ADMINISTRATIVE OBSOLESCENCE

Administrative systems are inherently liable to obsolescence to a greater or lesser degree. They can never be perfectly conceived so they are always called upon to be flexible. But flexibility is an attitude of mind of individuals and not a natural quality of a system. Systems accordingly respond erratically when found not to perfectly match changing issues. By the time the misfit between the system and administrative priorities is so wide that political will has finally gathered to achieve reform, new issues are emerging. But the reform is likely to be matched more to the issues of the past than to the future.

'Administrative obsolescence is an inevitable consequence of the rapid rate of economic and technological development', suggests Bennett (1989, 303). But the history of territorial governance in Europe and in the US shows that the shape of established structures dies hard, persisting beyond the point at which they are clearly obsolescent.

Against a background of high technology and rapid economic change, Bennett compares late twentieth century tensions in Western Europe in obsolescent administrative structures designed to match the travel times of the horse, with tensions in Eastern Europe where functional regions introduced in the 1970s and based upon a planned economy had already been superseded by technological change by the late 1980s. After 1990, the tension in Eastern Europe was the greater with the collapse of not only strong central planning, but even of national frontiers.

In the US, Rondinelli (1975, 60) records the difficulty of establishing regional planning and development agencies in the 1960s in the face of vested, pluralistic interests. And while the US was still prepared to admit new states to the Federacy in the latter part of the twentieth century, it was not prepared to adjust the boundaries of older states and cities overtaken by the geography of the automobile and of the Californian and Boston–Washington megalopolitan regions.

Between ten and twenty years after being introduced, the English metropolitan county councils and such an exceptional experiment in regional governance as Strathclyde Regional Council had all become obsolete in their strategic planning functions. The GLC lasted over twenty years before being declared obsolete. So if events overtook these British cases which were also distinctive by comparison with most European and US strategic arrangements of their time, it must be questioned whether any system of regional governance can be expected to survive the dynamics of politics and of social and economic change.

Part of the answer must be to note that the GLC and the English metropolitan county councils were all much criticised at their creation. All encompassed much less area and fewer executive responsibilities than required to readily control their regions' physical development, let alone to execute an efficient regional transportation strategy or significant economic initiatives. No council covered anything like its recognised travel-to-work area. Nor did any council area include any of its satellite new towns. Indeed, not just the GLC of 1965 but the original LCC has been said to have been obsolescent at birth: 'the setting up of the LCC in 1889 was in many ways a response to the diagnoses made and the prescriptions offered back in the 1850s and before' (Cannadine 1990, 168).

So the areas and scope of England's innovations in metropolitan governance were all arbitrary from the start, and as time passed their limitations were confirmed. Similarly, despite the unique Strathclyde Regional Council reaching far beyond its travel-to-work boundary, encompassing three new towns and far more opportunities and executive powers than any English council has ever had, it was also soon obsolete in important aspects of the strategic planning for which it was conceived. As the significance of metropolitan regions to the European economy became better recognised by the EC and featured more strongly in European policy, it came to seem that metropolitan Glasgow's functional relationships with metropolitan Edinburgh might be more significant for regional planning than Glasgow's links with the rest of Strathclyde. A Central Scotland metropolitan region embracing Edinburgh and Glasgow was superseding Strathclyde.

The British experiments must accordingly be seen as already flawed at their inception, overcome by incipient limitations of political compromise in the case of the GLC and of the English metropolitan counties, and of the historic tradition of river basin planning in Scotland in the Strathclyde case. The changing context of central–local relationships added to the underlying instability of the experiments.

Central–local relationships have fluctuated also in mainland Europe and in the United States, although generally in the direction of greater local responsibility and opposite to the British tendency. Also, although the metropolitan level has been emphasised by special arrangements in Spain, France and Italy, and in a few instances in Germany and the Netherlands, there has been generally more promising progress in regional or provincial governance and planning in Europe. Britain perhaps moved too soon in the 1970s to an unstable reform of strategic local government. In the US, there has been no attempt at any comprehensive reform of metropolitan governance, and the major innovations in strategic planning since the 1960s have been through state governments, particularly in the 1980s.

ARE CONFLICTS NECESSARY? PARALLEL SYSTEMS OR ORGANISATIONAL REDUNDANCY?

Conflicts were taken by the Conservative government as reason to abolish the metropolitan county councils in 1986. But we have seen that regional planning and much regional governance has commonly been a response to conflicts. And as Flynn *et al.* (1985, 94) suggest, criticism of conflict begs three questions. How widespread has conflict been? On what has conflict arisen? And was the conflict over real interests or merely inter-organisational rivalry?

Reorganised governance may better articulate or resolve disputes over strategic issues, but not dissolve them. Yet, the degree of dispute in two-tier administration can be exaggerated. Studies of relations between the Greater London and West Midlands County Councils and their lower tier councils showed that, despite periodic outbreaks or longer periods of conflict over certain shared functions, there was more or less continuous harmony in a much larger number of these. Indeed, 'most of the time in relation to most functions, the relationship of the metropolitan counties with their districts is not a recipe for conflict and uncertainty' (Flynn *et al.* 1985, 94).

But initiatives in regional planning and governance do commonly arise from conflicts, which cannot be expunged by mere administrative reorganisation. Conflict between parts of a region customarily reflect inherent social and geographical differences, where different interests compete for economic or political advantage. And the issues of enduring difficulty will often be dominated by housing, which has deep political meanings, and by issues involving decisions about how status and wealth will be distributed between parts of a region. Conflict in the matter of status was widespread in England long before metropolitan counties, and will certainly long outlast them.

In Britain, the Conservative government based its drive against the GLC and metropolitan councils in the 1980s ostensibly on the argument of reducing duplication. The same argument was put subsequently against the counties of England and Wales and the regions of Scotland. But it has been argued elsewhere that duplication and competition by parallel public services can be productive, and this case for parallel systems can be applied to regional planning and governance.

The arguments for and against parallel systems are simply summarised by Bendor (1985). Against parallel systems is the principal argument that two systems are wasteful and inefficient, if each is for much the same purpose. In favour of parallel systems is the principal argument that administrative reliability is improved, since inevitable failures in part of one system will be covered by continued operation in the other system.

Studying experience of transportation planning in the Twin City and Bay Areas, Bendor concluded that whatever the apparent complexity of overlapping interests, having parallel systems produced a better and more reliable outcome than would have arisen otherwise. Bureacratic manoeuvring was rife, but it produced very satisfactory outcomes; these were not what any individual participant had intended, but had been refined and strengthened through conflict.

Implicitly accepting conflict is Lindblom's (1965) favouring of 'partisan mutual adjustment', because it should involve both a rational assessment of alternatives and a proper way of dealing with community interests. This view is supported by Wildavsky (1975), who considers it a matter of principle that power should be dispersed to local level where a 'crazy quilt' of different jurisdictions, governments and special authorities will generate most information about preferences, impose fewest costs, inculcate most dynamism and lead to integrative solutions.

These are views from the US, however, whose crazy quilt is associated with local solutions palpably unintegrated at the higher level of US metropolitan areas and regions. This suggests that Wildavsky's argument is limited in two respects. First, because it implies homogeneous interests within discrete local areas, jockeying with the interests of adjoining or overlapping territories. But no local area will be wholly homogeneous, which will tend to the suppression of minority interests which are small within any single area yet collectively significant across many areas; such interests will have a better chance of a hearing if, with collective strength, they can negotiate with a strategic jurisdiction of some kind. Secondly, because as Hambleton (1979) points out, fragmentation and decentralisation are different matters; decentralisation may be a surer guarantee of minority viewpoints than fragmented local governance.

POLITICAL AND COMMUNITY RELATIONSHIPS
Community issues of a political kind develop at three major geographical scales, Bennett suggests (1989, 43). First, where 'nationalist', ethnic or other regional identities are asserted. Second, locally where people are united by an alienation from large-scale administrative units. Third, where individual interests are being redefined in relation to public administration as a whole.

These three directions for the development of community issues bear differently on the regional question, and on the question of administrative reorganisation.

There is a long tradition of 'nationalist' or ethnic regionalism in Europe and Asia. It has been associated with the development of regional economic policy to – in part – balance the political instability towards which it tends. It has also been the source of bitter tensions, massacre and war. The United Kingdom, the Soviet Union, the Indian sub-continent, Indonesia, the Balkans and the Middle East bear the scars of the intolerance which can accompany it. It has been seen by some as a response to centralist domination by capitalist enterprise, which colonises the economic periphery. But it is a force which survived in communist economies and was asserting itself strongly in the old Soviet Union in the 1990s. It evidently transcends economic systems, and is sensitive to their spatial impacts rather than to their ideology.

Alienation from large-scale administrative units is a phenomenon perhaps more asserted than proven. Those who believe in its existence suggest that it arises from people's lack of effective representation and participation in the affairs of large-scale units, and from lack of decentralisation. But while these poor qualities may be at more risk of developing in a large unit, they are certainly evident in many small ones. Political analysis of small units demonstrates their frequent domination by sectional interests and their inability to respond to variegated needs. Nonetheless, small units have great appeal for sections of the population and there are forces strongly directed towards them.

Finally, the redefinition of the interests of individuals in relation to administrative systems inevitably focuses on the scale of central governments. The United Kingdom has no constitution, but other governments of the East and West do. The Conservative government of the 1980s and early 1990s was wholly opposed to the British enjoying the political rights contained in the Social Charter being offered by the European Community to its member states. Contrarily, the government emphasised the merits of consumer rights as the British were transformed from the owners of basic public services in the 1970s, to the consumers of the goods of private suppliers in the 1990s.

Bennett suggests that the dominant force is towards reinforcing a smaller scale of governance, which he desecribes as 'flexible decentralisation'. He recognises that in the course of the fundamental reassessment of competences, responsibilities and resources which this implies, there must be matching consideration of how small units can be linked to gain economic and technical efficiency. This he calls 'flexible aggregation'.

This argument is echoed by Barlow (1982, 283), whose study of metropolitan government in London, Toronto, San Francisco, Manchester and Melbourne suggested that it received no favours by way of devolved functions from central governments, who instead tended to appease local interests. Metropolitan governments were thereby caught in a squeeze between higher and lower levels of governance. But Barlow implies that these are grounds for preferring regional to metropolitan government, so his solution is opposite to Bennett's.

SOCIAL AND ECONOMIC DEVELOPMENTS

Government has a sustained task to maximise the fit between the scale of its organisation and societal needs, as Bours (1989, 74) emphasises. It 'requires continual adjustment of governmental structures and processes, as society is constantly undergoing renewal and changes in scale.' Adjustment can take the form of changes to processes and procedures, or of changes to the administrative structure they inhabit.

In Europe, continuous regional restructuring has been described as the outcome of the interaction of four processes: of changes in economic systems of production and services; of the behaviour of multi-national corporations; of people's lifestyles and their composition into labour markets; and of political reactions to economic restructuring (Hansen, 1990, 256).

The strength of restructuring varies in different regions and in different governmental systems. In the US, local government is not malleable as it has been in most European countries. In the UK, local government was brought to reorganisation twice in only 20 years – in 1974/75 and in 1996. Each time, full regional local government was rejected. Social and economic change provided three principal pressures destabilising larger scale structures of local governance in Britain by:

1. Continuing dispersal of urban activities, spilling over city and metropolitan
    boundaries into the areas of peripheral local governments. This tends to in-
    stability, even where there may be little growth or even a declining popula-
    tion. With many of the costs of servicing the dispersed people falling still
    on the major authority, financial concerns as well as civic status prompt its
    councillors to seek extensions to its boundaries or new influence beyond
    them. In their restructuring, even the conurbations and metropolitan areas
    have been dissolved by the formation of wider regional cities. This has sig-
    nificant implications for the spatial distribution of public costs and income,
    and for common interests in airports, surface transport, exhibition and con-
    ference facilities and other regional goods. The degree of restructuring has
    been different in different countries. Comprehensive planning has been
    able to dampen the force of restructuring seen at its most extreme in parts
    of the United States. While the efficiency of this kind of planning may be
    strongly criticised from the viewpoint of purist economics, it cannot be said
    that restructuring of the Bos–Wash region of the eastern seaboard of the
    United States or of the Bay Area of the West Coast has occurred on a Chris-
    tallerian landscape of perfect economic neutrality. The very fragmented pat-
    terns of local government have constrained the pattern of restructuring, as
    communities have induced development to their local advantage.

2. The redistribution of voters and a reducing number of 'marginal' councils
    and parliamentary seats. Since the 1970s, the consolidation of near-perma-
    nent majorities for either the Labour or Conservative parties amongst
    parliamentary constituencies and of the Labour Party in urban councils has
    become more evident in the UK. Particularly, selective emigration of the
    better-to-do from the principal cities has almost excluded the possibility of
    Conservative control being restored to many urban areas where it tended to
    alternate with Labour until the 1970s. This has been the stimulus for over-
    whelmingly Conservative government initiatives to reform local govern-
    ment, evident in both the creation and abolition of the Greater London
    Council. Since the abolition of the GLC, the political alternative to bound-
    ary changes has been refined in the London case, where a combination of
    policies to privatise the inner city has successfully consolidated or increased
    the Conservative vote in selected boroughs. Gerrymandering of voters
    where gerrymandering of boundaries is impracticable is, of course, a strat-
    egy familiar to all parties and not the prerogative of just one.

3. Change in political issues and in the balance of power between central and
    local government. Forceful intervention of central government to disturb
    settled relationships with local government reached unprecedented heights
    in the Conservative administration of the 1980s. The inner city issues to
    which it gave priority in this period led to direct government action in local
    affairs through urban development corporations, task forces and other in-
    itiatives in fields in which local authorities had led the way for a hundred

years previously. While through competitive tendering, opting-out of schools from local government control and other means the scope and size of local government affairs was reduced, its capacity to negotiate a programme and budget with its electors was curtailed by expenditure restraints, including the capping of rates and community charges.

WHAT CONDITIONS FOR CHANGE?

Despite their progressive instability, structures of governance commonly persist into prolonged obsolescence. The imprint of Jacobin administration has lingered in France and elsewhere in Europe for 200 years. The United States sustains as old and even less reformed a system of state and local governance.

Comprehensive reform of British local government has been rare, although powers have been shifted and altered at intervals and battles for boundary extensions have been painfully fought – and irregularly won. For almost a century, comprehensive boundary reform had been limited to the creation of county councils in 1889, with infrequent localised reorganisations such as the creation of the GLC in 1963 and the formation of the Teesside County Borough soon after. Although larger reform had been discussed by several governments, the prospect repeatedly faded. But since 1974 the frequency of British reform has accelerated. Comprehensive reorganisation including the creation of the metropolitan county councils came in England and Wales in 1974, and it came in 1975 in Scotland including regional and islands councils. The English reforms lasted only twelve years until the abolition of the GLC and the metropolitan councils in 1986. By 1996, it was the government's intent to reduce two-tier local government and many of the county and regional councils throughout Britain.

What conditions have brought local government reform? British experience shows two grounds, in essence. There has been central government's declared wish for rationalisation and greater efficiency and effectiveness, represented in the national reforms of the 1970s, 1980s and 1990s, and in occasional localised reforms in and outside London. There has also been central government's opportunistic seizure of party political advantage, particularly in London in both 1963 and 1986, and in the abolition of the metropolitan county councils in 1986 under the cloak of 'streamlining the cities'. But not only have governments seen efficiency and cost savings in opposite solutions at different times, but at each there have been probably more calculations arguing the opposite of than supporting whatever case a government has made at any time.

Better metropolitan although not regional planning was certainly a main purpose of the reorganisations of the 1970s, although authorities' boundaries and the distribution of responsibilities were also designed to the advantage of local Conservative Party interests. But the metropolitan reorganisations by a later Conservative government in 1986 gave no mind to strategic planning at all, and the continued reforms intended for 1996 put no significance upon it at either metropolitan or regional scale.

Nonetheless, it could be argued that the reorganisation of the 1970s was no longer appropriate to conditions in the 1990s, and that the metropolitan and regional councils were genuinely obsolete in the terms in which they were created. For whatever the obvious dose of political prejudice in the government's moves to dissolve councils which were less than twenty years old, the scale of traditional issues of physical regional growth had outgrown not only the metropolitan areas, but also several of the standard regions originally defined over 50 years before. Of course, the obsolescence of arrangements for strategic planning was no justification for abandoning a half-hearted system of strategic planning for little system at all, as seems likely to exist in Britain after 1996.

The strategic obsolescence of English local government, in particular, could have been at least partially overcome by effective local alliances. But the English conferences of planning authorities have always been less direct and effective than the best examples of regional authorities in other countries. The Joint Regulations Act for the Netherlands reinforced the ability of local governments to work together over mutual interests, thereby adapting their administrative territory without need for structural reform. The West German *Länder* have managed growing cross-boundary interests by standing conferences of ministers. The sub-regional planning studies in England in the 1960s were cooperative initiatives of this kind, although neither as comprehensive nor as successful as to provide a late alternative to local government reform in the 1970s.

Can Regional Governance be Perfected and Avoid Fresh Outbreaks of Regional Planning?

Regional physical planners in particular seem often to suppose that perfecting a formal system of regional governance would obviate future problems of uncoordinated regional policy. It is implied (e.g. Royal Town Planning Institute 1986) that regional government with substantial executive powers would be able to contain and resolve most of the issues which prevail in regional planning, of most varieties.

But it has not been universal experience that innovative regional governance perfects regional planning. Such cases as that of the Twin Cities in the US or of Strathclyde in Britain show how regional issues can persist, some lying between the plurality of participants existing in any region, and some stretching across the borders of even the best defined region.

A general logic can be suggested to explain the general impracticability of perfecting forms of regional governance, enabling them to indefinitely match the scale of issues in regional planning and to produce planning of the most imaginative kind.

This logic starts with the supposition that it *is* possible to identify regions according to geographers' rules, albeit with increasing complexity and changing criteria. Most remote and sparsely populated regions with only agricultural or mineral resources will remain inviolate. But regions of or close to the principal manufacturing, commercial or administrative centres of national economies will commonly grow and intermingle, with the spreading hegemony of key functions of major economic centres and the dispersal of other activities within their widening hinterlands. Previously separate regions may increasingly overlap as specialist and complementary services are accentuated, as with the city regions of Glasgow and Edinburgh in central Scotland.

As notable a regional concept as the Randstad was becoming obsolete in the 1980s, when the Dutch government saw it being replaced by a Central Netherlands Urban Ring including two-thirds of the Dutch people (Faludi 1994, 494). And new regions may emerge, as they have in the corridor of the M4 motorway between London and Bristol in southern England.

So, the city region of the 1960s has been frequently superseded by the regional city of the 1990s. The emergence of this more dispersed city has been associated with contradictory tendencies. In their daily lives, a majority of the population is likely to have become collectively *less* focused on the old regional centre, particularly women, those allied to the manufacturing and distribution sectors of the economy, and the young below the level of higher education. This is despite communications within the regional city being much improved for a significant proportion of people. For those going on to higher education and those working in the financial and administrative sectors, however, the old regional centre will remain the focus. And the influence of the media of the old centre is likely to be wider than ever.

It is significant for the question of regional governance that in respects the influence of the regional centre will have shrunk, while in others it will have widened and intensified. Whatever the arguments for common financing to pursue an equitable redistribution of resources for education and other local services across spreading regions, there are contrary arguments saying that widening regions may become arbitrarily large for such significant functions as schooling, social work, local planning or drains and sewers.

Reservations of this kind do not deny the proven merits of aspects of experience in elected regional governance. But where this is merely commensurately enlarged local governance, it risks a crystallisation of regional bureaucracies. Bureaucratic infighting is likely to dampen the fire of imaginative regional planning; the most imaginative and influential regional plans have only infrequently emerged from major organs of regional governance.

A significant alternative to the multi-purpose regional council is a range of single-purpose commissions, on the model particularly developed in the US. The Bay Area and the Twin Cities are differing examples, because although in both regions the commissions are agents of their states, only in the Twin Cities does a forceful planning commission stand alongside the others. The different commissions for the variety of purposes do, of course, represent different regions appropriate to specific purposes – recreation, water supply, air pollution, airports, transit and so on. Here and elsewhere, single-purpose commissions for transit, water supply or marine and water pollution may be wholly appropriate, however their areas differ in scale and shape.

The closeness of correspondence of these commissions' areas is likely to count for less in coordinating them than will be the leverage which can be exerted amongst them. So the status of the Twin Cities Council's planning advisers with the State Governor of Minnesota relative to other commissions and political issues will be the measure of how effective the Council's coordination can be.

Beyond planning commissions is the highly fragmented other extreme of regional local governance, that of councils of government. Those of the US show need for very heavy pressure on them to produce let alone implement regional plans. And although the experience of standing conferences in England is more encouraging, it is only at a slow rate and with generally modest ambitions and achievement. Probably the source of proportionately the greatest number of imaginative, bold but also frequently politically acceptable regional plans, has been the sector of consultants, commissions and other ad hoc arrangements. This sector has a notably successful record, despite its usually being briefly rather than regularly incorporated in established processes of regional planning. Its good record lies not just in its relative freedom from the constraints of vested interest, and in its readier severance of ties of convention and its greater imagination. It has also been able to exert deep influence for very long periods, as did the Greater London and Clyde Valley plans.

Why has this occasional sector of regional planners been so effective? Possibly it has been less due to any greater inherent ability of imagination than to the nature of its authority. Although advisory, plans by consultants or *ad hoc* planning teams have been commonly commissioned to break a political deadlock by ostensibly neutral proposals, prepared frequently at the instigation of central or federal governments. So the backing of central authority has been commonly inherent in the work of the consultant or *ad hoc* team, and even when there has been no encouragement to a particular direction of a plan and accompanying policies, the central authority will bear a certain responsibility for them.

There have been significant cases in which central governments have shelved regional plans for which they have been the principal sponsor, of course. But the independent supplier has been a relatively successful source of far-reaching and politically acceptable regional planning.

The independent supplier has also the advantage of flexibility when one or more regional planning issues outgrows a regional planning area. Most regional planning organisations are, sooner or later, inclined to discuss or argue cross-boundary issues with adjoining organisations. The flexible region is not always matched by flexible governance.

So the old joke about a region being an area rather larger than the last for which planning proved unsuccessful might be more respectably described as the *law of imperfection* in regional planning. As all regions and all forms of regional governance are imperfect in some respect, so no regional plan will be perfect. All regional plans will be overtaken by events, not least in politics and affairs of governance. Regional planning is a recurrent necessity in virtually all economic and political conditions.

But recurrent as its necessity usually is, regional planning can be managed in different ways. Matching and permanent arrangements for regional governance are *not* essential for effective action on a particular regional plan. This logic does not suggest that complementary, stable arrangements for regional governance will not potentially ease the way to effective implementation. But it does suggest that regional planning of the traditional physical kind should not be the driving purpose of regional governance, and in particular not the dominant criterion for elected regional government of any kind. The relative significance of different regional issues varies over time – between such matters as regional highways, rapid transit, housing overspill, inner city regeneration, major industrial development and other topics – and there may be different organisational and political ways of dealing with these suited to different approaches at different times.

So this logic concludes that the best laid regional governance cannot remove the tendency for new regional issues to face it, surmounting its boundaries at times and even shrinking them at others. An apparently perfect match between areas of governance and the capacity for autonomous action neither guarantees effective regional planning nor is a precondition for it.

Among the regional cases previously discussed, the German *Länder* and Spanish autonomous regions as fully as in any country match scale of governance with the capacity for direct and effective regional planning. But neither system has been perfect, being inevitably prone to strains within the regions. The metropolitan system in England between 1974 and 1986 was much further from perfection and was ripe for reform, although desirably not that begun in 1986 and to be completed in 1996 which has had no basis at all in regional or strategic planning. However, before any further and more effective system could be instituted, it is inevitable that outbreaks of *ad hoc* regional planning will develop. As periodically in the UK since 1920 and in most regions, emergencies will rise with unanticipated pressures for housing, industry or other new demands for land. Or there will be no agreement between local councils over common strategy.

But even where better arrangements exist than those which Britain will possess after 1996, other countries find periodic reasons to step outside established arrangements for regional governance. Reasons are found to compile regional plans or policies straddling the boundaries of even some of the best defined regions; national boundaries give rise to this commonly, as the initiatives of the Nord-Pas de Calais with adjoining regions in Belgium and England exemplify. So even the best fit between the boundary of a region of governance and of a functional region is unlikely to preclude reasons to be found for cross-boundary regional planning.

The Nature of Regional Planning

The Characteristics of Regional Planning

Regional and strategic planning are concepts more easily seen in practice than defined in the abstract. Neither is defined in legislation in the UK as are structure plans, local plans, unitary plans, development control and some other means of achieving planning objectives.

By covering cases and the broad development of regional planning in the UK, Europe and the US, we have shown that although regional planning in some countries has been succeeded by formal arrangements for the continuous governance and planning of geographical regions, it remains an activity also operating at and across the boundaries of established geographical areas of local administration and planning. Planning of this kind is frequently described as 'strategic', but that terminology is also widely used to describe policy frameworks within organisations, including some working in areas substantially smaller than could be reasonably described as 'regions'. So although regional planning is normally also strategic, strategic planning may only occasionally be regional.

Our accounts of cases and of its general history have shown regional planning to be often ephemeral. Some advocates of more and better organised regional planning have not recognised that inevitability; they have wished to too much institutionalise the process, and to judge it by wrong criteria. The nature of much of it is often – quite properly – more like a guerrilla operation than like mainstream public administration. Commonly, the purpose of the teams brought in to situations of crisis is to report and then to self-destruct. Seen in this light, much more regional planning has been highly successful than is often supposed. Some – the *Clyde Valley Plan*, the *Greater London Plan, the West Central Scotland Plan*, and planning in the Ruhr and the Nord-Pas de Calais – has been profoundly influential. Where it has seemed unsuccessful, it has often been because its sponsors have failed it by political weakness over its implementation.

It is characteristic of much regional planning that it arises from political crises, of varying kinds. In Britain, governments have turned to regional planning in wartime, to cover when established systems could not cope with the speed or directness or authority which emergencies required. It has arisen at times of economic crisis, as in the early 1930s. And it has arisen in political crises – commonly associated with economic failures – as in the early 1960s, and possibly again in the 1990s. It is a means of governments showing special political concern by going over and above normal administrative arrangements; it can be used to overcome the defects of local government or to by-pass it; and it is a means of asserting central control over provincial affairs.

We see how regional tendencies endure, as established boundaries and administrative and political systems are overtaken by pressures and events which do not match existing arrangements. And because regional planning and regional administrative initiatives so often re-emerge, we can see that they are an enduring necessity. The need for them repeatedly arises, however irregularly, however the forms and intensity vary, and however often the circumstances change. The regional imperative may be inconstant, but it is insistent. There is a recurrent demand for strategic planning between the established levels of government.

We can accordingly summarise eight characteristics of the nature of regional planning:

1. Regional planning is an often mercurial concept. It is frequently ephemeral and more like a guerrilla operation than mainstream public administration. Some of its advocates have wished to too much institutionalise it. Some of its critics have failed to appreciate its proper nature.

2. Much regional planning has been highly successful. Some plans, like the Clyde Valley Plan, have been profoundly influential. Where it has seemed to fail, it has often been because it was not followed up by a proper context for action or, as in the 1960s planning for South East England, because it proved to be technically flawed.

3. Because regional planning so repeatedly emerges, it is evidently an enduring necessity between levels of government and agencies of administration. However, it arises in different places at different times, in different forms and with varying intensity in often changing circumstances.

4. Regions are inconstant. Their size, shape and composition fluctuate with changing political circumstances, and with the changing dynamics of social and economic geography.

5. No sooner are planning or administrative arrangements fixed for any region, than new regional issues arise around its borders. Regional issues are often political in origin and are certainly political in their implications. So no perfect system can be devised for regional planning and governance, and any regional planning arrangements tend to instability.

6. While regional planning conferences of largely equal partners are invaluable for monitoring, interpreting and exchanging information, they are commonly inept at resolving strategic policy. Leverage on those who will implement strategy is normally essential to resolving one which is coherent and far-sighted.

7. The need for comprehensive redirection of most regional strategies is infrequent and the timing is irregular. The proper role of many strategic teams is to report and then to self-destruct. The time cycle of strategy-making does not match that of strategic implementation.

8. The technical methods appropriate to regional planning must be sensitive to its characteristics. An exceptional degree of risk surrounds much regional planning strategy, because it commonly looks to longer time-horizons and a more complex context for its implementation than do most other kinds of development planning.

If these characteristics truly define the nature of regional planning, its future is assured and is not closely dependent upon a matching structure of regional governance as many have supposed. Indeed, as defined by the experience of Europe and the United States, the most common form of regional planning has been where called for because administrative structures have poorly matched rising regional issues.

Only a few regions have the stability of those homogeneous regions of traditional geography, with stable physical or economic features. More common are regions driven by factors of politics or economic dynamics, in constant flux. Those can never be exactly matched by a stable system of governance; political issues will always spill over their boundaries. Indeed, regional issues are, in essence, those which fixed patterns of administrative areas are incapable of solving internally, because interdependencies so join their interests. So, for the reasons of inertia of systems of governance and of the dynamics of economic and social change, an inherent need for regional planning persists in most countries.

The Techniques of Regional Planning

But just as social scientists have challenged comprehensive planning and planners' assumptions about their significance, any deterministic role for regional planning has been particularly open to challenge. Rondinelli (1975, 240) would so reorient planning that regional planning might have only a tenuous place in any formalised heirarchy of policy and decision making. Although his views derive considerably from experience in newly industrialising countries, he suggests that planning must:

1. be inextricably linked to policy and decision making. Mere prescription is not enough; intervention and entrepreneurial action amongst a wide variety of actors is required

2. find a place in this complex process

3. recognise that much decision-making will be devolved amongst groups making mutual adjustments with one another, as it cannot be all centrally controlled

4. recognise that not only do a multitude of policy makers plan, but that a variety of functions contribute to urban change

5. employ regional planners educated in new and different ways.

With its distinctive characteristics, regional planning particularly demands techniques to cope with the uncertainties of longer-term futures and of changing political, economic, technological and social contexts. Far-sightedness, uncertainty, risk, flexibility and robustness are prominent keywords in the vocabulary of regional planning. The contexts and relative infrequency of major reviews of regional strategy and policy tend to require policies for long-time horizons, often of 20 years or more, and much beyond the time-scale of local, structure and other prevalent development planning. Regional planning attempts frameworks for investment and action by a wide range of agencies and of private interests, collectively likely to be even more beyond direct control than with other kinds of plan.

Regional plans and policy are therefore likely to be exceptionally vulnerable to circumstances beyond their control, of unforeseen events, or of political or other forces whose responses may be guessed at, but which planning cannot steer. This inherent and acute climate of uncertainty, flexibility and risk has led to progressive monitoring of events as a common element of regional planning. But it has also led to regular monitoring sometimes substituting for periodic regional plan-making. This derives from the fallacies which surround monitoring, most seriously applying to regional planning.

There are three principal fallacies. Monitoring rather than long-term planning is said to: allow flexibility through limiting the forward view that needs to be taken at any particular time; allow policy to be adjusted as better data becomes available; and to allow current problems to be tackled first, leaving the more distant future to be worried about when it actually arrives. Together, these fallacies are sometimes used to argue against long-term regional planning horizons of 20 years or more ahead.

Such an argument is understandable in the light of experience of some insensitive regional plans. But there is enough experience elsewhere of robust technical methods and of successful plans to show the depth of the fallacies. The technical tests of flexibility behind the sub-regional study for Coventry–Solihull–Warwickshire, the Delphi scenario-making of the strategy for East Anglia or the alternative growth assumptions made for West Central Scotland are examples of the way in which robustness has been built into plans.

The fallacies are unsound because: looking at such an insensitive regional programme as that of 1963 for Central Scotland, it was not impossible to have conceived of the scenario of events which actually developed in the region, although the programme made no attempt to do so; looking far ahead does not mean that all has to be committed to that distant prospect; monitoring is only a flimsy safety net, because as we wait for data the future moves relentlessly ahead; politicians prefer to stick to their adopted policies for a sustained period, it being hard to modify them as quickly and as irregularly as monitored data might suggest to be necessary; current decisions frequently involve investment only worthwhile if paying back long into the future, so decisions are best made in the context of a wide view of future possibilities; and many immediate decisions as over highways or power stations take many years to become construction projects.

The limitations of monitoring were summarised by a senior English civil servant involved in regional planning in the South East in the 1970s, following the *Strategy for the South East*:

> The reason why I dislike 'monitoring' as such... is because people are not interested in it! We have produced lots of papers on housing, unemployment, and the labour market in an effort to answer the question – 'are we on target'?

But people are not interested in that question, nor are they interested in the answer, partly because the targets are indeterminate and shifting and conditions are changing all the time. Statistical tracking is not, I find, a particularly fruitful form of activity. We all go around in regional planning and say that 'objectives' are all-important, but to try to translate them into any sort of reality, to measure them against trends or indices and to get anyone to read the results once you have written them down, is certainly extremely difficult. (Curry 1975, 31).

Monitoring is nonetheless essential to regional planning, but is no alternative to periodic major review, fundamental re-questioning and any necessary restatement of regional plans and policies. As others have noted (Bryson, Freeman and Roering 1986, 79), most models drawn of the process of strategic planning do not show how strategic issues are to be identified. Restatement of plans and policies will not be necessary at every review, but a process confined to monitoring data is not alone a sufficient means of regional planning.

Conclusion: The Regional Imperative

Much regional planning must inevitably continue to be a reticulist activity, operating at the margins of regular planning, repairing the inadequacies of regular governance and bridging its periodic strategic gaps. Administrative reorganisation may minimise the number of cross-boundary strategic issues, but cannot wholly eliminate them. The most nearly perfect geography of regional governance will not sate political tensions, for either nations or regions.

There is an irrepressible regional imperative.

CHAPTER NINE

The Future of Regional Planning and Governance

Preface: Not as Before

The long and recurrent experience of regional planning shows shifts and changes in priorities, in its politics, in its methods and in the nature of regions themselves.

The future of regional planning is likely to be constant only in the demand for it, whatever the different titles it will assume. And arrangements for regional governance are likely to be sustained and effective only if they are flexible to the variable nature of regional planning and of regions.

What is a Region Now and in the Future?

The Regional Confusion

Across most of Europe, and also in some countries outside, regions became increasingly the focus of new approaches to governance in the 1980s. There were generally also moves to metropolitan governance, better matching the spreading scales of regional economic and social affairs. There were two obvious national exceptions. The UK dissolved its English metropolitan local governments in 1986, and only in a few cases had the US overcome its reluctance to establish effective arrangements for strategic planning and governance. But even these two conservative countries were reawakening to the potential of effective regional planning to better manage the pressures of growth; their earlier experiences of regional planning were being renewed in the 1990s.

But contexts for regional planning in the 1990s have been fast changing. Regions are no more only parts of separate nations. They now transcend national boundaries. The Region-Nord Pas de Calais and Kent County Council had cooperated since the commencement of the Channel Tunnel to the point at which, in 1990, an initial joint pilot action programme was being presented to the EC for training, economic development and tourism, to be followed by a joint transboundary development programme. This kind of regional cooperation was far short of regional governance, but it was one of many such regional links traversing the territories of the twelve member countries of the EC. And the Community was stretching links right across eastern Europe into the extended membership of countries seeking accession around the end of the century.

As the mosaic of regions spreads, it creates an underlying dilemma for regional planning and governance. On the one hand, the EC defines regions in terms of economics. By 1992, it was fostering 37 networks linking local or regional economies ranging from a selection adjusting to decline of shipbuilding, to a selection mutually concerned with ceramics. And simultaneously it recognised eight supra-national regions such as Alpine Europe and the Maritime Periphery, each with economic characteristics in common. On the other hand, the EC's NUTS categorisation of regions is based where possible on regions of governance employed by the member countries. In France or Germany, the *conseils régionaux* and the *Länder* offer established units of elected regional government and formal planning, fitting well into the NUTS scheme. But governance in some other countries is not so compatible with the NUTS design, which for the UK resorts to the standard statistical regions and to groupings of local authorities, which do not correspond with any consistent or formalised system of integrated regional planning.

The dilemma is that economic regions do not always make suitable regions for the purpose of regional planning. They may not correspond with acceptable political regions. Few regions are likely to be perfectly composed on both counts, although the rules of politics will tend to dominate in designs for governance. But the rules of politics have to be frequently redefined as regional contexts. As Friedmann says, 'flexibility in the application of regional concepts is a corollary to the experimental character of planning... No one set of regions is ever completely satisfactory. Each problem must be analysed in its own terms' (Friedmann 1964, 500).

In looking at the future, therefore, we must look at two types of region.

The Economic Region

The number of ways in which economic regions can be defined has increased as the advanced economies have moved into their post-industrial stages. The economic region of much historic regional planning was commonly highly integrated. It was bound together by links of production, as between the many metal-working firms of the West Midlands, or as between the foundries, forges, and casting plants of Clydeside and its shipyards and locomotive works. The Geddesian region was a river valley with a relatively closed economy of complementary trades, from agriculture to manufacturing, self-sufficient to a degree now uncommon.

But until the 1960s, in the UK, economic issues were most usually only the background to regional problems of housing and of perceived congestion. Regional plans were dominated by proposals for housing spread, new communities or new towns, and green belts. Economic proposals were significant elements of Abercrombie's plans of the 1940s, but were relegated by governments at the expense of the physical elements of the plans.

There had been earlier cases of planning for economic regions, of course; Abercrombie's East Kent Survey of 1925 had been to plan for the development of the coalfield, and in the Ruhr in the same era there had also been regional planning to develop coal production; in the US, the great river valley programmes had been exceptional innovations in economic planning. But these approaches were apart from the mainstream of regional planning.

The rise of land use-transportation planning in the 1960s brought forward one economic element which had existed in much earlier regional planning, in the form of commuting problems within daily work-journey regions. But these were only narrowly economic plans, not to be classified with the parallel flurry of infrastructural programmes in the UK – for *Central Scotland* (1963) and *North East England* (1963) in particular – which conceived of economic regions in a wider way than had been customary before, spreading their economic analysis beyond individual metropolitan commuting areas. And from the 1970s, the scope of regional economic planning enlarged in several senses. It not only looked more closely at questions of training, innovation, financing, marketing and other indicators of the health and adaptability of regional economies, but it looked at the international contexts of specific regions.

So, regional economic planning has come to define regions not merely by the limits of their daily travel-to-work areas, but as much by the limit of their links with competitor regions, with their capital regions on which they depend for higher level services, or with adjoining and often trans-national regions with which they share common interests and complementary futures. The mosaic of regions recognised or fostered by the EC are the new economic regions of Europe. And trading communities in other continents are assembling similar overlapping patterns of economic region.

The regional economic planning of this developing kind is leading to regional planning for international exchange of knowledge, for cooperation in new electronic highways to transport data rather than office workers, to foster economic adjustment and expansion amongst associated regions in different countries. This kind of trans-national cooperation requires a new conception of what an economic region is, certainly not self-contained, not defined by the effective limit of daily commuting or the circulation area of an evening newspaper, nor even controlled by one national government. Not just spreading traditional metropolitan regions like Clydeside – now merging with the complementary facets of the economy of Edinburgh in a more significant Central Scotland economic region – but crystallising new economic regions spanning Europe, forming around common issues or complementary potential for change or growth.

So, the integrity of the traditional economic region is continuing to dissipate. There has been the rise of multi-national companies, the decline of regionally based banks and finance houses, the dissolution of local social elites and – in the UK – the frustration of local government, all in different ways weakening internal regional dependencies and turning regions to look outwards. This redefines regional planning as it does the the variety of economic regions.

The Political Region

Regional politics, suppressed in eastern Europe and the Soviet Union for at least 50 years, seem likely to remain vigorous around the world. In the Soviet Union since 1991, they have helped to pull apart what had been a centralised state since long before the Bolshevik revolution of 1919. Yugoslavia divided also in 1991, and continued to bloodily fragment in the years that followed. In Spain, Italy and several other European countries, regionalism has carried less far, but equally reflects ethnic and historical divisions persisting through nineteenth century nationalism and the treaties of the aftermath of the Great War of 1914–18. And in the United Kingdom, a treaty of 1707 between England and Scotland had been under threat since the 1960s. There were also seeming counter-tendencies. In Germany and France, racialism and the revival of the neo-fascist right from the 1980s drove a nationalist revival. In Germany, historic regional divisions were papered over by unification. But what was seen as regionalism in some countries and as nationalism in others was the same force. Its roots were in ethnic and cultural inheritances, misfitting with the boundaries created by passing powers, whether communist as in the Soviet Union or capitalist as through the Allies who restructured the Balkans after 1919.

The political force of regionalism may in some cases be its own worst enemy, launching some regions into damaging confrontation with other regions of greater strength. Whether the more powerful regions retaliate with armed aggression as in Yugoslavia, or with economic oppression as in Spain, a degree of autonomy in governance may trade political independence for new regional disadvantage. As Hudson (1993, 16) suggests, it is certainly true that some of the more rapidly advancing regions of Europe are associated with a strong degree of regional autonomy, yet this does not ensure success in all cases. In the past, Northern Ireland has had perhaps fuller regional autonomy than any other part of the UK, but its economy has remained the weakest of any part. And UK governments have progressively reduced Scotland's advantages in financial aid as other parts of the nation have been irritated by calls for Scottish devolution or independence. So autonomy which decouples a region from balancing national inter-regional economic policies may exact a heavy price.

It may be argued that if political regionalism leads to greater regional devolution or political autonomy in certain countries in the future, it may have two principal effects on economic regionalism. On the one hand it may run counter to the pattern of internal regional links within a country, separating different ethnic or religious regions which had been previously integrated within a national economy. On the other hand, it may establish new connections between regions in different countries which find themselves politically rather than economically compatible.

The politics of regional governance has also been changing in some countries. The UK is a prime case. Although in the US and in certain countries of mainland Europe there has been a longer tradition of partnership in regional planning between the public and private sectors, this has been a significant feature in the UK only since the mid 1980s. But both planning method and the practice of implementation is likely to much more involve private sector interests in the future (Roberts 1993, 765). The significance of networking which has become clear in local economic development has also its place in regional planning.

So, the future of both economic and political regions in Europe is highly dynamic. Perhaps less so in the US, which is as liable as is Europe to significant economic change, but whose ethnic melting pot has yet to boil over at the regional scale prevalent in Europe, however often it has done in the cities.

The Case For Regional and Strategic Planning in the UK

The Three Principles

It might be argued that there is little or no case for regional and strategic planning in a small country like the UK. In the 1980s, it was dismissed by the government as a fashion of twenty years before. But some more knowledgeable opinion also pointed in the same direction; Bennett (1989, 69) could assert that 'There is a decreasing need for a "strategic" view over regional or metropolitan areas.' Yet the record of evidence shows that only in ignorance can it be argued that regional planning is not in demand, or that regions cannot be a natural and effective basis for governance. The context may tend to be unstable, but governments in Britain have administered many functions at regional level for well over a hundred years. The reasons have been various, but they have been compelling and recurrent. The tendency was sustained even in the 1980s, when not just regions but planning were anathema to the governing ideology of the period. By the 1990s, the imperative for regional planning was incontrovertible.

There can be no question about the permanency of regional issues in planning, or of continued forms of regional governance. But as perfection of regional management is impracticable in possibly all countries, so room for debate about the future of regional planning lies only in *who* plans, coordinates and takes decisions on regional issues, *who* administers, and do they do so under control of a directly elected regional body?

Most advances in regional planning and the most outstanding strategic planning decisions in Britain have probably occurred outside any formalised system of regional governance. They have occurred at the insterstices of established administrative systems, through ad hoc initiatives, consultants' reports and from other often transitory sources of advice and policies. Strategic decisions have been implied by governments' consent, not necessarily through a decision on an individual plan but through a variety of individual initiatives or decisions. This was typified with the *West Central Scotland Plan* of 1974, never specifically approved by its sponsors in central or local government, but absorbed into actions ranging from the establishment of the Scottish Development Agency, the initiation of the GEAR project in Glasgow and the termination of Stonehouse New Town. As in this case, it may be difficult to separate various strands of influence on hidden political decisions.

This irregular and occasionally obscure context for decisions on regional planning reflects the sometimes transitory nature of regional issues, and also matches the definition of regional planning with which the book opened. So, if some of our most creative regional planning has arisen without benefit of structured regional administration or governance, do we need it? And if regional planning may be creatively achieved – in some cases at least – without formalised regional governance, do we need it to ensure effective implementation?

Simply put, the case for considered arrangements for regional planning and governance rests on three principles (RTPI 1986, 38):

1. The evolving and spreading complexity of the social and economic structures of most metropolitan urban regions and of many rural regions.

2. Direct electoral accountability to extend the responsibility of locally elected representatives over a wider range of public services.

3. The merits of distributing resources within regions so as to fairly reflect local aspirations, efficiency and equity.

The Spreading of Regional Cities and of Pressures on Rural Regions

There is a spreading complexity in both urban and rural regions. Cities which once dominated their hinterlands have now become dominated by them in important respects. Some of the major cities of Britain now house fewer people than live elsewhere within their commuting hinterlands. Regional cities have succeeded even city regions. Administrative boundaries are distorted by the influence of party political interests and untidily match the geography of economic and social affairs.

This growth of the regional city is part of the case (Self 1982, 150) for dismissing the possibility of metropolitan area governance in favour of regional governance. Self also argues that effective regional government would better match an accompanying level of unitary local government. The case is reinforced by analyses of ways in which the metropolitan areas are dissolving into diffuse regions. As said of metropolitan London:

> While it is still valid for certain purposes to regard London as a metropolis, the limitations of such a perspective need to be fully recognised. The passage of time has seen the metropolitan boundary lose much of its earlier significance in the organisation of space. (Mogridge and Parr 1994)

But this truth about the changing economic and social structure of great urban regions and the spreading of strategic planning issues does not mean that all large-scale public services are better organised and provided at regional scale. Although since the GLC and the metropolitan county councils of England were dissolved in 1986 no political party or significant interest group has proposed the restoration of metropolitan governance except in the case of London, this does not mean that there may not still be a role for metropolitan governance for some services in some areas.

Accountability

Lack of local participation in political approaches to regional problems must tend to ineffective or unpopular action. But local control does not guarantee local sensitivity and accountability. Rising action on many social aspects of inner city problems of the UK from the 1970s was possibly handled more constructively in the area of Strathclyde Regional Council than in the areas of the English metropolitan county councils. Strathclyde Regional Council had an incomparable strategic capacity, whereas in the English metropolitan areas social responsibilities lay with district councils which had smaller resources, and so had less scope to redistribute them within their narrower tax bases.

So, does regional governance necessarily imply remoteness, weak popular participation and lack of accountability? Bennett (1989, 308) identifies four criteria for acceptable participation:

1. *Identity:* maintaining of community interest and of mutual support between individuals and groups within areas.

2. *Legitimacy:* the extent to which administrative decisions are accepted by individuals or groups.

3. *Penetration:* the extent and effectiveness of administrative effects on individuals or groups.

4. *Distribution:* the degree of redistribution from those who have to those who have not.

In contemporary economies, a large scale of sub-national governance can be argued to be commonly justified on all these issues. Long resettlement of metropolitan populations to new towns and commuter villages has created two scales of identity for substantial numbers of people, who have a regional as well as a local community identity. In urban regions particularly, legitimacy cannot be merely the sum of many local responses to wider problems; there are wholly proper differences of interest to be raised between participants at local and regional levels. Penetration certainly requires local sensitivity, but fragmented governance will certainly be inequitable governance. And equitable distribution requires equitable resources, demanding a wide base of income to redistribute.

But if very local government cannot alone satisfy the criteria for acceptable participation, an exclusively top-down approach in strategic matters is likely to be similarly insensitive. Government is too high above the regional level and local governments are too numerous for the government to act as regional authority for all issues with a regional dimension. Also, governments' quasi-judicial role in planning and the proper interplay of local and central considerations are prejudiced by unifying regional planning in government hands. This does not rule out, though, indirect regional planning through a planning commission or some other form of intermediary.

There is a distinction to be drawn here between planning of the kinds we have discussed, and other public services. The case for regional administration of personal services and of the use of land and distribution of activities in detail certainly lies in the direction of local government. Only where exceptional calls for national resources may arise in localised parts of regions, or over a relatively short period of time, may the case for support by a national government agency be justified. However, the purpose of effective regions for local administration and action is to minimise need for national agency intervention.

There should certainly be public awareness of regional frameworks for investment and public expenditure, to give an opportunity for challenge. Government has sought this principle in local government budgeting, but has diminished it by imposing guidelines for structure planning but by leaving them devoid of detail on public investment.

Effective Resource Planning

Effective resource distribution has to rest on the principles of being able, first, to identify problems and conflicts and, second, to resolve them. Even without accepting the government's critique of regional planning before 'streamlining' the cities in 1986, it can be recognised that the system of strategic planning by local government in England and Wales was seriously flawed. The system did not effectively meet the RTPI principles, which were more evident in the Redcliffe–Maud proposals for local government reorganisation than in the subsequent Local Government Act 1972; the failings of foresight in the 1974 reorganisation were errors of administrative judgement, and not defects in the principles of regional and strategic planning.

Strategic decision-making and resource distribution becomes fair and necessary where significant quantities of people, activities and inequities of services and prosperity daily straddle local government boundaries. Public transport, highway building, recreation facilities and the costs of supporting business and industry justify it. So do the external costs associated with pollution, urban decay or waste disposal, which neither arise nor are attributable to discrete local government districts. Fragmented strategic responsibilities invite non-elected or representative bodies which, unless in the form of government agencies, are poorly equipped to take decisive action on inequities and priorities within regions. The experience of France and the United States shows this, as does considerable experience in Britain prior to 1974. The consequence may be wasted potential and ineffective use of land and resources.

Notwithstanding the assistance of LPAC in Greater London, dividing structure planning responsibility between the government and the unitary district councils in the 'streamlined' metropolitan areas since 1986 has inevitably risked inflexibility, poor anticipation of the effects of economic change and wasteful competition between authorities in spending on infrastructure. Locally fragmented structure planning can scarcely but be confusing to the private and public sectors alike, as was experienced in the West Midlands between 1971 and 1974. And the strategic guidance on structure planning issues subsequently provided by governments for most regions has been opaque, doing too little to clarify the future context for the private investment so eagerly sought in the guidance.

In all these circumstances, a fair critic must be satisfied that there is an enduring case for regional strategic planning. It is also clear that however frequently it has come to the rescue over regional problems, the system in most of the UK has been slow, weak in anticipation, and inadequate to realise the creative talents or economic potential of the regions. When lack of entrepreneurialism has been seen as a national failing, the Government has been highly equivocal about releasing it in the regions.

The Possibilities For a New Basis For UK Regional Planning

The Regional Imperative

The UK has made often sophisticated, and sometimes significant and influential, initiatives to introduce a regional dimension to planning and governance. But the stream of experience has been discontinuous. And in the 1980s it ran thin, was openly derided by the Government, and might have expired.

In important respects the Government has widened its interventions in regional development in the 1990s, although in hand with a rejection of regional participation in the shaping and execution of wider strategic policy. Government's invitation to local government to participate in land use planning for the regions was a small gesture against the broader trend. Centralisation was fragmenting policies for the regions because they were being applied by individual government departments, with little opportunity to consider their consistency and impact within specific regions.

It is true that past regional and strategic planning has too often achieved less than might have been wished for. Even where successful against original objectives, strategic policies have frequently had unanticipated side-effects creating new strategic problems. So, the decongestion programmes for UK cities up to the 1970s certainly led to improved housing for inner city residents, but may have exacerbated aspects of inner city unemployment and social stress at the same time. There have been similar side-effects from landscape and agricultural land conservation strategy, which commonly paid more regard to control of building land than to the safeguard of natural habitats or, frequently, to the social base and heritage of building in rural settlements.

The intensifying growth of environmental and social pressure groups since the 1960s has coincided with a failure to sustain continuous and sensitive strategic planning in issues of widespread public concern. The government's much-reduced emphasis in the 1980s on strategic planning by negotiation and consensus increased tensions with these groups. It threatened to reduce the capacity of executive agencies and authorities to anticipate strategic issues, and to mutually adjust their policies to achieve strategic ends. In the 1990s, rhetoric about a revived wish for consensus was too often diluted by entrenched political bias amongst those appointed to the agencies and commissions reponsible for negotiations.

But regional planning in the primarily physical tradition of Britain is no longer the dominant justification for regional governance. Strathclyde's experience shows regional local government to be administratively viable, and to be justified by the potential to plan and redistribute priorities for a wide range of services. And Strathclyde confirms how unsatisfactory were the English metropolitan counties and the Greater London Council – combining restricted areas with restricted impacts; their geographical scale was too close to that of their lower tier of districts and boroughs, and they were too far from central government in their resource capacities.

Strathclyde proved not too big a regional local government to effectively administer services as personal as schooling, social work and consumer advice, as well as more familiar strategic services like highways, water and sewerage or policing. It has been too large neither in its volume of administration nor in the area over which it has provided services; nor could any other local government in the United Kingdom be designed to have been more fragmented into islands, archipelagos and remote communities.

Accordingly, it would not be administratively impracticable to replace English counties by local government at a much larger scale. The fear of political remoteness in regional local government is often exaggerated; experience in 1988 when local influence overturned Strathclyde's region-wide proposals for school closures shows the continuing importance and strength of local politics, even within such a large and disparate region. And when it was estimated (*Scotland on Sunday* 1993) that spending through unelected agencies – the 'new magistracy' – had grown to 39 per cent of the Scottish Office budget by 1993, accumulating much finance and several responsibilities from local government, remoteness was more obviously a feature of central than of local government.

Where inner city and employment issues with strong local impact were being treated in the 1990s by action by central government and its array of new agencies, it clearly denied any argument that regional local government must inevitably be too distant, unresponsive and unaccountable. It cannot reasonably be argued that a regional council office would be more remote than a Whitehall ministry, or the headquarters of a government agency. A regional councillor would expect to have more influence on local action than a Member of Parliament.

It is proper and necessary that Westminster should retain a stake in and directly fund key elements of regional development. This is not merely the mark of a centralist government like the Conservative one of the 1980s and 1990s; it reflects the high profile which inner city and local employment issues in particular are likely to hold in national politics for the rest of the century. But this does not warrant exclusion of local and regional participation in key decisions. Lack of any form of regional local government accordingly largely removes regional planning and action from local hands and electors, exacerbating its remoteness.

The advancing role of central government and its agencies is likely to persist. Just as new towns became a regional issue demanding national resources and intervention in the 1940s, so after the 1970s urban regeneration came to be not just a local or regional issue, but a national one also.

But most regional issues are inextricably interwoven with national ones. What is required is that both dimensions of the weave are clearly seen, and that they are represented in the taking of decisions about and within regional strategies. So autonomous regional local government would be as unbalanced an approach to regional strategy as that by centralised government. Yet the near extinction of the historic Conservative English county at the county council elections of 1993 ensured that the counties were now as politically unacceptable to the government as regions always had been. The fragmentation of local government was leaving central government even more responsible for such regional planning as would be effective.

A most significant development in the progressively changing environment for regional planning was the replacement of local taxation through property rating by the introduction of the Community Charge. Local discretion in raising and redistributing revenues was reduced, meaning that a much larger share of the cost of maintaining, servicing and renewing the metropolitan areas of Britain fell on local residents. Commuters and others enjoying the facilities of the conurbations had to pay less to use them. The effect of the Community Charge was largely regressive. Local authorities had less scope than before to geographically redistribute resources, as there was a significant fall in revenues raised from areas of higher-income households. Replacing the Community Charge by the Council Tax in 1993 redressed the problem only to a degree, because it would persist for as long as a per capita payment remained a component of the tax.

When the scope for local governments to redistribute local revenues is severely restricted, the case for regional local government is undercut. But a case remains. What changes are the appropriate scales and depth of the regions which might be so governed.

The pressures from the European Commission for formalised sub-national regional government are well-established, and a 'Europe of the Regions' is regarded by many as if it already existed. Others see how far short of the cliché is the current state of Europe, and particularly that of Britain. They argue that regional politics can provide the experience of serious administration and policy from which presidents, chancellors and prime ministers can emerge, as they have in Germany, France, the Soviet Union or the United States; regions can bridge the gap facing opposition politicians in Britain, jumping often from municipal to national management with one bound. They above all see regions as bringing a new balance and a more fully-founded peace to Europe. Those who echo Proudhon, Geddes, Kropotkin and the anarchist-philosophers of the nineteenth and early twentieth century believe that regional self-determination will bring stability to the nations which are held together only by centralised power. The argument is beguiling, but it has to answer whether the bloody process of self-determination of the federal regions of the Soviet Union and of Yugoslavia is a worthwhile sacrifice for the possibly greater peace to come. And those mistrusting an enthusiasm for regions see it as the attempted re-creation of a Europe of peace that never-was, or the fantasy of a world which never-could-be. And they argue that self-determination may also be self-sacrifice, when centralised support for peripheral economies is diluted or severed. So the regional imperative has its perils.

Local Responsibility and Regional Potential

Reassembling a system of strategic and regional planning and development faces many political issues, particularly those of local representation in regional policy, and of the fuller harnessing of regional potential in national economic and social development.

On the one hand, increasing strategic control on public expenditure which government has exerted through actions including the abolition of the metropolitan counties has been criticised as overwhelming local choice. Government has also been criticised for spurning local knowledge and potential, wasting the energy, innovative and organisational capacity of the regions, fragmenting the local authority system and dissipating networks of self-support established in the regions. Not all of these tendencies may have been intentional, but they have been the frequent consequences of government policies with other purposes.

The government has been forced by circumstances to build a flimsy framework for regional planning and governance. Ramshackle as it may be, and reluctant as the government has been to give it integrated coherence, it has grown nonetheless. The government has known that it has itself been riding a Trojan horse. The dilemma surfaced clearly in 1993, when the Government was defeated in its attempt to displace local authority representatives from the 24 places which the EC intended for them on the new, consultative Committee of the Regions. Yet, because there was no appropriate scale of elected governance from which nominations could be made directly, the government was able to itself pick the UK membership. In England, at least, a basis for direct representation did exist in the eight regional conferences of local planning authorities covering England, but their weak record of compiling realistic programmes of regional priorities does not suggest that they might have been much better a source of members.

Exploiting and fulfilling the potential contribution of regional organisations, figures and politicians is, of course, not solely a political issue. It is an economic one too. It has long been a feature of regional plans and strategies. It was central to regional plans of the 1940s, and remained so in the 1990s. It has been a main emphasis in many appraisals of regional planning and economic development (RTPI 1986, Goddard 1992, Town and Country Planning Association 1993).

Elsewhere in Europe, attitudes to regional initiative have been generally quite different. In the provinces of France, there has been a growing emphasis on aggressive metropolitan planning strategy since 1985, backed by new planning organisations for the metropolitan agglomerations. The metropolitan strategies take their context as being the new Europe, in which social and economic opportunities are to be seized by infrastructure programmes and far-sighted but flexible planning. Connections between social progress, economic opportunity and land-use and infrastructural planning are understood in France, quite contrary to the insistence by the UK government that development plans should confine themselves to the use of land and to the condition of activities on it.

There are, therefore, two essential components in the task of reassembling a system of strategic and regional planning for the UK incorporating fuller participation. There has to be a readjustment of the central–local relationship, and there has to be both a functional and an areal reorganisation of the base for planning and governance. These essentials can be sought in a number of possible ways, all of which involve much more than a marginal tinkering with the patchwork system we possess.

The new system should reinforce local government's role in strategy-making and implementation, releasing capacities for regional self-help which are currently suppressed, and doing this within a framework possessing the stability, resilience and effectiveness lacking in earlier experiments in regional planning and governance.

There are four principal grounds which justify a better linkage of regional and strategic planning:

1. The UK government has notably expanded its own administrative arrangements in the regions since the mid 1980s. But it has insufficiently linked them, perpetuating departmentalism and contradictions in strategic policy.

2. Local government was fragmented by the abolition of the metropolitan county councils in 1986 and is threatened further by removal of many county and regional councils in the later 1990s. Thereby, local government's potential in strategic planning has been greatly diminished, and local democracy has been flouted.

3. Not only have regions been repeatedly proven to be a significant context for local planning issues, and for public agencies, public infrastructure and services, but the private sector has demanded strategic regional planning for its interests.

4. In the European Community, the collective interests of the member nations have been increasingly interpreted through regional plans and programmes.

At this point, questions rush in about the detail of the appropriate machinery. How would it be designed and how would it work?

First, what areas are appropriate? The principal options are for expanded metropolitan regions or for larger provincial regions. The former may be more cohesive and closest to the most familiar local problems, but the latter may be more appropriate if we are thinking of balance of development and of resources among local authorities. Even if we accept the continuing significance of the most serious major spatial policy issue of the 1970s and 1980s, being how to respond to problems allied to economic restructuring and the evacuation of industry and population from inner urban areas, a larger regional perspective may be needed for effective urban policy.

Second, there is the question of the powers and resources of regional planning machinery. A major problem in the past has been the establishment of policy-proposing machinery without powers to ensure implementation of its plans. Regional local authorities or development agencies could perform some functions in their own right and, for the rest, they could secure implementation of planning priorities through financial powers.

Third, the other important question in which regional planning machinery needs to be equipped with powers and resources is in terms of political weight. It takes an exceptional person in the chair to give coordinating committees the political clout of ministers and elected bodies. Standing conferences have rarely succeeded in transcending the interests of their constituent bodies or in becoming more than the sum of their parts. Yet, with long experience of their serious limitations, the Government and the Local Government Commission for England advising it on reorganisation for the 1990s chose to rely on voluntary standing conferences for regional planning. And this within what would be the most fragmented pattern of local government in contemporary Europe or since its rationalisation in Britain in the nineteenth century.

Those believing in administrative rationality tend to favour comprehensive regional governance. Others interpret that rationality quite differently. As Bennett (1989, 311) points out, those who have pursued territorial rationality in administration have often seemed to show the influence of simplified theory like that of Christaller's central place studies. Bennett suggests that the rationale of strict efficiency in designing administration is insensitive, because it neglects: the need for adaptation after rapid change; the conflict between natural areas for administrative functions and those of existing political units, as well as with areas of community identity; the different areas natural to different administrative functions; the inertia of bureaucracies which may supersede geographical rearrangement.

What Might be Lost by Single-Tier Reorganisation?

For most of Britain's people, their new local authorities for the late 1990s are to be nearer to the former district than to county or regional council scale. This will fragment the scales for which structure plans were adopted in the early 1970s. But county and Scottish regional structure plans have in practice seemed in respects often too close to the scale or the detail proper to local plans, while being too far from sensitive strategic analysis of regional change, e.g. telecommunications, integrated transport policy, warehousing, airports, reservoirs, power generation and distribution, urban regeneration programmes or future housing markets. And regional guidance from the Department of the Environment has been widely criticised as superficial and inadequate, while the Scottish National Planning Guidelines fell short of their potential by neglecting the issue of financial resources, in particular.

But the pattern of English and Welsh county and of Scottish regional councils has had serious intrinsic weaknesses. The counties of England in particular may have fitted the purposes of the eighteenth century from which they derived. They may still be relevant in the late twentieth century to the County Championship in cricket, but their relevance to housing markets, strategic transport problems, countryside management and other features of strategic planning has been greatly eroded. In many parts of England – Cheshire and Hertfordshire, as notable examples – the counties have been very arbitrary areas for structure planning. The same came to apply to parts of Scotland, and even to the case of Strathclyde.

Strathclyde has been an exceptional experiment in regional planning. It has succeeded beyond any other experiment in strategic local government in the UK. Even so, it has been overtaken by events. Its experience does not at all deny the argument for regional planning and regional governance but, significantly, confirms their economic and political dynamics. For the function of strategic physical planning for which it was established, and for much of the economic planning which it assumed, the Regional Council's more natural region grew from the late 1970s to link with that of Edinburgh. Its future and that of the Edinburgh region were complementary in significant ways, and their strength together promised more in competition with other European metropolitan regions than if they remained divided.

But no unified local government for the two city regions would be acceptable, for the combined population would comprise the majority of Scotland's population. So combined strtaegic planning for a central Scotland region would have to be initiated by central government. This would be as for the often more populous regions of England. It could be argued to be merely a rationalisation in contemporary circumstances of the strategic initiatives which government took in Scotland between 1944 and 1974. It would fill a partial vacuum rather than limit local government's role in strategic planning, although that has been much reduced by changes of circumstance since 1975. Regional councils have depended upon Scottish Office acceptance of their structure plans. They depended upon the Secretary of State to carry their objections to district councils' local plans, or to development applications where they disagreed with their partners in local government. And since the 1970s the Scottish Office has published national planning guidelines to which structure plans must conform. For even longer, the new town development corporations have displaced local councils in direct control over local planning matters, and the strategic roles of Scottish Enterprise and Scottish Homes are both permitted and encouraged by the government.

Restoring an all-Scottish scale of regional strategic planning would be exactly consistent with the development of strategic planning – or of elected assemblies – for the English regions. It would be a natural evolution of the dynamic Scottish regional tradition. Nor is it a solution which has come to seem feasible only in the circumstances of the 1990s. In 1973, John P. Mackintosh, the Scottish constitutionalist professor and member of Parliament, attacked the flaws he found in the proposals of the Bill even as the new Scottish local government system was being debated in the House (Drucker 1982, 39). Within six months of the inception of the new councils, Mackintosh was arguing that strategic planning should be a responsibility of an all-Scottish Assembly.

After decades of regional and political change since the British system of structure and local plans was originally designed for unitary local government, planning functions had become ripe for re-assignment in the 1990s. Some county functions were clearly better or as well exercised at a smaller scale, and some were clearly better undertaken at a larger, regional scale. Some county-style planning had clearly been of a kind which could be better absorbed into local or unitary plans by smaller authorities, and some was overdue to be absorbed into a more explicit and vigorous form of strategic regional planning – at or about the geographical level at which the DoE gives regional guidance, but to a standard above it.

But the new system in train under the local government proposals announced for Wales in 1992, for Scotland in 1993, and emerging sporadically for England from 1993, had little regard for planning of any kind. The unitary system being introduced was shaped primarily in the local interests of the Conservative Party, and most blatantly so in Scotland. No real significance was given to the serious issue of strategic issues and services. The result was a system of local government threatening the quality and efficiency of public and private services, causing some national economic damage. With the recent case of Greater London behind it, it was astonishing that the Government should have ignored the damage which would subsequently have to be repaired after such an incomplete reorganisation of local government.

What Regions?

There are five principal dimensions to current regional issues which should structure the geography of a new system, and guide the distribution of responsibilities within it:

1. *Strategic physical planning*, the classic British metropolitan concern over the shaping of growth and change in conurbation and city regions. Although overspill, new towns and large-scale redevelopment of people and activities are diminished in most urban areas in Britain, there are echoes still in South East England of cries which have faded elsewhere; in all areas, however, urban regeneration continues to have implications for strategic planning policy.

2. *Infrastructure planning and investment.* Transportation and the renewal of obsolescent public services raise strategic issues of planning and investment for major urban areas, and for connections with their markets across Europe. Regions of growth and change have emerged (e.g. the M4 corridor and the landfall of the Channel Tunnel) raising issues not neatly fitting traditional structures of UK regional planning.

3. *Equitable and efficient governance.* Equitable and efficient provision of public services (e.g. social work, education and public transport) may in elements be more readily provided for areas larger even than the conurbation areas to which the metropolitan counties approximated. Strathclyde's case suggests that service delivery may make at least as significant a case for regional governance as do more traditional planning grounds.

4. *Economic development.* The still rising wave of urban and rural development initiatives through agencies including development corporations, task forces and action teams, reflects both new economic problems and a new perception of some old problems. There are dimensions of these which have been intractable within any recent system of local government.

5. *Regional politics.* Nationalist movements in Scotland, Wales and Northern Ireland have induced a regional dimension to central government in these countries, dating back 100 years in Scotland's case. In the early 1980s, Merseyside and the West Midlands attracted special ministerial responsibility when their economic and social problems brought an emerging partisan regional identification, and London got its own Minister for transport affairs in the early 1990s.

The variety of these dimensions to regional planning suggests that there might be some diversity in a new system; the size of the different dimensions varies amongst the regions. Although a uniform system of regional local authorities throughout England and Wales might handle some of the dimensions completely, this would not be true of all dimensions in all regions. The Scottish economist, Donald Robertson, noted this during the resurgence of regional planning in which he was

heavily involved in Scotland in the mid 1960s. He observed that 'largish administrative regions are likely to be more important in future in some parts of the
country, though not everywhere' (Robertson 1965, 124). And he went on to
comment that 'The tendency to follow an omnibus treatment of regional issues is
in part due to a fatal wish for comprehensiveness which has produced some notably
artificial attempts to carve up the body of England into unnatural regions for
analysis' (Robertson 1965, 126). An aspect of this problem of requisite variety is
described by Hogwood and Lindley (1982, 46–47) in regard to government
functions:

> Set against possible potential benefits from greater standardisation of re-
> gional boundaries are the undoubted costs arising both from the process of
> standardisation and the continuation of standardisation... If the issue of
> devolution to English regional assemblies or even of regional assemblies to
> oversee the operation of the regional organisation of ad hoc bodies were ever
> to develop, then the question of standardisation of boundaries would
> inevitably emerge... In the North of England, the standard regions, perhaps
> with some modifications, are not obviously unsuitable as the basis for
> devolved regional assemblies. In the South East, however, there are no
> obvious regional boundaries based on administrative practice, nor is it even
> clear how many regions would be drawn.

Financing Regional and Local Government

Geographical coverage and administrative power do not alone guarantee effective
regional planning and action. There must be real scope to distribute or to influence
the distribution of revenues in accord with the planning strategy. Strathclyde's
experience suggests that redistribution may have been at least as significant in
achieving regional strategic objectives as has been its physical planning role.

There are other models for regional tax management than by such a dominant
revenue raising and controlling council as that for Strathclyde. The Twin Cities
revenue-sharing programme for metropolitan Minneapolis-St. Paul has been
notable in the US. Revenues of the state sales tax are returned to cities and schools
on the basis of population and of an increasingly complex equalising basis. Growth
in the commercial and industrial tax base is similarly redistributed by a formula
which is inversely proportional to valuation per capita, which has progressively
reduced the income disparities per capita amongst municipalities from 11:1 to
under 6:1.

Restructuring of the delivery of local services and technical and policy changes
introduced by the government after 1979 have some implications still to be
resolved, including the appropriate scale of administration with regard to the
financing and management of local services. For example, progressive extension
of local school management and transfer of schools from local to central government funding would, if sustained in the 1990s, much reduce the role and rationale

for the pattern of British local government. Privatisation is akin to the restructuring of local services. Under trends of these kinds, the consequences would be that not only shire county councils as constituted in the early 1990s but also metropolitan district councils would become less viable.

What Alternatives For a New Focus for Regional Planning?
PRECEDENTS AND ALTERNATIVES

There are many significant alternative forms into which strategic planning might be placed. Some forms have already been attempted; others remain proposals from different interests. A new focus might be located within:

1. Regional local government (the RTPI model of 1986)
2. Regional assemblies
3. The Labour Party model for metropolitan London; more direct than LPAC but less wide than SERPLAN
4. A directly elected single-purpose planning authority on the German metropolitan model (e.g. Hannover)
5. Standing conferences on the English model of the 1990s
6. An ad hoc team, appointed in a specific strategic crisis, as in the 1960s and 1970s
7. A Secretary of State for each region, as for Scotland, Northern Ireland and Wales
8. A Minister of State for each region, as briefly in the 1980s for the West Midlands and for Merseyside, and later for London
9. Regional development agencies on the model of Scottish Enterprise or the Welsh Development Agency
10. Regional enterprise companies on the model of the Scottish network of local enterprise companies
11. Regional planning commissions, either independent with power to take decisions or advising the government like the REPC's of 1964–79
12. As in the varieties of other countries, including:
    - Spanish autonomous regions
    - Italian regional councils
    - French *conseils régionaux*
    - US Councils of Government
    - the distinctive Twin Cities Metropolitan Council of Minneapolis-St Paul.

There is a great choice of models on which to draw, and there are many variants within those summarised above. But different models fit within different traditions of governance. Not all are interchangeable; certainly not between countries with different political contexts, and this may be so in respects even between parts of the UK.

Any creative model must incorporate the three main components of effective strategic planning: intelligence, data and analysis; strategy crystallisation; and implementation. How do alternative models stand in the light of circumstances in the UK?

If it is supposed that central government will always participate in regional planning, and will also always cooperate to some degree with locally elected government, the components of possible alternative systems for regional planning can be grouped under three headings: councils of government; regionally elected governance; and regional administration of government. There are different ways of arranging contributions from each heading, and that of regionally elected governance is the most contentious of the three and may not be present at all. But recognising the political context of regional planning, such headings are essential frames for discussion.

COUNCILS OF GOVERNMENT

The standing conferences of planning authorities covering all England and Wales by 1993 were councils of government. COGs can be indirectly elected or nominated by the local authorities in membership. They have included central government representatives and representatives of regional interest groups, helping bring together those most concerned with planning issues in a region in a forum debating and agreeing on appropriate strategies.

Indirectly elected planning councils representing local authorities first rose in the Manchester and District Joint Town Planning Advisory Committee of 1921, running erratically up to the North West Regional Association of 1992. Central government has frequently instigated and commonly manipulated the councils; their performance has been as variable as their history, as the record of South East England and the West Midlands shows.

More advanced models were raised by the Royal Commission (1973) on the Constitution under Lord Kilbrandon. A majority of the Committee recommended eight non-executive regional councils for England comprising local government councillors, replacing the then regional economic planning councils in advising governments. A minority report favoured directly elected regional assemblies, able to raise and spend revenues as would have the Scottish and Welsh assemblies recommended by the majority. The majority proposition had similarities with the form of non-executive provincial council proposed several years before by Derek Senior, in his dissenting memorandum to the report of the Royal Commission on Local Government in England (1969).

Non-executive regional councils from the Kilbrandon mould might seem to be an advantageous interface between central and local government, and between local authorities and regional interests. Those implementing strategy would be involved in making it. And a system of this kind could maintain pressure to coordinate or unify the presentation of government programmes for regions. It would provide a higher platform from which local authorities could advocate policies or priorities calling for government support. It would involve no real adjustment to established levels of decision-taking and action. As the government said in its Green Paper following the Kilbrandon report:

> The scheme is based on the view that it would not be right for the English regions to be given any legislative or executive powers now exercised by central government, and it would be illogical (following the reorganisation of local authorities) for them to take over powers from local government. Yet at the regional level it is believed that there is scope for more effective cooperation between local authorities and a need for more open discussion and democratic influence on those matters affecting the region which are decided by central government or by ad hoc bodies. To meet this need, and to give advice to the Central Government on regional problems, there would be regional councils primarily composed of local government councillors.

But COGs can only develop a genuinely regional perspective if members leave their loyalty to their authority at the door of the conference room. And voluntary coordination tends to ignore resource constraints because few will cede parochial interests; in Britain, the proof lies outstandingly in experience of transportation planning for the conurbations pre-1974.

So while offering the possible advantage of thus locking the regions into central government planning, advisory regional councils would little advance the cause of an accountable or representative regional tier of administration and action. But the dilemma for governments with accountable, executive regional councils is that electors will expect them to strive for a better deal and more resources from government.

This argument also supposes that resource transfers to poorer regions would be generally traceable, as is the case with certain elements of public expenditure in Scotland, Wales and Northern Ireland, but not customarily for the regions of England. Furthermore, several important components of inter-regional resource transfer are not customarily publicised, as with tax relief on mortgages and on cars purchased through private companies, together with other tax concessions for the private sector. Nonetheless, much mischief can be made over the inter-regional allocation of resources, and unless non-executive bodies are nominated by the government they will be tempted to cause it trouble. The annoyance which non-executive regional councils can cause governments is evidenced by the example of the *conseils régionaux* in France. In the 1970s, prior to being put on an elected basis with a budget to dispense, some like the *Conseil* for the Nord-Pas de Calais had vocal power but little responsibility, and shouted for resources to government's irritation.

Fourteen years of experience of regional economic planning councils from 1965 to 1979 leave only rare evidence of any substantial impact on strategic decisions about regional development. And experience in the UK and in France with indirectly elected regional councils and urban communities is that they favour proportional disbursement of funds and opportunities among the participating authorities, rather than an objective appraisal of strategic planning needs.

COGs swept the United States during the 1960s, reaching their zenith in the 1970s and subsiding in the 1980s. They were damningly characterised by Mogulof (1971) as 'clearing-houses', although a few rose to be more than mere tokens of cooperative regional planning and governance. Their rise and most convincing role was during the years in which federal support for local transportation, housing and other programmes depended upon local governments demonstrating that they were individually acting within a coherent regional framework.

Various currents underlay the spread of COGs in the US, and these run less deep in the UK. In some US metropolitan areas, some regional councils were thought to have been driven by those trying to counter the onset of black mayors in the cities, whereby regional coalitions of local governments could re-establish white control over some civic affairs. But the pace at which the councils grew, and their deflation after the arrival of Reagan's policies of new conservatism, shows that generally it was the carrot of federal aid which stimulated them and its withdrawal which saw them fade. As Mogulof (1971, 13) emphasised, 'It is federal money, federal staff assistance and federal policy that is largely responsible for the health/and or weakness of the COG.'

At their zenith, the scope of COGs in the US was fuller than that of the standing conferences of English planning authorities. So, they represent a relatively low-key model which can co-exist with a fine-grain pattern of local government. They offer a modest alternative to a central government reluctant or unwilling to create regional authorities, or to one sympathetic to regional coordination but also wishing to consolidate its policy influence.

One of the strains upon COGs is that if they work with an active central government, they are likely to be pulled in two ways. Their staff and leading representatives work closely with central government, and they cannot too vigorously bite the hand that feeds them. Nor can they too critically attack their more independent local governments, lest their collective strength crumbles. This strain was implicit in the regional road construction units established in England in the late 1960s, sponsored by the government but largely staffed from local authorities. However, although this strain may demand resilience and diplomacy of the highest order, it at least reflects some potential for an active mediating role.

Even a central government bent on using a COG to more readily spread national policies across a region may, of course, have to agree a trade-off to achieve most of what it wishes. The council may cooperate only at a price to the Government. Furthermore, because government inevitably comprises separate departments which will never be fully integrated, it may be as incapable of achieving a fully rationalised regional framework for action as the COG will be to perfectly implement it.

An advantage of COGs to established local governments is to at least defer their loss of power and status. To have more mayors, chairs and leaders of council can share around more positions of local distinction. And more independence for cities limits the extent to which they must submit to wider, regional tendencies. US cities with black majorities have been reluctant to lose control to regional organisations in which they would be minorities again; few US councils of government have been concerned with regional issues of employment, housing, schools, or health (Mogulof 1971, 45). Under the US councils, the amount of imaginative regional planning was slight. The councils were less a means of creating and managing regional plans than of passing information between local and central government; they could advise local governments about intended federal action, they could help federal agencies with information, and they could give technical support to smaller local governments. This is why they have been given the alternative description of 'clearing-houses'.

Whatever the real value of the 'clearing-house' role which analysts like Mogulof acknowledge, they argue that it must be matched by positive regional planning. Being clearing-houses and creating a sense of regional community is not enough. To ensure their widespread continuation, the councils have also to be able to prepare plans against which to evaluate proposals by both local and central governments. Without effective federal power to insist upon the production of real regional plans, Mogulof expected US COGs to remain curbed by the primary allegiance of members to their own local government areas. He saw no evidence that local governments would subsume local policy within contrary regional strategy. He considered that 'In the largest part, the new ground for decision making engendered by the COG produces the same results one can anticipate without a COG' (1971, 72). Substantially different results could be expected only if a council evolved into a new form.

From examining a variety of European metropolitan COGs, Norton (1983, 54) reached the view that shared decision-taking was a key to effective implementation in a turbulent world. When – in Norton's view – comprehensive rational planning had become discredited, consensus-building amongst authorities and sectors was the new route to strategic coherence. He thought Greater Copenhagen to have showed the process at its most lively best, associated with commendable transport and recreation systems; the Frankfurt Regional Union was a more disputatious but similarly exhaustive opportunity for public debate on strategy.

What then are the prospects for councils of government? Most senior politicians will think the councils unattractive if they offer no direct authority, failing to face up to problems demanding selflessness from their members. Yet councils may be an attractive berth for some politicians, offering them a regional forum lacking scope to take contentious decisions, but offering a higher profile without risk of controversy. Local governments know that decisions by COGs must be consensual, and that none will lose by participating. Success may be minimal, but it will be largely painless. If little may be gained by cooperating, more may be lost by not doing so. Yet, COGs are a far cry from dynamic models of regional planning and governance.

REGIONALLY ELECTED GOVERNANCE

The advantage of directly elected executive regional governments with revenues to spend is that they have political authority to devise regional priorities. And they have the means to implement them. They could also take over some tasks hitherto performed by regional offices of central departments, notably some of those of the DOE and DTI. They could draw various strands of policy together at the scale of economic regions. Objections would come from the parts of local government which would see elected regional governance as a threat to their independence. However, the abolition of the GLC, of some counties of England and of a tier of Scottish local government, presents the opportunity to regard regional government as the restoration of local government, rather than a new complication of relationships. Central government departments would be likely to oppose the idea, as it would represent a loss of power for some. However, that would be desirable to a degree, and particularly for the Department of the Environment where the dissolution of the metropolitan counties brought disabling problems in assembling guidance for strategic planning after years of running-down of staffing in the regional offices.

Regional governance could, of course, represent devolution of government responsibility and legislative capacity on the model of the Scottish and Welsh Assemblies, which were the basis of the Government's Scottish and Welsh referenda in 1979. On the other hand, it could be on the model of the Strathclyde Regional Council, and thereby represent a geographical and functional extension of the English metropolitan counties. And the administration could be of differing degrees of bulk. Strathclyde Regional Council has had a staff of around 100,000, primarily employed as schoolteachers. But Strathclyde's planning staff has reached little over 100, fewer than the the 115 of the Greater Copenhagen and 187 of the Frankfurt regional authorities (Hall 1989, 176). In the Ruhr region with twice the population of Strathclyde, the SVR has had only a handful of staff.

Within England, devolution on any Scottish model lacks the historical justification or political imperatives which created a regional parliament for Northern Ireland for 50 years of the present century, and took Scotland close to the brink of an Assembly in 1979. Whatever any assumption by regional assemblies of some of the responsibilities of government, however, they would remain under central control in important respects. In these circumstances, some would be tempted to displace local authority powers and discretion. But regional authorities can be of varying bulk, depending upon their responsibilities. Effectiveness of strategic planning depends not on the bulk of the planning organisation, but on its leverage on affairs. Direct responsibility for building highways, sewers, schools and other infrastructure is not essential. More effective may be an authority's capacity to partially fund regionally significant developments. Leverage through support funding is a highly flexible and effective means by which a regional authority can steer strategy. Otherwise, the authority may face an exaggerated condition such as that in which the metropolitan counties were placed after 1974, when in the case of West Yorkshire the district councils only belatedly accepted that district responsibilities like housing, the environment and recreation, also had metropolitan dimensions.

A 'slimline' authority without direct executive responsibility can better protect strategy from the sometimes distorting influence of powerful infrastructure-building departments. What is necessary is that the political status of the authority remains high, so that it continues to influence a budget large enough to buy accord with its strategy.

There must be doubts about the capacity of the Strathclyde model to continue to plan strategically in the new environment of strategic government agencies, and where a department of planning is just one amongst larger and more powerful service departments in a council with thousands of employees. The Strathclyde model is certainly incompatible with single-tier local government and, specifically, with a Scottish Assembly.

REGIONAL ADMINISTRATION OF GOVERNMENT

Regional dimensions to government administration are clear and very long established. The Scottish Office is the oldest and fullest example. There has been shadowy history of regional coordination amongst government departments in England, either by internal committees or in the form of the regional economic planning boards of the period 1965–79, or later innovations like the regional coordination of urban regeneration from 1993.

It might be suggested that the experience of the Scottish, Welsh and Northern Ireland Offices could be reproduced in England, with regional ministers to 'coordinate' the work of departments in the regions. Ministerial responsibility for Merseyside and the West Midlands was an innovation of the early 1980s, inspired by riots and acute economic difficulties, succeeded by a junior minister for London in the early 1990s. But the secretaries of state for Scotland, Wales and Northern Ireland do not coordinate the responsibilities of other ministers, they are fully responsible for a range of functions for which they alone answer in Cabinet and Parliament. Reproducing the Scottish experience in England would mean dismantling most government departments excluding the Treasury and Defence, replacing them with regional departments responsible through a minister direct to Cabinet. This would reduce problems of regional coordination but enlarge the problems of national coordination.

Regional ministers or officials on the Merseyside, West Midlands and London coordinating model would, of course, be a more modest alternative. However, power continues to lie with the main departments spending the money, dealing with their clients and answering to Parliament. The coordinating ministers have lacked the power and resources to make their weight felt, as even senior Secretaries of State for the Environment found on Merseyside and throughout the history of inner city initiatives. The same problem arises with regional coordinating officials or 'prefects', but to an increased degree as officials cannot ultimately prevail against functional Cabinet ministers. In any case, French experience shows that it is impossible for Prefects to impose horizontal control on the field services of major departments which, defying all decrees and circulars, continue to deal directly with Paris.

Consistent with either model would be the creation of regional development agencies for England, responsible to government as have been the Scottish and Welsh Development Agencies, the regional water authorities or the Highlands and Islands Development Board. Agencies like the Rural Development Commission, English Partnerships and the Countryside Commission have more dispersed responsibilities, but otherwise are in a similar relationship to local and central government. Some of these agencies adopted powers hitherto held by ministers or by the civil service, some assumed responsibilities newly enacted by Parliament and others displaced local authorities in their duties. The Scottish Development Agency was seen in some English regions as a model to be borrowed, on the supposition that it would bring them extra financial resources. Agencies have had terms of reference which were generally more generously and flexibly applied than those of regionally based government departments. Although by offering financial aid they have been able to coordinate both local authorities and the private sector through buying support for their own regional objectives, agencies of this kind have also the political strength to place themselves above established regional planning.

Although relatively free of long-standing commitments and more able than local government to rapidly direct financing to new and unexpected projects within regions, the agency model cannot offer extra resources to every region; in important respects, agencies may tend to lead strategy, and to displace local authorities in some of their roles. Yet, agencies have represented a significant and potentially progressive step in regional strategic planning and development. They have seemed to be innovative to a degree which standing conferences have rarely been. But they are unaccountable, and being so they require at least a balancing and parallel local authority influence, which may be reinforced by an effective standing conference.

The model of a planning commission is quite untried in regional planning in the UK, although there have been partial precedents as in the Roskill Commission's (1971) pursuit of a location for the Third London Airport, which finally settled at Stansted against the Commission's conclusions. In the US, the Twin Cities Metropolitan Council for Minneapolis-St. Paul is an outstanding model, although planning commissions are a very long established feature of the US system of local governments.

The conditions in which non-executive and not-directly-elected planning commissions could be effective are where a government is reluctant to accept elected regional authorities, or even where elected authorities have been established but require special arrangements for significant sub-regions. Following the abolition of most Scottish regional councils after 1996, there will be a strong case for a nominated planning commission to advise upon strategic planning in central Scotland. The case would be equally strong whether Scotland were to have an elected Assembly or continue to be administered by the Scottish Office. Similarly, Peter Hall (1989, 178) has outlined the scope in South East England for an advisory Metropolitan Planning and Transportation Commission – alternatively called a Regional Development Authority; this authority would plan strategically and then pass implementation to the hands of local New Community Development Corporations.

Resolving the Choice: by Whom and How Might Better Strategic Planning be Achieved?

Narrowing the choice, two possible forms of arranging regional planning can be quickly discarded. First, ministers for each of the English regions would be cumbersome and ineffective; ministers for Merseyside, the West Midlands and London have seemed to be short-term political gestures which have gained little measurable advantage for their regions, and their scope of operation has been very limited. Second, federalist regional government for the English regions is unsought by any significant movement. Regional ministers with significant executive capacity would be a possible adjunct of regional government, as in the proposals for Scottish devolution several years ago, but this would imply reconstruction of UK government inconceivable except on a scale consistent with federalism.

But there is a continuing and essential role which government will wish to and should play in regional planning and strategic development. The relative needs of regions change with time; social and economic problems and urgent justifications for special financing do not follow a wholly predictable pattern, arising unevenly between regions in space and time. In seeking to much improve the regions' capacities to help themselves and to contribute to national development, it is not possible to fix a formula for a block grant by which each region would be covered for not only its permanent baseload of administrative responsibilities, but also for all irregular, short-run but intense economic and social problems or disasters. Many of the latter kinds of problem will be a national priority, calling for additional national resources.

The real choice for a new system therefore narrows to models in which local government capacity at regional scale would be much increased, but where central–local relations in England would continue to involve regional offices of government and departmental rather than regional ministers. But this leaves much scope for the Government to innovate to improve its responsiveness to the reinforced regional strategic focus of local government.

The choice for local government is simply between a two-tier system of local authorities, in which the upper tier would cover regions larger than the abandoned

English metropolitan county councils or the threatened shire counties, and a single-tier system of unitary authorities collectively supporting standing regional conferences. Either system would incorporate a major reorganisation of local government. The choices are not wholly new. They straddle the field debated by Redcliffe–Maud (Royal Commission 1969). Many rejected the Government's subsequent modification of the Redcliffe–Maud proposals, objecting not only to the inherent failings of the proposed metropolitan counties, but also to the division of planning between two tiers of local government. But with new experience of much economic, social and physical change in the long period since Redcliffe–Maud, the difficulties of two-tier planning in reorganised local government seem to have been due less to the principle of two tiers than to the faults of boundaries and of the balance of functions other than planning. Accordingly, a two-tier planning system below national level is perfectly feasible.

The issues to be finally resolved surround the power and way of working of the strategic regional level of planning; that is, how close should it be to an executive authority? Should it be in the form of a conference representative of participants but directly deploying minimal resources – of either finance or persuasion – or should it have substantial executive authority, and either precept funds from participants or be elected and have substantial revenue-raising and disposal powers? The criteria by which to prefer a new system must, above all, be the three principles for effective and democratic regional planning and governance previously cited:

1. The evolving and spreading complexity of the social and economic structures of most metropolitan urban regions and of many rural regions.

2. Direct electoral accountability to extend the responsibility of locally elected representatives over a wider range of public services.

3. The merits of distributing resources to reflect a considered balance between local aspirations, efficiency and equity within the regions.

Applying these criteria, the line of argument raises the question of whether they could be satisfied by a regional conference, joint committee, joint board or collective of nominated or indirectly elected representatives of single-tier local authorities. If they could not, it would point to the superimposition of a directly elected regional authority.

The preceding arguments might seem to point to a new focus for regional planning wholly in local government, rather than an arrangement to strengthen the government's role *vis-à-vis* local authorities. But long experience of the inability of local authorities to act both effectively and at the speed of regional issues, suggests that government may be the better level from which to force the pace and foresightedness of regional planning.

Government has at least on occasions in the past been able to drive the effort of regional planning at a rate to match the scale of current issues. This has been rarely the case with conferences and joint committees; however, they have improved upon an otherwise fragmented system of regional planning by local authorities. So without ignoring their value in past conditions, their limitations have been clear in resolving contentious inter-authority differences or in re-allocating expenditure to changing regional priorities.

As envisaged by government, the merit of ad hoc and voluntary inter-authority cooperation in place of the metropolitan county councils has seemed to be to help reduce local government expenditure and staffing. But standing conferences and joint committees have only rarely cast more than a pale shadow. Neither the Government nor even some of the principal and most respected defenders of local government have sufficiently recognised that the regional dimension is not one for mere coordination of administration; it is for planning, priorities and the flexible execution of strategic policy.

So, standing conferences cannot alone meet the criteria for effective and democratic regional planning. Nor can even strengthened regional offices of government. Nor has either been consistently able to match the inspiration more characteristic of an independent person or small team, which has been the most consistently successful means of reconciling regional issues into a far-sighted strategy. Government's civil servants suffer the pressures of inter-departmental politics, and find it almost as difficult to exercise strategic daring as have local government planners. We can reflect how the ad hoc strategic planning teams and irregular reviews of strategy of the past were quite often outstandingly successful, speedy and imaginative, benefiting by a degree of detachment from day-by-day local government affairs.

Accordingly, the production of perceptive regional and strategic plans does not depend upon an elected level of regional local government. Nor does effective implementation necessarily call for direct control by the planning agency over the arms of implementation. Compliance with plans can be ensured by other means, for which there is sufficient evidence from such as the *Clyde Valley* and *West Central Scotland* plans in Scotland, and the *Greater London Plan* in England, the Minneapolis-St. Paul Metropolitan Planning Commission in the US, or some of the *conseils régionaux* in France.

The report to the Royal Town Planning Institute (1986) envisaged a much reinforced Strathclyde model throughout the UK, with additional powers devolved from government. But events have overtaken the circumstances of 1986, and a Strathclyde planning region – specifically – may now be obsolete, made so by the changing economic and social geography of central Scotland and by the new world of government agencies with strategic roles. So before deciding for the kind of regional governance effectively practised in Strathclyde, it should be recognised that that Council's greatest success has probably lain in fields of administration other than strategic physical planning.

Certainly more successful in regional planning than its predecessor councils were for most of their history, Strathclyde's record in social work, education, and in redistributing priorities and resources in its major service responsibilities has been probably more outstanding. The Council's performance can be more clearly measured and its role has been more distinct in those respects. But in regional planning, the Council has shared the field with other partners. And necessary as the role of the *Strathclyde Structure Plan* has been, it is not clear that it has comprehensively led rather than reflected the sum of others' policies and actions. So, whatever case there might be to continue the Strathclyde model for regional administration and initiatives in education, water and sewerage supply, social care, transport or policing, circumstances in regional planning have greatly altered since the model was designed in the 1960s. Regional planning has to seek a less cumbersome and even better model elsewhere.

The elements of an improved regional planning system thus narrow down to one in which:

- *Government necessarily and properly dominates in principal elements of regional strategy;* it would determine regional allocation of national resources, and would retain the right to modify regional structure plans where national interests arise.

- *There is greater effectiveness in the local authority contribution to regional planning;* by a reinforced capacity to inform and advocate regional strategies and policies.

- *Earmarked shares of national resources would be allocated to be assigned to regional planning priorities,* to be determined within the regions.

- *Plans and programmes for regional priorities would be published,* through which the variety of public and private investors in regional investment could anticipate future demand and change for their services.

A New Model For Regional Planning in the UK

Assembling the new model, it would incorporate the three essential components of effective strategic and regional planning:

- *intelligence, data and analysis,* which is a job for a full-time team and which planning conference staff do excellently.

- *strategy crystallisation,* which is a periodic task but of irregular frequency, requiring imagination, detachment and occasional bravery. Planning consultants were called in to do the job prior to 1947, and *ad hoc* teams in the 1960s and 1970s. But planning conferences find the task hard.

- *implementation,* which is a painstaking, week-in and week-out job for local authorities, government, public agencies, private water and power monopolies, and the private sector at large.

These components need not be all under one roof. Although strategy and implementation are inseparable in concept, they need not be so in authorship. The pressures of implementation can drive out strategic thinking, as the history of corporate planning in local government shows clearly. But how can it be ensured that the strategy has adequate leverage on the implementers?

If it is reasonably supposed that any form of elected regional government for the UK could not exist until the late 1990s, then any earlier new model for regional planning would have to fit with a system of unitary, single-tier local government for most of the UK, and certainly for its major urban areas. A model doing this but also adaptable to any future organisation of governance in the UK would be a dual system, in which two complementary bodies participated in each region. There would be a *standing conference* of the local authorities, and a *planning commission* responsible to the Government. And the planning commission would lever support for strategy through a budget to fund strategic initiatives.

Each *standing conference* of local authorities would:

- have such committees and a secretariat as appropriate to conference interests, which could vary between regions
- maintain and interpret data and intelligence, and challenge strategic regional guidelines as it might choose
- implement strategy through development plans, and by member authorities' direct functions
- nominate UK representatives to the EC Committee of Regions.

Each *regional planning commission* would:

- be appointed by the Government and consist of perhaps eight members
- have a small professional staff and secretariat
- advise government by periodic review of strategy as a basis for regional planning guidelines
- advise on the strategic implications of investment programmes of government departments – perhaps to a Secretary of State for Regional Development
- appoint temporary staff or consultants as required
- hold public hearings prior to submitting strategic reviews and major recommendations to the Secretary of State
- be annually funded to the order of perhaps £75m for a region of 1 million population, to be dispensed in grants or loans for projects supporting or leading regional strategy

It might be argued that such a system of complementary bodies would portend rivalry, duplication and conflict. In some regards it certainly could, but this might desirably reveal some regional issues otherwise suppressed. It might also be argued that this system would be undemocratic. But it would do nothing to lessen the effective role of local authorities or to increase the power of central government or of the Secretary of State for the Environment. And it would make British regional planning both more sophisticated and more effective.

Europe: The New Regional Planning and the European Future

Between 1977 and 1987, the population of the European Community grew by over 7 million (ARL/DATAR 1992, 146), although in most EC countries and regions there was no natural increase in population. But in future, the scales and directions of internal migration are likely to be the most significant feature in the dynamics of European regions. And the prospects of large internal migrations within a larger Community will greatly influence policies within it, the rate at which new members are admitted, and the significance of regional planning.

The new Europe will remain dominated by the large metropolitan areas, even as tertiary services displace secondary manufacturing as the major employer in national economies. Without new policies, peripheral regions and smaller traditional manufacturing towns are likely to be increasingly overshadowed by the major metropolises; disparities of infrastructure and wealth will tend to widen.

Scenarios of the future metropolitan and urban structure of Europe vary, even as do the several ways in which the current structure can be interprteted. The metropolitan axis from London to Milan, curving through Brussels, the Ruhr and Zurich, vividly christened the 'blue banana', is the most memorable symbol in the current European urban system. But there will also be new regional groupings and shifting alliances. Marine issues faced by the Baltic countries and by those around the Aegean and Black Seas will link current and prospective Community members. Berlin's growing significance for the European economy will distort the perceived shape of the 'blue banana'. Other regional forces will bear on regional economies and alliances. In this dynamic situation, the European Commission argues that it must actively lead in spatial planning, because best correcting regional disparities depends on efficient urban and regional networks to maximise economic growth.

Some of the proliferating networks amongst European cities and regions may have little more than social value, entertaining civic officials and exchanging schoolchildren. But they are argued to have economic as well as political and cultural importance (Berg and Schaafsma 1991, 25). Networks induce exchange of information, helping participants to be amongst the first to gain significant knowledge. This is as true for those in public administration as for those in industry and in commercial multi-nationals. And the intersections of networks are favoured locations in the competition between city and metropolitan economies; here is fertile ground for multi-national companies, for international organisations, for research institutions, for marketing and for regional distribution and services.

Networking has economic significance not only in mutual support and exchange between regions across Europe, but also within regions. In Britain, the regional economic planning councils of the period 1965–1979 were a pale reflection of the kinds of regional network between industrial, business, research, training labour and social interests which have been formalised and longer sustained in other European nations, where the economic significance of regional networking has been better understood.

Belatedly, the idea of networking seemed to be implicit in some UK initiatives of economic and social rehabilitation in the 1990s, beginning with the City Challenge scheme and extended to the idea of Regional Challenge. But 15 years of erosion of regional networks had occurred in the UK during the naive era of non-consensual political ideology in the 1980s. And the privatisation of so many public services further weakened the possibility of the UK emulating the success of regional networks elsewhere in Europe, which have seemed to play a real part in some exceptional economic growth (Bachtler, Downes and Yuill, 1993; Cooke and Morgan 1991). Networking probably endured rather better in Scotland than elsewhere in the UK, but not with quite the intensity of the regions of France, as in Baden-Württemberg, or as in Emilia Romagna where networking was stimulated by Ervet, the regional development agency. Apart from the British Government's very equivocal support, the UK also lacked the local networking force of the Chambers of Commerce in France or of the regional business associations of Italy.

And in France, for example, the advantages of scale in international competition were being recognised where regions were being encouraged to cooperate for added economic strength, as with the 'Grand Sud' consortium of as many as five *conseils régionaux*.

Some from eastern Europe (Kuklinski 1993) look to their countries being absorbed into a Europe of comprehensively structured regions, which would take a rapidly growing role in an institutionalised system of European planning. But the new regional planning would not be merely the allocation of resources from the centre, as in the past; it would arise from within the regions. It would be 'innovative, strategic and pluralistic planning' (Kuklinski 1993, 29). So, regional planning is a potential means of reinforcing the European Community, and more necessary than before to release wider prosperity.

After its 'Europe 2000' appraisal, the Commission expected to proceed to complementary regional programmes amongst member states. Regular review of the European Regional Development Scheme containing national and regional planning objectives would influence the Community's priorities for its own programmes. A European statement would be prepared identifying national policies and programmes affecting other Community members, and indicating Community development priorities. The new Committee of the Regions and Local Authorities would be employed to advise the European Parliament in all this, and the Parliament would assume a decision-making role equivalent to that of the Council of Ministers:

> A regional development policy for Europe... must put forward a comprehen-
> sible and credible approach to the future spatial distribution of activities on
> the Continent. It must also suggest concrete programmes of reorientation
> with respect to the available resources. (ARL/DATAR 1992, 193)

Institutionalising regional planning within a European framework will not be easy. No uniform pattern can be drawn to serve all the purposes of regional planning in Europe equally well. Yet, as Kuklinski (1993, 29) suggests, revised analysis is required to develop a comprehensive regional system across the new Greater Europe. Devising a systematic level and pattern of regions would be complicated by the several regional systems already used by the EC: its 66 regions at NUTS 1 level, 174 regions at NUTS 2 level and 829 regions at NUTS 3 level; or the Objectives regions defined for Structural Funding; or the number of regions appropriate to the Committee of Regions and Local Authorities, to which the UK, France, Germany and Italy each contribute 24 of a total membership of 189. Only Germany amongst EC nations has a system of elected sub-national government at the NUTS 1 level; Belgium, Spain, France and Italy have elected councils at NUTS 2 level. The highest level of elected UK council is at NUTS 3 level, where there are around 100 metropolitan district, county and regional councils. Nor have member states been waiting for the Community to develop their regional structures. Late in 1992, Belgium agreed that its historic schism would be further rationalised by creating directly elected parliaments in Flanders and Wallonia.

Priorities in regional plans in western Europe have shifted greatly since 1945. Post-war reconstruction and satellite communities to relieve metropolitan congestion were priorities up to the late 1950s, when came the advance of the economists with their policy hypotheses to exploit the potential of the peripheral regions. Growth centres soon studded regional plans in both Europe and the developing countries. Later, growth centres fell into disrepute. Political critics accused them of being Trojan horses for the advance of international capitalism, and of being as much tools of colonialism as any employed in the historic subjection of tropical countries. Later, economists found them to be of variable and often disappointing performance, and sociologists found them to work against the best of liberal ideals.

Out of the turmoil of experience and progressive understanding of the developing impacts of the international economy, new priorities for regional planning are still being formed. After long practice in newly industrialising countries, John Friedmann (1979, 207) came to argue that although traditional regional planning might continue for many years, the cutting edge of professional thinking and practice now lay in helping assert regional interests against those of transnational economic forces. This assertion was the underlying purpose of the European Community for many political leaders, and regional planning was one of the proliferating weapons of intercontinental economic defence.

The US

The United States has not commonly been regarded by Europeans as a source of models for regional planning and governance, however frequently techniques for planning and urban policies have been borrowed since the 1960s.

But regional planning has repeatedly occurred in the US, perhaps disguised by the reluctance to reform local and regional government as has been done so signicantly in Europe on occasions. Consolidation of US city and county governments to reinforce the potential for effective strategy and resource allocation for combined functions has been limited, only sixteen cases being approved by referenda up to 1980 (Lim 1983, 10). An alternative approach has been to strengthen the county by lifting functions and tax-raising powers to it, as in Los Angeles County. Two-tier government has been notable only in the case of the Dade County government for Miami. Forms of regional governments have been created only for Portland, Oregon, and for Minneapolis-St. Paul.

Yet, despite the seemingly chaotic context for regional planning in such metropolitan regions as Chicago, decisions of a kind are reached by processes which might be described as those of an ideal pluralist democracy (Hemmens and McBride 1993, 144), or otherwise described as 'muddling-through'. But the long experience of regional issues and pressure for regional planning in the US has been shown previously. An imperative for regional planning has been inherent in US conditions, as the fragmented complexity of its local governments has suffered sustained pressures of development and of servicing from water supply and sewage disposal to traffic gridlock. Other recurrent motivations can be foreseen for regional planning and governance in the US. They have been repeatedly sought by: the economic interests of industry and commerce in metropolitan America; Presidents seeking to ameliorate national domestic political crises; environmental pressure groups; the US civil service when advancing federal intervention and support to the cities and metropolitan regions; professionals extending new techniques for strategic land use and transportation planning; the states, when there has been a retreat of federal intervention and of Presidential sympathy for the problems of the cities and metropolitan regions.

So although the source of the stimulus changes with national politics and preoccupations, the regional dimension persists in US public affairs. The scales and the titles change, but there is a continuing imperative for US regional planning and governance. Its more rationalised future shape might come from one of three moulds (Hemmens and McBride 1993, 147): a regional state commission like the Twin Cities Council or the proposed consolidated Bay Area Commission; reinforced sub-regional planning focused on county governments, which would commonly call for a regional council of sub-regional governments; or a strong regional agency with responsibilities deriving more from regional than from state government. The rise of growth management is likely to see more US experiments in regional planning and governance.

Finale

Ad hoc as it has often been, regional planning and governance in the UK, Europe and the US has not been superfluous or inadequate as some hypothesise that it must be. It has been not anomolous but a recurrent part of the mainstream of public affairs in most advanced countries. It has often been highly influential and appreciably successful, even in such countries as the UK where it has been irregularly conceived.

Although experience suggests that effective regional planning is entirely possible without a wholly complementary system of regional governance, this does not deny convincing arguments for a recognisably regional scale of governance. It may be justified on other grounds of public administration and enterprise, or of politics.

By defining regional planning as being most commonly a process arising from tensions and gaps within systems of governance, it will always be with us. So much of regional planning arises because of cross-boundary issues and tensions inevitable with any pattern of governance, regardless of whether or not it matches geographical regions.

There is a regional imperative.

References

Abercrombie, P. (1926) 'The preservation of rural England'. *Town Planning Review* Vol. XII No. 1, May.

Abercrombie, P. (1934) *North Riding: Outline Report for the County Council.*

Abercrombie, P. (1945) *Greater London Plan 1944.* London: HMSO.

Abercrombie, P. and Adshead, S.D. (1925) *South Teesside Regional Planning Scheme.*

Abercrombie, P., Adshead, S.D. and Earl of Mayo (1929) *Thames Valley Amenity Survey.* London: University of London Press.

Abercrombie, P., Adshead, S.D. and Earl of Mayo (1931) *Regional Planning Report on Oxfordshire.* London: Oxford University Press.

Abercrombie, P. and Archibald, J. (1925) *East Kent Regional Planning Scheme, Preliminary Survey.* London: University of Liverpool Press/Hodder and Stoughton.

Abercrombie, P. and Brueton, B.F. (1930) *Bath and Bristol Regional Planning Scheme.* London: University of Liverpool Press/Hodder and Stoughton.

Abercrombie, P. and Forshaw, J.H. (1943) *County of London Plan.* London: Macmillan.

Abercrombie, P., Fyfe, T. and Kelly, S. (1923) *Deeside Regional Planning Scheme.*

Abercrombie, P. and Jackson, H. (1948) *West Midlands Plan.* Unpublished draft report for Ministry of Town and Country Planning.

Abercrombie, P. and Johnson, T.H. (1922) *The Doncaster Regional Planning Scheme 1922.* London: University of Liverpool Press/Hodder and Stoughton.

Abercrombie, P. and Kelly, S.A. (1930) *Wye Valley Regional Planning Scheme.*

Abercrombie, P., Kelly, S.A. and Johnson, T.H. (1931) *Sheffield and District Regional Planning Scheme.* London: University of Liverpool Press/Hodder and Stoughton.

Abercrombie, P. and Kelly, S.A. (1932) *Cumbrian Regional Planning Scheme.* London: University of Liverpool Press/Hodder and Stoughton.

Abercrombie, P., Kelly, S.A., Trew, T. and Falconer, T. (1932) *Gloucestershire Regional Planning Scheme.*

Abercrombie, P. and Kelly, S.A. (1933) *North Wales Regional Planning Scheme.*

Abercrombie, P. and Kelly, S.A. (1935) *East Suffolk Regional Planning Scheme.* London: University Press of Liverpool Press/Hodder and Stoughton.

Abercrombie, P. and Kelly, S.A. (1935) *Lincolnshire Coast: Outline Planning Scheme.*

Abercrombie, P. and Matthew, R. (1949) *The Clyde Valley Regional Plan 1946.* Edinburgh: HMSO.

Ache, P. and Kunzmann, K. (1991) 'Towards a new national planning concept for Germany?' *Joint ACSP and AESOP International Congress*, Oxford, UK, July 1991.

Adams, T., Thomson, F. and Fry, M. (1930) *North East Kent Regional Planning Scheme*. North East Kent Joint Town Planning Committee.

Adams, T., Thomson, F. and Fry, M. (1931) *West Surrey Regional Planning Scheme*. West Surrey Joint Town Planning Committee.

Adams, T., Thomson, F. and Fry, M. (1931) *Mid Northamptonshire Regional Planning Scheme*. Mid-Northamptonshire Regional Planning Committee.

Adshead, S. (1927) *The Chesterfield Regional Planning Scheme*. Chesterfield: Wilfred Edmunds.

Adshead, S. (1931) *The South Essex Regional Planning Scheme*. London: J. Alexander.

Adshead, S. (1933) *The West Essex Regional Planning Scheme*. London: J. Alexander.

Advisory Commission on Intergovernmental Relations (1973) *Regional Decision Making: New Strategies for Substate Districts Vol. 1 Substate Regionalism and the Federal System*. A-43. Washington, D.C.: US Government Printing Office.

Advisory Commission on Intergovernmental Relations (1982) *State and Local Roles in the Federal System*. A-88. Washington, D.C.: US Government Printing Office.

Alden, J. and Morgan, R. (1974) *Regional Planning: A Comprehensive View*. Leighton Buzzard: Leonard Hill Books.

Allen and Potter (1932) *Leicestershire Regional Town Planning Joint Advisory Committee Regional Planning Report*.

Altes, W.K. (1992) 'How do planning doctrines function in a changing environment?' *Planning Theory* No.7/8, Summer/Winter.

Arcangeli, F. (1982) 'Regional planning in Italy'. In R. Hudson and J.R. Lewis *Regional Planning in Europe*. London: Pion.

Archibugi, F. (1986) *La politica dei sistemi urbani*. Roma: Centro Studie Piani.

Area 8 Study Team (1975) *Reading, Wokingham, Aldershot, Basingstoke Sub-regional Study*. Reading: Berkshire County Council.

ARL/DATAR (1992) *Perspectives of Regional Development Policy in Europe*. Hannover: Akademie für Raumforschung und Landesplanung.

Aron, J.B. (1969) *The Quest for Regional Cooperation: A Study of the New York Metropolitan Regional Council*. Berkeley: University of California Press.

Assembly of Welsh Counties (1992) *Strategic Planning Guidance in Wales – Overview Report*. Mold: Clwyd County Council.

Association of Bay Area Governments (1990) *A Proposed Land Use Policy Framework for the San Francisco Bay Area*. Oakland, CA: ABAG.

Bachtler, J., Downes, R. and Yuill, D. (1993) *The Devolution of Economic Development: Lessons from Germany*. Glasgow: Scottish Foundation for Economic Research, Glasgow Caledonian University.

Bahrenberg, G. (1989) 'West Germany: from decentralisation in theory to centralisation in practice'. In R. Bennett *Territory and Administration in Europe*. London: Pinter Publishers.

Barlow, I.M. (1991) *Metropolitan Government*. London: Routledge.

Barlow, I.M. (1993) 'Large city reforms'. In R.J. Bennett (ed) *Local Government in the New Europe*. London: Belhaven Press.

Bay Area Council (1988) *Making Sense of the Region's Growth*. San Francisco: Bay Area Council.

Bay Area Vision 2020 Commission (1991) *Bay Vision 2020: The Commission Report*. San Francisco: Bay Vision 2020 Commission.

Bendor, J.B. (1985) *Parallel Systems*. Berkeley: University of California Press.

Bennett, R.J. (1980) *The Geography of Public Finance*. London: Methuen.

Bennett, R.J. (1989) *Territory and Administration in Europe*. London: Pinter Publishers.

Bennett, R.J. (1993) (ed) 'Local government in Europe: common directions of change'. In R.J. Bennett (ed) *Local Government in the New Europe*. London: Belhaven Press.

Berg, M. and Schaafsma, M. (1991) 'Cities endangered, chances for urban regions'. *Dokumente und Informationen zur Schweizerischen Orts-, Regional- und Landsplanung*, DISP 105, April 1991, ETH Zürich.

Blaas, H. and Dostal, P. (1989) 'The Netherlands: changing administrative structures' In R.J. Bennett (ed) *Territory and Administration in Europe*. London: Pinter Publishers.

Bollens, S.A. (1992) 'State growth management: intergovernmental frameworks and policy objectives'. *Journal of the American Planning Association* Vol.58 No.4, Autumn.

Borras, S. (1993) 'The "Four Motors for Europe" and its promotion of R&D linkages: beyond geographical contiguity in interregional agreements'. *Regional Politics and Policy* Vol. 3 No. 3 Autumn 1993.

Boudeville, J.R. (1966) *Problems of Regional Economic Planning*. Edinburgh: Edinburgh University Press.

Bours, A. (1989) 'Management by territory and the study of administrative geography'. In R.J. Bennett (ed) *Territory and Administration in Europe*. London: Pinter Publishers.

Bours, A. (1993) 'Management, tiers, size and amalgamations of local government'. In R.J. Bennett (ed) *Local Government in the New Europe*. London: Belhaven Press.

Boyce, D.E., Day, N.D. and McDonald, C. (1970) *Metropolitan Plan Making*. Philadelphia: Regional Science Research Institute, University of Pennsylvania.

Boyer, M.C. (1986) *Dreaming the Rational City*. Cambridge, MA.: MIT Press.

Breheny, M.J. (1991) 'The renaissance of strategic planning?'. *Environment and Planning B: Planning and Design* Vol.18.

Brighton, Hove and District Joint Town Planning Advisory Committee (1932) *Report on the Regional Planning Scheme*. Mitcham, Surrey: Cook, Hammond and Kell.

Brindley, T., Rydin, Y. and Stoker, G. (1989) *Remaking Planning*. London: Unwin Hyman.

Brown, G. (1971) *In My Way: the Political Memoirs of Lord George-Brown*. London: Gollancz.

Bruce, R. (1929) *Regional Report for the NE Lancs. Joint Town Planning Advisory Committee*. Blackburn: J. Dickinson.

Bruce, R. (1945) *First Planning Report to the Highways and Planning Committee of the Corporation of Glasgow*. Glasgow: Corporation of the City of Glasgow.

Bruce, R. (1946) *Second Planning Report to the Highways and Planning Committee of the Corporation of Glasgow*. Glasgow: Corporation of the City of Glasgow.

Bryson, J., Freeman, R. and Roering, W. (1986) 'Strategic planning in the public sector: approaches and directions'. In B. Checkoway (ed) *Strategic Perspectives on Planning Practice*. Lexington, MA: Lexington Books.

Buchanan, J.M. (1966) *The Demand and Supply of Public Goods*. Chicago: Rand McNally.

Buchanan and Partners (1966) *South Hampshire Study*. London: HMSO.

Cannadine, D. (1990) *The Pleasures of the Past*. London: Fontana.

Central Unit for Environmental Planning (1969) *Humberside: A Feasibility Study*. London: HMSO.

Chelmsford Committee(1931) *Interim Report of the Departmental Committee on Regional Development*. Ministry of Health Cmnd. 3915. London: HMSO.

Cherry, G. (1974) *The Evolution of British Town Planning*. Leighton Buzzard: Leonard Hill.

Cherry, G. (1980a) 'Interwar regional planning schemes in Britain: an interim review'. *Planning History* Bulletin 2.

Cherry, G. (1980b) 'Prospects for regional planning – a review of metropolitan strategies for the West Midlands'. *Local Government Studies* May/June 1980.

Cherry, G. (ed) (1981) *Pioneers in British Planning*. London: The Architectural Press.

Cherry, G. (1993) Review of *Making the Right Choices, The West Midlands: Your Region, Your Future*. In *Town Planning Review* Vol.64 No.4 October.

Cheshire, P., D'Arcy, E. and Giussani, B. (1991) 'Local, regional and national government in Britain: a dreadful warning'. *Discussion Papers in Urban and Regional Economics* No.70, Department of Economics, University of Reading.

Claval, P. (1990) 'The new map of France'. In M. Hebbert and J.C. Hansen. *Unfamiliar Territory*. Aldershot: Avebury.

Cleveland, Durham and Northumberland County Councils (1992) *Regional Planning Guidance for the North East: Advice to the Secretary of State for The Environment*. Morpeth, Northumberland: Cleveland, Durham and Northumberland County Councils.

Commission des Communautés Européennes (1992) 'Les politiques régionaux dans l'opinion publique'. Luxembourg: Direction Générale des Politiques Régionaux, CEE Bruxelles.

Cooke, P. and Morgan, K. (1991) *The Intelligent Region, The Network Paradigm*. Regional Industrial Research Reports 7 and 8. University of Wales College at Cardiff, Cardiff.

Council of Europe (1991) *Assisting the Regions: A New Structural Policy*. Strasbourg: Council of Europe Press.

Council of Europe (1993) 'The challenges facing European society with the approach of the year 2000'. *European Regional Planning*, No.54. Council of Europe Press, Strasbourg.

County Planning Officers' Society (1989) *Metropolitan Strategic Guidance: The Experience of Neighbouring Counties*. London: County Planning Officers' Society.

County Planning Officers' Society (1990) *Regional Guidance and Regional Planning Conferences*. Aylesbury: Buckinghamshire County Planning Department.

County Planning Officers' Society (1992) *Competent Strategic Planning*. Ipswich: Suffolk County Council.

Coventry, Solihull and Warwickshire Sub-regional Study Team (1971) *A Strategy for the Sub-Region*. Warwick: Warwickshire County Council.

Cowling, T.M. and Steeley, G.C. (1973) *Sub-Regional Planning Studies: An Evaluation*. Oxford: Pergamon Press.

Credit Suisse First Boston Bank(1992) 'Europe: core vs periphery'. *CSFB Economics*, Geneva, December .

Crosland, A. (1974) 'Planning at the regional level'. *Built Environment* Vol.3 No.9.

Cullingworth, J.B. (1960) *Housing Needs and Planning Policy*. London: Routledge and Kegan Paul.

Cullingworth, J.B. (1979) *Environmental Planning 1939–1969*. Volume III. London: HMSO.

Cullingworth, J.B. (1991) 'The role of the states in urban growth management' *Regional Studies Association Newsletter* No.172, April, London.

Curry, C. (1975) 'Implementing and monitoring regional plans – the experience of the South East'. In J.M. Shaw (ed) *Regional Planning in East Anglia*. Discussion Paper 7. London: Regional Studies Association.

Damesick, P. (1982) 'Strategic Choice and Uncertainty: Regional Planning in Southeast England'. In R. Hudson and J. Lewis (eds) *Regional Planning in Europe*. London: Pion.

Darling, F. (ed) (1954) *West Highland Survey*. Oxford: Oxford University Press.

Davidge, W.R. (1927) *Report on the Regional Planning of West Kent*. North West and South West Kent Joint Regional Town Planning Committees.

Davidge, W.R. (1927) *Hertfordshire Regional Planning Report*.

Davidge, W.R. (1928) *South Bucks and Thameside Region Report*. Regional Joint Town Planning Committee.

Davidge, W.R. (1930) *Berkshire Regional Planning Survey*. Reading: Berkshire Regional Joint Town Planning Committee/Bradley and Son.

Davidge, W.R. (1934) *Cambridgeshire Regional Planning Report*. Cambridge: Cambridge University Press.

Davidge, W.R. (1934) *Buckinghamshire Regional Planning Report*. County Planning Advisory Committee.

Davidge, W.R. (1937) *Bedfordshire Regional Planning Report*. Bedfordshire Advisory Joint Town Planning Committee.

Davies, H.W.E. (1993) 'Europe and the Future of Planning'. *Town Planning Review* Vol.64 No.3, July.

Davies, H. (1993) 'Free markets and centralised political power: a British paradox'. In R.J. Bennett (ed) *Local Government in the New Europe*. London: Belhaven Press.

Davies, L. (1993) 'An Assessment of Regional Planning Guidance'. *The Planner*, 8 February.

Davis, M. (1990) *City of Quartz: Excavating the Future in Los Angeles*. London and New York: Verso.

DeGrove, J.M. (1991) 'Regional agencies as partners in state growth management systems'. *Proceedings of Joint ACSP and AESOP International Congress*, Oxford, UK, July 1991.

Department of Economic Affairs (1965a) *The North West: A Regional Study*. London: HMSO.

Department of Economic Affairs (1965) *The National Plan*. Cmnd.2764 London: HMSO.

Department of Economic Affairs (1965b) *The West Midlands: A Regional Study*. London: HMSO.

Department of the Environment (1971) *Long Term Population Distribution in Great Britain – A Study Report by an Inter-Departmental Study Group*. London: HMSO.

Department of the Environment (1976) *Development of the Strategic Plan for the South East, Interim Report*. London: Department of the Environment.

Department of the Environment (1978) *Strategic Plan for the South East, Review. Government Statement*. London: HMSO.

Department of the Environment (1988a) *Regional Guidance for the South East*. Planning Policy Guidance Note 9. London: HMSO.

Department of the Environment (1988b) *Strategic Guidance for the West Midlands*. Planning Policy Guidance Note 10. London: HMSO.

Department of the Environment (1988c) *Strategic Guidance for Merseyside*. Planning Policy Guidance Note 11. London: HMSO

Department of the Environment (1989a) *Draft Strategic Planning Guidance for London*. London: Greater London Regional Office, DoE.

Department of the Environment (1989b) *Strategic Guidance for London*. Regional Planning Guidance 3. London: HMSO.

Department of the Environment (1989c) *Regional Guidance for the South East* (PPG 9). London: HMSO.

Department of the Environment (1989d) *Strategic Guidance for Tyne and Wear* (RPG1). London: HMSO.

Department of the Environment (1989e) *Strategic Guidance for West Yorkshire* (RPG2). London: HMSO.

Department of the Environment (1989f) *Strategic Guidance for Greater Manchester* (RPG4). London: HMSO.

Department of the Environment (1989g) *Strategic Guidance for South Yorkshire* (RPG5). London: HMSO.

Department of the Environment (1990) *Regional Planning Guidance, Structure Plans and the Content of Development Plans* (PPG15). London: HMSO.

Department of the Environment (1991) *Regional Planning Guidance for East Anglia* (RPG 6). London: HMSO.

Department of the Environment (1992) *Planning Policy Guidance Note: Development Plans and Regional Policy Guidance* (PPG 12). London: HMSO.

Department of the Environment (1993) *Regional Planning Guidance for the Northern Region* (RPG7). London: HMSO.

Department of the Environment (1994a) *Regional Guidance for the South East* (RPG 9). London: HMSO.

Department of Physical Planning (1991) *Putting the Pieces Together: The Case for Maintaining the Function of Strategic Planning in the West of Scotland*. Glasgow: Strathclyde Regional Council.

Diamond, D. and Spence, N. (1983) *Regional Policy Evaluation: A Methodological Review and the Scottish Example*. Aldershot: Gower.

Dolphin, G. (1993) Report in *Planning Weekly*, 7 October.

Drucker, H. (ed) (1982) *John P. Mackintosh on Scotland*. London and New York: Longman.

East Anglia Consultative Committee (1969) *East Anglia: A Regional Appraisal*. Bury St. Edmunds: East Anglia Consultative Committee.

East Anglia Economic Planning Council (1967) *East Anglia: A Study*. London: HMSO.

East Anglia Regional Strategy Team (1974) *Strategic Choice for East Anglia*. London: HMSO.

London East Midlands Economic Planning Council (1966) *East Midlands Study*. London: HMSO.

East Midlands Economic Planning Council (1969) *Opportunity in the East Midlands*. London: HMSO.

East Midlands Regional Forum (1992) *Regional Strategy for the East Midlands*. Leicester: East Midlands Regional Forum.

Elson, M. (1986) *Green Belts*. London: Heinemann.

Estall, R. (1977) 'Regional planning in the United States'. *Town Planning Review* Vol.48 No.4, October.

European Commission (1991) *Europe 2000*. Brussels: EEC Directorate of Regional Policy.

Evans, A. (1988) *No Room! No Room!* Occasional Paper 79. London: Institute of Economic Affairs.

Faludi, A. (1992) 'Understanding Dutch strategic planning'. *Planning Theory* No.7/8 Summer/Winter.

Faludi, A. (1994) 'The Randstad Concept'. *Urban Studies* Vol.31 No.3.

Fawcett, C.B. (1930) 'Regional planning in England and Wales'. *Report of the Proceedings of the International Geographical Congress*, Cambridge 1928. Cambridge: The Executive Committee of the Congress.

Ferguson, E. and Wylie, R. (1993) 'Someone to watch over you'. *Scotland on Sunday*, 5 December.

Fitch, R. (1993) *The Assassination of New York*. London: Verso.

Flynn, N., Leach, S. and Vielba, C. (1985) *Abolition or Reform?* London: George Allen and Unwin.

Foley, D.L. (1972) *Governing the London Region: Reorganisation and Planning in the 1960s*. Berkeley: University of California Press.

Forshaw, J.H. (1927) *Lancaster and Morecambe Regional Planning Scheme*. London: University of Liverpool Press and Hodder and Stoughton.

Foster, C.D. (1988) 'Accountability in the development of policy for local taxation of people and business'. In R.J. Bennett (ed) 'Local fiscal crises: the policy imperative'. *Regional Studies*, 22.

Fraser Darling F. (1950) *West Highland Survey*. Oxford: Oxford University Press.

Freeman T.W. (1968) *Geography and Regional Administration*. London: Hutchinson University Library.

Friedmann, J. (1964) 'The concept of a planning region – the evolution of an idea in the United States'. In J. Friedmann and W. Alonso (eds) *Regional Development and Planning*. Cambridge, MA: MIT Press.

Friedmann, J. (1963) 'Regional Planning as a Field of Study'. *Journal of the American Institute of Planners* Vol.29.

Friedmann, J. (1979) 'The recovery of territorial life'. In J. Friedmann and C. Weaver. *Territory and Function: The Evolution of Regional Planning*. London: Edward Arnold.

Friedmann, J. and Bloch, R. (1990) 'American exceptionalism in regional planning 1933–2000'. *International Journal of Urban and Regional Research* Vol. 14, No. 4.

Friend, J. and Jessop, N. (1969) *Local Government and Strategic Choice*. Oxford: Pergamon Press.

Friend, J., Norris, M. and Carter, K. (1979) *Regional Planning and Policy Change: The Formulation of Policy Guidelines in Regional Strategies*. London: Department of the Environment.

Friend, J., Power, J. and Yewlett, C. (1974) *Public Planning: The Inter-Corporate Dimension*. London: Tavistock Publications.

Fürst, D. (Undated) 'The system of regional planning in Germany'. Unpublished mimeo., University of Hannover.

Gale, D.E. (1992) 'Eight state-sponsored growth management programs'. *Journal of the American Planning Association* Vol.58 No.4, Autumn.

Gappert, G. and Knight, R. (1987) 'The future of the winter cities'. *Urban Affairs Annual Review* Vol.31. London: Sage Publications.

Garden Cities and Town Planning Association (1918) Memorandum submitted to the Greater London Housing Conference, called by the London County Council, 30 October 1918.

Gardner, K. (1993) Report in *Planning Weekly*, 7 October.

Gaskin, M. (1969) *North East Scotland: A Survey of its Development Potential*. Edinburgh: HMSO.

Georgiou, G. (1993) 'From policy to action: the implementation of European Community regional programmes in Greece'. *Regional Politics and Policy* Vol.3 No.2, Summer.

Gilbert, G. and Guengant, A. 'France: shifts in local authority finance'. In R. Bennett *Territory and Administration in Europe*. London: Pinter Publishers.

Gillingwater, D. and Hart, D.A. (1978) *The Regional Planning Process*. Farnborough: Saxon House.

Glasson, J. (1980) *An Introduction to Regional Planning*. London: Hutchinson.

Glasson, J., Lloyd, M.G., McMillan, A. and Wood, C. (1990) *Models of Regional Planning*. Working Paper No.124. Oxford: Oxford Polytechnic School of Planning.

Gloucester County and City Councils (1970) *North Gloucestershire Sub-regional Study*. Gloucester: County Planning Department, Gloucester.

Goddard, J. (1992) 'Structural economic change and the regions'. *Proceedings of the Annual conference of the Regional Studies Association*, London, November 1992.

Government of Northern Ireland (1970) *Northern Ireland Development Programme 1970–75*. Belfast: HMSO.

Governors' Task Force on the Future of the Tri-State Regional Planning Commission (1981) *New Directions for Regional Planning: The New York–New Jersey–Connecticut Metropolitan Area*. New York, NY: Tri-State Regional Planning Commission.

Graham, O.L. (1976) *Toward a Planned Society*. New York: Oxford University Press.

Grassie, J. (1983) *Highland Experiment*. Aberdeen: Aberdeen University Press.

Greater London Regional Planning Committee (1929) *First Report of the Greater London Regional Planning Committee*.London: Knapp, Drewett.

Greater London Regional Planning Committee (1933) *Second Report of the Greater London Regional Planning Committee*. London: Knapp, Drewett.

Gripaios, P. and Mangles, T. (1993) 'An analysis of European super regions'. *Regional Studies* Vol.27 No.8.

Grodzins, M. (1978) 'The federal system'. In D.S. Wright (ed) *Understanding Intergovernmental Relations*. North Scituate, MA: Duxbury Press.

Gunn, L.A. (1978) 'Why is implementation so difficult?'. *Management Services in Government* Vol.33 No.4.

Hailsham, Lord (1992) *On the Constitution*. London: Harper Collins.

Hall, P. (1966) *The World Cities*. London: Weidenfeld and Nicholson.

Hall, P. (1969) *London 2000*. London: Faber and Faber.

Hall, P. (1989) *London 2001*. London: Unwin Hyman.

Hall, P., Gracey, H., Drewett, R. and Thomas, R. (1973) *The Containment of Urban England*. London: George Allen and Unwin.

Hambleton, R. (1979) *Policy Planning and Local Government*. New York: Universe Books.

Hansen, J. (1990) 'Epilogue'. In M. Hebbert and J.C. Hansen *Unfamiliar Territory*. Aldershot: Avebury.

Hardy, D. (1991) *From Garden Cities to New Towns: Campaigning for Town and Country Planning, 1899–1946*. London: E. and F. Spon.

Harrogate and District Regional Planning Committee (1937) *Preliminary Report and Planning Proposals*.

Haywood, S.C. and Elcock, H.J. (1982) 'Regional health authorities: regional government or central agencies?'. In B. Hogwood and M. Keating (eds) *Regional Government in England*. Oxford: Clarendon Press.

Healey, P., McNamara, P., Elson, M. and Doak, A. (1988) *Land Use Planning and the Mediation of Urban Change*. Cambridge: Cambridge University Press.

Hebbert, M. (1987) 'Regionalism: a reform concept and its application to Spain' *Environment and Planning C: Government and Policy* Vol.5, No.3.

Hebbert, M. (1990) 'Spain: A Centre–Periphery Transformation'. In M. Hebbert and J.C. Hansen *Unfamiliar Territory*. Aldershot: Avebury.

Hemmens, G.C. and McBride, J. (1993) 'Planning and Developemnt Decision Making in the Chicago Region'. In D.N. Rothblatt and A. Sancton (eds) *Metropolitan Governance: American/Canadian Intergovernmental Perspectives*. Berkeley: Institute of Governmental Studies Press, University of California.

Hickling A., Friend J. and Luckman J. (1979) *The Development Plan System and Investment Programmes*. Coventry: COOR.

Highlands and Islands Development Board (1967) *First Report of the Highlands and Islands Development Board*. Inverness: Highlands and Islands Development Board.

Hogwood, B. (1982) 'Introduction'. In B. Hogwood and M. Keating (eds) *Regional Government in England*. Oxford: Clarendon Press.

Hogwood B. and Lindley P.D. (1982) 'Variations in regional boundaries'. In B. Hogwood and M. Keating (eds) *Regional Government in England*. Oxford: Clarendon Press.

Holmes J. (1968) *The Moray Firth: A Plan for Growth in a Sub-Region of the Scottish Highlands*. Glasgow: Jack Holmes Planning Group.

Horan J.F. and Taylor G.T. (1977) *Experiments in Metropolitan Government*. New York: Praeger.

House of Commons (1980) *The DOE and the West Midlands Region*. Report of the Environment Committee. House of Commons Papers, Session 1980/81.

Hudson R. (1989) *Wrecking a Region*. London: Pion.

Hudson R. (1993) 'Retreat into regional fantasy'. *Times Higher Education Supplement* March 19.

Hufschmidt M.M. (1969) 'A new look at regional planning'. In M.M. Hufschmidt (ed) *Regional Planning: Challenge and Prospects*. New York: Praeger.

Huntingdon and Peterborough County Council (1970) *Peterborough Sub-Regional Study*. Huntingdon: Huntingdon County Council.

Interim Report of Departmental Committee on Regional Development. Cmnd. 3915, 1931. London: HMSO.

Jackson K.T. (1985) *Crabgrass Frontier*. New York: Oxford University Press.

Johnson-Marshall P. and Wolfe J.H. (1968) *The Central Borders: A Plan for Expansion*. Edinburgh: HMSO.

Johnston, T. (1952) *Memories*. London: Collins.

Joint Center for Urban Studies (1964) *The Effectiveness of Metropolitan Planning*. Washington D.C. : U.S. Government Printing Office.

Joint Committee of Wirral Local Authorities (1926) *The Wirral Regional Planning Scheme*. Birkenhead: Willmer Bros.

Jones G. (1988) 'Against regional government' *Local Government Studies*, September/October.

Jones V. and Rothblatt D.N. (1993) 'Governance of the San Francisco Bay Area'. In D.N. Rothblatt and A. Sancton (eds) (1993) *Metropolitan Governance: American/Canadian Intergovernmental Perspectives*. Berkeley: Institute of Governmental Studies Press, University of California.

Kalk E. (ed.) (1971) *Regional Planning and Regional Government In Europe*. The Hague: International Union of Local Authorities.

Keating M. (1982) 'The debate on regional reform'. In B. Hogwood and M. Keating (eds) *Regional Government in England*. Oxford: Clarendon Press.

Keating M. (1988) *The City that Refused to Die*. Aberdeen: Aberdeen University Press.

Keating M. and Jones. B (1985) *Regions in the European Community*. Oxford: Clarendon Press.

Keating M. and Rhodes M. (1982) 'The status of regional government: an analysis of the West Midlands'. In B. Hogwood and M. Keating (eds) *Regional Government in England*. Oxford: Clarendon Press.

King, R.L. (1987) 'Regional government: the Italian experience'. *Environment and Planning C* Vol.5, No.3.

Klemmer P. (1988) 'Adaptation problems of old industrial areas: the Ruhr area as an example'. In J.J. Hesse (ed) *Regional Structural Change and Industrial Policy in International Perspective: United States, Great Britain, France, Federal Republic of Germany*. Baden-Baden: Nomos Verlagsgesellschaft.

Kuklinski A. (1993) 'Socio-political changes in Central and Eastern European countries: territorial and economic repercussions and transformations in Europe'. In *The Challenges Facing European Society with the Approach of the Year 2000. European Regional Planning, No.54*. Strasbourg: Council of Europe Press.

Kunzmann K. (1990) 'Regional policy and regional planning in the Federal Republic of Germany'. *Proceedings of the Town and Country Planning Summer School 1990*. London: Royal Town Planning Institute.

Kunzmann K. (1990) 'Reuse policies in the Ruhr'. *Rassegna* No.42/2.

Labour Party (1991a) *Democracy and Devolution*. London: Labour Party.

Labour Party (1991b) *London: A World Class Capital*. London: Labour Party.

Leach, S. and Game, C. (1991) 'English metropolitan government since abolition: an evaluation of the abolition of the English metropolitan county councils'. *Public Administration* Vol.69, Summer.

Leicester–Leicestershire Sub-regional Planning Team (1969) *Leicester and Leicestershire Sub-regional Planning Study*. Leicester: Leicester City and County Councils.

Lewis, S. (1991) *Managing Urban Growth in the San Francisco Bay Region*. Hayward: Centre for Public Service Education and Research, California State University.

Lichfield, N. and Darin-Drabkin, H. (1980) *Land Policy in Planning*. London: George Allen and Unwin.

Lim, G.C. (ed) (1983) *Regional Planning: Evolution, Crisis and Prospects*. Totowa, N.J.: Rowman and Allanheld.

Lindblom, C.E. (1965) *The Intelligence of Democracy: Decision-Making Through Mutual Adjustment*. New York: The Free Press.

Lindley, P.D. (1982) 'The framework of regional planning 1964–79'. In B. Hogwood and M. Keating (eds) *Regional Government in England*. Oxford: Clarendon Press.

Lloyd, T.A. and Jackson, H. (1949) *Outline Plan for South Wales and Monmouthshire*. London: HMSO.

Local Government Boundary Commission (1947) Report, 1947. House of Commons Paper 86 (1947–48).

Lock, M. (1943) *Hull Regional Survey*. London: Housing Centre.

London Boroughs Association (1993) *All Aboard! Attractive Public Transport for London*. London: London Boroughs Association.

London Planning Administration Committee (1949) Report. London: HMSO.

London Planning Advisory Committee (1988) *LPAC Strategic Planning Advice for London – Policies for the 1990s*. London: London Planning Advisory Committee.

London Planning Advisory Committee (1989) *LPAC Review 1989 – Strategic Trends and Policy*. London: London Planning Advisory Committee.

London Planning Advisory Committee (1991) *London: A World City Moving into the 21st Century*. Report by Coopers and Lybrand Deloitte. London: HMSO.

London Planning Advisory Committee (1992) *Strategic Planning Issues for London*. London: London Planning Advisory Committee.

London Planning Advisory Committee (1993) *Draft 1993 Advice on Strategic Planning Guidance for London*. London: London Planning Advisory Committee.

London Planning Advisory Committee (1994) *LPAC Strategic Planning Advice for London*. London: London Planning Advisory Committee.

Long, J.R. (ed) (1961) *The Wythall Inquiry: A Planning Test-Case*. London: Estates Gazette.

Lysenko, V. (1993) 'Development of local government in Russia and the CIS'. In R.J. Bennett (ed) *Local Government in the New Europe*. London: Belhaven Press.

Mackaye B. (1962) *The New Exploration: A Philosophy of Regional Planning*. Urbana: University of Illinois Press.

Mackintosh, J. (1972) 'Evidence to the Commission on the Constitution'. *Written Evidence* Vol.9. London: HMSO.

Manchester and District Joint Town Planning Advisory Committee (1926) *Report upon the Regional Scheme*. Manchester: Blacklock.

Manchester and District Regional Planning Committee (1945) *Regional Planning Proposals*. Norwich and London: Jarrold and Sons.

Mann J. (1942) 'Scotland – to-morrow, lost horizons'. In *The New Scotland*. Glasgow: The London Scots Self-Government Committee.

Marcou, G. (1993) 'New tendencies of local government development in Europe'. In R.J. Bennett (ed) *Local Government in the New Europe*. London: Belhaven Press.

Markusen, A. (1987) *Regions: The Economics and Politics of Territory*. Totowa, NJ: Rowman and Littlefield.

Marshall, F. (1978) *The Marshall Inquiry on Greater London: Report to the Greater London Council*. London: GLC.

Martin, D. (1992) 'Europe 2000: community actions and intentions in spatial planning'. In *Proceedings of the Town and Country Planning Summer School 1992*. London: RTPI.

Martin, J.A. (1993) 'In fits and starts: the Twin Cities metropolitan framework'. In D.N. Rothblatt and A. Sancton (eds) *Metropolitan Governance: American/Canadian Intergovernmental Perspectives*. Berkeley: IGS Press, University of California.

Martins, M.R. (1986) *An Organisational Approach to Regional Planning*. Aldershot: Gower.

Massey, D. (1989) 'Regional planning 1909–1939: the experimental era'. In P.L. Garside and M. Hebbert (eds) *British Reginalism 1900–2000*. London: Mansell.

Matthew, R. (1964) *Belfast Regional Survey and Plan*. Belfast: HMSO.

Mattocks, R.H. (1930) *The Lake District (South) Regional Planning Scheme, The Report*. Kendal: Atkinson and Pollitt.

Mawson J. and Skelcher C. (1980) 'Updating the West Midlands Strategy'. *Town Planning Review*, Vol.51 No.2, April.

Mawson, T.H and Son with Crossland J. (1937) *Amounderness: being the Report of the Regional Planning Committee for the Area of the Fylde*. Fylde Region Joint Planning Advisory Committee. London: Batsford.

Mazza, L. (1991) 'European viewpoint: a new status for Italian metropolitan areas'. *Town Planning Review*, Vol. 62 No.2.

McDowell, B. (1985a) 'federal development policies and the adaptive regional council'. *Paper to the 1985 Federal Briefing, National Association of Regional Councils*, 5 February.

McDowell, B. (1985b) 'Strategies for adapting regional councils to new federalism. *Paper to the 27th Annual Conference of the Association of Collegiate Schools of Planning*, 3 November.

McDowell, B. (1985c) 'Regional planning without federal aid'. *Paper to the 27th Annual Conference of the Association of Collegiate Schools of Planning*, 1 November.

McDowell, B. (1986) 'Regional councils in an era of do-it-yourself federalism'. *Paper to Regional Council Executive Directors of the Southeastern States*, 20 March.

Mears, F. (1949) *A Regional Survey and Plan for Central and South East Scotland*. Edinburgh: Regional Planning Advisory Committee.

Mid Cheshire Joint Town Planning Advisory Committee (1929) Report. Liverpool: C. Tinling.

Midland Joint Town Planning Advisory Council (1931) *Report Upon the Regional Scheme*. Birmingham: Midland Joint Town Planning Advisory Council.

Midwinter, A., Keating, M. and Mitchell, J. (1991) *Politics and Public Policy in Scotland*. London: Macmillan.

Minay, C., Cross, D., Gillingwater, D., Shaw, T., Coombs, T., Filder, P., Hathaway, A. and Alden, J.. (1992) 'Developing regional planning guidance in England and Wales'. *Town Planning Review*, Vol.63 No.4, October.

Ministero dell' Ambiente (1992) *Piano Decenniale per l'Ambiente* (DECAMB). Rom Minstero dell' Ambiente.

Ministry of Health (1921) *Report of the South Wales Regional Survey Committe*. London: HMSO.

Ministry of Housing and Local Government (1963) *London – Employment: Housing: Land*. Cmnd. 1952. London: HMSO.

Ministry of Housing and Local Government (1963) *The North-East: A Programme for Development and Growth*. Cmnd.2206. London: HMSO.

Ministry of Housing and Local Government (1964) *South East England*. Cmnd. 2308. London: HMSO.

Ministry of Housing and Local Government (1964) *South East Study. 1961–1981*. London: HMSO.

Ministry of Housing and Local Government (1968) *Bedford, Milton Keynes, Northampton and Wellingborough Sub-Regional Study*. Unpublished, London.

Mogridge, M. and Parr, J.B. (1994) *Metropolis or Region: On the Development and Structure of London*. Unpublished paper, University of Glasgow.

Mogulof, M.B. (1971) *Governing Metropolitan Areas*. Washington, D.C.: The Urban Institute.

Morphet, J. (1994) 'In search of a strategy'. *Planning Week*, 10 March.

Morrison, H. (1993) Speech to the Scottish Council, Development and Industry, Glasgow, 10 November.

Morton, A. (1993) Speech to the Institution of Mechanical Engineers London, 6 March.

Motte, A. (1991) 'The challenges of European integration for urban planning: the French case'. *The Planner*, 13 December.

Mumford, L. (1946) *City Development*. London: Secker and Warburg.

Naftalin, A. (1986) *Making One Community Out of Many*. St. Paul: Metropolitan Council of the Twin Cities Area.

National Resources Committee (1935) *Regional Factors in National Planning and Development*. Washington, DC: US Government Printing Office.

Netherlands Scientific Council for Government Policy (1990) *Institutions and Cities: the Dutch Experience*. Report to the Government, 37. The Hague: Netherlands Scientific Council.

Newman, P. (1994) 'Paris planners try to close door on regional runaway'. *Planning*, 6 May.

Nicholas, R.J. (1945) *Manchester and District Regional Planning Proposals*. Norwich and London: Jarrold and Sons.

Nicholas, R.J. and Hellier, M.J. (1947) *Advisory Plan for South Lancashire and North Cheshire*. Manchester: Richard Bates.

North West Economic Planning Council (1966) *An Economic Planning Strategy for the NW Region*. Manchester: North West Economic Planning Council.

North West Economic Planning Council (1968) *The North West of the 1970s: Strategy II*. London: HMSO.

North West Joint Planning Team (1974) *Strategic Plan for the North West*. London: HMSO.

North West Regional Association(1994) *Greener Growth*. Wigan: North West Regional Association.

Northern Region Economic Planning Council (1966) *The Challenge of the Changing North*. London: HMSO.

Northern Region Economic Planning Council (1969) *Northern Region: An Outline Strategy of Development to 1981*. London: HMSO.

Northern Region Strategy Team (1977) *Strategic Plan for the Northern Region*. Newcastle: Northern Regional Strategy Team.

Norton, A. (1983) *The Government and Administration of Metropolitan Areas in Western Democracies: Survey of Approaches to the Administrative Problems of Major Conurbations in Europe and Canada*. Birmingham: Birmingham University, Institute of Local Government Studies.

Nottinghamshire and Derbyshire Sub-regional Planning Team (1969) *Nottinghamshire and Derbyshire Sub-regional Study*. Nottinghamshire County Council.

Novak T. (1974) 'Twin Cities regionalism: a local perspective'. *Public Management*, No.56, January.

Nuffield Foundation (1986) *Town and Country Planning: A Report to the Nuffield Foundation*. London: Nuffield Foundation.

O'Connor, J. (1973) *The Fiscal Crisis of the State*. New York: St. Martins.

Ostrom, V., Tiebout, C.M. and Warren, R. (1961) 'The organisation of government in metropolitan areas: a theoretical inquiry'. *American Political Science Review*, Vol.55, December.

Painter, C. (1972) 'The repercussions of administrative innovation: the West Midlands Economic Planning Council'. *Public Administration*, Vol.50.

Painter, M. (1980) 'Policy co-ordination in the DOE, 1970–76'. *Public Administration*, Vol.59, summer.

Palard, J. (1993) 'Structural and regional planning confronted with decentralisation and European integration'. *Regional Politics and Policy*, Vol. 3 No. 3, Autumn.

Parry Lewis J. (1974) *The Cambridge Sub-Region*. Cambridge: Cambridge County Council.

Payne, G.E. (1949) *The Tay Valley Plan: A Physical, Social and Economic Survey and Plan for the Future Development of East Central Scotland*. Dundee: East Central Scotland Regional Planning Advisory Committee.

Payne, J. (1978) 'Regional planning and water authorities'. In P. Drudy (ed). *Water Planning and the Regions*. RSA Discussion Paper No.9. London: Regional Studies Association, London.

Pepler, G. and Macfarlane, P.W. (1949) *The North East Development Area Outline Plan*. Unpublished report to the Ministry of Town and Country Planning.

PIEDA (1993) *A Regional Economic Development Strategy for the North West*. Wigan: North West Regional Association and North West Business Leadership Team.

Planning Advisory Group (1965) *The Future of Development Plans*. London: HMSO.

Powell, A.G. (1960) 'The recent development of Greater London'. *Advancement of Science*, Vol.XVIII No.65, May.

Powell, A.G. (1978) 'Strategies for the English regions'. *Town Planning Review*, Vol. 49 No.1, January.

Priemus, H. (1994) 'Planning the Randstadt: Between Economic Growth and Sustainability'. *Urban Studies*, Vol.31 No.3.

Ravetz, A. (1980) *Remaking Cities*. London: Croom Helm.

Regulski, J. (1993) 'Rebuilding local government in Poland'. In R.J. Bennett (ed) *Local Government in the New Europe*. London: Belhaven Press.

Report of South Wales Regional Survey (1920) Ministry of Health, London.

Rhodes, G. (ed) (1972) *The Government of London: The First Five Years*. London: Weidenfeld and Nicholson.

Rhodes, R. (1974) 'Regional policy and a "Europe of Regions": a critical assessment'. *Journal of Regional Studies*, Vol.8 No.2.

Ringli, H. (1991) 'Swiss national development concepts'. *Paper to the Joint ACSP and AESOP Congress*, Oxford, UK, July.

Roberts, P. (1993) 'Managing the strategic planning and development of regions: lessons from a European perspective'. *Regional Studies*, Vol.27 No.8.

Robertson, D.J. (1965) 'A nation of regions?'. *Urban Studies*, Vol.2 No.2.

Robertson, D.J. and Matthew, R. (1966) *Lothians Regional Survey and Plan*. Edinburgh: HMSO.

Robertson, D.J. and Matthew, R. (1968) *The Grangemouth/Falkirk Regional Survey and Plan*. Edinburgh: HMSO.

Robson, W.A. (1945) 'The Greater London Plan'. *Political Quarterly*, No.16, April.

Rondinelli, D. (1975) *Urban and Regional Development and Planning – Policy and Administration*. London: Cornell University Press.

Roskill Commission (1971) *Report of the Commission on the Third London Airport*. London: HMSO.

Rothblatt, D.N. (1971) *Regional Planning: The Appalachian Experience*. Lexington, MA: Heath Lexington Books.

Rothblatt, D.N. and Jones, V. (1991) 'Policy-making for metropolitan development: American and Canadian perspectives'. *Joint ACSP and AESOP Congress*, Oxford, UK, July.

Royal Commission (1940) *Report of the Royal Commission on the Distribution of Industrial Population*. Cmnd. 6153. London: HMSO.

Royal Commission (1960) *Report of the Royal Commisssion on Local Government in Greater London 1957–60*. Cmnd. 1164. London: HMSO.

Royal Commission (1969) *Report of the Royal Commission on Local Government in England 1966–69*. Cmnd. 4140. London: HMSO.

Royal Commission (1969) *Report of the Royal Commission on Local Government in Scotland 1966–69*. Cmnd. 4150. Edinburgh: HMSO.

Royal Commission (1973) *Report of the Royal Commission on the Constitution*. Cmnd.5460. London: HMSO.

Royal Town Planning Institute (1986) *Strategic Planning for Regional Potential*. Royal London: Town Planning Institute.

Royal Town Planning Institute (1991) *The Regional Planning Process*. London: Royal Town Planning Institute.

Royal Town Planning Institute, North West Branch (1990) *North West 2010: The Pressing Case for Strategic Planning*. Liverpool: Department of Civic Design, University of Liverpool.

Saunders D.L. (1977) 'The Changing Planning Framework'. In F. Joyce (ed) *Metropolitan Development and Change*. Farnborough: Saxon House.

Saunders, P. (1983) *The Regional State*. Working Paper No. 35, Urban and Regional Studies. Falmer: University of Sussex.

Schofield, A. (1929) *The West Sussex Coast and Downs Report of the Arundel, Littlehampton, East Preston and District Town Planning Advisory Committee*. Arundel, Sussex.

Scotland on Sunday (1993) 'Someone to watch over you'. *Scotland on Sunday*, 5 December.

Scott, M. (1959) *The San Francisco Bay Area: A Metropolis in Perspective*. University of Berkeley: California Press.

Scott, M. (1971) *American City Planning Since 1890*. Berkeley: University of California Press.

Scottish Council on Industry (1961) *Report of the Committee appointed by the Scottish Council (Development and Industry), Inquiry into the Scottish Economy 1960–61*. Edinburgh: Scottish Council (Development and Industry).

Scottish Development Department (1963a) *Central Scotland: A Programme for Development and Growth*. Cmnd.2188. Edinburgh: HMSO.

Scottish Development Department (1963b) *The Modernisation of Local Government in Scotland*. Cmnd.2067. Edinburgh: HMSO.

Scottish Development Department (1970) *Tayside: Potential for Development*. Edinburgh: HMSO.

Scottish Development Department (1970) *A Strategy for South West Scotland*. Edinburgh: HMSO.

Scottish Homes (1994) *Response to the Scottish Office Consultation Paper on Progress in Partnership*. Edinburgh: Scottish Homes .

Scottish Office (1966) *The Scottish Economy 1965 to 1970: A Plan for Expansion*. Cmnd.2864. Edinburgh: HMSO.

Scottish Office (1993) *The Structure of Local Government. Shaping the Future – the New Councils*. Cm. 2267. Edinburgh:HMSO.

Secretaries of State (1990) *This Common Inheritance*. Cmnd.1200. London: HMSO.

Secretary of the State for the Environment (1983) *Streamlining the Cities:Government Proposals for Reorganising Local Government in Greater London and the Metropolitan Counties*. Cmnd.9063. London: HMSO.

Self, P. (1962) *Town Planning in Greater London*. Greater London Papers No. 7. London: London School of Economics.

Self, P. (1971) *Metropolitan Planning Greater London*. Greater London Papers No. 14. London: London School of Economics.

Self, P. (1975) 'Organisation for regional planning'. *Town and Country Planning* Vol.43 No.11.

Self, P. (1982) *Planning the Urban Region*. London: George Allen and Unwin.

SERPLAN (1985) *Developing South East Regional Strategy: South East England in the 1990s: A Regional Statement*. RPC 450. London: SERPLAN.

SERPLAN (1986) *Regional Strategic Guidance*. RPC 602. London: SERPLAN.

SERPLAN (1989) *Into the Next Century: Review of the Regional Strategy*. RPC 1500 SERPLAN, London.

SERPLAN (1989) *Progress on the Review of South East Regional Strategy*. RPC 1580. London: SERPLAN.

SERPLAN (1990) *Shaping the South East Planning Strategy*. RPC 1660. London: SERPLAN.

SERPLAN (1990) *A New Strategy for the South East*. RPC 1789: E10. London: SERPLAN.

SERPLAN(1992) *SERPLAN Thirty Years of Regional Planning 1962–1992*. London: SERPLAN.

Shankland Cox and Associates (1970) *Deeside Planning Study*. London: Shankland Cox and Associates.

Sieber, S.D. (1981) *Fatal Remedies: The Ironies of Social Intervention*. New York: Plenum Press.

Simmons, M. (1990) 'London through the eyes of LPAC'. *Report of Proceedings: Town and Country Planning Summer School 1990*. London: Royal Town Planning Institute.

Simmons, M. (1991) 'Is the planning system now up to the job?' *Paper to the Joint Planning Law Conference on 'The Planning Balance in the 1990s'*.

Simpson, M. (1985) *Thomas Adams and the Modern Planning Movement: Britain, Canada and the United States 1900–1940*. London: Mansell.

Smith, B.C. (1969) *Advising Ministers*. London: Routledge and Kegan Paul.

Smith, B.C. *Regionalism in England*: (1964) *Regional Institutions: A Guide*. (1965) *Its Nature and Purpose*. (1965) *The New Regional Machinery*. London: Acton Society Trust.

Smith, P.M. (1966) 'What kind of regional planning?'. *Urban Studies*, Vol.3 No. 3, November.

Smith, R. and Wannop, U. (1985) *Strategic Planning in Action*. Aldershot: Gower.

Solé-Vilanova, J. (1989) 'Spain: developments in regional and local government'. In R. Bennett (ed) *Territory and Administration in Europe.* London: Pinter Publishers.

South East Branch RTPI (1991) *Report of Working Group Study on Good Practice in the Preparation of Regional Planning Documents*. London: RTPI.

South East Economic Planning Council (1967) *A Strategy for the South East*. London: HMSO.

South East Joint Planning Team (1970) *Strategic Plan for the South East*. London: HMSO.

South East Joint Planning Team (1976) *Strategy for the South East: 1976 Review*. London: HMSO.

South West Economic Planning Council (1974) *A Strategic Settlement Pattern for the South West*. London: HMSO.

South West Economic Planning Council (1967) *A Region with a Future: A Draft Strategy for the South West*. London: HMSO.

South West Lancashire Joint Town Planning Advisory Committee (1930) *The Future Development of South-West Lancashire*. Liverpool: University Press of Liverpool.

South West Regional Planning Conference (1991) *Towards a Regional Strategy*. Taunton: Somerset County Council.

Standing Conference of East Anglian Local Authorities (1989) *Regional Strategy for East Anglia*. Ipswich: Suffolk County Council.

Standing Conference on London and South East Regional Planning (1968) *Framework for Regional Planning in South East England*. London: Standing Conference.

Steeley, G. (1991) 'Viewpoint: The regional component'. *Town Planning Review Vol. 62 No. 1*.

Stodart, J.A. (1981) *Report of the Committee of Inquiry into Local Government in Scotland*. Cmnd. 8115. Edinburgh: HMSO.

Strathclyde Regional Council (1976) *Regional Report 1976*. Glasgow: Strathclyde Regional Council.

Strathclyde Regional Council (1981) *Strathclyde Structure Plan 1981*. Glasgow: Strathclyde Regional Council.

Swiss Federal Council (1987) *Federal Spatial Planning Report*. Berne: EMDZ.

Teesside Survey and Plan (1969) *Final Report to the Steering Committee*. London: HMSO.

Teixidor, L.F. and Hebbert, M. (1982) 'Regional planning in Spain and the transition to democracy'. In R. Hudson and J. Lewis (eds) *Regional Planning in Europe.* London: Pion.

Ter Heide, H. (1992) 'Diagonal planning'. *Planning Theory* No. 7/8, Summer/Winter.

Thompson, F.L. (1945) *Merseyside Plan 1944; A Report Prepared in Consultation with a Technical Committee of the Merseyside Advisory Joint Planning Committee.* London: HMSO.

Thompson, W.H. (1934) *Somerset Regional Report: A Survey and a Plan.* London: University of London Press.

Town and Country Planning Association (1993) *Strategic Planning for Regional Potential.* London: TCPA.

Town Planning Regional Survey (1926) Liverpool: Liverpool University Press.

Travers, T., Jones, G., Hebbert, M. and Burnham, J. (1991) *The Government of London.* York: Joseph Rowntree Foundation.

University of Wales (1993) *Quangos in Wales.* Cardiff: Department of City and Regional Planning.

Ushkalov, I.G. (1993) 'Regional development in the former USSR'. In R.J. Bennett (ed) *Local Government in the New Europe.* London: Belhaven Press.

Van den Berg, L., Van Klink, H. and Van der Meer, J. (1993) *Governing Metropolitan Regions.* Aldershot: Avebury.

Van der Heiden, N., Kok, J., Postumu, R. and Wallagh, G. (1992) 'Consensus building as an essential element of the Dutch planning system'. *Planning Theory* No.7/8 Summer/Winter.

Voogd, H. (1982) 'Issues and tendencies in Dutch regional planning'. In R. Hudson and J. Lewis (eds) *Regional Planning in Europe.* London: Pion.

Waniek, R.W. (1993) 'A new approach towards decentralisation in North-Rhine Westphalia'. *Regional Studies,* Vol. 27 No. 5.

Wannop, U. (1985a) 'The practice of rationality: a case study'. In M. Breheny and A. Hooper (eds) *Rationality in Planning.* London: Pion.

Wannop, U. (1985b) 'The Strathclyde new towns'. In J. Butt and G. Gordon (eds) *Strathclyde: Changing Horizons.* Edinburgh: Scottish Academic Press.

Wannop, U. (1990) 'The Glasgow eastern area renewal project'. *Town Planning Review,* Vol.61, No.4.

Wannop, U. and Cherry, G. (1994) 'The development of regional planning in the United Kingdom'. *Planning Perspectives,* Vol.9 No.1.

Weaver, C. (1984) *Regional Development and the Local Community: Planning, Politics and Social Context.* Chichester: John Wiley and Sons.

Weaver, C. (1990) 'Concepts and theories of regional development planning'. In K. Kunzmann, U. von Petz and K. Schmals (eds) *20 Jahre Raumplanung in Dortmund.* Dortmund: IRPUD, Universität Dortmund.

Welch, R. (1993) 'Economic restructuring and the capitalist periphery: implications for eastern Europe'. In R.J. Bennett (ed)*Local Government in the New Europe.* London: Belhaven Press.

Wells, H.G. (1903) *Mankind in the Making.* London: Chapman and Hall.

Welsh Economic Planning Council (1967) *Wales: The Way Ahead.* London: HMSO.

Welsh Office (1993) Circular No. 42/93 *Strategic Development Scheme: Bids for 1994–95*. Cardiff: Welsh Office.

West Central Scotland Plan Team (1974) *West Central Scotland: A Programme of Action*. Glasgow: West Central Scotland Plan Steering Committee.

West Midlands County Council (1974) *A Time for Action*. Birmingham: West Midlands County Council.

West Midlands Economic Planning Council (1967) *West Midlands: Patterns of Growth*. London: HMSO.

West Midlands Economic Planning Council (1971) *The West Midlands: An Economic Appraisal*. London: HMSO.

West Midlands Forum of County Councils (1981) *The State of Housing in the West Midlands Region*. Report of Housing Working Group. Birmingham: West Midlands Forum of County Councils.

West Midlands Group (1948) *Conurbation: A Planning Survey of Birmingham and the Black Country*. London: Architectural Press.

West Midlands Regional Study (1971) *A Developing Strategy for the West Midlands*. Birmingham: West Midlands Regional Study.

Wildavsky, A. (1975) *A Bias Towards Federalism: a Review Essay on Planning, Organisation Theory and Government Structure*. Working Paper No. 40. Berkeley: Graduate School of Public Policy, University of California.

Wilson, H. and Womersley, L. (1965) *Northampton, Bedford and North Bucks Study: An Assessment of Inter-Related Growth*. London: HMSO.

Wilson, H. and Womersley, L. (1968) *Teesside Survey and Plan: Final Report to the Steering Committee*. London: HMSO.

Wright, M. and Young, S. (1975) 'Regional Planning in Britain'. In J. Hayward and M. Watson (eds) *Planning, Politics and Public Policy*. Cambridge: Cambridge University Press.

Yorkshire and Humberside Economic Planning Council (1966) *A Review of Yorkshire and Humberside*. London: HMSO.

Yorkshire and Humberside Economic Planning Council (1968) *Halifax and Calder Valley: An Area Study*. London: HMSO.

Yorkshire and Humberside Economic Planning Council (1969) *Huddersfield and the Colne Valley: An Area Study*. London: HMSO.

Yorkshire and Humberside Economic Planning Council (1969) *Doncaster: an Area Study*. London: HMSO.

Yorkshire and Humberside Economic Planning Council (1970) *Yorkshire and Humberside: Regional Strategy*. London: HMSO.

Yorkshire and Humberside Economic Planning Council (1975) *Yorkshire and Humberside: The Next Ten Years*. London: HMSO.

Young, K. and Garside, P. (1982) *Metropolitan London: Politics and Urban Change 1837–1981*. London: Edward Arnold.

Young, K. and Kramer, J. (1978) *Strategy and Conflict in Metropolitan Housing*. London: Heinemann.

Young, S. (1982) 'Regional offices of the Department of the Environment: their roles and influence in the 1970s'. In B. Hogwood and M. Keating (eds) *Regional Government in England*. Oxford: Clarendon Press.

Subject Index

Author Index